873.01(VIR)/OU...

VIRGIL'S A

Also available or forthcoming in the IGNIBUS Paperbacks series from Bristol Phoenix Press:

Samuel Butler: *The Authoress of the Odyssey* (with new introduction by Tim Whitmarsh) (reissued 2004)

B.C. Dietrich: *The Origins of Greek Religion* (reissued 2004)

A.F. Garvie: *Aeschylus' Supplices: Play and Trilogy* (second edition 2006)

Arthur Keaveney: *Rome and the Unification of Italy* (second edition 2005)

A.W. Verrall: *Euripides the Rationalist* (with new introduction by Peter Burian, forthcoming)

T.P. Wiseman: *Clio's Cosmetics: Three Studies in Greco-Roman Literature* (reissued 2004)

VIRGIL'S *AENEID*

A Critical Description

Kenneth Quinn

BRISTOL
PHOENIX
PRESS

Cover illustration: 'The Trojan Horse': engraving by Fourdrinier from *The Works of Virgil* by John Dryden (1748).

First published in 1968
by Routledge and Kegan Paul Ltd

Reissued in 2006 by Bristol Phoenix Press
an imprint of The Exeter Press
Reed Hall, Streatham Drive,
Exeter, Devon EX4 4QR
UK
www.exeterpress.co.uk

© Kenneth Quinn 1968

The right of Kenneth Quinn to be identified as author
of this work has been asserted by him in accordance
with the Copyright, Designs and Patents Act 1988

British Library Cataloguing in Publication Data
A catalogue record for this book is available
from the British Library.

ISBN: 1 904675 52 2

Printed in Great Britain by Booksprint

To
GAMBY

Contents

			page
PREFACE			ix
ABBREVIATIONS			xi
1.	THE HEROIC IMPULSE		1
2.	GENESIS		
	I.	What is the *Aeneid* about?	23
	II.	The Task and its Problems	26
	III.	The Problems Solved	34
3.	STRUCTURE		
	I.	General Description	59
	II.	Structure of the Twelve Books	64
	III.	The Episodes	71
	IV.	Projection of the Narrator into his Narrative	77
	V.	Parallel and Suspended Narrative	84
	VI.	Tempo of the Narrative: Tenses	88
4.	THE TWELVE BOOKS		
	Book 1		99
	Book 2		112
	Book 3		121
	Book 4		135
	Book 5		150
	Book 6		160
	Book 7		174
	Book 8		189
	Book 9		198
	Book 10		212
	Book 11		233
	Book 12		252
5.	FORM AND TECHNIQUE		
	Part 1: Form		277
		I. Not Only Homer	278
		II. Difference in Attitude between Virgil and Homer	284
		III. The Exploitation of Form	288
		IV. Impure Poetry	293

Contents

Part 2:	Technique	299
I.	Gods	300
II.	Characterization and Motivation	307
III.	Parallel Divine and Psychological Motivation	316
IV.	Fate	320
Part 3:	The Contribution of Tragedy	323
I.	Tragic Attitude	324
II.	Tragic Suspense	327
III.	Tragic Irony and Insight	330
IV.	Implicit Comment	339

6. STYLE
- I. Words Alone — 350
- II. Words in Action — 353
  - (i) The Tradition — 355
    - (a) Ennius and the Old Poets — 355
    - (b) Catullus and the New Poets — 370
    - (c) A Common Style — 375
  - (ii) Innovation—*callida iunctura* — 384
    - (a) Latent Metaphor — 391
    - (b) Archaism brought out by Context — 393
    - (c) Etymological Puns — 393
  - (iii) Ambiguity — 394
  - (iv) Syntactical Ambiguity — 405
- III. The Virgilian Sentence — 414
  - (i) Metre — 415
  - (ii) Theme and Variation — 423
  - (iii) Subordinate Clauses — 428
  - (iv) Imagery — 431

LIST OF PASSAGES DISCUSSED — 441
INDEX — 445

Preface

The purpose of this book is not hard to state: broadly speaking my aim, *mutatis mutandis*, has been Mackail's:

> ... to present the poem in a single volume of manageable size, and with just so much of explanatory, introductory, or critical matter as may enable it to be read continuously with intelligent appreciation.

Naturally, that is easier said than done: the ever-present temptation to explain too much has to be kept in check; what one feels to be the important, relevant things usually turn out to be exasperatingly difficult to discuss. The fact remains that, in intention at any rate, this is a book whose object is to help in reading Virgil's poem 'continuously with intelligent appreciation'.

Chapter 1 attempts a preliminary exploration of what seems to me an important theme. Chapter 2 pieces together the circumstances, literary and historical, in which the poem took shape. Chapter 3 deals with the outlines of the poetic structure. Chapter 4, the longest, provides a fairly full analysis of the text; the twelve books are taken in order, Books 10 to 12—partly because they are less familiar, partly because of their importance to the plot—being discussed more fully than the rest. Chapter 5 deals with Virgil's use of form and some related theoretical problems. Chapter 6 returns to the text for a closer examination of the verbal fabric than was appropriate earlier.

To keep a big book within bounds I have had to be ruthless about footnotes. Those that remain mostly point to a more detailed treatment of things dealt with summarily, or warn the reader of an unconventional opinion. For the same reason I have given line-by-line translations only where I felt this helped in bringing out a point. Elsewhere (except in Chapter 6, which is of interest chiefly to those who have at any rate some Latin and where the quotations are mostly brief) Latin quotations are preceded by a paraphrase, more or less full,

Preface

in the text. Very serviceable translations of the *Aeneid* are available—such as the prose translation by W. F. Jackson Knight, which is both clear and accurate, if somewhat over-explicit, or the verse translations by F. O. Copley and C. Day Lewis.

A little reluctantly I have abandoned the idea of a critical bibliography. Some of the well-known books on the *Aeneid* will be found in the list of Abbreviations, while on many points it seemed sufficient to refer the reader to the admirable commentaries on Books 2 to 5 of R. G. Austin and R. D. Williams. Those who wish to take the matter further will be well served by Professor Jacques Perret's eminently sane and forthright critical bibliography in his *Virgile: l'homme et l'œuvre* (Paris, Boivin & Cie, 1952), pp. 168–88. A survey by Mr R. D. Williams of more recent important work on Virgil and of modern attitudes to his poetry is to be published, I understand, as a supplement to *Greece and Rome* about the same time as this book. Teachers in the United States will be familiar, of course, with the bibliographies by Professor G. E. Duckworth in *Vergilius* and *Classical Weekly*, and British teachers with the bibliography prepared for the Joint Association of Classical Teachers by Professor R. G. Austin.

I began writing this book in Melbourne in 1962 while preparing a special course of lectures for advanced students, which later formed the basis for Chapter 4. Chapter 1 was given as the annual lecture in Classics at King's College, London, and, in an Italian version, at the Istituto di filologia classica e medievale in Genoa in 1964; a first draft of Chapter 2 was delivered in lecture form at the universities of Reading and Liverpool in the same year. Parts of Chapters 4 to 6 have appeared in *Aumla, Greece and Rome* and *Maia*. When I returned to Melbourne at the end of 1964, the book had taken shape. During 1965–66 it was largely rewritten in Melbourne and in Dunedin.

My warm thanks are due to the many friends in many countries who have so freely put me in their debt. It would be invidious to single out the one or two who have struggled through the whole, and unfair to incriminate those who have not seen more than disconnected fragments.

K. Q.

Dunedin, Easter 1967.

Abbreviations

WORKS REFERRED TO BY AUTHOR ONLY

Austin
Conington
Conway
Mackail
Maguinness
Norden
Williams

The Commentaries by R. S. Conway on *Aeneid* 1 (1935), by R. G. Austin on *Aeneid* 2 (1964) and 4 (1955), by R. D. Williams on *Aeneid* 3 (1962) and 5 (1960), by Eduard Norden on *Aeneid* 6 (3rd edn 1927), by W. S. Maguinness on *Aeneid* 12 (1953), by J. W. Mackail on the complete poem (1930) and by J. Conington on the complete works of Virgil, vol. 1 (4th edn 1881), vol. 2 (4th edn 1884), vol. 3 (3rd edn 1883).

Bardon Henry Bardon, *La littérature latine inconnue* (1952–6).
Boyancé Pierre Boyancé, *La religion de Virgile* (1963).
Büchner Karl Büchner, article on Virgil in Pauly-Wissowa, *Real-Encyclopädie der classischen Altertumswissenschaft*; also published separately (1955).
Heinze Richard Heinze, *Virgils Epische Technik* (3rd edn 1914).
Otis Brooks Otis, *Virgil: a Study in Civilized Poetry* (1963).
Perret Jacques Perret, *Virgile: l'homme et l'œuvre* (1952).
Pöschl Viktor Pöschl, *Die Dichtkunst Virgils* (1950), quoted where possible from the English translation, *The Art of Vergil* (1962).

OTHER ABBREVIATIONS

AJA *American Journal of Archaeology*
AJPh *American Journal of Philology*
CQ *Classical Quarterly*
CR *Classical Review*

Abbreviations

GR	Greece and Rome
HStCPh	Harvard Studies in Classical Philology
LEC	Les études classiques
Mn	Mnemosyne
OCD	Oxford Classical Dictionary
REL	Revue des études latines
TAPhA	Transactions of The American Philological Association

The ancient lives of Virgil are quoted from Augusto Rostagni, *Svetonio* De Poetis *e biografi minori* (1944).

The fragments of Ennius are quoted from F. H. Warmington, *Fragments of Old Latin*, vol. 1 (1935), other fragments from W. Morel, *Fragmenta Poetarum Latinorum* (2nd edn 1927).

1

The Heroic Impulse

Like all the great classics of European literature, Virgil's *Aeneid* confronts the modern reader with a problem. The major works of contemporary literature are a different case. For a year or so, a decade, a generation perhaps, the critical debate that greeted their appearance produces a feeling of familiarity, some understanding of what the writer has tried to do and how far he has succeeded; even when the work is one about which there is no agreement, the reader feels at any rate aware of the issues involved; contemporary works, moreover, do not require that effort of the historical imagination on which a just appreciation of the great European classics depends; nor do they make the same demands on the reader's literary and linguistic knowledge. The masterpieces of the past tend to be hard to understand, or easy to misunderstand. What is worse, perhaps, than their strangeness or their difficulty is that there are so many of them. That kind of easy intimacy which is still possible with the major works of European music is out of the question in literature. A hundred years ago such an intimacy was still a common accomplishment. The concept of a classic in a large measure presupposes it. Our problem is: what substitute is there for this intimacy, and how may we acquire it?

Till quite recently Virgil occupied a privileged position. So long as he remained alive on the lips of men, a general understanding of the nature and quality of his poetry remained widespread among people who regarded literature as important. His greatest poem, the *Aeneid*, enjoys still a partial exemption from the fate that has overtaken many masterpieces. The number of people who possess a nodding acquaintance with the *Aeneid* is considerable. Many of course have read the poem in translation; but many, too, have worked their way through a portion of the original text; and quite a few still read the whole of the poem in Latin. Understanding and appreciation of the poem, however, have seriously deteriorated. We are near the point where the poem is read for its past reputation. The next stage is oblivion.

It is possible to find out a very great deal indeed about the *Aeneid*, as a visit to any moderately well-equipped reference library will demonstrate. An immense amount continues to be written. But most who write about the poem assume the intimacy that few readers now possess. Or else their interest is so highly specialized that the general understanding of this long and difficult poem which the reader needs if he is to read it as poetry is dispensed with. Into the critical vacuum easily flow ideas that the reader has picked up from odd places. Often they are ideas which are out of date, in the sense that they reflect tastes and prejudices we no longer share, the sensibility of an age whose judgments about literature are not ours. Or they may be the *obiter dicta* of learned men, worth attention because they are prompted by informed intuitions, but not necessarily carrying weight or enlightening, for the common reader may know better than the scholar what poetry is and how it works.

This book is for readers who like Virgil, or feel they are on the verge of liking him—or might like him if they knew something about him. It is also for readers who think they dislike or despise Virgil, but want to give him another chance. Its purpose is not to intrude in a growing friendship between poet and reader, still less to offer the reader a substitute for the *Aeneid*. But if these readers are to get far they need help —not before reading the poem, or when they've finished reading it, but time and again during the process of coming to understand the *Aeneid* and making it something they possess and value.

Let us assume the nodding acquaintance. We are beyond the point where our pleasure is a matter of lines, phrases, memorable scenes, brilliant images, striking characters. We feel we want to fit the bits of the poem together and make out of them something coherent. The way the bits begin to hang together is naturally something that depends on the particular reader. But before long the poet should take over from the reader. We should begin to see what he is driving at; or, to put it another way, the poem should begin to assert itself: we should start to see it as a structure, one whose shape we can grasp, or in which we see themes recurring.

The Heroic Impulse

The object of the remainder of this chapter is to explore one such recurrent theme. I believe it is the most important theme in the poem, but my intention isn't to foist an interpretation of the poem prematurely upon the reader. I only want to get him interested in the idea that Virgil has something to say.

Our starting point is in Book 2—the well-known episode of the death of King Priam (2.506–58). The dramatic setting is the great feast arranged by Queen Dido in honour of the famous and handsome adventurer who has come to her shores. Against a background of royal splendour (described at the end of the previous book) Aeneas tells the tale of the night six years before when Troy fell to the Greek invader. His story reaches its climax as Neoptolemus, the son of Achilles, bursts into the palace of King Priam accompanied by Agamemnon and Menelaus (2.499–502):

> uidi ipse furentem
> caede Neoptolemum geminosque in limine Atridas,
> uidi Hecubam centumque nurus Priamumque per aras
> sanguine foedantem quos ipse sacrauerat ignis.

> *I saw Neoptolemus myself*
> *murder-mad in the doorway, the Atrid brothers with him.*
> *I saw Hecuba, the hundred princesses, Priam by the altar,*
> *defiling with his blood the fire that he had consecrated.*

The exile pauses to ask the queen (506):

> forsitan et Priami fuerint quae fata requiras?

> *You ask perhaps how Priam met his destined end?*

His question marks the end of the tight-lipped recital of destruction which began 250 lines earlier. Aeneas now takes his hearers back over the events of the night through Priam's eyes (507–8):

> urbis uti captae casum conuulsaque uidit
> limina tectorum et medium in penetralibus hostem....

> *When he saw the captured city's fall, the palace-gate*
> *hacked down, the enemy within the central shrine....*

First his city taken, then his palace overrun, then the enemy within the inner sanctuary itself—we can feel how the march of events creates the emotional pressure that spills over in Priam's sudden impulse to fight back, to die a soldier's death (509-11):

> arma diu senior desueta trementibus aeuo
> circumdat nequiquam umeris et inutile ferrum
> cingitur, ac densos fertur moriturus in hostis.

> *Upon shoulders age-enfeebled the old man sets*
> *unavailing armour long unused, straps on futile*
> *steel, makes for the invading horde, there to die.*

His wife Hecuba tries to restrain him, but at that moment Neoptolemus appears, in pursuit of one of Priam's sons, Polites, whom he has already wounded. Polites falls dead at Priam's feet. The old man hurls his spear at Neoptolemus in a pathetic gesture of defiance (544-6):

> sic fatus senior telumque imbelle sine ictu
> coniecit, rauco quod protinus aere repulsum,
> et summo clipei nequiquam umbone pependit.

> *With these words the older man cast his harmless spear, no*
> *force behind it. Checked quickly with a brassy clang,*
> *it hung unavailing, lodged in the shield's centre.*

Neoptolemus deals with the father as ruthlessly as he had dealt with the son (550-3):

> altaria ad ipsa trementem
> traxit et in multo lapsantem sanguine nati,
> implicuitque comam laeua, dextraque coruscum
> extulit ac lateri capulo tenus abdidit ensem.

> *he dragged shaking Priam, his feet*
> *slithering in his own son's blood, up to the altar;*
> *twined left hand in his hair; with right, in a flash of steel,*
> *drew and hilt-deep in Priam's ribs plunged his sword.*

The death of Priam is one of the great show-pieces in Virgil's poem.[1] Though old age debars the king from giving his life for Troy in the front rank of the city's defenders, he does his feeble best to live up to the heroic ideal, familiar throughout antiquity. Tyrtaeus' seventh-

[1] For a full analysis of the episode see my *Latin Explorations* (1963) 229-38.

The Heroic Impulse

century formulation of it comes from a poem filled with Homeric echoes, but he intends it as a statement of the Spartan soldier's code:

τεθνάμεναι γὰρ καλὸν ἐνὶ προμάχοισι πεσόντα
ἄνδρ' ἀγαθὸν περὶ ᾗ πατρίδι μαρνάμενον.

Death in the front line of fighters is a noble thing when a brave man falls fighting for his country.

Only a cynical reader, surely, would point out that Priam behaves rather foolishly; that both his first impulse (to spring to the defence of a city he cannot hope to save) and his second impulse (to strike down an assailant he cannot hope to harm) are more a caricature of the hero's death than the real thing; can ensure only that Priam will die sooner, and more piteously, than he might have done if a rational assessment of his powers had stayed his hand, or if he had listened instead to Hecuba.

Tragedy, of course, is something that does not happen to ordinary people. It is easy to feel an element of irony in Virgil's narrative of the death of King Priam, as in his narrative of the death of Queen Dido in Book 4—a recognition that tragic magnanimity exposes noble man or noble woman to anguishes or disasters from which the more lowly are protected by common sense. To those who argue that the sublime folly of Dido is something we need no more than sense, while the uselessness of each of Priam's heroic gestures is stressed explicitly by Virgil (510 and 546: *nequiquam*; 510: *inutile*; 544: *imbelle, sine ictu*; etc.), we can answer that Priam's death is symbolic as well as tragically pathetic. Certainly the episode is no idly purple passage: the uselessness of Priam's resistance symbolizes the uselessness of Troy's resistance, finally revealed to Aeneas by his divine mother (588–633) when she banishes the mist that dims merely human sight and allows him to see the gods standing over Troy, engaged on its destruction. Priam's death gives dramatic order to the fighting of that night, which advances through the city to the palace and through the palace to its king. The death of the king is the pitiful embodiment of the city's overthrow; Priam's headless corpse lying on the beach the symbol of a city that has lost its gods. The horror of Priam's death stresses the impious brutality of the Greek army and its young champion Neoptolemus—a true son of his father, as Virgil drily observes, implying an assessment of Achilles that is intended to challenge the traditional image of Homer's hero (491–5):

> instat ui patria Pyrrhus: nec claustra nec ipsi
> custodes sufferre ualent; labat ariete crebro
> ianua, et emoti procumbunt cardine postes.
> fit uia ui; rumpunt aditus primosque trucidant
> immissi Danai et late loca milite complent.

*Pyrrhus fought forward like his father of old: bolts, guards
even, are powerless to check him; ceaselessly battered,
the door totters and the uprights give, torn from their sockets.
Nothing resists brute force; bursting inside, the Greeks
butcher the first rank of defenders, pack palace with soldiers.*

These are all facets of the Priam episode, planned dimensions of an important unit in Virgil's complex poetic structure. But there is, I think, a further aspect, no less planned than the others; a quality of the episode that neither supplants nor destroys its other qualities, even if it makes us question the assumption of most critics, that Priam's heroic gesture is designed to elicit our approval—an approval mixed of course with pity, but uncontaminated by any kind of condemnation.

Aren't we in short intended, however gently, however compassionately, to censure Priam? I do not mean merely that Virgil is good enough to want us, though we pity Priam, to understand what drives him to his death, while not wholly identifying ourselves with him. The reaction expected seems a more precise reaction: a clearly formulated, detached judgment that Priam's heroic gesture is not merely futile because he lacks the strength to make it effective, not merely inadequate, but irrelevant—irrelevant to the point of being wrong, the conditioned response of one trained to meet every emergency by an act of reckless bravery, unable to make any other response, unable to cope with situations that cannot be dealt with by fighting it out, sure it is *always* nobler to take up arms against a sea of troubles, unaware one might, by *enduring*, at any rate do less harm.

Naturally, we must not expect Virgil to put it quite like that, in as many words. He leaves it to us to formulate, if we choose, the moral implications of his narrative; his form does not deal in express moral judgments. He expects of us what any poet expects of his readers. It is a matter of adjusting our reactions to the text till we feel they are the reactions the poet's fiction prompts, not our personal reactions, which may be irrelevant; or reactions the poet anticipates and wishes perhaps to challenge by his fiction.

We should notice that, if Virgil makes Priam die a soldier's death, he apparently did not cast Hecuba in the same heroic mould. Her

The Heroic Impulse

behaviour does nothing to suggest the old story, recounted with approval by both Greeks and Romans, of the Spartan woman who bade her menfolk return from battle either *with* their shields (that is victorious, or at any rate without throwing them away in flight like cowards) or *on* them (that is dead).[1] Hecuba tries to restrain Priam from buckling his armour round his aged shoulders. She leads him back from his first impulse to join the fighting to the altar where she and her daughters are huddled like doves in refuge from the storm. When Neoptolemus comes, the situation passes from her control.

But wait a moment, you say. We can hardly expect Virgil to show Hecuba encouraging poor old Priam to rush off and get himself killed. Actually, if this were Statius, or Seneca, you could imagine just that happening. And, after all, why not? Virgil's story, admittedly, is less grotesquely rhetorical than Statius, or Seneca. But if Priam and Dido are painted larger than life, why not Hecuba, too? Isn't Virgil's very human Hecuba perhaps out of place?

We misunderstand Virgil if we think so. Priam and Dido are not less *human* than Hecuba. They ring true as people. They are simply more *heroic*, more the stuff that tragic heroes are made of. We should give Virgil the credit for perceiving the challenge his un-sublime Hecuba implies to his sublime Priam and ask ourselves whether her function is not to prompt a comment on Priam's heroic impulse.

The conclusion is hard to avoid when we observe that Virgil makes Hecuba talk as though it were not pity for Priam's age alone that moved her. Her opening words (519-22):

> 'quae mens tam dira, miserrime coniunx,
> impulit his cingi telis? aut quo ruis?' inquit.
> 'non tali auxilio nec defensoribus istis
> tempus eget.'

> *'What sorry purpose, my most unhappy husband,*
> *has made you arm yourself thus? Where so fast?' she said.*
> *'For such aid, for protectors of your sort*
> *there's no need now.'*

sound for a moment as though she meant that *old* men like Priam are not needed; but when she goes on (522):

> 'non, si ipse meus nunc adforet Hector'

> *'no! not even if my son Hector himself were here'*

[1] Plutarch, *Lacaenarum apophthegmata*, 16 (*Mor.* 241 F).

The Heroic Impulse

it is clear that by 'protectors of your sort' (*defensoribus istis*) Hecuba must mean *all* who would spring to fight a useless fight.

This is not to say that Hecuba is put wholly in the right and Priam wholly condemned. Virgil is too good for that. He is rarely completely on the side of any character in his poem and completely against the character opposing him. And here he makes it clear (by using of Hecuba in 515 the same word, *nequiquam*, that he used of Priam in 510 and 546) that Hecuba's trust in the gods to save them is as misplaced (for the gods protect Troy no longer) as Priam's conviction that the impulse to meet force of arms with arms is so absolutely right that the attempt must be made even when it must fail.

But lest we are troubled still by Priam's age and the memory of Homer's Priam and his pathetic reference to the shame of an old man killed in battle (*Il.* 22.71–6)—and perhaps, too, by the sneaking thought that Virgil has staked more on the sentimental appeal of a piece of sublimely useless heroism than on bringing us to scrutinize the ideals that heroism implies—let us turn to an episode where age does not come into it. Book 12 of the *Aeneid* opens with Turnus suddenly hesitant no longer to meet Aeneas in single combat. The decision taken, Virgil shows him all impatience, unreasonably impatient, for the fight. He wants to meet Aeneas at once; persuaded it is too late to fight that day, he takes himself off for an inspection of his equipment that quickly degenerates into a mock duel (12.81–106).[1] Before that, in an angry, unjust speech, he hurls back at his own men the reproaches he sensed in their eyes as long as he hesitated to meet Aeneas (11–17):

> 'nulla mora in Turno; nihil est quod dicta retractent
> ignaui Aeneadae, nec quae pepigere recusent.
> congredior. fer sacra, pater, et concipe foedus.
> aut hac Dardanium dextra sub Tartara mittam
> desertorem Asiae, sedeant spectentque Latini,
> et solus ferro crimen commune refellam,
> aut habeat uictos, cedat Lauinia coniunx.'

> *'There's no delay in Turnus, no cause for Trojan cowards*
> *to bandy words anew, to take back their pledged word.*
> *I go to meet him. Father, bring the holy things, fix the truce.*
> *Either with this right hand I shall send the Dardan to his*
> *death, this Asian runaway (let the Latins sit and look!)*
> *and sword in hand alone refute the common guilt,*
> *or he can have a beaten people, and Lavinia for his wife.'*

[1] For a discussion of these episodes see Chapter 4.

The Heroic Impulse

The old king, Latinus, and the king's wife, Amata, try hard to dissuade the fiery young prince. Latinus even takes on himself, in a plain distortion of the narrative of Book 7, the whole responsibility for the war. Why? Well, a full answer is not easily given; Virgil's situations are seldom simple. But one wrong answer can surely be rejected. We can scarcely suppose that Virgil, for the sake of rhetorical effect, threw to the winds the image he had built up of Latinus in Book 7 as the helpless victim of war hysteria. We must be meant to realize that Latinus is distorting the facts. Why he does so is clear enough: he regards Turnus as a wilful youngster whom he must humour, so that he can be talked out of a rash impulse; not as a hero who has made a courageous decision that should be upheld and commended.

I imagine an enlightened interpreter of Virgil, if asked to comment on the roles of Turnus, Amata and Latinus in this opening episode of Book 12, might say something like this: 'Yes, Virgil *has* opposed the heroic and the unheroic, the sublime and the common-sense, attitudes to life, just as Homer does when he makes Priam warn Hector against meeting Achilles in single combat in *Iliad* 22. It is the heroic attitude, of course, that Virgil approves of and wants us to approve of; though he wants us to feel for Amata and Latinus, too, while recognizing that they are weak, incapable of the heroic ideal.'

But does he? Virgil's sympathy for the frail and timorous is undoubted. Yet there are situations—the Priam episode and the opening scene of Book 12 among them—where I think we are meant to feel that the heroic is not necessarily the nobler ideal; that it is even the *shallower* of the two. In Homer the situation is different; it is as easy to admire Hector as to pity Priam—there is something worth fighting for. Turnus acts on an angry impulse to continue, at the risk of his life, a war that no one now wants except himself, for peace on fair terms is available. Contrast the way Pallas faces Turnus (10.445–63)—not on blind impulse, but after a clear reckoning of the outcome: Pallas knows the odds are against him, but he thinks he has a chance. Is that not more like bravery?

Plainly, when we reflect upon it, the heroic ideal is not so much a philosophy of life as a pattern of behaviour which equips the soldier well for most emergencies, but equips him rather ill for others—it is not in fact so much an ideal at all as a conditioned reflex. Is it not likely that this had become plain to Virgil, too, as a result of the decades of bloodshed and civil strife he lived through before he began his poem?

On the whole in war the heroic impulse, the urge to meet any emergency, any challenge, with unreflecting personal bravery, is obviously a good thing. Virgil would be a cheap cynic and a poor poet if his purpose were to deride one of the qualities which had made Rome great. Instead he describes with evident approval scores of brave men, Italians as well as Trojans, who die heroically. Admittedly, heroism alone brings small reward: in Virgil's Valhalla, those who fell in war (6.481: *bello caduci*), those even who distinguished themselves in war (6.478: *bello clari*), are numbered among the unhappy shades who roam through the ghastly gloom (6.462: *loca senta situ*) of the Plains of Grief; merely to have died a hero's death does not ensure admission to the Elysian fields. But cowards get short shrift from Virgil in his battle scenes. The unthinking bravery of Helenor, the ignoble bastard who dies a hero's death—upon which the simile provides an implicit comment (9.551–5):

> ut fera, quae densa uenantum saepta corona
> contra tela furit seseque haud nescia morti
> inicit et saltu supra uenabula fertur,
> haud aliter iuuenis medios moriturus in hostis
> inruit et qua tela uidet densissima tendit.

> *Like an animal that faces frenzied the close-packed armed band*
> *of hunters who hem it in, then hurls itself deliberately to*
> *death in a leap that brings it down on their spears,*
> *so the warrior, wanting death, throws himself at the thick*
> *of the enemy, heading where he sees their missiles massed tightest.*

is favourably contrasted with the prudent self-thought of Lycus, who runs away and gets killed just the same—an illustration of Horace's famous precept (*Odes* 3.2.13 f.):

> dulce et decorum est pro patria mori:
> mors et fugacem persequitur uirum.

Nor can we doubt that we are meant to despise the shifty Arruns of Book 11 who shoots down Camilla from cover, instead of meeting her in open fight—though Arruns is a patriotic coward, a vividly portrayed, bizarre, almost pathetic character, one of a fanatical sect of fire-walking priests; for Arruns himself, like Aeneas in the Helen episode, recognizes there is no glory in what he does (11.791–2: *mihi cetera laudem facta ferent*).

Yet, however much in the thick of the fight we admire the hero and condemn the coward, there are situations where the heroic impulse appears in a less favourable light. While the battle rages, there is seldom time for an ideal higher than the conviction that it is better to fight than run away. It is only when there is scope for initiative that moral responsibility and moral judgment become significant. Then, as we today know from experience, the trained soldier's mind, the trained general's even, does not always spring to the wisest decision. We may be sure, given the times in which he lived, that Virgil knew that, too; though we may be surprised to discover Virgil, in a heroic poem, stressing this deficiency in the hero's make-up.

Sometimes the heroic impulse leads to an action that is sublimely brave, as when Lausus (10.789–832) intervenes in the duel between Mezentius and Aeneas and saves the life of his father, a man all men hated, by throwing away his own. Sometimes the act of heroism is sublimely trivial, as when Phegeus (12.371–82) plants himself in the path of Turnus' chariot and grabs the reins as he hurtles past. As he careers all over the battlefield in his chariot, mowing down his opponents, Turnus is having a glorious time, without much risk, really, to his own life. The display of heroics is just too much for Phegeus (371):

> non tulit instantem Phegeus animisque frementem.

To put an end to it, he throws his own life away in a vain, contemptuous gesture of defiance.

But extreme cases are less instructive than those where judgment is not straightforward. Let us turn our attention to episodes where we can feel that the poet wishes us to perceive behind the act of self-sacrifice something more than Phegeus' empty gesture of defiance—something less exempt from the dictates of common sense that Lausus, understandably and commendably, leaves unheeded.

In *Aeneid* 2 one of the handful of companions who join Aeneas in the night of fighting that leads him to the royal palace is Coroebus, a young man who had come only a few days before to Troy and who was madly in love with the most tragic of Priam's daughters, Cassandra (342–3):

> illis ad Troiam forte diebus
> uenerat insano Cassandrae incensus amore.

Not long after he and the others have joined forces with Aeneas in the night battle, they come upon Cassandra, her hair wildly flying, as she is dragged from the temple of Minerva where she had sought refuge,

The Heroic Impulse

'turning burning eyes in vain to heaven for her soft hands were already bound' (405-6):

> ad caelum tendens ardentia lumina frustra,
> lumina, nam teneras arcebant uincula palmas.

The sight was more than Coroebus could stand (*non tulit*—the phrase Virgil uses of Phegeus), and on a mad impulse he plunged to his death among the Greeks who surround her (407-8):

> non tulit hanc speciem furiata mente Coroebus
> et sese medium iniecit periturus in agmen.[1]

And within moments he lies dead beside the altar where his bride had sought sanctuary in vain (424-6).

All readers of Virgil recall with pleasure the tale of Nisus and Euryalus in *Aeneid* 9, a story as charming and pathetic as it is at other moments ruthless and savage. Nisus is twice represented as acting on impulse, at the beginning and again at the disastrous conclusion of the adventure. The tale begins with the two on guard together in the Trojan camp. Nisus feels the urge to perform some spectacular act that will bring him glory—or at any rate free him from the boredom of routine (184-7):

> Nisus ait: 'dine hunc ardorem mentibus addunt,
> Euryale, an sua cuique deus fit dira cupido?
> aut pugnam aut aliquid iamdudum inuadere magnum
> mens agitat mihi, nec placida contenta quiete est.'
>
> *Nisus spoke: 'Is it the gods set men's mind on fire,*
> *Euryalus, or do we make gods our own imperious desires?*
> *To fight, to undertake some great deed, this is the thought*
> *that stirs in my mind impatient of idleness and calm.'*

---

[1] The force of *periturus* is something like 'wanting to die'. Strictly, the future participle has a purely temporal force—'about to die', as in the well-known *morituri te salutant*. But Virgil often uses it with something approximating to a final force, e.g., 5.107-8:
> laeto complerant litora coetu
> uisuri Aeneadas,

i.e., 'intending to see', or 'wanting to see'. This ambiguity inherent in the form is exploited in several of the 11 occurrences of the form *moriturus* in the poem: cf. its use of Priam in 2.511 (he does not die till later); of Dido in 4.308, 415, 519, 604; of Nisus in 9.400; of Helenor in 9.554; in 10.811 Aeneas says to Lausus '*quo moriture ruis?*'; in 10.881 Mezentius says to Aeneas '*uenio moriturus*'; cf. also Tarchon, 11.741 (he does not die), and Amata, 12.55.

The Heroic Impulse

We learn (192–3) that there has been a call for volunteers to make their way by night through the enemy lines to warn Aeneas, who is with King Evander, that the Trojan camp has been besieged. Nisus and Euryalus offer to go. They depart, the eager hopes of the Trojan leaders pinned on the success of their venture. It fails. A party of Italian cavalry on a night patrol surprises them, and Euryalus is captured. As he is about to be killed, Nisus, who had remained undetected and could have got away, cannot bear to see his friend killed before his eyes and do nothing. He shouts out an appeal to the Italians to kill him instead (427); but he is too late even to delay the deathblow. So, in a way that closely resembles the Coroebus-Cassandra episode—except that more is at stake—Nisus hurls himself on the group, strikes down with his sword the Italian commander, who had ordered the death of Euryalus, and then collapses in the peace of death on the body of his friend (438–45).

We can see each time the same psychological mechanism spring into action. And I think we may be sure that Virgil, though he could hardly have put it like that, means us to make some such appraisal of these episodes and those like them. Circumstances, however, alter cases, and I think Virgil intends to prompt this thought, too. For if Coroebus' life was his to give freely—one more life lost in a night when so many died—Nisus had a responsibility to his commander and to all his friends still alive but in danger: he should have restrained his impulse to die uselessly. Similarly, Turnus in Book 9 disregards the sensible course of action. He is presented with a chance to end the war, as Virgil explicitly comments (9.759: *ultimus ille dies bello gentique fuisset*). He managed to get inside the Trojan camp before the Trojans got the gates shut again after an ill-considered sortie; all he has to do is to open the gates and let the Italians into the Trojan camp, for the Trojans fell back at the sight of their terrible opponent. Instead, he lets himself be distracted by a mad impulse to slaughter all before him (9.760–1):

> sed furor ardentem caedisque insana cupido
> egit in aduersos.

Turnus is like that. He lets his chance slip again in Book 11 (11.896–902): at the news of Camilla's death he throws away an opportunity to catch the Trojans in an ambush and inflict a decisive defeat, in order to rush back to the scene of her death, thus setting in train the chain of events that ends with his own fated death.

The Heroic Impulse

Let us postpone the question of moral responsibility, and consider instead the motivation of the heroic impulse. Two elements keep recurring in these scenes where the emotions involved are more complex than in Lausus' act of pure heroism, or in Phegeus' act of pure bravado. The first is something that we may call, I suppose, the death-wish. The second is something less sentimentally or romantically attractive, the simple desire to kill. Either may be associated with what we should call a sense of guilt—an emotion which we might hesitate to identify, because it sounds too modern, if Virgil had not pointed to it himself in the words he puts on Nisus' lips (9.427–9):

> 'me, me, adsum qui feci, in me conuertite ferrum,
> o Rutuli! mea fraus omnis, nihil iste nec ausus
> nec potuit; caelum hoc et conscia sidera testor.'

'No, me, I did it! Here, turn your steel on me!
Rutilians! I am the offender, he planned nothing,
did nothing. Heaven is my witness and the stars that know.'

The *death-wish* we find in its simplest form in *Aeneid* 10 when Mezentius learns that his son Lausus has given his life for his father. It is the humiliation, more than the grief, that Mezentius cannot bear (846–8):

> 'tantane me tenuit uiuendi, nate, uoluptas,
> ut pro me hostili paterer succedere dextrae,
> quem genui?'

> *'Did such love, lad, for living hold me fast*
> *that in my stead I let face a foe's right hand the son*
> *that I begot?'*

Though wounded, he rushes out to meet Aeneas again in a hopeless encounter (870–1):

> sic cursum in medios rapidus dedit. aestuat ingens
> uno in corde pudor mixtoque insania luctu.

> *Whereat he headed headlong into their midst. A terrible*
> *shame rages in his heart, mixed with a mad confused grief.*[1]

But the feeling that it is better to die than survive occurs in many forms. We have it in Turnus' statement of the soldier's ideal in his speech in the Council of War (11.416–18):

---

[1] These words occur again at 12.666–7 of Turnus, when he is reproached by Saces.

> 'ille mihi ante alios fortunatusque laborum
> egregiusque animi, qui, ne quid tale uideret,
> procubuit moriens et humum semel ore momordit.'

> *'To him, I hold, fate allots the happiest role of all,*
> *his is the stoutest heart, who, to avoid such a sight,*
> *fell in battle, bit the dust, ended it all.'*

The same feeling overtakes Aeneas at the moment of his first appearance in the poem when all hope of reaching Italy seems once again thrust aside by the onset of a terrible storm (1.94–101). It strikes Aeneas again in Book 5, at what seems to him a more personal crisis, when the women revolt and set the ships on fire, endangering the whole expedition on the eve of the last stretch of their journey. Baring his shoulders as if to stand defenceless before his god, Aeneas beseeches Jupiter to spare the fleet, or else to strike him dead if his decision to continue the voyage to Italy is at fault. Other examples are Andromache (3.321–4) and the mother of Euryalus (9.493–7). The clearest case of all, of course, is Dido in Book 4. Sometimes the heroic impulse is frustrated of any opportunity for action. At others a character sees some recompense in death—Turnus, for example, when, his decision to fight Aeneas taken, he says to Latinus (12.48–9):

> 'quam pro me curam geris, hanc precor, optime, pro me
> deponas letumque sinas pro laude pacisci.'

> *'Lay aside, good sir, I pray, your care for me;*
> *let me take death as the price I pay for glory!'*

The feeling is more clear-cut later in the same book, when Turnus learns, after the chariot episode and his long respite from the realities of the duel, that his failure to meet Aeneas has resulted in the suicide of Queen Amata. In this crisis Virgil grants Turnus a moving insight into his own predicament. He knows he must fight Aeneas, he senses he cannot win, but he wants to commit one last mad gesture of heroism (12.678–80):

> 'stat conferre manum Aeneae, stat quidquid acerbi est
> morte pati, neque me indecorem, germana, uidebis
> amplius. hunc, oro, sine me furere ante furorem.'

> *'It's settled I face Aeneas, settled I endure whatever's harsh*
> *in death; you'll not see me disgrace you, sister,*
> *longer. Grant me, I entreat, this last act of madness.'*

The Heroic Impulse

It is interesting that Virgil lets both Mezentius and Turnus outlive the death-wish. Mezentius is swept back into battle on the maelstrom of the heroic impulse, but does not die, as he hoped, in the hot cut-and-thrust of combat. Instead his horse falls under him, he is thrown to the ground at Aeneas' mercy. As he waits for the death-blow, blind emotion subsides, rational thought regains control (10.899: *mentemque recepit*) and Mezentius dies a death more admirable, however grudging our admiration, than the typical hero's death, in icy, contemptuous acceptance of the calculated risks of war. The external circumstances of Turnus' death are similar. Again there is a delay: the truce arranged for the duel is broken. Again we feel the impetus of the heroic impulse falter, the need for a fresh decision to face death when death is at hand. And we should not fail to note that the resolution to back up a decision taken on impulse comes less readily to Turnus than it did to Mezentius.[1]

The *desire to kill* is a necessary component of the hero. But, while it must therefore normally win from us something approaching approval, it can also take an ugly twist. Nisus feels, we may suppose, he must kill someone, even if nothing is achieved thereby, even if the consequences to his side may be disastrous. But in rushing to kill he rushes to certain death, and we can feel that he regards death as a form of expiation. His useless, pathetic suicide perhaps expiates also an earlier stage in their adventure when Euryalus joined Nisus in indiscriminate slaughter of the sleeping Rutuli and the desire to kill got out of hand (9.342–4):

> nec minor Euryali caedes; incensus et ipse
> perfurit ac multam in medio sine nomine plebem
> ... subit. ...

> *Euryalus no less freely dealt out death. Alike aflame*
> *in drawn-out frenzy to the undistinguished rank and file*
> *... he addressed himself. ...*

Their own death is the price they pay for this carnage—it is the glint of moonlight on a looted helmet that betrays them to the Italian cavalry patrol.

Or take the long fugue of Turnus in Book 12. The exultant, random slaughter is no more pretty, no less psychologically revealing. When the truce is broken and the pitched battle which ensues postpones for Turnus the need to act out his decision to face Aeneas in single combat,

---

[1] See the discussion of the death-scene in Chapter 4.

Turnus, whom we saw a little earlier pale and silent (219–21), calls for the horses (326) in whose company he had sought comfort the night before (81–6); now he races back and forth in his chariot taking life in the sheer delight of combat. A situation where Turnus feels at home has been substituted for one he decided on impulse to face and had then awaited with apprehension, when the exhilaration of impulsive decision had evaporated.

But it is to the hero of the poem, to Aeneas, that Virgil ascribes the urge to kill in its ugliest form. We can hardly doubt it is done deliberately; that Virgil's intention is to show Aeneas, despite his struggle for *pietas*, a soldier still by training and liable to lapse into the conditioned reflexes of that training.

In Book 2 Aeneas is the typical soldier, who cannot resist a battle (337–8):

> in flammas et in arma feror, quo tristis Erinys,
> quo fremitus uocat et sublatus ad aethera clamor.

I rush to the fire and the fighting, answering the call of grim revenge, the din of battle and the shouts raised skyward.

He reacts to all crises in the same way. When his father refuses to leave Troy, Aeneas' first instinct, despite all that he has been told by Hector and Venus, is to rejoin the battle and die fighting (655):

> rursus in arma feror mortemque miserrimus opto.

When he realizes Creusa is no longer with them, his reaction is the same (747–51). Only by Book 12 has he learned to temper courage with reason, and he joins in the fighting after the truce is broken with reluctance.

If the urge to kill is made understandable each time it comes to Aeneas, it is sometimes hard to forgive. More than once the situation is impregnated with a bitter irony. Brutal as the killing of Priam is, it is an act of brutality the like of which Aeneas himself comes close to committing when, with Priam's body by the altar of his gods still before his eyes, he catches sight of Helen and raises his hand to strike down the woman who seems to him, in one of those stark simplifications that passion imposes, the cause of all that has happened that night. He feels the blaze of anger, the impulse to an act of revenge that is itself, he acknowledges it, a crime (576: *sceleratas sumere poenas*)— Helen, like Cassandra, had sought sanctuary in a holy place; if Aeneas kills her, he must defile the altar of the gods with an act even more openly sinful than the killing of Priam which he has just witnessed. His mother Venus holds him back in time. It is an episode that so far strained the sensibility of his contemporaries that Virgil, or his executors, hesitated, it appears, to let it stand.[1]

Rather worse is the impulse that comes to Aeneas when the young prince Pallas, who had been sent to fight under Aeneas' protection by his father Evander, is killed—in fair fight and after Pallas himself has shown little mercy for those he kills (see, for example, 10.385-96). It is Aeneas' one great battle-scene (apart from the duel in Book 12), his *aristeia*, but it is dominated by a sense of guilt and a lust for revenge which lead him even to contemplate offering eight young men whom he has taken prisoner as a living sacrifice to the dead Pallas. Virgil makes no attempt to analyse his character's psychological state in abstract terms (such as *ira, dolor, furor*, etc.). Instead he gives us the picture that dominates Aeneas' thoughts—or rather his eyes (10.515-17):

> Pallas, Euander, in ipsis
> omnia sunt oculis, mensae quas aduena primas
> tunc adiit, dextraeque datae.

> *Pallas, Evander, it is all there*
> *before his eyes, the first meal he had that day he came*
> *as a stranger, the pledges exchanged.*

It is as though Aeneas saw nothing of the carnage he creates about him. We might say Aeneas fought in a blind rage: Virgil graphically and economically reveals to us what blind rage felt like. As he sweeps on in pursuit of Turnus, he strikes out at all who stand in his path, until he meets Lausus, the young man who steps between Aeneas and his wounded father. Impatiently Aeneas kills Lausus too—and as he looks down on the young man's lifeless body we realize, if Aeneas does not, that the deed he is supposed to be avenging cannot be considered worse than the deed he has now himself committed. It is one of the great moments in the poem and surely a considered expression of the poet's judgment on the glamorized barbarity of war.[2]

---

[1] For this interpretation of the Helen episode see L. R. Palmer, '*Aris invisa sedebat*', *Mn* 3rd s. 6 (1938) 368–79. The needless doubts which are often raised about the authenticity of the episode are well dealt with by R. G. Austin, 'Virgil, *Aeneid* 2.567-88', *CQ* 11 (1961) 185-98.

[2] This episode is also dealt with in Chapter 5, 'Tragic Insight'. For the death of Lausus see also Chapter 5, 'Implicit Comment'.

C. M. Bowra, 'Aeneas and the Stoic ideal', *GR* 3 (1933-4) 8-21, though arguing that the character of Aeneas is drawn with Stoic principles in mind,

The Heroic Impulse

Aeneas checks himself and regains his uneasily achieved humanity, but the trauma caused by Pallas' death and Aeneas' reaction to it leaves behind a festering scar that flares up again at the very end of the poem when—at last—Aeneas has Turnus' life in his hands. He sees on his knees before him the enemy he has so long pursued and would, in conscious humanity, spare. An unhappy accident (the fact that Turnus is wearing an ornamented belt he had stripped from the body of Pallas) touches off the subconscious lust and the hand Aeneas had held checked a long moment (12.939–41) descends to take a life which need not, should not, be taken.

Then there is the ugly scene in Book 12 that follows the interruption of the duel. As Aeneas chases vainly after Turnus, looking, and feeling, more and more foolish, he first abandons, in an outburst of righteous indignation, his earlier decision to abstain from the fighting (494); then hits on a way of punishing the Latin city, near which the duel was to take place, for his humiliation instead of Turnus, whom he cannot catch. In an instant he appraises the opportunity the city presents (558–60):

> aspicit urbem
> immunem tanti belli atque impune quietam.
> continuo pugnae accendit maioris imago.

> *He catches sight of the city,*
> *uninvolved in all the fighting, scot-free, undisturbed;*
> *at once the image inflames him of battle on a larger scale.*

The key-word is *accendit*: in this context it suggests not merely the flash of thought but the flare-up of emotion aroused by the thought, and also how resentment flares up within Aeneas. It all sounds unpleasantly like the professional soldier who nurses a grudge against civilians, and is exhilarated at the thought of a spectacular act of destruction. A moment later Aeneas and his men are launched upon this act of destruction.

The sudden assault upon the undefended city causes the queen to commit suicide in despair. Her death brings Turnus to his senses and

---

claims that, in describing Aeneas' conduct after the death of Pallas, Virgil endorses a contemporary deviation from the Stoic doctrine that anger and the desire for revenge are to be condemned. If it is true that the 'view of anger as a legitimate passion was part of the Augustan ideal' (p. 17), Virgil's narrative seems to me to challenge that view, not endorse it.

back to the duel, so that the episode has a structural purpose. But it is hard to escape the feeling that Aeneas has surrendered to an impulse which disgraces his humanity. And I think Virgil makes Aeneas share our disquiet: his curt rallying speech to his men strikes a disagreeably righteous note (565: *Iuppiter hac stat*), and betrays an odd uneasiness that they may hesitate to obey his orders (566); he blames Latinus quite unjustly, and then descends to self-conscious rhetoric mixed with images of destruction (for example, 569).

Undoubtedly, some of these episodes leave an unpleasant taste in the mouth. Yet what Virgil wants from us is surely understanding rather than condemnation. The episodes are designed to stress the inadequacy of the hero's code, not its depravity; to show that the soldier's training, though it provides a ready answer to the situations of battle, is a poor guide when the situation is not clear-cut, but demands moral or humane insight, an ability to reckon with the more far-reaching consequences of our first response to an emergency.

In such situations the heroic impulse often provides wrong answers. Not merely answers that reveal an ugly streak in the hero, or suggest the shallowness of his moral make-up, while leading all the same to an outcome we can approve of; but answers that are plainly wrong. Nisus' action—however forgivable the impulse to which he yields—is an irresponsible action, one that might have led to disaster—and would probably have led to disaster if fate had not ensured by other means that Aeneas received prompt warning of the Italian attack and returned prepared to meet it.[1]

Are we making too much fuss about this action of Nisus, and introducing considerations Virgil did not foresee, much less seek to prompt? I think not. The mistake he makes Nisus commit he makes Aeneas commit also in much more serious circumstances. The night of Troy's destruction, Aeneas is visited by Hector in a vision: Troy's dead champion has come to appoint his successor. Hector commits to Aeneas' keeping the city's gods to take with him to a new home, the great city he will found across the sea (2.293-5). Aeneas is no sooner roused from his sleep than Panthus, the priest of Apollo, appears, carrying the images of the city's gods which he had taken with him when he fled from the citadel. But Aeneas fails to recognize this clear confirmation of his vision. With no thought for what Hector has just told him he surrenders to his soldier's training (314-16):

[1] The ships which are turned into sea nymphs meet Aeneas as he returns with the Etruscan fleet and warn him (10.219-48).

The Heroic Impulse

> arma amens capio; nec sat rationis in armis,
> sed glomerare manum bello et concurrere in arcem
> cum sociis ardent animi.

*Distraught I snatch up arms, though there's little sense in arms;
but to build a band for battle, to rush with comrades to the
citadel—thus the hot impulse.*

The heroic impulse could hardly be more clearly described, and it sweeps Aeneas along, reckless of his great new responsibilities, for 275 lines—until his mother appears before him to remonstrate with him for his folly and set him back on the path of destiny: his mission to save the Trojan race by other means than fighting.

This is the message of Book 2. The poet puts his intentions beyond doubt. His analysis of Aeneas' emotions is almost clinically exact (316–17):

> furor iraque mentem
> praecipitat, pulchrumque mori succurrit in armis.

*A mad anger tumbles over
reason, and the quick thought comes: how fine a fighting death!*

Aeneas' surrender to impulse is as futile as Priam's pathetic, foolish gesture, with which we began. We may hesitate, all the same, to assume it can be the business of a heroic poem to judge in this harsh light the hero who responds heroically to catastrophe. Yet is it so very surprising a conclusion—provided we understand the poem's purpose and the poem's structure? For both have been obscured by a century and a half of Romantic criticism; anxious to soft-pedal the *Aeneid*'s purpose as a national epic because they confused patriotism with jingoism, critics have forced on the poem a sentimental interpretation unable to cope with the discerning clarity of Virgil's analysis of the nature of heroism. Dryden, who lived in an age that was more realistic about patriotism, was nearer the mark when he stressed the conflict in the *Aeneid* between heroism and piety:

> That quality, which signifies no more than an intrepid courage, may be separated from many others which are good, and accompanied with many which are ill. A man may be very valiant, and yet impious and vicious. But the same cannot be said of piety, which excludes all ill qualities, and comprehends even valour itself, with all other qualities which are good.[1]

[1] *The Works of Virgil, Translated into English Verse*, ed. John Carey, vol. 1 (1819) 266.

The Heroic Impulse

The purpose of the *Aeneid* is clear enough. The poem commemorates a great victory, the battle of Actium, which came soon to symbolize the end of decades of bloody civil war. The victory itself is commemorated in a long showpiece in *Aeneid* 8. Among the scenes upon the wonderful shield of Aeneas is a stylized symbolic picture of the battle. At the formal core of its structure the *Aeneid* fulfils its purpose as a patriotic poem.

But about the outcome of a civil war any man who is honest will feel reservations he might not make about a war with a foreign enemy. For a nation whose rise to greatness was due to the success of its armies this was the moment of truth. Philosophers had long taught that courage is not always admirable, or always enough.[1] The time was ripe to see more clearly what war is and what it does to human nature. The *Aeneid* is one of those works of literature that derive their artistic impetus from the fact that a stage has been reached in the history of ideas where a whole society can be brought through literature to the imaginative realization of a moral truth which a recent traumatic experience has equipped it to grasp. So, round the formal core is woven the heroic legend of Aeneas, ennobling the victory of Augustus, of which Actium is the symbol, but providing at the same time a many-sided, subtle, humane, moral comment upon it. For if in the legend, as at Actium, the right side won, victory came only after a struggle that generated needless bitterness; that brought unhappiness and death to many for whom we could wish a better fate; and that, by the hour of final victory, left the hands and the conscience of no man, not even the champion of the victorious cause, clean.

---

[1] The question of the extent to which courage can be considered admirable is raised in Plato's *Laches*, and frequently debated; the Stoics in particular were concerned to point out the inadequacy of courage unstrengthened by wisdom.

2

Genesis

I. WHAT IS THE AENEID ABOUT?

Chapter 1 set out some of the reactions those who have read the poem through once or twice might have, as they start to get their bearings and to reflect on the meaning of what they have read. It suggested, in short, one way of looking at the poem as a whole.

When we are dealing with a complex work of art, some such preliminary orientation is desirable before we submit ourselves, prudently but responsively, to the long process of getting to know the work of art with that mixture of pleasure, enlightenment and affection which is the reward of accurate, intimate acquaintance. A first look must be hasty, the conclusions suggested by it no more than provisional. Most of the episodes glanced at in the previous chapter will need, therefore, to be considered with more care in their context when we come to Chapter 4.

This means going over some of the same ground again. But it is not to be expected that a poem, or a part of a poem, however intense the immediate appeal, however strong the interest aroused, will surrender its full meaning quickly or easily, or out of context. Moreover, in Chapter 1 a lot had to be taken for granted. To describe the *Aeneid* as an imaginative study of the heroic impulse is—like any other simple generalization about a complex work of art—at best a first step in what we hope will prove the right direction. To be of value, such a generalization needs clarification, amplification, substantiation. The whole question of Virgil's purpose in writing his poem has been no

Genesis

more than touched on. Perhaps this is the best point to begin a consolidation of first impressions. Some consideration of why Virgil wrote the *Aeneid*, some understanding of the historical context in which the poem took shape, are likely to prove useful preliminaries to a critical description of it.

From the confused versions that have come down to us of Virgil's dying wishes with regard to the poem he had not lived to complete one fact stands out: Virgil did not want his poem published; under pressure from Augustus, the poet's known feelings were disregarded.[1] A further scrap of evidence suggests there was more in Virgil's reluctance than the coyness of a finicky perfectionist. This is a letter Virgil wrote five or six years before his death to Augustus. It looks like a reply to one of the letters of Augustus referred to by Suetonius,[2] in which Augustus asked Virgil for a sample from the work in progress. Virgil's answer is that there is really nothing to send. And he adds:

> What I have undertaken is of such magnitude that I think I must have been almost out of my mind to embark upon so great a task,

---

[1] So the epigram of Sulpicius of Carthage, preserved by Suetonius, 160–8R: De qua re Sulpicii [Carthaginiensis] extant huiusmodi uersus:

> Iusserat haec rapidis adoleri carmina flammis
>   Vergilius, Phrygium quae cecinere ducem.
> Tucca uetat Variusque; simul tu, maxime Caesar,
>   non sinis et Latiae consulis historiae.
> Infelix gemino cecidit prope Pergamon igni,
>   et paene est alio Troia cremata rogo.

The first four lines of the epigram are also quoted in the biography attributed to Probus (Probus, 25–31R), who ascribes them to Servius Varus. Virgil's will, according to Suetonius, repeated his wish not to have the *Aeneid* published, though in vague terms (174–9R):

> Ceterum eidem Vario ac simul Tuccae scripta sua sub ea conditione legauit, ne quid ederent, quod non a se editum esset.
> Edidit autem auctore Augusto Varius, sed summatim emendata, ut qui uersus etiam imperfectos, si qui erant, reliquerit.

Suetonius' own account makes a lame attempt to gloss over what took place (169–73R):

> Egerat cum Vario, priusquam Italia decederet, ut si quid sibi accidisset, Aeneida combureret; at is facturum se pernegarat. Igitur in extrema ualetudine assidue scrinia desiderauit, crematurus ipse; uerum, nemine offerente, nihil quidem nominatim de ea cauit.

[2] 120–4R. Rostagni assigns these letters to the time of Augustus' Cantabrian expedition, 27–25 B.C.

What is the Aeneid about?

particularly since it involves me, as you know, in other much more important studies.[1]

Then, when the task was, according to Suetonius, virtually complete, Virgil set out on a voyage to Greece and the middle east, announcing his intention to devote three whole years exclusively to revising his poem; after that he proposed to concentrate on philosophy.[2] If Virgil's words are correctly reported (after all, Suetonius is only recording tales current in his own day), they betray surely the frame of mind of a man who feels serious misgivings about what he has written, misgivings about what he has done.

What was the reason for such misgivings? It can hardly have been the *scale* of the *Aeneid* that intimidated Virgil, as Professor Brooks Otis suggests,[3] for the nagging doubts seem to have persisted after the *Aeneid* was well on its way to completion—when, according to Suetonius, it lacked only the *summa manus*. Did Virgil, then, believe he had somehow failed fundamentally to accomplish what he had attempted? The question prompts another: what was it that Virgil attempted? What, in other words, is the *Aeneid* about?

We can answer that question with a summary of the narrative. The poem, we may say, tells how Aeneas led the remnants of his people from the smoking ruins of Troy round the Mediterranean through a series of adventures, in search of a new home in Italy which they find under his guidance and hold under his leadership in war. But it is a poor poem whose meaning can be comprehended in a prose paraphrase: while purporting to tell us what the poem is about, a para-

[1] Virgil's letter has been preserved for us by Macrobius, *Sat.* 1.24.11:
Ego uero frequentes a te litteras accipio . . . De Aenea quidem meo, si mehercule iam dignum auribus haberem tuis, libenter mitterem, sed tanta incohata res est, ut paene uitio mentis tantum opus ingressus mihi uidear, cum praesertim, ut scis, alia quoque studia ad id opus multoque potiora impertiar.

[2] Suetonius, 140–3R:
Anno aetatis quinquagesimo secundo impositurus Aeneidi summam manum statuit in Graeciam et in Asiam secedere triennioque continuo nihil amplius quam emendare ut reliqua uita tantum philosophiae uacaret.

[3] Otis, p. 2:
We do not even require Donatus' famous description of Virgil's method of composition—the prose outline, the utter lack of continuity in the actual writing, the tiny daily quota of verses, the constant revision—to understand the terrible difficulty of the task. It was not, to judge by all the appearances, the kind of reluctance that delayed the completion of *Faust*—a sheer inability to come to terms with the poetic *daimon*—but the very magnitude and scope of the work itself.

Genesis

phrase inevitably sheers off elements by which the poem's meaning, in any adequate sense, is created and determined. Yet the moment we attempt a more accurate answer, we become entangled in the provocatively complex structure of the *Aeneid*. It is often said that the poem is a national epic, that it celebrates the achievements of Augustus. But how, and where, and why does it do these things?

The question 'What is the *Aeneid* about?' is best answered in two stages. First, let us ask what the poem was that people *expected* Virgil to write—before news leaked out, that is, of what he was actually doing; what, in other words, was the task, and what were the problems the task imposed? When we have got that straight, let us consider his *solution*. We cannot hope, of course, to arrive at a chronological reconstruction of the way the poem took shape, but we can attempt an analysis of the main elements that compose it. I shall suggest five such elements. When we have isolated these, we should have a better idea of what the poem is about.

II. THE TASK AND ITS PROBLEMS

On 2 September 31 B.C., Octavian, the nephew of Julius Caesar and his adopted son and heir, inflicted a crushing defeat on the forces of Mark Antony and Cleopatra of Egypt in a naval battle off the promontory of Actium in north-west Greece. The fire of civil war that had ravaged Italy for nearly twenty years was at last extinguished. It was understandable, therefore, if the naval engagement of Actium came to assume a symbolic significance out of proportion to the actual victory won by Agrippa on the day of battle. For perhaps a decade, while the memory of the years of conflict in which thousands had perished was fresh and while the illiberal character of the new regime had not yet emerged, it was possible, because victory brought peace and stable government, to believe that right had triumphed. We might say the *Aeneid* was written only just in time.

The battle was not long over before there were signs that Augustus (to give Octavian the more familiar name he assumed in 27 B.C.) was looking for a poet who could put his achievements in their proper light. He wanted, in short, an epic poem with himself as the hero. It was not an unreasonable ambition for a successful statesman to entertain. Rome was full of epic poets; the historical poem extolling the achievements of a general or politician was an established instrument of public relations.[1] The best known recent example was probably Furius Bibaculus' epic on Julius Caesar; the most notorious, Cicero's poem on his own consulship.[2] Propertius indicates, briefly but pretty clearly, what the poem Augustus wanted would have been about. 'If I had any talent for heroic epic,' he says to Maecenas, 'I'd not waste my time on stories from mythology . . .; I'd write about Caesar's wars and achievements' (2.1.19–25):

> non ego Titanas canerem. . . .
> bellaque resque tui memorarem Caesaris. . . .

He goes on to give a list of battles: Mutina, Philippi, the defeat of Sextus Pompey and his fleet, the siege of Perugia, the war in Egypt—above all Actium . . . this would have been the subject, one to be treated (the tone of Propertius' summary implies) as a series of glorious feats of arms, with the why's and the wherefore's pushed into the background by the conventions of panegyric. Lucan represents a spectacular survival of this tradition.

The object, however, of Propertius' poem is to decline Maecenas' offer of such a commission. It was a task no poet seemed anxious to tackle. Horace, Propertius, Virgil to begin with, all declined politely, backing up whatever they may have said in private by carefully phrased evasions in verse, which they published. Horace told Agrippa he was just not the man to write an epic poem—about Actium or about anything else—and maintained that to the end.[3] When he com-

---

[1] See Bardon, vol. 2, p. 61, and T. W. Dickson, 'Lost and unwritten epics of the Augustan poets', *TAPhA* 63 (1932) lii-liii. Dickson finds evidence for more than 24 epics now lost by minor Augustan poets; 7 dealt with historical themes.

[2] Cicero also wrote a poem on the achievements of Marius and we find him keeping an eye open for poets who might write about himself: see *Att.* 1.16.15 and 1.19.20. On Furius Bibaculus see Bardon, vol. 1, pp. 350–1. On Cicero see Otis, p. 25. For an account of the history of what he calls panegyric epic, beginning with Choerilus of Iasos in the fourth century B.C., see Otis, p. 16.

[3] *Odes* 1.6. Actium is not named, but the reference was to naval exploits and Agrippa commanded the fleet at Actium. Cf. *Epistles* 2.1.250–9:

> nec sermones ego mallem
> repentis per humum quam res componere gestas,
> terrarumque situs et flumina dicere, et arces
> montibus impositas et barbara regna, tuisque
> auspiciis totum confecta duella per orbem,
> claustraque custodem pacis cohibentia Ianum,
> et formidatam Parthis te principe Romam,

Genesis

promised, in the Roman odes and elsewhere, it was with uneven success: the Regulus ode is a revealing mixture of fine imagery and bad rhetoric, though better than the final pathetic, 'laureate' (Virgil was dead) poem *Odes* 4.15. But an epic poem was another matter. Propertius, in addition to the refusal in the elegy to Maecenas just quoted, wrote an elegy which he dedicated to Augustus, that begins with ringing promises (2.10.1–4):

> Sed tempus lustrare aliis Helicona choreis, . . .
> iam libet et fortis memorare ad proelia turmas
> et Romana mei dicere castra ducis.
>
> *But it is time to range Helicon in a different dance, . . .*
> *I want now to commemorate squadrons brave in battle*
> *and the campaigns of Rome, and him who is my leader.*

But he is quick to add a warning that the poem is not likely to be much good (2.10.5–6):

> quod si deficiant uires, audacia certe
> laus erit: in magnis et uoluisse sat est;
>
> *Yet were my powers to fail me, praise for daring*
> *is assured: when the task is big, to have wanted is enough;*

and a dozen lines of cautious procrastination end with the words, 'May I live to see the day!' (*seruent hunc mihi fata diem!*)—a clear enough hint, surely, that if Augustus is in a hurry he would do well to look for somebody else.[1] Virgil also showed little heart, to begin with, for the job. It is just possible he attempted a historical poem early in his career and gave it up, but his remark in the opening lines of the sixth Eclogue more likely refers to a mythological epic—the civil war was not yet over.[2] In the flowery prooemium to Book 3 of the *Georgics*, written

---

> si quantum cuperem possem quoque; sed neque paruum
> carmen maiestas recipit tua, nec meus audet
> rem temptare pudor quam uires ferre recusent.

[1] In 2.34.59–66 he hands the responsibility gratefully over to Virgil, but eventually Propertius too compromised with a respectably eloquent elegy on Actium (4.6).

[2] *Eclogues* 6.3–5:
> cum canerem reges et proelia, Cynthius aurem
> uellit et admonuit: 'pastorem, Tityre, pinguis
> pascere oportet ouis, deductum dicere carmen.'

Suetonius' assertion, 75–6R (*Mox cum res Romanas inchoasset, offensus materia ad Bucolica transiit*), that Virgil early began some kind of Roman epic, then lost interest, is probably (as Rostagni suggests) only Suetonius' inference from *Eclogues* 6.3–5.

The Task and its Problems

probably within a year or so of Actium, he comes closer than Propertius to acceptance of the task; he sketches a plan for a poem to celebrate the exploits of Augustus, but in terms of a project for the future.

Yet the three poets were all members of the circle of Maecenas. Their rejection of the hint they received to turn their attention to a patriotic epic can hardly have implied a rejection of the new regime. Why, then, were they reluctant?

They were reluctant, I think, because the task confronted them with two problems, one an artistic, the other more a moral problem. Let us attempt to formulate these two problems.

Any poem represents a task, proposed or imposed by a patron or a master, or it may be self-imposed. Merely to carry out a task is the work of an artisan and there have always been such poetic artisans. When Horace made his polite *recusatio* to Agrippa he referred him to Varius Rufus, who seems to have produced what was required.[1] If Varius hadn't, plenty of other epic poets—of a kind—were available. They might pride themselves on a job competently executed. But the result was not anything we should call poetry. A true poet is reluctant to accept a task unless he can see in it the accomplishment of some creative act; it may be only a way of making new out of old that presents a challenge which can absorb him; or a way of using a traditional theme as a display of learning or wit. To find how he can do this is the poet's *artistic problem*. If the task does not present an artistic problem, the labour, the ordeal even, of writing the poem offers little attraction. On the other hand, the attraction exercised by the artistic problem may be enormous. Indeed, many Hellenistic poets saw little more apparently in their art than the challenge of technique.

---

[1] Agrippa may have wanted an epic poem for himself, but it seems likely that Horace addressed his *recusatio* to the commander of the fleet rather than to Augustus (Augustus and Agrippa appear side by side in Virgil's stylized narrative of Actium in *Aeneid* 8). At any rate, Varius seems to have written some sort of hexameter poem celebrating the achievements of Augustus. The scholiast on Horace, *Epistles* 1.16.27-9:

> 'tene magis saluum populus uelit an populum tu,
> seruet in ambiguo qui consulit et tibi et urbi
> Iuppiter,' Augusti laudes agnoscere possis,

ascribes the quoted words to Varius. They represent perhaps the competent rhetoric and the facile disregard of integrity that characterized the poem. Bardon, vol. 2, p. 33, remarks: 'Plus qu'en Virgile, Auguste a trouvé en Varius le poète du principat.'

Virgil and other serious poets among his contemporaries were, in the first place, reluctant, therefore, to accept the task of an epic poem because they did not regard the task as an act of artistic creation. Epic seemed to them a form too worn out for genuine poets to find congenial; the derision poured on epic by the Alexandrians for its turgid pomposity could not fail to impress those Roman poets who were responsive to the challenge imposed by new standards of technical sophistication. All the same, Horace, or Propertius, or Virgil might have found a way of bringing the form to fresh artistic life if that had been all that was involved.[1] But from Catullus onwards the best Roman poets had come to feel that technical virtuosity was not enough. Their attitude shows the characteristic preoccupation of the time—and to some extent of the Roman mind at all times—with the moral function of art. Poetry had become linked with morality; despite their enthusiasm and respect for the artistic achievements of Hellenistic poetry, poets were no longer satisfied with the Hellenistic concept of art for art's sake. The moral function of poetry and the moral responsibilities of poets were issues that were hotly debated; they seem to have worried Horace, for example, all his life. The task accepted had therefore to be as well an expression of one's personality, or one's ideas about right and wrong, the poet's view of things. But how could the sort of epic poem that Augustus wanted, however skilfully contrived, however satisfying artistically, be made an expression of the poet's own views; not merely the vehicle of a moral comment, but, in itself, the expression of a moral attitude? This is what I have called the *moral problem*: it seemed insoluble.

We are speaking all the time of serious poets. For it is a striking feature of Augustan poetry that a clear cleavage had come about between the serious poets and the poetasters. The former were distinguished from the latter by more than ability, a Hellenistic preoccupation with the highest standards of craftsmanship and the wish to write poetry that invited the informed approval of their fellow poets rather than the undiscriminating approbation of a wider public. They were determined also to maintain a high standard of personal integrity and independence. Their standards were the outcome of an artistic revolution, the new status won for poetry by Catullus and the *poetae novi*.[2] Alongside these serious poets, there were a host of poetasters

---

[1] Otis (Chapter 2) overrates, I think, the difficulty of the artistic problem.
[2] I have discussed this change in the poet's status in *The Catullan Revolution* (1959).

content to do the old sort of thing in the old sort of way. For a good, short specimen (212 hexameters) of the fulsome panegyric that would pass muster with an eminent statesman, and of the evident corruption of honesty involved, we may take the pseudo-Tibullan encomium of Messalla.[1] Augustus could without much difficulty have got a poet of this sort to write his epic for him—Varius perhaps did. The trouble was Augustus wanted an epic by a real poet. Likely enough he was puzzled, for the concepts of artistic and moral integrity must have been still novel, at the reluctance of real poets to produce the required article.

The kind of poem Augustus wanted not merely precluded self-expression; it necessarily involved the expression of sentiments that were a contradiction of conscience. What was needed was not simply the glorification of a general or a politician, but the justification of a cause. The civil war brought the problem raised by propaganda to a head. Caesar had shown in his memoirs on the Gallic War and the Civil War how the genuine achievements of a leader could be made to seem more praiseworthy, and his more suspect actions represented as forced upon him by circumstances, or by the intransigence or malevolence of his opponents. What was needed was more than a poem that sang the praises of a hero in the traditional fashion—a kind of writing necessarily rendered artistically frivolous by its simplification of the issues, but comparatively innocuous. The poet who took on the job might set out intending to do only this, but he would soon find it necessary not merely to simplify truth but to distort truth. Horace and Propertius foresaw this. Small wonder if to them, if not to Augustus and Maecenas, the task seemed incompatible with integrity.

It was not just that the basic issues would have to be presented in a way distasteful to the other side, though this was a serious matter: the opponents of Augustus included men of distinction and sincere conviction; to see them represented as knaves or opportunists would be repugnant to many. The rights and wrongs of thirty years of political manoeuvring and two decades besmirched with repeated acts of bloodshed were so complicated that even a historian anxious to discuss them impartially must think of himself, as Horace warned Asinius Pollio, as a man picking his way across the scene of a recent conflagration, liable at every step to plunge through what looks like inert ash to the fire that still smoulders beneath (*Odes* 2.1.1–8):

---

[1] Tibullus, 4.1.

Genesis

Motum ex Metello consule ciuicum
bellique causas et uitia et modos
   ludumque Fortunae grauisque
      principum amicitias et arma

nondum expiatis uncta cruoribus,
periculosae plenum opus aleae,
   tractas, et incedis per ignis
      suppositos cineri doloso.

The troubles of our state from consul Metellus' day,
the causes of war, the crimes, the phases of it,
*   the play of chance, the harm that great*
*   friends did, the swords*

flecked with gore for which the guilt remains—
risky as a throw of dice is what you take
*   in hand: you walk on ashes; but below,*
*   fires smoulder still.*

The hidden fires are those that smoulder in the hearts of the survivors. Comment of any kind on the events of the past 35 years[1] was likely to fan them into the open flame of hatred and anger. But that is not all: through Horace's words runs the clear hint that even those who were close to Augustus could not shut their eyes to the burden of guilt lying on all who had participated in the war. Writing to a prospective historian, Horace puts the case boldly; the carefully worded ambiguity *grauis principum amicitias* even hints at the greatest enormity of all, the wanton bloodshed of the proscriptions.[2]

So long as he is declining the job, Propertius can evade the basic issues with a polite string of victories. When the talk is of the realities of civil war, his feelings about the suffering that is the price of victory are sharply expressed—he grew up near Perugia, where Octavian besieged the forces of L. Antonius in 41 B.C., and exacted a bloody vengeance when finally he took the town (1.22.3–5):

---

[1] Pollio's history was to begin with the consulship of Metellus in 60—the year of the triumvirate of Caesar, Pompey and Crassus. Horace is writing about 25 B.C.

[2] The primary allusion, picking up the reference to the first triumvirate in the opening line, is to the dire consequences of that understanding between so-called friends; but the reference readily transfers to the second triumvirate; moreover the words chosen suggest the dire consequences to others of having friends among the great: with each shift of power, along with those who fell from power hundreds of their associates and friends also perished.

si Perusina tibi patriae sunt nota sepulcra,
  Italiae duris funera temporibus,
cum Romana suos egit discordia ciuis. . . .

*If you know our country's graveyard at Perugia,
where Italy's dead lay those cruel days
when a divided Rome hounded her people on. . . .*

In the preceding elegy, the siege of Perugia forms the scene of a bitter tableau (1.21.1–8):

'Tu, qui consortem properas euadere casum,
  miles ab Etruscis saucius aggeribus,
quid nostro gemitu turgentia lumina torques?
  pars ego sum uestrae proxima militiae.
sic te seruato, ut possint gaudere parentes: 5
  ne soror acta tuis sentiat e lacrimis—
Gallum per medios ereptum Caesaris ensis
  effugere ignotas non potuisse manus. . . .'

Commentators have bedevilled the interpretation of this extraordinarily powerful trifle: whose are the parents (5: *parentes*), whose the sister (6: *soror*)? The difficulties disappear if we assume, as Fraenkel laid it down for Horace, that 'everything that is relevant to the understanding and appreciation of a poem' is contained in it.[1] A soldier, struck down while trying to escape through the enemy lines, addresses a comrade-in-arms, who has been wounded and is now running away. Line 5 makes sense only if we assume the *parentes* are those of the man making his escape. The *soror* is also most likely to be his, but obviously some relationship between her and the dying man is implied as well. She might be his wife or his fiancée, but the most natural explanation (in the absence of either *tua* or *mea*) is that the two men are brothers, which satisfactorily explains *proxima* in line 4.[2] Chance has brought one brother past where the other lies. Hearing the dying man's groans, the survivor turns his gaze in terror toward the sound. The dying man reassures him; but in wishing his brother a safe

---

[1] Eduard Fraenkel, *Horace* (1957) 26.
[2] Camps, p. 99, oddly remarks:

there seems no reason why he should stress the *closeness* of their association, and no reason to suppose that any special relation existed between the two men, as their present encounter is obviously fortuitous.

But the fortuitous encounter of the two men who are closely related, only to be separated by death, is part of the irony of the poem.

Genesis

escape, he attaches a condition (5: *sic te seruato*), in which irony and shame are mixed with a force that is an index of Propertius' greatness as a poet: let the survivor spare their sister the truth, let her think her brother was killed by Caesar's army, not by an unknown assailant while running away.[1]

When we read lines like these we begin to understand how much lay behind such phrases as Horace's *bella matribus detestata* (*Odes* 1.1.24–5), or Virgil's *horrida bella* (*Aeneid* 7.41), how strong the feeling must have been that war was hateful and that it was wrong to glamorize it. It is the feeling which dominates (almost drowning the compliments to Octavian) the concluding lines of *Georgics* 1.

III. THE PROBLEMS SOLVED

Two problems, then, the one an artistic problem, the other a moral problem, confronted Virgil. From the outset he rejected the task less lightly than Horace or Propertius; perhaps he felt the challenge more keenly. But in the proem to the third book of the *Georgics*, where he offers his first sketch of a solution to the artistic problem, he seems as yet more concerned to evade the moral problem than to solve it. The epic he promises to write is spoken of, with a display of Hellenistic allegory aimed, one feels, at disguising the absence of real enthusiasm, as a temple of the Muses which Virgil will erect at Mantua by the river Mincius. There he will celebrate games that will rival those of Greece. On the doors of the temple the exploits of Augustus will be depicted in gold and ivory, and near them will be statues of Octavian's ancestors, Trojan and divine. A naval battle and the river Nile are briefly mentioned among the scenes that will be represented, but the stress is on Octavian's foreign conquests and his multiple triumph in 29 B.C.

The link with epinician poetry, in which formal praise is perfunctorily attached to real poetry, is apparent. Equally apparent is the way in which the civil war is underplayed and the emphasis thrown on foreign conquest. At the same time there are hints of things to come.

---

[1] Some editors, determined to make prose out of poetry, read *ut* for *ne* in line 6.

The Problems Solved

A connexion between Troy and Augustus and Actium is already adumbrated, the device finally used by Virgil in *Aeneid* 8 of reducing the encomium of Actium to a formal tableau on a work of art is foreshadowed. But in the form Virgil roughs out at this stage, it is an uninspiring programme for a poem. If Virgil genuinely hoped to find a solution to his moral problem, and wasn't just playing for time, the lukewarm, clever tone of the proem suggests the solution was still a long way off.[1]

A poem that played up foreign conquests and soft-pedalled the civil war meant side-stepping the moral problem instead of facing it. If Virgil was to accomplish what was expected of him, if his epic was to be intellectually honest—if in short the poem was to be any good—he must make a serious attempt to justify Augustus' conduct of the civil war to his fellow-citizens. Genuine *contemporary relevance* was a *sine qua non*.

To this inescapable *first element* of Virgil's epic others could naturally be added—with a twofold gain. A broader context might win a more sympathetic reception from those not bitterly committed to the lost cause. At the same time the polemical aspect of the poem could be made less strident; it might even be possible to imply reservations that Augustus would scarcely have accepted in a poem whose acknowledged subject was his conduct of the civil war.

A better way out than playing up foreign conquests was to make the poem more a historical epic of the type written by Naevius and Ennius. Naevius had written a history in verse (saturnians, not hexameters) of the first Punic War, preceded by some sort of introduction connecting Aeneas with the legendary origin of Rome; about twenty lines of his story of Aeneas survive; it seems to have included a first version of the great storm and the colloquy between Venus and Jove which we have in *Aeneid* 1 (see analysis of Book 1 in Chapter 4). Ennius had attempted a full-scale history of Rome (omitting the first Punic War which had been dealt with by Naevius) from its beginnings in legend down to his own day, starting with the fall of Troy and a brief account of the coming of the Trojans to Italy. It is the plan Livy followed in his great prose history, the first book of which appeared (with Livy's version of Rome's beginnings) about the time Virgil began work on the *Aeneid*.

---

[1] See Walter Wimmel, *Kallimachos in Rom: die Nachfolge seines Apologetischen Dichtens in der Augusteerzeit* (1960) 167 ff., and Otis, p. 39 n.

Genesis

In both Naevius and Ennius the subject was of course Rome, not an individual, and the method historical, or rather annalistic, with some desultory use of epic machinery.[1]

A poem that took in a wide sweep of history culminating in the present age would look less controversial, yet might reasonably represent the achievements of Augustus as crowning a complex and glorious historical process, while at the same time dissociating itself from the suspect, contemptible genre which historical epic had become in Virgil's day, in order to attach itself to the honourable tradition of Naevius and Ennius. Moreover, the broader context permitted the incorporation of such themes as the fundamental identity of the Roman and Italian characteristic virtues—Virgil after all was not a Roman, but an Italian—and the glamorous historical diversity of a people that was now one.

But this *second element*, history, if it was some solution to the moral problem, was no solution to Virgil's artistic problem. An annalistic framework was likely to result in versified history, at best good in purple passages. The movement of a poem is hard to reconcile with the linear chronological structure of history. Actual historical events resist the stylization that poetry imposes; they sound even less convincing if allowed to remain as historical events versified. If we feel inclined to attribute Ennius' lapses into prosiness to inexperience, we should think of the trouble Lucan encountered when he tried to versify history.

Ennius, of course, was still popular—remember Cicero's praise of him.[2] The *stylistic* debt under which Virgil places himself in the *Aeneid* to Ennius (and Naevius) shows his appreciation of the rugged, simple grandeur of the old poetry (see Chapter 6). But Virgil's sympathy was too much with the *cantores Euphorionis* and the new poetic tradition which had supplanted the old epic-tragic style, at any rate for serious poets, for him to find congenial the loose fabric of old Roman epic and its homespun characters.[3] In the proem to *Georgics* 3 we see him, with ideas of a historical poem already in mind, toying with ways

---

[1] See Otis, pp. 22–3.

[2] Cf. Cicero's well-known remark after quoting a couple of passages from Ennius' *Andromacha* (*Tusc. Disp.* 3.45): *O poetam egregium! quamquam ab his cantoribus Euphorionis contemnitur.*

[3] Suetonius' story that Virgil began a poem about Roman history and gave it up is, as we have seen above, probably based on *Eclogues* 6.3–5. But if Virgil did begin some kind of epic poem, he may well have given it up, finding the material intractable (*offensus materia*) according to his poetic standards.

round these difficulties: the pageant of Augustus' ancestors upon the wall of the temple is a device that will reappear in the *Aeneid*.

Another way out was a retreat into legend. In Greek literature, a tale of heroes or a story from mythology was the normal subject for an epic poem, as it was for tragedy. We mustn't of course think of a continuous epic tradition: epic begins with the Homeric poems, but the tradition lapsed till it was artificially revived in Hellenistic times by Apollonius and other bookish poets. Roman *historical* epic is really an offshoot: it represents an early attempt (guided by Greek experiments with historical epic)[1] to give the epic form native roots, rather as the early Roman tragedians, as well as following the traditional themes from legend, attempted to build tragedy round themes from Roman history.

Historical epic proved more successful than the *fabula praetexta*, but in Virgil's day it was tending more and more to serve practical ends. Heroic or mythological epic had become the favourite form of the dabbler in verse—the sort of poem any man who fancied he could write would have a go at. One was a *Thebaid* by Propertius' friend Ponticus; Propertius (1.7) politely compares his friend to Homer, but the way he talks to Ponticus about his epic gives us a pretty clear hint of the degree of Ponticus' artistic commitment to his theme.

In the Hellenistic age, a more compact, more sophisticated type of poem than mythological epic had come into existence. This was the epyllion—a term that has been much argued about; it has no ancient authority, but beyond doubt labels a recognized genre, of which Catullus' Poem 64 is the best known example.[2] Here higher standards of craftsmanship prevailed. The poets who wrote epyllia transferred to the Roman literary scene the contempt Callimachus had expressed for the flabby structure of old Greek epic. But if the general level of technical competence was higher, the epyllion seems by Virgil's day, no less than the full-length mythological epic, to have been stultified by a lack of creativity; in both, the same old subjects were worked to death—as Virgil himself drily observes in running through a string of

---

[1] Otis, pp. 9–10, dates the invention of historical epic from the *Persica* of Choerilus of Samos (not to be confused with Choerilus of Iasos) in the middle of the fifth century B.C. See also Otis, p. 16, for epics about the campaigns of Alexander.

[2] For a convenient summary of the controversy over the term 'epyllion' see C. J. Fordyce's commentary on Catullus (1961) 272–3. For details of epyllia by Cinna and others see Otis, p. 27.

Genesis

stock themes in the proem to *Georgics* 3.[1] Retreat into legend was not in itself therefore a solution: neither the full-length mythological epic nor the epyllion as it was currently practised offered much incentive, unless Virgil could reach out beyond the jaded incompetence of his contemporaries and recover the standard set by Catullus.

Legend could, however, contribute a *third element*. There was an obvious legend to choose, the one both Naevius and Ennius had used as an introduction to their historical epics: how Aeneas, the son of Anchises of Troy and the goddess Venus, after the sack of Troy by the Greeks had led a band of refugees to a new home in Italy. The story was a very old one: terracotta figures ascribed to the sixth and fifth centuries B.C. have been found at Veii representing Aeneas carrying his father Anchises on his shoulders, as Virgil makes him do when they flee into the night from the flames of Troy at the end of Book 2; an Etruscan amphora of the fifth century shows the same couple accompanied by Aeneas' wife Creusa and his son Ascanius. The legend of Aeneas was very likely linked with the story of Rome's foundation by Hellenistic historians in order to give the city by the Tiber a respectable start in life by integrating it into the existing fabric of myth and history. But long before that the main features, at any rate, of the story had acquired the prestige of genuine Italian folk-lore: King Latinus, his daughter Lavinia, Turnus, Mezentius—all were familiar figures; Virgil did not have to invent them. Many of Virgil's contemporaries no doubt accepted the stories quite uncritically. They would have regarded Virgil's recasting of them as a poetic presentation of things that actually happened. Virgil himself, we may be sure, while priding himself on the accuracy of his research into points of detail, felt for his material something closer to the tolerant scepticism which Livy extends to the legends of early Rome in his Preface.[2]

---

[1] *Georgics*, 3.4–8:
>   quis aut Eurysthea durum,
> aut inlaudati nescit Busiridis aras?
> cui non dictus Hylas puer et Latonia Delos,
> Hippodameque, umeroque Pelops insignis eburno,
> acer equis?

Of the themes referred to here some (e.g., *cui non dictus Hylas?*) suggest epyllia, others full-length epics.

[2] Livy, *Preface*, 6–7:
> Quae ante conditam condendamue urbem poeticis magis decora fabulis quam incorruptis rerum gestarum monumentis traduntur, ea nec adfirmare nec refellere in animo est. datur haec uenia antiquitati, ut miscendo humana diuinis primordia urbium augustiora faciat; et si cui populo licere oportet

The Problems Solved

We find Lucretius beginning his great poem with a formula (*Aeneadum genetrix, hominum Diuomque uoluptas*) that takes for granted familiarity with the legend that the Romans were descendants of Aeneas and through him of the goddess Venus. Some years earlier, probably, than Lucretius' poem, Julius Caesar, in a funeral oration in praise of his aunt Julia which he pronounced while quaestor in 68 B.C., reminded his audience that, whereas his late aunt was descended on her mother's side merely from kings, on the Julian side she was descended through Venus from the immortal gods.[1] If Caesar was consciously ironical, Octavian took more seriously the divine origin which he had acquired by adoption. Already as triumvir we find him issuing coins repeating, as a kind of family crest, the symbolic embodiment of the legend—a figure of Aeneas carrying Anchises—which the soil of Etruria has yielded up to modern archaeologists from a period four to five centuries earlier.[2] Before long the legend is caught up in an official assertion of divinity; the assassinated dictator is styled a god, Octavian styles himself (as early as 42 B.C.) *diui filius*, and we find ourselves moving in the queer world of official make-believe, in which the old legends of the divine origins of leading Roman families became articles of public cult, to be accepted, even by sophisticated Romans (however much tongue-in-cheek), as literally as the divine origins of Hellenistic kings had been accepted by their most credulous subjects.

At some stage the possibility must have occurred to Virgil of a poem which might avoid the prosiness of historical epic by a major reversal of emphasis: instead of a poem beginning in legend and moving forward through history, might not the legend of Aeneas be made the formal subject of an essentially mythological epic? This much of the solution, it seems, came to Virgil quite early. At any rate, about six

---

consecrare origines suas et ad deos referre auctores, ea belli gloria est populo Romano.

Livy then goes on (Book 1, Chapters 1–2) to give a non-committal recital of the basic facts of the story of Aeneas; his account closely resembles the plot of the *Aeneid*, except that Virgil, in Books 7 to 12, appears to have made a number of fairly drastic rearrangements in the sequence of events for the sake of his plot.

[1] Suetonius, *Div. Jul.* 6.

[2] He was following in his uncle's footsteps: on a *denarius* of c. 48 B.C. we find on one side a head of Venus, on the obverse Aeneas holding the Palladium (which figures so prominently in *Aeneid* 2) and carrying Anchises, with the inscription CAESAR. See also Lily Ross Taylor, *The Divinity of the Roman Emperors* (1931) and Fritz Taeger, *Charisma: Studien zur Geschichte des antiken Herrscherkults* vol. 2 (1960).

Genesis

years before Virgil died, Propertius was able to announce that, while he preferred himself to stick to love poetry, Virgil was engaged upon a work greater than anything ever written before—greater even than Homer's *Iliad*—in which he was going to deal with both the naval victory at Actium and the legend of Trojan Aeneas.[1] A full-length epic dealing with the legend of Aeneas, and somehow at the same time discharging honestly the inescapable obligation to commemorate the achievements of Augustus (making them perhaps the culminating point of some kind of historical pageant)—here was a poem it could be a challenge to write.

Two more elements were still to be introduced, and it was their introduction that brought the poem to life. One enabled Virgil to overcome his artistic problem: he found a way of making the poem worth writing technically. The other enabled him to overcome his moral problem: he found a way of making the poem say something worth saying.

Virgil's solution to his artistic problem is already foreshadowed in the opening lines of the poem (1.1–7):

> Arma uirumque cano, Troiae qui primus ab oris
> Italiam fato profugus Lauinaque uenit
> litora, multum ille et terris iactatus et alto
> ui superum, saeuae memorem Iunonis ob iram,
> multa quoque et bello passus, dum conderet urbem
> inferretque deos Latio, genus unde Latinum
> Albanique patres atque altae moenia Romae.

My poem is of war and a man: from Troy's shore originally he came, fated to be a refugee, to Italy and the Lavinian coast, much buffeted across lands and the deep sea

---

[1] Propertius, 2.34.59–66:

> me iuuet hesternis positum languere corollis,
>   quem tetigit iactu certus ad ossa deus;
> Actia Vergilium custodis litora Phoebi,
>   Caesaris et fortis dicere posse ratis,
> qui nunc Aeneae Troiani suscitat arma
>   iactaque Lauinis moenia litoribus.
> cedite Romani scriptores, cedite Grai!
>   nescio quid maius nascitur Iliade.

Suetonius' comment (116R), *Aeneidos uixdum coeptae tanta extitit fama*, etc., need be no more than a reasonable inference from Propertius' words, but it is consistent with the statement (94–100R) that Virgil began by laying the *Aeneid* out in a prose draft.

The Problems Solved

*by the divine will, by cruel Juno's unforgetting wrath,
in battle also much enduring, till he built a city
and introduced his gods to Latium, whence the Latin race,
the Alban fathers and the walls of high Rome.*

The formal subject of the poem is summarized in these seven lines. But through them, despite the insistence on Rome and Latium, run clear echoes of the two most famous epics of antiquity, the *Iliad* and the *Odyssey*.[1] The lines amount in fact to an assertion that the poem is itself both an *Iliad*—a story of war and fighting (*arma*)[2]—and an *Odyssey*—the story of a man's adventures.

This assertion, latent in the opening three words, is made more definite by repeated echoes of Homer's two opening sentences. 'Man' is the first word of the *Odyssey*, and the man meant is defined by Homer, as Virgil defines his man, in a relative clause, beginning in the first line and flowing over into the succeeding lines in a series of expansions, while the circumstances that launched the man on his adventures and the goal he kept before him are set out. But though the pattern is reproduced, the content is very different. There is, moreover, a small but interesting readjustment of the basic formula: where Homer surrenders to the Muse's inspiration (as he does in the *Iliad*), asking her for the words that will make his poem, Virgil begins with the confident first person *cano* of the conscious artist, contenting himself with an acknowledgment of the epic convention in a less emphatic position (line 8)—and there appealing to the Muse for information (*causas memora*), not adopting the role of her amanuensis.

The first five lines of Virgil's opening sentence thus reproduce the syntactical pattern of the opening sentence of the *Odyssey*. Virgil's sentence, however, is expanded to seven lines—the length of the first sentence of the *Iliad*. And like the first sentence of the *Iliad* it ends with a relative clause (*genus unde Latinum* . . . corresponds to Homer's ἐξ οὗ δή . . .); and, where the first sentence of the *Iliad* ends with the emphatic word Ἀχιλλεύς, Virgil's first sentence ends with the emphatic *Romae*—the climax of an ascending triad (*genus Latinum— Albanique patres—altae moenia Romae*), each member a syllable longer than its predecessor.

[1] See B. A. van Groningen, 'The proems of the Iliad and the Odyssey', *Mededeelingen der Koninklijke Nederlandsche Akademie van Wetenschappen*, Afd. Letterkunde Nieuwe Reeks, Deel 9 No. 8 (1946).
[2] The usual translation of *arma* as 'arms' is a mistranslatoin consecrated by tradition. For the Latin word has much stronger emotional connotations than the English; 'war' or 'fighting' is a more adequate translation.

Genesis

We have in fact a synthesis of Homer's two opening sentences, arranged in the form of a chiasmus. The first arm of the chiasmus picks up the opening phrase, *arma uirumque cano*; in it *uirum* is defined by a relative clause, describing the wanderings of the man, which is then summed up in a participial phrase (*multum ille et terris iactatus et alto*). In the second arm of the chiasmus, *arma* is expanded by a similar pattern, in reverse order: first comes the participial phrase summing up the *arma* theme (*multa quoque et bello passus*), then comes the relative clause (*genus unde Latinum* . . .); participial phrase and relative clause are separated this time by an additional member (*dum conderet urbem inferretque deos Latio*), to give a climactic surge to the final relative clause. The central line of the sentence (*ui superum saeuae memorem Iunonis ob iram*) we naturally take first with the preceding lines; but it belongs equally to the lines that follow, corresponding then to Διὸς δ' ἐτελείετο βουλή in line 5 of the *Iliad*. For if Juno leads the Greeks in the destruction of Troy and pursues them relentlessly in their exile, she is also the cause of the war in Italy.[1] Books 1 to 6 are Virgil's *Odyssey*, Books 7 to 12 his *Iliad*.[2] The two halves are tied together by a common hero: the *uir* defined by the relative clause is also the *uir* defined in lines 5–7.

But these seven lines also foreshadow Virgil's method of using Homer. Naevius and Ennius had borrowed phrases, bits of story, certain conventions of narrative and attitude, founding themselves on a tradition, but not hesitating to claim such freedom as they were capable of. Virgil consciously abdicates his freedom. His poem expressly recalls Homer's story and constantly evokes Homer's conventions. The storm in Book 1, the games in Book 5, the journey to the underworld in Book 6, Aeneas' shield in Book 8, the night raid of Nisus and Euryalus in Book 9, the avenging of Pallas in Books 10 to 12, the duel in Book 12—all these have their obvious antecedents in the *Iliad* and the *Odyssey*: the parallels are close and sustained. Then there are the small things: scenes, similes, numberless details of phrase, not merely influenced by Homer but modelled closely on Homer.[3] Finally, the structure of the poem is Homeric: the divine machinery,

---

[1] Our habits of punctuation tend to blind us to this type of syntactical ambiguity. For a discussion of this aspect of the opening lines of the *Aeneid* see Chapter 6.

[2] For the way the *Aeneid* falls into an *Iliad* and an *Odyssey* see Chapter 3.

[3] G. N. Knauer, *Die Aeneis und Homer* (1964), has attempted to gather together all Virgil's imitations of Homer and allusions to Homer. The result is a volume of 550 pages.

The Problems Solved

the rules Virgil imposes on himself for what may be said and what left unsaid follow Homeric practice. Yet for all this, Virgil's poem remains consciously, fundamentally, and unmistakably, Roman (see Chapter 5, Part 1, 'Form').

Rivalry with Homer was an important part of Virgil's poem: it represented the *fourth element* in the solution of his problem. It is, however, an aspect of the *Aeneid* of which most modern readers are barely conscious. Nor is it indispensable to our appreciation of the poetry to know that it is there, though this is vital to our understanding of the poet's attitude to his form. Indeed, knowledge can hinder appreciation. For when the frequency and explicitness of Virgil's 'imitations' of Homer are realized, the first reaction of the modern reader is apt to be one of bewilderment. This is not plagiarism. It is a subtle, sustained process of allusion and evocation and *challenge*. Virgil intended his fourth element to be as consciously present in the reader's mind (though less completely and less precisely—even the most learned reader must miss a lot) as it was in his own mind. In part its object is to give the narrative a new dimension, a peculiar illusion of depth; in part it is a special, complex way of making new out of old.

To some extent Virgil follows Horace's precept: you got material from the common stock; what mattered was to make the material your own by a new tightness of structure (*A.P.* 240–2—Horace is speaking of dramatic plot):

> ex noto fictum carmen sequar, ut sibi quiuis
> speret idem, sudet multum frustraque laboret
> ausus idem: tantum series iuncturaque pollet.

In constructing my poem I will take over known material, so that any man can hope to do the same, though he will sweat hard and to no avail if he dares the attempt: such is the importance of sequence and structure.

But this does not account for the constant incorporation of detailed verbal echoes. There is some similarity here with the modern artistic technique of *collage*. An artist makes a picture out of, say, bottle-tops and soup-tin labels. The picture that results is a picture in its own right. But full appreciation of its merit as a picture depends, in a way that is easily sensed but not easily accounted for, upon our recognition of the bottle-tops and soup-tin labels for what they are.[1] In art the technique

---

[1] Robert Graves accused T. S. Eliot of *collage* in *The Waste Land* ('These be your gods', in *The Crowning Privilege* [1955] 126). But Virgil's use of the technique is more sustained.

Genesis

is a comparatively crude one, because the process of association which the artist exploits depends on the use of actual physical materials. The correspondence can only be one of identity. In a poem more complicated degrees of relationship are possible. A characteristic Homeric syntactical pattern may contain an idea that is wholly Virgil's, or a Homeric idea may be given a new form. A very sophisticated tension is possible between the ways in which Virgil's words correspond to Homer's (because they are the Latin equivalents, because they say the things Homer says, or say things in the way Homer says them) and the ways in which they do not correspond (because they are *Latin* words, the units of a simple, vigorous vocabulary—whereas Homer's vocabulary is archaic and literary—impregnated, both as words and combinations of words, with associations with the two great Latin poetic traditions, the old epic-tragic style and the new compact, dense style of Catullus, out of which Virgil has created a diction of his own). (See Chapter 6, 'Words in Action'.)

Virgil is in fact carrying to a new pitch of refinement a technique evolved by Callimachus and other 'learned' Hellenistic poets who made it a point of honour to incorporate in their retelling of a legend nothing for which no precedent existed (the famous ἀμάρτυρον οὐδὲν ἀείδω),[1] however obscure the source and however unexpected or ironical the resultant synthesis. It is one more way in which Virgil shows that his sympathies are more with the new poets than with the writers of traditional epic.

We shall have more to say on this complicated question of the exploitation of a distinctive form in Chapter 5. For the present, we must confine ourselves to a brief example. In Book 10, when Mezentius replaces Turnus in battle, the long recital of Mezentius' victims (10.689–746) concludes with the 15-line episode of Orodes. As Mezentius stands over him poised for the death-stroke, Orodes warns Mezentius that his day, too, will come. Mezentius replies (742–4):

> ad quae subridens mixta Mezentius ira:
> 'nunc morere, ast de me diuum pater atque hominum rex uiderit.'

> *Smiling, but angry too, Mezentius replied,*
> '*Now die. As for me the king of gods and men may give the matter his attention.*'

---

[1] Cf. fragment 612Pf., and Norden on 6.14 and 6.445 ff.

The Problems Solved

This is practically what Achilles says as he kills Hector who had warned *him* to think of his own fate (*Iliad* 22.365-6):

'τέθναθι· κῆρα δ' ἐγὼ τότε δέξομαι, ὁππότε κεν δὴ
Ζεὺς ἐθέλῃ τελέσαι ἠδ' ἀθάνατοι θεοὶ ἄλλοι.'

'*Die. I shall meet my fate, when to bring that to pass
shall be the will of Zeus and the other immortal gods.*'

But in Homer this is merely the customary heroic exchange, rendered more memorable because it comes at the climax of the poem and by the stark τέθναθι ('die!')—imitated also by Virgil in 2.550. In Virgil the reference to fate nettles the unbeliever Mezentius, finds perhaps a chink in his agnostic armour; hence the elaborate irony of his reply to Orodes. Before long it *will* be Mezentius' turn to die and we shall remember then his words now. Note also how Virgil, in recasting Achilles' words, employs the idiomatic *uiderit*—a semi-colloquialism used in declining responsibility which sharpens the irony by undercutting the solemnity of the preceding formula *diuum pater atque hominum rex*.

Virgil accepts, in short, the challenge to be a Roman Homer; not merely to be a second Homer, but to write a poem which, though modelled on Homer, was essentially different. Propertius' couplet (2.34.65-6):

cedite Romani scriptores, cedite Grai!
nescio quid maius nascitur Iliade,

*Yield, Roman writers, yield, Greeks,
something is being born greater than the Iliad,*

is as accurate a statement of Virgil's intentions as the lines which precede. Comparison with Homer was the stock compliment.[1] For once it is meant seriously. There is more involved than Hellenistic ingenuity. One thing gained is that, in addition to the Homeric material actually incorporated by Virgil, a huge fund remains, to be drawn on by a process of allusion which challenges our recollection and suggests ramifications of Virgil's more tightly woven tale that give it complexity and a kind of three-dimensional quality.[2] But there is a more serious purpose still. Virgil's characters and situations keep reminding us of Homeric characters and situations and then revealing themselves as different. We keep seeing first a significant likeness, then

[1] Cf. Horace, *Odes*, 1.6.1-2, and Propertius, 1.7.3.
[2] See *Latin Explorations*, Chapter 8.

Genesis

a significant dissimilarity. Aeneas and Turnus both recall Achilles. Turnus has Achilles' unthinking bravery, a virtue we are led to admire and then to reject. Aeneas like Achilles is invincible, but morally he transcends Achilles to a degree that is rendered all the more apparent by occasional lapses to Achilles' level: his blind rage, for example, after the death of Pallas in Book 10 recalls the blind rage of Achilles after the death of Patroclus. Virgil seems to be aiming at something to take the place of the kind of analytic comment on character and motivation that he would have found cumbersome to express even in prose and artistically unachievable in any kind of poetic form known to him. He bends the Homeric tradition to his purpose. If Turnus reminds us at different stages of Achilles, Hector and Paris, it is a kind of graphic substitute for psychological analysis.[1]

There is, moreover, a danger in reducing Virgil's rivalry with Homer to an ingenious reshuffling of Homeric phrases and narrative elements. The danger is that of overstressing Virgil's cleverness, of seeing in the *Aeneid* a kind of clever puzzle. For, though so much of the *Aeneid* is taken from the *Iliad* and the *Odyssey*, nothing is any longer the same. Virgil's words constantly recall Homer, only somehow to challenge, even to reject Homer. It is not merely that the plot and the line of narrative have a new tightness about them; or that, while Homer is the formal model, he is not the only one: Greek tragedy, Plato, Apollonius, nearly every important department of Greek literature are pressed into service. (See Chapter 5, 'Not only Homer'.) There is that note of confident nationalism which we detect in the *Odes* of

---

[1] William S. Anderson, 'Vergil's second *Iliad*', *TAPhA* 88 (1957) 17–30, argues for a much more sustained synthesis of Homeric prototypes. While Virgil goes out of his way to keep the Trojan War before us, there is a kind of systematic turning inside out of Homer's story. (1) The Trojans assume more and more the role of the Greeks. (2) Aeneas and Turnus become composite characters. Aeneas = (a) Agamemnon (the commander-in-chief); (b) Achilles (the invincible warrior, absent during an attack on the camp); even (c) Menelaus (the rightful husband of Latinus' daughter). Turnus = (a) Achilles (the handsome, impulsive warrior, cf. 6.89: *alius Latio iam partus Achilles*); (b) Paris (saved from death by divine intervention in Book 10, he comes between Lavinia and her rightful husband); (c) Hector (the champion of his people killed by the opposing champion). The duel of Book 12 evokes (1) the duel of Menelaus and Paris in *Iliad* 3–4 (including the breaking of the truce); (2) the duel of Achilles and Hector in *Iliad* 22.

Anderson argues his case well, though he perhaps makes Virgil's reshuffling of the Homeric elements over-systematic. For further discussion of Virgil's relationship to Homer see W. A. Camps, 'A second note on the structure of the *Aeneid*', *CQ* 9 (1959) 53–6, and R. D. Williams, 'Virgil and the *Odyssey*', *Phoenix* 17 (1963) 266–74.

The Problems Solved

Horace: Actium and the conquest of Egypt symbolized for the Romans not only the final political triumph of Rome over the Hellenistic world, but the coming of age of Rome as a cultural power with a national literature of her own, able to rival and outdo the Greek masterpieces of the past.

So much for Virgil's solution of his artistic problem. The moral problem remained, unless he could make his solution of the artistic problem subserve his solution of the moral problem.

An intelligent contemporary of Virgil, hearing or reading the *Aeneid* for the first time, must surely have been surprised. Everyone in Rome interested in literature knew that Virgil had spent ten years writing a poem to celebrate the victory at Actium. Aware of the ticklishness of the task, our ideal contemporary reader would have been curious to see what solution Virgil had found to the problems that confronted him. Yet on a first hearing or reading, the poem can hardly have failed to seem more an evasion of the problems than a solution of them. Augustus' achievements and the victory at Actium are given a place, or rather three places; there are as well a few incidental references. But when everything that is said about Augustus is put together, it amounts to precious little. Virgil's discharge of his obligation must have seemed curiously perfunctory.

The first of the three passages in which specific mention is made of the events of recent history comes at the end of the brilliant stylized epitome of Roman history which Jove unfolds for Venus to console her after the great storm in Book 1 (1.286–96). Virgil's neat mathematics (Aeneas will reign for three years, Ascanius for thirty, his descendants for three hundred, the descendants of Romulus and Remus for an infinite period over an infinite empire—1.278: *nec metas . . . nec tempora pono*), the circular composition of his historical pageant (we start with a son of Venus who becomes a god and finish with a distant descendant who also becomes a god—then after him peace) establish that politely, ingeniously panegyrical tone which we assume when we wish to deprecate too serious commitment to the grandiloquence that is *de rigueur* on ceremonial occasions. According to the most likely reading of them, lines 286–90 refer to Julius Caesar.[1]

---

[1] 1.286–90:
        nascetur pulchra Troianus origine Caesar,
        imperium Oceano, famam qui terminet astris,
        Iulius, a magno demissum nomen Iulo.   [*Note contd. p. 48.*

Genesis

In that case there is no direct mention at all of Augustus; the return of peace, the imprisonment of sinful Madness (*Furor impius*) behind the locked doors of the Temple of War, and the resumption of the rule of law are not presided over by Augustus, but by white-haired Faith, Vesta, and the brothers Romulus and Remus, their quarrel finally ended. The imagery of the concluding lines is finely executed and plainly symbolic. But there is a notable reserve, even a coolness, implied about the rights and wrongs of the war that has at last come to an end.

In Book 6, Anchises makes a comparable prophecy to Aeneas (6.756–886). This time there is a specific reference to Augustus (789–805). The tone is highly laudatory. Indeed, where the other two passages display a very decent restraint and dignity, the note struck here is fulsome, as it is also in the sentimental reference to Marcellus, Augustus' nephew and son-in-law (868–86)—a passage that has been much overrated, though it contains some genuine pathos.[1] Augustus' praises are sung over a space of seventeen lines. But apart from one

---

> hunc tu olim caelo spoliis Orientis onustum
> accipies secura; uocabitur hic quoque uotis.

Many hold that these lines refer to Augustus. Conway's arguments, pp. 65–6, seem to me conclusive:

> 286–90 are certainly to be taken (with Serv., whose authority on such a point is paramount) as a prophecy of Julius Caesar, despite the inclination of some moderns (Heyne, Ctn., Sabb.) to link it with Augustus. The Emperor could well wait for the tributes paid him in Books VI and VIII; at this point, his useful but mainly peaceful distinctions would give Venus little comfort and would also be premature in the structure of the Epic, which must reserve for a climax the glories of its patron the Emperor. On the other hand Julius, whose character and conduct were a grave difficulty in the sublime Revelation of Book VI, is well qualified for the present context as representing the largest military triumphs of a race at present conquered, fugitive and in danger. In VI, 835 he is entreated by Anchises to behave well as being *sanguis meus* (a phrase never applied by V. to Augustus), just as here *nascetur pulchra Troianus origine*; which would be merely a cumbrous elaboration of compliment to a man whose father was not a Julius but an Octavius, and who could claim Julian blood only through the mother of his mother Atia. Those who see Augustus in these lines overlook (or mistake) the fact that to prophesy his apotheosis was to prophesy his death, which Horace was slow to do (e.g. *Od.* I. 2, 45–50), and which V. had avoided with some care in *G.* I. 24 (*habitura*), 36 (*eris*) and 42 (*iam nunc*); they also disregard *tum* (291), which is rightly used in the case of the Dictator, since his death left another 13 years of Civil War; whereas it was the *pax Augusta* which gave the first Emperor his power and his name.

[1] There are some curious factual discrepancies between the line of descent from Aeneas as foretold to Aeneas by Anchises and that foretold to Venus by Jove. For details see Mackail, Appendix E.

The Problems Solved

brief reference to the civil war in line 800, he is extolled as the divine general whose conquests cover a wider expanse of the earth than that traversed by Hercules in his labours, or by Bacchus in his migration westwards from the slopes of Nysa in India. Later in Anchises' speech (826–35), and separated from this panegyric by twenty lines of historical pageantry, comes a tableau in more sombre colours depicting Julius Caesar and Pompey as the future instigators, equally guilty, of the civil war. But in these lines there is no hint of Augustus; after the incomplete hexameter (835—Anchises breaks off in the middle of an appeal to Caesar to lay down arms: *'proice tela manu, sanguis meus . . .'*) Virgil sweeps back into events of the previous century, the conquest of Corinth and the overthrow of Perseus of Macedon. Then we come to Marcellus.

The third passage, the longest of the three, consists of a detailed description of the battle of Actium (8.671–713), followed by a 15-line passage (714–28) showing Octavian celebrating his multiple triumph on his return to Rome from the East two years after the battle. Actium is assigned a sequence of scenes in the series of stylized tableaux of Roman history (626–728) worked in gold, silver and enamel upon the magic shield which the fire-god made for Aeneas at Venus' request in his workshop beneath Mount Etna. The emperor is accorded one of the battle tableaux, but has to share it with Agrippa; his main appearance is in the triumphal tableau following. The other tableaux are devoted to the battle scene, the opposed divinities presiding over it, and the flight and death of Cleopatra.[1]

That is all, apart from glancing references to Augustus or Actium (such as 3.274–5, 6.69–74, 7.99–101, etc.). Of the three long passages, only the last (the sequence of tableaux representing Actium and the triumph upon Aeneas' shield) can be said to have been successfully integrated in the architecture of the poem. The section of Jove's speech in Book 1 that alludes to recent events is too brief for such a claim—it is the fine image of Madness enchained that carries it off. Anchises' panegyric of Augustus, the conqueror of the world, looks like something lifted from just the sort of epic poem Virgil did not want to write. The description of the shield is an incomparably finer piece of writing, striking in its stylized imagery. Its function as propaganda, however, is qualified by its context.

The shield, being a magic shield, the work of a god with fore-

---

[1] The layout is in fact very similar to **Horace's** Cleopatra Ode (1.37), which critics have found oddly equivocal in the attitudes implied.

Genesis

knowledge of the future, could, *ex hypothesi*, have anything on it. In fact, the pictures, we are told (626–9), illustrate two themes: (1) the descendants of Aeneas through his son Ascanius (not the descendants of Aeneas by Lavinia); (2) the wars that they will fight. The relevance of the first theme is that this is Aeneas' shield, got for him by his mother Venus; the relevance of the second is that it is a shield for use in war made by the god of armaments. We must assume that Virgil describes only a selection of the pictures on the shield—not all the descendants, not all the wars; some of the pictures described, moreover, (for example, the religious scenes) are somewhat loosely related to the two stated themes; references at intervals to the materials used remind us it is an artefact which is being described, not historical reality. With these reservations, the various action shots have their own internal logic and are strung together in chronological order. The fact that the description of Actium is much the longest grates less than the fact that Catiline and Cato have to provide the sole transition from early history and legend to Actium.

It is important, however, to add to the implicit assertions made by the series of tableaux of Actium the qualifications which the fact that they are pictures on a magic shield imposes. The poet is not committed to the assertion that the forces depicted (Rome's gods pitted against the gods of Egypt) were in fact at work, for the poem moves in a world where everything is caused by gods. The Romans can have their thrill of pride at a victory over a foreign queen, and Augustus his personal thrill of pride. But the poet's integrity is preserved. The hypothesis, in short, on which the poet's fiction rests may be stated as follows. If Vulcan had made a magic shield for Aeneas, and if he had foretold the future on it in pictures, then the scenes he would have depicted might well include those Virgil describes. The only trick Virgil plays on his readers is the trick he plays also in Book 1, that of making the events of recent history the culmination of a historical process. It is a trick the Roman mind, prone always to regard history in terms of a family chronicle, could easily accept, and a very pardonable trick to play in an occasional poem.[1] (See Chapter 5, 'Impure Poetry'.)

In none of the three passages, however, is the name of Augustus

---

[1] See Friedrich Klingner's interesting remark, *Römische Geisteswelt* (3rd edn 1956) 293, about the ancient concept of cycles of history as opposed to our idea of history as a continuum.

W. H. Auden, who had used the idea of a shield that foretold the future himself in an earlier poem, 'The Shield of Achilles', later, in a poem, 'Secondary

The Problems Solved

directly linked with the civil war, and one cannot help a first reaction that the omission is deliberate and disappointing. The battle of Actium had quickly, of course, come to be regarded as the symbol of the end of the war; victories less glorious have often since been treated by historians as turning-points in history. In a sense, therefore, the sequence of scenes on the shield can be regarded as discharging the poet's formal obligation. But if the first element in our analysis of Virgil's solution has really been reduced to these three passages, Virgil can hardly be said to have faced squarely his central task.

What about our second element, the history of Rome? Let us look at the immediate context of the three passages in which reference is made to the recent past. In each the dramatic moment of the narrative is left behind while the legend of Aeneas is linked to Virgil's own day by a graphic presentation of selected historical events. The theme of the first is the future greatness of Rome as a world power; the second singles out some of Rome's future heroes; the third is a series of tableaux depicting crises in Rome's history. But, in addition to these set pieces or pageants—Professor Perret has likened them to the cadenzas of a concerto[1]—our second element gets a good deal of incidental attention. Indeed, we may say that it is more closely woven into the structure of the poem, in the sense that it is always present as a kind of background to the events taking place in the foreground—a future, more or less distant, that is repeatedly foreshadowed. It is, in short, an organic part of the whole. Sometimes the name of a person or place within the narrative touches off an echo, an association with subsequent history. Sometimes a fated connexion between narrative present and historical future is asserted—the most famous example is when Dido calls down upon Aeneas' head the curse that anticipates the Punic Wars and the hatred they generated in historical times between the two peoples. Sometimes the association of past with future is more sustained—for example, in the picture of primitive Italy and the evocation of national types in the catalogue at the end of

---

Epic', objected violently to Virgil's use of the idea:

> No, Virgil, no:
> Not even the first of the Romans can learn
> His Roman history in the future tense,
> Not even to serve your political turn;
> Hindsight as foresight makes no sense. . . .

His objections do not seem to me relevant, once one grasps the care Virgil has taken to anticipate them.

[1] Perret, p. 91.

Genesis

Book 7, or the catalogue of Etruscan types in Book 10, or the conducted tour on which Aeneas is taken by Evander round the future site of Rome in Book 8. The connexion between past and future may be pointed to by Virgil, or left unstated for the reader to sense for himself—this is particularly so with details of religious ritual. As a result, the reader acquires an imaginative conviction of the fundamental unity of the peoples of Italy—a unity which at the time of the battle of Actium had been a political fact for little more than fifty years.

But, though this second element is something which has been made truly part of the poem, it does not form a large part. The *Aeneid* is, before anything else, a story—the story of one man; of our five elements, the third, legend, is the most obvious. In a prose summary, it would be hard to find any space at all for our first and second elements. Reading such a summary, and reading then what all the handbooks tell us, that the *Aeneid* is a national epic, we could well be forgiven for wondering how this can be so.

When Virgil dismissed the idea of a historical epic linking legendary past and recent events in a chronological sequence, in favour of a tale from legend, the fundamental reversal of emphasis which resulted was possible only if Virgil's audience could feel that the story of Aeneas' wanderings and his struggle with Turnus was related to the present occasion. But what had Aeneas to do with Actium? The *Aeneid* is, of course, a tale about Augustus' ancestor; nor was it inappropriate, at the close of a war which had threatened Rome's existence, to look back across history and recall how Rome came into existence in the first place. But these are excuses, not reasons: pegs on which to hang the legend of Aeneas, and not meant to be taken for more than that. Plainly, if Virgil decided to tell the story of a war and a man, it was because he knew his audience would read the *Aeneid* with another war and another man in mind.

We saw that in one sense our fourth element, rivalry with Homer, makes of the *Aeneid* a *tour de force*. Virgil had sailed as close as possible to plagiarism, had produced a poem which imitated other poems to an extent that, one would have thought, must preclude creativity. If instead Virgil succeeded in producing an imaginative fiction that arouses and holds our attention, one major reason for his success is that he has transcended Homer's objective. In one important respect the *Aeneid* differs from all preceding epic poems: it is no longer a story told for the story's sake. It is a poetic myth, appealing more to

The Problems Solved

our fancy than to our taste for adventure. The *collage* technique, the stylization of the narrative, create an atmosphere remote from reality; the narrator's voice acquires a tone, a mannered, serene inflexion, that underlines his detachment from the normal objectives of narrative. The *Iliad* and the *Odyssey* are stories of the recent past, old soldiers' yarns, retold by a poet rather larger than life and with a degree of imaginative surrender that only just outruns contemporary belief. The *Aeneid* is a tale about the distant, legendary, magical past, written for a sophisticated, rational audience able to evoke and appreciate a setting dissociated from their actual beliefs about what men can do and how the world works. Where the *Iliad* and the *Odyssey* are tales told for their narrative excitement, rendered moving and memorable by a genuine if loosely formulated pathos, the *Aeneid* reaches out towards a clearly visualized moral objective.

This is the *fifth element*. Virgil's myth fulfils on an epic scale the function that Horace in his odes often assigns to a two- or three-line vignette from mythology,[1] that of turning a well-known story, or a detail of it, into an imaginative statement of a moral problem. Horace himself experimented with this use of mythology on a larger scale in *Odes* 3.4: not only is his *longum melos* designed as a comment on the events of the civil war (*uis consili expers mole ruit sua*), the battle of the Giants is a symbolic restatement of the battle of Actium—and is commonly so taken by scholars;[2] Horace perhaps intended the ode, the longest of the Roman odes, as some compensation for the epic he refused to write.[3]

Another way of putting it is to say that what Virgil did was to transfer to epic some of the techniques of the animal fable famous from Aesop onwards. Take Horace's story of the town mouse and the country mouse (*Satires* 2.6.79–117). A pastiche of epic style encourages the illusion that the mice are human beings: the town mouse behaves like a city bourgeois expounding his sham culture; the country mouse, with the good sense of a humble, unspoilt rustic. At the same time, Horace keeps dispelling this illusion by details which stress that his characters are really mice. It is good fun, but there is more to it than fun: by forcing the reader to preserve an illusion that keeps threatening to disintegrate, Horace strengthens the moral

---

[1] See, for example, my discussion of the final stanza of *Odes* 1.8 in *Latin Explorations*, pp. 139–40.

[2] E.g., Wickham, and Commager, p. 200.

[3] So Agathe H. F. Thornton, 'Horace's Ode to Calliope (III, 4)', *Aumla* 23 (1965) 96–102.

effectiveness of his narrative. Our understanding of the human types satirized is enhanced by the effort we must make to disentangle the ways in which Horace's characters behave like mice and the ways in which they behave like men.[1]

Equally, Virgil's narrative can be regarded as a kind of Platonic *myth*, a story intelligible on a purely narrative level, but designed primarily to suggest intuitions of things not easily put into ordinary words; it was a form that had recently been given fresh currency by Cicero's use of it in the *Somnium Scipionis*.

Catullus attempted to introduce this element in comparatively naïve fashion into his epyllion Poem 64; in the *Aeneid* it becomes the final integrating element that holds all five in a valid artistic synthesis, and it solves Virgil's moral problem. The ideal contemporary reader we postulated earlier would take it for granted that, somehow or other, Aeneas was Augustus. Educated, by art even more than by literature, to a high degree of perceptivity in the recognition of symbols, he would quickly realize that the poem only made sense if, while seeming hardly to be about Augustus and the war at all, it was somehow about them all the time.

We have to keep saying 'somehow'. Any thoroughgoing equation between Aeneas and Augustus, or between the war through which Aeneas led his people and the civil war, is obviously impossible. Both are 'wrong' wars; both, wars that keep breaking out afresh when all seems over; in both, the right side wins and a just peace follows. But beyond that, the strength of the poem as a comment upon recent events depends on avoiding too close a correspondence. Clear-cut equations would have meant an end of frankness. The *Aeneid* is a poem about a leader who has to learn to lead, who makes the mistakes that leaders make. Because his is the more just cause, he inevitably overcomes his opponents—as fairy-tales always work this way, the sharp edge of propaganda is softened. But his opponents remain worthy of our sympathy, even of our affection. Situations that are never quite the same as situations in the civil war keep reminding us none the less of the civil war, because they involve similar decisions and reveal similar inadequacies in those who must make decisions.[2]

[1] See my discussion of this question in 'Horace as a love-poet', *Arion* 2 (1963) 59–77, especially 65–7.
[2] Take, for example, the episode that begins at 12.311. The situation is obviously close to that which we have in Horace's 7th *Epode* and the link is further suggested by an obvious verbal echo. (See the discussion of this passage in Chapter 4.) At the same time there are obvious differences.

The Problems Solved

Symbolism, unlike allegory, depends on a lack of precise identification, on a refusal of the fairy-tale to be reduced to a retelling of reality with only the names changed.[1] Symbolism differs from allegory in two other important respects. First, the symbolic fairy-tale exists in its own right. It is independent of its symbolic meaning. The tale does not fall apart, or lapse into vapid obscurity, because the correlations of the characters and situations in the tale with characters and situations in reality have not been grasped by the reader. Second, the correlations are never simple or mechanical.[2]

Thus in the *Aeneid*, even on the most fundamental points more than one correlation is possible. Though one thinks first of the civil war, it is often the problems and the situations of the social war that are illuminated by Aeneas' war. Though one thinks first of Augustus, the correlation of the story of Dido and Aeneas in Book 4 is as much with Cleopatra and Julius Caesar (who tried to break free) as with Cleopatra and Mark Antony (who didn't). The presence of all these possible transfers of significance cannot be made explicit. An element of uncertainty always remains, to intrigue the reader and arouse his responsiveness to the text; it permits a degree of guarded frankness otherwise unachievable, and it guarantees the integrity of the poet by enabling him to stop short of final one-sided judgments.

When the mere difficulty of fixing the direction and the limits of the symbolism has stimulated the reader to a more discerning scrutiny of the fairy-tale and the moral situations which it creates, he sees that practically everything is placed in a context that suggests complex attitudes to it; not only multiple possibilities of a transfer of significance to real persons and situations, but the difficulty of judging

---

[1] See Perret, pp. 93–6. His argument is well restated by R. D. Williams in his review of Perret, *CR* 4 (1954) 34–5:

... symbolism is the poet's way of suggesting different levels of significance at which his words may be taken, while allegory is the cruder method of equating. ... In the *Aeneid* symbolism is ever present. ... We read of Dido on one level of significance as the tragic queen who fell in love with Aeneas, on another as the personification of Carthage, symbol of the Punic Wars, and on another as Cleopatra, symbol of the allurements of the East. ... There are in Aeneas, it is true, many of the traits of a future Emperor of Rome; there are symbolized in him many of the virtues of Rome and some of those of Stoicism; but there is also the weakness and weariness of human flesh and blood.

[2] Cf. Pöschl, pp. 36–7:

... das Symbol besteht auch ohne den Bezug auf das andere, das sich in ihm gestaltet, die Allegorie nur durch diesen. Das Symbol gestattet, ja verlangt mehrere Deutungen, die Allegorie nur eine einzige.

persons and situations. We realize that the poet wishes to convey a whole range of attitudes to events—sympathy for the losing cause, for example, as has often been remarked, but also sympathy with the victors: victory can cost them so much. Then there is the complex motivation of events. On one level, events are caused by the gods; but one soon senses these are a plastic embodiment of instinct, impulse, character, and the indefinable something that makes people what they are and renders what they do impossible to account for rationally. On another level, events represent the unfolding of destiny: in the end Aeneas does not beat Turnus by a superhuman effort—Turnus is rendered incapable of fighting by Jove in order to bring about the fulfilment of fate; at the same time we are made to feel the moral or psychological reasons for Turnus' physical failure. On a third level, events are the symbol of things to come. What happens in Books 7 to 12, though its most direct correlation is with the events of recent history, represents also a kind of symbolic foreshadowing of the whole course of Roman history down to Virgil's day.

The large-scale transfers of significance are backed up and made possible by a constant, more incidental play of symbolism.[1] Let us take one brief example, the simile which compares the uproar of lamentation that breaks out when Dido's suicide becomes known, to a city thrown into confusion by an enemy pouring in to destroy it (4.669–71):

> non aliter quam si immissis ruat hostibus omnis
> Karthago aut antiqua Tyros, flammaeque furentes
> culmina perque hominum uoluantur perque deorum.
>
> *Just as if an enemy within the gates were bringing all*
> *Carthage down in ruins, or old Tyre, while the mad flames*
> *roll over the tops of the homes of men and gods.*

The simile is also a symbol. While it helps us to realize imaginatively the confusion of the actual scene in the poem, we realize, too, that Dido's death does represent the overthrow of the hopes of the city over whose construction she had presided—as Anna will say in a moment (682–3):

> 'exstinxti te meque, soror, populumque patresque
> Sidonios urbemque tuam.'

[1] Pöschl's book is mainly devoted to the study of this more incidental use of symbolism. See also Michael C. J. Putnam, *The Poetry of the Aeneid: four studies in imaginative unity and design* (1965), *passim*.

The Problems Solved

'*You have stamped me out, sister, your people, too, your Sidonian elders and your city.*'

The image here also integrates with the other symbolic images of the material fabric of Carthage that each mark turning-points in the narrative of Dido and Aeneas. When Dido first appears in Book 1 (1.503–4), it is to superintend the construction of her city which has just been described in detail. At 4.74–6 we see her escorting Aeneas round the city still under construction, wishing she could ask him to share the task with her. Only a few lines later—the narrative moves so quickly at this point—the disintegration of Dido's sense of responsibility to her city is capped by the memorable image of the unfinished walls stripped of their work force, the cranes and scaffolding looming motionless over them (4.86–9). At line 259, Mercury on landing finds Aeneas, wearing the purple cloak and the sword in its bejewelled scabbard which Dido had given him and with which she was to kill herself, presiding in Dido's stead over the construction of her city (260: *Aenean fundantem arces ac tecta nouantem*)—an image that tells us a great deal very economically about the extent to which Aeneas has acquiesced in the liaison.[1]

This synthesis of five elements—(1) contemporary relevance, (2) history, (3) myth, (4) rivalry with Homer, (5) symbolism—gives the *Aeneid* its peculiar status as a mixed or composite work of art. (See Chapter 5, 'Impure Poetry'.) Any serious attempt at understanding the poem must take cognizance of the constant tension between the story told and the implications of that story—what we may call, if we like, the poem's message. The fairy-tale of war and a man and its continual transfer of significance to a real war and a real man are set against a pattern of implications of which the most constant perhaps are these three. First, that war corrupts; that, as we saw in the previous chapter, no man emerges with his hands clean. Second, that guilt is forgivable: *tout comprendre c'est tout pardonner*. Third, that we are all caught up in a pattern of events beyond our control which it is useless to resist: *fata uiam inuenient*. This is, of course, the transcending Stoic mysticism: whatever a man does, he remains the instrument of the

---

[1] For the symbolism of this sword see *Latin Explorations*, p. 201, note 1. It is worth noting that both Dido and Aeneas free themselves from the tangle of bonds that holds them with the stroke of the sword—Dido by her suicide, Aeneas by the symbolic stroke with which he slashes through the cable that holds his ship to the shore (4.580).

world's purpose.[1] But the poem, I think, was intended to be less creative in its theology than in its anti-militarism and its pervasive humanity. The Stoic doctrine of *fata uiam inuenient* would fall upon ears that were in the main receptive. The function of the poem is rather to spell out a lesson which a people who had taken pride in military glory and in unthinking discipline must have found hard to learn, but which those who had survived the civil war had to learn if they were to look back on the events of recent history with compassionate understanding, or rightly judge the conduct of the victor.

[1] Or, as Edwyn Bevan, *Stoics and Sceptics* (1913) 55, states it: whatever one did would subserve the divine plan. The phrase *fata uiam inuenient* occurs twice in the *Aeneid* (3.395 and 10.113). For Aeneas as the Stoic hero who achieves insight by trial and error see C. M. Bowra, 'Aeneas and the Stoic ideal', *GR* 3 (1933–4) 8–21.

3

Structure

I. GENERAL DESCRIPTION

Our modern texts of the *Aeneid* contain 9,896 lines. The figure includes a number of lines, mostly single lines, which occur in more than one place in the traditional text. Though repetitions of lines and passages are common enough in Homer and also fairly frequent in Lucretius, modern editors tend to assume that the repetitions in the *Aeneid* are more often due to textual corruption or the incompletely revised state of Virgil's manuscript than the result of a wish on Virgil's part to follow Homeric practice, or to adapt it to fresh effects of his own.[1] Some repetitions are surely intentional. The last line of the poem, for example, which describes the death of Turnus:

uitaque cum gemitu fugit indignata sub umbras,

occurs also at 11.831, where it concludes the narrative of the death of Camilla. The Homeric 'model' also occurs twice, of the death of Patroclus (*Iliad* 16.856–7) and of the death of Hector (*Iliad* 22.362–3). Moreover, Camilla and Turnus have much in common: both are young romantics, contemptuous of death—till it stares them in the face.[2]

Much depends on the weight we attach to ancient tradition. We are told that Virgil first prepared a prose draft of his poem, then worked at it piecemeal and in no particular order, often completing the sense of a

---

[1] The question of incomplete and repeated lines is fully discussed by J. Sparrow, *Half-lines and Repetitions in Virgil* (1931).
[2] For a list of possible cases of 'epic' repetition see Sparrow, pp. 79–87.

Structure

passage with a draft line or lines to be worked up later. There is general agreement among ancient authorities that, because of its unfinished state, the poem was revised to some extent by Virgil's literary executors, but that they kept editorial interference to a minimum.[1] Scholars nowadays are less willing to find evidence of uncompleted and incoherent work than they were a generation ago.[2] A particular situation in the poem naturally often resembles another, and it is not improbable that in such cases Virgil occasionally noted down the second time the words he had used previously, leaving the re-formulation of his idea till later. A tendency to re-formulate recurring situations in similar turns of phrase was, moreover, clearly characteristic of the way Virgil's mind worked.[3] But while this seems a reasonable explanation of the repetition, practically without change, of 3.192–5 at 5.8–11, the analysis of Turnus' emotions at 12.666–8 is just as likely to be intended to recall to the reader the analysis of Mezentius' emotions at 10.870–1.[4]

[1] For the prose draft see Suetonius, 94–100R:
   Aeneida prosa prius oratione formatam digestamque in XII libros particulatim componere instituit, prout liberet quidque et nihil in ordinem arripiens: ac ne quid impetum moraretur, quaedam imperfecta transmisit, alia leuissimis uersibus ueluti fulsit, quos per iocum pro tibicinibus interponi aiebat ad sustinendum opus donec solidae columnae aduenirent.
The story of how the *Aeneid* was revised for publication is best preserved in the life prefixed to Servius' commentary:
   postea ab Augusto Aeneidem propositam scripsit annis undecim, sed nec emendauit nec edidit; unde eam moriens praecepit incendi. Augustus uero, ne tantum opus periret, Tuccam et Varium hac lege iussit emendare, ut superflua demerent, nihil adderent tamen: unde et semiplenos eius inuenimus uersiculos, ut 'hic cursus fuit'.
Cf. Suetonius, 177–82R:
   Edidit autem auctore Augusto Varius, sed summatim emendata, ut qui uersus etiam imperfectos, si qui erant, reliquerit. Quos multi mox supplere conati non perinde ualuerunt ob difficultatem, quod omnia fere apud eum hemistichia absoluto perfectoque sunt sensu, praeter illud 'quem tibi iam Troia'.
A similar account is given in the verses attributed by Suetonius to Sulpicius of Carthage (quoted in Chapter 2), and by Macrobius (*Sat*. 1.24.6) and Pliny (*NH* 7.30), in lines attributed to Augustus.
[2] Mackail, for example, in his commentary constantly finds signs of unfinished work; Perret, pp. 140–5, on the other hand concludes:
   Il se peut que l'*Enéide* n'ait pas reçu la dernière main de son auteur; nous n'en pouvons être assurés et il nous est particulièrement impossible de reconnaître en quoi Virgile, le cas échéant, l'aurait rendue plus parfaite.
[3] See Austin on 2.314.
[4] Some editors even restore 12.668 after 10.871, where it is not found in the primary MSS. On such stylized descriptions of emotions see Chapter 5, 'Characterization and Motivation'.

General Description

A more interesting problem is that of the 'half-lines' (*hemistichia*)—lines which are complete in sense but break off, usually at one of the principal caesurae.[1] There are about sixty cases. Whether Virgil proposed to complete any or all of these lines is a much debated question.[2] There is a famous anecdote according to which Virgil completed two half-lines (6.164–5) on the spur of the moment during a reading.[3] But this seems to conflict with the story,[4] also told by Suetonius, that it was his practice to put in draft lines where a passage remained to be completed. All that can be said with certainty is that there is no known precedent for half-lines in a hexameter poem, and that no subsequent Roman poet used half-lines.

Once or twice a whole passage recalls another. The clearest case is that provided by the Sinon episode (2.57–198) and the Achaemenides episode (3.588–691). Mackail regards the latter passage as a quarry used in the construction of the former; others find in the parallel proof of poverty of invention. But it is also possible that the echo is *meant* to be caught and that the similarity between the two situations is an example of *implicit comment* (see Chapter 5, 'Implicit Comment', and the discussion of the Achaemenides episode in Chapter 4). Virgil may want us, in other words, to read between the lines of Aeneas' narrative, instead of taking it at its face value. Certainly a hint of delicate irony in Virgil's description of the appearance of the blind Cyclops suggests an assessment of the situation in conflict with that made by Aeneas, and the final tableau (3.675–81) is one of the finest things in Virgil. Aeneas speaks with horror of the towering figures of Polyphemus and his giant brothers who line the ridge above the beach. But for the reader the horror is softened and a more compassionate attitude prompted by the concluding simile (3.677–81):

cernimus astantis nequiquam lumine toruo

---

[1] The break in mid-sentence at 3.340 is sometimes quoted as an example of a half-line which is incomplete in sense. But the break is probably deliberate—Andromache cannot bring herself to speak of Troy. Cf. 1.135.

[2] See Sparrow, pp. 21–52; F. W. Shipley, 'Problems of the Latin hexameter', *TAPhA* 69 (1938) 134–60; and Perret, pp. 142–4.

[3] Suetonius, 132–9R:

Erotem librarium et libertum eius exactae iam senectutis tradunt referre solitum, quondam eum in recitando duos dimidiatos uersus complesse ex tempore. Nam cum hactenus haberet 'Misenum Aeolidem', adiecisse: 'quo non praestantior alter'; item huic 'aere ciere uiros', simili calore iactatum subiunxisse: 'martemque accendere cantu', statimque sibi imperasse ut utrumque uolumini adscriberet.

[4] See Suetonius, 94–100R, quoted above.

Structure

Aetnaeos fratres caelo capita alta ferentis,
concilium horrendum: quales cum uertice celso
aeriae quercus aut coniferae cyparissi
constiterunt, silua alta Iouis lucusue Dianae.

*We see standing close, uselessly, angry-eyed, the brothers
reared on Etna's slopes, their lofty heads clapped against
the sky, a terrifying band, as when tall-topped oaks,
rising high in the air, or cone-bearing cypresses,
have fallen still, Jove's forest tall or Diana's glade.*[1]

The manuscript tradition is in the main extremely good. There are three primary manuscripts, usually designated in modern editions by the letters M, P and R; M (early fifth century) is complete, P (fourth century) has gaps amounting in all to 879 lines of the *Aeneid*, and R (fifth-sixth centuries) gaps amounting to 2,245 lines. Mackail remarks that there are perhaps not more than a dozen passages, in the 10,000 lines of the *Aeneid*, where an emendation has been generally accepted against the unanimous reading of the primary manuscripts.[2]

There are none the less passages (for example 1.636, 12.648) where the text is corrupt beyond certain repair, though usually the sense is not seriously affected, and rather more passages where minor variations are found between the manuscripts. In a few places (e.g., 4.436, 4.464) we are told the reading was already a matter of dispute in antiquity. More serious than these comparatively trivial uncertainties are a number of passages (e.g., 4.244, 9.486) where it seems hard, or impossible, to attach satisfactory sense to Virgil's words, though there is no tradition of textual corruption and no convincing repair is easily pointed to. We are not, of course, taking into account places where the interpretation of Virgil's words is obscure though the literal meaning is clear, or places where his words are intentionally ambiguous. (See Chapter 6, 'Ambiguity'.) One long passage, the Helen episode (2.567–88), is not found in the manuscripts; the 22 lines are quoted by Servius, who tells us that they were removed from the published text by Virgil's literary executors; once held to be spurious, they

[1] The personification implied by the verb *constiterunt* makes the simile more effective: the trees are merely motionless, i.e., not waving in the breeze, but we are invited to read into their lack of movement some emotion akin to that felt by the Cyclopes, frozen in their tracks in indecision.

[2] Mackail, p. lx. He goes on to cite four instances of departures from the reading of M, P and R which have been generally accepted (though in two of the four cases Mackail prints the MS. reading). For further comment on the text of the *Aeneid* see Büchner, pp. 1476–7.

General Description

are now generally accepted as authentic.[1] With this story we should compare the tradition, reported by Suetonius (183-5R), that Varius (as literary executor) reversed the order of two books—either Books 2 and 3, or, more probably, Books 1 and 3. Such an alteration would require a degree of editorial intervention that seems hard to credit.

What is said in one place in the poem occasionally clashes with what is said in another. Few of the inconsistencies to which attention has been drawn are important. They involve the sort of thing Virgil would probably have tidied up in final revision.[2] A handful have become notorious. Some result from approaching the text in the wrong frame of mind. Palinurus' account of the way in which he met his death, for example (6.347-71), seriously conflicts with that given by the narrator at 5.833-61; but the conflict is almost certainly not inadvertent (see analysis of Book 5). Two are more puzzling: the conflict between the version at 1.267-74 of the line of succession after Aeneas' death and the version at 6.760-70, and what looks like a muddle over the number of years occupied by the wanderings of the Aeneadae—six years at 1.755 and still only six (something like a year later) at 5.626.[3]

Almost all we know about the manner and circumstances of composition of the poem is told us in a short biography of Virgil (220 lines in a modern printed text) by the fourth-century grammarian Aelius Donatus; the biography, intended as part of an introduction to a commentary on Virgil (now lost), is usually taken to represent a reworking of a life of Virgil by Suetonius, and is often referred to (as in this book) simply as if it were the actual work of Suetonius.[4] A second, shorter biography (30 lines), usually attributed to the grammarian Probus, a contemporary of Suetonius, adds little, except some confusion.[5]

For the interpretation of the text of the *Aeneid* we can turn for assistance to a detailed commentary (on Virgil's three major works) by

---

[1] The case for authenticity is carefully stated by R. G. Austin, 'Virgil, *Aeneid* 2.567-88', *CQ* 11 (1961) 185-98.

[2] For a list of inconsistencies see A. Guillemin, 'L'originalité de Virgile', *REL* 8 (1930) 168 ff.; cf. Perret, pp. 140-1.

[3] On this hotly debated question see, e.g., E. de St Denis, 'La chronologie des navigations troyennes dans l'*Enéide*', *REL* 20 (1942) 79-98. For what seems to me a simple explanation see my '*Septima aestas*', *CQ* 17 (1967) 128-9.

[4] Aelius Donatus should not be confused with Tiberius Donatus (also fourth century), who also wrote a commentary (on the *Aeneid*). It survives and is occasionally quoted, but is almost valueless.

[5] We know a good deal, of course, about the *life* of Virgil—e.g., from Horace. See Büchner, pp. 1037-61.

the fourth-century grammarian Servius. It has reached us in two versions. The longer was first printed in 1600 by Pierre Daniel. It is customary to refer to sections of the commentary found only in this longer version by the formula 'Servius Danielis', or 'Servius D.' (occasionally 'Servius Auctus'), to distinguish such references from references to what is considered to be the actual text of Servius. The provenance of these additions is a matter for dispute, but most scholars now regard them as sections of the commentary (which Servius often refers to) of Aelius Donatus mentioned in the previous paragraph which later became assimilated into Servius' text.[1]

Servius' commentary, being the work of a native speaker of considerable erudition, is naturally very valuable indeed. Servius can blunder, however; and he often shows a limited understanding of Virgil's intentions. Our respect for critics nearer than ourselves to the time when an ancient author lived needs to be restrained by thoughts of what eighteenth-century critics made of Shakespeare (Servius is better regarded as a Theobald than a Johnson) and by bearing in mind that after a certain lapse of time (more than four centuries separate Servius from Virgil) greater proximity in time hardly means, on many scores, freer access to the truth.

II. STRUCTURE OF THE TWELVE BOOKS

The twelve books constitute a structure possessing evident harmony in its proportions. Each book is also a structure complete in itself; the narrative units which compose it are easily pointed to, and yet together they form a coherent whole. These are features of the poem the reader needs to grasp—much as discerning appreciation of a well-designed building involves an awareness of its proportions. The lasting power of a work like the *Aeneid* to hold our interest and affection has much to do with the complex relationship of the different parts of the total structure to one another and to the whole. Changes in mood, tempo and narrative technique form a continually varying pattern comparable to that formed by the different movements and parts of movements of a symphony. In addition to the more straightforward, immediate pleasure afforded by the individual parts, there is the more

---

[1] For a summary of this complex question see the article on Servius by J. F. Mountford in *OCD*.

Structure of the Twelve Books

refined pleasure we experience in perceiving the interplay of the parts, and the pleasure produced by our apprehension of the whole as a single, coherent, yet almost infinitely diverse structure.

Alexandrian scholars established the practice of dividing an epic poem into books when they divided the *Iliad* and the *Odyssey* into 24 books each, for convenience of reference. In taking over the practice, Virgil makes it the basis of a series of carefully organized structural patterns. As the poem has come down to us, the books vary in length a good deal: Book 4 (705 lines) is the shortest; Book 12 (952 lines) the longest.[1] In the second half of the poem, a clear break in the narrative separates each book except the last from that preceding. Each time, there is a distinct change of scene; between Books 7 and 8 there is also a lapse of time filled in by a short *Bridge Passage*; Books 9 and 10 each go back in time to the concluding action of the previous book with a change of scene (*Parallel Narrative*—see Section V below). The absence of a break, therefore, between Books 11 and 12, where the narrative flows on with no slackening of the tension and no real change of scene (except that, instead of a distant prospect of both armies, we have a sharply focused close-up of Turnus), is dramatically more effective than if the dividing point had been made at 12.112, where the narrative sequence that began with the Council of War at 11.225 comes to an end. The first six books have a more complicated structure. Dramatically the narrative is continuous. But in Books 2 and 3 the forward flow of the narrative is broken while we look back through Aeneas' eyes over the events of the previous six years; moreover Book 3, though it adheres closely to Book 2—both books are part of Aeneas' long account of his adventures—begins with a marked change of tempo from that of Book 2 and makes only a somewhat half-hearted attempt at narrative continuity.

Each of the twelve books ends with a *Tableau* (see Section III below). The Tableaux are of two kinds. Five times (at the end of Books 2, 3, 4, 6[2] and 9) there is a kind of rallentando of the action (*Tracking*

---

[1] Once again we must remember the poem may not be finished as it stands. On the other hand Mackail, influenced by M. M. Crump, *The Growth of the Aeneid* (1920), seems to me to go far beyond what is necessary or plausible in his detection of incomplete work and his consequent suggestions for tidying up the structure of individual books.

[2] The end of Book 6 looks as though it may not have received the *summa manus*. The rallentando line (899):

> ille uiam secat ad nauis sociosque reuisit

is followed by two lines, one of which is a repetition of 3.277 while the other (reading disputed) forms a rather flat transition to the beginning of Book 7.

Structure

Away—an effect not, of course, confined to ends of books), marked by one or more perfect tenses following a narrative in the historic present (see 'Tenses', Section VI below). Rather more often the action ends in historic presents (Books 7, 8, 10, 11 and 12) or with direct speech (Books 1 and 5), and either runs on into the next book (Books 1, 5, 11) or breaks off with no relaxation of the tension (Books 7, 8, 10).[1]

In each of these final Tableaux there is a central figure. In five (Books 2, 3, 5, 6 and 8) it is Aeneas, and in two more he is in the background while the centre of the stage is taken by another character (Dido in Book 1, Mezentius in Book 10); at the end of Books 11 and 12 the stage is equally divided between Aeneas and Turnus. Aeneas is missing at the end of only three books: in Book 4, the central figure of the Tableau is Dido; in Book 7, Camilla; in Book 9, Turnus. Indeed, the number of appearances in final Tableaux offers a kind of index to the importance of Virgil's major characters (Aeneas: 9; Turnus: 3; Dido: 2; Camilla and Mezentius: 1 each).

Less need be said about the way the books begin. Either there is a brisk continuation of the narrative (Books 2, 4, 6, 9, 10 and 12), or else a short Bridge Passage picks up the threads (*Tracking Forward*) before the narrative is resumed at its normal tempo in historic presents (Books 3, 5, 7, 8 and 11)[2]; this is also the pattern followed when the narrative proper begins at 1.34 after the Introduction. In Books 2, 5, 6, 7 (after the 4-line apostrophe of Caieta) and 11, Aeneas is the central figure, and in Book 3 he is the speaker. Book 1 begins, after the Introduction, with a glimpse of the Aeneadae, before concentrating on Juno, reserving Aeneas for his dramatic entry at line 92; Book 4 begins with Dido; Book 8 with a Tableau of the Italians preparing for war; Books 9 and 12 with Turnus; and 10 with the War Council of the gods.

It is at once apparent that the twelve books can be thought of as two groups of six, and the first half of the poem is often described as Virgil's *Odyssey*, the second as his *Iliad* (see Chapter 5).[3] Both halves have, of course, a common hero and a constantly maintained final objective. Books 1 to 6 contain the narrative of the journey to Italy; in them the

---

[1] The perfects at 5.868 are instantaneous perfects (see Section VI below).
[2] For the opening of Book 5 see *Latin Explorations*, pp. 227–9.
[3] The observation that the *Aeneid* is both an *Iliad* and an *Odyssey* is already foreshadowed by Suetonius (85–6R: *argumentum . . . quasi amborum Homeri carminum instar*) and has been repeated countless times by critics, most recently by Otis, who makes it the basis of his analysis of the poem. Mackail, upset apparently by the implied denial of Virgil's originality, rejects what most find a convenient truism (p. xlv). 'No misconception', he says, 'could be more profound.'

scene changes continually, and there is considerable variation in the tempo of the action (Books 1, 2 and 6 each occupy a day or so, Book 5 several weeks, Book 4 several months, and Book 3 several years). In Books 7, 9, 10, 11 and 12 (after a short Bridge Passage, 7.1–36, describing the final stage of the journey up the coast of Italy) the scene hardly shifts from the mouth of the Tiber. Variety is provided by Book 8, which follows Aeneas up the Tiber to the future site of Rome; near the end of the book we see Aeneas setting out for Etruria, and near the beginning of Book 10 we see him returning to the Tiber and the Trojan camp with the Etruscan fleet. The tempo of the action also varies less in the second half of the poem; though the whole action of Books 7 to 12 extends over a matter of weeks, this time is largely accounted for by the interval needed for the marshalling of the Italian forces between 7.622 and 8.18 and by the twelve-day truce declared at 11.133, which has presumably expired by the time of the Trojan advance announced at 11.445. Leaving out of account the Bridge Passage 8.1–17, Books 7, 8 and 9 each occupy a day or so, while Book 10 (from line 256 onwards), the last 471 lines of Book 11, and Book 12 (except for the first 112 lines) each tell the story of no more than a few hours of fighting. We are hardly expected, of course, to keep track of the passage of time with this degree of prosaic exactness; indeed, a precise chronology is sometimes hard to fix. All the same we should note that—apart from minor variations to avoid monotony—a progressive acceleration takes place in the tempo of the narrative: the poem moves slowly during the first half, quicker in Books 7 to 9, fastest at its climax (Books 10 to 12).

But almost as apparent as the division into two groups of six books is a division into three groups of four.[1] Within this *tripartite structure*, Books 1 to 4 form a closely cohering structure, organized around the long flashback of Books 2 and 3—the dramatic moment of the beginning of Book 4 is the same as that at the end of Book 1; though the narrative ranges over the whole of Aeneas' wanderings, Carthage remains the dramatic setting. Books 5 to 8 form an interlude between the drama of 1 to 4 and the fighting of Books 9 to 12 (foretold for the reader from the opening lines of the poem, more specifically at 1.263, and for Aeneas at 6.86–92 in the Sibyl's prophecy of *bella, horrida bella*). Books 9 to 12 contain the story of the war in Italy: the war is declared at 7.601–22, but the first advance on the beleaguered

---

[1] Noted by Mackail, p. 298. Cf. G. E. Duckworth, 'The architecture of the *Aeneid*', *AJPh* 75 (1954) 1–15.

Structure

Trojans does not begin until 9.25, the actual fighting not until 9.503. There is a lot less fighting in Virgil's *Iliad* than is sometimes assumed. Excluding the skirmish that touches off the war (7.519–39), the Italian advance on the Trojan camp, where no actual fighting takes place (9.25–175), and the night raid on the Italian camp by Nisus and Euryalus and their subsequent death (9.176–458), the narrative of combat is concentrated in five very different groups of episodes: (1) The attack on the Trojan camp (9.459–818)—the war begins at 9.503 with a reminiscence of Ennius:

> at tuba terribilem sonitum procul aere canoro
> increpuit. . . .

A crisp, melodious blast of brazen trumpet sent forth far and wide its terrifying sound. . . .

(2) The pitched battle which follows the simultaneous arrival of Aeneas with the Etruscan fleet and Pallas with the Arcadian reinforcements (10.308–908). (3) The cavalry battle, in which Aeneas and Turnus take no part (11.597–895). (4) The confused fighting which stops the duel (12.266–592). (5) The duel itself (12.681–952). This makes a total of 1,859 lines—something like one third of the total length of Books 7 to 12. (In Books 1 to 6 the only fighting comes in the central section of Book 2—about 200 lines—in which Aeneas relates the destruction of Troy.) There are also, of course, in Books 7 to 12 passages describing preparations for battle, the advance of troops and so on—Virgil does not compose in episodes unrelated to their context and detachable from it.

In none of the five battle-scenes is the fighting continuous. In Book 10, for example, the narrative of battle is interrupted by the episode in which Turnus is spirited away from the scene of battle (633–88) and by the episode in which the body of Mezentius' dead son is brought to him while he rests wounded by the Tiber (833–70). Elsewhere the narrative fabric is varied by vivid brief descriptive passages, often of great beauty, such as the description of the twin giants Pandarus and Bitias, whose foolhardy bravery makes them throw open the gate of the Trojan camp (9.672–82), or the colourful Tableau of Chloreus (11.768–77). Or else a few biographical lines suspend the narrative of battle, filled with a concentrated pathos eliciting our sympathy at the moment of his death for some minor character, such as the unwarlike tenant-farmer's son Menoetes (12.517–20):

Structure of the Twelve Books

et iuuenem exosum nequiquam bella Menoeten,
Arcada, piscosae cui circum flumina Lernae
ars fuerat pauperque domus nec nota potentum
munera, conductaque pater tellure serebat.

*And the young man Menoetes who hated war in vain,
an Arcadian, who on the banks of Lerna where they fish
had plied his art; a poor house he had, no known gifts from
powerful friends; his father rented the land he sowed.*[1]

Even when Virgil is describing the cut-and-thrust of full-scale battle in patent imitation of Homer, there is often an ironic purpose behind his stylized narrative of slaughter. Take, for example, the following bloodthirsty Tableau which ends with a grisly touch, sometimes quoted, by those who have not sensed its purpose, as evidence of Virgil's uncertain taste in the description of battle-scenes (10.379–96):

haec ait, et medius densos prorumpit in hostis.
obuius huic primum fatis adductus iniquis
fit Lagus. hunc, magno uellit dum pondere saxum,
intorto figit telo, discrimina costis
per medium qua spina dabat, hastamque receptat
ossibus haerentem. quem non superoccupat Hisbo,
ille quidem hoc sperans; nam Pallas ante ruentem
dum furit incautum crudeli morte sodalis
excipit atque ensem tumido in pulmone recondit.
hinc Sthenium petit et Rhoeti de gente uetusta
Anchemolum thalamos ausum incestare nouercae.
uos etiam, gemini, Rutulis cecidistis in aruis,
Daucia, Laride Thymberque, simillima proles
indiscreta suis gratusque parentibus error.
at nunc dura dedit uobis discrimina Pallas:
nam tibi, Thymbre, caput Euandrius abstulit ensis;
te decisa suum, Laride, dextera quaerit
semianimesque micant digiti ferrumque retractant.

*So speaking, he rushes into the enemy's midst.
His first opponent, led on by unkind fate,
is Lagus, whom he catches snatching up a mighty rock,
hurls his spear, transfixes him right where the spine
held the ribs apart and then withdraws his spear from the
bones where it had lodged. Hisbo moves in, hoping to
surprise him, but fails; for Pallas, as Hisbo charges*

---

[1] For this interest in common people, cf. the honest widow of 8.407–13.

Structure

> *made careless by frenzied grief for his dead friend,*
> *gets in first and plunges his sword in Hisbo's heaving lung.*
> *He heads next for Sthenius and a man of Rhoetus' ancient stock,*
> *Anchemolus, who dared defile his stepmother's marriage bed.*
> *You fell also, twins, upon the Rutilian plain,*
> *Larides and Thymber (sons of Daucus so alike*
> *their parents knew them not apart, joyful when mistaken).*
> *But now harshly has Pallas differentiated you;*
> *your head, Thymber, Evander's sword has taken off,*
> *your right hand, Larides, seeks you parted from its owner;*
> *the fingers not yet dead twitch around the sword they grasp.*

The final detail of the twitching lopped-off fingers has an interesting pedigree. In Homer (*Iliad* 5.79–82) Eurypylus lops off Hypsenor's arm as he kills him. Ennius goes one better, and adds some real pathos (epic fragment 501–2W—quoted by Servius on *Aeneid* 10.395–6):

> oscitat in campis caput a ceruice reuulsum
> semianimesque micant oculi lucemque requirunt.

> *His head torn from the neck gapes on the plain;*
> *his eyes, half alive, flicker and seek the light of day.*

Lucretius (3.634–69), arguing that part of the *anima* can be cut off along with a limb, recalls that 'stories are often told' (642–3) of chariots lopping off limbs which continue to show evidence of the *anima* trapped in them. Among the examples Lucretius gives is that of a head (654–5) and toes (652–3):

> inde alius conatur adempto surgere crure,
> cum digitos agitat propter moribundus humi pes.

> *Then another tries to rise though he has lost an ankle,*
> *while the dying foot nearby on the ground twitches its toes.*

But we are less concerned with the pedigree of Virgil's lines than with the irony of this scarcely veiled caricature of a heroic battle-scene, accentuated by the concentrated, tantalizing pathos of small, elusive touches: the twins, so alike, their fond parents could not tell them apart, who are distinguished now in death by mutilation; Anchemolus, who 'dared defile his stepmother's marriage bed'—it is the one thing we shall ever know of him. (See Chapter 5, 'Implicit Comment'.) These are the first victims of Pallas, that handsome, courageous young prince for whom we shall shortly want to feel only sympathy. Our

Structure of the Twelve Books

sympathy for Pallas will be justified—can we suppose Virgil felt less deeply than we do for the character he has created? But he wants that sympathy uncontaminated by sentimentality: we should remember, if Aeneas could not, that Pallas was as ready to kill as Turnus.[1]

As we get to know the *Aeneid* better, in fact, it becomes clear that the poem is more about its *uir* than about *arma*—more about a man than about a war. Though Aeneas is absent throughout Book 9 and for most of Books 7 and 11, the story is essentially his story. The three parts of it show him successively as the handsome adventurer (Books 1 to 4), the leader of his people (Books 5 to 8), and the commander in war (Books 9 to 12). We see the increasing load of responsibility that lies on a leader's shoulders, the self-control that responsibility demands, the sacrifices and the anguish of decision that it imposes, the flaws in Aeneas' character that it discovers.

Virgil's mind perhaps liked working in threes. Many of the individual books also fall readily into a tripartite pattern. In Book 4 we have practically the three acts of a tragedy; in other books the divisions are less clear-cut. The recurring patterns may be no more than an unconscious mannerism, but they are sufficiently apparent for us to wonder, in dealing with a writer whose artistry is as self-conscious as Virgil's, whether they were not consciously present in Virgil's mind. In the tabulated analyses of individual books in Chapter 4, each book has been divided into three *Sections*. These divisions should be regarded merely as suggestions, offered more to help the reader with a complicated narrative structure than in any hope of reconstructing the plan to which Virgil worked.

III. THE EPISODES

The tabulated analyses of the twelve books in Chapter 4, as well as the division of each book into Sections, suggest a further division of the poem into 167 *Episodes*. This figure excludes the *Introductions* to Books 1, 2, 3, 6 and 8, formal *Invocations* within books (1.8–11, 6.264–7, 7.37–45 and 7.641–6), the two *Catalogues* (7.647–817 and 10.163–214) and two independent *Tableaux* (9.159–75 and 9.459–72).

[1] For other detailed descriptions of killings by characters of whom we in general approve see 9.324–38, 411–19, 442–5.

Structure

The Episodes fall, roughly speaking, into two types.

The first type have a well organized, coherent structure. At the same time they are units of the total structure, and could not in most cases be removed from the poem without textual surgery; short *Bridge Passages* normally link one Episode to another, making the point of division between Episodes, like the division between paragraphs in a printed text, a matter for editorial whim.[1] These are the Episodes that stick in the memory, because in them some one thing which is important or exciting takes place (Laocoon throws his spear at the horse, Priam is killed, Dido and Aeneas quarrel, Palinurus is lost overboard, a Council of War takes place, Venus heals Aeneas' wounded leg); we are left in no doubt where the action takes place and who is present. Some of the Episodes are long (the Council of War, 11.225–444, is 220 lines in length), some quite brief (the first Laocoon Episode, 2.40–56, occupies only 17 lines).

The second type comprises Episodes which are less tightly coherent. Their function most often is to provide a narrative link between Episodes of the first type. We are told in them the things we need to be told for the story to possess continuity, depth and variety. They seem often, therefore, to lack unity of structure and the divisions made in the analyses are sometimes arbitrary. For example, the burning of the ships, 5.604–99, shown in the analysis as a single Episode, might equally well be divided at line 664 or even at line 685 because the Episode really only provides a narrative framework for a series of Tableaux: the false Beroe, the arrival of Ascanius, Aeneas before his god.

Two other terms need to be defined. One is *Tableau*. This denotes passages, usually a dozen lines or so in length, which highlight a particular situation or moment in the action. Normally a Tableau forms part of an Episode, but occasionally it is independent, serving as an introduction to a book (for example, 2.1–13) or to a Section of a book (for example, 9.159–75, 9.459–72). The second term is *Vignette*. This designates a still smaller unit, usually a line or so, which is made to stand out from a narrative context by a single vivid image.

In any complex work of art, it is easy to point to variations in the size and nature of the units composing it. Variety is a basic requirement

---

[1] For example 1.418–20: at some point in these lines the Episode in which Aeneas meets his mother ends and the Episode in which he arrives at Carthage begins. Some editors make a new paragraph at 418, some at 419. Cf. 1.656: does this line begin an Episode or conclude one?

The Episodes

of all large-scale composition. The proposed division of the individual books of the *Aeneid* into Sections, Episodes, Tableaux and Vignettes is intended primarily to facilitate analytical description of the poem. The reader is not offered the results of a piece of detective work; it is not suggested that the tabulated analyses represent a reversal of the actual process of composition.[1] There are reasons none the less for believing that some such hierarchy of structure was present in Virgil's mind. One reason is that the patterns recur and are easily sensed. Another is that what we are told about Virgil's methods of composition implies he thought of his poem in terms of comparatively small structural units, whose place was determined by a preliminary prose draft, to be composed individually and in no particular order.[2] The different principles guiding large-scale composition and detailed composition were understood and discussed by the ancient critics, as Horace's well-known precept shows (*Ars Poetica* 361–2):

> ut pictura poesis: erit quae si propius stes
> te capiat magis, et quaedam si longius abstes.

As in a picture, so in a poem: one attracts you more when you stand closer to it, another if you stand back some distance from it.

A structural hierarchy has an important function. By giving the story a constantly changing, sharply focused centre of interest, it keeps the story from rambling; the centre of interest dictates each time what is relevant and what may be omitted. As a result a high degree of concentration and economy is possible. Moreover, each time we pass from one unit to another, an opportunity arises for varying the pace: the tempo of an Episode may be reduced, to extract the maximum of pathos or excitement from a situation; or it may be accelerated, to pass quickly over a complicated series of events, pausing for a moment in the process, to pick out a vivid Tableau or Vignette. By a ruthless rejection of incidentals, so that only those details are narrated which

---

[1] G. E. Duckworth, *Structural Patterns and Proportions in Vergil's Aeneid* (1962), has argued that the poem is composed of units constructed so as to bear an exact mathematical relationship to one another—that of the golden section. His calculations necessarily depend on just the kind of clear-cut independence of one Episode, etc., from another that Virgil seems to me to have taken pains to avoid.

[2] See Suetonius, 94–6R, quoted above. Virgil's system of starting from a prose draft has been much derided, but he is not the only major poet to employ this technique. W. B. Yeats also began from a prose draft, followed by various, often numerous, rough verse drafts before reaching a fair copy; see Jon Stallworthy, *Between the Lines* (1963).

Structure

subserve the central interest of the unit in which they occur, the poem acquires a fast-moving, efficient vitality very different from traditional epic.

Because of these characteristics it is tempting, and in many ways appropriate, to call Virgil's technique dramatic. But if we do so we must remember that any use of the term 'dramatic' to describe a text not specifically designed for stage presentation (or purporting to be so designed) is apt to confuse us unless we fix carefully the meaning we wish to attach to it. There are Episodes which may be usefully described as *essentially dramatic*: in them dialogue preponderates almost to the exclusion of narrative; with very little adjustment Virgil's text could be staged. But it is not often that the term can be regarded as —with a little licence—properly descriptive of the structure of an Episode. Rather more often it seems useful to say that an Episode is *dramatic in spirit*; though the structure is, strictly speaking, narrative, perhaps with some dialogue, the Episode has an obvious theatrical quality which is not so much due to the events narrated, as to the way the Episode is constructed. We may perhaps say that the situations are described in such a manner as to ensure that the reader visualizes what is related with a clarity and a sense of excitement that can reasonably be likened to the dramatic experience in its strict sense; sometimes it is only part of an Episode—a single Tableau, say—that stands out because of its dramatic quality. For there are also Episodes which we must describe as *narrative in spirit*, and Episodes finally which we must describe as *essentially narrative*, though they may contain dialogue.

Let us consider these different types.

The Quarrel Episode in Book 4 (4.296–396) provides probably the best example of an Episode whose structure is essentially dramatic. A short Bridge Passage of 9 lines weaves the Episode into the preceding narrative and sets the scene—the equivalent of the stage directions which a modern dramatist builds into his text. A second Bridge Passage, also 9 lines in length, relates the *coup de théâtre* with which the Episode ends (Dido faints before she can finish her speech) and provides a lead-in to the narrative following. Brief narrative comments of 2 to 3 lines (more stage directions) link the three long speeches. Virgil's *technique*, moreover, is thoroughly dramatic: the dialogue reveals character, and creates a clash of personalities that advances the action. Compare the opening Episode of Book 12 (12.1–80), in which the efforts of Latinus and Amata to dissuade Turnus from fighting Aeneas in single combat only increase Turnus' intransigence (see the

The Episodes

detailed discussion of this Episode in Chapter 4); here, too, dialogue preponderates and the technique is thoroughly dramatic. On a larger scale is the Episode of the Council of War in Book 11 (11.225–444); after a rather longer Bridge Passage (225–42) the remainder of the Episode is taken up (except for 15 lines of stage directions) with four long speeches, amounting in all to 187 lines (see the detailed discussion of this Episode in Chapter 4). We may find dialogue used on this scale in Homer; but Homer's speeches are not designed, like Virgil's in the Episodes just mentioned, to effect a theatrical clash of personalities, nor is the narrative context in which Homer's speeches are embedded designed to subserve their theatrical effect.

We may with equal appropriateness call essentially dramatic Episodes of a rather different kind, in which the emphasis falls upon situation more than upon the interplay of character. Take the Episode in Book 1 (1.520–636) where a party of Trojans from the ships damaged in the storm, headed by Ilioneus, is received by Dido while Aeneas watches unseen. There are four fine speeches in this Episode and two *coups de théâtre*: first, the magical revelation of Aeneas (586–93), and then the passage in which Aeneas, after his eloquent promise of eternal gratitude to Dido, strides forward to clasp the hands of the comrades he had believed dead (610–12). (See Chapter 4.)

Compare these Episodes with that of the death of Priam (2.506–58). Structurally this Episode is largely narrative, but it is pure theatre in spirit. Or take the sequence of Episodes that ends with the Trojans dragging the horse within the walls of Troy (2.13–249). It is not the speeches or the incidental dialogue that make these Episodes dramatic in spirit, but the fact that things happen which the text impels us to visualize sharply. The Episodes are constructed with a constant attention to the effect upon the other characters of Sinon's sudden appearance, his able rhetoric, and the apparent confirmation of his lies by the spectacular removal of Laocoon. The two Laocoon Episodes are completely theatrical in spirit, though the second contains no dialogue at all.

But there are also plenty of Episodes which are just as clearly narrative in spirit. A preponderance of dialogue need not make us feel we want to describe an Episode as dramatic. The dramatic structure may be no more than a convenient convention, as in the Episode in which Jove makes his great prophecy to Venus (1.223–304), or that in which Aeneas meets his mother disguised as a huntress (1.305–417). Too little happens in these Episodes for us to want to call them dramatic; there is no particularly striking portrayal, or conflict, of character. We are closer to Homer or Apollonius.

Last of all, there are Episodes which we must describe as essentially narrative, though they may contain dialogue and often individual Tableaux which are brilliant and exciting. Take the Episode describing Aeneas' arrival at Carthage (1.418–519). In the course of a hundred lines the scene changes half a dozen times. We first see Aeneas climbing the hill that dominates Carthage; a few lines later he has come down into the town and we see him looking up at the tall buildings rising among the huts (438: *fastigia suspicit urbis*); next we watch him mix unobserved with the crowd till he comes to the temple; while he is contemplating the scenes that commemorate the Trojan War, Dido arrives and for 13 lines (496–508) the centre of interest shifts to her; then Ilioneus and the other Trojans arrive, a scene which we watch through the eyes of Aeneas and Achates. All this is excellent vivid writing, but it cannot usefully be described as dramatic in structure or in spirit. Short Tableaux light up the Episode, but the Episode as a whole has the characteristic linear movement of narrative: the story moves forward step by step, scene follows scene, event follows event. The characteristic movement of drama is circular: the action revolves around a single situation, while we watch the reactions of the characters, as in the Quarrel Episode or the Council of War; or while we wait for the inevitable to happen—we know from the outset that Priam must be killed, that the horse will be admitted; the relationship of the parts in these Episodes is an organic or cumulative one. Compare the Episode of Nisus and Euryalus in the sleeping Italian camp (9.314–66) or the Episode of the banquet in Book 1 (1.697–756). In these Episodes, the number of separate steps in the story is not in any way dictated by the structure of the Episodes. They could be multiplied or reduced without structural harm. We may guess that in the end Nisus and Euryalus will be killed; when they have finished eating, it is natural that Dido should ask Aeneas to tell the story of his adventures. But these things are not foreseeable in the way events are foreseeable in tragedy. This is particularly the case in the battle Episodes in the second half of the poem.

IV. PROJECTION OF THE NARRATOR INTO HIS NARRATIVE

When we say of a passage of *narrative* that it is dramatic, what we are pointing to isn't most often just the fact that Virgil's technique is unusually vivid, or subjective, or designed to play upon our emotions.[1] These qualities are the consequences of the very extensive use of what is in itself a simple enough device.

There are broadly speaking two procedures open to the writer whose form is not pure drama. The most obvious role for him to adopt, or so it seems to us, is that of the chronicler of past events who contents himself with putting on record what occurred (in fact or in fiction) along with his own comment on the events he records. This is the technique generally adopted nowadays by historians and in most sophisticated forms of narrative. There is, however, an alternative procedure which has a distinguished ancestry. The writer who adopts this procedure projects himself into the past (or into his fiction), relating the events as if they were actually taking place as he writes—or rather as he speaks, for this type of narrative usually preserves, or simulates, the narrator's speaking voice. To put it more simply, description is substituted for report. The speaker re-lives the past, recapturing as he does so the emotions originally aroused by the events described in those who saw them happen; the reactions of the original participants become the narrator's reactions. We might suppose that this is a technique which has existed from the beginnings of literature. In fact in its literary form it is a good deal more sophisticated than it appears. It is unknown to Homer, who always adopts the standpoint of one who is recording past events. We first find the graphic description of the past as still present in Herodotus, in whom it is an occasional technique, used in those parts of his story which he wishes to make particularly exciting.[2]

An essential feature of this more dramatic or graphic form of narrative is the use of the present tense. But by Virgil's day the present

[1] Otis stresses the subjectivity of Virgil's style. Heinze remarks on what he calls '*die überwiegende Richtung Virgils auf das Psychische*' (p. 362, see especially the following paragraph), a feature repeatedly stressed by Pöschl; the vividness of Virgil's narrative style is obvious to all. For the differences recognized by ancient critics between the conventions of history and tragedy in the treatment of emotion see Austin on 2.486 ff., and also on 2.195–8 and 2.554. I am not concerned to reject these assertions, but to draw attention to their structural basis.

[2] See J. Humbert, *Syntaxe grecque* (2nd edn 1954) 137–8.

tense in the narration of past events (what grammarians call the historic present) had become so usual that it amounted to little more than a stylistic mannerism: no real projection of the writer into his narrative accompanied the use of the present tense and none was invited from the reader. Roman writers, indeed, had always preferred the present tense in narrative, perhaps because the forms of the perfect tense were often cumbersome, but originally, one suspects, out of sheer linguistic ingenuousness.

Naturally we cannot tell what led Virgil to lend an old technique a new stringency and effectiveness. Perhaps it was his fondness for restoring to words their full, precise meaning (often eroded away in current usage) that made him ask what would be the result if the historic present, instead of being merely a stylistic variation, were treated as a tense that actually meant something different from the perfect tense. Perhaps it was his practice of composing in small-scale units that led him to exploit ways of making them graphic and self-sufficient. Or perhaps it was a natural flair for the dramatic, a habit of thought which made him visualize events in terms of situations (how the thing looked, how it affected the participants—what we call empathy) instead of thinking in abstract terms of events as things to be recorded. Most likely all these factors were involved.

The next chapter will provide many examples of the dramatic Tableaux and Vignettes that stud the narrative fabric of the poem. As a consequence of them the narrative proceeds in a series of described scenes with a minimum of connecting reportage. Where there is reporting, it usually takes the form of a short summary linking Tableaux—recording the arrival of a character in a scene that is then described, or reporting his departure from that scene, or providing some kind of recapitulation or brief comment on motivation or appearance.

The success of such Tableaux depends on a rigorous selection of detail, the basis of which needs to be understood. The writer who attempts a compressed, detached *record* of past events bases his selection upon an intellectual analysis of the events to be described; the details chosen are those which are either factually important, or those which it seems logically slovenly to omit—details the reader expects to be recorded even where it is obvious that they must have occurred. Virgil's method is completely different. He concentrates on the things he finds visually interesting (things which are themselves spectacular, or which serve as an index of inherent emotion—what

Projection of the Narrator into his Narrative

Eliot called the objective correlative of the emotion), leaving it to the reader to fill in the rest for himself. Take the Tableau of Aeneas crossing Acheron (6.410–16):

> caeruleam aduertit puppim ripaeque propinquat,
> inde alias animas, quae per iuga longa sedebant,
> deturbat laxatque foros. simul accipit alueo
> ingentem Aenean: gemuit sub pondere cumba
> sutilis et multam accepit rimosa paludem.
> tandem trans fluuium incolumis uatemque uirumque
> informi limo glaucaque exponit in ulua.

He turns the dark blue hull round and comes alongside the bank,
then thrusts the rest, the souls, aside from the long benches
where they sat and lets the gangways down, taking aboard as he does so
the mighty Aeneas. Beneath his weight the patched-up craft
groaned and the holes let the marsh flood in.
Safely across the river at last, he disembarks priestess
and warrior among the shapeless slime and the grey-green sedge.

The first two and a half lines sketch in the background: Charon was already on his way; he turns back to pick up Aeneas, dumping a cargo of souls to make room for him. The next two and a half lines are devoted to recapturing a single moment in the journey: Charon's ghostly tub creaks as Aeneas climbs aboard (it was not built to take the weight of a living hero) and the marshy waters of the Styx pour in at the seams. No time is wasted in telling us that the Sibyl somehow got aboard, too; she is glanced at in the next line, but the alliteration *uatemque uirumque* is aimed at stylization of the narrative more than factual completeness; we are not told whether any of the other passengers remained—if only to help with the rowing (compare line 320); or did Aeneas, like Aristophanes' Dionysus, have to work his passage? There is no description of the boat getting under way; nothing is said of the journey itself; the disembarkation is cut to a terse statement that both passengers arrived safely; if *tandem* suggests the trip was a slow and painful business, coupled with *incolumis* it reflects the passengers' feelings more than it states a fact. We do not see them take their leave of Charon—all the details of arrival are eliminated so as not to detract from the impact of the last line and the impression the slime and sedge convey of the horror of Aeneas' reaction as he sets foot upon the farther shore. The principle guiding Virgil's selection of detail is that we are told what catches the eye of the

Structure

narrator. The first sentence is the most detailed because something unusual has happened: each of Charon's actions interests the observer, until the scene is dominated by Aeneas. In the second sentence, everything is concentrated on the moment of Aeneas' embarkation; in the third sentence, on making us feel what it must have felt like to be Charon's passenger at the moment of arrival: relief that the journey is safely over, horror at what confronts him. There is no temptation to the reader's misguided curiosity to let his attention stray.

Until he becomes accustomed to Virgil's technique, the reader has to be on his guard against a tendency, inculcated in the schoolroom, to take it for granted that he is being offered an account aimed at helping him to get the facts straight. Take the lines which begin Virgil's description of the naval race (5.114–23):

> prima pares ineunt grauibus certamina remis
> quattuor ex omni delectae classe carinae.
> uelocem Mnestheus agit acri remige Pristim,
> mox Italus Mnestheus, genus a quo nomine Memmi,
> ingentemque Gyas ingenti mole Chimaeram,
> urbis opus, triplici pubes quam Dardana uersu
> impellunt, terno consurgunt ordine remi,
> Sergestusque, domus tenet a quo Sergia nomen,
> Centauro inuehitur magna, Scyllaque Cloanthus
> caerulea, genus unde tibi, Romane Clüenti.

Commentators usually assume that they are dealing with an intellectual analysis of the basic facts, presented with the degree of ornate obliqueness prescribed by the conventions of the Common Style of Augustan verse. (For the term 'Common Style' see Chapter 6.) Acting on this assumption, they translate the first two lines somewhat as follows: 'Four ships entered for the first event, selected from the whole fleet and well matched with their heavy oars.' This corresponds so well to their expectation of how a naval race *should* begin, they are liable to blind themselves to the violence they have done to Virgil's poetry. In fact what we have is a dramatic Tableau, related in the present tense as though by an eye-witness. We are told what the observer notices; the details that attract his attention in the spectacle he is watching are not necessarily those he would consider the most important, the most worthy of record, if he set out subsequently to recollect in tranquillity what had occurred. Virgil's *ineunt certamina* is not the abstraction suggested by our translation, but the narrator's description of the actual progress of the ships up to the starting-point.[1] At this stage the four hulls advance abreast in column (*pares*[2]). The detail that catches the spectator's eye in this scene is the ponderous movement of the oars; when the race begins, the rapid motion of the oars will disguise their weight, now they thud into the water at each stroke: *grauibus remis* is therefore instrumental ablative with *prima ... ineunt ... certamina*; we might paraphrase, 'they row ponderously up to the starting-point of the first event', but Virgil's words are of course more clipped, more graphic than any prose equivalent. The usual interpretation (to take *grauibus remis* as descriptive ablative with *pares carinae*) involves the editors in all manner of implausibilities in explaining away how the ships can be described as 'well matched' in rowing-power when we are later told specifically (line 153) that they were not; again modern notions tend to intrude, causing us to suppose that Virgil means the organizers took trouble to ensure fair play, when all he means by *ex omni delectae classe* is that the organizers selected the four best ships in the fleet.

A series of spectator's impressions follows. The keenness of the rowers on one ship strikes him; the size of another—it is not in fact the largest,[3] but his eye lingers on its three banks of oars, though all the ships are triremes; the colour of the third. There is no logic behind the selection of detail. It just happens that these are the things the observer notices in each case. At the same time the spectator remains, of course, the ideal, omniscient narrator of epic, able therefore to know the future history of the houses that later claim descent from the captains of the ships, and preserving the tone, syntax and diction appropriate to epic relation. There is the same conflict between psychological realism of context and non-realism of form that we find in the speeches of Virgil's characters, the same tension between psychological truth and the poetic artificiality of the verbal fabric.

We shall find in the *Aeneid* innumerable instances of this technique of presenting narrative in visual, elliptical form. It explains what must otherwise seem the curiously arbitrary nature of Virgil's narrative in the catalogue in Book 7 of the forces which march to the assistance of Turnus under their various commanders, the way a piece of vivid imagery is often left tantalizingly unclear (because Virgil

[1] Cf. 7.647–8:
primus init bellum Tyrrhenis asper ab oris
contemptor diuum Mezentius agminaque armat.
[2] For this use of *pares* cf. 5.580.
[3] *Scylla* is heavier than *Chimaera*—see line 153.

Structure

is not concerned with explaining clearly, but with capturing the dramatic possibilities of quick action-shots), or the way descriptive detail and narrator's comment are constantly intermingled (because the comments are those that spring from the poet's reaction to the scene into which he has projected himself). It explains also Virgil's fondness for what is apt to appear irresponsible exaggeration—his Trojan horse is 'as big as a mountain' (2.15: *instar montis equum*): for the excited spectator (in this case Aeneas) naturally exaggerates—he communicates his reactions to what he sees, not a dispassionate assessment of reality.[1]

Another interesting consequence of this projection of the narrator into his narrative is that the distinction between past and present is obscured. The more fanciful parts of Virgil's narrative acquire as a result a kind of implied reality that is not actually asserted. Dido's seduction by Aeneas in the cave, for example, is followed by an Episode in which we see Rumour spreading her report of scandalous goings-on at the royal palace. The narrative of Rumour's activities begins in the present tense (4.173):

> extemplo Libyae magnas it Fama per urbes
>
> *Straightway Rumour goes through Libya's great cities*

(where *it* is graphic, like *ineunt* at the beginning of the naval race)—and then breaks off for an elaborate description, first of the appearance of this monstrous creature (4.174–83), and then of the way she operates (4.184–7):

> nocte uolat caeli medio terraeque per umbram
> stridens, nec dulci declinat lumina somno;

---

[1] Compare 1.510–11: the names are those of the three men whom the narrator, or perhaps Aeneas, caught sight of at first glance. Ilioneus is not named (he is simply among *Teucrorumque alios*); though he will be the most important (the spokesman) of the group, he is not at first noticed. Or take the description of the attack of the serpents on Laocoon and his sons—*depascitur* (2.215), for example, does not mean (as some have improbably supposed) that the serpents consume the boys on the spot, or even that they devour their limbs (*artus*); the narrator observes the serpents' hungry assault, then his gaze switches to Laocoon as the serpents turn to attack him—he is their real objective. We are never told what happened to the boys because the narrator did not take in at the time what happened to them—his attention was directed elsewhere.

For further theoretical discussion of this technique of selective detail see *Latin Explorations*, pp. 202–11, 'Elliptical Narrative'.

Projection of the Narrator into his Narrative

>   luce sedet custos aut summi culmine tecti
>   turribus aut altis, et magnas territat urbes.

By night she flies midway between sky and earth, hurtling through
the darkness, not closing her eyes in the pleasure of sleep;
by day she sits on guard, high on a roof-top
or on lofty towers, bringing terror to mighty cities.

We then return from this general statement about Rumour for a description of her activities in the case of Aeneas and Dido; and as we do so, we actually move back (while Virgil picks up the thread, as it were, of what he was saying) into the imperfect tense (4.189–90):

>   haec tum multiplici populos sermone replebat
>   gaudens, et pariter facta atque infecta canebat. . . .

Now she began to spread among peoples all manner of talk,
rejoicing, filling her recital equally with things done and not done. . . .

We come forward again into the present for the Bridge Passage connecting this Episode to the Episode of Iarbas among his altars (4.195–7):

>   haec passim dea foeda uirum diffundit in ora.
>   protinus ad regem cursus detorquet Iarban
>   incenditque animum dictis atque aggerat iras.

Such the talk the obscene goddess spreads everywhere on men's lips.
Without delay she turns aside to King Iarbas,
inflames his thoughts with her words and piles his anger up.

What has happened? Suppose Virgil had used the perfect tense in his narrative. For the monster's appearance and habitual activities he would have had then to shift to a tense appropriate to description—either the imperfect, or the present. The imperfect would have left Rumour a creature within the fairy-tale. The present would have warned the reader that a statement was being made allegedly true also of the present time, and he might have been disposed to reject the assertion. By using the present for the *events* in his story, Virgil can get away with the present for description, though this amounts to an assertion that the monster Rumour actually exists in the present—the historic present is exclusively a narrative tense, not available for description. But in projected narrative, where past becomes present, the encroachment of fairy-tale upon reality is so unobtrusive that it hardly occurs to us to challenge it.

Structure

V. PARALLEL AND SUSPENDED NARRATIVE

In the simplest form of story everything takes place in a single setting. Next in order of structural complexity comes the story which follows a single character or group of characters from scene to scene, simply discarding other characters when they have served their purpose; last, the story in which the interest is divided to describe things happening to different people in different places at the same time.

This third type of story involves structural considerations which do not arise with the other two types. Interrupting the linear progression of a story for the parallel relation of simultaneous events, though it marks the beginnings of sophistication in story-telling, is a device as old as Homer. So long as the larger units of structure are involved, Virgil's use of *Parallel Narrative* hardly calls for comment. Clearly the events narrated in Book 9 run roughly parallel to those narrated in Book 8, and the two sets of Parallel Narrative join with the return of Aeneas to the Trojan camp at 10.256; the reader is warned of the switch from the first set of events to the second by the opening line of Book 9. Yet even here Virgil's artistry should not be underrated. Consider the point selected to effect the switch—the first set of events is not followed through to its conclusion before reverting to the second; though we return at 9.1 to the beleaguered Trojan camp, Aeneas' task (to find allies in the coming war) is still unaccomplished as we leave him lifting on to his shoulder the wonderful shield on which is represented the destiny and glory of his descendants (8.731: *attollens umero famamque et fata nepotum*). Consider, too, the point of juncture of the second narrative with the original narrative: instead of another *atque ea diuersa penitus dum parte geruntur* at the beginning of Book 10, we follow the besieged Trojans into the events of a fresh day (10.118–45); then a second shorter, more fast-moving piece of Parallel Narrative carries us back to the point where we left Aeneas at the end of Book 8; this narrative in its turn is suspended for the catalogue of Etruscan ships (10.163–214), and then resumed to conclude with the *coup de théâtre* at 10.261, when from the leading ship Aeneas raises aloft his magic shield as a signal to the Trojans lining the walls of the besieged camp. (See Analysis of Book 10 in Chapter 4.)

What has happened is that Virgil has combined the device of

Parallel and Suspended Narrative

Parallel Narrative with another device, that of suspending the narrative at a crucial point.

This second device of *Suspended Narrative* can occur independently: an unexpected turn of events may simply continue the linear progression of the narrative. For example, when Laocoon at 2.52 strikes his spear against the flank of the wooden horse and the Greek stratagem seems on the verge of discovery, the attention of all is distracted by a group of shepherds and their prisoner Sinon. Here we have, as Heinze remarked, a typical Virgilian structural device.[1] The device of projected narrative allows actually a slight overlap in the two actions: the imperfect *trahebant* suggests the shepherds had been approaching for some time before the observer noticed them. Then, 150 lines later, with this second action complete the centre of interest reverts to Laocoon.

But naturally the two devices occur often in conjunction with one another. Consider the structure of the narrative in Book 10 following the death of Pallas. The run of the narrative which relates the trail of blood Aeneas leaves behind him in his wild pursuit of Turnus is suspended at line 605, and we do not return to Aeneas until three Episodes later at 769 (after the Bridge Passage 762–8). What takes place in the interval? First we hear Jove and Juno arrange to put Turnus out of his pursuer's reach (606–32); next (633–88) we follow the Episode of Turnus' eerie escape through to the point where the ship on which he is trapped carries him back to his own city of Ardea; next (689–761) we move back in time to the point immediately following Turnus' departure from the battlefield for a narrative of the exploits of Mezentius. Then at 769 Mezentius meets Aeneas and the suspended narrative of Aeneas' exploits is resumed, though not at the point in time where we left him at 605, but at some later point—thus permitting a judicious curtailment of Aeneas' bloodthirsty pursuit of revenge.

Quickly a second pattern of interlocking Episodes begins. Mezentius is wounded in his duel with Aeneas, saved from death by the intervention of his son, and assisted from the battlefield (762–832). But we do not follow him; for though this Episode began with Mezentius at the centre of interest, he was displaced from the leading role by Aeneas at 800 and we now remain with Aeneas until he has killed Lausus. After Lausus' death, the narrative of Aeneas' exploits is suspended a

---

[1] Heinze, p. 20:
Auf dem Höhepunkt der Aktion Eintreten der Gegenaktion: das ist echt virgilische Struktur der Handlung.

second time while we move back again to rejoin Mezentius as he washes his wound in the Tiber and waits anxiously for news of his son (833–70). But meanwhile his son has been killed by Aeneas and the sequence of events which we had followed through to their climax now impinges at 841 on the new sequence of events to which our attention has been switched; finally, Mezentius, having brought us back to Lausus, rides out to meet Aeneas and to his death (870–908).

Parallel and Suspended Narrative can both occur within a single Episode. By their use the opening Episode of the second Section of Book 2 (2.250–67) is given a neat, circular structure. A short descriptive passage ends with a Vignette—in Troy all is silent; exhausted by the excitement of a day of rejoicing, the Trojans have fallen silent and now lie sprawled in sleep (2.252–3):

> fusi per moenia Teucri
> conticuere; sopor fessos complectitur artus.

The centre of interest shifts to the Greeks—the Greek fleet is already on its way back to Troy. The Greeks give the pre-arranged signal— and the centre of interest reverts to Troy: at the signal Sinon unbolts the horse's flanks; the Greeks within slide down a rope and 'pour into the city buried in wine and sleep' (2.265):

> inuadunt urbem somno uinoque sepultam.

We are back at the point where we left the Trojans at line 253, and the parallel streams of narrative now join.

Usually the reader is warned of the parallel relationship between successive Episodes by the use of a word or formula that points to their contemporaneity.[1] Within an Episode, where the overlap of parallel events is seldom more than partial, the only indication is often that provided by a change of tense. The overlap is often missed therefore by the modern reader as a result of a natural tendency to assume that events following one another in the narrative also follow one another in time. Take the opening Episode of Book 12. Since Amata's words follow Turnus' reply to Latinus (12.48–53) we may be tempted to suppose that the intervening Bridge Passage (12.54–5):

> at regina noua pugnae conterrita sorte
> flebat et ardentem generum moritura tenebat

---

[1] See O. W. Reinmuth, 'Vergil's use of *interea*, a study of the treatment of contemporaneous events in Roman epic', *AJPh* 54 (1933) 323–39.

Parallel and Suspended Narrative

But the queen, dismayed by the new turn of the fighting,
was in tears, as wanting death she clung to her eager son-in-law

relates a reaction to Turnus' words which does not take place till he has finished speaking. In fact, as the imperfects *flebat* and *tenebat* make plain, what Virgil means is that at the moment when Turnus finished speaking, Amata had already for some time been clinging tearfully to Turnus in an agony of despair provoked by his mood of passionate truculence. It is as if the narrator only now becomes aware of Amata: she was there all the time; but till now the narrator's attention was focused on Turnus. Compare 1.748–52:

> nec non et uario noctem sermone trahebat
> infelix Dido longumque bibebat amorem,
> multa super Priamo rogitans, super Hectore multa;
> nunc quibus Aurorae uenisset filius armis,
> nunc quales Diomedis equi, nunc quantus Achilles.

> *Moreover ill-fated Dido had been making the night last*
> *with talk of every sort, drinking love in a long slow draught,*
> *piling up questions about Priam and about Hector, too,*
> *now how armed the son of Dawn had come, now*
> *what Diomede's horses were like, now how big Achilles was.*

We underestimate the artistry of Virgil's conclusion if we suppose that Dido does not begin to ask her questions till Iopas has finished his song—right at the end of the book. The imperfects unobtrusively imply a quite different situation, which we may perhaps fill out somehow like this: Dido has been talking to Aeneas throughout the banquet—and falling more and more in love with him; the narrator has not missed what has been going on, but hitherto there have been more important things to describe; their conversation now becomes important because Aeneas' account of his adventures will follow out of what they have been talking about; a quick recapitulation of what has been happening becomes necessary, to explain what is about to happen.[1]

[1] Compare 1.579–81; 4.238–9; 8.152–3; 12. 247–50; sometimes the overlap is pointed to explicitly by the wording of a short Bridge Passage, as in 4.362–4 or 12.938–41, but often Episodes which overlap only slightly are linked by the use of imperfects in the Bridge Passage (see next Section, *Tracking Forward* and *Tracking Away*).

Structure

VI. TEMPO OF THE NARRATIVE: TENSES

The narrative units differ in tempo no less than the books which they compose. At one end of the scale come those most nearly dramatic in structure—the hundred lines of the Quarrel Episode represent an action that might well last no longer than it takes to read. In the Introduction to Book 3, on the other hand, the narrative sums up in the space of twelve lines events we must suppose to occupy something like twelve months. We expect, of course, some variation of speed in a long poem;[1] but in the *Aeneid* the variation is particularly marked, and something needs to be said about the principles to which Virgil works and his technique for putting them into effect.

The first point to observe is that the allocation of space bears little relation to what might seem to us the inherent dramatic or narrative possibilities of the situation. If in Book 4 Virgil allots 101 lines to the quarrel and cuts down the seduction to a 7-line Tableau, it cannot be said that this was the only way to go about it. Or take two cases which seem more strictly comparable—the departure of the exiles from their homeland at the beginning of Book 3 and their departure from Buthrotum later in the same book (3.472–505). The first is a harrowing occasion, full of possibilities for pathos; the second little more than a touching incident. Yet Virgil allots 34 lines to the departure from Buthrotum and only 4½ lines (8–12) to the departure from Troy.

His decision may be said to be dictated primarily by a sense of what is appropriate: a seduction, a departure into exile are things easily overplayed; so Virgil deliberately plays them down. To say that is already to point to a principle of composition—a fastidious avoidance of effects cheaply secured. But structural considerations are also involved. In Book 4 the main weight of interest falls upon the disintegration of the affair between Aeneas and Dido; everything before the Quarrel Episode is preliminary to the main action of the book.[2] In Book 3 Virgil is compressing the events of something like five years into the space of little more than seven hundred lines. Obviously, unless the book is to read like a dull epitome, certain scenes—not too

---

[1] Otis, Chapter 2, gives the name 'asymmetry' to this feature of what he calls the 'subjective' style.
[2] See *Latin Explorations*, 'Virgil's Tragic Queen', pp. 32–5.

many—must be played up. But the scenes must be carefully distributed. One chosen for fuller treatment is the departure from Buthrotum: it brings the book to life again after the long prophecy of Helenus, in readiness for the accelerated tempo and marked increase in narrative interest of the final Section of the book.

But techniques evolved to achieve a poet's architectural intentions can become ingrained habits of thought. In lesser artists they degenerate into mannerism; in the case of really great artists they can form the characteristic stylistic basis of a way of writing that constantly furthers the poet's capacity for creative expression. As a result of Virgil's keen dramatic sense, his experiments with tempo acquire a quite exceptional importance, affecting not only the overall layout of his epic, but his handling of individual Episodes, Tableaux and even Vignettes.

Virgil is thus led to exploit, to an extent not found in other writers, the resources of connotation which the Latin tenses had inherited or acquired as the literary language evolved. There were five forms at his disposal: the historic present, the perfect, the imperfect, the pluperfect, and the historic infinitive. Of these five, the historic present is easily the commonest in the *Aeneid*, as it is in most types of narrative in Latin.[1] Where Virgil differs from other writers is in the care he takes to make the historic present subserve his technique of projected narrative. He limits the historic present, in short, to those parts of his narrative where the implication inherent in the form (that past events are being narrated as though they were taking place before the speaker's eyes) is brought out by the context. (See Section IV, above.) The graphic, essentially *dramatic* structure of such passages is enhanced by a contrasting employment of one or more of the other narrative tenses, to which roles are assigned that are also in some ways peculiar to Virgil and need careful definition.

In English we worry less about the distinctions Latin makes as a matter of course between different kinds of past action; the interplay, for example, between perfect (or historic present) and imperfect is not at all deeply ingrained in those who speak English. The fact that we have to resort to clumsy periphrastic forms discourages precision: 'he

---

[1] On an average the historic present is about three times as frequent as the perfect in the narrative sections of the poem. (Some forms, e.g., *soluit*, are of course ambiguous, but one may conjecture that they would be felt by the Roman reader as belonging to the same tense as adjacent verbs.) The incidence of perfects rises markedly in the more dramatic sections of the narrative. For some statistics see *Latin Explorations*, p. 222.

always said' is the natural English for *semper dicebat*, not 'he used always to say', or something similar. Many writers use the periphrastic forms only when they are driven into a syntactical corner: we have to say, 'while she was reading, he came in'; but most of us would say 'he smoked while she read', more often than 'he was smoking while she was reading'. The Romans were less free: in Latin—as in Greek—every past action involved a decision between rival tenses. But the fact that the system existed and functioned smoothly enabled a Roman to make distinctions which we can only make less readily, and to appreciate distinctions instinctively that we are apt to miss in reading Latin.

Despite its name, the Latin perfect serves more often in all classical writers as a simple past tense (referring to a single occasion—whereas the English simple past tense is often used instead of the more cumbersome past continuous) than as a true perfect, though it has this function also. This is not to say that Virgil or his contemporaries felt that the tense meant different things in different contexts. Many of them would have been aware, it is true, that the Latin perfect corresponded to two separate tenses in Greek, and we should never discount the effect of Greek syntax on the usage of literary Latin. But it is better to say that Virgil's choice of the perfect depends on the connotations the tense imparted to a context rather than on any consciously assessed temporal significance. Since, however, no English tense offers a range of connotation corresponding to the Latin perfect, some form of analysis must take the place of instinctive feeling—until the Latin way of thinking becomes natural to us.

Occasionally the perfect tense is used in the *Aeneid* where we should use a perfect in English. In 1.118–23, for example, the surrounding historic presents and the use of *iam* make us want to translate *uicit* by a perfect verb:

> apparent rari nantes in gurgite uasto,
> arma uirum tabulaeque et Troia gaza per undas.
> iam ualidam Ilionei nauem, iam fortis Achatae,
> et qua uectus Abas, et qua grandaeuus Aletes,
> *uicit* hiems; laxis laterum compagibus omnes
> accipiunt inimicum imbrem rimisque fatiscunt.[1]

Here and there men are visible swimming in the swirling sea, their equipment too, planks, Trojan treasure floating.

[1] Compare 2.180, 253, 332, 505; 4.582; 6.215; etc.

Tempo of the Narrative: Tenses

Already Ilioneus' ship, already stout Achates',
she that carried Abas, she in whom aged Aletes sailed,
have been beaten by the storm; through loosened joints all
let in the hostile flood, gaping at the seams.

But much more frequently our instinct is to render Virgil's perfects by a past tense. And here a close inspection of Virgil's usage reveals what at first appear to be two oddly incompatible sets of connotations.

Often the flavour of the perfect is exactly that of the aorist in Greek. It implies a sudden development, an unexpected turn of events, something that was over and done with in a moment. Usually in such cases a single verb in the perfect (at most two or three) interrupt the main flow of the narrative in historic presents. Take the opening line of Book 2:

>Conticuere omnes intentique ora tenebant.

When Aeneas rises to speak, a hush falls suddenly upon the buzz of conversation, followed by an expectant silence during which all keep their gaze fixed on Aeneas.[1] Or take the following lines (1.453–60):

>namque sub ingenti lustrat dum singula templo
>reginam opperiens, dum quae fortuna sit urbi
>artificumque manus inter se operumque laborem
>miratur, uidet Iliacas ex ordine pugnas
>bellaque iam fama totum uulgata per orbem,
>Atridas Priamumque et saeuum ambobus Achillem.
>constitit et lacrimans 'quis iam locus,' inquit, 'Achate,
>quae regio in terris nostri non plena laboris?'

As he takes in each detail of the temple that towers above him,
waiting for the queen, as he wonders what is this city's story,
and admires the bands of workmen and their
organized labours, he sees Troy's battles all in order
and the war that now the whole world knows of,
the Atrid brothers, Priam and their common foe, Achilles.
He stopped short and weeping, 'What place now,' he says, 'Achates,
what region of the earth is not full of our travail?'

As Aeneas and Achates make their way round the great temple at

---

[1] Compare 1.82, 84 and 90 where the three instantaneous perfects *impulit, incubuere* and *intonuere* each introduce a fresh dramatic turn of events in the storm; other examples are: 1.588; 2.575; 4.164, 167 and 168—three fresh turns of events in a context of historic presents; 6.204, 559; 8.530 and 531; 10.103, 453, 843; 11.150, 551; 12.300 and 301, etc.

Carthage, taking in all the details of the scene, they come upon a series of tableaux depicting things that are only too familiar to them. Aeneas stops short (*constitit*): what had been a casual inspection abruptly acquires a plangent personal relevance.

Because of its use in such contexts we are apt to feel that the perfect is a more exciting tense, more emotionally charged than the historic present. It comes as a surprise to find that Virgil also uses the perfect in situations where a relaxation of the emotional tension seems intended. A common pattern is a sentence in perfects after an exciting or dramatic passage in direct speech, expressing a character's reaction to that speech or an action taken by him at its conclusion. Usually the narrative resumes at once in the historic present.[1]

Clearly it is out of the question to pin down the effect Virgil aims at to any clear-cut meaning attaching to the perfect tense. Often, therefore, the switch from one tense to another is dismissed by editors without comment, on the assumption that it is meaningless and arbitrary—or dictated by metrical convenience ('*metri causa*'). Usually, it is true, in a given line a present could not be substituted for a perfect, or *vice versa*. Certain forms of certain verbs are metrically intractable. It is also probable that Virgil liked particular forms because of their expressiveness (for example the ending -*uere*). But Virgil's actual practice is all against the supposition that such factors led him regularly to write a perfect instead of a historic present, or *vice versa*. Probably the best way to describe the phenomenon is to say that the change of tense imposes a change of tempo. The function of the perfect is more to *mark* the change than to state its nature. A signal is given to the reader by the change of tense; but it is left to him to interpret the signal in the way that seems to him appropriate to the context. Sometimes, if he is reading aloud, he will respond to the signal by an acceleration of the tempo—as though, upon the graphic recital of events taking place before the narrator's eyes, an event were superimposed so abrupt or so unexpected that it has occurred before the narrator realized it was taking place. At the other extreme, the force of the perfect may perhaps be best described as a kind of laying aside of the narrator's pose of actual participation in the action while something that does not deserve the full excitement of graphic description is sketched in; or while we withdraw to place an occurrence in its proper perspective (something over and done with and now

---

[1] See 2.524–5; 4.54–5; 6.76, 155; 10.495, 867–70, 882; etc.

remote); or while we retreat to a decent distance because the events are too horrible to need enhancement by graphic presentation.[1]

The force of the Latin imperfect is more easily defined. This tense is used of a past action the duration of which is regarded as significant by the speaker; where the duration of the event is not regarded as significant by the speaker, the perfect is used. Thus the imperfect is the past equivalent of the present indicative—both tenses add to the notion of occurrence the connotation of 'going on'. If Latin does not provide in present time for the distinction which it regularly makes in the past, this is because all present actions are normally regarded as 'going on'. Occasionally of course a speaker may wish to stress that an action takes place quickly; in that case he has to treat the action as over in a flash, and use the instantaneous perfect. But though the present may take over the *narrative* function of the perfect tense (our 'historic present'), Latin usage does not allow it to assume the *descriptive* function of the imperfect. Where the situation requires an imperfect, the only substitute usage permitted was the historic infinitive.

Clearly an effective contrast in tempo is easily secured by imposing on the background of events related in the imperfect an event, or events, related in the instantaneous perfect. For example, 7.25-8 (as dawn was beginning to break over the sea, the winds suddenly fell):

> iamque rubescebat radiis mare et aethere ab alto
> Aurora in roseis fulgebat lutea bigis,
> cum uenti posuere omnisque repente resedit
> flatus.

Actually Virgil often prefers the historic infinitive to the imperfect. For example, 8.215-18 (as Hercules drives his oxen off, their calls are suddenly answered by one of the oxen which Cacus has stolen):

> discessu mugire boues atque omne querellis
> impleri nemus et colles clamore relinqui.
> reddidit una boum uocem uastoque sub antro
> mugiit et Caci spem custodita fefellit.[2]

---

[1] The perfect is often used in this last way in describing the death of a character—e.g., Priam, 2.550-3; Euryalus, 9.432; Lausus, 10.817-20; etc.

[2] The historic infinitive, though equivalent in meaning to an imperfect, is much less common. Virgil apparently introduced the construction to epic. There are seldom more than a handful of examples in any one book; usually two or three infinitives occur together, as in the example just quoted. The high proportion of passive infinitives (10 out of 32) is remarkable. J. J. Slicher, 'The historical infinitive', *CPh* 9 (1914) 279-94 and 374-94, remarks (p. 380) that

Structure

Such a switch from imperfect (or historic infinitive) to perfect is of course quite normal Latin, though Virgil constructs his sentences with more attention than most writers to the dramatic possibilities inherent in the events he relates. A use of the imperfect which is more characteristically Virgilian is a switch from imperfect to historic present. This is essentially a device for getting graphic narrative started or restarted—the narrator moves closer to the events he is describing, till the past becomes for him the present. The effect may be compared to a technique of film-making: the camera starts at some distance from a scene and moves progressively closer to it, securing not only greater detail, but an illusion of participation in the action. For that reason, and to underline dramatic intention, I shall call this narrative device *Tracking Forward*. Observe how we can feel the camera move closer to Dido and Anna at the conclusion of Anna's speech (4.685–9):

> sic fata gradus euaserat altos,
> semianimemque sinu germanam amplexa fouebat
> cum gemitu atque atros siccabat ueste cruores.
> illa grauis oculos conata attollere rursus
> *deficit*; infixum *stridit* sub pectore uulnus.[1]

> *Still speaking she had reached the topmost steps,*
> *and was fondling in her embrace her sister now near death,*
> *groaning as she tried to dry the dark blood with her dress.*
> *Dido, attempting to lift again her heavy eyes,*
> lacks *the strength. A sharp sound* comes *from the wound*
> *inflicted in her breast.*

Tracking Forward is common in Bridge Passages where it establishes a temporal overlap between successive Tableaux or Episodes (see Section V above, 'Parallel Narrative'). The converse effect, *Tracking Away*, is secured by the use of perfects; for example, after a graphic list of Camilla's victories (9 historic presents in 12 lines) the narrator withdraws from the scene in a summing-up sentence (11.676–7):

> quotque emissa manu contorsit spicula uirgo,
> tot Phrygii cecidere uiri.[2]

Virgil's fondness for the passive 'follows naturally from the frequency with which he uses the infinitives to express the awe or helplessness of human beings in the presence of what occurs to control their destiny'.

[1] Compare the opening lines of Book 5, discussed in *Latin Explorations*, pp. 227–9.
[2] Compare 7.23–4, 600; 12.593–4.

Tempo of the Narrative: Tenses

> *For each shaft that the maiden cast*
> *a Phrygian warrior fell.*

These are the basic types. Naturally the number of patterns involving two or more of the four main narrative tenses is very large.[1] Take the Palinurus Episode at the end of Book 5 (5.827–71). After a Bridge Passage the narrative proper begins with a distant shot (Tracking Forward) of Palinurus aboard the leading ship (833–7). Normally we would now pass to the main line of the narrative in historic present. But here a *coup de théâtre* intervenes—the God of Sleep suddenly appears through the darkness (838–41). To this the perfect tense is appropriate. The main line of the narrative follows in historic presents (842: *fundit*; 847: *fatur*; 855: *quassat*), except for the imperfects (852–3) which *describe* Palinurus' actions while he was speaking. Then the tempo changes again for the second *coup de théâtre*—Palinurus falls overboard and the God of Sleep vanishes (two perfects). The historic present is resumed for a couple of lines (the fleet sails on as though nothing had happened) and then we move back for a distant shot in imperfects (Tracking Away) of the fleet heading for a reef (864–6). Finally at 868 the tempo changes again to the perfect as Aeneas intervenes to bring the flagship back on course.

What has been said should help to interest the reader in an aspect of Virgil's narrative technique which has received less attention than it deserves. Further examples of the use of the tenses to secure a constantly varying tempo will be discussed in the analyses of individual books in Chapter 4. An example of the kind of distortion that inattention to Virgil's tenses can lead to is provided by the commentators on 9.250–1 (Aletes is congratulating Nisus and Euryalus on their courage):

> sic memorans umeros dextrasque tenebat
> amborum et uultum lacrimis atque ora rigabat.

Conington translates as though two successive actions were involved: 'he threw his arms round their necks and grasped their hands'—a scene that sounds vaguely comic. But if Virgil had meant two successive actions, he would have used two historic presents, or more likely two instantaneous perfects. Two imperfects build up, fortunately, a

---

[1] There is nothing especially characteristic about Virgil's employment of the pluperfect; its main use is in formulae like *dixerat, uix ea fatus erat*, etc., after direct speech, and in clauses followed by clauses beginning with inverted *cum*— see Chapter 6.

different picture: while Aletes is still making the speech we have just read (247-50), he goes up first to one of the pair and then the other; as he comes alongside each, he claps his left hand on the young man's shoulder, taking him as he does so by the right hand with his own right hand.[1]

Let us conclude with a rather longer example. Here is Virgil's description of the preparations for the duel between Aeneas and Turnus (12.113-33):

> postera uix summos spargebat lumine montis
> orta dies, cum primum alto se gurgite tollunt
> Solis equi lucemque elatis naribus efflant.   115
> campum ad certamen magnae sub moenibus urbis
> dimensi Rutulique uiri Teucrique parabant
> in medioque focos et dis communibus aras
> gramineas, alii fontemque ignemque ferebant
> uelati limo et uerbena tempora uincti.   120
> procedit legio Ausonidum, pilataque plenis
> agmina se fundunt portis, hinc Troius omnis
> Tyrrhenusque ruit uariis exercitus armis,
> haud secus instructi ferro quam si aspera Martis
> pugna uocet, nec non mediis in milibus ipsi   125
> ductores auro uolitant ostroque superbi,
> et genus Assaraci Mnestheus et fortis Asilas
> et Messapus equum domitor, Neptunia proles,
> utque dato signo spatia in sua quisque recessit,
> defigunt tellure hastas et scuta reclinant.   130
> tum studio effusae matres et uulgus inermum
> inualidique senes turris ac tecta domorum
> obsedere, alii portis sublimibus astant.

The 21 lines form four sentences. First comes a poetic evocation of sunrise—the most fanciful of Virgil's many descriptions of dawn and incorporating a reminiscence of Ennius.[2] The switch in tense from the opening imperfect (113: *spargebat*) to the graphic historic presents (114: *tollunt* and 115: *efflant*) is then repeated on a grander scale in the two succeeding sentences. The second sentence (5 lines), which describes the officials as they go about their work of getting all ready for the duel and the opening ceremony, is in imperfects (117: *parabant* and 119: *ferebant*). Then comes a graphic 10-line sentence (6 historic

---

[1] Mackail gets the picture almost right, but misses the force of the imperfects.
[2] See Chapter 6 for Virgil's descriptions of dawn.

presents). The change of key is marked by the tense of the opening word, *procedit*; upon this scene of activity in progress is superimposed the spectacle of the two armies advancing towards one another; the senior officers move to and fro among their men, until at a given signal both armies halt in the positions marked out for them and pass from movement to immobility as they drive their spears into the earth and set their shields against them.[1] Finally, a 3-line sentence: the tempo accelerates for a moment (marked by the instantaneous perfect *obsedere*, 133) to describe the rush of women and non-combatants for good positions on the towers and roof-tops; and then the camera focuses for a final lingering vivid shot (historic present *astant*, 133): against the tall gates of the Latin city a crowd of spectators stands motionless.

[1] As a result of Virgil's free use here of asyndeton, the organization of these two sentences is obscured by the punctuation of our modern texts. Virgil's use of tense contrast is among other things a substitute for punctuation. (The perfect *recessit* in 129 is in a frequentative temporal clause.)

4

The Twelve Books

This chapter contains a short paraphrase of each book of the *Aeneid* (printed in italics), followed by a tabulated synopsis of the structure of the book, and a fairly full restatement in prose of Virgil's text. Naturally, in such a restatement there is a good deal of tidying up: unimportant aspects of the story, left at the point where they can be made to work if we care to concentrate our curiosity on them, are here straightened out; actions are explained that Virgil chose not to explain. The object is to help the reader. But a different emphasis results. Any feeling that Virgil's text needs this assistance must be resisted. Indeed the tempo of Virgil's narrative depends on rigorous economy of detail;[1] similarly, the study of motivation in the following pages will often make explicit what is more effectively hinted at in the text by brief, stylized clues (see Chapter 5, 'Characterization and Motivation', and 'Implicit Comment').

No attempt has been made to accord equal treatment to each of the 167 Episodes into which I have divided the poem. Some call for little comment. Some are better dealt with in other chapters. Among the

---

[1] See *Latin Explorations*, pp. 202–11, 'Elliptical Narrative'.
Perret remarks wisely (p. 141):

> La vérité est que l'*Enéide* répond très mal à plusieurs des questions qu'on lui pose lorsqu'on la prend comme un livre d'histoire.

And he adds (p. 142):

> La perfection artistique n'inclut pas que l'œuvre d'art apparaîtra toujours parfaite de quelque biais qu'on la considère. Telle statue donne une étonnante impression de perfection, de réalisme même; ira-t-on reprocher à l'artiste d'avoir fait blanches, dures et froides des chairs qui sont roses, souples et tièdes?

Book 1

rest I have selected for full discussion here those that seemed to me the most interesting, or the most difficult.

All passages dealt with at any length in other chapters will be found in the *List of Passages Discussed*, which precedes the *Index*.

Most of the technical terms—e.g., Episode, Suspended Narrative, Tragic Irony—are defined in Chapters 3 and 5. All such terms are listed in the Index.

BOOK 1

In Book 1 a great storm overtakes Aeneas and his men on the last stage of their journey, scattering the ships of the fleet; Aeneas with seven ships manages to make the coast of Africa.

He is met there by his divine mother Venus, disguised as a huntress; relying on the reassurances she has just received from Jove about her son's destiny, she tells him to make for Carthage, where he is reunited with his companions and welcomed by Queen Dido.

A great banquet is arranged, to which Venus sends Cupid, disguised as Aeneas' son Ascanius, with instructions to make Dido fall in love with Aeneas.

Note: The sentences in the short summary above correspond to the division of the book into Sections in the following tabulated synopsis.

Introduction:		
The poet's prologue		1–7
Invocation		8–11
Hypothesis		12–33
I 34–222	*The Storm:*	
	(i) Juno-Aeolus	34–83
	(ii) Aeneas	84–123
	(iii) Neptune	124–156
	(iv) The landing in Africa	157–222
II 223–636	*Interlude:*	
	(i) Jove-Venus; Jove's prophecy	223–304
	Arrival in Carthage:	
	(ii) Venus-Aeneas	305–417
	(iii) Aeneas arrives; the temple; Dido	418–519
	(iv) Ilioneus' speech; Aeneas-Dido	520–636

The Twelve Books

	The Banquet:	
III	(i) Preparations	637–655
637–756	(ii) Venus-Cupid; Ascanius kidnapped	656–696
	(iii) The banquet	697–756

A 7-line prologue (discussed in Chapter 2) and a brief formal invocation (8–11) are followed by a more elaborate statement of the hypothesis upon which the story of the poem will rest (12–33). The starting point is Carthage and the remote past (12: *urbs antiqua fuit, Tyrii tenuere coloni*)—a city devoted to war and aggression (14: *studiisque asperrima belli*) and the home of Juno in her role as a goddess of war (16–17: *hic illius arma, hic currus fuit*). After this solemn beginning, there is a marked change of tone. The present tenses *tendit* and *fouet* (18) project us into the distant past (Projected Narrative) and Virgil glides away from the ancient historical enmity of Rome and Carthage into an increasingly whimsical summary of Juno's role in the legend of the Trojan War. Juno's hatred of the Aeneadae is thus given a double basis, the legendary basis being, however, subordinated (29: *his accensa super*) to the historical one. Because of their Trojan past, because of the future that awaits the city they will found, the Aeneadae have been kept far from their promised home in Italy while year after year they wander the seas, driven on by fate (31–2).

Having embedded Rome's struggle for the accomplishment of her destiny (33: *tantae molis erat Romanam condere gentem*) in a context of romance, Virgil launches upon his narrative at line 34. A tripartite arrangement of the narrative readily suggests itself. What marks off the three Sections from one another is chiefly the change in mood. The first ends on a note of gloom and stoic resistance to despair reminiscent of Teucer's words in Horace *Odes* 1.7—it is remarkable how often Virgil seems to owe to Horace the germ of an idea or a Tableau.[1] The second Section ends on a note of hope, aroused for the reader by Jove's prophecy and for Aeneas by Venus' words at 387–401. In the third Section, a spirit of optimism pervades the participants in the main action, overshadowed on the divine level and therefore for the reader (Tragic Irony) by a foreboding of disaster: the happy, hospitable queen is doomed to destruction (712: *pesti deuota futurae*).

The narrative proper begins with a 2-line Vignette that sharpens the general statement of lines 31–2 into a visual image (34–5):

---

[1] Among other examples are the Episode of Aeneas in the storm (1.84–123—cf. *Odes* 1.14 and *Epode* 7) and the Episode in which Vulcan leaves Venus to begin his day's business at the forge (8.407–53—*Odes* 1.4).

Book 1

uix e conspectu Siculae telluris in altum
uela dabant laeti et spumas salis aere ruebant.

*Scarce out of sight of the Sicilian land, out upon the sea,
they were happily setting sail, driving bronze through salt spray.*

It is a good example of Virgil's technique of evocative imprecision. The place, the dramatic moment, the mood of the characters are all fixed; but the actual scene is reduced to an impressionistic sketch—we are tempted to say that the details are left to the reader's imagination. We shall be nearer the mark if we say that the reader's imagination is challenged to produce its own vivid private image from words (*aere* and *spumas salis*) which do little more than provide the raw materials.[1]

The Aeneadae do not reappear till 50 lines later, in the middle of the narrative of the storm. Reverting to the divine level, Virgil resumes the tone of playful fantasy which we detected in the hypothesis. He allows himself now more than a trace of irony. Any lingering feeling that we are somehow expected to take it all seriously is dispelled by the Hellenistic pretence of casual realism in the treatment of Juno's speech and her colloquy with the God of the Winds (36–80). In the following Episode (84–123) the same tone dominates the narrative of the storm that overwhelms the Aeneadae when Aeolus unleashes his monstrous charges. The winds are personified, or rather half-personified—Virgil stops short of any description of their appearance; they are wild creatures, kept chained up by Aeolus in his mountain dungeon, which reverberates with their angry protests as they crowd around the bars of their prison while their keeper attempts to quieten them (54–7). When at Juno's request he releases them, they pour forth in formation (82: *agmine facto*) like soldiers launching an attack. Conway describes these lines as a fanciful, humorous expansion of Lucretius 6.189–203. A better way of putting it is to say that what Lucretius presents as a series of formal similes (his clouds only *look* like caves, his winds only *sound* like wild beasts) Virgil restates as a fantasy in which the words that are evocative of imagery are to be taken at their full value.

[1] We find this impressionistic technique also in Horace—cf. my remarks on the opening lines of *Odes* 1.5 in *Arion* 2 (1963) 64–7. What is *aere*? W. F. Jackson Knight is wrong, I think, in two respects in his Penguin translation, 'The bronze-plated oars churning the salt water to foam'. (1) *Georgics* 1.105 seems to make it tolerably clear that what we are intended to visualize is the ploughing action of the ship's prow, not the tips of the oars; (2) he spoils the poetry by making a deliberately vague phrase precise (in 6.165 *aere* refers to a trumpet). Cf. 10.214 and 223. For another example of evocative imprecision see 11.768–71.

Abruptly we turn to the storm scene itself. The first part of Virgil's description (before Aeneas' speech) is highly dramatic, organized into three stages round three instantaneous perfects, each beginning a line and each followed by a series of graphic historic presents. The first came in the preceding Bridge Passage (82: *impulit*—Aeolus gives the signal for attack). Now we have *incubuere* (84—the winds descend upon the sea) and *intonuere* (90—a crack of thunder marks the climax of the storm). (See Chapter 3, Section VI, 'Tempo of the Narrative: Tenses'.) After Aeneas' speech the winds surround the fleet like so many gigantic assailants. While he is still speaking, the north wind strikes at the sail of Aeneas' ship (102); the south wind drives three ships against a reef (108); the east wind drives three more against a sandbank (110-12). In part this is an ironic intellectual expansion of such simple pieces of poetic fancy in Homer as the bag of the winds given by Aeolus to Odysseus in *Odyssey* 10 and the storm in *Odyssey* 5.291-6, strained as a challenge to the reader's imaginative response.[1] At the same time the imagery is underpinned by the actual nature of cyclonic storms in the Mediterranean in which the wind shifts constantly (as in 2.416-19; cf. *Iliad* 9.4-8); what we are offered is naturally a stylization of this phenomenon; missing this, ancient critics (belonging to an age more familiar with rhetoric than with poetical fantasy) complained of the impossibility of a simultaneous onslaught by several winds.[2]

At line 92 comes Aeneas' first appearance in the poem, and it is a *tour de force*. The opening line of the poem spoke merely of 'a man' (*uirum*), defined only through his *labores*; the second reference to him was equally underplayed (10: *insignem pietate uirum*); now we have the hero at last, named for the first time—and he is almost in tears. Black night lies upon the sea (89: *ponto nox incubat atra*). A series of flashes of lightning reveal Aeneas to us, while to him and to his men the flashes reveal death on every side (91: *intentant omnia mortem*[3]). Aeneas' nerve almost fails him. His short speech, the first words he pronounces in the poem (94-101—mostly taken up by a curiously touching apostrophe of Diomede, the enemy Aeneas respects as he does not respect Achilles), is a reminiscence of Odysseus' speech in

---

[1] Compare the conflict aroused in the reader's mind by the simultaneous description of Atlas as a mountain and as a giant (4.246-58).
[2] See Mackail on 1.85. Compare Horace *Epode* 10.
[3] Note the ambiguity of *intentant*: (1) 'everything displays death'; (2) 'everything aims death at them'. By a slight change Virgil has sharpened and made his own a phrase from Catullus (64.187: *ostentant omnia letum*).

Book 1

Odyssey 5.306 ff., tuned to betray Aeneas' crumbling endurance of a responsibility that seems never-ending. The storm redoubles in frenzy. We watch it for a while through Aeneas' eyes (114: *ipsius ante oculos*) before returning to the world of fantasy for the following Episode (124–56), in which Neptune, after reprimanding the winds for their unauthorized incursion upon his territory, proceeds to put the damage right: with his fairy-tale assistants he dislodges Aeneas' ships from the reef we saw them strike against at 108, scoops out channels for others; then, work over, he takes a joyride in his chariot across a placid ocean (156).

We see no more of Aeneas till line 170, but an extraordinary emphasis has been thrown upon the poem's hero by his first appearance. A careful introduction of the poem's hero is a major function of Book 1. Showing him in action presents him to the reader more effectively than talking about him; our sympathy for him is more readily gained if we see him in scenes that provide an objective correlative for his mood of resignation and near-despair. Similarly in the final Episode of the first Section (157–222) Aeneas' gloomy landing with a remnant of his followers on a strange, deserted African coast, their scratch meal, Aeneas' forced words of reassurance—all make convincing a state of mind that can be summed up (not merely asserted) in line 209:

> spem uultu simulat, premit altum corde dolorem.[1]
>
> *His face feigns hope, his heart represses deep grief.*

We see again the very human Aeneas created by these contexts at the moment where hope starts to commingle with despair at 451–2:

> hic primum Aeneas sperare salutem
> ausus et adflictis melius confidere rebus.
>
> *Here first Aeneas dared hope for
> safety, to place more trust in his crippled fortunes.*

We witness his spontaneous outburst of gratitude to Dido (597–610). We see him finally in easy conversation with the queen who is fast

---

[1] Observe that Virgil's comment in this line corrects what is often taken, by those who quote it out of context, to be the facile optimism, or the easy sentimentality, of Aeneas' words to his men (203): '*forsan et haec olim meminisse iuuabit*'.

The Twelve Books

falling in love with the handsome adventurer she has befriended (748–9).[1]

A second function of the book must be to assert, at as early a stage as possible, the relevance of the poem's formal subject: how is it that a poem all expected to be about Rome and Augustus has turned out to be about Aeneas? On one level this has been plainly hinted at already by the storm Episode. The contemporary reader, prepared by his expectation of what the poem must really be about, whatever its *apparent* subject, and alert therefore for an implied equation between Aeneas and Augustus, could hardly fail to have recognized the applicability of the central Tableau (the leader, to whom the easy way out has been denied, beset by crisis after crisis) to the events of the civil war; the ship of state was a familiar metaphor and one that had been utilized in just this context by Horace (*Odes* 1.14: *O nauis, referent . . . te . . .*). But (like much of the symbolism of the poem) this is a level of significance never more than delicately adumbrated by Virgil, one poetically complementary to the narrative with which it is logically incompatible. The ostensible relevance of the story of Aeneas must lie elsewhere. It is twofold. First, the story is part of the legend of how Rome came into being (33: *tantae molis erat Romanam condere gentem*, cf. 5–6). Second, it is part of the legend of the Julian house: the dynasty that started with Aeneas ends with Julius Caesar and (through the fiction of adoption) with Augustus. To retell, therefore, the story of Aeneas is a compliment both to Rome and to Augustus.

But it must remain a somewhat perfunctory compliment unless the data upon which it rests can be made a significant part of the poem's structure. Virgil now addresses himself to this problem. The second Section begins with an Episode that is in effect an interlude. In it the

[1] Less successful is the more formally heroic Aeneas of the second Episode of the second Section who proclaims himself to his mother, whom he does not recognize (378–85):

> 'sum pius Aeneas, raptos qui ex hoste penatis
> classe ueho mecum; fama super aethera notus
> Italiam quaero patriam; et genus ab Ioue summo.
> bis denis Phrygium conscendi nauibus aequor,
> matre dea monstrante uiam data fata secutus;
> uix septem conuulsae undis Euroque supersunt.
> ipse ignotus, egens, Libyae deserta peragro,
> Europa atque Asia pulsus.'

We can sense the bitterness that underlies this factual recital of his misfortunes; all the same it is hard to suppress a feeling that the attempt to exploit Sophocles (*OT* 8) has introduced a touch of priggishness. Oedipus is a much more formal character, never drawn with the realism Virgil uses in creating Aeneas.

Book 1

reader is invited to contemplate a Roman pageant linking legendary past and the events of recent history. This interlude has an organic connexion with the narrative it suspends (Suspended Narrative). Catching Jove at the moment when the landing of the Aeneadae in Africa is causing him anxious thought (226–7), Venus pleads the case of her son, the man to whom 'the whole world is denied for Italy's sake' (233: *cunctus ob Italiam terrarum clauditur orbis*—i.e., he may not make his home elsewhere), and asks for an assurance that the *labores* (241) of Aeneas will have their promised happy ending. To comfort her, the father of gods and men, 'unwinding further than usual the secret book of fate' (262), foretells to Venus the deification of Aeneas and the future of the dynasty he will found in Italy down to the lifetime of Augustus. We are dangerously close to propaganda, but, as we saw in Chapter 2, the prophecy is made a geometric progression, to keep it within the atmosphere of fairy-tale: Aeneas, after fighting a great war against the peoples of Italy, will reign in Latium for three years; his son Ascanius will reign for thirty years, and then transfer the seat of his kingdom to Alba Longa; there, after three hundred years, Romulus and Remus will be born and they will found Rome;[1] to their descendants Jove has assigned unlimited dominion (278–9)— Juno will abandon her persecution, retribution will come to the descendants of the Greeks who destroyed Troy, under a mighty Julius Rome's conquests will stretch from west to east; after his death and deification (290: *uocabitur hic quoque uotis*—i.e., like Aeneas) peace will reign, the dread iron-bound Gates of War will be shut upon a monstrous allegorical creature, the spirit of civil war, mad, unholy, savage, bloody-mouthed, held in a hundred brazen chains (293–6):

> 'dirae ferro et compagibus artis
> claudentur Belli portae; Furor impius intus
> saeua sedens super arma et centum uinctus aenis
> post tergum nodis fremet horridus ore cruento.'

The events of recent history are not evaded, but they are dextrously skated over and subordinated to this final powerful image, based, we are told, on a painting of Apelles representing War in chains (*belli imaginem restrictis ad terga manibus*) which was placed by Augustus in his own forum,[2] but described in terms more like those a modern pacifist might be expected to choose than a Roman. Moreover it is

---

[1] Notice that these three stages are already implied in lines 6–7.
[2] Elder Pliny, *NH* 35.93. See Conway on 1.294.

The Twelve Books

not War who is imprisoned, but 'unholy madness'—plainly civil war. Virgil had of course to tread carefully. When the Gates of War were shut in 29 B.C. by Augustus, officially it was to mark the end of Rome's external wars. But by linking that occasion implicitly with his imaginary opening of the Gates of War of Latinus' city in Book 7, Virgil contrives to suggest that at last under Augustus an age of internal peace has arrived.[1]

His prophecy concluded, Jove despatches Mercury, in case Dido, 'unaware what fate requires' (299: *fati nescia*), accords Aeneas a hostile reception. We might expect the narrative to resume with the arrival of Aeneas in Carthage. Instead we find him confronted, during a dawn reconnaissance, by his mother, in heavy disguise. By this long Episode (305–417) two things are achieved. First, Dido is presented (in Venus' long account of her misfortunes, 340–68) as a character with an initial claim upon our sympathy: like Aeneas, she is a refugee who has had to start life afresh in a new country. Second, when Venus sends him on his way magically wrapped in a cloud (411–14—an echo of Odysseus' encounter with Athena in *Odyssey* 7[2]), the ground is laid for Aeneas' dramatic appearance at 586. There are also some nice touches: Venus' gruff assumed personality; the trace of irony in her final epiphany—her short hunting skirt suddenly flows down to her feet (404). All the same, this is an unsatisfactory Episode. The *sang-froid* with which Venus sends Aeneas on his way to Carthage clashes awkwardly with her sudden alarm at 657. Nor can the Episode bear comparison with the brilliant Episodes that precede and follow it; even as a relaxation of the action it hardly earns its keep in a book where the general standard is so high.

Heartened by his mother's words and enveloped in a protective cloud, Aeneas, accompanied by Achates, makes his way to Carthage. There he is first filled with melancholy and envy by the happy activity of an exiled people whose wanderings are over (437: '*o fortunati, quorum iam moenia surgunt!*') and then startled to see depicted on the walls of a temple scenes all too familiar from the Trojan War. Quickly the sorrow of recollection is displaced by hope; these scenes are a

---

[1] For the theory held by some editors that the Julius mentioned is Augustus, see Chapter 2.

[2] In Homer Athena first puts a mist round Odysseus and then meets him. Virgil has separated these two actions, reversed their order and used them in separate Episodes. The device of a cloud or mist is also used by Apollonius, 3.210–14.

Book 1

guarantee that he has come among a people who honour nobility of character and whose minds are accessible to pity (461-2):

> 'en Priamus: sunt hic etiam sua praemia laudi,
> sunt lacrimae rerum et mentem mortalia tangunt.'[1]

And indeed against the general background of fighting (briefly sketched in in 488-93) scenes stand out that seem, in Virgil's description of them, prompted by feeling for human suffering: the chaos wrought in the camp of Rhesus by Diomede (469-73); the death at the hands of Achilles of Priam's young son Troilus (474-8); the women of Troy in supplication before Minerva who averts her gaze from them (479-82); the barbarous treatment by Achilles of Hector's body and its ransom by Priam (483-7).[2]

While Aeneas is absorbed in the contemplation of these scenes, the queen appears, to take her seat in the temple (494-506). She has just begun the day's business when there is an uproar. Aeneas sees faces he recognizes—caught up in an advancing crowd are men from the lost ships, come to beg the queen for help for themselves and their companions. Resisting an impulse to rush forward, Aeneas and Achates prudently await developments.

The spokesman Ilioneus makes a vigorous, common-sense speech (522-58): the Trojans have lost their leader, their ships need repair, will the queen help?[3] Dido's reply (562-78) is equally to the point: the Trojans must excuse the treatment they received on landing—it was a necessary security measure; of course she will help in any way she can. To clearheadedness and humanity she adds generosity: will the Trojans consider staying in Carthage? They will be welcome, on equal terms with her own people. As for Aeneas, a search-party will be despatched at once.

---

[1] Virgil leaves it to us to guess what the Tableau was in which Priam figured. Was it his death (to be related in Book 2)? Or the Tableau mentioned at 486-7 of Priam begging for the body of Hector from Achilles? On the famous phrase *sunt lacrimae rerum*, see p. 407.

[2] For a detailed discussion of these scenes see R. D. Williams, 'The pictures on Dido's temple', *CQ* 10 (1960) 145-51.

[3] Two points are interesting in Ilioneus' speech. First, he clearly feels no compulsion to reach Italy—Aeneas' sense of mission is something personal; his men do not share it. Left to himself, Ilioneus would be quite content to settle in Sicily. Second, Ilioneus treats as a natural phenomenon the storm which has been described to us in fairy-tale terms. Compare the apparent clash between Virgil's description of the death of Palinurus at the end of Book 5 and Palinurus' own account of what happened to him in Book 6.

The Twelve Books

It is the moment for Aeneas to reveal himself. Magically the cloud that had enveloped him and Achates evaporates, and Aeneas confronts Dido with all the splendour of a divine epiphany. He thanks the queen profusely (595–610), evading, however, for the moment (610) any talk of settling in Carthage. (For an analysis of Aeneas' speech see Chapter 6.) The Episode ends with a formal speech of welcome from Dido (615–30), in which she sums up her feelings in a fine rhetorical line (630):

'non ignara mali miseris succurrere disco.'

'*No stranger to ill-fortune I am learning to help those who suffer ill.*'

The third Section begins with a short narrative Episode relating the preparations on both sides for the great banquet which Dido now arranges to welcome the Trojans (637–55). At this point Venus reappears. Somewhat surprisingly (it might seem more natural if Juno sensed danger first) she is alarmed at the turn events have taken. She is sure Juno will not be long in intervening at so critical a juncture (672: '*haud tanto cessabit cardine rerum*'; in fact Juno does not act till 4.90). Her solution is to kidnap Ascanius. In his place she sends her own son Cupid to the banquet with instructions to see to it that Dido falls in love with Aeneas. A vivid, selective description of the banquet follows (697–756): first the lavish spectacle (697–708) and the central figures, Aeneas, Dido and Cupid (709–22); then the talk that followed the eating (723–40); finally the minstrel Iopas (740–7—does his song of the wandering moon and the toiling sun, though rooted in the tradition of cosmological poetry, symbolize the parallel destinies of Dido and Aeneas, this mortal Diana and Apollo whom fate has thrown together?[1]) This third Episode and the book conclude with Dido asking Aeneas to tell her (and the assembled guests) the story of his adventures—an example of Virgil's fondness for structural parallelism: the first and the third Sections both end with a Tableau of people eating and reminiscing. The purpose of this is clear enough: to emphasize how much circumstances have altered between the two occasions.

We have pointed to two major functions of Book 1: it introduces the hero in circumstances that put us on his side; and it puts the legendary story in a context of contemporary relevance. A third

---

[1] See Pöschl's discussion of the song of Iopas, Eng. edn 150–2. For Dido as Diana see 1.498–504; cf. the parallel simile of Aeneas as Apollo, 4.143–50.

Book 1

function is to make clear the stance Virgil adopts with respect to the Homeric tradition. This is accomplished partly by the open, sustained challenge of direct allusion (no other book recalls Homer more plainly); partly by a deployment on an unprecedented scale—one that Virgil himself will not attempt to keep up[1]—of an apparatus of gods, goddesses and minor powers intervening in human affairs. We shall see in Chapter 5 that there is more to this assertion of Virgil's allegiance to Homer than at first meets the eye. A preliminary word, however, is in order here on Virgil's divine machinery because the question is of very direct relevance to our understanding of how Virgil's story works.

Given the circumstances—Dido's sympathy for Aeneas in his misfortune (she is reminded of her own past misfortune), the shock of their first encounter, the glamour of the banquet—it is easy to imagine her falling in love, and easy to imagine that Aeneas' young son might innocently help in bringing this about.[2] Equally well, things might *not* have turned out so. Without his divine machinery Virgil would have been obliged to tell us how Dido fell in love with Aeneas. He might have done so at the end of Book 1 or at the beginning of Book 4. In either place, however, explanation would have slowed up the narrative; and in the latter place it might have had the further inconvenience of suggesting that Virgil was making up his story as he went along. As it is, a sense of expectancy, a presentiment of trouble, exist at the end of Book 1, ready to overshadow the action of Book 4, so that Dido's helpless love for Aeneas is something we can accept from the opening line of that book (see Chapter 5, 'Tragic Suspense').

The structural gains are clear, but many modern readers are disturbed, feeling they cannot overlook the unreality of Virgil's data: instead of being free agents in whose moral struggles we can interest ourselves, Virgil's characters seem the helpless puppets of omnipotent, wrangling divinities. How can we discuss them as though they were normal human beings? Almost equally disturbing is the thought that the whole poem appears to involve belief in Rome's historical mission; it seems an intolerably narrow, deterministic view of history.

The difficulties are less grave than they have been made to appear. To begin with, we are not actually asked to believe anything about the way the world works. No assault is attempted by Virgil upon the

[1] In Apollonius the divine action is pretty desultory and it does not seem to have been a prominent feature of early Roman epic. In Catullus 64 the gods take part freely in the wedding scenes, but in the Theseus-Ariadne story there is only one perfunctory divine intervention—that of Bacchus.

[2] Cf. Dido's wish for a son, 4.327–30.

reader's private convictions. The *Aeneid* is not a philosophical textbook but a work of imaginative fiction. We may, if we like, call it a romance. I prefer the term 'fairy-tale', as a convenient, if rather inaccurate, label for a story which is in certain respects fantastic, but in the main manifestly about the kind of world we know. The suspension of disbelief (to use Coleridge's phrase) invited from us by a writer who challenges us to accept, for the duration of his fiction, things he does not himself believe in any more than we do, must be distinguished from that imposed by our historical sense—pretending to ourselves we believe in the things the writer believed in, in order to read him sympathetically. Virgil, we may be sure, did not believe that human beings were manipulated by gods in anything approaching the way in which his gods manipulate his characters in the *Aeneid*.

At first sight this reassurance may appear to arouse more misgivings than it allays. Conscious distortion of reality is surely worse than that due to mistaken belief. Oddly enough in literature this is not so. It is possible to construct a fiction that depends on a hypothesis palpably false to human experience, in which none the less, except for the consequences necessarily deducible from that hypothesis, everything corresponds to human experience.[1] Ghost stories usually take this form; so do countless tales which depend on the hypothesis that human beings continue to behave and appear after death exactly as they did in life. Such fictions can give the impression of being profoundly true in all respects save the implausibility posited. The thing is easier if the implausibility falls in an area where popular belief, superstition, wishful thinking, or the like, introduces an element of uncertainty even in the minds of those who normally regard themselves as inaccessible to such influences. For the duration of a good ghost story, we are all prepared to think ourselves into a frame of mind we at other times consider ourselves to have outgrown.

Many of Virgil's contemporary audience no doubt accepted his

---

[1] H. G. Wells, in a preface to the collected edition of his *Scientific Romances* (1933), remarks, pp. vii–viii:

In all this type of story the living interest lies in their non-fantastic elements and not in the invention itself. They are appeals for human sympathy quite as much as any 'sympathetic' novel, and the fantastic element, the strange property or the strange world, is used only to throw up and intensify our natural reactions of wonder, fear or perplexity. . . .

For the writer of fantastic stories to help the reader to play the game properly, he must help him in every possible unobtrusive way to *domesticate* the impossible hypothesis. He must trick him into an unwary concession to some plausible assumption and get on with his story while the illusion holds.

Book 1

apparatus of gods and goddesses as a substantially true explanation of the realities underlying human experience. After allowance is made for obviously fantastic embellishments and simplifications, we have an explanation of the world that more or less corresponds to that given by the Stoics. Equally, many of Virgil's contemporaries rejected outright all belief in the intervention of the gods in human affairs. This was of course the Epicurean position; but, of educated Romans in the time of Augustus, a majority probably were, like Cicero in his considered view of the world at the end of his life, pretty thoroughgoing agnostics in their private thinking, prepared, for reasons of social convenience, to support a state religion they did not believe in.[1]

As far, then, as the motivation of his characters is concerned, Virgil invites us to accept for the duration of his fiction a common, though not universally held, conventional explanation of human experience. In return, he offers us heightened poetic and intellectual pleasure. The fantasy makes for vividness and stimulates reflection. It is not why Dido falls in love that matters (why do people fall in love anyway?), but the subsequent disintegration of her personality as a result of pressures brought to bear on her by circumstances. Taken in this spirit, Virgil's study of Dido is realistic and profound.

An indifference to the external causes of misfortune (i.e., those that operate from outside our conscious will), while it is characteristic of what we may call the tragic outlook, is apt to appear offensive to those who approach literature with a strong moral sense. These are the people who want somebody to be to blame when things go wrong, who expect a story to be constructed in such a way as to enable the reader to apportion responsibility for what occurs. It worries them to see the good suffer for being good, as Dido suffers for the warmth of her generosity, even if, once trapped by circumstances, she brings that suffering on herself by her impetuosity and self-deception (see Analysis of Book 4); though these readers see this happen frequently in real life, they expect things to be different in a book. The *Aeneid* offers little satisfaction to any who approach it in this frame of mind. Virgil was more concerned, probably, with the reality of human suffering, the tragic spectacle it provided. He does not, of course, reject morality: *pietas*, a man's recognition of responsibilities to his

---

[1] The *De Natura Deorum* and the *De Diuinatione* reveal more, probably, of Cicero's personal beliefs than his speeches. See M. L. Clark, *The Roman Mind* (1956) 18. The *Somnium Scipionis*, though it avoids poetic fantasy, is as much a conscious fairy-tale as the *Aeneid*.

gods and to his fellows, is a quality to be prized. His poem contains admirable characters and characters less admirable. But the idea of a just world, though common enough in popular thinking in antiquity, *is* implicitly rejected. Virgil seems almost to challenge it openly in this book when he makes Aeneas ask (603–5) that Dido be rewarded for her generosity by divine justice, by mortal justice, and by her private sense of virtuous action (604: *mens sibi conscia recti*—an allusion to the Stoic doctrine that virtue is its own reward), for in the end she is denied all three sources of comfort. (For a discussion of the passage see Chapter 6.)

A final word about Virgil's apparent historical determinism. An external determination of human behaviour, once made one of the poem's hypotheses, makes it easier for us to accept the same hypothesis in those sections of the poem where we move out of a legendary context into a historical context. His audience might otherwise have found the implied invitation to suspend their disbelief in the destiny of Rome (if they did disbelieve) unacceptable. Jove's prophecy to Venus, Anchises' second speech to Aeneas in Book 6, the pageant of Roman history upon the shield of Aeneas in Book 8, are nonsense unless we accept a deterministic view of history—either in fact or simply as a hypothesis granted for the duration of Virgil's fiction. But the moment we relate these three great 'historical' cadenzas to the divine apparatus of the poem, we realize the probability that the one is no more, and no less, intended to be taken seriously (i.e., as an assertion of the poet's actual convictions) than the other. The 'historical' cadenzas, in other words, are part and parcel of the world of make-believe in which the poem moves. They take advantage of a public occasion (the commemoration of the end of a war), on which reflections upon the greatness of Rome and her divine mission are pardonable, almost mandatory; the object, however, is not to assert that greatness and that destiny, but to use the occasion as a starting point for a meditation upon the effects of war on human nature.

BOOK 2

In Book 2, Aeneas begins his story by telling how the Trojans in their folly listened to Sinon instead of Laocoon and took the wooden horse within the walls of their city amid scenes of rejoicing.

Book 2

That night Aeneas is visited by Hector in a vision and entrusted with his mission to save the Trojan people; he joins the fighting in the streets and then finds his way to Priam's palace in time to see the old king killed by Neoptolemus; he is about to murder Helen in revenge when Venus, revealing to him the gods joined in the destruction of Troy, persuades him to concentrate on escape.

Returning home, Aeneas manages, after the double miracle of the flame and the comet, to get Anchises to consent to exile; they depart, but on the way to the assembly point Aeneas' wife Creusa is lost; the book ends with the refugees gathering on Mount Ida.

We leave Book 1, our minds captivated by the splendour of the concluding Episode. Against the background of the banquet, the two main characters stand out, their affinity for one another and their common destiny underlined, perhaps, by the symbolism of the song of Iopas. But we remember, too, the sinister, sensually thrilling image of the love god disguised as Aeneas' son, his face glowing with fire (1.710)—the fire that is already consuming the doomed queen (1.712: *pesti deuota futurae*).

No contemporary reader would have been much in doubt about the outcome. Eventually Aeneas must reach Italy—the legend requires it. He might have been more unsure about Dido; Virgil's version differs anyway, in a number of respects apparently, from tradition.[1] But there was little room for an element of surprise. Indeed Virgil scarcely seeks to surprise. The function of the divine action is, as we saw, more to sharpen the reader's expectation of disaster than to bring disaster about. Instead of surprise Virgil offers us that special kind of suspense which is characteristic of Greek tragedy; it is not *what* is going to happen that arouses the suspense, as in a modern adventure story, but *how* what we sense must happen does happen. (See Chapter 5, 'Tragic Suspense'.)

But with the tragic action imminent, the narrative is broken off (Suspended Narrative). Books 2 and 3 form a long flashback; in Book 2, Aeneas tells the story of the night Troy was destroyed by the Greeks; in Book 3, the story of the six years of wandering around the Mediterranean that followed. The structural effectiveness of introducing the story of Aeneas' *labores* at this point is obvious. We come to them with

---

[1] For what is known, or can be conjectured about the Dido legend see Heinze, pp. 115-19.

The Twelve Books

our interest in the personality of Aeneas aroused by Book 1. By breaking the forward, linear movement of the narrative and switching from the third to the first person, the danger of monotony, inherent in any very long narrative, is reduced. A new unity is given the old story of the destruction of Troy by making the narrative centre round one person and restricting it (after a more general first Section) to what that one person did and saw on that night.

The story of Book 2 is exciting in itself—incomparably more exciting than that of Book 3. The first Section is almost melodramatic, a kind of prelude in the manner of Euripides to the more Sophoclean pathos of the second and third Sections, though the pathos is heightened and made more complex by a very Euripidean sense of irony and futility. But it is not the primary function of Book 2, either as a unit in the total structure or as a structure in its own right, to provide excitement.

As a unit in the total structure its main functions are three. First, to fill in the past. Second, to put us on Aeneas' side: in Book 4 he will not cut an attractive figure; a fund of sympathy is built up for him in Book 2 which can be all but exhausted in Book 4—reading Book 4 by itself, taking it as a detached episode, is unfair to Aeneas; at the same time the magnitude and inevitability of the mission Aeneas must carry out are graphically impressed upon us: in Book 4, Aeneas' talk of his mission has little effect on Dido; having read Books 2 and 3, we feel differently. Third, to put Aeneas in a situation where, for all the sympathy he arouses in us, we must feel that his conduct is patently misguided: Book 2 is a series of illustrations of the human weakness of a leader, his inadequacy to the task abruptly thrust upon him; before he can be a true leader of his people, he will have to learn, as we shall see again in Books 4 and 5, to control himself.

As a structure in its own right Book 2 also deserves close attention. The following tripartite arrangement readily suggests itself:

	Introduction	1–13
I 13–249	*The Horse:* (i) The horse inspected (ii) Laocoon A (iii) Sinon A, B, C (iv) Laocoon B (v) The horse admitted	13–39 40–56 57–198 199–233 234–249

Book 2

II 250–633	*The Night Troy Fell:* (i) The attack begins (ii) Hector visits Aeneas in a vision (iii) Aeneas-Panthus; Aeneas gathers a force *Fighting:* (iv) In the streets (v) At the temple of Pallas; Cassandra (vi) At Priam's palace (vii) The death of Priam (viii) Helen (ix) Venus and the vision of the gods destroying Troy	250–267 268–297 298–369 370–401 402–434 434–505 506–558 559–587 588–633
III 634–804	*Preparations for Exile:* (i) Anchises; miracles of the flame and the comet (ii) Aeneas' party sets out (iii) Creusa lost; Aeneas returns (iv) Vision of Creusa (v) On Mount Ida	 634–704 705–729 730–770 771–794 795–804

More tightly organized than the others, the first Section has a more important function than has been supposed. The most colourful part of the narrative is Virgil's retelling of the ancient, familiar story of the horse.[1] But the main function of the Section is to provide a neat illustration of the parallelism of the divine and heroic actions. (See Chapter 5, 'Parallel Divine and Psychological Motivation'.) Troy falls because the gods withdraw their protection; but the city falls equally through the folly of the Trojans. Virgil's starting point is the old legend of the *fata Troiana*—prophecies of events, the occurrence of which spelt the fall of Troy.[2] One such event was to be the removal of a small statue of Minerva (the Palladium) from the temple of the goddess in Troy; at 163-75 we learn that the statue *has* been stolen by Diomede and Ulysses.[3] But the Trojans, instead of remaining on their

---

[1] The story of the horse is already found in Homer (*Od.* 8.499–515—Virgil follows closely the summary of the legend given by the Phaeacian minstrel Demodocus, adding Laocoon and Sinon). See Austin on 2.15. For a magnificent representation of the horse on a seventh-century pithos from Mykonos see *AJA* 67 (1963), plate 66. For the currency of the legend at Rome see, e.g., Cicero's elaborate pun in *Pro Caelio* 67.

[2] See Austin on 2.163.

[3] For an early fourth-century kylix showing Diomede carrying off the Palladium see G. M. A. Richter, *Greek Art* (1959) 343.

guard, are reassured by the story Sinon tells them of the misfortunes that ensued for the Greeks. When Virgil makes Sinon describe the scene in the Greek camp (172–5):

> 'uix positum castris simulacrum: arsere coruscae
> luminibus flammae arrectis, salsusque per artus
> sudor iit, terque ipsa solo, mirabile dictu,
> emicuit parmamque ferens hastamque trementem.'

> *'Scarce was the statue set up in the camp when its eyes
> turned upwards flashing flame, salt sweat bathed its limbs,
> and, wondrous to relate, three times the goddess stood
> resplendent on the earth, bearing shield and fearful spear.'*

we are expected, I think, to feel that the epiphany did occur, but that it meant that Minerva was lending the Greeks her aid in battle; not, as Sinon pretends, that she was angry with them.[1]

The layout of this first Section looks complicated but is designed for dramatic effect. After their first excited inspection, the Trojans are undecided what to do with the horse. Laocoon intervenes (50–3):

> sic fatus ualidis ingentem uiribus hastam
> in latus inque feri curuam compagibus aluum
> contorsit. stetit illa tremens, uteroque recusso
> insonuere cauae gemitumque dedere cauernae.

> *So speaking, with all his strength he hurled his great
> spear into the side of the beast's curving jointed belly:
> it lodged there quivering; and, when the shock reached
> the cavernous hollow womb, it shivered and gave a groan.*

His action might have saved the Trojans if their attention had not at that moment been distracted by the arrival of Sinon. (For this example of Suspended and Parallel Narrative see Chapter 3; the two Episodes overlap, as the tenses *trahebant* in 58 and *obtulerat* in 61 show; Aeneas' exclamation in 54–6 links the two Episodes, implying it was the *fata deum* that produced Sinon at this critical juncture to act upon the *mens laeua* of the Trojans.) He makes three long speeches. The first (77–104) is devoted to winning pity for himself. In the second (108–44), he builds up his tissue of falsehoods, taking care to avoid offering any explanation of the horse (it is merely mentioned in

---

[1] For a similar example of something said by a speaker to deceive an audience when what is said should instead give the game away, see 5.636–8: if Beroe had been genuine she would not have believed Cassandra.

passing, 112–13). Finally, invited by Priam to tell the Trojans what the horse was for, he spins his tale. By the time he has finished (194), Sinon has the Trojans completely on his side. Our attention now reverts to Laocoon (again the imperfect *mactabat* in 202 marks an overlap). The sole doubter left is eliminated, and the Trojans are only too prone, as a result of Sinon, to misconstrue the portent.

When in his third speech Sinon connected the horse with the Palladium (183), the Trojans should have scented danger. Then Laocoon, the priest of Neptune (201)—the other guardian divinity of Troy—is destroyed by the two great snakes while he is sacrificing to Neptune for guidance (202). The snakes emerge from the sea (the domain of Neptune), strangle Laocoon and his two sons, and then make off to the temple of Minerva to conceal themselves beneath the feet and the shield of the goddess (226–7—not of course the Palladium). The reader could hardly expect a clearer symbolic statement of the fact that Minerva and Neptune have joined forces against Troy. Aeneas knows all this now when he tells his story to Dido (though Virgil naturally cannot allow him to underline things too heavily); but he had to wait for his mother to lift from his eyes the mist that dims ordinary human sight and make manifest to him Minerva and Neptune joined with Juno in the destruction of Troy (608–16).

The two Laocoon Episodes and the three speeches of Sinon are thus interlocked, so that Sinon's final words are followed closely by the death of Laocoon.[1] And hard upon the lesson of the second Laocoon Episode come two more, which the Trojans also misinterpret. As they strain at the horse, 'it sticks four times in the very gateway and four times from its belly comes the ring of arms; yet we Trojans persist and thoughtless, blind with folly, install the portent of disaster in the holy citadel itself' (242–5):

> quater ipso in limine portae
> substitit atque utero sonitum quater arma dedere;
> instamus tamen immemores caecique furore
> et monstrum infelix sacrata sistimus arce.

---

[1] Mackail, p. 47, misses this:

Both [parts of the Laocoon story] are insertions, which have only a slight organic connexion with the main current of the story. Either, or both, could be omitted without leaving any gap, and in fact with some added continuity; and the latter and longer of the two has a touch of overloadedness which suggests a comparatively early date of composition, and the absence of final revision after it had been inserted in its present place.

The Twelve Books

Even then it might not have been too late if they had listened to Priam's daughter Cassandra, but she was cursed to know the truth and never to be believed (246–7). Instead they deck the horse with garlands (249).

We should be careful to avoid saying that the Trojans are given four *warnings* and neglect them. It is not the intention of the gods to *warn* the Trojans. Their interpreting the signs as they do interpret them was, in the emotional circumstances, inevitable. But looking back through Aeneas' eyes, we can see how the Trojans were made the instruments of their own destruction. This is how tragedy works (see Chapter 5, 'Tragic Attitude').

Naturally, the interplay of divine and heroic action teems with philosophical questions which it is not the business of the poem to raise, much less settle. The Trojans, Aeneas will maintain, did not *deserve* their fate (3.1–2: *gentem immeritam*). If they had been more prudent, fate would presumably have had to resort to other means to destroy Troy—*fata uiam inuenient*. At most, it seems, they might by prudence have *delayed* the fall of Troy (see Vulcan's odd remark to Venus, 8.398–9). Without concerning himself with such philosophical issues, Virgil exploits the irony inherent in a situation where men seem the instruments of their own misfortune.

We pass from this concluding scene heavily impregnated with Tragic Irony, the certainty of Troy's destruction impressed upon us, to the second Section of the book. After a brief narrative (250–67) of the return of the main body of the Greeks in their fleet and the opening of the gates to them by the Greeks within Troy, the second Section begins, as it will end, with a vision. In the first, Hector appears to Aeneas, who like the rest of the Trojans is sleeping soundly following the day's rejoicings (265: *urbem somno uinoque sepultam*), to warn him that resistance is useless, to entrust him with the city's gods, and to charge him with his mission to take his gods and his people to their new home in the city which he is to build across the seas (289–97). The second vision, which is of a rather different kind, has already been referred to —the revelation granted Aeneas by his divine mother of the gods bent on the destruction of Troy. Its purpose is the same; Aeneas is warned a second time, and more emphatically, that it is useless to resist.

Between the two visions we see Aeneas abandon himself to a protracted, senseless gesture of resistance, preferring death to defeat, forgetful how important it is that he should not be killed, now that a new responsibility has been laid on his shoulders, one more onerous than that incumbent upon the soldier to show himself a brave man. It is the

Book 2

first sustained study in the poem, the first of several in this book, of the Heroic Impulse (see Chapter 1).[1]

The second Section, therefore, has the circular structure characteristic of drama: it moves around a situation; at the end Aeneas is back where he was at the beginning. But during these 384 lines the pathos and the horror of Troy's destruction have their effect upon us. The actual narrative of the night of fighting is cut to 136 lines—three Episodes organized around Aeneas: we see the fighting through his eyes, following him and the band he scrapes together through the streets. First, success: they put on Greek armour and exploit the resultant confusion (370–401). Then defeat, the brutal capture of Cassandra and the death of most of Aeneas' followers, destroyed by their own stratagem (402–34). Finally, separated from the rest, Aeneas makes his way to the scene of destruction at the royal palace (434–505). The first two of these three Episodes are also linked by the character Coroebus: he is introduced at 341–6 and his fated death forecast; he is then glimpsed at 386–93, when he initiates the stratagem of the stolen armour; at 407–8 he surrenders to the Heroic Impulse; at 424–6 he is killed beside the altar of Minerva.[2]

The death of the old king forms an Episode by itself outside the main framework of the narrative of this Section. (For a detailed discussion of this Episode see Chapter 1.) Aeneas' arrival at the palace is timed so as to make him the helpless spectator while Neoptolemus kills Priam. An element of frustration, therefore, sharpens Aeneas' anger when he catches sight of Helen (like Priam she had sought the protection of an altar); his mood in fact is curiously like that which follows the death of Pallas in Book 10 (see Analysis of Book 10 and Chapter 5, 'Implicit Comment') except that here Venus intervenes before Aeneas can complete the cycle by killing Helen.[3]

The third Section brings almost a relaxation of the action after this intensely rapid and moving second Section. It opens with yet another illustration of the Heroic Impulse—Aeneas' father Anchises, determined, like Priam, to throw away his life in battle rather than see Troy destroyed (645–6):

---

[1] Cf. *Latin Explorations*, pp. 207–11.
[2] Coroebus is an example of Interweaving; see *Latin Explorations*, pp. 212–16.
[3] See Chapter 1, and, for the dispute about the authenticity and significance of the Helen Episode, the references there to Austin and Palmer.

The Twelve Books

> 'ipse manu mortem inueniam; miserebitur hostis
> exuuiasque petet. facilis iactura sepulcri.'

> '*I shall find death for myself in action. One of the enemy will
> pity me, or want loot. Loss of burial matters little.*'

The pathos is heightened by the mixture of bitterness and surrender to the irrational in the last words—for no ancient did the loss of proper burial matter little. Unable to sway Anchises, Aeneas again forgets his mission in the heat of a further Heroic Impulse (655–72). Neither listens to Creusa, who, like Hecuba in the previous Section, plays the role of the unheeded exponent of common sense. To convince Anchises that he was wrong when he declared that the gods would have spared his house for him, if they had wanted him to go on living (641–2), a double miracle is needed. A strange flame plays around the head of Ascanius, but leaves him unharmed (679–86); a comet crashes through the night sky to land on Mount Ida—pointing to the place where the exiles should assemble (692–8).

The function of this Episode is to suggest that the destruction of Troy by the gods was not a purposeless act of malevolence, but the working-out of a divine plan which is constructive as well as destructive: Troy falls, Rome rises. On this level, however, the Episode is less successful (we can accept the miracles, but Anchises' surrender to them smacks too much of rhetoric to be convincing) than on its more purely dramatic level—the portrayal of the frenzy of despair and the fine panache of Aeneas' speech (657–70) with its conscious irony (659–63), overlaid by the unconscious Tragic Irony the reader senses as he dissociates himself from Aeneas' assessment of the situation.

The party set out after a succinct evocation of the traditional scene: Aeneas; on his shoulders, his father carrying their city's gods; by his side, his son; behind him, as they move into the darkness, his wife Creusa (721–5). We might then have passed without further ado to the final Tableau on the slopes of Mount Ida (795–804). Why does Virgil give such prominence to Creusa? She could have been disposed of without fuss in a number of ways. Clearly one function of the two Creusa Episodes is to add further to our sympathy for Aeneas before Virgil proceeds to whittle that sympathy away in Book 4. There he must seem almost devoid of feeling; his despair when he misses Creusa, his frantic dash back to the burning city (730–70), help to prevent too harsh a judgment of him. But Creusa has another hardly less important function: when Aeneas meets her ghost (771–94), she

Book 2

too, like Hector and his mother (but in a way that is more simply moving), can assure him that all that has happened that night represents the accomplishment of a divine purpose in which room is left for hope.[1]

Some of the writing in this third Section is of a very high order—the Tableau of Troy, for instance, with its obvious reminiscences of Euripides' *Trojan Women* (752–67). We can imagine the empty heart with which Aeneas returns to the unhappy herd of refugees who had gathered in his absence (798: *collectam exsilio pubem, miserabile uulgus*). Judged, however, by the very high standards of the first two Sections, the third is uneven, particularly in the treatment of Anchises, but also in the treatment of Creusa; we can see why she is there, her speech (776–89) is good; but she does not quite come off. The short passages of real poetry stand out a little uncomfortably among the rhetoric of the rest.

BOOK 3

In Book 3, the Aeneadae, after a winter spent in preparation, set out on their wanderings round the Mediterranean in search of their promised new home; following unsuccessful attempts to settle in Thrace and Crete, they reach Buthrotum in Epirus; several years have passed.

They spend some months in Buthrotum and from Helenus, who rules over the former dominions of Achilles in Thrace, Aeneas receives a detailed prophecy about what lies ahead.

At length they make the crossing from Epirus to Italy and sail straight on to Sicily; after a night near Mount Etna, they pick up one of Ulysses' men, Achaemenides, then make their way round the south coast of Sicily to Drepanum, where Anchises dies.

A quiet book is needed between the close-packed structures of Books 2 and 4; all the same, Book 3 must be regarded as a failure. It has, as we shall see, some fine scenes; there is much more to Book 3 than dry chronicle; but the problem of accommodating a space of five or six years to Virgil's dramatic manner is not solved. The trouble is not that the story of the wanderings in Virgil's adaptation of it from

---

[1] In Book 3, Aeneas apparently forgets, or disregards, what Creusa tells him. It is usually taken as one of Virgil's slips. But the conflicting prophecies of 3.4–5 intervene. Moreover, Aeneas is at cross purposes with his destiny throughout Book 2; is this perhaps a final instance?

chronological form to dramatic form has lost precision.[1] Precision is not what Virgil is after. His object is selective evocation, at a constantly varying tempo, of the traditional story; fullness of detail, even clarity of exposition, within the space Virgil allows himself (a single book) would result in scrappiness. What is wrong is that the attempt at dramatization of the narrative fails. The Aeneadae do not come to life; Aeneas, Anchises, Palinurus (see 202, 513–19, 561–2), perhaps Andromache, are the only characters we can visualize (compare the living minor characters in Book 5). Too often we cannot sense even the presence of the others in the narrative, let alone the alternation of hope and despair to which we should feel them exposed.

Obviously, once Virgil made the destruction of Troy part of the narrative structure of his poem, he had to include some account of how the Aeneadae got to Sicily. Legend supplied the basic facts; but some weaving of at any rate a selection of these into the fabric of the story (along with fresh details devised by Virgil) was necessary to provide narrative continuity. It was not something that could be got over quickly without the risk of imbalance after a whole book devoted to the events of a single day. Book 3 attempts, unsuccessfully, to provide this continuity.

Another obvious function of Book 3 is to rival Homer. Odysseus

---

[1] Mackail complains (p. 89):
Further, the story of the Wanderings, while it retains more of the annalistic handling than suits dramatic or epic structure, has in the reshaping lost a good deal of the precision and continuity of a chronicle. The chronology is vague, and is made more confusing still by the references to it in Books I and V.

For the tradition that the order of Books 1 and 3 was reversed by Virgil's original editors, see Suetonius 183–5R (referred to in Chapter 3). If the present Book 3 originally came first, it is likely it would have been written in the third person.

The chronology of the wanderings is a notorious problem. At 1.755–6 (the concluding lines of Book 1) Dido, after asking Aeneas to tell her the story of his wanderings, adds:
'nam te iam septima portat
omnibus errantem terris et fluctibus aestas.'

At 5.626 Iris, disguised as the Trojan woman Beroe, laments:
'septima post Troiae excidium iam uertitur aestas.'

Yet an interval of upwards of a year, apparently, separates the two occasions; already by 4.193–4 the winter is well advanced; at 5.46 Aeneas tells his men that exactly a year has elapsed since Anchises' death—the last event (3.714: *hic labor extremus*) narrated in Book 3. Dido's words, therefore, and those of the false Beroe are commonly held to be irreconcilable. See E. de St Denis, 'La chronologie des navigations troyennes dans l'*Enéide*', *REL* 20 (1942) 79–98. For a suggested solution see my note, '*Septima aestas*', *CQ* 17 (1967) 128–9.

Book 3

spends four books relating his travels (*Odyssey* 9 to 12—including his colloquy with the spirits of the dead at the edge of the world in *Odyssey* 11). Virgil retains the formal feature of a flashback, but drastically reduces the length of it, transfers *his* Nekyia to Book 6, and incorporates a number of details from the second book of Apollonius' *Argonautica*.[1] The challenge to make new out of old is accepted. But if the traditional material is really to earn its keep, it must be given a form that will enable it as well to discharge a useful function in the structure of the poem as a whole.

What this function, the main function of Book 3, is, is fairly clear: it is to make more intelligible Virgil's concept, in the poem, of the relationship between man and fate. The poem takes it for granted that fate is all-powerful. If the Aeneadae are destined to reach Italy, they could be got there, therefore, without a hitch. But if the gods did everything for man, human existence would become meaningless. Jove makes this point when he refuses Cybele's request to grant Aeneas a journey without risk (9.95-7):

> 'mortaline manu factae immortale carinae
> fas habeant? certusque incerta pericula lustret
> Aeneas? cui tanta deo permissa potestas?'
>
> *'Shall ships made by mortal hand take on
> immortal status? Is Aeneas to have sure passage
> through unsure perils? What god is granted power like this?'*[2]

Virgil has not, of course, explicit answers to these problems and is not interested, I think, in providing answers—the poem, as I have said, is not a philosophical textbook. He merely utilizes, as part of the hypothesis upon which his poem is constructed, the sort of answers many people would give.

Pretty clearly, Virgil's intention in the first half of the poem is to show Aeneas undergoing a series of *labores* to prove (or rather to develop) his *pietas*—a sort of transference from the physical to the psychological level of the old story of the labours of Hercules. One thing a leader has to learn is the folly, sometimes, of surrender to the

---

[1] Apollonius has the encounter with the Harpies and Phineus, a long prophecy by Phineus, an encounter with savage birds on the island of Ares, and a rescue of the sons of Phrixus which sounds a little like the Episode of Achaemenides. There is also an echo of Theocritus, perhaps, in Virgil's description of Polyphemus (see below).

[2] Cf. also Aletes' remark, 9.246-50, that a nation's fate is in part determined by the quality of its men.

heroic impulse (Book 2); another is endurance in adversity (Book 3); a third is the need to subordinate passion to duty (Book 4); a fourth is confidence in himself and in the rightness of his mission when that confidence is lost by those under his command (Book 5); a fifth is the deeper understanding, the mystic insight, that can underpin such confidence (Book 6). Each of Books 2 to 6 represents an ordeal, or rather an experience, the result of which is a more mature grasp by Aeneas of himself; having undergone these *labores,* he is fit to assume the leadership of his people in war.[1]

In Book 3, Aeneas' men, too, have to endure, as well as their leader, in order to reach their fated goal. Observe, however, that Virgil concentrates, not on their adventures or the details of their hardships, but on their eager, fumbling search for a new home. Where Book 2 showed the Trojans the instrument of their own misfortune, Book 3 will show them the instrument of the regeneration of their hopes. Fate, we are to assume, prefers the collaboration of man in working out his own destiny for good or evil. This much makes sense and is sound Stoicism, so long as we remember that Virgil is making imaginative use of a doctrine, not enunciating it. Where he gets into difficulties is over the mechanics of deciding what guidance the Aeneadae are to receive. The idea that fate will find a way (395: *fata uiam inuenient*— Helenus' words to Aeneas)[2] is straightforward enough. But what role should prophecy play in such a system? Helenus, for example, makes the very odd remark at the beginning of his prophecy that not only are there things that he does not know himself, but there are others which Juno forbids him to tell (379–80):

[1] C. M. Bowra, 'Aeneas and the Stoic ideal', *GR* 3 (1933–4) 11, remarks:

When Augustine condemns Aeneas as a Stoic [*Civ.D.*9.4], he gives us a clue to the solution. Aeneas is a Stoic, but like all Stoics he has to go through a period of probation, and during this his temptations and difficulties are often too much for him, and he fails. The Stoics, like the Christians, believed that virtue was impossible without trial, and Virgil, adapting himself to the current Stoicism of his age, set himself to describe the development of such a man. He was not so bad an artist as to make him triumph over all his temptations, nor so precise a Stoic as to confine himself to the letter of the doctrine. But unquestionably in the first six books the clue to Virgil's treatment of Aeneas is that he is using not only the doctrine but in some cases the terminology of Stoicism. He takes his hero through a course of tests and trials, which are the indispensable condition of his moral development, and it is only after he has passed through them and found in them his moral weaknesses that he is allowed the vision of the destined glories of Rome.

[2] Jove says the same as Helenus at 10.113. Cf. what Helenus says of the power of Juno at 3.433–40.

Book 3

'prohibent nam cetera Parcae
scire Helenum farique uetat Saturnia Iuno.'[1]

*'As for the rest the Fates forbid
Helenus to know, nor does Saturnian Juno allow me to speak.'*

Once again this is primarily a philosophical question. But it is one that starts to concern the reader of the poem, if the feeling troubles him that Virgil's use of prophecy is arbitrary, or artistically unconvincing.

	Introduction		1–12
I 13–293	To Buthrotum (several years):		
	(i) Thrace		13–72
	(ii) Delos		73–120
	(iii) Crete		121–191
	(iv) Storm at sea; island of the Harpies		192–269
	(v) Leucas		270–283
	(vi) To Buthrotum		284–293
II 294–505	At Buthrotum (about a year):		
	(i) Andromache—Helenus		294–355
	(ii) Prophecy of Helenus		356–471
	(iii) Departure		472–505
III 506–718	To Sicily (i–iii = 3 days; iv = ? a month or so):		
	(i) To Italy		506–567
	(ii) Near Etna		568–587
	(iii) Achaemenides and Polyphemus		588–691
	(iv) Round Sicily to Drepanum; short summary of events to date		692–718

After the quiet, simple ending of Book 2, the formal opening of Book 3 marks a change of tempo from detailed, tight-lipped narrative to a more detached narrative that has no time for detail because there is more ground to cover[2] (1–3):

---

[1] The insistence on Apollo in Book 3 is remarkable—see 90–101, 154, 371, 395, 434, 474. The Sibyl in Book 6 is also, in her prophetic function, priestess of Apollo.

[2] Mackail (pp. 91–2) claims the change of tone betrays rearrangement of Virgil's text:
> In support of this conjecture it may be noted that the opening lines of Book III are not merely in their stately rhythm and exalted diction strikingly different in tone from what succeeds them, but are not a quite natural resumption of the narrative broken off at the end of Book II, and suggest the possibility that as originally composed they were meant to begin the whole poem.

The Twelve Books

> Postquam res Asiae Priamique euertere gentem
> immeritam uisum superis, ceciditque superbum
> Ilium et omnis humo fumat Neptunia Troia. . . .

> *After the overthrow of Asia and Priam's undeserving house*
> *by decision of the gods above, after proud Ilium's*
> *fall, when Neptune's Troy lay a smoking ruin. . . .*

The tone of the book is fixed in the concluding sentence of the introductory paragraph (11–12):

> feror exsul in altum
> cum sociis natoque penatibus et magnis dis.

> *An exile I put to sea,*
> *my comrades with me, my son, the Penates and the great gods.*

This is to be the story of a man without a land (Virgil clearly connects *exsul* with *solum*—cf. *extorris*; as it happens, it is a false etymology[1]). Observe how line 12 is built round an ambiguity in *penatibus*. The primary reference is to the images they carry with them; but *magnis dis* imposes the non-concrete sense, which is helped by the echo of Ennius.[2] It is, of course, the non-concrete sense that is required when an echo of the line comes back, in the picture upon Aeneas' magic shield, of Augustus leading the Romans into battle at Actium (8.679):

> cum patribus populoque, penatibus et magnis dis.

> *with Senate and People, Penates and great gods.*

The first Section tells the story of how the Aeneadae wander about from place to place, hoping each time they have reached their goal. Already before they set out, they are plunged into uncertainty (4–5):

> diuersa exsilia et desertas quaerere terras
> auguriis agimur diuum.

> *a life of exile in all manner of distant, empty lands*
> *the gods to us in prophecy commended.*

Virgil with his usual economy implies the Aeneadae consulted the gods more than once, but with results which seemed to them contradictory (*diuersa* means 'utterly different', not just 'different'). We have heard only the prophecy of Creusa (2.780–4). Did they seek confirmation

---

[1] Virgil is fond of using words in a slightly odd way that stresses what he takes to be their etymology. See Chapter 6, 'Etymological Puns'.
[2] Ennius, epic fragment 193W.

Book 3

and get instead answers which seemed to them to conflict with what Creusa told them? Anyway, they head first for Thrace and are driven from that lonely, barbarous land by the eerie warning of Polydorus. The first clear clue comes when they retreat to Delos for further prophetic guidance (93–6):

> summissi petimus terram et uox fertur ad auris:
> 'Dardanidae duri, quae uos a stirpe parentum
> prima tulit tellus, eadem uos ubere laeto
> accipiet reduces. antiquam exquirite matrem.'[1]

> *Bowed down we fall to the ground and to our ears a voice comes:*
> *'Tough sons of Dardanus, that same land which first bore you*
> *through your parents' stock, will with glad breast*
> *greet you on return. Seek out your ancient mother.'*

They decide this means Crete. There the first broken glimpse of hope is dashed by the pestilence that descends upon their new city after only a few months. They are on the point of returning to Delos to consult Apollo afresh when the god sends the Penates to Aeneas in a vision warning him that they must move on again (161–71).[2]

Virgil's meaning seems to be that the Aeneadae, human and fallible, keep missing their destiny: Aeneas disregards Creusa as he had disregarded Hector; Anchises misinterprets Apollo.[3] The alternative names that keep recurring (Ausonia, Hesperia, Italia) accentuate the uncertainty. Even now they hesitate and move up the western coast of Greece and become involved with the Harpies, whose leader Celaeno issues the prophecy of the tables (fulfilled at 7.112–29)—a not very successful Episode, even if it has a structural purpose and represents a careful integration of traditional material. Continuing their voyage, they reach Leucas where they find a temple of Apollo (Virgil takes the opportunity of establishing a link with Actium), coming eventually to Buthrotum in Epirus.

---

[1] When we come to Book 7, we shall see again this insistence on the antiquity of Italy. Note how *matrem* revivifies the metaphor latent in *ubere*.

[2] Note how the play between the concrete and non-concrete sense of Penates is exploited in this passage—e.g., in the beautiful line (157):
> nos tumidum sub te permensi classibus aequor.

[3] Though it appears from 180–5 that Anchises (1) knew that his people had a double origin; (2) had been told by Cassandra (but had not, of course, believed her) that the Trojans would go to Italy, Virgil seems to intend us to understand that Anchises now connects the two facts for the first time. Of course the Trojans easily appear more stupid than Virgil intended, unless we remember that the Aeneadae could not possess our grasp of Mediterranean geography.

The Twelve Books

Unlike Sections 1 and 3, where the scene changes constantly, the second Section of Book 3 has a single setting. At Buthrotum, the political situation is a little complicated. Helenus, a son of Priam of Troy, rules over what was once the dominion of Achilles, having succeeded to it by virtue of his marriage to his twice-widowed sister-in-law Andromache, formerly wife of Hector, and then in exile wife of Achilles' son Neoptolemus (or Pyrrhus), whom we met in Book 2 as one of the leaders of the Greek invaders and the murderer of Priam, and who was later murdered by Orestes. (The details of this slightly improbable sequence of events would have been familiar to Virgil's audience from the *Andromache* of Euripides and other plays, Roman as well as Greek.) The Section begins with the first real highlight of the book—Aeneas' meeting with Andromache. He comes upon her as she is pouring a libation to her dead husband Hector. In a glade by a river called Simois, which is not the real Simois, lies the grave of Hector, but it is not his real grave—all is make-believe in this touching Tableau (300–13):

> progredior portu classis et litora linquens,   300
> sollemnis cum forte dapes et tristia dona
> ante urbem in luco falsi Simoentis ad undam
> libabat cineri Andromache manisque uocabat
> Hectoreum ad tumulum, uiridi quem caespite inanem
> et geminas causam lacrimis sacrauerat aras.   305
> ut me conspexit uenientem et Troia circum
> arma amens uidit, magnis exterrita monstris
> deriguit uisu in medio, calor ossa reliquit;
> labitur et longo uix tandem tempore fatur:
> 'uerane te facies, uerus mihi nuntius adfers,   310
> nate dea? uiuisne? aut, si lux alma recessit,
> Hector ubi est?' dixit, lacrimasque effudit et omnem
> impleuit clamore locum.

I set out from the harbour, leaving ships and shore behind,
and chance upon a solemn festival and a joyless offering
outside the city, in a glade by a stream falsely named Simois—
Andromache, pouring libation to the dead, summoning Hector's ghost
to an empty tomb; she had decked it with green turf,
set up twin altars to make a proper place for tears.
When her eye lit on me approaching, distraught at the
sight of Trojan battle rig, shocked by so great a marvel,
she froze as she looked, her bones lost their warmth.
She falls faint, then, after a long time, with an effort, speaks:

Book 3

> '*Is it real the shape I see? Do you really come and bring news,*
> *goddess-born? Do you live? Or, if life's light has gone,*
> *where is Hector?*' *As she spoke, she burst out weeping and filled*
> *the whole place with her crying.*

Observe how the pathos of the scene is drawn out by delaying the key word *inanem*, line 304 (with its usual ambiguity—(1) 'empty'; (2) 'useless'). The following sentence contains a good example of Virgil's evocative imprecision. It has long been debated what is meant by *Troia circum arma* (306-7).[1] Yet Virgil surely intends no precise meaning; he is out to capture Andromache's sudden confused recognition of a sight that was once familiar (men in Trojan armour) but that she no longer expects to see about her. She is not really sure indeed what she has seen, for the shock freezes her (308: *deriguit uisu in medio*—note the use of contrasting tenses in this Tableau). Then the thought comes to her that Aeneas must be a ghost, that she, too, is dead perhaps; and, crowding in on that thought, the feeling of the wrongness of it if that were so: why, if they are all dead, does Aeneas come to her? why not her own dead husband Hector?[2] It is little wonder that the scene captured the imagination of Racine.

In addition to providing a rest from the constant movement of the other two Sections, the second Section has a structural function. The first and third Episodes of the Section form a frame round the long prophecy of Helenus, the central Episode of the book as it is of the Section. By now, the Aeneadae know that their goal is Italy, and they know where Italy is—it is the country they can see across the Adriatic. The function of Helenus' prophecy is to add fresh pathos to the narrative of the wanderings by disclosing to the Aeneadae that their goal is still much further off than they think: their future home lies not in the Italy they can see and which they feel within their grasp, but on the west coast, and to reach it they must make the long journey round Sicily. Helenus' opening words emphasize this dramatically and effectively (381-7):

> 'principio Italiam, quam tu iam rere propinquam
> uicinosque, ignare, paras inuadere portus,

---

[1] Williams, e.g., says ' "Trojan warriors accompanying me", rather than "Trojan armour I was wearing".'

[2] There is a similar imprecision in Andromache's words to Aeneas (310-12). If we are to pin her down, we must agree with Williams against Mackail that *si lux alma recessit* means 'if you are dead', rather than 'if we are all dead'. But it is a mistake to impose this kind of precision upon her words.

longa procul longis uia diuidit inuia terris.
ante et Trinacria lentandus remus in unda
et salis Ausonii lustrandum nauibus aequor
infernique lacus Aeaeaeque insula Circae,
quam tuta possis urbem componere terra.'

*'To begin with, Italy, which you think close,
innocently preparing to make port near by,
lies in a land far off, the way to it long and hard.
First with Sicily's waters must your oars wrestle,
the broad western ocean you must sail across,
the lake of Hell approach, Aeaean Circe's isle:
not till then may you raise your city in a safe land.'*

When the point is rammed home at 396–8, and then again (477–8) in Helenus' short farewell speech to Anchises, we can feel the intermingling of despair with hope that uncertainty has brought. It provokes Aeneas' rueful parting words to his hosts (495–7):

'uobis parta quies: nullum maris aequor arandum,
arua neque Ausoniae semper cedentia retro
quaerenda.'[1]

*'You have won peace. You have no sea to plough,
no quest for a western land that ever moves
away.'*

But despite its structural function, despite its central position in the book, the prophecy of Helenus comes near failure. Helenus remains too colourless to assume dramatic life. Virgil for once has not overcome the self-imposed limitations of his form. He has chosen to observe the epic convention which normally precludes explicit delineation of character, or even appearance, though these were things his contemporaries were intensely interested in and things it was not beyond their power to describe—think, for example, of Sallust's word portrait of Catiline, or the vivid individuality of Roman portrait sculpture. Virgil occasionally describes appearance as an index of character, especially in the Vignettes of minor characters in the battle scenes of the second half of the poem (e.g., Chloreus, 11.768–77). But mostly character is left to emerge from action, and still more from dialogue; it is, after all, the method of tragedy, and on the whole this dramatic technique serves Virgil well—his skill in

[1] Cf. Aeneas' words to the Sibyl (6.61):
'iam tandem Italiae fugientis prendimus oras'.

Book 3

revealing personality through dialogue is impressive. (For fuller discussion see Chapter 5, 'Characterization and Motivation'.)

Helenus, however, takes little part in dialogue. His long prophecy imposes an impersonal, oracular tone which might matter little if he were to remain a minor figure. Given the major role which the structure of the book requires, sandwiched as he is between the very moving Episode which precedes and the equally moving, convincing Tableau of Andromache's words to Ascanius at the moment of departure (482–91), the woodenness of Helenus becomes something of a disaster. There is no description of Andromache either; but *her* character is created by her reaction to situation; however much individual readers differ in the Andromache they inwardly visualize, her personality must fall within the limits fixed by action and dialogue.

Another structural function of the second Section is to create a kind of Tragic Irony that overshadows the opening Episode of Section 3. When the Aeneadae leave Epirus, we have a detailed description of their overnight halt at Ceraunia (506–20):

> prouehimur pelago uicina Ceraunia iuxta,
> unde iter Italiam cursusque breuissimus undis.
> sol ruit interea et montes umbrantur opaci.
> sternimur optatae gremio telluris ad undam
> sortiti remos passimque in litore sicco   510
> corpora curamus: fessos sopor inrigat artus.
> necdum orbem medium nox Horis acta subibat:
> haud segnis strato surgit Palinurus et omnis
> explorat uentos atque auribus aera captat;
> sidera cuncta notat tacito labentia caelo,   515
> Arcturum pluuiasque Hyadas geminosque Triones
> armatumque auro circumspicit Oriona.
> postquam cuncta uidet caelo constare sereno,
> dat clarum e puppi signum: nos castra mouemus
> temptamusque uiam et uelorum pandimus alas.   520

We make the open sea hard by neighbouring Thunder Point—
from there to Italy is no distance across the water.
The sun plunges meanwhile, the hills are wrapped in shadow.
Each man is given his oar and we stretch out by the water's edge
upon the welcome earth; all along the dry shore we seek
comfort for our bodies; sleep flows through tired limbs.
Night was not yet half way round her journey through the hours
when Palinurus (never slack) rises from his bed, marks every
puff of wind, turns his ears to catch the air, takes in

the whole gliding motion of the stars through silent sky,
Arcturus, the rainy Hyades, the two Bears,
observes Orion in his panoply of gold.
When he sees all in order, the sky serene,
from his poop he gives the signal loud. We break camp,
and venture on our way, spreading our canvas wings.

This terse narrative—it reads like an extract from some Roman historian—contrasts sharply with the tempo of the first Section of the book. We feel vividly the anxious wait, the quick decision to depart, the excited thought of all—Italy at last. Note especially the vivid Tableau of Palinurus (513–19). Nowhere else in Book 3 are the events of a few hours allotted so continuous a narrative. But we feel throughout the note of irony imposed on the scene by Helenus' prophecy; all the time the thought is fresh in our minds that reaching Italy does not mean the end of the *labores* of the Aeneadae. Their real homecoming is not till four books later at 7.25–36. The resultant pathos is most effective. And it is heightened by the spectacle which confronts the Aeneadae when they reach the Italian coast: all they see are the temples of hostile goddesses; their first omen is that of the white horses that spell war, with peace only later (537–43). Then comes the horror of Charybdis and the terrifying spectacle of Etna in eruption at night (570–82). Naturally they take Sicily and Italy as one. What a welcome to their new world!

Why does Virgil devote so much space to the Episode of Achaemenides and Polyphemus? The character of Achaemenides, though modelled to some extent on the rescue of the sons of Phrixus in Book 2 of Apollonius' *Argonautica*, seems to be Virgil's invention. Is it only 'a passage of rhetorical and grandiose writing, detached from the immediate world of human experience', 'a stitched-on piece of brilliant colours'?[1] Is it early material which Virgil later used as a quarry for the Sinon Episode when he came to work up Book 2?[2] A little reflection, I think, reveals Virgil's intentions. One function of the Episode is to accentuate the magic and the strangeness of the new world to which the Aeneadae had come: Charybdis,[3] Etna, Polyphemus. The night of uneasy rest which the Aeneadae pass near Etna

---

[1] Williams on 3.588 ff.
[2] This is Mackail's opinion (p. 516). (See Chapter 3, Section I.)
[3] Scylla we hear about only from Helenus, apart from the passing reference at 684.

Book 3

(583–7) is particularly telling. Achaemenides is the first human being they meet, and he comes to them with a tale of horror. Then Polyphemus appears, accompanied by his brother giants. Small wonder if the Aeneadae run away in panic from the place where they have first set foot. Only a miraculous change of wind saves them from disaster (682–9).

Here we have a magical, uncanny setting that prepares the reader for the fantasy of Book 6 and for the picture of Italy as a land ancient and bizarre which Virgil draws in the first Episode of Book 7 and again in the catalogue at the end of Book 7. But there is another element in the Achaemenides Episode, easier to sense than to account for. Virgil's treatment of the Cyclops story is most effective. Achaemenides, in a summary of Homer's cave scene, makes Polyphemus cruel and revolting. His judgment is nowhere explicitly contradicted, and when the giant appears he strikes terror into the Aeneadae. But Virgil's actual description of Polyphemus (put, of course, on Aeneas' lips) makes him sound vaguely pathetic (655–61):

> uix ea fatus erat summo cum monte uidemus
> ipsum inter pecudes uasta se mole mouentem
> pastorem Polyphemum et litora nota petentem,
> monstrum horrendum, informe, ingens, cui lumen ademptum.
> trunca manum pinus regit et uestigia firmat;
> lanigerae comitantur oues; ea sola uoluptas
> solamenque mali. . . .
>
> *Scarce had he said this when on the mountain-top we see*
> *the massive figure itself moving along the flocks,*
> *shepherd Polyphemus seeking for the beach he knows,*
> *monstrous, terrible, shapeless, huge, deprived of sight.*
> *A pine-trunk guides his hand and makes his steps firm.*
> *The fleecy ewes follow him—his only joy*
> *and comfort in misfortune. . . .*

The details of the imagery more than counterbalance Aeneas' explicit assertions (658: *monstrum horrendum, informe, ingens*—and even this line ends with the curiously touching phrase *cui lumen ademptum*).[1]

There is more than an echo here of Theocritus' Polyphemus.[2] Even the whole band of Cyclopes seem not so much menacing as pathetic,

---

[1] Part of the effect of the phrase depends on an ambiguity: (1) 'whose (single) eye had been lost' and (2) 'who had been deprived of the light of day'.
[2] The transformation of Homer's figure of horror into a figure of pathos may, of course, be due to Philoxenus and Hermesianax who precede Theocritus.

particularly in the final image (677–81—already quoted in Chapter 3, Section I) where the simile of the cypresses and pines on a mountain ridge implies a scene of innocence and beauty that cuts across the asserted attitude of Aeneas. Virgil wishes, I think, to suggest that the first reaction of the Aeneadae to the strangeness of the western land is natural but mistaken. And perhaps here is the key to the Structural Parallelism of the Sinon Episode and the Achaemenides Episode. For it is their general similarity that is more disturbing than the recurring details of phrase. Both Achaemenides and Sinon come forward as Greeks connected with Ulysses. Both tell a tale and win the Trojans' acceptance of their tale. We feel some sort of Implicit Comment is intended. Is perhaps the real despair of Achaemenides contrasted with the feigned despair of Sinon? Is it some kind of retribution? We should remember that these Episodes stand almost at the beginning and at the end of Aeneas' narrative.[1] Are we meant to feel that Achaemenides' version of the encounter in the cave (which is Homer's) has something of Greek perfidy about it, too?[2]

All this sounds, and must sound, speculative; but there are points in a poem of the stature of the *Aeneid*, some of them key points, where the poet must choose not to reveal his meaning too plainly; where the suggestion that there is another side to something, another way of looking at things, must be no more than hinted at.

The final Episode of the third Section strikes us as rather unsatisfactory and underplayed by comparison with the rest of the Section. Virgil wants perhaps to let things calm down after the extremely graphic Episode of Achaemenides and Polyphemus (whatever we make of it), in order to make a fresh, strong start at the beginning of Book 4. Moreover, it is psychologically sound for Aeneas to underplay the death of his father (710–14), and then to break off his narrative as though he were no longer in the mood to talk (715):

> hinc me digressum uestris deus appulit oris.
>
> *When I departed thence the god drove me to these shores.*

There is no call for Aeneas to tell the story of the storm which brought

---

[1] Note, too, how the last lines of Book 3 echo the opening lines of Book 2.

[2] Heinze (pp. 112–13) points out how the similarity of the Episodes is underlined rather than concealed by Virgil. He takes Virgil's intention to be to lay stress on the humanity of the Trojans who, after having been led to destruction by their compassion and trust for Sinon, can still take pity on an enemy when he begs for protection.

Book 4

him to Africa; Dido knows about that already. But though one sees the need for a relaxation of the tension, just as one sees the need for the prophecy of Helenus, the feeling remains that Virgil's manipulation of his narrative at these two points is, as the poem stands, unsuccessful.

BOOK 4

In Book 4, tormented by her infatuation with Aeneas and frustrated in her hopes of marriage, Dido lets herself be seduced by Aeneas while they are taking shelter from a storm on the day of the great hunt, and accepts the liaison that follows as a substitute for marriage; when the liaison has lasted some time, Aeneas, reminded of his mission by Mercury, prepares to leave Carthage.

After a bitter quarrel, Dido, smothering her pride, begs Aeneas to stay a little longer; when he refuses, she decides to take her life.

She builds a great pyre within the palace and, after cursing Aeneas, kills herself on it as Aeneas sails out of Carthage with his fleet.

Book 4 is Virgil's masterpiece. Already in antiquity Ovid claimed it had more readers than any other part of the *Aeneid*.[1] Augustine's tortured admiration of it is famous.[2] It can stand comparison with the other great books in the qualities where they excel—it has the narrative power of Book 2, the imaginative power of 6, the tragic intensity and truth of the finest scenes in 10 and 12. But Book 4 overshadows these by its perfectly contrived synthesis of tragedy and epic.

The book is the shortest of the twelve and the most *dramatic* in form. A tripartite structure is more clearly discernible than in the other books: lines 1–295 recount the beginning of the affair; lines 296–503, the alienation; lines 504–705, the end of the affair—Aeneas' departure and Dido's suicide. Indeed we can hardly doubt that Virgil consciously intended this division, for each of the three Sections has its own clearly marked internal unity, each begins with the entry of the queen and the phrase *at regina*, and each time the word following that phrase (*graui, dolos, pyra*) strikes the keynote of the ensuing action.[3]

[1] Ovid, *Tristia*, 2.535: *nec legitur pars ulla magis de corpore toto*. Admittedly Ovid is establishing a case for the popularity of poetry about free love.
[2] Augustine, *Confessions*, 1.13.
[3] This perhaps sounds like praising Virgil as a cryptographer more than as a poet. What has happened is that Virgil begins each Section with a sentence that is a kind of précis: first comes the opening phrase *at regina*, then the key word of the opening sentence proper, thrown into prominence by the pause that follows it at the third-foot caesura.

The Twelve Books

But Virgil's *narrative* technique also reaches in this book its highest level of perfection and variety—the passage 74-89, for example, in which a close-packed succession of images suggests the compulsive, irresistible impetus of Dido's wild infatuation; or the serene, colourful, tightly organized narrative of the hunting Episode (129-72), its happy, relaxed realism and the terrifying, penetrating, ironic symbolism with which that Episode concludes; or the awful, sublime simplicity of the death Episode (630-92).

The following synopsis shows the structure of the book:

I 1-295	(i) Dido in love		1-89
	(ii) Juno-Venus		90-128
	(iii) The hunt, ending in the cave scene		129-172
	(iv) Fama		173-194
	(v) Iarbas	*Interlude*	195-218
	(vi) Jove—Mercury—Aeneas		219-278
	(vii) Aeneas decides to leave		279-295
II 296-503	(i) The quarrel		296-396
	(ii) *tempus inane peto*		397-449
	(iii) The plan		450-503
III 504-705	(i) Dido faces death		504-552
	(ii) Aeneas leaves		553-629
	(iii) Death		630-692
	(iv) Epilogue		693-705

We begin with a searching scrutiny of Dido's progressive surrender to infatuation, organized into three terse Episodes. Virgil displays all his usual gentleness, but each step that Dido takes away from honesty with herself towards degradation is plain. She is already deeply in love with Aeneas when the book opens. Because the third Section of Book 1 has ensured that the fact of Dido's love comes as no surprise, two lines suffice to assert her smouldering passion (1-2):

> At regina graui iamdudum saucia cura
> uulnus alit uenis et caeco carpitur igni.[1]

> *But the queen, stricken long since by a grievous passion,*
> *nurses the wound with her veins, is consumed by a hidden fire.*

From the opening words of the book we are concerned no longer with

---

[1] We should take *iamdudum* first with *saucia* and then with *alit* and *carpitur*. For a study of the ambiguities in these lines see my article 'Syntactical ambiguity in Horace and Virgil', *Aumla* 14 (1960) 43-4.

the onset of Dido's infatuation, but with the progress and consequences of it. Already we see her struggling to present the infatuation to herself in a form that need not involve its instant rejection (3–5):

> multa uiri uirtus animo multusque recursat
> gentis honos: haerent infixi pectore uultus
> uerbaque, nec placidam membris dat cura quietem.

In her mind the manliness of the man crowds ever back,
ever the honour of his house; in her heart his face, his words
stick fast; passion denies her limbs the peace of sleep.

The scene is not the same as at the end of Book 1. By now the banquet is over. On the less rational level of Dido's thoughts (4: *pectore*) linger a mental image of Aeneas and the echo of his words; neither will give her peace. But on a more rational level (3: *animo*), however much she rejects the idea of marriage (for she vowed not to remarry after the death of her husband), the thought keeps crowding back (3: *multa . . . multusque recursat*) that the man she loves is an ideal suitor—a courageous warrior, the descendant of a great house.[1]

It is part of the irony of Dido's character that a situation created by her own integrity can only be resolved, since her infatuation is irresistible, by the unconscious sacrifice of that integrity. This is of course, many would contend, the fatal flaw of Aristotelian tragic theory. (See Chapter 5, 'Tragic Attitude'.) She rejected at once any thought of Aeneas as a lover; it is only as her permanent consort, as the sharer and protector of her rule, that she allows herself to think of him. She toys with the possibility of marriage in her speech to Anna and pretends to herself to thrust it aside. It is left to Anna to state for her the arguments which prove marriage with Aeneas a sensible course: Carthage is a rising city in a hostile land; Dido needs Aeneas. There are, Anna admits, two obstacles to marriage. First, Dido has vowed she will not remarry; well, she must get the gods to agree to let her

[1] Note how the rhythm of line 3 (which should be read with second- and fourth-foot caesurae) emphasizes the repetition *multa multus* and imposes a slight hesitation between *uiri* and *uirtus*—it is as though Dido in her thoughts looks for another word to describe Aeneas but cannot find a better: this man is a real man. Virgil has made his own a well-known passage in which Lucretius describes the lover pining for his absent mistress (4.1061–9):
> nam si abest quod ames, praesto simulacra tamen sunt
> illius et nomen dulce obuersatur ad auris. . . .
> ulcus enim uiuescit et inueterascit alendo
> inque dies gliscit furor atque aerumna grauescit.

abandon her vow (50: *tu modo posce deos ueniam*). Second, Aeneas does not love her; but when the religious side of things has been attended to (*sacrisque litatis*), Dido can surely find ways of getting Aeneas to stay a while in Carthage (51: *indulge hospitio causasque innecte morandi*); that should solve the problem.

The obstacles are lightly stated by Anna—she has no wish to discourage Dido—but they must be faced; Dido is sane enough still to see this. But once marriage with Aeneas is presented as an objective that can be legitimately entertained, the smouldering fire of passion flares up (54-5):

> his dictis incensum animum inflammauit amore
> spemque dedit dubiae menti soluitque pudorem.
>
> *By these words she inflamed a mind on fire with love,*
> *gave hope to doubting thoughts, undid pride.*

It blinds her to a first sacrifice of integrity: even if the gods approve, for Dido to represent to herself her pursuit of Aeneas as an action dictated by political expediency is sheer self-deception.

But the next step takes her much further down the path of degradation, for the gods' approval is not secured—and Dido goes ahead without it (56-89). The priests are mystified when she starts each day with a fresh sacrifice and peers eagerly at the pulsating entrails for signs that she may go ahead (63-7):

> instauratque diem donis, pecudumque reclusis
> pectoribus inhians spirantia consulit exta.
> heu, uatum ignarae mentes! quid uota furentem,
> quid delubra iuuant? est mollis flamma medullas
> interea et tacitum uiuit sub pectore uulnus.

There *are* perhaps signs—note the Latent Metaphor in *reclusis*: the breasts of the sacrificial animals are unlocked by the priests' knives, to expose the secrets contained within. But the poor priests do not know what to make of it all, for Dido says nothing to them of the passion that consumes her.[1] She holds back a while in a frenzy of indecision, and

---

[1] The meaning of these lines has been much debated by those who fail to catch the significance of *tacitum*. Some take the phrase *instaurat diem donis* to mean that Dido goes on sacrificing throughout the day that began at line 6. To me it seems more likely that the meaning is 'she sets the day going with gifts'—a fresh sacrifice every morning, morning after morning. The period embraced by 56-67 overlaps, in other words, that embraced by 68-89, till by 86-9 the count of the days is lost. The phrase *instaurat diem donis* is an example of *callida iunctura* (see Chapter 6).

Book 4

perhaps never determines consciously to go ahead without making her peace with the gods: it is more important to be with Aeneas. She is like a deer, wounded by a hunter, who does not even know his arrow has found a mark (68–73—for a discussion of this simile see Chapter 5, 'Characterization and Motivation'). The simile is followed by a passage of brilliant, condensed narrative (74–89); a series of images dissolve into one another, as they do in a film when the director wishes to create the illusion of time passing rapidly but filled none the less with events we must know about. Her pursuit of Aeneas becomes more and more open. She escorts him round her city, over the construction of which we saw her preside with such happy pride (1.503–4: *laeta . . . instans operi regnisque futuris*). She tries to speak out, to say what is in her mind—and breaks off in the middle of a phrase (76: *incipit effari mediaque in uoce resistit*). She proposes another banquet, with another recital of his adventures and hangs on Aeneas' words when he tells his story. She roams the empty palace in the middle of the night. She detains young Ascanius to soothe her love for Aeneas of which she cannot speak (85: *infandum si fallere possit amorem*).[1]

What interval of time, how many separate occasions, do these scenes represent? How many days have gone by since she began her sacrifices at line 56? It is impossible to tell. Virgil wants the illusion of days that slip by unregarded. But when we come to the image that concludes the series (86–9):

> non coeptae adsurgunt turres, non arma iuuentus
> exercet portusue aut propugnacula bello
> tuta parant: pendent opera interrupta minaeque
> murorum ingentes aequataque machina caelo,

we realize several days at least must have elapsed. For at the beginning of this series of images all was activity of construction, and pride in that activity (75). Now we have only the stark picture of a crane towering motionless and untended over half-finished walls; without the queen to guide it the construction of her city has lost its impetus. Dido's degradation has progressed one stage further.

A short Episode follows in which we see Venus and Juno chuckling

---

[1] Dido's love is not to be spoken of (1) because it is not for her, a queen, to speak first; (2) because her love still lacks the gods' approval. There is no need to suppose, as some do, that Virgil means more than that; he is rather fond of using words in their literal, or etymological, meaning. Ascanius is Ascanius again; Cupid was to take his place for one night only (1.683).

over a plan to join forces in bringing Dido and Aeneas together. Juno is desperate, and prepared to stage a union that will pass for marriage (127: *hic hymenaeus erit*).[1] Venus, remembering what Jupiter has told her about Aeneas' destiny (1.257-66)—though she pretends not to know about it (110-12)—falls in with Juno's scheme for the fun of it (128), confident her protégé cannot come to much harm. The switch from tragedy to something not far from comedy is disconcerting for the modern reader—are we to take *this* for the divine approval that Dido has been seeking? Yet the Episode is as much a part of the structure of Virgil's fairy-tale as the Episodes of Juno, Aeolus, and Neptune in Book 1. One function of it is to suggest that somehow the universe now plays a trick on Dido. In a sense, divine approval is given her, but only in a way that throws final responsibility back on her own shoulders. Without the excitement and the glamour of the hunt,[2] the commotion caused by the storm, the accident (as it seems) that separates the two from the rest, and the further accident that brings them together at the entrance to the cave, Dido might still have held back. But the fact that she is the victim of a trick does not exculpate her. For, if the seduction is excusable, the way she lets it

---

[1] The editors usually reject the preceding line (126: *conubio iungam stabili propriamque dicabo*) on the grounds that it is a repetition from 1.73. But perhaps Virgil wishes us to feel that Juno has something of an obsession about marriage as a solution to difficulties—she was, after all, the goddess of marriage.

[2] A few words here about the structure of this brilliant Episode. It begins with a short, selective Tableau of the younger men (130-2). Next we see the nobles waiting for their queen to come out from the royal chamber and mount her horse, which waits less patiently (133-5). Then she emerges from the palace flashing with gold; her nobles swarm round her, and the Trojan nobles led by Iulus advance to meet her (136-41). Last of all Aeneas joins the company and assumes command (*agmina iungit*); a long simile (the pendant of the simile likening Dido to Diana, 1.498-502) likens him to Apollo leaving his winter home in Lycia to superintend the spring dances at Delos (143-50). As they advance into the foothills there is a sudden rush (*decurrere* is instantaneous perfect) of goats from the ridges, contrasted with the steady running of deer across the plain (151-5). Then a Tableau of Ascanius, all excitement, looking for lions where there are only goats and deer (156-9). Meanwhile the rumble of the gathering storm, and then the sudden rush for cover (*petiere* is instantaneous perfect) while the streams pour down in torrents from the hills (160-4). Dido and Aeneas make their way to the cave—*eandem deueniunt* implies they find their way separately to the entrance. Dido leads the way (*Dido dux*—see Chapter 6). An earthquake gives the sign for the eerie mock marriage (according to Servius an earthquake was an ill omen among the Etruscans). There is the same tense contrast between *fulsere ignes* (the sudden flash of lightning) and *ululnarunt* (the sudden wail of the mountain nymphs) and the main line of the narrative in historic presents (165-8). Finally the Bridge Passage with Virgil's comment (169-72).

Book 4

develop into a liaison and calls that liaison marriage, careless of how the thing looks to others, is not to be excused (170–2):

> neque enim specie famaue mouetur
> nec iam furtiuum Dido meditatur amorem:
> coniugium uocat, hoc praetexit nomine culpam.

> *Unmoved by talk, or how things look,*
> *Dido plans now no clandestine love:*
> *she calls it marriage, with this word cloaks her fault.*

Dido has receded one more step from reality to self-deception.

We might expect Act 1 of our tragedy to end at this point. But Virgil wants again, on a larger scale, the effect he secured in 74–89: the illusion of time passing without any clear narrative of what takes place. Dido's position is clear. What about Aeneas? He has seduced a beautiful queen who was perhaps only too anxious to be seduced. To a Roman, as to an English gentleman of the seventeenth or eighteenth century, if not to us, the act would not have seemed one that need lie heavily on the conscience.[1] But now he lets her sweep him along into a lasting liaison which she hopes will develop into marriage. He must sense this, perhaps he knows it.[2] Virgil avoids stating for us the case we can easily make ourselves against Aeneas. Instead, he takes us away from Carthage into a world of make-believe, irony, and fantasy where the lovers are talked about but from a distance. Rumour, a horrid, monstrous creature, spreads her tale (193–4):

> nunc hiemem inter se luxu, quam longa, fouere
> regnorum immemores turpique cupidine captos.

> *Now they keep the whole long winter warm, the wantons,*
> *no thought of those they rule, prisoners of a shameful lust.*

We are left to guess how much truth there is in her report. Some,

---

[1] Dryden's comment is a useful corrective to misplaced sentimentality (ed. John Carey, *The Works of Virgil, Translated into English Verse* by John Dryden, vol. 1 [1819] 272):
> I need say no more in justification of our hero's courage. . . . But he is arraigned with more show of reason by the ladies . . .; . . . to say the truth, it is an ill precedent for their gallants to follow. Yet, . . . they may learn experience at her cost; and, for her sake, avoid a cave, as the worst shelter they can choose from a shower of rain, especially when they have a lover in their company.

[2] For the relevance here of the Roman usage of consensual marriage, see *Latin Explorations*, pp. 38–9.

clearly; for Rumour, though she 'lays hold on what is false and twisted as often as she reports the truth' (188), 'mixed in the tale she told things done with things not done' (190). Eventually Jove himself steps in (219–20)—in answer to the complaint of Iarbas (whom Dido had rejected as a suitor) that his heavy investment in right religion has gone unrewarded.

We come back to Aeneas at the moment when Jove's messenger Mercury alights to warn him he must leave Carthage—and see him wearing a sword studded with jasper which Dido had given him and a purple cloak which she had worked with gold,[1] presiding over the construction of the city rising among the huts (259–64):

> ut primum alatis tetigit magalia plantis,
> Aenean fundantem arces ac tecta nouantem
> conspicit, atque illi stellatus iaspide fulua
> ensis erat Tyrioque ardebat murice laena
> demissa ex umeris, diues quae munera Dido
> fecerat, et tenui telas discreuerat auro.

Mercury's arrival gives vivid, fairy-tale form to Aeneas' abrupt realization of the extent to which he has compromised himself and the decision he takes to extricate himself before it is too late. The evident symbols of command, the fact that Aeneas has taken Dido's place in superintending the building of Carthage, make the situation plain, while avoiding the condemnation of explicit statement; it is left to the reader to conjecture how far Aeneas allowed himself, as time went by, to acquiesce in Dido's interpretation of their relationship. The first Section concludes with the end of the liaison in sight.

In the second Section Virgil adheres more closely to tragic form than anywhere else in the poem. Of the 208 lines, 120 are dialogue. The Quarrel Episode is almost pure drama in structure. Dido comes to Aeneas in a mood of blazing, uncomprehending anger—how can he think of going? At line 314 she switches to an appeal for pity, so confident in her complete innocence of blame that our sympathy is left untroubled, while she speaks, by the thought that she *is* largely to blame for her misfortune. Swept on by the impetus of her appeal, she inadvertently condemns herself more fully than she realizes (321–2: *te*

---

[1] The sword is the one Aeneas leaves behind in the *thalamus* after the quarrel Dido places it on the pyre at 507 and then takes it to kill herself at 646. The cloak is one of the two that Aeneas produces at 11.72, selecting one of them to wrap round the body of Pallas.

Book 4

propter eundem exstinctus pudor);[1] even then, the abjectness with which she throws herself upon Aeneas' pity (if only he had left her with a son to help her remember) leaves us for the moment wholly on her side. Dido deserves pity, and receives it—ours, and Aeneas' (though she cannot see it). But she wants more than pity: she wants love, and she wants Aeneas to stay with her in Carthage.

In Aeneas' hesitant rejoinder Virgil is less concerned with stating a case (this is not the moment for reason, moreover Aeneas' case is far from watertight) than with creating through dialogue a portrait of Aeneas as a decent, feeling man, struggling to control himself, anxious to say nothing that will wound, aware of his share of responsibility, but ill at ease because he cannot really understand the violence of Dido's reaction to his departure. He loves Dido, but to him that seems beside the point.[2] He begins determined to say as little as possible in reply to her charges of faithlessness and ingratitude (333: *tandem pauca refert*; 337: *pro re pauca loquar*) and then wanders on in a long, vain attempt to make Dido understand the overriding, inescapable importance of his mission. Many have complained that Virgil fails to make Aeneas' case convincing. But it is not intended to convince us. We are meant even to feel that it does not convince Aeneas and certainly it does not convince Dido: his protest that personal feelings must be subordinated to duty is beyond her comprehension.

Dramatically Aeneas' speech has several functions. First, it provides, alongside Dido's speech, a study in contrasting personalities. Second, it advances the action by deepening the rift of incomprehension which now separates Dido and Aeneas. Third, Aeneas' forced restraint has a sobering effect upon the reader. When Dido's anger blazes forth again, we immediately feel less identified with her point of view than we did at the end of her previous speech. She begins on a flamboyant, rhetorical note (365–73), then restates her claim for pity (373–6):

> 'eiectum litore, egentem
> excepi et regni demens in parte locaui;

---

[1] Dido means the shame, or rather the pride, she quenched in going back on her promise not to remarry—see her words in line 27. But there is already a note of irony in Virgil's echo of that line in his comment at line 55; and the Dido we see now is indeed a woman whose sense of pride and shame is utterly quenched. See Chapter 5, 'Tragic Irony and Insight'.

[2] For Aeneas' love for Dido see 4.395 and *Latin Explorations*, p. 36. Mackail oddly contends (lxv): 'His entanglement at Carthage brings him no pleasure while it lasts'.

> amissam classem, socios a morte reduxi;
> heu furiis incensa feror. . . .'

> *'I befriended the needy
> castaway, shared my kingdom with him in my madness,
> restored his lost ships, saved his men from death—
> alas! a burning frenzy bears me along. . . .'*

We feel she condemns herself inadvertently twice over. When she says *regni demens in parte locaui*, she means 'I was mad to share my kingdom' (mad, that is, to share it with somebody who could not be trusted). But we take the words as Tragic Irony: 'in my madness (the madness of infatuation) I shared my kingdom with him'. Then the words *heu furiis incensa feror*, a kind of sigh of self-pity, elicit condemnation instead of pity. There is irony also in the scorn with which she rejects the participation of the gods (376–80) in what *we* know to be their concern. Only in the final threat of revenge (384–7) does she regain dignity.

But the possibilities of narrative are also exploited in this second Section. In a developing emotional situation time is needed for a character to reach, or go back on, a decision. A dramatist can fill in the appropriate time with dialogue or suggest it by an actual break in the dramatic action. Virgil's method, as we have seen, is to use a passage of narrative to create the illusion of time passing. He now does this twice. Time is needed, first, for Dido to back down from the indignant dismissal of Aeneas at the end of the Quarrel Episode to a frame of mind in which she is prepared to beg Aeneas to stay. A short passage of rapid tempo narrative describing the preparations of the Aeneadae for departure fills in this interval (397–411) without any real relaxation of tension. For Dido, too, watches the preparations for departure (408–11), and this provides an objective correlative for the sudden final surrender of dignity (412: *improbe Amor, quid non mortalia pectora cogis!*). She cannot face Aeneas, so she sends Anna to beg him, as a favour—not to stay, but to wait a little longer (433: *tempus inane peto*). When Aeneas refuses, Dido's humiliation is complete. She must come to terms with reality or find some fresh way of retreating from reality. In either case time is needed. A narrative block of 41 lines tells us how the situation develops: lines 437–49 are a terse statement of the repeated ineffectual comings and goings of Anna, crowned by the great tree simile and its vivid imaginative portrayal of Aeneas' anguished determination;[1] lines 450–77 narrate the mental struggle

---

[1] For this Episode see *Latin Explorations*, pp. 40–1 and 49–51.

Book 4

which brings Dido from despair to the decision to take her life. The outcome is a triumph of unreason over reason, but by it she masters her grief (474–5):

> ergo ubi concepit furias euicta dolore
> decreuitque mori . . .
>
> *So when, overcome by grief, she conceived her mad plan*
> *and determined she would die . . .*

and goes to her sister with that serenity (477: *spem fronte serenat*) which the mad display in the execution of their plans (478–9):

> 'inueni, germana, uiam (gratare sorori!)
> quae mihi reddat eum uel eo me soluat amantem.'[1]
>
> *'Sister dear, I have found a way (congratulate me, sister!)*
> *which will bring him back to me, or stop me loving him.'*

The last act opens with a short narrative Episode (504–52) in which we see Dido putting into effect the plan she described to Anna in the concluding Episode of the previous Section (504–8):

> at regina pyra penetrali in sede sub auras
> erecta ingenti taedis atque ilice secta,
> intenditque locum sertis et fronde coronat
> funerea; super exuuias ensemque relictum
> effigiemque toro locat haud ignara futuri.
>
> *But the queen, in an inner fastness of the palace, rears*
> *a great pyre skywards of pine brands and hewn ilex-oak;*
> *decks the place with garlands, crowns it with foliage*
> *of death; on it places the sword and harness he had*
> *left, and him in effigy, not in doubt of what will be.*

As the reader follows Dido through the grisly details of the ritual, he wonders, perhaps, why Dido has perpetrated so elaborate a hocus-pocus to deceive her sister. Even when 'she calls the gods to witness and the stars who know fate's secrets' (519–20):

> testatur moritura deos et conscia fati
> sidera . . .

and adds an appeal to 'whatever just and mindful power is concerned with those who love not on equal terms' (520–1):

---

[1] These lines are discussed in Chapter 5, 'Tragic Irony and Insight'.

The Twelve Books

> tum, si quod non aequo foedere amantis
> curae numen habet iustumque memorque, precatur,

we do not at first doubt that we are in the secret, too.

But in the calm of her last night on earth the icy resolution of madness cracks, her love for Aeneas wells up afresh, and with it a flood of anger (531–2):

> ingeminant curae rursusque resurgens
> saeuit amor, magnoque irarum fluctuat aestu.[1]

It is a resurgence of the *odi et amo* mood which earlier drove her to beg Aeneas to wait, however much she hated him for his treatment of her. To regain her calm she must convince herself there is no alternative to her plan.[2]

At this point the narrative breaks off (Suspended Narrative), and we return to Aeneas. As he lies asleep on the poop of his ship, everything ready for departure, he has a vision of Mercury returning to repeat his warning to leave Carthage on an unmistakable note of urgency (560–1):

> 'nate dea, potes hoc sub casu ducere somnos,
> nec quae te circum stent deinde pericula cernis?'

> *'Goddess-born, can you go on sleeping in this crisis,*
> *do you not see the perils that will soon surround you?'*

It is in Dido's plan for suicide that Mercury sees danger (563–5):

> 'illa dolos dirumque nefas in pectore uersat
> certa mori, uariosque irarum concitat aestus:
> non fugis hinc praeceps, dum praecipitare potestas?'

> *'She is turning over in her heart a dreadful cunning deed,*
> *bent on death, and stirring waves of anger up, more than one.*
> *Do you not fly fast from here, while the chance of flight remains?'*

Plainly we are meant to piece together the hints Virgil gives here and those he gave at 519–21. And when dawn comes and from her vantage point (586: *e speculis*—the point perhaps from which she had looked down each day on the preparations for departure) Dido sees the

---

[1] Dido is the subject of *fluctuat*. Those who make *amor* the subject spoil the metaphor—latent in *resurgens* and brought out by *fluctuat* and *aestu*. For an analysis of these lines see Chapter 5, 'Characterization and Motivation'.

[2] For an analysis of her speech see *Latin Explorations*, pp. 55–6, and Chapter 5, 'Tragic Insight'.

Book 4

Trojan fleet already under sail—and Aeneas beyond her grasp—her tirade reinforces the feeling that something has gone wrong with her plans. In some mad way that must elude us, since Aeneas' precipitate departure forestalls her, she was aiming at revenge, or vindication, as well as suicide.[1]

After her long outburst of frustrated anger, which ends in the famous curse of Aeneas (615-21) and then of his descendants (622-9—foreshadowing the Carthaginian Wars), the Death Episode (630-92) begins. What is the function in this Episode of the nurse Barce? She cannot be there simply to be sent out of the way—Virgil need not have had her in the narrative at all. Her structural function is to arrange for the appearance of Anna when it is just too late; the instructions Dido sends Anna ensure Dido the time she will need. But Barce has also a dramatic function, as the recipient of Dido's last ambiguous reference to her intentions (639-40):

> 'perficere est animus finemque imponere curis
> Dardaniique rogum capitis permittere flammae.'

When Dido first spoke to Anna of the pyre, she said its purpose was 'to bring him back to me, or to stop me loving him' (479). Now that Aeneas has gone, to say that lighting the pyre will bring him back might strain credulity. Dido concentrates therefore on the second reason she gave for the construction of the pyre: 'she is in a mind to carry the matter through and put an end to her suffering.' To us her words point plainly to suicide, but she conceals her purpose from Barce by the way she goes on: she is going, she says, to put an end to her suffering by 'committing to the flames the pyre which holds the Trojan's life'. She can call the pyre *Dardanii rogum capitis* because it has Aeneas' effigy on it, as we learned at 508. Barce knows this of course, and departs, satisfied she understands what is in train: by destroying the effigy Dido hopes to shake off her infatuation and regain her happiness; no more is intended, she supposes, than common witchcraft.

We know better. But we must wait, in horrified expectancy, while Dido puts her plan into effect. We had perhaps forgotten about the effigy, and may feel that Virgil might have made the point clearer, since it is an important one. But that is not his way. Moreover our uncertainty and our expectancy are heightened if our mental picture of

[1] There is no clear clue, I think, to her intentions in 600-6—this is the wild raging of a frenzied woman.

the details of the death scene is not made clear-cut by precise description at this stage.

As Dido prepares to mount the pyre, she is afraid (642: *trepida*); but a wild exhilaration, provoked by the very monstrosity of her plans (*coeptis immanibus effera*), sweeps her on. This analysis of her emotions is followed by a description, in chiastic order, of the symptoms: her rolling, bloody gaze reveals the exhilaration, her quivering, blanching cheeks reveal the fear. In this state of mind she reaches the top of the pyre[1]—and sees there, among the *exuuiae* placed beside the effigy, the sword ornamented with jasper which she had given to Aeneas as a present and which at 261–2 we saw him wearing as one of the symbols of consortship; after the quarrel, when Aeneas went back to his ships (396), he left the sword in the royal *thalamus* (cf. 495 and 507). Now it is to serve as the death-weapon.[2] She unsheathes her lover's sword—'a gift not sought out for such a use' (647: *non hos quaesitum munus in usus*)—and pauses while 'her gaze takes in the Trojan raiment and the bed she knew'. Before her lies a macabre reconstruction of all that she has lost, and it is impossible to escape a feeling that Dido somehow believes, or half believes, that death means restoration. A mere effigy of Aeneas occupies the bed they had shared[3]—but the scene makes her 'linger a moment in memory and in tears' (649: *paulum lacrimis et mente morata*) before she 'takes her place upon the bed, to pronounce the words which were her last'. In a final assertion of her royal rank she strikes a formal note (651–2):

> 'dulces exuuiae, dum fata deusque sinebat,
> accipite hanc animam meque his exsoluite curis. . . .'

[1] I feel certain that the *gradus* of lines 646 and 685 refer to some sort of steps on the pyre, and that Austin is wrong in supposing the pyre was placed on top of a turret which had to be gained by a stairway.

[2] The sword can only be Aeneas' sword, even though Ovid (*Her.* 7.187) and Silius (8.148) seem to have remembered Virgil carelessly. Conington in a detailed discussion of the passage admits it should be the sword which Dido gave Aeneas and of which we learn in lines 261–2, but his courage fails him when it comes to accepting the logic of his own argument: 'In that case however we should have expected Virg. to have made more of the thought of Dido perishing by her own gift.' By the same token we might expect Virgil to make more of the fact that the effigy which is placed on the pyre at line 508 was still there when Dido climbed upon the pyre at line 646. Virgil's technique of relying on the active collaboration of his reader just does not allow for such jogging of his reader's memory.

[3] Cf. the story of Laodameia, and Euripides' Admetus. Virgil's use of *notum* is a superb example of the ordinary word that looks like a throw-away but should pull us up with a start. Cf. 3.657 and 11.195.

Book 4

*'Relics sweet as long as fate and god allowed,
accept this life and free me from my suffering. . . .'*

It is Aeneas' sword that will free her. But the second person plural *exsoluite* unites the sword with the other *exuuiae*, and with his effigy: all are bidden to 'accept the life' that Dido now discards. She goes on to state her claim to be remembered (655–8):

> 'urbem praeclaram statui, mea moenia uidi,
> ulta uirum poenas inimico a fratre recepi,
> felix, heu nimium felix, si litora tantum
> numquam Dardaniae tetigissent nostra carinae.'

> *'I founded a city of renown, I saw my walls rise.
> I avenged a husband's death (a brother was our foe).
> Fortune favoured—ah! too much: if but these shores
> had never felt the touch of keels from Troy.'*

At the last, it is a queen again who speaks. Her record of achievement contains much that Aeneas has still to achieve. She would have been happier if she had never seen the Trojan, for his coming meant the surrender of pride and fame to passion. It is a harrowing contrast with Aeneas, for whom the outcome of the conflict between love and duty, much though the struggle hurt, was never in doubt. Her brief epitaph complete, she presses her face against the bed, averting her gaze before bringing down the sword.

The death-stroke itself is left undescribed. Virgil describes instead the uproar that follows shocked realization of what has happened (663–71). At this point Anna arrives and takes her dying sister in her arms. The book ends with a little sad, fantastic tailpiece, relating how Juno sends down Iris to free Dido's soul from her body, which will not release it (696–7)—'because she was not dying by fate, nor earned death, but pitifully before her time in a sudden blaze of madness':

> quia nec fato merita nec morte peribat,
> sed misera ante diem subitoque accensa furore.

It is the nearest Virgil comes to explicit comment.[1]

[1] For the tailpiece see Chapter 5, 'Fate'.

The Twelve Books

BOOK 5

In Book 5 we come back to Aeneas and his men as they sail away from Carthage watching the flames of Dido's funeral pyre on the horizon; a storm forces them to put in again at Drepanum in Sicily, and it is decided to hold a day of games there to mark the anniversary of the death at Drepanum of Anchises.

After a naval race, a foot race, a boxing match, and an archery contest, the games are rounded off with a ceremonial cavalry parade, interrupted when the Trojan women try to set fire to the fleet.

Aeneas is undecided whether to continue the voyage to Italy, but eventually the ships set out escorted by Neptune; Palinurus is lost at sea during the night.

Once again the narrative can readily be divided into three Sections —a central Section of nearly 600 lines, preceded and followed by much shorter Sections.

I 1–103	(i)	To Drepanum	1–41
	(ii)	Games proclaimed; at the tomb of Anchises; the snake	42–103
II 104–699		The Games—interrupted by vi:	
	(i)	Naval race	104–285
	(ii)	Foot race	286–361
	(iii)	Boxing	362–484
	(iv)	Archery	485–544
	(v)	The Troy Game	545–603
	(vi)	Burning of the ships; Aeneas' failure of nerve	604–699
III 700–871	(i)	Indecision; vision of Anchises; departure	700–778
	(ii)	Venus-Neptune	779–826
	(iii)	Under way; Palinurus lost during the night	827–871

When, at 5.777, the Aeneadae set sail from Drepanum for Italy, we can hardly avoid a feeling of *déjà vu*: we saw them do just this at 1.34–5, immediately after the formal introduction to the poem, in the opening lines of Virgil's narrative. What Virgil has gained, however, by turning his hero aside from the attainment of his objective for more

Book 5

than four books is easily seen. The narrative has acquired an impetus and a depth Virgil could scarcely have given it if he had passed straight from 1.35 to 5.774—even if he had substituted for the colloquy between Venus and Neptune, which now suspends the narrative at the outset of the third and final attempt to reach Italy (5.779–826), the grander Episode (1.223–304) in which Jove assures Venus of her son's glorious destiny and the future greatness of the city he will found in Italy.

All the same, when the Aeneadae set out from Carthage at the *beginning* of Book 5, we may still wonder why Virgil does not allow them to reach Italy unmolested. Why another storm—the third they meet with in their wanderings?[1] Admittedly, the storm allows the return to Drepanum and the narrative of the games; and a quiet book is clearly desirable between Books 4 and 6—a slackening of the tension, such as that provided by Book 3 between Books 2 and 4. Admittedly, too, some kind of build-up of Anchises is needed. In Book 2 he played an ineffectual role; in Book 3, though deferred to by Aeneas, he hardly proved an effective counsellor; some sense of his importance must now be created in preparation for the role he will play in Book 6. Furthermore, the games give Virgil an opportunity for his most sustained piece of rivalry with Homer: the first 440 lines of the second Section follow closely the games in *Iliad* 23.[2] And Virgil's concluding pageant, the *Lusus Troiae*, connects the legendary past with the present day, providing at the same time a neat transition to the burning of the ships: Ascanius, the leader in the *Lusus Troiae*, arrives on the scene first, Aeneas' more dramatic appearance follows.

Here, then, are a number of ways in which Virgil has exploited the possibilities of Book 5, but they hardly justify the book. However, in addition to these incidental functions, Book 5 has others which are more important.

Perhaps the main function of the book is to focus our attention on Aeneas. In Book 4 it was Dido who, from the outset, held our attention. We come back to Aeneas feeling no longer the unqualified

[1] The first (in time) is the storm which precedes their encounter with the Harpies (3.192–208)—the first 4 lines of which are repeated (in the third person instead of the first) at 5.8–11. The second storm is the one that takes them to Carthage, 1.34–222.
[2] Homer has 640 lines. Virgil simplifies and tidies up Homer's narrative: he has four contests instead of eight.
Virgil's contemporaries probably found the narrative of the games full of interest: Williams, Bk 5, p. x, points out that a revival of interest in athletics was encouraged by Augustus.

sympathy he aroused in us in Book 1, from his first appearance on the verge of despair (1.92–101). Virgil's technique with Aeneas is almost the opposite of the technique he uses in drawing Dido. She too, to begin with, wins our admiration and our pity; but it is an increasingly qualified admiration that we extend to her, and in the end our pity is accompanied by a clear sense that she has brought her suffering upon herself. As we watch her devise and execute her spectacular suicide, the pity she arouses is mixed with horror; it is more the pity we feel for those who are mad than the purer pity we feel for innocent suffering. With Aeneas, however, the reservations, the qualifications come early. He is an ascending character, Dido a descending one. Book 2 showed him a courageous leader, but unthinking, and therefore ineffectual: it is a component of his character—the Heroic Impulse—against which he must struggle to the end. Book 3 showed him the instrument of fate, commanded by prophecy, but uncomprehending: he will remain so till Book 6. Book 4, like Book 2, put him clearly in the wrong: he showed himself better than Mark Antony (who could not tear himself free from Cleopatra) but no better than Julius Caesar (who did escape, but only, like Aeneas, after a compromising delay). Book 5 has as its first major function to create a situation in which our dwindled sympathy for the poem's hero can flow back. Ordinary, decent behaviour, the behaviour of a humane commander, helps. And then a moral crisis at the climax of the second Section repairs the alienation more completely.

Nor is it only the reader who feels this alienation. Aeneas' own men feel as we do. Virgil has had the courage, not only to expose his hero to our condemnation, but to enact that condemnation in his narrative. There is a hint of it in the note of embarrassment we detect at 4.288–95, when Aeneas, after an agony of indecision (283–6), calls his captains together to give them their orders for leaving Carthage . . . and admits he has not told the queen—he will tell her, he says, when he gets the chance.[1] The second hint comes at 4.573–9, when the men are told by their agitated commander that the time has come 'to cut the tangled ropes and run for it' (575: *festinare fugam tortosque incidere funis*).[2] The men's job is, of course, to obey orders and they spring into action (581).

---

[1] This Episode is studied in Chapter 5, 'Implicit Comment'.
[2] The emphatic position of *tortos* after the caesura and the obvious symbolism make it clear that the word is not an ornamental epithet (all ropes are twisted in their manufacture) and that the proper translation is 'tangled' not

Book 5

These two short scenes, each constructed to tell against Aeneas (even though in each he acts upon a peremptory warning from the gods), provide a background to the emotions we sense in Aeneas' men in the opening Tableau of Book 5 (1–7):

> Interea medium Aeneas iam classe tenebat
> certus iter fluctusque atros Aquilone secabat
> moenia respiciens, quae iam infelicis Elissae
> conlucent flammis. quae tantum accenderit ignem
> causa latet; duri magno sed amore dolores
> polluto, notumque furens quid femina possit,
> triste per augurium Teucrorum pectora ducunt.

Meanwhile Aeneas was well on his way with his fleet,
ploughing grimly through waves black from a north wind,
gazing back at walls on which the fire unhappy Dido lit
casts flickering flames. Though what caused such a conflagration
remains obscure, aware how harsh the grief
when great love is defiled, what frenzied woman can attempt,
the Trojans feel forebodings of disaster in their hearts.

By focusing the camera first on Aeneas, Virgil suggests his isolation. His men are in the background; they do not know the rights and wrongs of the situation—they merely sense that something terrible has happened after their departure, and the feeling weighs them down.[1]

In the central Section of Book 5 it seems natural, therefore, for the rank and file of the Trojans to advance into the limelight, while Aeneas withdraws temporarily into the background, coming forward only to award prizes and to treat unlucky competitors with good-humoured generosity (282–5, 358–61; compare his intervention 461–7). We see here a second major function of Book 5—to draw the rank and file of the Aeneadae a little more in the round. Unlike Homer's games, where the contestants are all major characters, those who take part in Virgil's games all play minor roles; even Acestes (519–44) is hardly an important character. Not more than a dozen Trojans are

---

'twisted'. It should also be observed that both Aeneas and Dido get out of their predicament by a stroke of the sword.

[1] Virgil is careful to avoid explicit comment—it is not his way, and moreover the obvious partial identification of Aeneas with Augustus precludes anything like open condemnation. But the last line points the way: why should Aeneas' men feel uneasy forebodings about what they have left behind them, unless they feel their commander is responsible for what has occurred?

The Twelve Books

delineated at all fully;[1] but these stand out; the whole weight of the narrative in the first three contests is thrown on the emotions aroused and the clash of personalities.

A short analysis of the narrative of the naval race, the first contest and the one described at greatest length, will show the stress laid on emotion, and also the care Virgil has expended on the structure of his narrative. Four triremes take part;[2] the contestants have to row out to a rock in the bay, round the rock, and then sail back to land—on a calm, sunny day they would naturally have a light sea breeze behind them on the return journey.[3] This permits an exciting beginning to the race as the rowers churn up the water to get under way (136-50), and then an opportunity for seamanship when the captains jockey for position on approaching the rock. On the outward leg the leader, Gyas, loses his head and throws his helmsman overboard (172-5)—an incident which permits an exquisite little Vignette of the helmsman Menoetes (178-82):

> at grauis ut fundo uix tandem redditus imo est
> iam senior madidaque fluens in ueste Menoetes
> summa petit scopuli siccaque in rupe resedit.
> illum et labentem Teucri et risere natantem
> et salsos rident reuomentem pectore fluctus.

When at last he returns waterlogged from the bottom,
Menoetes, who is getting on in years, his clothes streaming,
makes for the top of the reef; now he has sat down where the rock is dry.

---

[1] The following characters are given some prominence in the four contests:
(1) *The Naval Race*—the four captains and Gyas' helmsman Menoetes (all Trojans).
(2) *The Foot Race*—seven contestants are named (Virgil remarks that there were *multi praeterea*), but the spotlight falls on Nisus, Euryalus, Salius and Diores (all Trojans) and the Sicilian Helymus.
(3) *Boxing*—only two contestants: one Trojan, Dares, and one Sicilian, Entellus.
(4) *Archery*—Prince Acestes and three Trojans, Hippocoon, Mnestheus (who also appears in the naval race) and Eurytion.
Total—12 Trojans and 3 Sicilians.

[2] For the opening Tableau see Chapter 3, 'Projection of the Narrator into his Narrative'.

[3] It is sometimes doubted whether sail is used at all as a result of a misunderstanding of the narrative at 280-1. But Virgil means there that despite Sergestus' difficulties in rounding the rock with damaged oars he manages to make sail eventually like the others. The image of the dove (213-17) puts the use of sail beyond doubt. (See Chapter 6, 'Imagery'.) For details of the techniques used see S. L. Mohler, 'Sails and oars in the *Aeneid*', *TAPhA* 79 (1948) 46-62.

Book 5

The Trojans laughed at him when he fell and again while he was swimming, and now they laugh as he spews up waves of salt water from his lungs.

The narrative is constructed to elicit our sympathy for the old man so roughly handled by his captain, but the crowd see only the comic side as Menoetes flounders round in the water and then scrambles up on the rock; 'waves' (182: *fluctus*) is not poetic diction, but the exaggeration of an excited narrator (Projected Narrative)—and an echo of Homer (*Odyssey* 5.322-3). As a result of his thoughtlessness, Gyas drops to second, and then to third place, while Cloanthus (whose seizure of the inside position at the rock had provoked Gyas' angry impulse) goes on to win; so that, even though Cloanthus successfully appeals for a push from the god of harbours on the last stretch, we can feel that the race has gone to the best seaman.

Meanwhile, Sergestus has taken the turn too close and got his inside bank of oars entangled with the rock: we shall see him sail in a bad last after an ungainly piece of rowing—his ship is like a snake that has been run over by the wheel of a cart (273-9). Mnestheus, despite his spirited urging on of his rowers (189-97), is last to come up to the turning point. He seizes the advantage offered by Sergestus' mishap, gets quickly round the rock, and sweeps out into open water under sail —like a dove frightened in a cave; its wings beat against the roof as it tries to escape; once safe outside, it glides along with its wings motionless (213-17). Flushed with this initial success, Mnestheus now overtakes Gyas on the home run and comes in second.

The pitch of excitement reached is based on an assertion of speed which we can hardly accept—by modern standards Virgil's triremes, whether rowed hard or under sail, move pretty slowly. But we forget this, drawn into the narrative by the economical vividness of the Tableaux, the fineness of the similes, and the clash of personalities. We are left to visualize for ourselves the individual rowers, and the crowd which roars its encouragement, or its approval of a popular decision; yet we feel the *collectam exsilio pubem, miserabile uulgus*, of 2.798 begin to acquire the stature that will be needed of them for the events of Books 7 to 12. The process is continued in the following Episodes: a foot race, which serves as a first introduction of Nisus and Euryalus, whom we shall meet again in Book 9; a boxing match (an acute psychological study, despite the lighter tone assumed);[1] and an archery contest—probably the least successful, as a piece of writing.

---

[1] For a study of the boxing match see *Latin Explorations*, pp. 203-6.

of the four events. Even if by the end of the fourth contest we have in fact got to know only a handful of the Aeneadae, a vivid sense has been acquired of the reality of the whole number.

Aeneas had not failed to sense his loss of moral authority over his men. When the storm overtakes the fleet in the opening Episode of the first Section, Palinurus is for the moment the real commander; he takes emergency action on his own initiative (15–16), then tactfully suggests a change of course; Aeneas merely acquiesces (17–31).[1] Throughout the central Section, Aeneas' anxiety to repair the damage is emphasized by the self-effacing tact with which he conducts the games and shares his authority with Acestes—a local princeling (though of Trojan descent) as is indicated by his rustic appearance (35–41). Above all, Aeneas' utter prostration in the final Episode of the central Section when confronted with the crisis of the burning of the ships betrays his feeling of alienation.

The rebellion of the Trojan women is stirred up on the divine level of motivation by Iris (under instructions from Juno), disguised as one of the women, Beroe. But on the human level it is psychologically convincing. While the men have been at the games, the women have remained behind on a lonely stretch of beach mourning Anchises; before them they see the ocean that they must cross again (613–17):

> at procul in sola secretae Troades acta
> amissum Anchisen flebant, cunctaeque profundum
> pontum aspectabant flentes. 'heu tot uada fessis
> et tantum superesse maris!' uox omnibus una.
> urbem orant, taedet pelagi perferre laborem.

> *Some distance away, all alone on the lonely beach,*
> *the Trojan women wept for Anchises, and as they wept*
> *all looked out on the deep ocean. 'Alas, all that water,*
> *so much sea still and we are tired'—all voice the same thought.*
> *They pray for a city, loath to face their sea toil out.*

A third attempt to reach Italy confronts them; a second time they will have to depart from a land where they could be happy. Aeneas' sense of a mission imposed by fate is something entirely personal. His men do not feel it (remember how Ilioneus, in his speech asking for Dido's assistance, 1.522–58, showed no inkling of an inescapable task im-

---

[1] I have made explicit what Virgil's technique enables him to convey implicitly (see Chapter 5, 'Implicit Comment'): the fact that the spotlight falls first on Palinurus, the importance given to the Episode by the interchange of dialogue, stress without the need of comment the unusualness of the situation.

Book 5

posed on the survivors of Troy by destiny; even Venus is more concerned with protecting Aeneas than with the accomplishment of his mission[1]); how can we expect the women to feel what the men do not?[2]

The rebellion marks a fresh challenge to Aeneas' moral ascendancy over those he leads, an ascendancy which he has been slowly recovering but which is still precarious after the alienation of Book 4. This new, unexpected threat to the success of the journey to Italy at its final stage provokes a moral crisis in Aeneas himself. Is he right to drive his people on? Is he fit to be their leader after all? These are the feelings that underlie the desperate, dramatic gesture of 685–92:

> tum pius Aeneas umeris abscindere uestem
> auxilioque uocare deos et tendere palmas:
> 'Iuppiter omnipotens, si nondum exosus ad unum
> Troianos, si quid pietas antiqua labores
> respicit humanos, da flammam euadere classi
> nunc, pater, et tenuis Teucrum res eripe leto.
> uel tu quod superest infesto fulmine morti,
> si mereor, demitte tuaque hic obrue dextra.'

Then good Aeneas began to tear the clothing from his shoulders,
calling on the gods for help, lifting his hands to heaven:
'Almighty Jove, unless by now you hate us Trojans
to a man, if somehow as of old fair reward awaits
man's labours, grant the fleet escape from fire
now, father, snatch from ruin the little left of Troy.
Else do what's next to do: despatch to death with cruel bolt
if I deserve death, let your right hand destroy me now.'

Aeneas bares his shoulders, not in order to throw himself into the task of saving the fleet from destruction by the fire, but to show himself defenceless before his god as he asks for a sign from heaven: let Jove either snatch from destruction the Trojans' slender chattels that remain, or take the logical alternative and strike down Aeneas with his thunderbolt if he does not deserve to be their leader.[3]

---

[1] See her words to Jove (1.231–3) and her willingness to let Aeneas abandon Italy (10.44–50).

[2] Traditionally the rebellion occurred at the mouth of the Tiber. Virgil's placing of it here is, as Mackail remarks (p. 165), 'a piece of real constructive genius'.

[3] The compressed, almost colloquial style of Aeneas' words has caused some doubt about the sense. The object of *demitte* is not *quod superest* (which is used adverbially, as Servius says) but a pronoun understood. (For the omission of

The Twelve Books

The Episode marks Aeneas' failure of nerve. *We* know there can be no doubt that the Trojans will reach Italy—this is fated. But Aeneas cannot have our certainty. Virgil shows the sudden anguish, the impulse which assails Aeneas when he can no longer believe that he is working in harmony with fate to resolve by self-destruction a situation he finds intolerable.[1]

Once we realize the psychological weakness which the crisis uncovers, we can understand better the extent to which Aeneas is prostrated by it. For, though the sign he asked for comes quickly and the fire is quenched, doubt continues to obsess Aeneas, a feeling that his people *would* be happier where they are, even if staying meant forgetting his mission (700–3). He knows that war awaits them (3.458–60) if they persist in the struggle to reach Italy. Old Nautes suggests a compromise—let those remain in Sicily who have had enough, or for whom there is no longer room, while the others follow Aeneas to the bitter end (709–18). His words serve only to redouble Aeneas' misgivings (719–20). It takes a vision of his father Anchises (who backs up Nautes' suggestion) to restore his confidence; observe, however, the different emphasis given by Anchises. Nautes makes the lot of those who choose to go sound unattractive (710: *quidquid erit, superanda omnis fortuna ferendo est*); for Anchises they are *lectos iuuenes, fortissima corda* (729), men who have a job to do—the conquest of Italy.

Nine days more go by (762), and then the reduced expedition sets sail. Neptune himself sends it on its way accompanied by a pageant of nymphs (816–26), after a colloquy with Venus, in which he promises the Aeneadae, with one unnamed exception, a safe journey to Italy (779–815). Finally in this long book (827–71) comes the beautiful, eerie narrative of the loss of Palinurus as the fleet glides through the calm, moonlit Mediterranean night. The symbolism of Palinurus' disappearance is evident. Aeneas needed him when the dark storm stood over his head (10: *caeruleus supra caput astitit imber*) after

---

the pronoun as a colloquialism see Austin on 4.383; cf. 4.320–1 and 4.493.) (1) The order of the words *si mereor, demitte* makes *me* the natural pronoun to understand—'destroy *us*,' (regarded by Williams as equally probable) 'if I deserve it' would surely require a pronoun to be expressed; (2) 'destroy us, if I deserve it' is poor sense—why should all be destroyed because the leader is at fault? (3) Aeneas' stance, shoulders bare, is surely an invitation to the gods to strike *him* down. For *leto* (690) in the sense of 'destruction' see Chapter 6, 'Etymological Puns'.

[1] This Episode is also discussed in Chapter 1.

Book 5

leaving Carthage; in that crisis he seemed incapable of action. Now the storm is past, and in the crisis which follows Palinurus' disappearance Aeneas jumps to deal with the situation like a true commander (864–8).

As well as the symbolism we note the careful fusion of divine and realistic levels of motivation (see Chapter 5, 'Characterization and Motivation'). On the divine level Sleep seeks out Palinurus, beguiles him, makes him unconscious, and throws him overboard. But on the other level sleep comes to Palinurus bringing a woeful dream (840: *somnia tristia portans*)—the drowsy illusion which comes to Palinurus on the threshold of sleep that Phorbas is by his side. He struggles against it, then falls asleep (on the divine level, the god touches him on the temples with his wand), loses his balance and plummets overboard, the tiller still in his hand. When Aeneas meets Palinurus on the banks of the Styx (6.337–83), despite the echoes of 5.858–60 in 6.349–51, Palinurus insists on a natural explanation of what happened to him. (Compare the account Ilioneus gives of the storm in 1.534–8 with the fairy-tale account we are given by Virgil, 1.34–222.)[1]

If Book 5 is a quiet book, it is also one in which much is achieved. Relaxation of the tension permits the rehabilitation of Aeneas. He had no choice but to leave Carthage; it was the right course of action, however uneasy his own conscience. But he should not have allowed a situation to develop from which it was necessary to escape, and in which his conduct was inevitably exposed to misunderstanding, even by his own men. During this period of relaxation, Virgil devotes himself to sustained, detailed rivalry with Homer, to adding to Anchises' stature in preparation for Book 6, and to bringing to life the mass of the Trojans in preparation for their struggle with the hard tough people (730: *gens dura atque aspera cultu*) with whom they will have to contend in Italy. But the book is not all relaxation. The flare-up of rebellion and Aeneas' reaction to the crisis, though they occupy only two Episodes, complete the lesson of the book—that a commander needs not only the confidence of those he commands, but confidence in himself.

---

[1] For this and other apparent discrepancies in the two Palinurus Episodes see E. de St Denis, 'Où situer les écueils des sirènes et la chute de Palinure?', *LEC* 7 (1938) 472–91.

BOOK 6

Book 6 brings the Aeneadae to Italy: they land at Cumae, and Aeneas at once consults the Sibyl; after she has made her prophecy, Aeneas asks for help in reaching his father in the underworld; she tells him he must first find the golden bough, and also that he will have to bury the body of a comrade when he returns to the ships; these tasks performed, Aeneas, escorted by the Sibyl, begins his descent into Hades.

Aeneas and the Sibyl, after passing through the entrance to the underworld, get Charon to take them across Acheron, then make their way through the Plains of Grief; a Bridge Passage follows, in which Tartarus (not visited by Aeneas) is described by the Sibyl.

Finally, they reach Elysium; Aeneas is reunited with his father and receives from him a mystic revelation and a prophecy, then returns to the world above and his fleet.

The narrative is continuous throughout. However, the beginning of the descent, marked off by the short invocation 264–7 from the approach to the entrance to Hades, can fairly be regarded as the end of one Section, while the Bridge Passage 548–636, in which the switch from normal narrative to description by the Sibyl marks a break between two very different groups of Episodes, can conveniently be considered the end of a second Section.

	Introduction:	
	Arrival at Cumae	1–8
I	(i) The Sibyl A: at the temple of Apollo	9–155
9–263	(ii) Misenus A	156–182
	(iii) Aeneas finds the golden bough	183–211
	(iv) Misenus B	212–235
	(v) The Sibyl B: at Avernus; departure	236–263
	Invocation	264–267
	(i) At the entrance; the entrance to the underworld described	268–294
	(ii) Crossing Acheron: Charon A—Palinurus—Charon B—Cerberus	295–425

Book 6

II 268–636	(iii)	*Various Tableaux of the* lugentes campi: Children who died in infancy; the unjustly condemned; suicides; those who died of love	426–449
		Dido	450–476
		The *bello caduci*	477–493
		Deiphobus	494–547
	(iv)	Tartarus (not visited, but described by the Sibyl); the golden bough deposited	548–636
III 637–901	(i)	Arrival in Elysium	637–678
	(ii)	Aeneas meets Anchises	679–702
	(iii)	Anchises' first speech: doctrine of the souls	703–751
	(iv)	Anchises' second speech: Rome's men of destiny	752–892
	(v)	Return to life	893–901

The landing in Italy with all its easy opportunities for rhetoric is underplayed. Virgil leaves unasserted the excitement of arrival, and allows the emotions of the Aeneadae to emerge from a brief but brilliant opening Tableau, almost Breughel-like in its rugged, stylized simplicity (3–8):

> obuertunt pelago proras; tum dente tenaci
> ancora fundabat nauis, et litora curuae
> praetexunt puppes. iuuenum manus emicat ardens
> litus in Hesperium; quaerit pars semina flammae
> abstrusa in uenis silicis, pars densa ferarum
> tecta rapit siluas inuentaque flumina monstrat.

They turn the prows of their ships to face the sea (they must be ready for departure—who knows what may happen in this strange land?); its anchor then held each ship fast in that position and, one by one as we watch, the sterns embroider a border of semi-circles along the beach.[1] A group of men jump eagerly ashore, then set about exploring the country that is to be their home. Observe how *emicat* draws out the metaphor latent in *ardens* and prepares for the actual flash of flame in the next line; how the routine operations of making fire and effecting a first reconnaissance of the hinterland are described analytically (in language shot through with echoes of Lucretius), as though, in this

---

[1] Note how *curuae*, apparently the stock epithet, is given a fresh, sharp significance by its context.

strange, primitive land, no action could be taken for granted. And notice how *monstrat* unobtrusively captures the emotions inherent in the scene—they are eager (*ardens*) to show one another what the new land is like.[1]

After these six lines, the description of the scene on the beach breaks off (Suspended Narrative). Aeneas is impatient—he must consult the Sibyl, as Helenus had warned him to (3.441–60),[2] and enlist her aid in reaching the underworld, in order to consult his father about the coming war as Anchises had told him he should (5.731–6). For this first landing in Italy is not the end of their journey.

With Achates he enters the Sibyl's magnificent temple—and again the narrative is suspended: upon the walls of the temple, Daedalus, the architect, recorded the story of the Minotaur and his own unhappy escape from Crete. The reader embarks upon this elaborate, Hellenistic description in something like the mood of casual appraisal with which we may suppose Aeneas lets his eye wander over the pictures while he waits for the Sibyl—and is then absorbed, as Aeneas is absorbed, by the story and the associations it touches off, until the priestess (whom Virgil draws as an austere, aloof figure) appears, to recall him crisply to the task in hand (37: *non hoc ista sibi tempus spectacula poscit*).

Her terrifying trance begins and Aeneas, with a simple formal dignity that unobtrusively marks a rise in stature in Virgil's hero at this point, puts his request: now that he has escaped the incubus of Troy,[3] may he hope for a settled home in Italy? As Virgil introduces his new, more confident Aeneas, he makes the first specific equation between him and Augustus. For the temple that Aeneas will build to Phoebus (69–70) is a clear allusion to the great temple of Apollo on the Palatine, dedicated by Augustus in 28 B.C. The Sibyl's answer, given in an interval of lucidity, is a grim prediction of war (86: *bella, horrida bella*), expressed in terms establishing a series of detailed, explicit correspondences between the narrative of the following books and the *Iliad*. The Aeneadae will be besieged in Italy as they were at Troy. The Tiber will flow with blood as did the rivers of Troy. A second Achilles, likewise goddess-born, awaits the Aeneadae in Italy (89–90):

---

[1] Mackail, missing Virgil's intentions, strongly complains (p. 207) that these lines 'are in the rather crude annalistic manner of the epitomized episodes of Book III'.

[2] The prophecy of Helenus is specifically recalled by the reference to Helenus' words in 3.445–51 at the end of Aeneas' speech to the Sibyl (74–6).

[3] I owe the phrase 'the incubus of Troy' to William S. Anderson, 'Vergil's second *Iliad*', *TAPhA* 88 (1957) 18.

Book 6

> 'alius Latio iam partus Achilles,
> natus et ipse dea'.

A woman and a foreign marriage will again be the cause of misfortune. Once more Virgil accepts the challenge to rival Homer. But the correspondences are dramatically appropriate, too: for naturally the Sibyl speaks to Aeneas of what is to come in terms of what he has already passed through at Troy.[1]

His reply suggests again the new, soberly confident Aeneas (103–5):

> incipit Aeneas heros: 'non ulla laborum,
> o uirgo, noua mi facies inopinaue surgit;
> omnia praecepi atque animo mecum ante peregi.'[2]

> *Aeneas the demi-god began: 'No feature of these tasks,*
> *O maid, is new to me, none unexpected;*
> *I have learnt about all, and have forearmed my mind.'*

He passes to his second request: will the Sibyl help him make his way down to Hades, to meet his father? In her reply, the Sibyl, speaking now as priestess of Diana-Hecate, assumes a note of sombre irony in marked contrast with her earlier frenzy as priestess of Apollo (125–9):

> 'sate sanguine diuum,
> Tros Anchisiade, facilis descensus Auerno:
> noctes atque dies patet atri ianua Ditis;
> sed reuocare gradum superasque euadere ad auras,
> hoc opus, hic labor est.'

> *'Trojan son of Anchises,*
> *born of blood divine, easy is the way down to Avernus:*
> *day and night black Pluto's portal yawns,*
> *but to retrace your steps, to escape to free air,*
> *there's the rub, that's a task.'*

No longer prophetic, she has little interest in Aeneas' reasons for the journey, but is prepared to help him (133–6). He must seek a golden branch, she tells him, to take as an offering to the Queen of Hell: when he has found it, if it allows itself to be plucked, that will show his plan is approved of by fate (146–8). She adds that one of Aeneas' comrades

---

[1] For the Sibyl's prophecy and the relation of Books 7 to 12 to the *Iliad* see Anderson, op. cit.

[2] The reference is to 3.458–60, where Helenus says of the Sibyl:
> 'illa tibi Italiae populos uenturaque bella
> et quo quemque modo fugiasque ferasque laborem
> expediet, cursusque dabit uenerata secundos'.

The Twelve Books

has died during his absence and will have to be buried before Aeneas can make his journey to the underworld. In conclusion she gives details of a sacrifice that must be made before the journey begins. The interview over, Aeneas leaves the temple.

The death of Misenus is spoken of by the Sibyl (149–52) merely as a pollution of the fleet to be removed before the descent begins; but an implicit connexion between his death and the discovery of the golden bough is created by the narrative structure of the remainder of the first Section. It is the preparations for the funeral that lead Aeneas to the golden bough; the narrative of the funeral is broken off (Suspended Narrative) by a bridge Episode (183–211) in which Aeneas finds the golden bough, then the narrative of the funeral is resumed; the funeral over, Aeneas returns to the Sibyl, performs the ordained sacrifice, and sets out with her for Hades. Virgil makes no connexion between the death of Misenus and the discovery of the golden bough. Indeed Misenus' death is explained quite independently—he was swept off a rock and drowned by Triton for boasting about his prowess on the conch (171–4). As for the golden bough, it is Venus' doves that lead Aeneas to it (190–204). But the feeling is hard to resist, in view of the Sibyl's specific reference to Misenus and her opening words, that a life must be lost so that Aeneas, having entered Hades, can return to life again.

But the two Misenus Episodes are more than a structural device. After the fantasy of Misenus' death (171–4), a Tableau of the Aeneadae hewing timber for the funeral pyre in the first of the Episodes re-establishes the rugged, primitive tone we saw in the opening Tableau of the book (180–2):

> procumbunt piceae, sonat icta securibus ilex
> fraxineaeque trabes cuneis et fissile robur
> scinditur, aduoluunt ingentis montibus ornos.[1]
>
> *They fell the pitchy pines, an ilex rings beneath their axes,*
> *great beams of ash and splintery oak are split*
> *with wedges, from the hills they roll the huge trunks down.*

We follow Aeneas away from this starkly simple Tableau back into fantasy and the discovery of the golden bough. When we return with

---

[1] The lines are an echo of Ennius 181–5W (also a funeral scene), as we know from Macrobius (*Sat.* 6.2.27) who quotes them, pointing out Virgil's imitation. Both passages go back to *Il.* 23.114 ff. Once again Mackail (p. 219) misses Virgil's intentions and complains of awkwardness.

Book 6

him, the funeral has already begun (212 ff.), and the same grim, archaic note is resumed for a detailed description of the ceremony.

Two imperfects (213: *flebant, ferebant*) give the illusion of Tracking Forward as we pass from one Episode to another (Parallel Narrative). Then six historic presents (216–19) mark the beginning of the ritual:[1] the pyre, which has already been constructed (215: *struxere* is perfect), is decked with sombre foliage, and the cypresses of death set in position in front of it; water is boiled and the body washed and anointed.[2] Then come two instantaneous perfects (222: *subiere*, 224: *tenuere*) as the tempo of the ceremony changes, contrasting with the present *cremantur* (224) which describes the spectacle of the burning pyre. The tempo changes again while the *postquam* clause with its perfect verb (226) and the five following perfects (227–31) describe the ritual acts that conclude the funeral ceremony. Finally the burial: the historic present *imponit* (233) marks the transition from description of scene into history (234–5).

The descent to the underworld may now begin, and the scene shifts to the uncanny silence of Lake Avernus (236–40). A four-line invocation by the poet is followed by a short Tableau of Aeneas and the Sibyl dimly visible in the gloom as they approach the entrance to the underworld. Line 268 (*ibant obscuri sola sub nocte per umbram*) is often praised, if not always rightly understood. The simile which follows (270–2) fixes the degree of darkness—that gloom when things can still be seen but lose their colour. Aeneas and the Sibyl are dimly visible (*obscuri*) as on a night in which there are no stars and no moon—only the gloom of night (*sola sub nocte*).[3]

---

[1] In 216 *ante* is spatial not temporal. See Varro's interesting note, quoted by Servius, on the custom of placing cypresses around a funeral pyre.

[2] Again Virgil builds on Ennius. Ennius' line, quoted by Servius, is *Tarquinii corpus bona femina lauit et unxit*. Virgil has added an evocative three-word image *aena undantia flammis* (bronze cauldrons, seething water, leaping flames), and the wonderful pathos of the genitive participle *frigentis:* (1) Misenus, though dead, remains a person; (2) the chill of his body contrasts with the flames beneath the cauldrons and the fire that will consume him.

[3] Cf. 453, where Dido is described as *obscuram*—a sort of pale glow (in life she was *candida*) which makes one feel the moon is about to rise through cloud. Jackson Knight's Penguin translation 'they were walking in the darkness, with the shadows round them, and night's loneliness above them' is an attempt to state explicitly in prose what he thinks the line implies. But he is wrong, I feel, about *obscuri*. His translation of *sola sub nocte* depends on an old theory that *sola* is a transferred epithet; in good poetry there is often a tendency for the force of one word to spread along the line; no more than that is involved here.

The Twelve Books

We are at the entrance. The narrative has hardly begun before it is interrupted (Suspended Narrative) by an allegorical description (273–89) of the scene at the entrance. Here at the jaws of Death (273: *uestibulum ante ipsum primisque in faucibus Orci*) are stationed various agencies of death (hunger, disease, war, old age, etc.), their symbolic attendants (*Luctus, Curae*), and assorted monsters. At the sight, Aeneas reaches for his sword (and the narrative resumes), but the Sibyl stays his hand.

The long Episode of the crossing of Acheron is held together by the same device of Suspended Narrative, which separates the first Charon Tableau from the second by Aeneas' colloquy with Palinurus—the first of a series of characters from previous books met by Aeneas in the underworld.[1] In Aeneas' first encounter with him (295–336), Charon is made to sound like a dirty, ill-kempt slave, his boat a battered tub. One terrifying touch turns the squalor into menace—the unwavering glare of Charon's burning eyes (296–300):

> turbidus hic caeno uastaque uoragine gurges
> aestuat atque omnem Cocyto eructat harenam.
> portitor has horrendus aquas et flumina seruat
> terribili squalore Charon, cui plurima mento
> canities inculta iacet, stant lumina flamma.[2]

> *Here a great, swirling stretch of water, thick with mud,*
> *seethes, belching sand out everywhere into Cocytus.*
> *A dreadful ferryman the waters of these rivers guards,*
> *filthy, loathsome Charon; from his chin sprouts an unkempt,*
> *greying mass, his eyes are steady and on fire.*

The stylized realism—apart from this one touch—contrasts admirably with the allegorical symbolism of 273–94, providing at the same time a most effective context of irony for the description, which now follows, of the pitiful horde of men, women and children—as numerous as the leaves that fall at the first chill of autumn in a forest, or as the birds that pack together for their winter flight across the sea to sunny lands—clamouring for preference on their last journey, arms reaching out toward the opposite shore for which they long (305–14):

> huc omnis turba ad ripas effusa ruebat,

---

[1] Other characters from earlier books are: Orontes from Book 1, Dido from Book 4, Deiphobus from Book 2; at 630 there is an allusion to the Cyclopes from Book 3.
[2] See W. F. Jackson Knight, *Roman Vergil* (1944) 209.

Book 6

>matres atque uiri defunctaque corpora uita
>magnanimum heroum, pueri innuptaeque puellae,
>impositique rogis iuuenes ante ora parentum:
>quam multa in siluis autumni frigore primo
>lapsa cadunt folia, aut ad terram gurgite ab alto
>quam multae glomerantur aues, ubi frigidus annus
>trans pontum fugat et terris immittit apricis,
>stabant orantes primi transmittere cursum,
>tendebantque manus ripae ulterioris amore.

These pathetic creatures are at the mercy of a shabby, unsmiling, sinister tramp. Some he takes; others he waves aside, while the Sibyl explains to Aeneas that the rejected passengers are the unburied dead, condemned to haunt the banks of Acheron for a hundred years before they can be taken on board.

As Aeneas stands stricken with pity (331–2), he sees more than one of his comrades, among them the gloomy figure of Palinurus (340). We thus pass easily away from the main Charon narrative, though the interchange with Palinurus ends a little stiffly—the Sibyl intervenes to chide Palinurus for asking Aeneas either to bury his body or to escort him personally across Acheron, assuring him that his body will receive proper burial and that the place will bear his name.[1] At 384 the narrative of the approach to Acheron is resumed. Aeneas and the Sibyl come down to the river, and Aeneas is at once challenged by Charon. A colloquy between Charon and the Sibyl follows which one may perhaps be excused for finding a trifle forced: she tells Charon it is in order for him to take Aeneas, even though his previous live passengers brought him trouble, and clinches the matter by pointing to the golden bough; Charon immediately puts his ship about (he was on his way across with the cargo of souls we saw him embark at 315–16 when he challenged Aeneas from mid-stream at 385); he comes in alongside again and hustles his passengers ashore, to make room for Aeneas. But with the embarkation of Aeneas (410–16), Virgil recovers the balance between irony and horror achieved in his earlier picture of Charon: even the touch of the leaky tub groaning beneath the weight of the live Aeneas comes off. (See the analysis of this scene in Chapter 3, 'Projection of the Narrator into his Narrative'.) On the

---

[1] For apparent discrepancies between Palinurus' account of how he met his death and Virgil's narrative in Book 5 see the analysis of the Palinurus Episode in Book 5.

other side they meet Cerberus. But a doped biscuit disposes of him and Aeneas and the Sibyl slip quickly off (417–25).

As Aeneas makes his way through the foul region (462: *loca senta situ*) of the Plains of Grief (441: *lugentes campi*), various Tableaux of the unhappy dead confront him.[1] Two passages of rapid-tempo narrative, in which a string of characters flash before us (445–9 and 479–93) are each followed by a Tableau taken at a slower pace with dialogue; the first group, those who in various ways died before their time, leads up to Dido; the second, those who died in war, leads up to Deiphobus.

The wailing of children who died in infancy greets Aeneas as he arrives.[2] He comes then to Minos, busy reviewing the cases of those unjustly condemned to death, and next to those who took their own lives—how they regret it now!—(436–9):

> quam uellent aethere in alto
> nunc et pauperiem et duros perferre labores!
> fas obstat, tristisque palus inamabilis undae
> alligat et nouies Styx interfusa coercet.

> *How they wish now they could*
> *face hard work and poverty in the world above!*
> *Divine law bars the way, the gloomy, unlovely waters of the marsh*
> *hem them in, confined by Styx also, nine times interfused.*

Then, as the Plains of Grief open out before him, he sees, in a great forest (451), those who died of love—'tortured still by love's anguish even in death' (444: *curae non ipsa in morte relinquunt*). This grim

---

[1] There appear to be three divisions of the dead: (1) Elysium—the only happy place; (2) Tartarus, where the *mali* are punished by Rhadamanthus; (3) the *lugentes campi*—apparently the permanent abode of all who do not win admission to Elysium and are not condemned by Minos (431–3) to Tartarus. Like Aeneas, the dead presumably arrive at (3), and either remain or move on to (1) or (2) after judgment by Minos, choosing either the left- or the right-hand road (540–3). Minos, we gather, does not judge obvious cases—those who die in infancy or commit suicide. Admission to (1) is open to the classes specified in 660–5, but not easily gained: even *bello clari*, e.g., can remain in (3); I take 713–14 to mean simply that reincarnation is selective; imprisonment in (2) is reserved for hardened criminals. But obviously Virgil has worked out a loose framework of fantasy, the details of which he has not space to incorporate in the tight structure of his poem; immense controversy, therefore, rages over many points.

[2] For another example of a switch of narrative introduced by the sound that precedes it cf. 12.617–19—Turnus hears the uproar in the city which Aeneas has just attacked. Also 12.869.

Book 6

Tableau of the utter misery of death is relieved by a short Hellenistic passage (445–9), in which a series of heroines who in one way or another died through love flash before us. Among them Aeneas sees Dido, 'dimly visible—like the first glow of the new moon' (453–4):

> obscuram, qualem primo qui surgere mense
> aut uidet aut uidisse putat per nubila lunam.

Their meeting is famous. Aeneas, tears in his eyes, speaks to Dido with earnest, embarrassed affection, caught off his guard almost—the eager longing of the souls who crowded the bank of Acheron beseeching Charon for passage is cruelly belied by the dank horror of what Aeneas sees around him (455–66):

> demisit lacrimas dulcique adfatus amore est: 455
> 'infelix Dido, uerus mihi nuntius ergo
> uenerat exstinctam ferroque extrema secutam?
> funeris heu tibi causa fui? per sidera iuro,
> per superos et si qua fides tellure sub ima est,
> inuitus, regina, tuo de litore cessi.   460
> sed me iussa deum, quae nunc has ire per umbras,
> per loca senta situ cogunt noctemque profundam,
> imperiis egere suis; nec credere quiui
> hunc tantum tibi me discessu ferre dolorem.
> siste gradum teque aspectu ne subtrahe nostro.   465
> quem fugis? extremum fato quod te adloquor hoc est.'

He wept as he addressed her with loving affection:
'Unhappy Dido, it was true then, the news I
heard, that you were dead, with the sword had ended things?
Alas, was it I caused your death? By the stars I swear,
by the gods above, by any oath that deep beneath the earth obtains:
it was not my doing, Queen, when I quit your shore.
By order of the gods, the same that send me now through
the shadows, through murk-strewn places and the depths of night—
by their commands was I driven on. Yet could I not believe
my departing spelt for you unhappiness like this.
Stay your step, withdraw not from my gaze.
Whom do you flee? Never after this does fate allow us speech.'

His case is the same as it was in Book 4, and it strikes us still as weak—though not as weak as it is sometimes made to sound. When Aeneas says 'Yet could I not believe my departing spelt for you unhappiness like this' (463–4: *nec credere quiui hunc tantum tibi me discessu ferre*

The Twelve Books

dolorem), his uneasy but sincere compassion is not the result of *discovering* that Dido had taken her life (he tells us at 456–7 he had heard about her death), but the realization, freshly gained from the evidence he sees about him as he passes through the *loca senta situ*, of what death means.[1] Dido does not even look at him as he speaks (the imperfects of 468–9 emphasize the Parallel Narrative); her face expressionless (historic present, 470), she wheels around (instantaneous perfects, 472) to join Sychaeus, who comforts her lovingly.

But what is Dido doing in the group of those who died for love and are 'tortured still by love's anguish' (444: *curae non ipsa in morte relinquunt*)?[2] Usually, when Virgil is less than clear, it is in order to elicit the reader's collaboration. Surely what he wants to suggest here is that Dido, though she turns in scorn from Aeneas to Sychaeus, loves Aeneas still, with that turmoil of love mixed with hate (the *odi et amo* complex) which tortured her in the second and third Sections of Book 4.[3]

At the far end of the Plains of Grief Aeneas comes to those who died in battle (477–8). Among them are the former enemies of the Trojans, who take to flight at the flash of Aeneas' armour in the gloom (490).[4] Whether they were famous warriors (478: *bello clari*) like Tydeus (the father of Diomede and one of the Seven against Thebes) or Parthenopaeus (another of the Seven against Thebes) or Adrastus (the father of these two who saw them both die),[5] or whether they were less dis-

---

[1] T. S. Eliot, 'Virgil and the Christian World', *On Poetry and Poets* (1957) 129, in an otherwise sympathetic and sensitive discussion of this passage, makes Aeneas say: 'I am sorry that you took it so hard', and then complains that Aeneas is made to sound a worm.

[2] What, for that matter, is Sychaeus doing here? Shouldn't he be among those who were condemned to die unjustly? It seems best to assume that *his locis* at 445 does not mark off one special group, but refers to the *lugentes campi* in general; the group of those who died for love and the suicide group at any rate clearly overlap—lines 445–8 include several suicides as well as at least one murder and one accidental death. Phaedra committed suicide, Procris was accidentally killed, Eriphyle was killed by her son because she betrayed her husband, Euadne committed suicide, and Laodamia committed suicide; the fates of Pasiphae and Caeneus (who changed his sex) are obscure. See Norden on 6.445 ff.

[3] This leaves a minor puzzle, the interpretation of 473–4:
　　coniunx ubi pristinus illi
　　respondet curis aequatque Sychaeus amorem.
Does Dido love Sychaeus too? Or does Virgil mean that Sychaeus loves her as much as Aeneas does?

[4] It flashes because Aeneas is alive—a touch of magic rather than good physics.

[5] Observe Virgil's studied avoidance of Homeric heroes.

Book 6

tinguished—those who merely fell in war (481: *bello caduci*) like the eight obscure comrades-in-arms of Aeneas whom Virgil cites in passing—prowess in battle earns small reward, it seems. (See Chapter 1.)

We come now to Priam's son Deiphobus, his body hacked to pieces (494–5). As with Palinurus, the account given Aeneas of his death differs from Virgil's earlier narrative.[1] He tells Aeneas that Helen (she was Deiphobus' consort, it seems, after Hector's death) had disarmed him while he slept, and then admitted Menelaus and 'that scoundrelly bastard Ulysses' (529: *hortator scelerum Aeolides*), who had shown Deiphobus no mercy. Similarly what we are now told of Helen hardly squares with the narrative of Book 2 (2.567–87). Virgil's purpose is partly, perhaps, to emphasize the elusiveness of truth—it is so hard to find out what happened; partly, to compress his narrative, by leaving out details the reader can easily supply for himself, or about which he wishes to imply something less than certainty. Did Menelaus reject his faithless wife, despite the assistance she gave the Greeks in getting into Troy? Did she have to seek refuge from Greek and Trojan alike in the temple of Minerva? This notion of the manysidedness of truth has its relevance to the Deiphobus Tableau with its reversal of Homer's account of his death (amplifying the anti-Greek note of 489–93).[2]

This is in effect the end of the second Section of the book. A bridge Episode, whose main function is to prepare for a change of tone in the third Section, is, however, woven in at 535: the Sibyl intervenes to break off Aeneas' conversation with Deiphobus—in the world above it is past midday and they must not lose time. Her remark helps to make plausible the fact that they do not visit Tartarus—we have to be content with her lurid description of what takes place there as they pass by. But the device has several other structural functions. First, it enables Virgil to exploit the endless tangle of legend about the underworld: Dido and Deiphobus are made to stand out from the quickly sketched-in Tableaux of the great mass of the dead, so that the choice of these two seems less arbitrary than if they had been left unsupported. Second, the transition from narrative by the poet to first-person narrative in the Sibyl's description of Tartarus (562–627) makes for variety and a change of tempo. Third, her description creates a buffer passage between the legendary Hades of Section 2 and the

---

[1] At 2.310 we simply saw Deiphobus' house crashing in flames, though Aeneas says he had heard that Deiphobus had died in the fighting that night.
[2] *Latin Explorations*, pp. 216–17.

The Twelve Books

philosophical Elysium of Section 3, with its echoes of Platonic myth.

Aeneas surrenders the golden bough to the Queen of Death (636) and he and the Sibyl pass from the Plains of Grief to Elysium, to emerge from a region of darkness and misery into a region bathed in light (it has its own sun and its stars and planets) where all is happiness (637-41). From the *lugentes campi* they have come to the *campi nitentes* (677). But even in this very Greek Valhalla, where the dead devote themselves to *musike* and *gymnastike*, the call of life is as strong as it was in the Plains of Grief—compare Aeneas' surprised exclamation (721: *quae lucis miseris tam dira cupido*?) with 436-7. There is a difference, however. Here in Elysium reincarnation is not an idle longing but a duty.

Making his way through Elysium (637-78), Aeneas is reunited at last with his father. While they are talking happily, he catches sight of a group of dead awaiting reincarnation, and Anchises gives him a very Platonic-sounding discourse, with Stoic overtones, on the doctrine of the souls.[1] After the theoretical lecture, Anchises takes Aeneas and the Sibyl over to the throng of souls and names some who will bring glory to Italy in the future.

In his review of Rome's men of destiny, Virgil eschews a chronological arrangement, in order to keep the Tableau of Augustus (791-805) distinct from that of the other participants in the civil war, Julius Caesar and Pompey (826-35).[2] The pageant ends with Anchises' famous formulation of Rome's historical mission (847-53):

> 'excudent alii spirantia mollius aera,
> credo equidem, uiuos ducent de marmore uultus,
> orabunt causas melius, caelique meatus
> describent radio et surgentia sidera dicent:
> tu regere imperio populos, Romane, memento,
> hae tibi erunt artes, pacique imponere morem,
> parcere subiectis et debellare superbos.'

---

[1] Few lectures can have aroused more controversy. As I have said, it seems easiest to suppose that only deserving souls reach Elysium, not the souls of all who die, or all who escape Tartarus. Naturally this creates all kinds of difficulties. In the pageant of souls returning to earth that now follows, those named will all be good men; where do evil men come from? Are all who graduate to Elysium reincarnated? It is pointless to probe Virgil's text for answers to such questions.

[2] For the treatment of Augustus and the other participants in the civil war and the conflict between the account given here of the successors of Aeneas and that given in 1.267 ff., see Chapter 2.

Book 6

'Others will force on breathing bronze a softer line,
I well believe, tease from marble the living face,
plead cases better, plot with rod orbits
in the sky, predict the planets' rise.
You, Roman, remember that to govern nations
will be your culture, and to add to peace a way of life,
mercy for conquered, unending war with the proud.'

As in other passages which have become famous, we are apt to overlook the extent to which context limits the meaning of Virgil's words. Anchises' prophecy is less an injunction than a statement of fact, the conclusion pointed to by the pageant of soldiers and politicians Aeneas has witnessed: Rome's peculiar contribution to culture will lie in her concern with government (851: *regere memento*), to crown peace with a way of life (852: *pacique imponere morem*)—fair treatment of those she has defeated, but unrelenting war against those who arrogantly resist her mission to rule;[1] Virgil's contemporaries, looking back on several centuries of reasonably enlightened conquest could feel the boast backed up by history. But this is at the same time the policy Aeneas will follow in his war with the Italians, and, by implication, the policy Augustus followed when his uncle Julius, disregarding Anchises' appeal to throw arms aside (835: *proice tela manu, sanguis meus*), forced upon *him* a war that had to be fought to the bitter end. But the care, the embarrassment almost (betrayed by the false note struck in the final *superbos*), with which Virgil voices even a veiled comment upon the civil war is evident. Quickly he slides away from his true climax into the security of history (Marcus Claudius Marcellus, the consul of 222 B.C.) and the pathetic but somewhat fulsome panegyric of Marcellus' descendant, the young Marcellus, Augustus' nephew's son-in-law and heir, who had died in 23 B.C. at the age of twenty.

The pageant fades and Anchises' last words to his son are of the tasks that lie ahead and the war to be fought in Italy. Though it was Aeneas' main objective to learn about these things,[2] in Virgil's narrative only three lines (890-2) are now devoted to them. Aeneas then makes his way to the twin Gates of Sleep, and takes his farewell of Anchises and the Sibyl, passing through the Gate of Ivory (by which

---
[1] In 852: *hae tibi erunt artes, hae* has the idiomatic force of *hic* which we see at 4.347 when Aeneas says: *hic amor, haec patria est*. It amounts almost to 'this will have to serve instead of culture'. On *pacique imponere morem* see R. D. Williams, *GR* 11 (1964) 61.
[2] Anchises does say at 5.737 that he will tell him about *genus omne tuum* as well.

the shades send up false dreams to the world above) to rejoin his waiting comrades and resume his journey.[1]

A note of haste is apparent in the concluding lines of Book 6; one cannot help wondering whether it is the result of unfinished work, or of a problem Virgil could not solve, created by the imbalance imposed by the conflict between the book's structural purpose (the enlightenment of Aeneas about the tasks that confront him and the symbolic statement of some kind of mystical experience) and its function as propaganda.[2] It is tempting to regard the Marcellus passage as a misguided, despairing attempt by Virgil to honey the pill of his references to the civil war. The possibility is suggested by the disagreeably insincere note which we sense at many points in this third Section. We notice it first when only Trojans (apart from Orpheus and Musaeus) figure in the opening Tableau. It is apparent again in the cursory statement of qualifications for admission to Elysium at 660–5. We cannot expect Virgil to tidy up every loose end when he passes from the pure fairy-tale atmosphere of Section 2 to a Section in which we are clearly meant to catch undertones of genuine belief (Stoicism blended with Platonic and Orphic ideas). But in this more moral fiction a practical objective (propaganda) is unpleasantly evident, and it is not assimilated as it should be into the fiction. Virgil's myth lacks the poetry, the pathos, and the wonderful fantasy of his legendary Hades. After reading the former, we cannot suppose the successful realization of the latter was beyond his talents; it is easier to suppose his heart was not in it.[3]

BOOK 7

Book 7 brings the Aeneadae to the Tiber and the omen of the tables is fulfilled; next day an embassy a hundred strong is sent to King Latinus, who receives them hospitably, promises to give his daughter Lavinia in marriage to Aeneas, and sends the Trojans back with gifts.

[1] Why does Aeneas take the gate of false dreams? On this famous crux, see Wendell Clausen, 'An interpretation of the *Aeneid*', *HStCPh* 68 (1964) 146–7.

[2] The story of the effect Virgil's reading of the panegyric of Marcellus produced at court is well known. Suetonius' version (120–9R) is that, in response to increasingly pressing requests from Augustus, Virgil, after considerable delay, gave a reading of three complete books (Books 2, 4 and 6), and that Octavia, the mother of Marcellus, broke down at the words *tu Marcellus eris*.

[3] See L. A. MacKay, 'Three levels of meaning in *Aeneid* VI', *TAPhA* 86 (1955) 180–9, and Brooks Otis, 'Three problems of *Aeneid* 6', *TAPhA* 90 (1959) 165–79. For a more favourable evaluation of Book 6 than mine see R. D. Williams, 'The sixth book of the *Aeneid*', *GR* 11 (1964) 48–63.

Book 7

Juno intervenes, sending the Fury Allecto, who fills Amata, the king's wife, and Turnus (who hopes to marry Lavinia) with mad anger; she then incites a group of peasants over the killing of a stag; the war hysteria spreads; Latinus finds it impossible to resist it, and Juno herself opens the Gates of War.

After a formal invocation of the Muse, Virgil lists, with sketches of the forces under their command, thirteen Italian leaders, including Turnus, who rally against Aeneas.

I 1–285	Landing:	
	(i) Arrival at the Tiber	1–36
	Invocation A	37–45
	(ii) Résumé of local situation	45–106
	(iii) The omen of the tables fulfilled	107–147
	Embassy to Latinus (next day):	
	(iv) Departure	148–169
	(v) At the palace of Latinus; speech of Ilioneus; the Trojans sent off with gifts	170–285
II 286–640	(i) Juno—Allecto A	286–340
	(ii) Amata aroused by Allecto	341–405
	(iii) Turnus aroused by Allecto	406–474
	(iv) The peasants aroused by Allecto (incident of the stag)	475–539
	(v) Juno—Allecto B	540–571
	(vi) War hysteria: the peasants—Turnus—[Amata]—Latinus	572–600
	(vii) Juno opens the Gates of War	601–640
III 641–817	Invocation B	641–646
	Catalogue of the Italians:	
	(1) Mezentius	647–654
	(2) Aventinus	655–669
	(3) Catillus and Coras	670–677
	(4) Caeculus	678–690
	(5) Messapus	691–705
	(6) Clausus	706–722
	(7) Halaesus	723–732
	(8) Oebalus	733–743
	(9) Ufens	744–749
	(10) Umbro	750–760
	(11) Virbius	761–782
	(12) Turnus	783–802
	(13) Camilla	803–817

The Twelve Books

In Book 7 events move fast. The Aeneadae land happily by the Tiber, and are royally received by Latinus; yet by the end of the book war has broken out. It is hardly surprising if the structure of Virgil's narrative creaks at first under the strain imposed by so rapid a reversal of fortune. When the Aeneadae seek out at once the local king to make over to him the symbols of authority (243–8), our eyebrows quiver. When Latinus in return offers Aeneas his own daughter's hand in marriage, though he acts in obedience to a prophecy, we feel this is just too good to pass for truth, even in a fairy-tale. On the other hand, the second Section, in which the events that lead to war are set out, is brilliantly contrived; it is in some ways the finest piece of sustained narrative in the poem. Hardly less brilliant is the magnificent, colourful, bizarre pageant of the Italians marshalling for war in Section 3.

The book begins quietly, and a little oddly, with the death of Aeneas' nurse Caieta, who is disposed of in four lines.[1] Now that the Aeneadae are within reach of their goal, Virgil must rise to the occasion. A fine, solemn sentence (5–7) gives his narrative the required impetus, and then two beautiful lines show us the Aeneadae sailing through the night before a steady breeze, beneath a pale moon, over a moonlit sea (8–9):

>   aspirant aurae in noctem nec candida cursus
>   luna negat, splendet tremulo sub lumine pontus;

aspirant aurae in noctem ('the breezes breathe into the night') is one of Virgil's most memorable phrases. The hint, moreover, of the supernatural in these lines unobtrusively sets the stage for the ensuing Tableau of the Trojans' eerie last night at sea: they skirt the shore of the island where Circe, the rich daughter of the sun-god, sings in her inaccessible glades as she spins the night through, surrounded by angry, roaring lions, swine, bears and wolves—all men once, reduced to beasts by her magic potions, and imprisoned; the Aeneadae hear their cries, and pick out shapes (18: *formae*) in the light of Circe's cedar torches (10–20):

>   proxima Circaeae raduntur litora terrae,
>   diues inaccessos ubi Solis filia lucos

---

[1] The four lines are a short Bridge Passage from the end of Book 6 with which editors have often expressed dissatisfaction. Caieta, of course, is yet another piece of antiquarian geography (like Misenus and Palinurus); but we may wonder whether Virgil had settled the transition from Book 6 to Book 7 in his mind.

Book 7

    adsiduo resonat cantu, tectisque superbis
    urit odoratam nocturna in lumina cedrum
    arguto tenuis percurrens pectine telas.
    hinc exaudiri gemitus iraeque leonum
    uincla recusantum et sera sub nocte rudentum,
    saetigerique sues atque in praesepibus ursi
    saeuire ac formae magnorum ululare luporum,
    quos hominum ex facie dea saeua potentibus herbis
    induerat Circe in uultus ac terga ferarum.[1]

The magical, vaguely sinister Italy that greeted the Aeneadae at the end of Book 3 is instantly recreated.

At dawn the Aeneadae reach the Tiber. During the night the wind had increased in strength to carry them past the *uada feruida* (24) which swirl round the coast where Circe dwelt. Suddenly it drops (instantaneous perfects, 27: *posuere, resedit*). They start to row, but their oars seem to make no progress in the calm sea. Then Aeneas gets his first sight of the Tiber as it flows out, swift and tawny with sand, into the sea, while, on either side of the river and above it, the birds that inhabit its banks or live in the river itself circle overhead and charm the air with their song. Aeneas gives orders to alter course and joyfully passes from the gathering light of dawn into the sombre mouth of the river (30–6):

        hunc inter fluuio Tiberinus amoeno
    uerticibus rapidis et multa flauus harena
    in mare prorumpit. uariae circumque supraque
    adsuetae ripis uolucres et fluminis alueo
    aethera mulcebant cantu lucoque uolabant.
    flectere iter sociis terraeque aduertere proras
    imperat et laetus fluuio succedit opaco.[2]

At line 36 Virgil passes abruptly (Suspended Narrative) from this

---

[1] A rather complex ambiguity is built round *formae*: (1) the wolves are not really wolves, but men in the *shapes* of wolves; (2) a zeugma links *formae* with *exaudiri*—the Aeneadae 'hear from afar' the cries of the animals, and pick out from afar shapes they recognize as wolves. Virgil, moreover, particularizes (what he says explicitly of wolves holds good of the lions, bears and swine) in a way quite usual in poetry, though incompatible with the logic of prose. Circe is also structural—she married Picus, Latinus' grandfather, and the horses Latinus gives Aeneas are descended from the magic horses which Circe stole from her father the sun.

[2] The river is sombre because of the foliage that overhangs it (the birds who are *adsuetae ripis* imply trees, etc.). But the antithesis *laetus* ... *opaco* is also a symbol of the war that is to follow happy arrival.

smiling scene to formal invocation of the Muse and a prediction of war that echoes the Sibyl's prophecy at 6.86 (41–2):

> dicam horrida bella,
> dicam acies actosque animis in funera reges.

> *I shall tell of dread war,*
> *I shall tell of battles, of princes driven to their deaths by passion.*

Not, observe, driven to their deaths by fate: the war that now begins is a needless, pointless war, as the careful narrative of the second Section stresses repeatedly.

Many hold that Books 7 to 12 are duller than Books 1 to 6. I think they are wrong. But if they are right, then Virgil has failed. For it is a 'greater cycle of events', he claims, that now begins, a 'greater work' upon which he is embarking (44–5):

> maior rerum mihi nascitur ordo,
> maius opus moueo.

His story, as he told us at the beginning of the poem, is the story of a leader in war (1.1: *arma uirumque cano*); not two narratives juxtaposed, but a single narrative, built round the leader who will conduct the war, and whom we had first to get to know—not casually, but intimately. Books 1 to 6 are intended as a preparation for Books 7 to 12.

The invocation is followed by an Episode of 62 lines, in which Virgil sketches in the hypothesis upon which his plot will rest. An old, peace-loving king, Latinus, descended from Saturn himself (the Italian god of agriculture, identified in Hellenistic times with Cronus), has a daughter. Among the suitors for Lavinia's hand—and the kingdom that goes with it[1]—a handsome prince, Turnus, is the choice of Queen Amata. Latinus, however, has been warned by portents that his daughter must not be married to Turnus, but to a foreign husband.

Where he wants facts which are not part of the familiar common stock of legend, Virgil's usual practice is to weave them in beforehand, so that they can be drawn out, when needed, from the reader's recollection.[2] Here the switch of the narrative to a completely new setting rules this out. He makes the best of a bad job by relating as vividly as possible the portents which cause Latinus to reach his odd-sounding decision: first, the swarm of bees that foretold the arrival of a

---

[1] Cf. Pandarus' sneering reference to the *dotalis regia* at 9.737, repeated by Drances at 11.369.
[2] On *interweaving* see *Latin Explorations*, pp. 212–16.

Book 7

foreigner (59–70); then, the fire that played round Lavinia's head, portending fame for her and war for her people (71–80); lastly, the prophecy which came to Latinus out of the night as he lay in the temple of his oracular father (81–103).

We left the Aeneadae at line 36 preparing happily to land in their new home. We return to them at 104, to find them snatching their first scratch meal on the grassy bank of the Tiber (106–11). Famished, they eat the large, square spelt cakes they have placed on the grass, as well as the fruit they have gathered and piled on top. Young Ascanius ventures a joke: 'We're eating the tables, too.' His father seizes on the remark: the prophecy of the tables which has hung over the Aeneadae since it was hurled at them in anger by the Harpy Celaeno at 3.255–7 has been confirmed; their new home has indeed been reached. Aeneas calls for a libation to Jove, and Jove endorses Aeneas' interpretation of what has taken place: a triple clap of thunder rings out—it is Jove himself hurling his bolts at a cloud, to set it flaming with rays of golden light (141–3). The prophecy, mentioned also by Helenus at 3.394, is traditional material. We may suppose Virgil kept it out of respect for tradition. But it falls a little flat, despite the studied verbal poetry of 141–3.[1]

The next day Aeneas sends a hundred Trojans on an embassy to the city which has been discovered in a dawn reconnaissance, to ask for peace, while he himself sets about fortifying the camp (148–59). They are received in the ancient, awe-inspiring, rustic palace of Latinus (172: *horrendum siluis et religione parentum*), lined with cedar images of Latinus' ancestors—Italus, Sabinus, Saturn, Janus, and 'the other kings from the earliest times who fought and were wounded in battle for their country's sake' (181–2: *aliique ab origine reges, Martiaque ob patriam pugnando uulnera passi*). Last named is Latinus' grandfather

---

[1] The prophecy is found in Lycophron 1250 and elsewhere. See Williams on 3.256f.

Aeneas, not mentioning Celaeno or Helenus' reference to the prophecy (3.394), says (122–3):

'genitor mihi talia namque,
nunc repeto, Anchises fatorum arcana reliquit',

and this is usually taken to be one of Virgil's inconsistencies. But it is hard to believe that he would have written the present passage without reference to the passage in Book 3. Mackail, denying inconsistency, says:

Anchises 'bequeathed' (*reliquit*) to Aeneas, before his own death, . . . the injunction to let the omen, when it should occur, determine the exact place for his first settlement.

It is also easily assumed that Anchises made some reference to the prophecy in his advice to Aeneas in 6.888–92.

The Twelve Books

Picus, tamer of horses. He sits dressed in the Roman short State toga and carries the Quirinal augury staff and the sacred shield. Hard on these objects of an almost holy antiquity for a Roman comes a touch of fantasy: Picus had married Circe, and she had turned him into a bird (*picus* is the Latin for 'woodpecker'), splashing his wings with colour (187–91):

> ipse Quirinali lituo paruaque sedebat
> succinctus trabea laeuaque ancile gerebat
> Picus, equum domitor, quem capta cupidine coniunx
> aurea percussum uirga uersumque uenenis
> fecit auem Circe sparsitque coloribus alas.

Ilioneus makes his speech (213–48), urging the equal antiquity of the Trojan race, stressing that fate has sent them to Italy, and offering Latinus the symbols of Priam's rule over the Trojans—a gesture which we can only take (Virgil does not explain it) as an expression of the Trojans' willingness to recognize the authority of Latinus, if they are allowed to live in peace in a city of their own; this kind of joint authority is proposed again by Aeneas in stating the terms of the duel at 12.189–94, and finally imposed by Jove at 12.834–7.[1] Latinus, realizing Aeneas must be his portended son-in-law (255–8), happily grants the Trojans what they ask, tells them of the prophecy and his daughter, and sends the ambassadors back with a present of 300 horses, adding as a personal gift for Aeneas a chariot drawn by two horses from the special divine stock surreptitiously bred by Circe from the horses of her father, the sun-god, for Latinus' grandfather Picus. The Trojan ambassadors ride off 'high in hope' to carry back peace (285).[2]

But we know that war threatens and, of course, Aeneas knows it, too, despite his present happiness (288: *laetum*); the burden of knowledge he cannot share is part of the load a leader must always carry. Virgil's narrative of the course of events that lead to war is perhaps his most sustained attempt at representing interlocking levels of motivation. (See Chapter 5, 'Parallel Divine and Psychological Motivation'.) On one level, the war is instigated by Juno, after an in-

[1] See Pöschl, Eng. edn, p. 149. There is a curious echo of this passage in Latinus' speech, 11.330–5.

[2] For an analysis of this fine line see Chapter 6, 'Ambiguity'. There is more than one echo in this Episode of the Episode in Book 1 (1.520–636) where Ilioneus makes his speech to Dido, who receives the Trojans with a generosity that is thwarted by the subsequent course of events.

Book 7

dignant speech (293–322) very like her opening speech in 1.37–49 and notable mainly for the famous line (312):

'flectere si nequeo superos, Acheronta mouebo.'

'*If I cannot budge the gods above, I shall stir up Hell.*'

She enlists the monstrous Fury Allecto. Each time Allecto causes the mischief. But each time the situation is ripe for mischief. A wave of hysteria sweeps through the Latins—a phenomenon of which history affords many examples. On one level, we are offered fantasy. On another, we are given an uncomfortably realistic picture of the way in which war does in fact often break out.

Allecto's first victim is the queen. Finding Amata in that turmoil of rage and anxiety a woman feels (345: *femineae ardentem curaeque iraeque coquebant*) when her daughter's happiness appears threatened, Allecto slips a snake from her head between Amata's breasts; unnoticed, it becomes first the great snake-shaped necklace that Amata wears, then one of her long head-bands; next it entwines itself in her hair, gradually poisoning her whole being (349–53). We can take Virgil's lines as a fanciful, poetical description of Amata's gathering madness, or we can take them at their face value, as part of his fairytale. Eventually, Amata breaks out in a frenzy of unreasoning, imaginary fears (359–72). When her words have no effect upon Latinus, she careers about the city, like a top whipped by boys around an empty courtyard (378–80), before putting into execution the mad plan she has conceived. Under the pretence of a Bacchic rite, she takes her daughter off into the mountain forests; there, as the news spreads, she is joined by other mothers, while she sings a mad marriage hymn for her daughter and for Turnus.

Allecto now turns her attention to Turnus. But whereas Amata had to be made mad to make her act irresponsibly in flagrant disregard of her duty as wife and queen, Turnus is an easier case: the irrational element is already there; all Allecto needs to do is to touch it off (Heroic Impulse) by representing to Turnus that his honour has been affected. She appears disguised as Calybe, the ancient priestess of Juno, as he lies asleep in his father's city of Ardea. Juno has sent her, she says, to tell him he must take up arms against the Phrygians and insist on justice from Latinus (429–34). The young prince laughs at her in his dream: he has heard all about the arrival of the Trojans and he knows Juno has not forgotten him; Calybe is a doddering old woman

The Twelve Books

(440: *uicta situ uerique effeta senectus*); let her stick to her temples and leave war to those whose business war is. (See Chapter 5, 'Tragic Irony'.) Blazing with anger, Allecto reveals herself in her true form, and cracks her whip at the terrified Turnus (454-5):

> 'adsum dirarum ab sede sororum,
> bella manu letumque gero . . .'

> '*From the home of the dread sisters I come,*
> *I carry in my hand war and death . . .*'

As she speaks, she thrusts a smoking torch into Turnus' heart. He jumps from his sleep, crazy with the lust for battle, his mind seething like a cauldron over a blazing fire (460-6). A summary of a speech to his men (467-70) reveals the muddle in his thoughts. First, he says that peace has been threatened and that they must march to the king under arms, to protect Italy and drive the invader away; then, that they will give Latins and Trojans alike a run for their money. Observe, however, that nothing is said of Lavinia: though muddle-headed, Turnus wants a righteous-sounding case. He does not much mind what that case is; it is action he wants, and action for Turnus means fighting; the rights and wrongs of the matter concern him less. As for his men, they ask nothing better than to follow their brave, handsome young prince into battle (472-4).[1]

The structure of Allecto's third exploit is more complicated. Sweeping down to the Trojan camp on the banks of the Tiber (477: *litore*) where Ascanius is hunting,[2] she throws a fresh scent into his dogs' nostrils which sets them in pursuit of a particular deer. The narrative is suspended while the deer is described. It had been taken from its mother and reared by Tyrrhus, custodian of the royal herds, his sons (we are told at 532 that the eldest was called Almo) and his daughter Silvia; she particularly had lavished her affection upon the animal; it wandered in the woods by day, but every night returned to the house. Ascanius' hounds start it while it is resting in the shade after enjoying a swim down the Tiber. Excitedly, Ascanius hurls a spear at the beast, and Allecto ensures that it does not miss (496-9). The deer flees, bleeding and whimpering like a human being, to its stable in Tyrrhus' house. In no time a band of peasants gathers, armed with the

---

[1] How are we to explain this sudden reversal of attitude in Turnus from inactivity to belligerence without Allecto? Presumably Turnus had relied on justice, and then on impulse decides to take justice into his own hands.
[2] Cf. 4.156-9.

Book 7

first thing that came to hand—stakes, cudgels, whatever they find—led by Tyrrhus brandishing an axe he had been using to split an oak (500–10).

The care Virgil expends on the details of this moving story shows how seriously he wants us to take the motivation of it, even though that motivation is constantly adapted to the conventions of his fairy-tale. From a rooftop Allecto now blows a blast upon a horn which vibrates through the forest and causes mothers in a twinge of anxiety to press their sons to their breasts (511–18).[1] Peasants and Trojans alike rally to the sound. In the ensuing mêlée Almo is killed, struck by an arrow in the throat—the blood from the wound chokes him (531–4). Among other casualties is an old man Galaesus, a wealthy farmer noted for his fair dealing, who is killed while trying to intercede between the two sides (535–9):

> corpora multa uirum circa seniorque Galaesus,
> dum paci medium se offert, iustissimus unus
> qui fuit Ausoniisque olim ditissimus aruis:
> quinque greges illi balantum, quina redibant
> armenta, et terram centum uertebat aratris.

It is a good example of Virgil's quiet, ironical pathos.

Allecto reports the success of her mission to Juno and returns to the underworld via the gloomy gorge of Amsanctus. We now see, in reverse order, the outcome of each of her exploits. The peasants pour into the city carrying their dead—we get a glimpse of the boy Almo, and of old Galaesus, his face disfigured (575: *Almonem puerum foedatique ora Galaesi*); while they are protesting to Latinus, Turnus arrives with his soldiers; the crowd is swollen by the menfolk whose wives have joined Amata in the mountains. The resultant, general hysteria drives everybody into a war which is contrary to their destiny (583–4):

> ilicet infandum cuncti contra omina bellum,
> contra fata deum peruerso numine poscunt.

In vain the old king tries to withstand the tide of events that swirls round him like an angry sea (586–90); realizing he cannot bring his people to reason, he tells them the punishment for this unholy act will fall upon their own heads, and withdraws into his palace.

---

[1] Allecto's blast on the horn is an echo of *Il.* 11.1–14. The mothers and their instinctive fear of war will occur many times.

The Twelve Books

The narrative breaks off at line 600 (Suspended Narrative) for a description of the ancient Roman practice of opening the Gates of War, and is then resumed for the climax of the second Section of the book. Latinus will not open the gates, so Juno herself swoops down from on high and with a blow of her fist bursts apart the iron-clad rails and sends the gates swinging open (620–2):

> tum regina deum caelo delapsa morantis
> impulit ipsa manu portas, et cardine uerso
> belli ferratos rumpit Saturnia postis.[1]

Throughout Italy preparations for war commence (623–40).

The final Section of Book 7 begins with a formal invocation of the Muses, the second in the book (641–6), followed by a catalogue of the forces which pour together from all over Italy to ally themselves with Turnus, who has assumed command of the Latin forces. The parallel with the catalogue of the ships in *Iliad* 2 is evident; but the term 'catalogue', though traditional, wrongly describes Virgil's transformation of his model. Homer offers us the sort of list we might expect from a historian, except that it is given verse form and filled out with a wealth of picturesque detail. Virgil uses similar material but constructs from it a loose series of Tableaux and Vignettes, organized around the twelve leaders who join Turnus. Some of the Tableaux and Vignettes show us troops arriving in Latium; others, soldiers on their way; others, soldiers just setting out. Some describe the soldiers themselves; others, the towns from which they come. We have, in short, Virgil's usual technique of selective visual description, backed up by the kind of comment that seems to spring from the poet's reaction to the scene observed, instead of a formal chronicle filled out by discursive reminiscence.[2] (See Chapter 3, 'Projection of the Narrator into his Narrative'.)

The basic structure is a rapidly moving succession of lightly sketched-in scenes (the device Virgil uses in 4.74–89). Interspersed with the graphic description of visual detail (the tense is normally historic present, occasionally imperfect—e.g., 668, 698, 782) are blocks of comment, added, as though emerging naturally from the visual narrative, to explain points of special interest—the pedigree of a

---

[1] Line 622, which is taken from Ennius (see Chapter 6), helps to blend this composite picture of ancient Rome and fantasy.

[2] For an excellent detailed analysis of the catalogue and its function in the poem see R. D. Williams, 'The function and structure of Virgil's catalogue in *Aeneid 7*', *CQ* 11 (1961) 146–53.

Book 7

leader, details of appearance, the situation of a town. As in the Dido sequence, precise statement of what is happening and where it happens is sacrificed to speed; the Tableaux and Vignettes seem designed to build up a complex picture of the forces massing in Latium eager for war, the sketches being tied together when we come to Turnus (783–802) by suggestions that he is leading a fantastic fairy-tale parade. Once or twice the scene changes—Messapus and Halaesus are still rallying their peoples—while in the case of Oebalus, Ufens and Umbro no scene can be determined.

We begin with a short action Tableau of Mezentius on the march, accompanied by his son Lausus (647–9):

> primus init bellum Tyrrhenis asper ab oris
> contemptor diuum Mezentius agminaque armat.
> filius huic iuxta Lausus.

The adverb *iuxta* ('by his side') limits the meaning of the verbs—*init bellum* must be visual, not abstract; *armat* perhaps means that Mezentius is getting his troops into their battle equipment ready for the march. A comment follows in a relative clause, then another detail of the Tableau: Lausus leading his thousand soldiers (651–3); then a further comment: Lausus deserved a better father and a campaign he could have felt happier about.

Aventinus is next, introduced by a four-line action Tableau (655–8), in which we see him picturesquely dressed, giving a display with his chariot and horses. Then come five lines of comment (relative clause followed by temporal clause) giving his pedigree and linking his name with the Cacus legend which will be used in Book 8. Two lines of comment follow, and we turn for a moment from Aventinus to the men he leads, while Virgil tells us how they fight in battle (664–5). Finally an action Tableau (666–9): Aventinus dismounts, throwing back as he does so the terrible lion's head which serves as his helmet, before entering the palace of King Latinus. Aventinus is thus accorded two Tableaux, one at the beginning and one at the end.[1]

The next Tableau introduces Catillus and Coras (670–7). They arrive like a twin avalanche to take up their position right out in front of the front line—a single Vignette amplified by a simile: *Tiburtia*

---

[1] Some editors, not understanding Virgil's technique, reject 664–5. But the sudden switch from Aventinus to his men and then back again is only disconcerting so long as we assume that Virgil is attempting reportage. For the addition of a final Tableau in a different tense cf. 698 ff.

moenia linquunt (670) creates the illusion that we have followed their headlong progress all the way from their native Tibur.

Caeculus shows a slightly different arrangement of similar material. His fantastic pedigree comes first (678–81), introduced by the bare statement that he was not absent (678: *nec ... defuit*) from the massing of the forces. This is followed (681–90) by an action Tableau of his slingers and a description of their strange uniform.[1]

Messapus is introduced by two lines of comment (691–2), then the scene changes to present him in an action Tableau (693–4) still rallying his people—they have long lost the habit of war and are difficult to rouse. We then slip into three lines of comment on the places where his people live (695–7), followed by a second Tableau which is one of the highlights of the catalogue. Messapus' men sing of their prince as they march, like deep-voiced swans pressing purposefully forward through the air and pouring forth from their long necks a melody that echoes over the Asian swamp where they have been feeding—no one would think they were soldiers on the march ... (698–704):

> ibant aequati numero regemque canebant,
> ceu quondam niuei liquida inter nubila cycni
> cum sese e pastu referunt et longa canoros
> dant per colla modos, sonat amnis et Asia longe
> pulsa palus ...
> nec quisquam aeratas acies ex agmine tanto
> misceri putet. ...[2]

With Clausus we are back in Latium. He and his men are introduced in a Tableau (706–11), interrupted for a two-line pedigree (708–9). Then comes the comment (712–21), which develops into a series of evocative Vignettes of the places from which Clausus' troops come. Finally there is a single-line action shot (722):

> scuta sonant pulsuque pedum conterrita tellus.

They beat their shields, the earth trembles at the pounding of their feet.

---

[1] At first sight *spargit* (687) does not look like a visual detail: since the war has not actually started, why should they be using their slings? Perhaps Virgil leaves it to us to visualize them practising with their slings.

[2] Line 702 is an uncompleted line. Observe how Virgil has transformed *Il.* 2.459 ff. Ennius claimed descent from Messapus. It seems possible therefore that Virgil has built in a compliment to his predecessor. See Williams, 'The function and structure of Virgil's catalogue in *Aeneid* 7', *CQ* 11 (1961) 151.

Book 7

Halaesus, like Messapus, is still getting his men together. We start with a three-line Tableau (723-5) followed (726-30) by a series of shots of the places where they live, followed by a brief comment (730-2) on their appearance in war.

Oebalus shows a fresh variation of technique. This time there is no Tableau, only comment (733-43), introduced by a direct apostrophe, followed by a pedigree and a series of shots showing Oebalus' people and the towns where they live, and then three further lines of comment on their appearance in battle.

The same technique is followed for Ufens (744-9)—the shortest description of the thirteen. Neither Oebalus nor Ufens is set in any definite scene.

A further variation on the technique used with Oebalus and Ufens is used with Umbro (750-60). We see only Umbro, not his men. We are told simply that he came, and then given a vivid description of his appearance, his powers as a soothsayer, to which is added a comment of mingled irony and sympathy (752-8):

> ... fortissimus Umbro,
> uipereo generi et grauiter spirantibus hydris
> spargere qui somnos cantuque manuque solebat,
> mulcebatque iras et morsus arte leuabat.
> sed non Dardaniae medicari cuspidis ictum
> eualuit neque eum iuuere in uulnera cantus
> somniferi et Marsis quaesitae montibus herbae.

> ... *Umbro most valiant,*
> *who used to put vipers and fiercely hissing water*
> *snakes to sleep by song and motion of his hand,*
> *soothing their anger, treating their bites with skill.*
> *But the blow he took from a Trojan's lance he could*
> *not treat; against that wound his sleep-inducing charms,*
> *his herbs gathered on Marsian hills, had no power.*

Virbius gets the longest mention. He is introduced by a four-line pedigree (761-4), branching out into the story of his connexion with Hippolytus (765-80), followed by a two-line action Vignette of Virbius training his horses on the parade-ground ready for war (781-2).

After the eleven princes who rally to his side (Camilla is still to be mentioned—she is placed at the end of the book), Turnus himself is described as he moves about among the gathering host, towering above it (783-4), a magical figure of flame (785-8):

cui triplici crinita iuba galea alta Chimaeram
sustinet Aetnaeos efflantem faucibus ignis
(tam magis illa fremens et tristibus effera flammis
quam magis effuso crudescunt sanguine pugnae).[1]

His tall, triple-plumed helmet displays aloft
a Chimaera breathing fire of Etna from its jaws.
The cruder the lust for battle grows now blood is spilt
the more it rages, rearing high on savage flames.

His attachment to a fairy-tale world is further underlined by the detailed description of his shield which follows: it bears a picture of his ancestor Io transformed into a heifer; Argus watching her, her father, the river-god Inachus, busy at work, complete the picture.

In the action Tableau of Camilla leading her cavalry at the gallop with which the catalogue ends, fantasy is blended with realism: she is not merely fleeter than the winds but could fly across a field of corn without harming it; or across the sea, suspended on the wavetops, without wetting her feet.[2] The series of sketches, therefore, ends, as it began, with a figure who later plays an important part in the narrative —Mezentius in Book 10, Camilla in Book 11; the one repulsive, the other attractive. All the young men scramble out from their houses to watch Camilla in wonder as she passes at the head of her Amazons, a figure of purple and gold, carrying a shepherd's staff of myrtle with a spearhead fixed to it. They are joined by the mothers, whose feelings about war we can guess from the glimpse of them in line 580; their more reluctant admiration is something we are left to think about as the book comes to an end.

Aeneas is kept pretty much in the background in this book—he appears briefly in two Episodes in the first Section. One function of the book is to create an imaginative picture of the peoples of Italy in primitive times. The magic and the strangeness of the country which the Aeneadae first glimpsed near the end of their wanderings in Book 3 find their counterpart in the people who dwell there. But the main function of the book is to get the war started. While our sympathy is

---

[1] On these lines see Pöschl, Eng. edn, p. 96. Jackson Knight's introduction to the Penguin translation (p. 20) is anxious to play down the magic of these lines ('On the whole, Virgil, and Homer still more, were very moderate with their exaggerations.').

[2] Mackail (p. 295) strangely comments (on this Tableau which concludes a series of Tableaux filled with magic and fantasy) that lines 808–11 'have been criticized, not without reason notwithstanding their beauty, as hyperbolical and out of tone with their surroundings'.

Book 8

aroused for these strange, spirited tribes who will one day form a nation, responsibility for the war is placed squarely on their shoulders. War breaks out as the result of their surrender to hysteria, and then spreads like wildfire: the eagerness with which leader after leader marches to join the coming battle implies a comment that Virgil chooses to leave unstated.[1]

BOOK 8

Book 8, after a short recapitulation of the events of the third Section of Book 7, covers the events, on earth and among the gods, of three days and two nights.

On the first day, the river-god Tiber comes to Aeneas in his troubled sleep to prophesy the fulfilment of the prodigy of the white sow (predicted by Helenus, 3.389–93), and to tell him that he must make his way upstream to ask for reinforcements from King Evander; the prodigy is fulfilled, and Aeneas sets out on his journey up the Tiber, whose course is magically stilled.

After travelling throughout the night, Aeneas and his companions arrive late the next day, to find Evander and his Arcadians busy with rites commemorating the visit of Hercules. Evander welcomes Aeneas and in explanation of the rite relates the story of Hercules' visit and how he killed the monster Cacus. That evening he takes Aeneas round his humble city, which occupies the future site of Rome.

A divine action now starts and runs parallel to the heroic action: that night, before they go to sleep (see 405–6), Venus asks her husband Vulcan to make magic armour for her son; rising before dawn the next day, he goes to his forge to give the Cyclopes their instructions. Shortly after dawn Evander goes to Aeneas, promises him the assistance Aeneas has asked for, and tells him that he will send his son Pallas with him; as he finishes speaking there is a flash of lightning and the reverberation of thunder, and the magical arms of Aeneas are seen in the sky. Aeneas prepares to leave for Etruria (where Evander has advised him to seek further reinforcements) taking Pallas with him. After an affectionate parting between father and son, Aeneas and Pallas set out and are met by Venus who gives Aeneas the armour Vulcan has made for him, including the wonderful shield.

---

[1] See Chapter 5, 'Implicit Comment'. On the structure of Book 7, as a movement into darkness out of light, see Pöschl, Eng. edn, pp. 167–8.

The Twelve Books

		Introduction: Italy rises in arms	1–17
I 18–101	{	The First Day: (i) Tiber visits Aeneas in a vision; the white sow (ii) Aeneas sets out to visit Evander, travelling through the night	18–85 86–101
II 102–369	{	The Second Day: Evander A— (i) welcomes Aeneas (ii) tells the story of Cacus (193–279); the rite (iii) shows Aeneas his city	 102–183 184–305 306–369
III 370–731	{	Interlude: (i) Venus-Vulcan (ii) Vulcan at his forge The Third Day: Evander B— (iii) farewells Aeneas; signs in the sky (iv) Aeneas and Pallas prepare to leave; Evander farewells Pallas (v) Departure The Shield: (vi) Venus gives Aeneas the shield; the shield described (see below for detailed analysis of scenes)	 370–406 407–453 454–540 541–584 585–607 608–731

One function of Book 8 is to suspend the narrative of the gathering tide of war in order to show us the other side of the picture—the forces, human and divine, that will assist Aeneas in the coming battle. In Book 7, the spotlight was on Turnus; now it returns to Aeneas. It will continue to alternate between the two leaders in the following books: in Book 9, Aeneas is absent when Turnus leads the attack on the Trojan camp; in Book 10, Aeneas is at the centre of events—Turnus, though present for a time, is removed from the battle by Juno before he can meet Aeneas. In Book 11, both leaders play a minor role—a kind of respite, before their confrontation in Book 12.

Another of the main functions of the book is to discharge the poet's obligation to write a poem celebrating Rome. However, this function is prominent in two Episodes only—that in which Aeneas is taken by

Book 8

Evander round the area where Rome will rise centuries later (306–69), and that in which the pageant of history upon the great shield of Aeneas is described (608–731).[1]

Book 8 is remarkable for the smoothness of its plot construction. Aeneas needs assistance—so Tiber takes him to Evander. He arrives in the middle of a festival, and cannot therefore that day transact his business with Evander—so Evander takes the opportunity to tell Aeneas the story of Cacus and then takes him for the evening stroll round what will one day be Rome. Meanwhile the divine forces gather, and in the third Section the two lines of narrative, divine and heroic, run side by side, till they meet when Venus hands the magic shield over to Aeneas. Moreover Pallas, who is going to play a key role in the unspringing of the plot of Book 10, is woven into the story with an unobtrusive technique very unlike that employed in introducing Turnus. It is Pallas who first receives Aeneas—he darts forward at the approach of Aeneas' ships (his father is too old). But at this first glimpse of him nothing is asserted about Pallas' appearance or his character beyond the single word *audax* (110), which backs up Pallas' action in rushing to confront the Aeneadae. Pallas then fades into the background: he is mentioned in passing by his father at line 168; when Aeneas and Evander meet the next morning, Achates accompanies Aeneas, and Pallas accompanies Evander (466); again little is said of him when his father announces to Aeneas that, as he is too old to fight himself, he will send his son with Aeneas to learn the art of war, accompanied by four hundred cavalry (514–19). Virgil leaves it to his father's affection for Pallas to elicit our sympathy for the young man: if Pallas is fated not to return, Evander prays he may die now while he has his son, his only comfort, in his embrace, 'while anxiety leaves room for doubt, while the future is uncertain' (580: *dum curae ambiguae, dum spes incerta futuri*). The old king falls in a faint, and his servants carry him into the palace. As Aeneas and the others depart, our eye lights for the first time on this young man who has inspired such affection, conspicuous as he rides among his men in brightly painted battle-rig, like Lucifer, the favourite star of Venus, when he raises his face from the ocean to dispel the darkness of night from the sky (587–91):

> inde alii Troiae proceres, ipse agmine Pallas
> in medio chlamyde et pictis conspectus in armis,

[1] Romulus (according to the chronology set out at 1.261–77 in Jove's speech to Venus) is to be born 333 years after the events narrated in the *Aeneid*. Not till then do the Aeneadae settle in Rome.

> qualis ubi Oceani perfusus Lucifer unda,
> quem Venus ante alios astrorum diligit ignis,
> extulit os sacrum caelo tenebrasque resoluit.

These lines and their implied assertion of the glory of war are followed by a two-line Vignette, in which we see the mothers standing all anxiety on the walls as they watch the squadrons in their shining bronze armour disappear in a cloud of dust (592–3):

> stant pauidae in muris matres oculisque sequuntur
> pulueream nubem et fulgentis aere cateruas.

Without comment Virgil juxtaposes the two sides to war. (See Chapter 5, 'Implicit Comment'.)

The groundwork for this plot is laid in a crisp, efficient first Section after a recapitulation of the events of the previous book and an analysis of Aeneas' reaction to them. His mind is calm though deeply anxious; the clear, bright light of his intellect plays on every possibility, like the shimmering light of the sun or the moon reflected upon water in a cauldron, which flits all round the room, then rises and strikes against the ceiling (18–25):

> talia per Latium. quae Laomedontius heros
> cuncta uidens magno curarum fluctuat aestu,
> atque animum nunc huc celerem nunc diuidit illuc
> in partisque rapit uarias perque omnia uersat,
> sicut aquae tremulum labris ubi lumen aenis
> sole repercussum aut radiantis imagine lunae
> omnia peruolitat late loca, iamque sub auras
> erigitur summique ferit laquearia tecti.[1]

Father Tiber appears to Aeneas in a vision, picturesquely dressed—he is wearing a filmy, grey-coloured cloak and a garland of reeds on his head (33–4):

> eum tenuis glauco uelabat amictu
> carbasus, et crinis umbrosa tegebat harundo.

As he often does, Virgil introduces a playful note where we might expect only solemnity, by exploiting the dual status of Tiber as a river-god and the river itself.[2] His prophecy concluded, the god dives back

---

[1] The simile is an Implicit Comment upon the simile in the previous book that describes Turnus' state of mind when he breaks into his heroic impulse (7.462–6).

[2] Cf. Atlas, 4.246–58, and the catalogue of Etruscan ships, 10.163–214.

Book 8

into his own waters. Aeneas says his prayer of thanks (71–8), discovers the white sow, then busies himself with preparations for the journey Tiber has told him to undertake to Evander.

In the second Section, a more leisurely tempo succeeds this urgent note. Relationships are built up between the major characters, and a situation created in which the reader can be led naturally to the scene of pre-historic Rome. Excitement in this quietly moving Section is provided by Evander's story of how Hercules killed the monster Cacus (193–279); the narrative, which occupies 87 lines and is, incidentally, an excellent example of Virgil's exploitation of tense-contrast, forms a short, carefully constructed, highly dramatic tale within a tale in the best tradition of the epyllion.

At this point Virgil's picture of primitive Italy fades. With the third Section we move into the world of magic, treated on Virgil's usual note of gentle irony. The colloquy between Venus and Vulcan, however momentous in its significance, however stylized the imagery, follows the typical pattern of a conversation between a husband who is more a man of action than a talker and his quick-witted wife. Venus is well practised in achieving her purpose by arousing Vulcan's massive, flaming passion (388–93) and she knows, too, how to exploit her husband's previous generosity to attractive goddesses (383–4). This bedroom conversation has upset Romantic critics, to whom the reminiscences of Homer have seemed one more instance of Virgil's poverty of invention.[1] The function of the Episode is as a preliminary challenge to Homer, in anticipation of the more ambitious challenge of the Shield Episode later in the Section. There is nothing surreptitous about Virgil's borrowings from Homer—they are openly flaunted (for example, by the allusion to Thetis' appeal to Vulcan at 383).[2] At the same time the borrowed material is transformed: instead of Homer's homely picture of Thetis making a social call, we

---

[1] Heyne observed (italics mine):

Qui sequitur locus meo iudicio artis magis quam ingenii laudem habet: *nimis manifesta imitationis sunt vestigia* simulque ieiunae istius copiae quae fere imitationis studium prodere solet.

Mackail, quoting Heyne, adds:

To this admirable criticism it has only to be added that even from the point of view of workmanship the episode is ragged, and clearly awaits the artist's final remodelling.

[2] William S. Anderson, 'Vergil's second *Iliad*', *TAPhA* 88 (1957) 26, points out how Virgil goes out of his way to remind us that he is borrowing from Homer.

have a stylized picture, in which realism and fantasy are ironically juxtaposed.

The interlude continues with Vulcan's visit before dawn to his forge under Etna, staffed by the Cyclopes. This Episode opens with the fine simile of the woman (a virtuous wife, or more likely a widow who wishes to remain *uniuira*) who rises from bed in the middle of the night to get on with her spinning (407–15):

> inde ubi prima quies medio iam noctis abactae
> curriculo expulerat somnum, cum femina primum,
> cui tolerare colo uitam tenuique Minerua
> impositum, cinerem et sopitos suscitat ignis
> (noctem addens operi) famulasque ad lumina longo
> exercet penso, castum ut seruare cubile
> coniugis et possit paruos educere natos:
> haud secus ignipotens nec tempore segnior illo
> mollibus e stratis opera ad fabrilia surgit.
>
> *Then when night was half-way past and his first sleep
> had driven off fatigue—the time when a woman, who must
> make life bearable with her distaff and some modest
> weaving, fans the ashes of her dying fire (adding
> the night to her labours) and by its dim light busies
> her slaves with their drawn-out task, to keep chaste
> her husband's bed and rear his little sons—
> so the fire-god, no less alert at that hour,
> rising from his soft couch, makes off to the smithy.*

Here we have a reversal of the normal mythological simile: divine action is illustrated by human action, instead of the other way round.[1] Vulcan's arrival at his forge, like Charon in Book 6, is a superb piece of ironic fantasy. He finds the Cyclopes busy on three jobs—a thunderbolt for Jove, a chariot for Mars, and an aegis for Minerva. 'Put all that stuff aside,' says Vulcan, 'and listen to me. We have to make armour for a real man' (439–41):

> 'tollite cuncta' inquit 'coeptosque auferte labores,
> Aetnaei Cyclopes, et huc aduertite mentem:
> arma acri facienda uiro.'

---

[1] The simile too comes from Homer—it is an expansion of *Il.* 12.433–5.

The first line of Virgil's simile has been oddly misunderstood by critics from Servius onwards, who complains *'quies expulerat somnum paene nihil est: quid enim quies nisi somnus?'* What Virgil means, of course, is that after her first deep slumber she can manage without further sleep.

Book 8

Notice the emphasis on *uiro*—Vulcan does not usually work for mortal customers.

The Cyclopes throw themselves into the task and from a mass of molten metal begin to shape the great shield, but the fanciful account of their labours (445–53) is suspended to bring us back to Aeneas and Evander. It is dawn. The old king has donned battle regalia (sword and panther skin) in honour of the occasion. He promises help and tells Aeneas how to get more. The Etruscans have revolted from the inhuman rule of Mezentius. A prophet having told them a foreigner must lead them, they came to Evander and he would have accepted, old as he was, if there had not been Italian blood mixed in his mother's stock. Let Aeneas be their leader. As with the prophecies in Book 7, we may feel the machinery creak.

Aeneas is weighed down with thoughts of the war that lies ahead (520–2) when Venus gives her sign from the sky and displays the armour that Vulcan has made for her son. It is the sign that Aeneas has been waiting for, and his mood changes to one of compassionate confidence (537–40). Escorted by Evander, he heads for the ships to select the men who will ride with him and Pallas into Etruria on the horses provided by Evander—the rest are to return downstream to the Trojan camp. The old king, much distraught, says good-bye to his son, and the party ride off amid a clatter of hooves (596). They have almost reached the Etruscan camp when Venus meets them in a valley and hands over the magic armour to Aeneas (608–16).

A short Tableau follows, in which we see Aeneas examining his new armour in wonder (617–25). It includes a helmet that pours forth flame, a death-dealing sword (621: *fatiferum . . . ensem*—the sword with which Aeneas will kill Turnus at 12.950), a great gleaming cuirass, greaves of gold and electrum, a spear, and a 'shield the manner of whose construction is beyond description' (625: *clipei non enarrabile textum*). We leave the scene at this point for a description of the shield, returning just over a hundred lines later for an exquisite three-line tailpiece (729–31):

> talia per clipeum Volcani dona parentis
> miratur, rerumque ignarus imagine gaudet
> attollens umero famamque et fata nepotum.[1]

[1] Observe both the ambiguity in 731, based on a common metaphor (e.g., Cicero, *Pro Flacco* 37.94, *rem publicam umeris sustinere*), and the syntactical ambiguity of *rerum*: (1) with *ignarus*; (2) with *imagine gaudet*, i.e., 'having no knowledge of the reality, it gives him pleasure to see the things depicted'. (See Chapter 6, 'Ambiguity' and 'Syntactical Ambiguity'.)

The Twelve Books

Such are the scenes on Vulcan's shield, his mother's gift:
he looks at the pictures in happy, uncomprehending wonder
as he takes on his shoulders the future of his people.

As with the catalogue in Book 7 and the pictures on Dido's temple in Book 1, Virgil's description of the shield resolves itself into a series of action Tableaux; the individual themes are represented sometimes by a single shot, sometimes by a sequence of shots. Virgil asks us to imagine that the shield carried a complete pictorial representation in chronological order of the descendants of Ascanius and the wars which they would fight (626–9). From this whole, he picks out a handful of well-known events in Roman history, to prepare the way for a full-scale description of the battle of Actium. As it happens, only three groups of scenes are connected with war. (For a discussion of the hypotheses on which Virgil's description of the shield rests see Chapter 2, Section III.)

First comes a fine single Tableau of the she-wolf lying in the cave of Mars, giving suck to the twins Romulus and Remus and turning her head to lick them as she does so (630–4):

> fecerat et uiridi fetam Mauortis in antro
> procubuisse lupam, geminos huic ubera circum
> ludere pendentis pueros et lambere matrem
> impauidos, illam tereti ceruice reflexa
> mulcere alternos et corpora fingere lingua.

Adjoining this picture is a sequence of four Vignettes (635–45) representing the rape of the Sabine women: first, the rape itself in the theatre; second, the war that ensued with the Sabine king; third, a Vignette of the peace ceremony; fourth, the terrible punishment of the Sabine Mettus Curtius for subsequently breaking faith with Rome— his body was bound to two chariots and torn apart when they were driven in different directions; King Tullus then dragged the bloody remains through a forest, bespattering the undergrowth with blood (642–5):

> haud procul inde citae Mettum in diuersa quadrigae
> distulerant, at tu dictis, Albane, maneres!
> raptabatque uiri mendacis uiscera Tullus
> per siluam, et sparsi rorabant sanguine uepres.

Next comes the war with Porsenna, represented by two Tableaux (646–51)—one of the descendants of Aeneas rushing to fight for

Book 8

liberty, the other Cocles resisting Porsenna at the bridge while Cloelia (a Roman girl who had been given as a hostage to Porsenna) swims back to Rome in the river beneath. Next a single Tableau (652–62) of the entry of the Gauls into Rome in 390 B.C., in which the eye lights on three details: first, Manlius defending the Capitol; second, a goose in flight, representing the geese which warned Manlius; third, a party of armed Gauls advancing in the darkness (we see their golden hair and clothing, the glitter of their striped cloaks). Next a short religious Tableau (663–6)—the Salii, the Luperci, and a procession of mothers. Next a Tableau of the underworld (666–70) showing Catiline being punished in Tartarus and Cato (the younger) legislating in Elysium.

Something less than half Virgil's description of the shield is occupied with these Tableaux. After this highly selective pageant, the remainder (671–728) is devoted to a more detailed series of Tableaux of the battle of Actium, in which the poet discharges his obligation to commemorate the conclusion of the civil war.

Virgil begins with a stylized picture of the battle scene itself (671–97), and concludes with a description of the presiding gods (698–706—the yelping gods of Egypt on one side; Neptune, Venus, Minerva on the other; Mars, the Furies, Discord and Bellona in the middle; Apollo above it all, bow in hand), merging into a second Tableau (707–13) of the flight of Cleopatra and her fleet (709–13):

> illam inter caedes pallentem morte futura
> fecerat ignipotens undis et Iapyge ferri,
> contra autem magno maerentem corpore Nilum
> pandentemque sinus et tota ueste uocantem
> caeruleum in gremium latebrosaque flumina uictos.[1]
>
> *Amid the slaughter, pale at death's approach,*
> *the fire-god had shown her, a north-west wind astern;*
> *facing her the great grieving mass of Nile,*
> *spreading his flowing robes to fold the vanquished in*
> *and conceal them in the waters of his azure lap.*

Last of all (714–28) comes a series of scenes from Octavian's triumph in 29 B.C. two years after the battle.[2]

In Homer, the shield of Achilles is quickly lost sight of and we pass to typical scenes from the Greek countryside. Virgil keeps strictly to

---

[1] Virgil exploits the ambiguities inherent in the double image of Nile as a god and as an expanse of water.

[2] Compare the similar sequence of scenes in Horace's Cleopatra Ode (1.37).

The Twelve Books

his hypothesis. He has a craftsman's pride in triumphing over self-imposed limitations: though he never allows us to forget that it is an artefact which he is describing,[1] his highly stylized Tableaux live. At the same time he wishes, we may be sure, to keep his readers within the framework of fantasy within which his poem moves, lest propaganda spoil the poetry. (See Chapter 5, 'Impure Poetry'.)

BOOK 9

Book 9 comprises the action of two days and the intervening night. On the first day Juno sends Iris to advise Turnus to attack the Trojan camp while Aeneas is away; the Italians advance; when the Trojans do not emerge, they turn their attention to the Trojan fleet, but Cybele transforms the ships into sea nymphs, and the first Section concludes with an angry speech by Turnus.

During the night Nisus and Euryalus make a sortie through the sleeping Italian camp to take word to Aeneas of the Italian attack; they are discovered by a night patrol and killed.

The following day the Italians advance again, displaying the heads of Nisus and Euryalus; the narrative of the ensuing siege is organized into four short Episodes, followed by a detailed description of the havoc caused when Turnus gets inside the Trojan camp, from which he is eventually expelled.

I 1–158	The First Day—the Trojans besieged: (i) Juno sends Iris to tell Turnus to attack (ii) The Italians advance (iii) Cybele transforms the ships into nymphs (flashback Cybele-Jove, 80–106) (iv) Speech of Turnus	1–24 25–76 77–125 126–158
II 159–458	Night Sortie: Opening Tableau (i) Nisus and Euryalus volunteer (ii) Council of War; they depart (iii) In the Italian camp (iv) They are discovered and killed	159–175 176–223 224–313 314–366 367–458

---

[1] E.g., *fecerat*, 628; *addiderat*, 637; *aspiceres*, 650; *extuderat*, 665; *addit*, 666; *in medio . . . cernere erat*, 675–6; *uideres*, 676; *fecerat*, 710; *finxerat*, 726. He keeps naming the materials from which Vulcan constructed the scenes (see especially the elaborate statement which introduces the Tableaux of Actium—they are in gold, silver and blue enamel, 671–3); gold is the material most often alluded to, but Mars is worked in iron (701: *caelatus ferro*).

Book 9

	The Second Day—the Italian attack:	
	Opening Tableau: heads of Nisus and Euryalus	459–472
	(i) Euryalus' mother	473–502
	Siege:	
III	(ii) The attack	503–524
459–818	(iii) Turnus and the collapsing tower	525–568
	(iv) Scene at the gate	569–589
	(v) Remulus taunts the Trojans and is killed by Ascanius; Apollo	590–671
	(vi) Pandarus and Bitias open the gate; Turnus in the Trojan camp	672–818

In the first Section, the least dramatic of the three, there is a careful interlocking of the heroic and divine actions in an atmosphere of fairy-tale, to which the realistic narrative of fighting in the second and third Sections stands in striking contrast. The four Episodes which make up the first Section form a neat pattern. In the first, Juno sends Iris to tell Turnus an opportunity is at hand (6–13), though Turnus could easily have discovered what Iris tells him and Iris' injunction *'nunc tempus equos, nunc poscere currus'* can represent an impulse that is very characteristic of Turnus (see Analysis of Book 12). In the second, the Italians attack. A countering divine action follows in the third Episode, as Cybele springs to save the ships.[1] Turnus is unabashed (126: *at non audaci Turno fiducia cessit*) and in the fourth Episode we see him haranguing his men to persist with the siege of the camp, even though the Trojans do not offer battle—they had been instructed by Aeneas, in the event of trouble, to stay within the walls of the camp (40–6). Turnus' speech (128–58) is notable for two things. First, the sustained comparison with events at Troy, in which he casts himself first in the role of a second Menelaus (138–9), then builds up

---

[1] The flashback explaining her intervention is interesting. The Trojan fleet had been built from wood from her sacred grove. Cybele had asked Jove that the fleet therefore be immune from harm. Jove had replied that a thing made by mortals could not enjoy immortal status—moreover it would mean that Aeneas' journey would be free from hazard (96–7: *certusque incerta pericula lustret Aeneas?*). But Jove was prepared to grant that the ships which succeed in reaching Italy shall be turned into sea nymphs when their duties are over.

Once again the fairy-tale atmosphere makes Mackail uneasy (p. 335):

> The episode of the change of the Trojan ships into sea-nymphs fails to carry conviction: Virgil himself half apologizes for it, and many of his readers are inclined to wish that he had discarded the incident and its sequel in x. 219–55, and left it to be treated by the hand of Ovid as a fairy tale.

to a climax which is almost a summary of the *Iliad*: Turnus will not need Vulcan to make him arms as Achilles did, nor will he need a fleet of a thousand ships to get at the Trojans; there will be no stealing of statues (as the Greeks stole the Palladium—see Analysis of Book 2), no hiding in horses, no Hector to make the war drag on for ten years (148–55):

> 'non armis mihi Volcani, non mille carinis
> est opus in Teucros. addant se protinus omnes
> Etrusci socios. tenebras et inertia furta
> Palladii caesis summae custodibus arcis
> ne timeant, nec equi caeca condemur in aluo:
> luce palam certum est igni circumdare muros.
> haud sibi cum Danais rem faxo et pube Pelasga
> esse ferant, decimum quos distulit Hector in annum.'

It is a little hard to see the point of this tirade. The allusions to the *Iliad* come less naturally than those in the Sibyl's speech to Aeneas, 6.86–94; the reference to the arms of Vulcan (in a context which implies Achilles) is particularly unhappy now that we have just seen Aeneas receive arms from Vulcan. Equally odd is the ranting, truculent tone of Turnus' speech. Are we meant to feel, when Turnus brushes aside the miraculous saving of the ships which Trojans and Italians alike have witnessed (133: *nil me fatalia terrent*), that he should have known better, that he has deliberately coarsened himself in the face of a warning? The tone of the passage seems to imply Turnus is half aware that fate is against him, and dismisses his misgivings with the dishonest argument of 136–7 (*sunt et mea contra fata mihi*).[1] Is the long string of parallels with the Trojan War perhaps *meant* to fall flat? Turnus in any case ends his speech lamely: 'The better part of the day is over,' he says, 'so let us take things easy' (156–8).

The second Section, comprising just 300 lines, is devoted to the night escapade of Nisus and Euryalus. This is not an isolated showpiece, but the first action of the war. If originally composed as an independent epyllion, as some suppose, it has been carefully adapted in tone and implication to form an integral part of the poem. It begins with a Tableau of great beauty (159–75):

> interea uigilum excubiis obsidere portas
> cura datur Messapo et moenia cingere flammis.   160

[1] Servius remarks that the argument is dishonest, but explains the dishonesty as a permissible rhetorical device.

Book 9

bis septem Rutuli muros qui milite seruent
delecti, ast illos centeni quemque sequuntur;
purpurei cristis iuuenes auroque corusci,
discurrunt uariantque uices, fusique per herbam
indulgent uino et uertunt crateras aenos;   165
conlucent ignes, noctem custodia ducit
insomnem ludo . . .
haec super e uallo prospectant Troes et armis
alta tenent, nec non trepidi formidine portas
explorant pontisque et propugnacula iungunt,   170
tela gerunt. instat Mnestheus acerque Serestus,
quos pater Aeneas, si quando aduersa uocarent,
rectores iuuenum et rerum dedit esse magistros.
omnis per muros legio sortita periclum
excubat exercetque uices, quod cuique tuendum est.   175

Fine, terse descriptive writing brings out vividly the details of the scene as night descends on the besieged camp. The Trojans are hemmed in by the ring of the Italian camp fires. Fourteen companies of Italians besiege the camp, each with its own commander, the whole operation entrusted to Messapus (159–62). Their red and gold helmets glitter as they march to and fro each time the guard is changed; those not on duty sprawl on the grass and pass the night drinking and gambling by the camp fires instead of sleeping (163–7). (The Italians display immediately a lack of discipline in which Nisus will see his opportunity.) Looking down on the scene from above, the Trojans uneasily check their defences without laying down their arms (168–71). Aeneas' lieutenants, Mnestheus and Serestus, move among them, and every man is alert and attentive to his task (171–5).

Four Episodes follow, each with its distinct structure, mood and purpose.

In the first (176–223) we are introduced again to Nisus and Euryalus (whom we met originally in the foot race in Book 5[1]), and told of the impulse that comes to Nisus, Euryalus' reaction, and their decision. The different characters of the two men are clearly shown. Nisus is the elder—though both are young (235)—the more cynical (184–7; 194–5; 208–9), and the more sensible (211–12; 216–18). Euryalus is ready to throw his life away for glory (205–6):

'est hic, est animus lucis contemptor et istum
qui uita bene credat emi, quo tendis, honorem.'

[1] It is characteristic of Virgil's technique of never over-explaining that no reference is made here to the foot race.

The Twelve Books

*'Mine is a spirit that holds life cheap, a fair
price to pay for honour such as you now seek.'*

But Nisus wants a tangible reward (194); this is a calculated risk which he is ready to face, because there is a job to be done (193: someone must take word to Aeneas) and because he frets at the inactivity of the siege (187). Nisus' plan is to go alone, but Euryalus will have none of it; he brushes aside Nisus' objections (219), even Nisus' reluctance to be responsible to Euryalus' mother for her son's death (216–18). They call for men to replace them at their post and ask to be taken to Ascanius. One function of this first Episode is to show that the Trojans are not cowards; they do not engage the Italians because Aeneas had ordered them not to, but even a realist like Nisus prefers danger to inactivity. Another function is to get the plot under way, and this is achieved mainly through dialogue.

The structure of the next Episode is rather more complicated. It begins with a Tableau of Ascanius and the other Trojan leaders (229–30):

> stant longis adnixi hastis et scuta tenentes
> castrorum et campi medio.

It is a good example of Virgil's ability to evoke a scene in a few words: these legendary figures, leaning on their long spears and holding their shields as they debate late into the night, suggest a council of war very different from any Virgil's readers might have taken part in. Nisus and Euryalus enter nervously, and Nisus presents his plan: the Italians are by now in a drunken sleep (236–7—we can readily believe this after the opening Tableau of the Section); Euryalus and he should be able to get through the lines—they'll bring back a load of loot while they're about it.[1] Nisus' offer is received by old Aletes with an outburst of congratulation (246–50): virtue is of course its own reward, but Aeneas and Ascanius will not forget such bravery (252–6). Aletes' two remarks are separated by a short Vignette in which we see him go from one to the other of the two young men, slapping each on the back while he shakes him by the hand.[2] Ascanius takes the hint and offers the most extravagant rewards to Nisus and Euryalus if they succeed in their mission—not only valuable presents, but Turnus' horse,

---

[1] Even with the transposition of 241 to follow 243 (adopted by some editors, following Servius, who noted it as an alternative) 242 implies Nisus' original intention was to complete his mission and then worry about loot afterwards.

[2] For the tenses in 250–1 see Chapter 3, 'Tempo of the Narrative: Tenses'.

Book 9

prisoners-of-war for slaves, and King Latinus' land (269–74). Virgil must surely have intended us to notice that the promises are not only lavish, but barbarous, quite out of keeping with Aeneas' view of his mission in Italy. Euryalus asks for one thing more: if he does not come back, will they look after his mother?—he has not told her, because he could not endure her tears (283–92). Ascanius promises Euryalus that, if he does not come back, the rewards will be paid to his mother (299–302).[1] Gifts are exchanged, and the Episode ends with a Tableau of the scene at the gates of the camp: the Trojans, young and old alike, crowd round the two young men to wish them a safe return, while Ascanius, whose sense of responsibility belies his years, gives them a detailed message for Aeneas; but good wishes and message are scattered by the winds and wafted to the clouds (308–13):

> protinus armati incedunt: quos omnis euntis
> primorum manus ad portas iuuenumque senumque
> prosequitur uotis, nec non et pulcher Iulus,
> ante annos animumque gerens curamque uirilem,
> multa patri mandata dabat portanda; sed aurae
> omnia discerpunt et nubibus inrita donant.[2]

The next Episode shows the two threading their way through the sleeping Italian camp. Nisus, unable to resist the opportunity (320: *nunc ipsa uocat res*), tells Euryalus to keep watch, while he wreaks havoc among the sleeping Italians. These are the first killings of the war, and they are presented in a series of three wonderfully sharp Vignettes set against a supporting cast of half a dozen other victims. Rhamnes, prince and prophet, snoring loudly on a great pile of bedding, is the first to be dispatched—his prophetic gifts availed him nothing (324–8). Next is Remus,[3] along with his retinue (329–34); this time not only the prince is highlighted (we see his headless corpse spurting blood over ground and bedding), but also his charioteer: Nisus slices through the man's drooping neck as he sleeps by his horses. Finally, after a couple more victims named but left un-

---

[1] Has Virgil blundered, perhaps, with this promise? Or does he intend us to understand that the promise is valid only if Nisus and Euryalus get word to Aeneas: trying and failing would not be enough?

[2] The winds scatter both the good wishes and the instructions: the good wishes are in vain, Nisus and Euryalus do not really listen to Ascanius' instructions—they are more concerned with the adventure ahead.

[3] In 330 *premit* equals *opprimit* (the common use of the simple verb where the verb plus preverb is usual in prose), but the result is a kind of understatement.

The Twelve Books

described, it is the turn of Serranus: he was strikingly handsome, he had gambled far into the night and now lay in a drunken sleep—if only he had gambled the night through he would have lived to see the dawn! The narrative of the ten killings occupies fifteen lines (324–38):

> simul ense superbum
> Rhamnetem adgreditur, qui forte tapetibus altis   325
> exstructus toto proflabat pectore somnum,
> rex idem et regi Turno gratissimus augur,
> sed non augurio potuit depellere pestem.
> tris iuxta famulos temere inter tela iacentis
> armigerumque Remi premit aurigamque sub ipsis   330
> nactus equis ferroque secat pendentia colla;
> tum caput ipsi aufert domino truncumque relinquit
> sanguine singultantem; atro tepefacta cruore
> terra torique madent. nec non Lamyrumque Lamumque
> et iuuenem Serranum, illa qui plurima nocte   335
> luserat, insignis facie, multoque iacebat
> membra deo uictus: felix, si protinus illum
> aequasset nocti ludum in lucemque tulisset.

This will be Virgil's normal technique in describing battle scenes: a series of Vignettes set against an unfocused background of killing, here and there a terse comment, ironic or pathetic, or a thumbnail sketch of the dead man's ancestry, aspirations or appearance.

The spectacle of Nisus striding through the camp like a hungry lion through a sheepfold (339) arouses Euryalus' lust for killing (342–3), and he joins in the slaughter. Three of the four Italians he kills are merely named, the fourth is allotted a Vignette: Rhoetus was awake, had seen everything, was trying in terror to hide behind a great winejar when Euryalus plunged a sword deep in his chest, just as Rhoetus was springing to his feet, killing him instantly. With his dying breath he belched up a bright red foam of blood mixed with wine (345–50):

> ... Rhoetum uigilantem et cuncta uidentem,
> sed magnum metuens se post cratera tegebat;
> pectore in aduerso totum cui comminus ensem
> condidit adsurgenti et multa morte recepit.
> purpuream uomit ille animam et cum sanguine mixta
> uina refert moriens.

Observe the terrible realism of the last sentence. Observe, too, how delicately Virgil manipulates our attitude to Nisus and Euryalus

Book 9

during this slaughter. At the point where he wants our sympathy to recede from Nisus, he places the Vignette of Serranus (335–8). Then Euryalus joins in but, before our pity for the victims becomes too strong, we are put on Euryalus' side again by Rhoetus, who meets a coward's death (345–50), then alienated once more when Euryalus presses on, greedy for loot (350: *furto feruidus instat*) and heads for Messapus and his followers—out beyond the last camp fire he can see their horses tied and grazing.[1]

Nisus, the older, more sensible soldier, realizes the danger of forgetting their mission if they let themselves be carried away by the twin passions of murder and loot (354: *sensit enim nimia caede atque cupidine ferri*). Euryalus selects a few pieces—the *phalerae* (an ornament worn on the breastplate) and the swordbelt of Rhamnes (Nisus' first victim) and the helmet of Messapus, the leader of the besieging Italians, stolen while he sleeps—and puts them on and the two go on their way (359–66).

Euryalus has inadvertently sealed the fate of both.[2] The reader can hardly suppress the comment which Virgil does not make—that those who deal out death with so little thought for their victims are perhaps not so greatly to be pitied after all when death overtakes them too. (See Chapter 5, 'Implicit Comment'.) A flash of moonlight on the helmet Euryalus is wearing gives them away to a passing patrol of Italian cavalry. They are challenged and flee into a thicket.[3] Nisus has almost made his escape—remember that in Book 5 he had shown himself the better runner—when he stops and looks round for his companion: Euryalus is nowhere in sight. He picks his way back, guided by the uproar, to find that Euryalus, nervous, unsure of the way and laden with loot (384–5), has fallen into the hands of the enemy. He loses his head and, unable to resist the impulse to do something, throws a spear into the group killing one of the Italians;[4] he takes a second shot and strikes down a second victim. The only result is that the Italians, frustrated by an assailant whom they cannot see,

---

[1] Virgil takes the opportunity to challenge Homer's account in *Il*. 10 of the raid by Odysseus and Diomede on the horses of Rhesus.
[2] Rhamnes' *phalerae* and his swordbelt are described in detail (359–63) in preparation for the warning line (364):
        haec rapit atque umeris nequiquam fortibus aptat.
Both the *phalerae* and the helmet of Messapus are picked out in the final Tableau at the end of the Section (457–8).
[3] Observe the interplay of the narrative tenses in 371–80.
[4] In 411–15 Virgil seems to dwell on the suffering Nisus causes by his impulse to save Euryalus.

take their revenge on Euryalus. Nisus cannot endure to see his young companion killed before his eyes. He reveals himself with a cry, but it is too late: the sword has come down on Euryalus (433-7):

> uoluitur Euryalus leto pulchrosque per artus
> it cruor inque umeros ceruix conlapsa recumbit:
> purpureus ueluti cum flos succisus aratro
> languescit moriens lassoue papauera collo
> demisere caput, pluuia cum forte grauantur.[1]

*Euryalus stumbles, dead; his lovely limbs are covered
in gore and his neck slumps on his shoulders,
like some bright flower, its roots sliced off by a plough,
that goes limp as it dies, or like poppies whose heads,
weighed down by heavy rain, droop on tired necks.*

In a useless gesture of self-immolation and destruction he charges into the group to strike down the leader Volcens (who had ordered Euryalus' death), plunging his sword in Volcens' face as he is killed himself (441-5):

> instat non setius ac rotat ensem
> fulmineum, donec Rutuli clamantis in ore
> condidit aduerso et moriens animam abstulit hosti.
> tum super exanimum sese proiecit amicum
> confossus placidaque ibi demum morte quieuit.

*None the less he presses on, whirls his sword
as if it were a thunderbolt, plunges it in the Rutulian's
mouth, open in a shout, taking as he dies his enemy's life,
then hurled his transfixed body on his lifeless
friend, finding there at last the peace of death.*

The poet's promise of immortality which suspends the narrative for a moment at this point (446-9) strikes an almost openly ironical note before the final Tableau. Reaching the Italian camp, the cavalry patrol find it a scene of carnage. At the same time a crowd assembles in the camp. While they inspect the bodies of Nisus and Euryalus (454-5: *ipsa corpora*) and the wounded lying bloody on the ground, the spot-

---

[1] Virgil remembers Catullus (11.22-5) but characteristically makes the reminiscence more precise (Catullus' flower is 'touched' by the plough, Virgil's is *succisus*—'cut beneath', i.e., its roots are sliced off, but it is left standing), and adds a reminiscence of Homer (*Il.* 8.306-8). For some misdirected criticism of Virgil's simile see Robert Graves, 'The Anti-poet', in *Oxford Addresses on Poetry* (1962) 43.

Book 9

light falls on the gleaming helmet of Messapus and the *phalerae* of Rhamnes which have been recovered at such cost (457–8):

> agnoscunt spolia inter se galeamque nitentem
> Messapi et multo phaleras sudore receptas.

The third Section opens with a description of dawn in three serenely lyrical lines (459–61), introducing a Tableau (462–72) sufficiently like the opening Tableau of the second Section and the Italian advance at the beginning of the book (25–76) to emphasize how the situation has changed: the Italians advance, angry now and in a mood for battle, displaying the heads of Nisus and Euryalus fixed upon spears, while the Aeneadae receive, in a mood of gloomy resolution (471: *maesti*; 468: *duri*), this grim revelation of disaster and frustration of their hopes.

Their mood provides an effective foil to the Episode of Euryalus' mother (473–502). When the news reaches her, she throws down her spinning and runs wailing along the wall in uncomprehending, uncontrolled grief (why did her son not tell her he was going? how can she be deprived of her right to bury him?), heedless of the danger to which she exposes herself—and indeed inviting death:[1] like Aeneas after the burning of the ships (5.685–92), she invites Jove to strike her down from on high. She is led away, leaving the men shaken and with little taste for battle (499: *torpent infractae ad proelia uires*).

The siege now begins, announced by a peal of trumpets and an onomatopoeic flourish, modified from Ennius (503–4):

> at tuba terribilem sonitum procul aere canoro
> increpuit.[2]

The trumpet gave from afar its terrible, sonorous, brazen rattle.

Three short Episodes launch the narrative of the siege. First of these (503–24) is an action Tableau—a general picture of various aspects of a typical Roman siege operation, ending with glimpses of two of the Italian commanders: Mezentius, a firebrand in his hand, and Messapus, leading an attack on the *uallum*.

The next Episode (525–68) brings us back to Turnus who again leads the attack. Here the narrative is more detailed and is introduced

---

[1] For the death wish see Chapter 1.
[2] Ennius (143W) went a little too far for Virgil:
> at tuba terribili sonitu taratantara dixit.

by a short formal invocation. Turnus sets fire to one of the Trojan towers and it crashes forward, spilling out the defenders in it. Only two escape unmaimed, and the remainder of the Episode highlights the different reactions of these two when confronted with Turnus: the courageous bastard Helenor surrenders to the Heroic Impulse, like a wild animal that rushes at the hunters who have trapped it (545–55); Lycus runs away, but Turnus contemptuously snatches him from the wall as he is trying to scale it, like an eagle seizing its prey (556–68). Observe how vivid this scene is made to appear to the reader; yet only two killings are described, and each time more space is devoted to the simile than to direct narrative of the fighting.

In the next Episode (569–89), the scene shifts to the main gate of the camp, where we see eleven Trojans and Italians fall in rapid succession; the manner of death of three of the first four is tersely described, the last seven—Trojans killed by Turnus—are a string of names. The narrative then slows down to highlight the death of one Italian and one Trojan. Privernus is the Italian (576–80): a spear grazes his left side; unthinking he drops his shield and claps his hand to the wound— and an arrow pins the hand to his flank before biting its way deep into his body.[1] The Trojan is the son of Arcens. Virgil's technique this time is more elaborate: first he describes the appearance of the son of Arcens—his bright, rust-coloured, embroidered cloak, his striking features; next he gives a thumbnail biographical sketch (583–5); finally we see Mezentius dispatch him with a spectacular sling shot (586–9).

After these three battle scenes comes an Episode (Ascanius' first feat of arms) which falls outside the main narrative framework, rather as the account of the death of Priam falls outside the main narrative framework of Book 2—in both cases the actual event is narrated in the ordinary way, and then recapitulated in detail. Ascanius' victim is Turnus' brother-in-law Numanus, also called Remulus. Coming out in front of the other Italians, Numanus harangues the besieged Trojans in what Virgil calls a speech to be proud of in part and in part to be ashamed of (595–6: *digna atque indigna relatu uociferans*). In it he describes with pride the tough, simple life of the Italians (602–13):

---

[1] Housman's recasting of line 579, *et laeuo infixa est alte lateri* (adopted by Mackail), which removes *manus* and keeps *sagitta* the subject, is a remarkable example of Housman's misplaced ingenuity. One recalls Housman's own remark about those who timidly meddle with what they might, without rashness, have left alone. The only excuse for meddling with the line is the change of subject, but this is a Virgilian mannerism.

Book 9

'non hic Atridae nec fandi fictor Ulixes:
durum a stirpe genus natos ad flumina primum
deferimus saeuoque gelu duramus et undis;
uenatu inuigilant pueri siluasque fatigant,
flectere ludus equos et spicula tendere cornu.
at patiens operum paruoque adsueta iuuentus
aut rastris terram domat aut quatit oppida bello.
omne aeuum ferro teritur uersaque iuuencum
terga fatigamus hasta. nec tarda senectus
debilitat uiris animi mutatque uigorem:
canitiem galea premimus semperque recentis
comportare iuuat praedas et uiuere rapto.'

*'There are no Atrid brothers here, no false-tongued Ulysses.
A tough race by birth, we take our sons down to the river
and toughen them in the harsh chill of its waters.
Tireless hunters, our boys do not let the forests rest;
horsemanship is their play and the practice of archery.
They become men able to endure work and live on little,
who rake and tame the land, strike fear into towns in war.
We at no time quit our swords, with spears reversed
we belabour the oxen's backs. Old age does not slow us,
weakens not our strength of spirit nor our vigour;
we press our grey hairs into the helmet, ever glad to bring
home the freshly-won prize and to live by pillage.'*

With this picture of the simple life, reminiscent of Lucretius' picture of primitive society in Book 5 of the *De Rerum Natura*, Numanus contrasts the effeminacy of the Trojans (614–20). But one suspects that his contempt for the refinements of civilization was meant by Virgil to strike his contemporaries as doubled-edged.[1] Ascanius, with Jove's assistance, sends an arrow through his head, and Apollo then intervenes, praises Ascanius for his achievement and advises him to take no further part in the battle. It is not easy for the modern reader to feel sympathetic towards this flight of patriotic fancy, but we must remember the context is a fantastic one; despite the recurring concentrated realism, the atmosphere of magic is never absent in Virgil's narrative of the siege.[2]

---

[1] The word *desidiae* (615) was one much bandied about by the elegiac poets in self-defence of their sophisticated abandonment of the typical Roman way of life.

[2] Mackail (p. 335) is unfair. He complains, among other things, of the undue length of the Episode, not allowing that 23 of the 82 lines are taken up with Numanus' speech, which it would be a pity to miss.

The Twelve Books

Ascanius' exploit and Apollo's spectacular departure (656–60) put fresh heart into the Trojans (661–71), and the twin giants Pandarus and Bitias, tall as the fir-trees or the mountains of their native country, surrendering to the Heroic Impulse, throw open the gate they had been told to guard and stand on either side of the entrance, bristling with arms and inviting battle—they are like twin towers, or twin oaks that rear their shaggy heads on either side of a river (672–82):

> Pandarus et Bitias, Idaeo Alcanore creti,
> quos Iouis eduxit luco siluestris Iaera
> abietibus iuuenes patriis et montibus aequos,
> portam, quae ducis imperio commissa, recludunt,
> freti armis, ultroque inuitant moenibus hostem.
> ipsi intus dextra ac laeua pro turribus astant,
> armati ferro et cristis capita alta corusci:
> quales aeriae liquentia flumina circum,
> siue Padi ripis Athesim seu propter amoenum,
> consurgunt geminae quercus intonsaque caelo
> attollunt capita et sublimi uertice nutant.

Literal-minded commentators have been troubled by what seems to them Virgil's irresponsible exaggeration, disliking the comparison of the two giants twice to trees and once to mountains.[1] Two points are worth making. First, the scene is one of fantasy, and the fantasy is maintained—compare the description of the death of Bitias (703–16), especially the concluding simile. Second, the comparisons purport to record the reactions to the great size of the two giants of the narrator projected into his own narrative (see Chapter 3): they are the subjective utterances of an excited spectator, not the accurate objective statements of a detached narrator.

The news that the gate is open quickly brings Turnus. On arrival he kills Antiphates, who is allotted a Vignette (696–701), then three more Trojans before he reaches Bitias and strikes him down with a mighty sling shot that sends Bitias crashing to the ground with his great shield reverberating on top of him, gigantic in death as in life (703–16).

---

[1] Mackail remarks on 9.674:

The exaggeration of *et montibus aequos* is unpleasant, and the more so that Virgil returns from it to the comparison of the warriors with trees. The suggestion made by Jacob Bryant to Heyne that it should be altered to *in montibus* is very attractive, and we may all agree in Heyne's comment, 'ita utique malim Virgilium scripsisse'. There is, however, a similar exaggeration in *haud partem exiguam montis* of the stone used as a missile by Acmon x. 128.

Book 9

The Trojans retreat in panic. Pandarus gets the gate closed again, but in the confusion no one notices until it is too late that Turnus has been shut inside the camp; he confronts them, a terrible figure of fire and thunder, shield flashing, on his head a blood-red crest (731-3):

> continuo noua lux oculis effulsit et arma
> horrendum sonuere; tremunt in uertice cristae
> sanguineae, clipeoque micantia fulmina mittit.

Pandarus rushes at him, but is no match for Turnus; his death is related with traditional Homeric fullness, including the heroic exchange before the first blow (735-55).

As the Trojans flee in terror, it is Turnus' opportunity—he has only to open the gates and let the Italians in; but the lust for slaughter drives him on heedless of his opportunity.[1] He kills twelve Trojans, merely named or briefly described, till we come to the last, the martial poet Cretheus—a sort of Trojan Alcaeus (774-7):

> ... et amicum Crethea Musis,
> Crethea Musarum comitem, cui carmina semper
> et citharae cordi numerosque intendere neruis:
> semper equos atque arma uirum pugnasque canebat.

> ... *also Cretheus, friend of the Muses,*
> *Cretheus, the Muses' companion, ever concerned with song,*
> *and with fitting verses to the strings of his lyres:*
> *his poetry was all of horses and battles and fighting.*

Mnestheus rallies the Trojans and they gradually force Turnus back; fourteen heavily-moving lines (788-801) describe his reluctant retreat. Then Juno is forced by Jove to withdraw her support (802-4), and the book ends with an exciting, fast-moving Tableau—fourteen separate statements with no subordinate clause—describing Turnus' stubborn stand, till at last he turns and plunges into the Tiber, to emerge on the other side cleansed of the slaughter he has wrought (806-18—these lines are discussed in Chapter 6).

One function of Book 9 is to load the scales evenly, without doing this too obviously. Our sympathies are all for Nisus and Euryalus and we are properly filled with horror when the Italians fix their heads to stakes and carry them like standards as they advance (465-7). Yet we saw Nisus and Euryalus behave with equal callousness during their passage through the Italian camp. Another function of the book is to

---

[1] See Chapter 1.

make us feel how much the Aeneadae depend on Aeneas. But this is a vivid, exciting book, whose qualities far outrun its structural usefulness, a mixture of psychological insight, poetic fancy, narrative pathos and horror; it deserves a high place among the twelve.

BOOK 10

Book 10 represents the crisis of Books 7 to 12. The fighting which had begun the previous day at 9.459 is reduced temporarily to deadlock until the return of Aeneas with reinforcements and the establishment of a beachhead in the Italian rear.

At 10.362 the battle begins in which the blockade of the Trojan camp is broken by Aeneas, following the death of Pallas.

The events of the third Section really decide the issue of the war: the day's fighting ends with the death of Mezentius and the humiliation of Turnus; at the beginning of Book 11 we shall see the Italians anxious for peace—the flare-up at 11.445 is a senseless return of war hysteria.

The narrative of the battle (Sections II and III) is organized around the deaths of three important characters, Pallas, Lausus and Mezentius. Pallas is the first to be killed. His death turns the battle for Aeneas into a mad pursuit of personal revenge culminating in the death of Lausus. Finally, in the concluding lines of the book, Aeneas kills Mezentius.

I
1–361

Prologue—Council of the Gods:
  (i) Jove—Venus—Juno—Jove 1–117
The Return of Aeneas:
  (ii) Attack on Trojan camp resumed 118–145
  (iii) Aeneas on his way 146–162
Catalogue of Etruscan ships 163–214
  (iv) The nymphs 215–255
  (v) Aeneas arrives 256–307
  (vi) Struggle for a beachhead 308–361

II
362–605

The Battle—First Phase:
The death of Pallas:
  (i) Pallas rallies the Arcadians 362–425
  (ii) Pallas resisted by Lausus 426–438
  (iii) Pallas killed by Turnus 439–509
  (iv) Aeneas runs amuck 510–605

Book 10

III
606–908
	Interlude:
	  (i) Jove–Juno
	  (ii) Turnus spirited away
	The Battle—Second Phase:
	The death of Lausus:
	  (iii) Mezentius assumes command
	  (iv) Mezentius meets Aeneas A; Aeneas kills Lausus
	The death of Mezentius:
	  (v) Mezentius by the river
	  (vi) Mezentius meets Aeneas B; death of Mezentius
		606–632
		633–688
		
		689–761
		
		762–832
		
		833–870
		
		870–908

Virgil's divine Council of War, the only one in the poem, is a synthesis of four Homeric precedents (*Iliad* 4.1–72; 8.1–40; 15.1–167; 20.1–40). Yet it strikes the modern reader as a curiously inadequate prologue to a book which is structurally so important and in some respects the finest in the poem. We are not greatly upset by the ironical delineation of Venus and Juno; their bickering, their limited insight into the forces of destiny, are consistent with the way they are drawn in the rest of the poem; one function, plainly, of the prologue is to provide light relief, and a second to express Virgil's adherence to his Homeric form. What troubles us is the feeling that the prologue appears to have a third function: despite the bickering and the banter, something important, apparently, is decided and it is hard to see what.

The prologue begins quite grandly (1–5):

> Panditur interea domus omnipotentis Olympi
> conciliumque uocat diuum pater atque hominum rex
> sideream in sedem, terras unde arduus omnis
> castraque Dardanidum aspectat populosque Latinos.
> considunt tectis bipatentibus, incipit ipse.

> *Meanwhile almighty Jove's house is opened wide,*
> *the father of gods and king of men summons a council*
> *to his starry seat, whence he gazes down on all*
> *the earth, the Trojan camp and the Latin peoples.*
> *They sit in the palace that looks two ways. Jove himself begins.*

Yet already in Jove's opening speech things start to go wrong. How can he claim he forbade the war in Italy (8: *abnueram bello Italiam concurrere Teucris*) when at 1.263 he spoke of the war as part of fate's plan—as did the Sibyl at 6.86–97, not to mention Helenus and

The Twelve Books

Anchises? When he goes on to argue that the proper time to fight (11: *iustum pugnae tempus*) is not now, but in the coming war with Carthage, and that then hatred and rapine will be legitimate (14), this sounds like the sort of historical epic we believed Virgil determined not to write. The long, partisan summaries of the situation by Venus and Juno which follow are comparatively innocuous—they resemble the speeches Thucydides puts in the mouths of leading characters at an important juncture. We can even sympathize with Venus when, more moved by thoughts of her son's safety than the prospect of glory, she pleads to be allowed to remove him to one of her sanctuaries, where he can live in obscurity and retirement (52–3):

> 'positis inglorius armis
> exigat hic aeuum.'

But when Jove rises to pronounce judgment, a sudden solemn note (101–3) prompts us to attach weight to what he says, and this is confirmed by his actual words, and by what follows (113–17). What we are to make of his speech is by no means clear, however. After some pompous beating about the bush (104–11), Jove assumes a businesslike tone. He makes the intriguing pronouncement that 'the course of action embarked on by each man will decide what he must endure and whether he is to be lucky or unlucky' (111–12: *sua cuique exorsa laborem fortunamque ferent*). He backs this up with a reaffirmation of what he has said already at line 108: in the coming battle he will remain impartial (112: *rex Iuppiter omnibus idem*—a final reproof to the rival goddesses, rather than an echo of Zeus' edict of non-intervention in *Iliad* 8.5–17). Finally, he declares that, however things turn out, 'fate will find a way' (113: *fata uiam inuenient*—the phrase Helenus used in his prophecy to Aeneas, 3.395).

In themselves, the ideas are neither hard, nor inconsistent with the way the poem appears to work. They are expressed, however, with an involved, tortured compression that seems to invite closer scrutiny. Does Jove mean, we wonder, that today is somehow a special day, one on which men are freer than usual? The answer is almost certainly No. Jove's speech is better regarded as primarily an assertion that the story of Turnus, and to a lesser extent the stories of Pallas, Lausus and Mezentius (Aeneas is less easily fitted into the pattern) will be worked out upon tragic lines: each, by being himself, will bring about his own fate. (See Chapter 5, 'Tragic Attitude'.) To this a fresh dimension is added by an assertion of the Stoic belief that whatever men do will

Book 10

prove to subserve the plan of fate. Naturally, such an overriding pattern should not be imprinted too plainly upon events.

At 118 we return to earth and the beleaguered, dispirited Trojan camp for a short Episode that is apt to look pointless, since nothing happens in it. Its function is to provide a recapitulatory glimpse of the Trojans, back where they were at 9.468–72 before the ill-considered sortie of Pandarus and Bitias let Turnus within the camp and nearly brought certain disaster upon them. Virgil wants us to sense the Trojans' mood of helpless depression, so that Aeneas' imminent arrival with reinforcements, to which we pass at 146, will be dramatically more effective. But if this Episode, the function of which is to underline the stalemate reached, is to have some weight, it must also have some length; at the same time it must not include any important action to disturb our feeling that all depends on the return of Aeneas. So, after the opening Tableau, Virgil resorts to a string of Trojan names—individuals picked out from among the defenders (lightly sketched in at 130–1) who ring the walls of the camp. The list is relieved by two short action shots (at 127–8 the giant Acmon strains to lift a huge rock; at 139–42 Ismarus tips his arrows with poison). The whole passage is built round a central 7-line Tableau of Ascanius, the acting commander, conspicuous because of his fair skin and his long, flowing hair. What action there is in this scene (the Trojans are doing their best to repel the attackers) is underplayed.

At 146 the scene shifts away from the Trojan camp to Aeneas. We move back first of all to the previous night and then, in an explanatory parenthesis (148–56), to a quick summary of what has been going on since we left him at the end of Book 8: on leaving Evander he made his way to seek aid from the Etruscan king, Tarchon; realizing that Aeneas is the foreign leader foretold in the prophecy related by Evander to Aeneas at 8.497–513, Tarchon at once entrusts his fleet to him. After this summary comes a Vignette: Aeneas sits in the leading ship, preoccupied with thoughts of war, while Pallas at his side plies him with a youngster's questions about the stars, about landmarks that loom out of the night, and about Aeneas' adventures on land and sea (159–62):

> hic magnus sedet Aeneas secumque uolutat
> euentus belli uarios, Pallasque sinistro
> adfixus lateri iam quaerit sidera, opacae
> noctis iter, iam quae passus terraque marique.

The Twelve Books

One function of this moving little Vignette is to fix the dramatic moment at the end of the recapitulation, for this is the moment we shall come back to at line 215 after a bravura Hellenistic passage of 52 lines, beginning (after a short invocation) with a formal catalogue of the ships under Aeneas' command, and ending on the same formal note in a 2-line tailpiece (213–14). For as the catalogue progresses, full scope is given to the play of the intellect upon this simple theme. After a paragraph in which four Etruscan captains and the 3,200 men under their command are set out in the traditional manner, the fun begins at 185. A fifth captain, Cinyrus, is quickly disposed of, in order to focus attention on the sixth, Cupauo. The plumes on his helmet recall the legendary story of his father. In a flash we are in the middle of that story: Cycnus, out of grief for Phaethon whom he loved, while singing of his sad love beside Phaethon's sisters Phaethusa and Lampetia (who had been turned into poplars) was himself turned into an elderly swan and sailed into the air still singing (189–93). At 194 we come back to his son Cupauo and the great ship Centaur which he commands. And then the fireworks begin again. Intellectual irony intensifies the animation of a charming, vivid Vignette, in which the ship (it had a centaur as its figurehead) becomes itself a centaur for a moment, towering over the water and threatening the waves with a great rock—and then a ship again, ploughing the deep water with its long keel (195–7):

> ingentem remis Centaurum promouet: ille
> instat aquae saxumque undis immane minatur
> arduus, et longa sulcat maria alta carina.[1]

Virgil now plays this trick on us a second and a third time. But, as the next captain is Ocnus, the founder of Mantua, he pauses for a short eulogy of his own birthplace, before bringing us back to the Etruscan fleet with these hair-raisingly ingenious lines (204–6):

> hinc quoque quingentos in se Mezentius armat,
> quos patre Benaco uelatus harundine glauca
> Mincius infesta ducebat in aequora pinu.

From here also Mezentius arms five hundred against himself;
these Mincius, decked in grey-green reeds, was leading
from his father Benacus to the sea on war-like ship.

[1] For *minari* with accusative and dative see Lewis and Short II A β. Mackail wrongly takes *saxum* as the subject of *minatur*.

Book 10

Mezentius is said to arm the five hundred men of Mantua against himself because it is their hatred of Mezentius that has caused them to rally to the standard of Aeneas. Their ship is called the Mincius, but Mincius is also the river which flows past Mantua (since the Mincius has its source in Lake Benacus, the modern Lago di Garda, the river can be described as descended from his father Benacus). Equally Mincius is the god of the river, and the representation of the god which serves as the ship's figurehead. All four, the ship, the river, the god and the figurehead were leading (206: *ducebat*) the men of Mantua down to the sea from father Benacus.[1] Finally the spotlight rests on Aulestes abroad his great ship, the Triton. His rowers move so completely as one man that Aulestes himself is described as beating the waters with a hundred oars on either side. And Triton is, of course, both the figurehead of the ship threatening the sea with its great blue conch, and the living Triton, down to his flanks a shaggy human figure swimming in the water, the rest a sea-monster; beneath his semi-bestial breast the waves foam and roar (209–12):

> hunc uehit immanis Triton et caerula concha
> exterrens freta, cui laterum tenus hispida nanti
> frons hominem praefert, in pristim desinit aluus,
> spumea semifero sub pectore murmurat unda.[2]

By 215 night has long fallen on the armada which is now well on its way (under sail—see 218—whereas in the action shot of Aulestes they were still using their oars). The flashback is over and we are back in the scene we left at 162.[3] One function of the atmosphere of ironical fantasy created in the preceding lines is to prepare the reader for a

---

[1] It involves a needless introduction of geographical problems to ask how the men of Mantua could sail all the way from the Lago di Garda to the Etruscan sea.

[2] Of these eight Etruscan captains, only Abas (10.427), Asilas (11.620, 12.127 and 550) and Aulestes (killed at 12.289) are heard of again. Abas was also the name of a Trojan captain, presumably drowned with his ship at 1.121, whose shield (in that case a shield he had captured from the Greeks) was dedicated by Aeneas at Actium at 3.286. But one can never be sure to what extent Virgil is prepared for this kind of detective work. Tarchon, the Etruscan commander-in-chief, is not included in the catalogue.

[3] Failure to understand the flashback technique of 146–214 has caused some confusion. Büchner, p. 1411, maintains that the repeated description of Aeneas steering his ship is unparalleled and therefore inadmissible—apparently forgetting that we have the same technique and a similar double picture of Ariadne in Catullus Poem 64.

The Twelve Books

final challenge to his imagination. As Aeneas sails through the moon-lit night, he is met by the ships of his own fleet transformed by the great earth mother at 9.116–17 into sea nymphs. They now come dancing round his ship (224) and one of them, Cymodocea (she is a better talker than the rest—225: *fandi doctissima*), holding on to Aeneas' ship with one hand and paddling gently with the other, warns him to crowd on sail (229: *uelis immitte rudentis*), explaining who she and her companions are and the danger that lies ahead. Her warning complete, she sends Aeneas' ship on its way with an expert thrust (247: *haud ignara modi*) and she and her companions race off while the bewildered Aeneas pulls himself together for a prayer of thanks to the great earth mother.[1] This charming piece of whimsy has disturbed commentators who have not observed how well it is matched to its context, or understood what Virgil has achieved by the elaborately ingenious and highly artificial sequence of scenes which it concludes.[2] The sequence has two functions. The first is concerned with structure: Aeneas (and the great force he brings with him from Etruria) must not be produced out of a hat to save the Trojan camp. A feeling that they are on their way has to be given time to establish itself, a mood of suspense has to be created, so that the excitement and relief produced by their arrival can be shared by the reader. The second function is a matter of tone. At 256 a narrative of war and bloodshed begins that continues unbroken for 350 lines (until the spiriting away of Turnus at 606). If some of the atmosphere of magic and fantasy created in the hundred lines just concluded can overlie the battle-scenes to come, it will help to emphasize their essential *un*reality; the reader might otherwise suppose he was meant to take the battle-scenes at their face value.

Dawn breaks at 256 as Aeneas and the Etruscans, armed for battle, arrive in sight of the Trojan camp. Standing high on the stern of his ship, Aeneas raises the magic shield which his divine mother had given him at 8.616. A great shout arises from the walls of the camp, and the Trojans, their morale restored, launch a hail of fire at their besiegers; stretching forward to hurl their spears, and shouting as they do so, they are like a flight of squawking cranes sweeping through a sky black with clouds before an approaching storm (262–6):

---

[1] The great earth mother had been worshipped in Rome since the second Punic War. She perhaps helps to make the Phrygians sound less alien.

[2] The sequence should be compared to the interlude in Book 4: 4.173–278—also about 100 lines.

Book 10

        clamorem ad sidera tollunt
Dardanidae e muris, spes addita suscitat iras,
tela manu iaciunt, quales sub nubibus atris
Strymoniae dant signa grues atque aethera tranant
cum sonitu, fugiuntque Notos clamore secundo.

Turnus and the other Italian leaders turn round in astonishment to see the whole sea swimming with ships; Aeneas, like a blood-red comet in the night, or the sinister star Sirius, that spells fever and disease for mankind, dominates the scene; fire pours from his magic helmet and shield. The quality of the poetry, the magical setting which precedes, ensure that what we might otherwise take for rhetorical exaggeration is taken in the true spirit of fairy-tale: Aeneas' helmet and shield *do* vomit fire.[1]

In the narrative of the landing the spotlight falls alternately on Aeneas and Turnus. First Aeneas (256–75, with a glance at Turnus, 267–9). Next we see Turnus rallying his men in preparation for a rush to the beach as Aeneas and the Etruscans attempt to land (276–86). Then in 287–307 our attention is focused on Aeneas and Tarchon: Aeneas attempts an organized, disciplined landing; Tarchon flings his squadron on to a stretch of beach where the sea is less rough, losing his own ship in the process. Note the effective, terse, exciting, *realistic* descriptive writing in these 21 lines—there is no reason why parts of a fairy-tale should not be realistic. Excitement is not easily produced solely by an appeal to the imagination; it depends also on the graphic representation of things within our experience.

The battle to establish a beachhead now begins (308). Our attention is switched to Turnus as he rushes his men to meet the enemy. Aeneas rapidly dispatches a series of opponents, and at once stylization and poetry take the place of realism. A short Vignette makes each of Aeneas' first five victims sound strange or exciting: Thero, the giant; Lichas, who was cut from the body of his dead mother; Cisseus and Gyas, who wield the clubs their father had as a present from Hercules; Pharus, who is killed by a javelin that lodges in his mouth as he shouts his battle-cry. Aeneas is about to strike down a sixth opponent (Cydon—also economically picked out, 325–7), when the seven sons of Phorcus spring to the Italian's aid. Aeneas kills three of them, and then our attention is diverted by the arrival of three of the Italian

---

[1] Whereas Achilles' breastplate merely gleams as he rushes to meet Hector (*Il.* 22.25–32). For the star and the comet see Otis, p. 355.

The Twelve Books

leaders described in the catalogue at the end of Book 7 (7.707 ff., 723 ff. and 691 ff.): Clausus (345), Halaesus (352) and Messapus (354). The struggle for a beachhead begins in earnest and, after a simile in which the emotions of the men fighting are transferred to a gathering storm (one hears the roar of the wind, but all is motionless), three sinewy, ruggedly rhythmical lines sum up the deadlock, the Vignette stylized by the epic cliché with which it concludes (354–61):

> expellere tendunt
> nunc hi, nunc illi: certatur limine in ipso
> Ausoniae. magno discordes aethere uenti
> proelia ceu tollunt animis et uiribus aequis;
> non ipsi inter se, non nubila, non mare cedit;
> anceps pugna diu, stant obnixa omnia contra:
> haud aliter Troianae acies aciesque Latinae
> concurrunt, haeret pede pes densusque uiro uir.[1]

> *Each side strains*
> *to drive the other back. At Italy's very door the battle*
> *rages. Just as when high in the sky quarrelling winds*
> *contend, each as brave, each as strong, neither*
> *budging—nor does cloud or ocean budge:*
> *so the Trojan and the Latin battle-lines*
> *engage, foot pressed on foot, man packed against man.*

At 362 our attention is turned to the Arcadian cavalry contingent, and the battle proper and our second Section begin. These are the men who had set out with Aeneas and Pallas at 8.585 for Etruria; when Pallas and Aeneas came south with the Etruscan fleet, the Arcadian cavalry, reinforced by Etruscan cavalry, made the journey overland, reaching the Trojan camp (as we learnt from Cymodocea at 10.238–40) just before Aeneas.[2] They have had to bear the brunt of the Italian attack and have been driven into an area littered with rocks and brushwood uprooted by the river (362–3, presumably the flood area of the Tiber near its mouth). Their objective no doubt was to join forces with the landing party, but on this rough ground they have had to dismount and their morale has suffered as a consequence.

---

[1] For the cliché see Chapter 6, 'Ennius and the Old Poets'.
[2] Mackail's complaint (p. 374) of inconsistency is unfounded and his assumption that the Arcadian cavalry are separated from the landing troops by the Italian force mistaken. The camp is ringed round with besiegers, but the landing force under Aeneas and the cavalry contingent meet outside the ring. Pallas is therefore free to rejoin his cavalry on landing.

Book 10

Taking in the situation as he lands, Pallas rushes to assume command of his fellow-countrymen, rallies them with a typical Roman general's *contio*, and then hurls himself at the enemy. It is Pallas' first experience of action (see 508), but he quickly dispatches half a dozen Italians—two of them twins, one of whom he leaves decapitated, the other with the fingers of his amputated right hand still twitching (390–6; for a discussion of the passage and the significance of this gruesome detail see Chapter 3, Section II). Rhoeteus meets his death by accident (399–404), kicking his native soil with his heels as he dies—a second grisly touch; next Halaesus (already glimpsed at 352) meets his fated end: it had been foretold that he would die by the arms of Evander—which Pallas is wearing (411–25).[1]

Lausus steps into the breach. Virgil does not remind us who he is—he relies on us to recall the son of Mezentius who deserved a better father at 7.649–54. His first victim is Abas, one of the Etruscan captains (see 170), so presumably Pallas has now been joined by the main body. When Lausus kills this tough fighter (428: *pugnae nodumque moramque*) a rout ensues that brings Lausus and Pallas face to face—both young and handsome, neither destined to see home again (433–6):

> hinc Pallas instat et urget,
> hinc contra Lausus, nec multum discrepat aetas,
> egregii forma, sed quis Fortuna negarat
> in patriam reditus.

The comment is designed to emphasize their parallel destinies, for the parallelism is important to the structure of this Section, and also to establish Lausus in our minds in preparation for his big scene (790–832). Another comment follows: Pallas and Lausus are not to be allowed to join battle—a greater foe awaits each (436–8). (See Chapter 5, 'Tragic Suspense'.)

Pallas has not long to wait. Turnus rushes up in his chariot to help Lausus, takes in the situation, and shouts to his followers that he will attend to Pallas, adding a characteristic piece of braggadocio (442–3):

> 'solus ego in Pallanta feror; soli mihi Pallas
> debetur; cuperem ipse parens spectator adesset.'

> '*I go alone to meet Pallas; Pallas is mine
> alone; I wish his father were here to watch.*'

---

[1] In 412 *seque in sua colligit arma* is possibly ambiguous: (1) 'Halaesus braced himself behind his defensive armour'; (2) 'he launched himself against the arms of Evander and met his fate'.

It is all quickly over, but the narrative occupies some forty-five lines —each step is carefully and vividly described. First the Italians withdraw, leaving Turnus in his chariot in the middle of an open space (444). Pallas, who has heard Turnus' words (as 445 and 448 show), stops short, looks his opponent over from a distance undaunted (447: *truci uisu*), makes his response to the challenge ('death or glory—my father can cope with either'), and advances into the arena. The Arcadians' blood chills as Turnus jumps from his chariot—a lion matched against a bull. A simple exchange of spears decides matters. Pallas prays to his protector Hercules for victory ('let Turnus see me strip his bloody armour from his dying frame') as he makes his throw. Hercules weeps at the words, and is consoled by his father Jove—'all men are fated to die; Turnus' hour too is near at hand' (464–73). Pallas' aim is good, but his spear merely grazes Turnus (474–8). Turnus takes his time, then his answering throw whistles through the air. It hurtles through Pallas' shield to find its mark. Pallas rips the spear from his chest: his life-blood follows it and he falls upon his wound with a crash of armour (479–89).

Observe that, however much we pity Pallas, he met his death in fair fight matched against an antagonist he hoped he might beat, as the metaphor of the lion and the bull (454–6) suggests. Though the weaker (cf. 11.174), he is no weakling. If he had won, he would have shown no more thought for his victim than Turnus does now (462–3). It is a nice thrust: Virgil makes us feel that pity for Pallas is an inadequate response—just as Pallas' unthinking, heroic courage is an inadequate response. Naturally Virgil does not elaborate the point: he exploits instead the epic conventions, which rule out moral evaluations except those of the most incidental kind; he could not easily have said explicitly, anyway, what his verse prepares us to see for ourselves (see Chapter 5, 'Implicit Comment').

Standing over the body, Turnus turns to Pallas' men (491–5):

> 'Arcades, haec' inquit 'memores mea dicta referte
> Euandro: qualem meruit, Pallanta remitto.
> quisquis honos tumuli, quidquid solamen humandi est,
> largior. haud illi stabunt Aeneia paruo
> hospitia.'

> '*Arcadians,*' he said, '*mark the message you shall take
> Evander: I restore Pallas in the condition he has asked for.
> Such honour, such comfort as grave and burial bring*

Book 10

I make him present of: he will have to pay dear for friendship with Aeneas.'

Some would make Pallas the subject of *meruit*, but that is poor sense and contrary to the spirit of the passage. Turnus' jibe is directed at Evander—if he didn't want his son killed, he should have kept him at home. They are cruel words, but they are addressed to an old enemy (for the enmity between Evander and the Latins, see 8.55 and 8.146–7) and both words and action show more feeling (however ironically expressed) than we find in Homer's heroes.

Turnus then places his foot on the body and rips from it Pallas' heavy, ornamented belt. Virgil suggests it is covetousness rather than contempt that prompts the action (see 500). None the less Turnus has gone too far (502). The time will come when Turnus will repent this day (505: *oderit*). (For a discussion of these lines see Chapter 5, 'Tragic Attitude'; see also conclusion of Analysis of Book 12.) The Episode ends with a short Tableau: the Arcadians, grief-stricken, carry Pallas off on his shield; their only consolation is the thought of the carnage he wrought among the Italians on his first and last day in battle (508–9).[1]

We come now to Aeneas' reaction to the death of Pallas (510–601).[2] Something has been said in Chapter 1 of the significance of this Episode, which has shocked more than one of Virgil's commentators.[3] Let us now try to fix more precisely the nature of Aeneas' reaction, the response to it that Virgil wishes to elicit from his readers, and how he goes about securing the effect he wants.

R. S. Conway was perhaps the first to stress how the death of Pallas

---

[1] Line 509 is surely an ironic echo of Cymodocea's words to Aeneas at 245.

[2] How does Aeneas learn of Pallas' death? All Virgil says is (510–12):

> nec iam fama mali tanti, sed certior auctor
> aduolat Aeneae tenui discrimine leti
> esse suos, uersis tempus succurrere Teucris.

Is the *certior auctor* the spectacle of Pallas' body borne on the shoulders of his comrades? Compare the way Mezentius learns of Lausus' death, 841–3.

[3] Mackail (p. lxvi) says of Aeneas' decision (announced at 519) to sacrifice live prisoners:

> Of this shocking order ... one can only say that it is Virgil's single lapse into barbarism, and think or hope that the lines might have been cancelled in his final revision.

C. M. Bowra, 'Aeneas and the Stoic ideal', *GR* 3 (1933–4) 8–21, claims Aeneas' pursuit of revenge is an illustration of the Augustan ideal of anger as a legitimate passion—the antithesis of the orthodox Stoic view, from which Bowra maintains the Augustans openly deviated. If this was the Augustan view, I should prefer to say that Virgil here rejects it.

touches off emotions which transform Aeneas' attitude to the fighting.[1] The battle becomes a personal vendetta, and in his pursuit of Turnus Aeneas strikes down all in his path as he ranges back and forth through the enemy line (513–15):

> proxima quaeque metit gladio latumque per agmen
> ardens limitem agit ferro, te, Turne, superbum
> caede noua quaerens.

His fierce onslaught is opportune, for the death of Pallas started a rout (512). As a result of Aeneas' intervention the rout is checked and the blockade of the Trojan camp is lifted (604–5). But we are told this incidentally at the end of the Episode, almost as though the fact escaped Aeneas' notice. It will not be the only occasion in the war when the right end is attained for the wrong reasons. Aeneas behaves with a new ruthlessness: the sense of *caede noua quaerens*[2] is fixed by *ardens* (514, cf. 552: *ardenti*) and by *furit* (545, cf. 604: *furens*): Aeneas blazes with a mad anger that at first causes him to kill indiscriminately (513: *proxima quaeque metit gladio*) as though oblivious of his actions (see 515–17 and the comment on these lines in Chapter 1). And when the first blind frenzy passes, he descends to a vow of calculated, bloodthirsty vengeance: he will sacrifice at Pallas' funeral eight prisoners whom he has taken alive (nor does Aeneas back down on this—see 11.81–2). Throughout the Episode Aeneas treats his victims with a mixture of contempt and bitterness (556: *inimico pectore*; 591: *dictis amaris*). He is a sombre embodiment of death striding over the battlefield—across the priest of Apollo and Diana, Haemonides, a shining figure of light, falls the gigantic shadow of the assailant who has struck him down (537–41):

> nec procul Haemonides, Phoebi Triuiaeque sacerdos,
> infula cui sacra redimibat tempora uitta,

---

[1] R. S. Conway, 'Vergil's creative art', *Proc. Brit. Acad.* 17 (1931) 28–9:
So far as I know no commentator has yet realized ... the complete difference which the death of Pallas makes in Aeneas ...; he takes the offensive with fury, ... is merciless to his opponents, overwhelming one after the other, giving no quarter, and taunting them with their defeat, in the fashion of the Homeric warriors; ... and at the end Vergil compares the madness of his rage to that of a torrent or a whirlwind. This is the only place in the *Aeneid* in which the word *furens* ('raving') is applied to its hero.

[2] In *caede noua* we have an example of syntactical ambiguity (see Chapter 6): taken with *superbum*, it applies to Turnus (he is proud of his recent killing of Pallas); taken with *quaerens*, it applies to Aeneas (he seeks out Turnus with a display of slaughter not yet witnessed).

Book 10

totus conlucens ueste atque insignibus armis:
quem congressus agit campo, lapsumque superstans
immolat ingentique umbra tegit.

Only before Lausus' splendid, youthful courage does Aeneas hesitate; he tries to brush Lausus aside with a brusque warning (810: *increpitat ... minatur*); then, when the youngster stands his ground (as Pallas did when confronted with Turnus), he kills him in a fresh flood of anger (813–14: *saeuae iamque altius irae Dardanio surgunt*). The killing of Lausus, though it forms a separate Episode structurally, is the dramatic conclusion of Aeneas' fugue.

Killing in anger is common enough in war—today as in the Heroic Age; so too are lust for revenge, striking down victims who plead for mercy, the murder of prisoners as a reprisal (Achilles in *Iliad* 21.26–8 selects twelve live victims to be sacrificed in return for the death of Patroclus. But Virgil writes for readers who, while aware that such things (even perhaps the sacrifice of live prisoners[1]) are part of the horror of war, must take a different view of them from an audience in heroic times; they cannot see Aeneas, a character so drawn as to elicit their sympathy for him as a human being, sink to this level without discomfort and regret.

As in Book 4, we feel Virgil has pulled his hero wholly out of his heroic context, in order to invite us to assess his conduct by the standards of contemporary civilized men.[2] In neither case, naturally, should we allow sentimentality to condemn Aeneas out of hand. His wild pursuit of vengeance after the death of Pallas is as credible, as much within our experience of how decent human beings *can* behave, as his treatment of Dido. In both cases, moreover, we must allow the social context to modify our reactions: just as the Romans had different ideas about seduction and different marriage laws from ours,[3] so too their ideas about the propriety of revenge were likely to have been different from ours. A feeling that the violent taking of life called for a killing in return, that the need for vengeance amounted almost to a moral obligation, lies deeply embedded in men's minds, even in

---

[1] See *Oxford Classical Dictionary*, p. 788, s.v. 'Sacrifice'. A reference is sometimes seen to the story told by Suetonius, *Aug.* 15 and Dio, 48.15.4, of the offering of live sacrifices by Octavian after the siege of Perusia. Seneca knew, and seems to have accepted, the story: *De Clem.* 1.11.1. Modern scholars tend to dismiss it as part of the anti-Augustan tradition.

[2] The juxtaposition in 591 of *pius* with *dictis amaris* implies standards more civilized than those of the Heroic Age. Cf. the same technique in 4.393.

[3] See *Latin Explorations*, p. 38.

The Twelve Books

those societies where law, or enlightened thinking, rejects it.[1] Sympathy is a more relevant response than condemnation. More relevant than either is to ask *why* Aeneas behaves as he does.

As soon as we ask the question, we see that revenge is too simple an answer. The relationship between Pallas and Aeneas is more complicated than that between Patroclus and Achilles. Achilles lost his closest friend and felt the lust (which he saw no reason to control) of a primitive man to kill the man who had killed Patroclus. Aeneas' position is very different. A young prince whom he scarcely knows (though the Vignette 10.159-62 suggests a maturing relationship between them), who was entrusted to his care to learn the art of war (8.515-17), has been killed on his first day in battle. Aeneas' relationship to Evander enters as much into the reaction produced by Pallas' death as his relationship to Pallas; Virgil's more imaginative statement makes this clear (515-17):

> Pallas, Euander, in ipsis
> omnia sunt oculis, mensae, quas aduena primas
> tunc adiit, dextraeque datae.

> *Pallas, Evander, he*
> *sees it all, that first banquet to which he came*
> *a stranger, the right hands clasped.*

A sense of responsibility (cf. 11.45-8 and 55), a feeling of guilt for an obligation accepted (*dextrae datae*), work upon his emotions as strongly, more strongly perhaps, than grief. (All these complex feelings are aroused again at the end of the poem—see Analysis of Book 12.)

If despite these hints we still feel that Virgil has tried to depict a righteous anger of which we are supposed to approve, a moment's reflection suffices to suggest to us a less straightforward response is desired. Aeneas' assertion that the death of Pallas has changed every-

---

[1] Pöschl, Eng. edn, p. 86, remarks:

> To the ancient man, revenge meant restoration of his spiritual existence. Thus, Dido in her 'epitaph' glories in having avenged Sychaeus' death and, thus, Evander stays alive in order to bring the news of revenge to his son in the realm of the dead (XI.177 ff.).

For a more cautious statement of the problem in a similar context see Helen Gardner's comments on the relevance of Elizabethan ideas about revenge to our understanding of *Hamlet*: 'The Historical Approach', in *The Business of Criticism* (1959) 36-7. Evander at any rate feels entitled (11.176-81) to claim Turnus' life from Aeneas in return for his son's.

Book 10

thing (532–3) is wholly unjustified—Pallas was killed in fair fight—except by the intolerable pressure of Aeneas' own conscience: he should not have let the youngster get killed, how can he face his father to tell him? (In fact we see at 11.95–9 that Aeneas *cannot* face Evander.) Then, can it be accident that of Aeneas' eleven victims three (including the first and the last—the most prominent) surrender and beg for mercy? We should not miss the way Virgil reflects comment upon his characters by their treatment of their victims. In describing Pallas' victims we saw him underline the gruesome details (10.394–6 and 403–4), and we shall see the same technique employed with Camilla—to suggest the insensitivity of these two, of whom we want so much to approve, to the horror of war. Similarly, in describing Aeneas' victims, the emphasis falls on the way they implore Aeneas to spare their lives and the ruthless anger with which he disregards their pleading. Aeneas' denial of mercy here is fully within the conventions of heroic warfare.[1] But if Aeneas' anger allows him to do everything the heroic conventions permitted, then the justification for that anger is put in question. How was Turnus' conduct worse than Aeneas' conduct now? This is the comment that will be implied with even greater force when we come to the death of Lausus.

At 605, after a little less than a hundred lines of slaughter, we leave Aeneas until 769 when he strides to meet Mezentius; a glancing reference at 661–2 shows, however, that Aeneas continues *caede noua quaerens Turnum*. Had things gone on like this, he could hardly have failed to track down his quarry—and Virgil would have been faced with the difficulty (which faces him throughout the duel) of staging a contest between two invincible warriors and making it interesting to an audience who knows which must win. The inevitable is staved off here by a failure of nerve on the part of Turnus' protectress Juno who, with Jove's connivance, spirits Turnus away from the battlefield.

This eerie Episode, with which the third Section of the book begins, is preceded by a short divine interlude (606–32). For once Jove, not Juno, speaks first. It seems best to take his words as heavy irony—'Just as you thought, eh? it's Venus who is keeping the Trojans out of trouble, not their ability to fend for themselves and their tough courage' (607–10):

'o germana mihi atque eadem gratissima coniunx,
    ut rebare, Venus (nec te sententia fallit)

[1] And Magus' plea (10.524–9) echoes Hector's, *Il.* 22.338–43. Aeneas' refusal is hardly less callous than Achilles'.

227

Troianas sustentat opes, non uiuida bello
dextra uiris animusque ferox patiensque pericli.'

Jove refers, of course, to Juno's complaint of unfair assistance for Aeneas by Venus (10.63–95, especially 81–3). Now that Aeneas is showing how well he can look after himself (bearing out Jove's prophecy, 10.107–13, that each man will carve out his own destiny in the coming battle) Jove teases (612: *sollicitas*) Juno.[1] Aeneas is after all a soldier; somewhere in the poem Virgil must establish his hero's ability as a fighter (even though his achievements are laden with overtones), if he is to enter the duel with Turnus looking like a man who can be expected to win.

But though Virgil's intentions are not wholly frivolous, we must not take the divine interlude too seriously either. Its main function is to provide relief after 300 lines of fighting. At the same time we are invited to observe with ironic amusement that Juno—heedless, in her anxiety to save her favourite, of the harm she must do her own side—now asks for Turnus (613–16) just the sort of unfair protection she had complained of. Jove gives her permission to spirit Turnus from the battlefield, making it clear it is only a reprieve. She plunges down at once (633–4) and entices Turnus from the field in pursuit of a ghostly Aeneas on to one of the Etruscan ships (655; for the troops from Clusium, see 167), which Juno then causes to break away from its moorings and carry Turnus back to Ardea and his father Daunus (688). As the ship moves off, the ghost of Aeneas dissolves (664) and Turnus realizes he has been duped. Overcome with humiliation, he is swept past the battlefield (674–5); he tries three times to commit suicide, but each time he is restrained by Juno.

It might seem that Virgil goes to a great deal of trouble to get Turnus out of the way. But the Episode has at least two other functions. One is to re-establish the fairy-tale atmosphere (in the cut and thrust of battle there has been no space for atmosphere). Another is to undermine Turnus' confidence in himself. Turnus is never quite the same again; he realizes, perhaps, that he has been saved from certain death. Never again does he face Aeneas with the same brash self-assurance. He hedges when the question of the duel is raised in Book 11; then, at the beginning of Book 12, he abruptly screws himself up for the ordeal with an effort that betrays his lost confidence.

Meanwhile, prompted by Jove (689: *Iouis monitis*), Mezentius has

---

[1] Jove, or Virgil, overlooks Venus' intervention at 331–2.

Book 10

taken Turnus' place on the battlefield. Virgil likes this unobtrusive mixture of understatement and mystification. The phrase *Iouis monitis* looks like a casual formula (it is used of Aeneas at 4.331, a like formula of Tarchon at 11.727-8); we may feel that Virgil has nodded—forgotten that Mezentius is the last man to listen to the promptings of Jove. Virgil, of course, has not forgotten. He wants to make the point that even this rabid atheist (7.648: *contemptor diuum*, cf. 8.7) is under Jove's control. Mezentius has so far taken no part in what we have seen of the battle.[1] Jove brings him to the forefront of the action now, partly to even things up, partly to lead him to his fated death.

This fine Episode (689–761), which follows a new pattern, is organized around a series of similes. The Etruscans rush to confront their exiled prince whom they hate, but Mezentius withstands their hail of fire like a rock that juts out into the sea exposed to the full fury of the wind (693–6). This first simile introduces a piece of fast-moving narrative. Mezentius quickly kills two of his opponents and leaves a third, who had fled, writhing on the ground[2] while he hands his victim's armour to his son Lausus (an indication that Lausus is at his side). After a fourth victim, the tempo slows down in a pathetic vignette of Mimas, a close friend of Paris and born the same night; but while the dead Paris sleeps in the city of his fathers, Mimas lies unknown in a faraway land. The onslaught against Mezentius has slowed down too—though they hate him, the Etruscans are afraid of Mezentius. A second, longer simile (707–18) rounds off the scene: Mezentius stands, contemptuously shaking off his assailants' spears, like an angry boar at bay in the hunters' nets while the hunters stand around shouting and throwing their javelins from a safe distance.

The initiative passes to Mezentius. He first picks out Acron, 'a Greek who had fled abandoning his marriage' (Virgil's trick of the intriguing detail);[3] catching sight of the bright cloak Acron's bride had made for him, he descends on him like a hungry lion on a fleeing deer (third simile, 723–8). Next he picks out Orodes. Disdaining to hit him as he runs, Mezentius overtakes him and blocks his retreat, then strikes him down with an ironical shout to his men—Mezentius' first words in the poem (737):

---

[1] We see something of him in the attack on the camp the previous day. For Mezentius as an example of *interweaving* see *Latin Explorations*, pp. 212–14.
[2] Lines 697–700 are a curious echo of Horace, *Odes* 3.2.13–14.
[3] How had this Greek got to Etruria? Virgil leaves us to infer what we like from the scrap of information he gives us about Acron's broken marriage.

The Twelve Books

'pars belli haud temnenda, uiri, iacet altus Orodes.'[1]

'*Here lies tall Orodes, men, a warrior none should slight.*'

Orodes tells his unknown assailant that he will not have long to wait before fate overtakes him too. (These lines are discussed in Chapter 2, Section III.) A short, less dramatically intense piece of narrative follows—11 lines of general slaughter on both sides, for Mezentius has now quelled the rout started by Aeneas (and the departure of Turnus), and the Episode concludes with a 4-line Tableau of the gods looking down from Jove's palace on the scene of death and pointless (758: *inanem*) suffering.

Now that the tide of battle has turned again[2] it is inevitable that Mezentius and Aeneas should meet—the fate Orodes predicted for Mezentius is at hand. The Episode (762–832) is introduced by a fourth simile (763–8): Mezentius struts across the field of which he is for the moment master, like Orion wading through the sea and towering high above the water, or else striding on land with an ashtree wrenched from a mountain-top in his hands, his head in the clouds. The duel between Aeneas and Mezentius, which ends in Mezentius' death and the victory of the Trojans in the battle,[3] is, like the duel between Aeneas and Turnus in Book 12, divided into two separate parts (762–802 and 870–908). As Aeneas approaches for their first encounter, Mezentius awaits his opponent undismayed (770: *imperterritus*) and then hurls the first spear with a characteristic gesture of contempt for religion—his strong right arm and his spear take the place of gods for the *contemptor diuum*; if he wins he will deck out his son Lausus as a living trophy with the armour stripped from Aeneas (773–6):

> 'dextra mihi deus et telum, quod missile libro,
> nunc adsint! uoueo praedonis corpore raptis
> indutum spoliis ipsum te, Lause, tropaeum
> Aeneae.'[4]

---

[1] The remark is addressed to and well received by Mezentius' followers who have now taken heart and joined him (738).

[2] Observe how Virgil, while relating his story in the Homeric tradition in terms of personalities, keeps before us a clear overall picture of the course of the battle.

[3] Book 10 concludes with the death of Mezentius, but it is clear, from the beginning of Book 11, that the Trojans ended commanders of the field and that their losses were lighter.

[4] A trophy was an effigy dressed in the armour of a defeated opponent offered to the gods in discharge of a vow.

Book 10

The spear glances off Aeneas' shield and kills one of his companions. Aeneas throws his spear: it cuts through Mezentius' shield and inflicts a deep wound in the groin (785–6). While Aeneas reaches for his sword to dispatch Mezentius as he stumbles helplessly away (794–5), Lausus (who has been at his father's side throughout), rendered reckless by grief—he loves his father (789–90)—leaps between the two, to take the blow of Aeneas' sword on his own shield, then covers his father while Mezentius retreats under a protective hail of Italian spears (797–802). Aeneas angrily takes shelter behind his shield (normally the forces on either side do not intervene in a duel until one of the contestants is killed), issuing a brusque warning to Lausus as he does so. Undaunted, Lausus challenges Aeneas (813: *exsultat demens*), and in a sudden surge of anger Aeneas lunges at Lausus and drives his sword home to the hilt.

We are back where we began with the death of Pallas. The sight of Lausus' dead body causes Aeneas to stop short (821); without realizing the full significance of his own action, he is touched by the young man's sacrifice of his life to save his father's. He makes an uneasy, uncomfortable speech (825–30), then impatiently (830: *increpat*) bids Lausus' hesitant companions to come and take the body, armour intact, for burial, lifting Lausus from the ground himself as he does so. (This passage is discussed more fully in Chapter 5, 'Tragic Insight'.)

The scene switches, with Virgil's customary reticence, from this moving Tableau (the real climax of the book) to a contrasting Tableau, wonderfully compact in its description (833–40):

> interea genitor Tiberini ad fluminis undam
> uulnera siccabat lymphis corpusque leuabat
> arboris acclinis trunco. procul aerea ramis
> dependet galea et prato grauia arma quiescunt.
> stant lecti circum iuuenes; ipse aeger anhelans
> colla fouet fusus propexam in pcctore barbam;
> multa super Lauso rogitat multumque remittit
> qui reuocent maestique ferant mandata parentis.

His father meanwhile on the river-bank
was stanching his wounds with water as he rested,
leant against the trunk of a tree. Some way off his bronze
helmet hangs from a branch, his heavy armour lies on the grass.
Round him stand his bodyguard. Sick he gasps,
eases his neck, lets his long, combed beard flow over his chest.

He asks repeatedly of Lausus, keeps sending men to call him back, to bring a grieving father's orders.

But it is too late for orders. As Mezentius speaks, he catches sight of the men who are bringing his son's body to him and guesses what has happened. What follows is a masterpiece of unsentimental pathos. Mezentius is no monster; his sardonic cruelty is not worse than that of many professional soldiers. But even a tough realist cannot lose his own son (848: *quem genui*) unmoved. Mixed with grief is shame (870–1). According to Mezentius' code, killing in battle is nothing to make a fuss about (901). But running away and letting your own son get killed is another matter. He should have faced his enemies; it was his duty after the way he had treated them (852–3). He has betrayed his own code (851—the *crimen* is not his past conduct, but what he has just done), disgraced the name of his son (849–51). Only death can wipe out his humiliation. Aeneas has found the weak spot in Mezentius' moral armour (878–9). Wounded as he is, Mezentius doesn't stand a chance against Aeneas; but he has lost interest in life and is in the mood to give his enemy a run for his money. He staggers to his feet, clambers into his armour, climbs on to his horse and rides out, bristling with spears, to meet Aeneas.

The second encounter (870–908) is a wild, desperate affair, in which all the normal rules are disregarded by Mezentius. He rides three times round Aeneas showering his spears at him; Aeneas turns on the spot and allows the spears to lodge in his shield while he thinks what to do. At length he lowers his shield and drives his spear between the temples of Mezentius' horse. The horse rears up, tumbling its rider off and then falls on him amid the shouts of the onlookers on both sides. Aeneas advances for the death-stroke with a taunt on his lips. Mezentius raises his head and drinks in the sky above while he recovers his reason (899). 'What are you waiting for?' he says to Aeneas; 'why all these threats of death? There is nothing wrong in killing.[1] I did not start this fight expecting to get off, nor did my son Lausus strike such a bargain with you on my behalf.' His last words as he braces himself to receive the death-stroke are to ask Aeneas to have his body buried, and thus protect it from the hatred of his own people.[2]

---

[1] This amounts of course to a final oblique comment, from a point of view which Virgil does not perhaps fully share, on Aeneas' reaction to the death of Pallas.

[2] Contrast Mezentius' final unflinching acceptance of the realities of war with the protests of Camilla and Turnus.

BOOK 11

Book 11 begins with the Trojans in possession of the field o̲f̲ ̲.̲.̲ the return of Pallas' body to his father accompanied by a solemn procession; a twelve-day truce is concluded for the burial of the dead.

A Latin Council of War, begun in a mood of broken morale, is addressed successively by Venulus (reporting the failure of his mission to Diomede), Latinus (recommending peace), Drances (urging a duel between Turnus and Aeneas to decide the war), and Turnus, who argues for continuing the war; while they are still talking, news is brought of a Trojan advance and the war breaks out again.

The third Section is devoted mainly to a cavalry battle in which the Italians are led by Camilla; it ends with her death and the Latins on the defensive as night overtakes the two armies camped before the city of Latinus.

I 1–224	**Burying the Dead:** (i) Victory (trophy of Mezentius) and death; funeral procession of Pallas starts	1–99
	(ii) An Italian embassy arranges a 12-day truce	100–138
	(iii) Arrival of Pallas' body; Evander's speech	139–181
	(iv) The funeral of the Trojan-Arcadian dead; funeral of the Italian dead	182–212
	(v) Grief in Latinus' palace; talk of a duel Turnus-Aeneas	213–224

II
225–485
	Talk of Peace:
	(i) The Italian Council of War
	Speeches of:
	  Venulus (243–295)
	  Latinus (302–335)
	  Drances (343–375)
	  Turnus (378–444)
		225–444

	(ii) War breaks out again	445–485
	Preparations for Battle: (i) Turnus plans an ambush with Camilla	486–531
	Interlude: (ii) Diana recounts to Opis the childhood of Camilla	532–596

		The Cavalry Battle:	
III 597–915		(iii) Slaughter of minor characters on each side	597–647
		(iv) Camilla kills twelve (Ornytus and a Ligurian picked out for special mention)	648–724
		(v) A sudden charge by Tarchon, capturing Venulus, reverses the Etruscan rout	725–759
		(vi) Camilla killed by Arruns; Trojan victory imminent	759–835
		(vii) Arruns killed by Opis	836–867
		(viii) The routed Italian cavalry excluded from their own city	868–895
		(ix) Turnus abandons the ambush; the two armies camp overnight before the city	896–915

The narrative begins at dawn on the day after the battle in Book 10 with the erection by the Trojans of a trophy of Mezentius in thanks to the gods for victory. Aeneas' heart, however, is not in the ritual; he is obsessed by gloomy thoughts—victory is too heavily overshadowed by death, particularly, we shall see, the death of Pallas (2–4):

> Aeneas, quamquam et sociis dare tempus humandis
> praecipitant curae turbataque funere mens est,
> uota deum primo uictor soluebat Eoo.

The others are jubilant (13: *ouantis*), but Aeneas' speech (14–28) is businesslike and flat, his reference to Pallas (26–8) as formal as the rest; only the abruptness with which he breaks off in tears betrays his feelings. He goes to where Pallas is being prepared for his journey. When he sees the body he can hold back his grief no longer (41), nor the thought that he has let Evander down (45–8—compare the cry of self-reproach, 55: *haec mea magna fides?*).

Till now the narrative has been tight-lipped and underplayed. An intensely moving passage follows (59–99), describing the funeral procession which is to escort the dead Pallas home to his father. Aeneas spreads over the body an elaborately worked cloak—one of two given him by Dido (72–5—for these lines see Chapter 5, 'Implicit Comment'). The narrator's eye lights on the mass of captured equipment, the bound prisoners who are to be offered as a living sacrifice (81–2), the armour-bearer of Pallas (Acoetes—see 30–3) rolling on the ground in grief (85–7). Pallas' battle-charger also grieves—a Homeric reminiscence (*Iliad* 17.426 ff. and see Suetonius *Iul.* 81) that does not

Book 11

entirely come off, even in this context of fantasy.[1] As the procession gets under way, Aeneas abruptly (98: *nec plura effatus*) and uneasily detaches himself from it, and returns to the Trojan camp; again Virgil makes no comment, but the reader senses a sudden decision, taken because Aeneas cannot face Evander.

Having decided to keep Aeneas at the camp, Virgil makes good structural use of him. His return enables him to receive a Latin embassy, come to treat for the bodies of the Italian dead lying on the battlefield. This Episode provides a break in the tension between the description of the funeral procession and the narrative to come of the arrival of Pallas' body at its destination. It has another function too. When Aeneas, in granting the request, observes that it would have been better if matters had been settled by a duel between himself and Turnus (115–18), Virgil dwells on the reaction of the embassy (120–1):

> illi obstipuere silentes
> conuersique oculos inter se atque ora tenebant.
>
> *Surprised, they fell silent,*
> *and eyed one another without speaking a word.*

What leaves them speechless? Why the glances exchanged in silence? Are they moved by the magnanimous humanity with which Aeneas has received them? Or when Aeneas said (110–11):

> 'pacem me exanimis et Martis sorte peremptis
> oratis? equidem et uiuis concedere uellem!'
>
> '*You ask peace for those to whom the luck of battle*
> *has brought death? Would I could grant it to those who live!*'

did he voice the ambassadors' own thoughts?

Eventually, the Latin spokesman Drances replies: the ambassadors will do what they can to conclude a peace, if necessary one that excludes Turnus (129: *quaerat sibi foedera Turnus*). Drances is an old enemy of Turnus, but he advances the right policy, even if it is for the wrong reason; and the other ambassadors clearly agree with him (132). A twelve-day truce is arranged, and a short passage of rapid-tempo narrative relates the preparations for a mass funeral on both sides, concluding with a vigorously sketched Tableau filled with echoes of Homer and Ennius (135–8):

[1] Robert Lowell keeps the detail ('stately tears lather its teeth') in his 'Falling Asleep over the Aeneid', an evocation of the opening Episode of *Aeneid* 11.

The Twelve Books

> ferro sonat alta bipenni
> fraxinus; euertunt actas ad sidera pinus,
> robora nec cuneis et olentem scindere cedrum
> nec plaustris cessant uectare gementibus ornos.[1]

> *The tall ash rings beneath the*
> *two-edged axe; they lay low pines that touched the stars,*
> *while all the time they split oaks and sweet-smelling cedar*
> *with their wedges, load elm on groaning wains.*

The narrative breaks off (Suspended Narrative) to describe the scene at Pallanteum as the funeral procession, which we left at 99, approaches. A fine Tableau (139–50) begins the Episode, in which the spotlight falls first on the Arcadians rushing to the gates to receive the body with an escort of torch-bearers stretched out in a long line (143–4):

> lucet uia longo
> ordine flammarum et late discriminat agros

then on the Trojan mourners, the *matres* who fill the city with their lamentations, and finally on Evander as he throws himself on the body of his son.

Evander's formal speech (152–81) hardly seems to justify its position at the climax of this moving narrative sequence. In a situation frought with pitfalls for rhetoric, Evander makes all the stock points: 'Pallas should have been more careful, not let success go to his head—how fortunate my wife is not alive—if only *I*, not Pallas, had gone to fight the Rutuli—at any rate he died a glorious death—I could not have wished a better end—Turnus, not Pallas, would be dead now if they had been more evenly matched.' These are just the things a father *might* say when struggling to find what chill consolation words can offer. All the same, the rhetoric makes us uncomfortable (especially 167 and 173–4). The purpose of this speech comes at its end, when Evander gives the Trojans a message for Aeneas that amounts to a formal demand for Turnus' life in return for that of his son (176–81). We have seen Aeneas' surrender to the urge to take a life—Turnus' life—in return for Pallas'. Evander's demand for revenge is less ugly; it seems more excusable. But at the end of the poem his demand increases the strain on Aeneas' conscience, and provokes a final surrender to instincts he had struggled hard to master (see Analysis of Book 12).

[1] Cf. Ennius, epic fragment 181–5W, and *Il.* 23.114 ff.

Book 11

A fresh day dawns at 182 with Aeneas and Tarchon, the Etruscan leader, superintending the construction of the funeral pyres. At 202, night falls upon the Aeneadae standing guard all along the beach over the burning bodies of their companions. The day's events are compressed into 21 carefully organized lines, in which Virgil successfully exploits two simple devices. One is variation in tempo: the construction of the pyres, the placing of the bodies on them, are quickly dealt with (perfect tenses 185–6); the spectacle when the fires are lit and 'shroud the high sky in darkness with their murk' is drawn in a little more fully (historic present 187); then come the fast-moving spectacle of the ritual ride of the cavalrymen in armour three times round the pyres and the ceremonial cries of lamentation (instantaneous perfects 189–90); the remainder of the ceremony—the cries of grief, the throwing on the pyres of equipment belonging to the dead men or captured from the enemy, the killing of the sacrificial animals—is described at a more relaxed tempo in the next 11 lines; finally comes the long vigil over the burning bodies, but, instead of attempting to assert its length, Virgil says merely that the Trojans 'could not be torn away' till night had fallen. The second device is the juxtaposition of light and dark: the shining armour of the cavalry is contrasted with the sombre blackness of the smoke (187–8); the darkness of night is lit up by the stars burning in the sky and the pyres still burning on earth (200: *ardentis socios*, and 202: *stellis ardentibus*).[1]

A further contrast is achieved between the stark simplicity of this spectacle and the more disjointed description of the Italians dealing with their dead (203–12): some erect pyres, some bury the dead, others remove the dead from the battlefield for burial elsewhere. Meanwhile —the funerals occupy two whole days (210: *tertia lux*)—the palace of Latinus is a scene of grief, detestation of war, and anger: it is all because Turnus has lost his bride—the kind of simplification of the issues resentful people embittered by grief resort to. Sensing his opportunity, Drances puts about the story that Aeneas has challenged Turnus to a duel (Aeneas, in fact, had merely said it would have been more reasonable if Turnus and he had fought it out between them).

What is the function of the Italian Council of War which occupies nearly the whole of Section 2? To get the war restarted? But it is the Trojans who take the initiative (446–50—presumably at the end of the twelve-day truce). Turnus' fiery speech is largely to blame, however,

---

[1] In 195 the chariot-wheels are also described as 'burning' (*feruentis*). Is Virgil careless or is he being clever?

for the wave of hysteria aroused by the news of their advance; he was not the only man who wanted war: despite the mood of defeatism there were many Italians who felt as he did (222: *multa sententia*), or supported him on various grounds (222: *uariis dictis*).

But the main function of these 220 lines is not so much to advance the plot, as to give dramatic form to irreconcilable points of view. Virgil's contemporary audience, accustomed to this technique (it was a regular device of ancient historians from Thucydides onwards— used, for example, by Sallust), doubtless enjoyed the debate. What interests us are the skill and the sensitivity with which Virgil gives life, depth and reality to contrasting personalities.

The Episode begins on a muted note (a trick Virgil likes—compare the long slow prelude to the battle in Book 10) with two speeches whose main purpose is to render more effective the rich orchestration of the pair that follow. Since it is the return of Venulus which justifies summoning the Council, the proceedings begin with Venulus' account of his failure to draw Diomede into the war. He contents himself with a verbatim report presented almost without comment: Diomede will not join in the war (279–80); he advises the Italians to offer their gifts to Aeneas (281–2) and make peace while they can (292–3). For his refusal and his advice Diomede offers two reasons: it is wrong to oppose the Trojans; and it is not easy. His own experience is proof of both assertions.

Virgil represents Diomede, with an implied slight to Achilles, as the greatest of the Greeks who fought at Troy (Venulus says proudly, 245: *contigimusque manum qua concidit Ilia tellus*; compare Aeneas' words at 1.96: *o Danaum fortissime gentis*). The change that has come over this Greek warrior is an interesting, sustained example of how Virgil uses Homer. He takes the old legend, of which there are traces in Homer,[1] that after the sacking of Troy the gods' anger turned against the Greeks, gathers together references scattered through the *Odyssey* to the misfortune and disaster which overtook the leaders of the Greeks on their return from Troy, and adds a new moral emphasis of his own (255–9):

> 'quicumque Iliacos ferro uiolauimus agros . . .
> . . . infanda per orbem

[1] E.g., *Od.* 3.132-4—Nestor tells Telemachus that after the sack of Troy Zeus planned a sorrowful return for the Greeks since they were not all wise or just. Cf. *Od.* 1.326-7—the minstrel sings to the suitors the tale of the sorrowful return from Troy which Athena laid upon the Achaeans.

Book 11

>   supplicia et scelerum poenas expendimus omnes—
>   uel Priamo miseranda manus.'

> '*All of us who ravaged Troy with our swords . . .
>   . . . throughout the world have
> suffered beyond words in punishment of our crimes—
> a band Priam himself would take pity on.*'

Their guilt explains the great storm in which Ajax, the son of Oileus, perished,[1] the exile of Menelaus in Egypt, the wanderings of Ulysses (underplayed by Virgil), the shameful death of Agamemnon. And so on: the facts are in Homer, but what Homer presents as a tale of adventure and bad luck, with only the faintest adumbration of the notion of retribution, Virgil turns into a curse laid on guilty men.[2] Finally Diomede speaks of himself: an exile separated from his wife, he is still pursued by his lost companions in the form of horrible flying creatures whose mournful cries echo along the rocky river valleys of Apulia, his new home (269-74). Diomede's special guilt lay in his wounding of Venus—one of Homer's more light-hearted passages, the climax to the encounter between Aeneas and Diomede (*Iliad* 5.297-351), and a story that hardly reflects credit on Aeneas, who is laid out by Diomede with a great rock;[3] Venus rushes to the rescue, and gets a flesh wound from Diomede in the process. Virgil reinterprets this story as a grim, hard-fought duel between the greatest of the Greeks and a Trojan as great as Hector. Diomede's picture of Aeneas as a truly formidable antagonist (282-4) lacks conviction, however.[4]

The handling of the other three speeches is brilliantly successful. Diomede's concluding advice is not to risk battle with the Trojans, but to make peace instead (292-3):

>   'coeant in foedera dextrae,
>   qua datur; ast armis concurrant arma cauete.'

[1] Evoked with Hellenistic obliqueness by Virgil in 259-60.
[2] Virgil's principal source is the story Menelaus tells Telemachus (*Od.* 4.351-585) during his exile in Egypt. Menelaus wrung from Proteus, the wily old man of the sea, the story of the shipwreck. He knew, of course, what had happened to his brother Agamemnon (whose murder is mentioned a number of times in the *Odyssey*). Virgil seems to imply a link between the storm at sea and the theft of the Palladium, as in Lycophron.
[3] The detail of the rock, utilized again by Homer in the Aeneas-Achilles duel, *Il.* 20.285-9, is adapted by Virgil to his own purposes at 12.896-907.
[4] Moreover Virgil overlooks the encounter between Aeneas and Achilles (from which Aeneas had to be saved by Poseidon, *Il.* 20.159-339)—an episode given much more prominence by Homer.

The Twelve Books

After the uproar has subsided, Latinus addresses the assembly. His feelings are clear: he did not want the war in the first place, the prospect of its continuance fills him with gloom. He took Diomede's refusal of assistance on top of the recent disaster, to which the graves of the Italians who died in battle bear eloquent witness, as a clear sign that the Italians have provoked the anger of the gods in a hopeless struggle against Aeneas (231–3):

> deficit ingenti luctu rex ipse Latinus;
> fatalem Aenean manifesto numine ferri
> admonet ira deum tumulique ante ora recentes.

He attempts to convey these feelings as tactfully as possible: 'This is a bad time to have to deliberate,' he begins; and he ends with a neutral formula throwing open the discussion with the gentlest of warnings: 'Remember the situation is grave' (335). His tact, his consciousness of the way his own sympathies lie, above all his weakness (features of Latinus' character already drawn in by Virgil) make him fight shy of raising the rights and wrongs of the issue. 'The war is *ill-advised*' (305: *bellum importunum*), he starts to say—and leaves the word to imply a great deal more than the practical arguments with which he goes on to back it up: 'We are fighting against a people we cannot hope to beat, we can no longer expect outside assistance, our own losses are too evident.' Then, fearing that even so he has said too much, he ends this first section of his speech (his statement of the situation) with a nervous addition: 'I make no recriminations' (312: *nec quemquam incuso*); 'everyone has fought as bravely as he could.' But the allusion to Turnus is as plain as it is unfortunate; we shall see Drances does not let his opportunity slip.

The second, longer section of Latinus' speech (22 lines) makes concrete proposals: 'We have land we could give the Trojans; or we can offer them assistance in rebuilding their fleet' (lost when the ships were turned into sea nymphs at 9.107–25). The suggestions sound reasonable and dignified. But they amount to surrender, an admission which is withheld until Latinus' final proposal (330–4)—to send an embassy of a hundred petitioning for peace and offering the Trojans the throne of the kingdom and the royal robe of state. The situation has altered tragically since Book 7: then it was the Trojans who sent an embassy of a hundred (7.153–5) and Latinus who accepted the symbols of command (7.247) and granted peace in return.

Drances, who follows Latinus, is a fascinating personality. Perhaps

Book 11

because his character is so completely un-epic, Virgil allows himself for once a detailed thumbnail sketch more in the style of a prose historian. (See Chapter 5, 'Characterization and Motivation'.) Drances is the typical politician—a man to be reckoned with rather than liked or trusted. Virgil stresses the impurity of his motives—how Drances seizes his opportunity to work off his grudge against Turnus.[1] There is the same combination of personal dislike and clearsightedness in Cicero's passionate attack on Antony in the *Philippics*. Indeed, a suspicion that Virgil had Cicero in mind is hard to suppress—the description fits so well, even the reference to Drances' liberality (338: *largus opum*), for Cicero was an incorrigible spendthrift.[2]

At any rate Drances' technique is thoroughly Ciceronian. He begins on a bland note (343–4):

> 'rem nulli obscuram nostrae nec uocis egentem
> consulis, o bone rex.'
>
> '*Plain to all is the matter you raise, sire; no
> need for me to speak.*'

But a moment later he has brought into the open the undercurrents which Latinus' unfortunate *nec quemquam incuso* was intended to avoid. 'Everybody admits he knows what must be done, but nobody is prepared to speak out,' says Drances (344–5—Drances' *mussant* is picked up by Virgil at 454). Though politely framed as a generalization, the statement is clearly aimed at Latinus. After this preamble the first section of Drances' speech follows (346–51). It amounts to a carefully worded smear of Turnus, beginning on a note of elaborate irony ('I crave permission to speak from the author of our misfortunes . . .'),[3] then assuming a more challenging tone: 'I shall speak in any case and disregard his threats . . .: the most distinguished of our leaders have fallen, the whole city has been plunged into grief—while he tries his strength against the Trojan camp, relies on his ability to run away, and waves his armour at the sky' (Drances refers to Turnus' attack on the

---

[1] This, I think, is the meaning of the difficult phrase (342) *his onerat dictis atque aggerat iras*, rather than Mackail's (p. 435) fairly meaningless 'weights and heaps up his angry feelings'.

[2] Servius (on *Eclogues* 6.11) has a story, repeated by Petrarch (*Epist. de rebus fam.* 24.4 vol. 3, p. 265 Fracassetti—addressed to Cicero), that Cicero, meeting the young Virgil, pronounced him *magnae spes altera Romae* and that Virgil built the phrase into his poem (12.168—of Ascanius) as a compliment to Cicero.

[3] Cf. the elaborate suggestion of pressures militating against free speech at the opening of Cicero's *Pro Milone*.

The Twelve Books

Trojan camp at the end of Book 9 and his pursuit of the ghost of Aeneas in Book 10).

Abruptly Drances strikes at the heart of the matter (352–6): Latinus' proposals are all very fine, but they overlook one thing—the proposed marriage of Lavinia to Aeneas, Turnus' real reason for starting the war; without the marriage there can be no firm peace. Drances is of course completely right: Lavinia was part of the original settlement (7.268–73); she cannot be subtracted from it now.

Drances goes on, but he cannot resist the temptation to drag Turnus in again—still without mentioning his name: 'Since we are so afraid of *him*, we must go to him and entreat him to back down, and put his king and his country before his private interest' (357–9). Then, with the sudden inspiration of the born orator, Drances drops the show of leaving unnamed the object of his sneering irony and turns in a dramatic direct appeal to Turnus. It is the longest section of his speech (360–75) and its effect is gauged beautifully: 'Why do you persist with a hopeless war? Give us peace, Turnus, it is what we all want. And give us, too, the only inviolable pledge of peace' (362–3):

'pacem te poscimus omnes,
Turne, simul pacis solum inuiolabile pignus.'

'I know you think I hate you—well, let's not go into that.' (Drances is openly mocking Turnus now.) 'But, look, I come as a suppliant to you: pity your people, lay aside your anger; now that you have been beaten—go home'[1] (365–6):

'en supplex uenio: miserere tuorum,
pone animos et pulsus abi.'[2]

It is the kind of theatrical gesture that hoodwinks nobody, and yet nobody can resist it—or even want to protest at the cruelty of the concluding double blow. We, the audience, feel a malicious pleasure in Turnus' discomfiture, particularly as we are aware that there is a good deal in what Drances says. At the same time we know that rhetoric like this persuades nobody. When Drances goes on, therefore ('we have suffered enough; if you are so ambitious for glory and a royal dowry . . .'), we may wonder if Drances has not misjudged things, not gone too far. And then comes the second crack of Drances' whip: '. . . go and meet your enemy face to face,' he snarls at Turnus,

---

[1] Turnus, of course, belonged to the neighbouring city of Ardea.
[2] For the repetition of the phrase *miserere tuorum* by Saces see 12.653.

Book 11

'instead of letting us, the ordinary people, litter the battlefields, an unburied, unwept-for mass, to win a royal bride for Turnus' (371–3):

> 'scilicet ut Turno contingat regia coniunx,
> nos animae uiles, inhumata infletaque turba,
> sternamur campis.'

The gauntlet is thrown in Turnus' face. If he fails to pick it up (and really he does) the scene will work like a slow poison, gradually alienating even the most cynical about rhetoric from this glamorous figure whom Drances has exposed. Naturally, Drances does not expect Turnus will agree to a duel; Drances is content to wait, and we shall see at the beginning of Book 12 that he did not have to wait in vain.

For the moment Drances' object is to goad Turnus beyond endurance: 'If you are a man,' he continues, 'if you are a soldier, look, your challenger awaits you. . . .' Turnus jumps to his feet and cuts off Drances in mid-sentence with a shout of rage.

He goes on to make a fine, fighting speech, the longest of the four. We might fall for the glamour of its fiery phrases, if we did not have Drances' words at the back of our minds to expose their irrelevance.

The first of the three sections into which the speech falls is an angry tirade (378–409): 'You talk a lot, Drances, but this is a time for deeds not words. Why don't you try your hand at fighting?' Turnus has the soldier's contempt for politicians, but issues are seldom as simple as soldiers like to think them. Next (392–8) Turnus picks up the first part of Drances' cruel gibe (366: *pulsus abi*); but his defence only makes things worse. Everyone knows about Turnus' feats of bravery; but everybody knows, too, about his mysterious disappearance at the height of the fighting (10.633–88). 'A hopeless war, you say? Crazy, defeatist talk!' (399–400)—again he attempts to answer Drances (362) but muddles things by attempting to answer Diomede as well (403–5).

Contemptuously turning aside Drances' ironical protestations of fear (406–9), Turnus then directs himself to the proposals made by Latinus (410–33). In this central, longest section of Turnus' speech there is a sudden rise in dignity. His answer, carefully reasoned and well put together, is built around two long periodic sentences. The argument of the first is as follows: 'If we are defeated because we have lost one battle, well then, let us ask for peace—though I should prefer a soldier's death' (411–18). (Again the honest soldier's intolerable simplification of the problems of defeat.) The argument of the second is: 'But we still have men to fight. Our losses are no worse than the enemy's. Why are we afraid? In war there are always ups and downs' (419–27). (Put in as many words, this is obviously false, but the vague imagery of *parque per omnis tempestas* in 422–3 might have got by if we had been more fully on Turnus' side.) This second section concludes with a piece of even more patent wishful thinking: 'We can do without help from others' (Turnus refers again to Diomede) '—there are enough of us here' (428–33).

In a final section (434–44) Turnus takes up the suggestion of a duel: 'If you want me to fight Aeneas, I will—divine armour and all.' The end of Turnus' speech amounts to a formula of self-devotion which reminds the reader of Decius Mus in the First Samnite War,[1] and a last attempt to meet Drances' taunts: 'Aeneas challenges me?' (The reference is to the end of Drances' speech, 374–5.) 'I welcome the challenge—Drances shall not take my place.' Despite his words (442: *et uocet oro*), Turnus plainly does not welcome a duel. Chiefly, no doubt, because Drances has proposed it; but also, I think, because Turnus wants the war to go on: war is his element. We shall see, too, at the beginning of Book 12 that Turnus is no longer happy at the prospect of meeting Aeneas face to face—his eerie experience in Book 10, when Juno spirited him away from Aeneas' clutches, has perhaps left him with a feeling that he is not destined to survive an encounter.

At this point news is brought that the Trojans have broken camp and are advancing. There is pandemonium among the younger men and an angry rush to arms which their elders are powerless to check (445–54). Turnus strides contemptuously out of the Council of War, his undertaking to face Aeneas forgotten in the conditioned response to danger (459–62). He is not evading the duel, but war is what he wants and he seizes the opportunity to brush opposition aside. A moment later he is busy issuing instructions for battle to his men (463–7).

There is no resisting the impulse to arms and the wave of unreason quickly spreads, leaving Latinus helpless (469–72) as he was left when war first broke out (7.591–600). On one side we see frantic preparations to defend the city; on another a procession of *matres* headed by Amata with Lavinia at her side—a helpless victim perhaps of the prevailing hysteria (479–80); even the *matres*, to whom Virgil extends his pity so freely, are coarsened by war: lashed to a mood of hatred and vindictiveness, they are on their way to the temple of Minerva to

---
[1] Livy 8.9.

Book 11

pray for the destruction of 'the Phrygian bandit'. (See Chapter 5, 'Implicit Comment'.)

The third Section opens with preparations for the coming battle (486–531). As he scrambles into his armour, Turnus is in high spirits (491: *exsultat*). Two implicit comments suggest the quality of his mood. A simile conveys the first: the happiness that fills Turnus at the prospect of battle is so simple-minded it is almost as innocent as that of a stallion long kept locked up, which escapes at last to join the mares in the open fields, or tosses its mane in high spirits as it races to plunge into the familiar waters of a stream (492–7):

> qualis ubi abruptis fugit praesepia uinclis
> tandem liber equus, campoque potitus aperto
> aut ille in pastus armentaque tendit equarum
> aut adsuetus aquae perfundi flumine noto
> emicat arrectisque fremit ceruicibus alte
> luxurians, luduntque iubae per colla, per armos.

A second comment is implied by the arrival of Camilla and her squadron of Amazons. The charm of the Vignette (her whole squadron dismounts as one, 499–501), Camilla's joyful eagerness, are hard to resist. But Turnus loses some of his glamour; his unthinking courage impresses us less now that we see it matched by this light-hearted girl. For Camilla is no man-woman—recall the glimpse of her at the end of Book 7; if Virgil uses of her in 507 the daring epithet *horrenda*, it is the intensity of her mood more than her appearance which is frightening.[1] Camilla is a beautiful, impulsive, reckless girl. If she seems as heroic as Turnus, can it be so hard to be a hero?

Crisply Turnus gives Camilla her instructions. Patrols have reported that Aeneas' light-armed cavalry is advancing directly towards the city (which lies some distance south of the Tiber) from the Trojan camp at the Tiber mouth; Aeneas' plan is to distract attention by the cavalry advance and take the city unawares. Turnus will lie in wait, therefore, for the Trojan main body in a defile in the hills (an echo of the famous historical battle of the Caudine Forks in 321 B.C.), leaving Camilla to command the Latin cavalry, at present under Messapus, in addition to her own contingent of Volscians.

Camilla now becomes the centre of attention. We leave Turnus at 531, settling into his position in the pass. No more is heard of the

---

[1] Note, too, the undercutting effect of the reference to mares in the simile and the guarded suggestion that they correspond to Camilla and her cohort.

The Twelve Books

ambush till 896. The intervening 364 lines are taken up with the narrative of the cavalry battle and the consequences of defeat in it for the Italians. But first comes an interlude, in which Camilla's protectress Diana recounts Camilla's childhood to her aide Opis (532–96). Two long Episodes then relate Camilla's exploits in the battle (648–724) and her death (759–835). These three Episodes are separated by shorter Episodes in which Camilla does not figure, designed to give the reader some sense of the general run of the cavalry battle; a sixth Episode relates the death of the strange fanatic Arruns who kills her (836–67).

The first of these six Episodes leads us from the battle into fantasy—rather as the battle in Book 10 is preceded by a sequence of scenes establishing an atmosphere of fairy-tale. As they watch Camilla enter the battle, Diana tells Opis the story of this child of the woods—how her exiled father inured her to a lonely existence in the mountains (569) and trained her from infancy to handle the javelin and the bow (573–5). Confronted once by a raging river while making his escape, her father tied the child to a spear and, after dedicating her life to Diana, hurled the spear across the echoing waters (561–3):

> dixit et adducto contortum hastile lacerto
> immittit: sonuere undae, rapidum super amnem
> infelix fugit iaculo stridente Camilla.

Today's Camilla's life is drawing to its close (587). Diana cannot resist fate, but she instructs Opis to shoot down Camilla's assailant. Thus Diana sets the stage for the tragedy that now begins. We know before it starts that Camilla will die, and we know that whoever kills her will die too (see Chapter 5, 'Tragic Suspense').[1]

Meanwhile the Trojan cavalry have reached Lavinium and the two lines ride to meet one another, a manoeuvre that ends in a head-on charge by one horseman on either side, from which one of Tarchon's Etruscans emerges the victor. The Latins retreat to their walls, then wheel about and pursue the Trojans. This manoeuvre is repeated; and on the third advance battle is engaged, each horseman picking out his opponent as the two lines close (631–2). A scene of general slaughter follows, ending with a Vignette: the giant Herminius is killed by Catillus, one of the stranger figures in the catalogue in Book 7

---

[1] Mackail (p. 418) curiously objects to Diana's long speech (suggesting Virgil had composed it in an earlier draft as direct narrative) on the grounds that 'The exquisite detail is hardly relevant to the immediate occasion'.

Book 11

(7.672–7), as he rides bare-headed and bare-shouldered, scornful of danger.

Back to Camilla. She is exhilarated (648: *exsultat*—the word used of Turnus at 491) by the slaughter (648–52). Around her are the girls she has chosen as her companions, her advisers in peace as in war (658) —like the original Amazons (now described in a simile). We pass from this opening Tableau with its emphasis on the joy of battle to a catalogue of Camilla's victims. It is surely not accidental that the details of Euneus' death are made to sound so repulsive (668–9):

> sanguinis ille uomens riuos cadit atque cruentam
> mandit humum moriensque suo se in uulnere uersat.

He vomits streams of blood as he falls, chews the gore-drenched ground, spins on his wound as he dies.

Camilla dispatches seven more before the tempo slackens for a detailed, picturesque Vignette of the rustic warrior Ornytus (677–89— he wears a great wolf's head, teeth and all, as a helmet). Then, after two more victims, it is the turn of an unnamed Ligurian who attempts to escape from Camilla by a trick; she falls on him like a hawk. In less than 80 lines (648–724) she has killed twelve men.

Tarchon, the Etruscan commander, intervenes (sent by Jove) and rallies his men with a spectacular exploit—the capture single-handed of Venulus, whom Tarchon with a sudden charge sweeps off his horse on to his own horse, stabbing him to death after a fierce struggle— 'like a tawny eagle that has swooped down to snatch up a snake which now writhes in the eagle's talons; each time its hissing head rises, the eagle strikes at it with its beak, winging its way through the air as it does so' (751–9):

> utque uolans alte raptum cum fulua draconem
> fert aquila implicuitque pedes atque unguibus haesit,
> saucius at serpens sinuosa uolumina uersat
> arrectisque horret squamis et sibilat ore
> arduus insurgens, illa haud minus urget obunco
> luctantem rostro, simul aethera uerberat alis:
> haud aliter praedam Tiburtum ex agmine Tarchon
> portat ouans. ducis exemplum euentumque secuti
> Maeonidae incurrunt.

The narrative of this spectacular feat halts in mid-line (759) to introduce Arruns—it is as though we catch sight of him stealthily stalking Camilla as our eye wanders for an instant from the scene which has till now held our attention (759–61):

> tum fatis debitus Arruns
> uelocem iaculo et multa prior arte Camillam
> circuit, et quae sit fortuna facillima temptat.

But the narrator, being omniscient, can see more than we can, and Arruns is identified at once as 'fate's man' (*fatis debitus* is ambiguous—Arruns is both the man destined to kill Camilla and the man destined to be killed himself[1]). A sinister figure, he circles on his horse, always ahead of Camilla anticipating her movements with quick, unobtrusive changes of direction (765: *furtim celeris detorquet habenas*); in his hand quivers the spear that will not miss (767: *certam quatit improbus hastam*).

We leave Arruns after these eight and a half lines—no thumbnail sketch of his appearance, no brief biography; because we can only watch his movements, our ignorance makes Arruns a more sinister figure. At 768 the scene switches (Suspended Narrative) to Camilla's colourful last victim, the glamorous ex-priest Chloreus, resplendent in purple and red on a horse whose mantle is studded with bronze and gold; his bow and his helmet are of gold, his linen cloak is saffron, its tinkling folds held in place with a golden buckle, his tunic and his trousers are richly embroidered[2] (768–77):

> forte sacer Cybelo Chloreus olimque sacerdos
> insignis longe Phrygiis fulgebat in armis
> spumantemque agitabat equum, quem pellis aenis
> in plumam squamis auro conserta tegebat.
> ipse peregrina ferrugine clarus et ostro
> spicula torquebat Lycio Gortynia cornu;
> aureus ex umeris erat arcus et aurea uati
> cassida; tum croceam chlamydemque sinusque crepantis
> carbaseos fuluo in nodum collegerat auro,
> pictus acu tunicas et barbara tegmina crurum.

Striking as it is, the picture of Chloreus is far from clear—another example of Virgil's vague complexity in detailed description; it would have been easy to be clear, but Virgil works like the artist who prefers an intricate pattern of forms, textures and colours to representational

---

[1] The ambiguity is pointed out by Conington.
[2] The cloak tinkles, presumably, because of the metal ornaments attached to it: *crepantis* might mean 'rustling', but linen does not rustle.

Book 11

clarity.[1] Camilla cannot resist Chloreus' colourful accoutrements.[2] She pursues him, rendered oblivious of danger by her feminine covetousness (782: *femineo praedae et spoliorum ardebat amore*). And then the two arms of the Parallel Narrative join in the middle of a fine long sentence (778–90), as Arruns hurls his spear (783) with a prayer that reveals at last the kind of man Arruns is. He is a priest of Apollo, a religious fanatic—a member of a sect of firewalkers; for him Apollo is *pater omnipotens*, not Jove. He acts out of a kind of patriotism, 'to obliterate this disgrace to our arms' (789)—a higher motive certainly than greed, higher perhaps than glory; Arruns at any rate expects no glory this day (790–2):

> '... non ...
> uirginis aut spolia ulla peto, mihi cetera laudem
> facta ferent.'

He is content to return home unglorious (793: *patrias remeabo inglorius urbes*). It does not occur to him that he will be denied even this. (See Chapter 5, 'Tragic Irony'.) The spear finds its mark—Camilla does not even hear it come; but as she tumbles from her horse, the narrative deserts her, to follow Arruns in his panic-stricken flight—like a wolf that has killed a shepherd or a steer (806–15).

We return to Camilla for the death scene, which is taken at a slower tempo—it occupies 20 lines (816–35), including a short speech, and ends with a magnificent sentence, in which Camilla (not her soul, as we should have to say in prose) lays aside the reins, slips reluctantly from horse to ground, and then, devoid of life's warmth, slowly frees herself from her body, and lets her head slump in death while 'life with a groan flees protesting to the shades' (827–31):

> simul his dictis linquebat habenas
> ad terram non sponte fluens; tum frigida toto
> paulatim exsoluit se corpore lentaque colla
> et captum leto posuit caput, arma relinquens,
> uitaque cum gemitu fugit indignata sub umbras.[3]

---

[1] Conington, quoting Servius ('*Sane armorum longa descriptio illuc spectat, ut in eorum cupiditatem merito Camilla uideatur esse succensa*'), remarks:
We may add, that the very length of the description expresses the place which the spoils fill in Camilla's thoughts, and the length of time she spends in trying to obtain them.

[2] Though Virgil refuses to probe her thoughts, leaving it in doubt whether it is Chloreus' arms she wants as a spectacular temple offering or his clothes to wear herself.

[3] Line 831 is used again at the end of the poem, of Turnus.

The Twelve Books

The narrative returns at 836 to Arruns—Opis stands waiting for him as she was told to by Diana (591–2). His initial terror over, Arruns is starting to preen himself (854: *uana tumentem*) when she calls out to him and looses her arrow. Virgil devotes five lines (858–62) to the firing of the arrow—and then disposes unceremoniously of Arruns: unlike Camilla, he hears the arrow coming; it strikes; as he lies dying, nobody takes any notice of him (865–6). Her mission completed, Opis returns to Olympus.

Camilla's death brings about a full-scale retreat of the Italian cavalry. Their headlong rush for safety is graphically caught in a fine Vignette (874–8):

> sed laxos referunt umeris languentibus arcus,
> quadripedumque putrem cursu quatit ungula campum.
> uoluitur ad muros caligine turbidus atra
> puluis et e speculis percussae pectora matres
> femineum clamorem ad caeli sidera tollunt.

> *They carry unstrung bows across slumped shoulders,*
> *while four-footed hoof-beats batter a crumbling field.*
> *In a swirling black cloud the dust rolls up*
> *to the walls; the mothers on the watch-towers beat their breasts,*
> *raise to the stars in heaven the sound of women grieving.*

A moving picture of grief, despair and slaughter follows (879–90). The Italian cavalry attempt to force their way into the city. For their own people dare not open their gates to them, and repel them as they would an invading enemy. The result is general carnage (885–6). Doubtless those inside, remembering the havoc wrought by Turnus within the Trojan camp at the end of Book 9, believe they must keep the city's gates closed at whatever cost. Yet the Trojan cavalry are not, it seems, planning an attack on the city—they are not mentioned after 873; their mission was merely to create a diversion (512–13); having succeeded, they would naturally rejoin the main body.¹ Panic blinds all to the reality of the situation. Those outside hurl themselves to certain death (898–90), with a frenzy that in a real attack would pass

---

¹ Acca in her report to Turnus at 896–900 claims the Trojans are massing for an attack (*ingruere infensos hostis*), that fear (of an attack) is gaining the city (*metum iam ad moenia ferri*)—not that the city is being attacked. It rather seems from 911 that Virgil imagines the Trojan cavalry as joining up with the infantry when Aeneas comes down out of the hills (they could easily elude Turnus' infantry). This makes better sense of 911 than Conington's suggestion that the horses are chariot horses, though it hardly supports Acca; but hers may be taken as an alarmist report, based on the panic of 876–90.

Book 11

for heroism: in the confusion they forget they are running away; the hysteria of the onslaught touches off the familiar conditioned responses, and cowards start to behave like heroes. Those inside fight, with what would equally pass for heroism—if it were the enemy they were destroying. 'Inspired by true patriotism and the example of Camilla', the womenfolk hurl down a hail of improvised weapons, 'eager to be the first to die in the defence of their city's walls' (891–5):

> ipsae de muris summo certamine matres
> (monstrat amor uerus patriae, ut uidere Camillam)
> tela manu trepidae iaciunt ac robore duro
> stipitibus ferrum sudibusque imitantur obustis
> praecipites primaeque mori pro moenibus ardent.

Nowhere else in the poem are the consequences of war described with such poignancy as in this short study of perverted heroism; nowhere else does Virgil permit himself so patent and so telling a thrust of laconic irony.[1]

Meanwhile news of Camilla's death and the rout of the Italian cavalry has reached Turnus. At once he abandons the ambush—and his chance of catching Aeneas and the Trojans in the pass. He acts on impulse (901: *furens*). But alongside the psychological explanation Virgil sets the hand of fate: *saeua Iouis sic numina poscunt*. For not only is Aeneas saved from surprise attack: a chain of events is set in motion by Turnus that ends with his own fated death. The juxtaposition of Turnus' departure and the arrival of Aeneas at the entrance to the pass (underlined by the precise wording of 903: *uix e conspectu exierat campumque tenebat*) is sufficient Implicit Comment. Turnus is a brave soldier, but a bad general. He allows impulse to thrust aside accurate appraisal of the situation: the city is not actually being attacked, at most it is threatened; any Trojan forces on the plain are unimportant compared with those he can trap in the pass and destroy if he remains.[2]

---

[1] I find the fuss made over 892 largely needless. The meaning undoubtedly is that the *matres*, who hitherto have not taken part in the fighting, have watched Camilla (the cavalry battle takes place close to the city—see 597), and her example of true patriotism points the way—to a course of action that is a distortion of true patriotism. The omission of an expressed object for *monstrat* introduces no real obscurity; Virgil aims at the maximum of conciseness, to prevent his comment from becoming heavy-handed. (Some editors, supposing that *ut uidere Camillam* means the *matres* now see Camilla's body, complain that this conflicts with Diana's promise at 593–4.)

[2] No doubt we are meant to feel it is the death of Camilla that sweeps

The Twelve Books

Turnus reaches level ground first (903) followed by Aeneas, and the two armies find themselves in full view of one another as the commanders lead their men at a fast pace towards the Latin city (906–11). Since the sun is already setting, an immediate engagement is precluded, so the armies camp for the night in front of the city.

BOOK 12

In Book 12 Turnus, provoked by the attitude of his men, whose morale is low after the disastrous cavalry engagement of Book 11, announces he will fight Aeneas and refuses to listen to Latinus and Amata when they attempt to dissuade him.

The stage is almost set for the duel when there is a fresh outbreak of fighting, in which the leading role is played by Turnus in his chariot, until Aeneas wrenches the initiative from him by a sudden attack on the Latin city; this and the resultant suicide of Amata force upon Turnus the realization that the duel cannot be evaded.

After a spectacular first encounter Turnus loses his nerve and flees; Jove intervenes, and in a second encounter Turnus is quickly brought to his knees; Aeneas is at first inclined to spare Turnus, then kills him in a sudden angry impulse.

Book 12, the longest in the poem, possesses the tragic intensity but lacks the economical unity of Book 4. A more complex structure, it attempts to provide narrative excitement as well as tragic inevitability. None the less its structure is essentially tragic: the events that led up to the duel seem temporarily unimportant while we watch the stresses, brought to bear upon Turnus by this final, inevitable, hopeless encounter, torture and ennoble him—not beyond recognition, but beyond any expectation we could reasonably have had of him in Book 7. As I said in discussing Book 4, Turnus is an ascending, Dido a descending, personality. Like Book 4, moreover, Book 12 shows Virgil's most highly developed use of dialogue for the involuntary, ironic revelation of character, his most telling use of imagery, and some of his most economically intense use of language.

What distinguishes the two books most is the relationship of dialogue to narrative. In Book 12 only 280 lines out of 952 are dialogue (rather below the average for the twelve books), compared with 340

---

consideration of strategy aside. The news is a most bitter blow (896: *saeuissimus*); Turnus is overwhelmed (897: *ingentem tumultum*).

Book 12

lines out of 705 in Book 4. A long central Section, essentially narrative in structure, cuts off the compressed, highly dramatic account of the events leading up to the duel (Section 1, 112 lines) from the duel proper (Section 3, 225 lines). This central Section has two functions. The more obvious is to create suspense: the duel has been hanging over Turnus since the challenge was hurled at him by Drances early in the previous book (11.368–70); it must now provide the dénouement of Virgil's story. The end is in sight, but it is put off by a further outbreak of fighting, even more pointless than that which followed the Council of War in Book 11. (In similar fashion, the narrative of the duel is divided into two separate encounters in Section 3 at line 791.) Suspense is, of course, one of the most obvious devices at the disposal of the writer of a narrative poem, and one Virgil can scarcely avoid, once he has assigned a whole book to the story of the duel: the duel itself cannot be made to last too long or it will become boring or ridiculous.

At the same time, a diversionary action longer than the action it suspends must do more than provide suspense. This long central Section is not just a narrator's trick. The whole basis upon which the two contestants finally come to grips has shifted as a result of what happens in Section 2. The Turnus who eventually advances to meet Aeneas at line 681 is not the Turnus of the opening lines of the book; nor is he the Turnus we glimpse at lines 219–21, just before the preparations for the duel are interrupted. Equally, the Aeneas who advances to meet Turnus at line 697 has not remained throughout the interval the serene dispassionate instrument of fate we saw at 107–12, the just prince we saw at 175–94, concerned to respect his father's precept (6.853):

> parcere subiectis et debellare superbos.

Though it is the pathetic overthrow of Turnus that wins our first interest, we are shown also how the march of events in war can corrupt the character and motives of even the most high-minded of leaders till sometimes the good fight is fought for bad reasons. If the Aeneas of Book 4 suggested Julius Caesar or Mark Antony, the Aeneas of Book 12 points plainly to Augustus; and the portrait is hardly a flattering one.

I 1–112	*The Duel decided on:* (i) Turnus decides—against Latinus, Amata and Lavinia (ii) The combatants prepare	1–80 81–112

The Twelve Books

II
113–727
- *The Duel held up, then finally begun:*
  The duel scene—
    - (i) The ceremony prepared for — 113–133
    - (ii) Divine intervention foreshadowed — 134–160
    - (iii) The ceremony begins: speeches by Aeneas and Turnus — 161–215
    - (iv) Iuturna provokes an incident — 216–276
    - (v) Fighting again, Aeneas wounded — 277–323
  Aeneas and Turnus—
    - (vi) Fugue of Turnus in the chariot A — 324–382
    - (vii) Aeneas' wound is healed by Iapyx with Venus' help; he returns to the battle — 383–467
    - (viii) Fugue of Turnus in the chariot B; he is joined by Iuturna disguised as his driver Metiscus — 468–499
    - (ix) Various exploits of Aeneas and Turnus — 500–553
  Turnus decides again to meet Aeneas—
    - (x) Aeneas launches a sudden attack on the Latin city; Amata commits suicide — 554–613
    - (xi) Turnus, told the news by Saces, decides to meet Aeneas — 614–680
    - (xii) Turnus advances to meet Aeneas; Jove and the scales — 681–727

III
728–952
- *The Duel fought:*
  First encounter—
    - (i) Turnus' sword (not his own) is broken; he runs, Aeneas after him; Turnus gets his own sword and Aeneas recovers his spear; they confront one another again — 728–790
  Interlude—
    - (ii) Juno-Jove, the bird of death; Iuturna departs — 791–886
  The final encounter—
    - (iii) The rock; Turnus is defeated and not spared — 887–952

We begin with an Episode that is almost pure drama—comment cut to a minimum, the main stress on the revelation of character and motive through dialogue. Wasting no time on explanations or description of scene, Virgil leaves it to us to fill in the situation for ourselves. Book 11 ended with the two armies facing each other at sunset outside the Latin city. We must now imagine Turnus moving

Book 12

among his men as they go about their task of fortifying their camp for the night, little stomach left for fighting. Turnus sees them eye him as he passes, hears their muttered challenges to keep his promise to fight Aeneas. Less than three lines suffice to sketch in the scene; what interests Virgil is Turnus' reaction.

For Turnus is plainly not anxious to face Aeneas. No doubt, as when he sidestepped Drances' sneering challenge in Book 11, he wants the war to go on—war is his element. But Virgil neither makes too much of Turnus' reluctance nor fully explains it. We see him hang back until practically shamed into fighting. Then abruptly he decides he *will* fight Aeneas; but behind his angry, swaggering panache we quickly sense a confused awareness that his time is up.

Defeat, the failure of his men's morale, at first made Turnus only more determined not to listen to talk of peace (3: *ultro implacabilis ardet*). But it takes more than an angry commander to rouse a broken army. The impulse to do something, the pressure he senses round him, take control. He goes to the king and announces that he will meet Aeneas,[1] his stormy, contemptuous words (11–17) directed as much at his own men as at the king (the speech is quoted and discussed in Chapter 1). Self-deception, not effrontery, puts him in a mood to blame anyone except himself for the delay (11: *nulla mora in Turno*), to assume that the Trojans will want to back out of their challenge (12: *nec quae pepigere recusent*).[2] Like any man who has at last made an unpleasant decision, Turnus wants action. Of course, given the time of day, it is silly to talk of fighting Aeneas at once, but Turnus is in no mood for sense. 'The Latins can sit and watch,' he says (15–16), 'while Turnus does their fighting for them'—the cruel, unjust words of a man who has been trapped into a course of action he would have preferred to avoid. If he loses, Aeneas 'can have a beaten people' (17: *aut habeat uictos*—another angry cut at his own men) 'and Lavinia for his wife'.[3]

Latinus and Amata attempt to talk Turnus out of his decision. Latinus' thoughts are dominated by a hardening certainty about the way fate points: earlier he might have felt he had misread prophecy

---

[1] The fact that Amata and Lavinia are present shows Turnus is speaking in the palace. Reaching the plain first, his army camped between the Latin city and the army of Aeneas, rejoined now, presumably, by his cavalry. Turnus can therefore get in and out of the city without difficulty.

[2] In fact Aeneas did not make a formal challenge at all at 11.115–18; his words were twisted by Drances at 11.220–1 to make it appear so.

[3] Observe how each time the war resolves itself for Turnus into a personal feud over Lavinia. Cf. 7.470 (Turnus will take on Latinus too, if he does not get his rights), 12.80 and 12.937.

when he offered Aeneas his daughter; clearly he does not now; he overstates even (26-8) the weight of prophecy that was disregarded.[1] Both he and Amata take it for granted Turnus will be killed, and their conviction compels Turnus' admission (49) that the duel is a hopeless gesture. At the same time, his former reluctance and his present uneasy braggadocio are put in a fresh light: his feeling that he does not stand a chance is not the reaction of a coward, but a feeling others share.

To make it easy for Turnus to back down, Latinus avoids giving him a direct answer and stresses instead the wrongness of the war, shifting as he does so the responsibility for it on to his own shoulders (31: *promissam eripui genero, arma impia sumpsi*; in fact, Latinus had no hand in starting the war: he tried to resist the general mood of war hysteria but was swept aside by it—see 7.586-600). Turnus does not want a way out. He brushes Amata aside as impatiently as Latinus (54-63). Only Lavinia's tears affect him a moment (70-1).[2] All the same, their concern, their despair, cause a change in Turnus. When Latinus hinted that Turnus might be killed, Turnus replied that death is cheap at the price of glory (49: *letumque sinas pro laude pacisci*); he will give his opponent a run for his money. This is more ironic meiosis than reckoning with the consequences. But by the time he makes his reply to Amata, the steady pressure of their apprehension has begun to tell. 'Tears are ill-omened,' he says. But the way he puts it suggests a new uneasiness. 'Anyway, death is not something that can be put off'[3] (72-4):

---

[1] Some editors claim that line 28 is a rhetorical exaggeration. It is true the only prophecy we have heard of forbidding the marriage of Lavinia to Turnus and promising a foreign husband for her is that of Faunus (7.96-101). But at 7.268-72 Latinus speaks of *plurima monstra*. As for *homines* here, we are told at 7.102-5 that the prophecy was common knowledge.

[2] Whereas Amata had been crying (this is the force of the imperfect *flebat*, 55), Lavinia's is a sudden outburst (64: *accepit uocem lacrimis*) prompted by something her mother says (*uocem* = 'word' or 'phrase'). Pretty clearly it is the phrase *generum Aenean* that causes her to break down—as well it might. But then she blushes, and Virgil underlines the blush with a lovely simile. Why does she blush? Is Virgil suggesting she might not so much mind Aeneas as a husband? Many have commented on the fact that Virgil does not allow Lavinia to speak. In his own day young brides had often to serve as the helpless tokens that sealed political compacts; doubtless there is a hint at that practice here. Perhaps, too, he was following the rule of the Athenian dramatists which restricted the number of speaking actors in a scene to three. It is just the kind of respect for a detail of tradition that is characteristic of Virgil.

[3] The meaning of the words *neque enim Turno mora libera mortis* has been debated since antiquity—see Servius, and Mackail's note. They are best taken as an example of Tragic Irony (see Chapter 5). For Turnus, the words mean 'if

Book 12

'ne, quaeso, ne me lacrimis neue omine tanto
prosequere in duri certamina Martis euntem,
o mater; neque enim Turno mora libera mortis.'

Turnus tries to thrust his uneasiness aside with a sudden reversion to the rhetoric of his opening speech to Latinus (75–80). But he cannot fully recapture the mood in which he started out, as the pathetic opening lines of the following Episode show. Under the pretence of making sure that all is ready for the next day, Turnus goes to seek comfort from his horses, before trying to screw up his courage in an absurd mock encounter which restores to him—superficially—the angry confidence (based on the pretence that his enemy is a coward) that sent him clamouring for the duel at line 10. (For a fuller discussion of this Tableau see Chapter 5, 'Characterization and Motivation'.)

Hard on this Tableau (87–106), on which our pity for Turnus commands a judgment less severe than the precarious, distorted quality of his courage would otherwise impose, comes a shorter Tableau (107–12, concluding the Section), in which we see Aeneas steel himself for the coming battle (108: *acuit Martem et se suscitat ira*); he is confident, almost serene—anger seems the wrong word for wrath that remains so detached. The contrast is so pointed, we feel the second Tableau lacks Virgil's usual subtlety. I suspect it is the reaction Virgil planned, for soon we shall see a less detached Aeneas: there is no place in war for detachment. At the same time we sense an element of dishonesty in Virgil's procedure which we must find displeasing. The discerning reader sees that the portrait of Aeneas in 107–12 is undercut by Sections 2 and 3. But the comment is too telling for public circulation, while the portrait which is drawn here for general consumption is drawn a little crudely—one example of an uneasy compromise, deep in the poem's structure, between its acknowledged function as a work of propaganda and its more honest, but slightly surreptitious function as a penetrating comment, offered to a people sick of war, on the way war dehumanizes. (See Chapter 5, 'Impure Poetry'.)

A second Section is obviously now needed to carry us into the next

---

I'm to die there's nothing I can do about it'. It is the traditional soldier's attitude: death comes when it comes; there can be no question of trying to avoid it—only cowards do that. But Turnus says more than he means: for us, the words imply that he is not a free agent; a combination of fate and character drives him along a course Latinus and Amata beg him not to follow.

The Twelve Books

day and up to the point where the duel actually begins. Had all gone smoothly, the second Section need not have been longer than the first: if we were to take the description of the opening ceremony (113–33 and 161–215) and add to that the fine imagery describing Turnus and Aeneas as they advance to meet one another (681–703), we should have, after a very little recasting, an entirely adequate transition from Section 1 to Section 3. Events take, however, an unexpected turn: an incident sweeps aside preparations for the duel; quickly, it becomes a pitched battle, described on a scale comparable with the battle narratives of Books 10 and 11. The layout of this second Section is both complicated and effective. Pretty clearly the 615 lines fall into three main groups of Episodes. The first group begins at dawn with the preparations for the duel, and carries on after the truce is broken to the final short but vivid Tableau (311–22), in which Aeneas is wounded by the arrow of an unknown assailant while he stands bareheaded, right hand outstretched, vainly appealing to his men to hold back from the fighting. The second group ends with a description of pitched battle; overcome by the same indiscriminate anger as his followers, Aeneas is now as much embroiled in the fighting as Turnus. The third group ends with a Tableau of Jove holding his scales aloft to announce the foregone conclusion of the encounter.[1] Within each group the lines of division are naturally less apparent; the analysis given above is, as usual, intended to help the reader, not to reconstruct Virgil's draft.

Section 2 begins at a slow tempo. A certain magnificence in the proceedings, an exalted, elaborate narrative, intensify our sense of disaster when all the pomp and ceremony lead nowhere. We are forewarned of disaster by the Episode of Juno and Iuturna (134–60); but we must live with our foreknowledge for some time if it is to be dramatically effective for us to know that disaster is pending. After the fine descriptive passage which sets the stage for the duel, the reader is apt to be puzzled by the spectacle of the embarrassed efforts of the queen of the gods to enlist the aid for her own ends of her husband's former mistress, just as he is apt to be puzzled by the Episode of Juno and Venus in Book 4 (4.90–128), or by the intervention of Venus in the unexpected role of healer of the wounded later in the present Section

---

[1] The first group ends with a rallentando marked by the Tracking-Away perfect *iactauit* (323), after which the second group begins with an echo of the opening words of the book (*Turnus ut . . . uidit*). The beginning of the third group is marked by the sudden transition at 554 from impasse to the course of action which restores the initiative to Aeneas.

Book 12

(12.411–19). It is not so much that the divine intervention is unnecessary, or somehow spoils the story—we can easily adjust our thinking to Virgil's trick of Parallel Motivation (see Chapter 5). What leaves us uneasy is the hint of flippancy, though flippancy is not easily gauged in a language we do not speak; the stress laid on facts we might expect to have been soft-pedalled conflicts with the grand, majestic mood just established. But this is to misread the Episode: Virgil resorts to irony partly to relieve the tension; partly to avoid excessive commitment to what must remain a beautiful, challenging poetic fantasy. In such a fantasy it is often useful to have the reader in the know beforehand—so long as he can feel he is specially privileged by a convention of a fairy-tale, not receiving a lesson in philosophy.

We return after this divine interlude to the scene before the Italian city and the ceremony of the vows. Aeneas promises that, if Turnus is the victor in the duel, the Aeneadae under Iulus will admit defeat and depart; if Aeneas is the victor, he promises generous terms: he does not want a kingdom (190: *nec mihi regna peto*); the two peoples can live side by side, Latinus in enjoyment of the supreme temporal authority, Aeneas the spiritual head of the two peoples.[1] Latinus replies with a solemn oath to respect the terms Aeneas has proposed.

Our attention switches to Turnus as he comes forward (218–21) to the sacrificial altar. A glimpse of him a moment earlier (164–5) left little opportunity to divine whether his mood had changed or not from the night before. The figure we now see, so pale, so young as he advances to murmur a private entreaty to his gods is plainly that of a man who feels himself doomed. Now that he has Aeneas before him, he can no longer cling to his fiction of a cowardly, degenerate opponent. To his own men the contest looks pitifully unequal (216–17).

At this point the divine action begins to interlock with the heroic one: Iuturna, disguised as one of the Rutuli, moves among them working on their feelings. But the thoughts she instils are those that would naturally arise—shame at having forced the duel upon their commander, the evident numerical inferiority of the enemy. They are less concerned for Turnus (he will get his glory) than at the unfairness of it—why should they lose their freedom because he is no match for Aeneas? The mood spreads to the rest of the Italians and is fanned to action by what seems a favourable omen—a flock of birds force an eagle to drop a swan he has seized in his talons; an augur interprets

---

[1] There is an obvious reference in the words *nec mihi regna peto* to Julius Caesar, possibly also to the Augustan settlement of 27 B.C.

The Twelve Books

the sign for them and hurls the first spear. It strikes a handsome, young Arcadian, one of nine brothers (222–76).

The madness spreads fast. Angrily the Arcadian's brothers rush forward. So do the Italians, leaving Latinus to flee with his priests. Swords are drawn, chariots mounted (282–8). One of the Italian leaders, Messapus, rides down an Etruscan with his horse and sends him stumbling against the altars before dispatching him with a sacrilegious taunt (289–96). A Trojan snatches a burning torch from an altar and plunges it in the face of an assailant, then kills him (298–304). Another Trojan has his sword poised to strike when the Italian wheels round and splits his pursuer's head open with an axe (304–10).

The space Virgil devotes to these incidents underlines an Implicit Comment whose relevance to the continual recrudescence of violence in the civil war is obvious, and is sharpened by an interesting use of allusion in the opening lines of the following Episode. Aeneas' cry *quo ruitis?* (313) as he appeals to his men not to join in the fighting can hardly have failed to evoke in the minds of Virgil's contemporaries the beginning of Horace's seventh Epode (*Quo, quo scelesti ruitis?*)— Horace's impassioned appeal to his fellow-countrymen not to embroil themselves again in the horrors of civil war.

But no one listens to the voice of reason, and an arrow directed by an unknown hand renders Aeneas helpless.[1] Turnus' reaction is different. (We come now to the second group of Episodes, in which the spotlight moves backwards and forwards between Turnus and Aeneas.) A situation he can cope with sets Turnus on fire with hope (325: *subita spe feruidus ardet*). He calls for his horses (326: *poscit equos*—the repetition reminds us they are the horses from whom he sought comfort at 82–6), and with a wrench at the reins he is off in his chariot, dealing destruction all around him like the god of war himself. The names and the manner of death of his first three victims are curtly recorded, and then the narrator lingers a moment over two brothers, as though struggling to check pity and affection (343–5), before passing to a 16-line description of the death of Turnus' sixth victim. Six more follow—the last picked out in a vivid one-line Vignette as Thymoetes tumbles from the neck of his rearing horse. Turnus races on, sweeping all before him like the north wind. Only one man holds his ground—Phegeus, who throws his life away in a futile gesture of contempt for heroics: hurling himself at Turnus' chariot,

[1] At 815 Juno claims it was Iuturna's arrow that wounded Aeneas.

Book 12

he clambers on it, and, sword in hand, protecting himself with his shield, is working his way towards Turnus when he comes in contact with one of the wheels; Turnus strikes Phegeus' head from his body as he falls.

Virgil leaves it to this concluding 12-line Tableau (discussed in Chapter 1) to make its Implicit Comment on the distinction he would have us draw between two kinds of unthinking courage: the aimless heroics of Turnus, who kills for the joy of killing in an evasion of reality (so long as he can kill, it does not occur to him that he may be killed—compare Camilla), and the heroism of Phegeus, equally pointless, yet somehow easier to admire because he throws his life away in a gesture of spirited, reckless defiance.

More telling comment will come when the description of Turnus' flight from reality is resumed at line 468. For the moment the narrative is suspended, to take us back to Aeneas at the point where we left him at line 323. We follow the angry, limping figure into the Trojan camp and watch while the physician Iapyx (who had chosen the art of medicine in preference to all the skills offered him by his lover Apollo)[1] wrestles to extract the arrow from Aeneas' thigh. It will not come free. All the time the roar of battle grows louder, and the air is thick with dust.

Upon this Tableau of the Heroic Age (387–410) is superimposed a piece of whimsy: Venus intervenes to toss into the physician's gleaming basin a homely preparation called dittany, known to the wild goats of Crete (if not to Iapyx), where she had procured it no doubt before racing to Aeneas' aid. She laces it from her personal supply of ambrosia and panacea, remaining invisible throughout. The brew works. The arrow slips from the wound, the limb recovers, and Iapyx, recognizing the presence of a hand more skilled than his own, promptly pronounces Aeneas fit for active service (425: *arma citi properate uiro! quid statis?*). Just as suddenly the mood of whimsy evaporates and its place is taken by a formal, heroic Tableau whose moving simplicity is weakened by neither its evident symbolism nor its flamboyant rhetoric (432–40):

> postquam habilis lateri clipeus loricaque tergo est,
> Ascanium fusis circum complectitur armis
> summaque per galeam delibans oscula fatur:

---

[1] The music of line 397 seems to have haunted Gray. Surely in an age which cultivated the poetry of allusion his 'Mute, inglorious Milton' is a conscious echo of Virgil's *maluit et mutas agitare inglorius artis*.

The Twelve Books

'disce, puer, uirtutem ex me uerumque laborem,
fortunam ex aliis; nunc te mea dextera bello
defensum dabit et magna inter praemia ducet.
tu facito, mox cum matura adoleuerit aetas,
sis memor et te animo repetentem exempla tuorum
et pater Aeneas et auunculus excitet Hector.'[1]

When his shield was in place at his side, his corslet on his back,
throwing his arms round Ascanius, he takes him in his embrace,
with his lips touches him lightly through his helmet, speaks:
'Learn, boy, from me what courage is and true toil;
from others, what luck is. Now will my right hand in war
protect you and lead you where great prizes wait.
You must see that you remember; when soon you are a grown man,
let your father Aeneas, your uncle Hector stir your thoughts.'

Like any practised writer or psychologist Virgil knows the effectiveness of an unexpected return to solemnity after a relaxing jest. When Aeneas leads a charge from the Trojan camp, this time it is Turnus and the Italians who hear the uproar and see the dust of an advancing enemy, who feel a chill run through their blood. But while the others join in the fighting, Aeneas still holds back; he moves up and down through the dust of battle seeking out one opponent only—Turnus (466–7):

> solum densa in caligine Turnum
> uestigat lustrans, solum in certamina poscit.

Before the rest, Iuturna realizes the significance of the uproar (448–9). Substituting herself for his charioteer Metiscus, she takes Turnus on a wild dash whose only object is to keep her brother from Aeneas.

By making Iuturna intervene to put an end to Turnus' bout of slaughter, Virgil avoids making Turnus run away in full consciousness of what he is doing; that would be to make him too openly a coward. On the other hand Turnus is not unaware of what is happening: later he tells Iuturna that he was not deceived by her disguise (632–4); we must presume he notices that his charioteer tries to prevent him from joining battle with the enemy (480). The function of Iuturna is to bridge the gap between what we should call unconscious and conscious

---

[1] For a discussion of the symbolism of 435–6 see Perret, p. 138. Aeneas' concluding words (440) are an exact echo, with only the tone changed, of Andromache's words to Aeneas (3.343). The repetition is surely not pointless.

Book 12

thought. To begin with, Turnus is not conscious he is run[ning] from Aeneas. He may not fully realize what he is doing [ ] brings him to his senses at 664. Virgil would probably have had much more difficulty than we should in analysing this psychological phenomenon even if he had not limited himself to the conventions of his form. But he knew what it was like to be in a state of diminishing honesty with oneself. And this is, I think, his attempt at artistic representation of that state.

Circumstances now undermine Aeneas' mood of aloof high-mindedness. The Tableaux of Aeneas at 107–12, 311–17 and 464–7 show the increasing strain brought to bear upon a mind almost priggish at the outset in its confident detachment. A single spear shot by Messapus (488–90) now wrecks what remains of Aeneas' determination not to join in the fighting.[1] Unable to restrain his anger, he succumbs, with a prayer to Jove for pardon, to the universal lust for blood, and we are back where we were at 10.514–15.

For the rest of the Episode (505–53) the camera passes back and forth from Aeneas to Turnus. When Aeneas abandons his pursuit of Turnus, Turnus resumes his fugue in the chariot,[2] reaching a new peak of exultant slaughter at 509–12, in a Vignette which shows him attaching to his chariot the heads of the two brothers Amycus and Diores. The description of the exploits of the two leaders follows the usual pattern of an alternation between a terse recital of names and a highlighting of pathetic detail (for example, the young Menoetes who hated war, 516–20, or Aeolus, 542–7, both killed by Turnus; Murranus, 529–34, killed by Aeneas—his body is trampled on by his own horses). Meanwhile, what had begun as a series of isolated incidents has now become a hotly contested pitched battle, the narrative of which in the high style of heroic epic is rounded off with a reminiscence of Ennius (552–3):

> pro se quisque uiri summa nituntur opum ui;
> nec mora nec requies, uasto certamine tendunt.[3]

Each man for himself, they struggle with all their might;
no let-up, no respite, in a great, wild struggle they contend.

---

[1] Messapus is presumably the first to attack Aeneas, who has confined himself to pursuing Turnus. His intervention is perhaps intended to distract Aeneas from Turnus, which would explain Virgil's comment that Aeneas was provoked by being unfairly attacked (494: *insidiis . . . subactus*).
[2] We have to arrive at clarity by a juxtaposition of 479–83 with 509 ff.
[3] Cf. Ennius, epic fragments 164W and 394W.

By now, at the end of this second group of Episodes, any chance that the duel will take place seems remote. As Aeneas' gaze ranges up and down the field of battle—despite his anger, he remains on the alert for signs of Turnus (557–8)—his eye lights on the Latin city, in front of which they are fighting, and he senses at once the opportunity for a spectacular act of strategy—and a coup that will be some compensation for having been made to look a fool by Turnus (cf. 570–1).[1] (See the discussion of this Episode in Chapter 1.) A typical Roman *contio* follows (565–73): standing on a mound, Aeneas presents his plan to his men with that economy of words which, we are told, was characteristic of Julius Caesar. His brusque, businesslike tone conceals distortion of fact and the cynical, vindictive bloodthirstiness of what he proposes (567–9):

> 'urbem hodie, causam belli, regna ipsa Latini,
> ni frenum accipere et uicti parere fatentur,
> eruam et aequa solo fumantia culmina ponam.'

> *'The city which caused the war, Latinus' realm itself,*
> *unless they accept the curb, admit they are beaten, will obey,*
> *I shall this day raze, lay level with the ground its smouldering roofs.'*

Only the unarmed, innocent civilians (the *matres*, the *uulgus inermum inualidique senes*, whom we saw at 131–2) remain in the city. Aeneas' attempt to unload responsibility for an act of wanton destruction on to any shoulders but his own (compare also 572 and 580–2), his struggle to shelter behind the assertion of a righteous cause (565: *Iuppiter hac stat*[2]), should deceive no thinking reader; indeed, his opening words suggest they do not fully deceive *him*—why does he make so much fuss about being obeyed?

A full-scale onslaught on the Latin city follows, led by Aeneas with the same ruthless efficiency displayed by Neoptolemus in his attack on Priam's palace at 2.469–505 (Implicit Comment). One difference is that a minority of the Italians are for surrendering the city to Aeneas

---

[1] The city has been left defenceless, but it is of course protected at the front by the Italian army which had camped overnight between the city and the Aeneadae and had then been marched out before the duel to face the Aeneadae. Aeneas' plan, as we shall see at 621, involves taking advantage of the general confusion to withdraw a detachment of his men to attack beyond the Italian lines at the side or in the rear (*diuersa ab urbe*). Once the attack has been launched, the Italians withdraw from the battlefield into the city to defend it from within. (This explains 661–2.) The attack progressively absorbs the forces on both sides until Turnus is left by himself at 664.

[2] The words are a reminiscence of Ennius 253W.

Book 12

(584–5). Amid the general despair, the narrative first picks out Amata (believing the attack must mean that Turnus is dead, she commits suicide, taking on herself the blame for all that has happened), then Lavinia and Latinus, prostrate with grief, before it is suspended to return to Turnus at the moment when the uproar of the attack reaches his ears (Parallel Narrative). He grabs the reins from Iuturna and stops his chariot, unable to think clearly (622). His sister tries to keep him within the comparative safety of his fugue. But already before now his exhilaration had begun to evaporate (616: *iam minus atque minus successu laetus equorum*), its place taken by a mood of resignation and the beginnings of an honesty with himself that lend Turnus a new tragic stature. While it brought him comfort, he acquiesced in Iuturna's play-acting. But a growing sense of shame now makes him reject it. He begins to see in the deaths of the leaders of his own side an ironic vindication of Drances' taunt (11.360–73) that Turnus lets others fight his battles for him. Is death after all so terrible a thing? (646: *usque adeone mori miserum est?*) His speech to Iuturna (632–49) reveals, graphically and convincingly, this complex psychological process, without of course analysing it or pinpointing the transition from each state of mind to that succeeding it.

The movement towards honesty with himself is accelerated by the arrival of Saces—the typical tragic messenger. He tells Turnus the queen is dead, the king too muddled to act; the eyes of all are fixed on Turnus. For Turnus is alone—the fighting has left him behind; while the other Italian leaders put up a desperate struggle (661–2), Turnus is 'wheeling his chariot around in an empty field' (664: *tu currum deserto in gramine uersas*).

What Saces and the Italians want of Turnus is not plainly stated. The decision Turnus is about to take is dramatically more effective if it is his decision. But plainly what Saces wants, and perhaps dare not ask, is not that Turnus should join in the battle for the city, but that Turnus should fight his duel with Aeneas and, one way or the other, put an end to the suffering of all. His opening supplication is: 'Take pity on your people' (653: *miserere tuorum*)—a pathetic echo of Drances' ironical words to Turnus in the Council of War (11.365).[1] The faces and eyes directed toward Turnus (656–7) recall the looks of Turnus' soldiers—those which, at the beginning of the book, finally drove him into acceptance of the duel.

---

[1] Virgil prepares the reader for the echo, by Turnus' reference to Drances (644: *Drancis dicta refellam?*).

An agony of conflicting emotions tortures Turnus before he takes his decision. Turning, he has visible evidence of the impending destruction of the city: a great tower tumbling in flames. There seems only one honourable course to take: to seek out Aeneas and throw his life away in a last futile gesture. More surely than he sensed it before, Turnus knows that to meet Aeneas means death. But death faced, however pointlessly, is better than the shame of death evaded. (For a further discussion of this passage see Chapter 5, 'Tragic Insight'.)

Jumping from his chariot, he rushes toward the city (681). Now it is Turnus, not Aeneas, who appeals for an end to the fighting so that the duel can take place (compare 693-5 with 311-17). His headlong advance is like a crumbling mass of rock torn loose by a storm or the passage of the years to hurtle across the plain beneath, engulfing forests, herds and men (684-9); it symbolizes the disintegration of Turnus' personality and that self-destroying energy (*uiolentia*) which is characteristic of him—Horace's *uis consili expers* that *mole ruit sua*.[1]

A contrasting simile highlights the figure that confronts him. Abandoning the attack on the city, his assurance, his confidence in the rightness of his actions recovered, Aeneas stands firm, cool, resplendent, joyful even, in the path of his enemy, 'high as Mount Athos, or Mount Eryx, or Father Appennine with his shimmering ilex-oaks, rearing his flanks to heaven and rejoicing in his crowning mantle of snow' (701-3):

> quantus Athos aut quantus Eryx aut ipse coruscis
> cum fremit ilicibus quantus gaudetque niuali
> uertice se attollens pater Appenninus ad auras.

Both sides withdraw and lay down their arms to watch. An exchange of spears precedes the duel (711), followed by a charge in which the two shields strike against one another with a crash that fills the sky (724). As they lock, like two angry bulls watched apprehensively by the herds they lead, straining and grunting in the death struggle (715-22), Jove himself displays his scales in which he has placed the destinies of the two combatants, to proclaim to all the fated outcome of the contest.[2]

---

[1] Horace, *Odes* 3.4.65.
[2] The meaning of the concluding line of the Section has provoked endless argument; see Warde Fowler, *The Death of Turnus* (1919) 127-31, and the commentaries of Mackail and Maguinness. A more interesting question is the meaning of the Tableau: does Jove not know the outcome of the struggle? Of the two passages in Homer where the image of the scales occurs (*Il.* 8.68-72

Book 12

The narrative of the duel resolves itself into two encounters, each full of Homeric echoes,[1] separated at 790 (Suspended Narrative) by a long divine interlude that first relieves the tension and then sets the stage for tragedy. A change of tempo and mood distinguishes the two Episodes. The first (728–90) is fast-moving, full of excitement, remarkable for its compression and for the skill shown in the selection of detail and plot construction—by a series of simple devices the tables are turned spectacularly three times. The second Episode (887–952) is slow-moving and appeals to our sense of pathos and tragedy instead of our appetite for excitement.

It is Turnus who first seizes the initiative. An opportunity presents itself; his sword flashes out, and from his full height he strikes a blow at Aeneas (728–30). A great shout arises from both sides—and then they see Turnus' sword lying in shining fragments on the tawny sand (741: *fulua resplendent fragmina harena*); in his excitement when he

---

and 22.208–13) it is the latter, I think, that Virgil has particularly in mind: the scales are held up to *demonstrate* to the other gods where the burden of fate lies heavier. The image of the scales occurs also in Aeschylus, *Ag.* 439, and there is a well-known parody of the idea in Aristophanes' *Frogs*. Virgil introduces the concept of *labor*, presumably inviting us to connect this passage with 12.435–6 and 10.111–12.

[1] The first encounter *ends* in a chase that evokes the chase with which the duel between Achilles and Hector in *Il.* 22 *begins*. Virgil's deer simile (749–55) is an elaboration of Homer's (*Il.* 22.188–93). In Homer (*Il.* 22.276–7) Athene gives Achilles back his spear; in Virgil (786–7) Venus gives Aeneas *his* spear back. The second encounter is built round the incidents of (a) the rock (896–907), based on a conflation of *Il.* 12.445–50 (Hector during an attack on the Greek camp raises a rock that no two ordinary men could lift), *Il.* 21.403–6 (Athene strikes Ares with a *boundary*-stone), and *Il.* 5.302–8 (Diomede snatches up a rock in his duel with Aeneas), and (b) the paralysis of Turnus (908–12), in which the dream simile is based on the simile describing Achilles' pursuit of Hector (*Il.* 12.199–201). But the material taken from Homer is (1) a combination of many different passages; (2) an elaboration by Virgil of Homeric material until he has made it his own (e.g., the deer simile); or (3) a transformation of Homer: the dream simile in Homer (applied to the pursuit of Hector) is of a chase that never ends; the dream Virgil describes, as an illustration of the uncanny paralysis of Turnus, is the dream in which we are desperately anxious to run away, but are deprived of all ability to act and even of the power of speech. (Compare the dream in Lucretius, 4.453–6). And of course this adapted and transformed material is embedded in a rich fabric of fresh invention (e.g., the magic swords, the uncanny bird) and forms part of a new narrative which is quite remarkable for the skill of its plot construction and entirely different in tone and purpose from Homer.

For the way in which Virgil uses, by allusion, both the duel of Menelaus and Paris in *Il.* 3–4 and the duel of Achilles and Hector, see W. S. Anderson, 'Vergil's second *Iliad*', *TAPhA* 88 (1957) 29.

jumped on to his chariot at 326, he snatched up not the magic sword given to Turnus' father by Vulcan (described at 90–1) but an ordinary man-made sword belonging to Metiscus and no match for the immortal armour of Aeneas.[1]

Turnus takes to his heels in a mad attempt to escape, but has constantly to retrace his steps (742–3). A great marsh bars the way on one side, the tall walls of the city on another; he heads away from these, but the Trojans spring to hem him in (744–5).[2] The initiative has passed to Aeneas, but he cannot firmly grasp it: his wounded leg (though healed by Venus herself) hampers him in the pursuit; he is like a great dog that has cut off a fleet-footed deer but cannot catch it (750–5). Turnus as he runs calls out for his magic sword. Aeneas threatens instant death to the man who proffers it. The grim comedy continues (758–65).[3]

A double *coup de théâtre* restores the initiative to Turnus—and then wrests it from him again. Aeneas, despairing of catching Turnus, runs to where his spear fell when he cast it at Turnus in the exchange that preceded the hand-to-hand fighting (711);[4] a great olive-tree sacred to Faunus had been removed by the Trojans in clearing the ground for the duel; but a root had been left and in this the spear had stuck fast (766–73). Panic-stricken, Turnus appeals to Faunus not to release the spear. Then while Aeneas struggles vainly, Iuturna, once more disguised as Metiscus, runs forward and hands Turnus his magic sword. For an instant Turnus is on top. Then Venus wrenches the spear free from the root for her son (774–87).[5] The two rush forward for a second

---

[1] Note two characteristically Virgilian tricks here: (1) Virgil builds in earlier the information needed now about Turnus' sword so that it will not seem like something invented on the spur of the moment for the sake of the plot; (2) the story of the wrong sword is introduced by the distancing formula *fama est* (735) as though Virgil's story were not his own but a condensation of an ancient story endless in its ramifications. The shattered sword comes from Homer, *Il.* 3.361–3 (Menelaus breaks his sword on Paris' helmet). On these devices, see *Latin Explorations*, pp. 198–220.

[2] Note the tense contrast between *cingunt* and the instantaneous perfect *inclusere*; if Virgil had meant that the Trojans were *standing* in a circle, he would have written *includunt* or *includebant*.

[3] Lines 764–5 are based on a detail of the pursuit of Hector, *Il.* 22.159–61, but *ludicra* transforms the allusion. The pursuit of Hector is a straight race differing only from a normal foot race in the stakes; the pursuit of Turnus is a crazy race, like something staged for a prize that will raise the spectators' laughter when presented—but the prize is life itself.

[4] Again a detail built in earlier to be made use of later.

[5] The double divine intervention keeps up the atmosphere of fairy-tale, but in fact nothing happens outside the limits of plausibility: advantage is taken of

Book 12

encounter. Both have had their confidence restored (788: *animis refecti*), though both are feeling the strain physically (790: *certamine Martis anheli*). The initiative, however, has reverted to Aeneas: a man with a sword must get close to his opponent; a man with a spear can hurl it from a safe distance.

At this point comes a long divine interlude (96 lines). It begins on that gently mischievous note which Virgil assumes when the course of the heroic action is foreshadowed or revealed on the divine level. 'Come,' says the king of gods and men in effect to his wife, 'this sort of thing cannot be allowed to go on for ever.' And, after a little tactful flattery (800–2), Jove puts his foot down: 'I will have fate tampered with no further' (806: *ulterius temptare ueto*). Juno, after wriggling to extricate herself from the accusation of tampering ('Iuturna', she protests, 'exceeded her instructions'), asks a final favour: let this be an end of Troy and let the peace involve no obliteration of the race for whom she has fought (821–8). These are the terms that Aeneas had already proposed at 187–94 and Jove acquiesces in them with a smile.

Abruptly the tone changes: and a grim fantasy takes the place of whimsy. Jove sends his personal messenger of death, one of the two dread figures (*Dirae*) born of darkness that attend him in the chastisement of mankind. Hurtling down to the battlefield, the creature assumes the form of a small bird—the kind, says Virgil, that late at night sits on tombstones or lonely heights troubling us with its song (863–4):

> quae quondam in bustis aut culminibus desertis
> nocte sedens serum canit importuna per umbras.

When the bird flies in Turnus' face, beating against it with its wings, he is overcome with a fear like none he knew before (865–8). Recognizing the sound and knowing she can help Turnus no longer, Iuturna retreats lamenting the emptiness of the immortality granted her; what joy can it bring her if she may not save her brother?[1]

To what psychological reality does this lovely fiction of the awful bird of death correspond? It is a question we may fairly put without

---

Aeneas' distracted attention to give Turnus his sword; Aeneas, faced with a crisis, makes a supreme effort and frees his spear.

[1] Iuturna is the most pathetic of Virgil's female characters after Dido—a real person, not just a cog in the plot. Even so her speech (872–84) is apt to seem needlessly long to us at so intensely dramatic a juncture. Virgil perhaps wants to relax the tension before resuming the narrative of the duel.

treating Virgil's poem as though he had written a version in code of a textbook on human behaviour. We left Turnus at 790, sword in hand, his confidence restored. We return at 887 after the divine interlude to the same scene, no more than an instant later. But in that instant Turnus' confidence has been drained away. As he hangs back, Aeneas waves his great spear at Turnus, and mocks him, in an echo of Turnus' own words, for his hesitation.[1] The reason for the transformation in Turnus on what we may call the level of reality is plain. Turnus has hardly got back his sword when he catches sight of the spear that must put him at the mercy of an opponent he cannot reach to strike at with his sword. What pulls him up in his tracks is not fear of Aeneas, but a chilling realization that fate has again blocked his path to hope, as his sober reply to Aeneas' taunt shows (894–5):

> ille caput quassans: 'non me tua feruida terrent
> dicta, ferox; di me terrent et Iuppiter hostis.'

*Shaking his head he said, 'Your hot words do not
fright me, boaster; the gods fright me and mine enemy Jove.'*

It is this unseen, impenetrable barrier between him and hope which is symbolized by the flapping of the bird's wings in his face.

In a final, heroic effort of defiance he grasps a great boundary-stone —placed there of old, Virgil drily remarks, 'to keep these fields free from strife' (898). But as Turnus runs with it his strength fails him so utterly, he no longer recognizes himself; his knees give way and the missile falls short (903–7). He stands paralysed like a man in a nightmare (908–12). For a moment the divine level reimposes itself in a brief phrase (913–14):

> quacumque uiam uirtute petiuit,
> successum dea dira negat.

> *Wherever courage sought a way
> the dread goddess bars access.*

His mind in a turmoil, he looks about him, unable either to retreat or to advance. Aeneas bides his time. At length he gets his chance and hurls his great spear at his helpless opponent. It strikes Turnus in the thigh and he falls to his knees (927).

---

[1] Line 889:
  'quae nunc deinde mora est? aut quid iam, Turne, retractas?'
is an echo of Turnus' words (not heard, of course, by Aeneas) at 11:
  'nulla mora in Turno; nihil est quod dicta retractent.'

Book 12

Virgil's poem ends with a scene that is justly famous:[1] Aeneas towers over his defeated enemy, ready to strike the death-blow (938: *acer in armis*); touched, however, by Turnus' embarrassed plea for mercy, he is on the point of sparing him—and then strikes him down after all.

The ground is prepared for this concluding *coup de théâtre* in Book 10. For it is the sight of the belt stripped from the body of Pallas that turns Aeneas, when compassion and humanity are about to gain the upper hand, into a terrifying spectacle of mad, blazing rage (946–7: *furiis accensus et ira terribilis*). To the narrative of the killing of Pallas and the removal of the belt from his body by Turnus, Virgil added a comment (10.501–5):

> nescia mens hominum fati sortisque futurae
> et seruare modum, rebus sublata secundis!
> Turno tempus erit, magno cum optauerit emptum
> intactum Pallanta et cum spolia ista diemque
> oderit.

Man's mind knows nothing of fate and what will be his lot
when buoyed up with success, nor what limit he should keep.
The time will come for Turnus when he would give much
to have had naught to do with Pallas, when he will hate this day
and what he took.

The lines are an adaptation of Homer's comment on Patroclus' boast to Achilles (*Iliad* 16.46–7), but there are two things which are not in Homer: the statement that Turnus went too far, did not observe the proper limit, in his treatment of Pallas, and the statement that the time will come when Turnus would give a lot to have had nothing to do with Pallas.[2] We should not assume too hastily that the 'time' Virgil meant

---

[1] See, e.g., A. H. Thornton, 'The last scene of the *Aeneid*', *GR* 22 (1953) 82–4.

[2] We are discreetly reminded that Turnus has the belt—and that the time for his repentance has not yet come—by a detail in Virgil's description of the funeral procession in Book 11: at the end of the procession proper, before the long line of mourners, walks a group of men carrying Pallas' spear and helmet —'for', Virgil adds, 'victorious Turnus has the rest' (11.91–2):
> nam cetera Turnus
> uictor habet.

Three further points: (1) Turnus' wish is not a wish for something realizable —there is no suggestion of buying Pallas back from the dead; *emptum* is not for *redemptum*; (2) *intactum* has, I think, the general meaning I have given it— Turnus wishes he had had nothing to do with Pallas, not that he had not taken the belt; (3) *optauerit emptum* is a common idiom, almost a colloquialism—no possible transaction is contemplated.

The Twelve Books

is the moment when Aeneas now stands over Turnus. To make Turnus feel at this point that he would have given anything to have had nothing to do with Pallas comes too close to making him sound like a coward right at the end of the poem, makes us feel Virgil is cheating, blackening a character for whom he has aroused so much sympathy, instead of letting him die a hero's death; a spasm of regret on leaving life (cf. 952) is all right, but repentance forced out by the wish to save one's own skin is nasty. It is better to suppose the time begins earlier—at the point, perhaps, where Turnus realizes that he cannot get out of the duel, that Aeneas is out for his blood and looks (after the uncanny ghost Episode of Book 10) like getting it.

Yet Turnus' killing of Pallas can hardly, by itself, justify Aeneas' present awful anger. The blind lust for revenge that overflowed after the death of Pallas has by now been brought under control. In that rage Aeneas declared he would offer eight captured Italian prisoners as a living sacrifice at Pallas' funeral (10.517–20), and with still smouldering anger he sent the prisoners to Evander at 11.81–2; the Aeneas who stands over Turnus now listening to his words has recovered his hard-won humanity.

He listens, therefore, to Turnus when Turnus suddenly, unexpectedly, pleads for his life. Like Camilla, Turnus is a young romantic who thinks nothing of death—until it stares him in the face. (Compare the icy realism with which Mezentius accepts death, 10.900–6.) He cannot bring himself to ask openly for mercy (observe the equivocation of 935: *et me, seu corpus spoliatum lumine mauis*). Instead he talks of his father Daunus, entreats Aeneas not to widen further the circle of hatred (938: *ulterius ne tende odiis*). Aeneas stops short in the middle of the death-stroke.[1] While Turnus continues speaking, he stands motionless, letting his eyes run over Turnus (939: *uoluens oculos*). It is to begin with no more than that willingness to let the speaker have his say with which Dido receives Aeneas' justification of his actions (4.363–4); but gradually Turnus' words begin to take effect: more and more Aeneas' determination to go ahead when Turnus has finished (the usual epic convention) subsides into indecision.

Then Aeneas' wandering eye catches sight, high on Turnus' shoulder (941: *umero alto*—we see from 926–30 that Turnus is on his knees before Aeneas with his right hand extended in supplication), of

---

[1] The instantaneous perfects *stetit* and *repressit* emphasize the abruptness with which Turnus' words check Aeneas.

Book 12

the ornamental plaques upon the belt Turnus is wearing—and recognizes it for Pallas' belt. The reader feels the trap, set by fate for Turnus that day when it tempted him to go too far, snap tight now about its victim, in final fulfilment of Jove's ordinance to the gods before the battle that they must leave men free to decide their own fate, that 'the course of action each man has embarked upon will determine his destiny and what he will endure' (10.111–12: *sua cuique exorsa laborem fortunamque ferent*). (See Chapter 5, 'Tragic Attitude'.)

It is however on Aeneas that Virgil wishes us to concentrate our attention in the concluding lines. The reaction he wants to prompt is plain. We must condemn the sudden rage that causes Aeneas to kill Turnus when he is on the point of sparing him—and when his death no longer makes sense, for Turnus has acknowledged defeat (936–7); the war is over and the peace terms already agreed to (187–94). The killing of Turnus cannot be justified, this is beyond doubt the judgment expected of us. It is of course intolerable, from the point of view of plot construction, that Turnus should be left alive. But if he is a competent poet, aware of the implications of his own fiction, Virgil must make Aeneas' action both psychologically plausible and forgivable: we cannot be invited to condemn the poem's hero at the very climax of the poem.

We have seen it is the belt that decides Turnus' fate. But how?[1] Aeneas can scarcely have forgotten that Turnus killed Pallas. Why, then, is his reaction so violent? Has the fact, while remaining part of Aeneas' intellectual memory, lost, as the days went by, its grip upon Aeneas' emotions? It seems a reasonable explanation, but not the only explanation. For even if Aeneas began the duel in a spirit of revenge (as Virgil's text suggests), the fight quickly became like any other fight; in the participants' minds one thought predominated: the determination to win—sharpened in the case of this particular duel by the humiliation Aeneas felt at being unable to catch Turnus when he ran away from him.

When therefore Aeneas stands victorious over Turnus it would be understandable if Pallas were no longer in his thoughts; merely to be reminded of Pallas might be enough to rekindle the lust for revenge. Yet that is not really the way Virgil wants it either. For in that case

---

[1] The point has been made by more than one critic. E.g., W. S. Maguinness, *The Tragic Spirit of the Aeneid* (1955) 6, comments:

> ... the Trojan strangely notices for the first time that Turnus is wearing this most conspicuous ornament.

action, the death-blow, would have followed close upon the return of memory. Instead, Aeneas lingers a long moment—not now in indecision, but in recollection (945–6).[1] Why?

Virgil does not tell us what Aeneas thinks, or feels, or remembers: that would be to make things too cut and dried. He drops hints, hoping that scenes and words from earlier in the narrative will pass through our minds, so that we can feel they are passing through the mind of Aeneas too. The first hint lies in the word *pueri* at 943: it evokes the protective relationship that grew up so quickly between Aeneas and the young prince—inviting us to recall, not the battle scenes or the Tableau of Pallas riding off to war with Aeneas (8.585–96), but the charming Vignette in which we glimpsed Pallas at Aeneas' side as they sailed down the Etruscan coast through the night, talking (10.159–62). We remember next, perhaps, Aeneas' passionate distress when Pallas is killed on his first day in battle (10.513–17); how we saw in that distress a sense of guilt, a feeling of responsibility laid on his shoulders by Pallas' father, and betrayed. Our thoughts move back to the early morning scene when Evander accompanied by Pallas advanced to shake hands with Aeneas (8.465–8) before entrusting his son to Aeneas' care and promising help in the war to come. That was one of the scenes which flashed before Aeneas' eyes when the news of Pallas' death was brought to him (10.517: *dextraeque datae*); we may feel it flashes again through his mind now, and, with that scene, the old man's passionate farewell to his son (8.558–84—ending with the prayer that he may not outlive his son, if Pallas is fated to be killed) and his unequivocal demand, delivered to Aeneas' men when they bring him the body of his son, that Aeneas should kill Turnus in revenge for Pallas (11.176–81).[2]

Here are memories enough to explain Aeneas' action in killing Turnus after he has half decided to spare him, and to render his action forgivable by all who realize that Virgil has attempted to make his hero

---

[1] In 945–6, as with *uoluens oculos* in 939, Virgil takes over an idea, a piece of psychological observation he used in his study of Dido (4.648–50):

> hic, postquam Iliacas uestis notumque cubile
> conspexit, paulum lacrimis et mente morata
> incubuitque toro dixitque nouissima uerba.

In both, the *postquam* clause emphasizes the slow movement. See *Latin Explorations*, p. 220.

[2] Observe the ambiguity of *dextera causa tua est* in 11.178: (1) '(If I go on living it is because) I rely on the obligation you accepted when we shook hands'; (2) 'I rely on your strong right hand in battle'.

Book 12

a human being and not a superman or a saint. The memories might render plausible, too, his sudden, flaring anger. But there is, I think, another subtler explanation for that, built into the poem earlier, to be recalled now, like these scenes, by the reader who has read the poem carefully.

Impressed upon the plaques (*bullae*) by which Aeneas recognized the belt was a story of bloodshed and crime (10.497: *impressum nefas*), a scene from legend, or perhaps a series of scenes (10.499: *quae*), from the story of the daughters of Danaus: there were fifty of them, and they married the fifty sons of Aegyptus; on their wedding night all but one murdered their husbands. Virgil contents himself with evoking the story briefly (10.497–9), leaving it to his readers to recall details for themselves, and passing on to tell us the names of the artist and his patron, with that apparent disregard for relevance which is characteristic of his manner:[1] what looks like Homeric embellishment has a carefully thought-out purpose—to fix in our minds, not the details of the story, for his readers knew them, but the fact that the story was there on the belt of Pallas.

Three hints evoke the fact now. The first is contained in the words *notis fulserunt cingula bullis* in 942. Why were the *bullae* familiar? Because the story they told made them distinctive. We remember first there was a story; then we remember what it was. Second, to clinch our first suspicion that we have seen what Virgil is driving at, comes the intriguing phrase *saeui monimenta doloris*. A brief scrutiny reveals, and resolves, the ambiguity: in one sense the belt is 'a reminder of cruel grief'—Aeneas' grief at losing Pallas; at the same time it is 'a record of savage suffering'—the suffering of the husbands who were murdered by their brides. Finally a third hint: Aeneas did not merely catch sight of the belt; he 'drank it in' (*hausit*). Virgil's intention is surely plain: as the memories of Pallas and Evander flood back and the passions those memories arouse surge higher, the scene upon the belt abruptly puts any lingering feelings of humanity aside; in a mind already inflamed, the contemplation of a scene of violence proves the final incitement to violence.

It is in a mood approaching righteous indignation (the mood we have seen him in repeatedly in this book—with less and less justification) that Aeneas brings his sword down upon the kneeling, suppliant figure before him (947–51):

[1] Cf. 5.359–60. We are told that the story of the daughters of Danaus was among the scenes on Augustus' temple of Apollo on the Palatine.

The Twelve Books

'tune hinc spoliis indute meorum
eripiare mihi? Pallas te hoc uulnere, Pallas
immolat et poenam scelerato ex sanguine sumit.'
hoc dicens ferrum aduerso sub pectore condit
feruidus.

'Shall you who wear things ripped from those
I protect escape me? Pallas strikes you now, Pallas
takes your life, takes his vengeance on guilty blood.'
So speaking, incensed he plunges the sword in the breast
before him.

The very solemnity of the high style,[1] the assertion of self-exculpation (Aeneas claims for himself the role of a mere instrument of revenge), the accusation levelled at an opponent we can feel guilty of no real crime (Virgil's *infelix* at 941 unobtrusively contradicts Aeneas' *scelerato ex sanguine*—it was bad luck Turnus was wearing the belt, not the working out of just retribution), our understanding, above all, of how much more complex the motivation of Aeneas' action is than he himself is aware—all these factors contribute to that sense of alienation which is one of the devices of tragedy. We feel less and less that we can identify ourselves with a character, or with the point of view of a character. But as we observe this final failure of insight in Virgil's tragic hero we reflect that we too—or any man in that situation—might have acted thus and deceived ourselves thus about the degree of rightness of our action. The relevance of the death scene to the events of their own times can hardly have escaped Virgil's contemporaries.[2]

[1] E.g., the building of a phrase around the vocative participle (*indute*) where prose would use a relative clause.

[2] Cf. Lucretius' dry observation (3.307–10):

sic hominum genus est. quamuis doctrina politos
constituat pariter quosdam, tamen illa relinquit
naturae cuiusque animi uestigia prima.
nec radicitus euelli mala posse putandumst.

5

Form and Technique

Part 1: FORM

When we call the *Aeneid* an epic, what we have in mind is the *form* of the poem. According to Greek ideas, an epic poem had to be written in dactylic hexameters, it had to be a long poem divided into books, it had to tell a story—and not just any kind of story either; these were the traditional rules of the form: there was little room for argument or experiment. That was not the end of the matter, moreover. The form also aroused expectations with regard to what we call *technique*.

It is true that the first Roman epic poets relaxed these requirements. But their unorthodoxy was not the result of heretical zeal, except in so far as it was heresy to want to write an epic poem on a Roman subject; improvisation was forced on Naevius and Ennius by the need to make the best of a bad language in the virtual absence of a native literary tradition. Everybody still knew what an epic poem should be, and how, properly speaking, you went about writing one. The concept of form was fundamental and comprehensive; the conventions to be observed in the matter of technique, while not inflexible, were ancient, venerable, widely respected, not to be disregarded lightly.

Critics often talk, therefore, as though Virgil were the slave of his form; as though the form left him no choice but to accept limitations of story and technique he would gladly have discarded. Manifest dissimilarities between Virgil and Homer are swept aside with the explanation that they are no more than the differences one would expect to find between an oral and a literary epic. It will be the object of this chapter to argue that Virgil is more the master of his form than its slave; that, if he took his story largely from Homer, if he accepted limitations of technique evolved in a different intellectual context, it was because he hoped he could make all he took the expression of his own poetic will.

The distinction between oral and literary epic, commonly made by critics, though useful for certain purposes, is apt, indeed, to distort the position of Virgil's poem in the literary tradition to which it belongs. The modern reader naturally associates the *Iliad* and the *Odyssey* with other oral epics (the Chanson de Roland, the Icelandic sagas, Beowulf); though these are the products of widely different cultures, they look alike, in the ways that peasants of different countries resemble one another more than they resemble their sophisticated cousins in the big cities of their own countries. But this implies an attitude to Homer which we must not attribute to Virgil. For him, as for his contemporaries, the poems of Homer were the work of a poet who differed from later epic poets only in being incomparably greater. First, in all senses, came Homer; there were people who held that epic had had its day, but that was a different matter; if epic was what you wanted, Homer was the supreme master.

After Homer came the countless others. Among these Virgil is the exception—not because he was the only poet to cherish hopes of beating Homer at his own game, but because of the peculiarly complex, sustained intimacy of association he set out to establish. Virgil's *Aeneid* cannot claim to compete with Apollonius' *Argonautica* as a linguistic *tour de force*—it is after all written in a different language. But Apollonius' epic is only superficially Homeric; Virgil's evocation of Homer aims deeper, at the very core.[1] In returning to Homer, he returned, moreover, in no archaizing mood; he returned to challenge directly the greatest poet of antiquity.

1. NOT ONLY HOMER

The *Aeneid*, in short, is not pastiche. In the first place, what Virgil gives us is by no means only Homer. He does not limit himself to Homer's data, but borrows freely from every department of Greek literature.

[1] For Choerilus of Samos (5th cent.), Antimachus (late 5th cent.) and other Greek renovators of Homeric epic see Otis, Chapter 2. (But contrast Albin Lesky, *A History of Greek Literature* [1966] 305.)

Part 1: Form

From *post-Homeric epic* he takes, for instance, the story of the wooden horse and the fall of Troy—a legend briefly alluded to by Homer, but recounted in full by subsequent epic writers.[1] Characters and details of legend from post-Homeric epic crop up constantly. To take one example, Memnon and Penthesilea who figure among the pictures on Dido's temple (1.488–93) are leading characters in the lost *Aithiopis* of Arctinus.[2]

Virgil's next most important source, probably, is *Greek tragedy*, which took over the ancient myths and elaborated them. Also among the pictures on Dido's temple (1.474–8) is a representation of the encounter between Troilus, one of Priam's younger sons, and Achilles, a story related by Sophocles in his lost *Troilus*. Neoptolemus, the son of Achilles, who plays such a prominent part in the narrative of *Aeneid* 2, is only briefly alluded to in Homer but one of the main characters in Sophocles' *Philoctetes*.

Virgil draws also upon Apollonius' *Argonautica*, though more for entire minor episodes than for details of story. The scene in *Aeneid* 1 where Cupid is substituted for Ascanius (1.657–96) is a refinement on a charming, discursive scene in Apollonius (3.1–166 and then 275–98), in which Hera and Athena prevail on Aphrodite to send Eros to take a potshot at Medea.[3]

Among minor Greek sources, one worth mentioning is Lycophron, an obscure (in all senses of that word) Hellenistic poet said to be the author of the *Alexandra*, a dramatic monologue in 1,474 iambic trimeters, reporting Cassandra's prophecies about the survivors of the fall of Troy down to the rise of Roman power. A prophecy connecting Troy with Rome, and representing the connexion as the working-out of fate, was grist for Virgil's mill. But Virgil seems also to have amused himself by building into his poem brief allusions to Lycophron's text. Juno, for example, before launching the storm upon the Aeneadae says (1.39–41):

> 'Pallasne exurere classem
> Argiuum atque ipsos potuit submergere ponto
> unius ob noxam et furias Aiacis Oilei?'
>
> '*Was Athena able to burn the Argive*

---

[1] See Austin on 2.15.
[2] Memnon is alluded to briefly twice in the *Odyssey* (11.522 and 4.188), Penthesilea is not in Homer.
[3] Virgil makes his colloquy between Venus and Juno come later (at 4.90–128).

Form and Technique

*fleet and drown those who sailed in it for one
man's fault—and a madman, too, Ajax, son of Oileus?'*

The key to this bit of Alexandrian cleverness (hall-marked for the learned reader by the echo of ἑνὸς λώβης ἄντι in *unius ob noxam*) lies in Lycophron's story (365 ff.) that Ajax raped Cassandra in the temple of Pallas Athena at Troy; Lycophron (followed by Virgil) links this with the story (told by Menelaus to Telemachus, *Od.* 4.499–511) that Ajax was drowned by Poseidon while returning from Troy.[1] Later in the poem, the rape of Cassandra becomes one of the details selected by Virgil for his narrative of Troy's destruction (2.402–30).

Much material, finally, is taken over from Virgil's predecessors in *Roman poetry*, principally of course the earlier writers of epic. In some form the story of Aeneas' settlement in Italy was briefly recounted by both Naevius and Ennius, and perhaps the story of Dido too, in some form, by Naevius.

We must be less concerned here, however, with what the poem is made out of, than with what it is made into. Much that Virgil takes over from post-Homeric sources had become familiar, and lay waiting to be collected from the common quarry by all who told a legendary story; to demand the authority of Homer would have been overfastidious. A lot of Virgil's story remains pretty clearly his own. Though we must add the reservation 'as far as we can tell', we no longer take seriously the source-hunters who supposed that Virgil could invent nothing. Horace's prescription (*Ars Poetica* 119) reflects the practice of the day: *aut famam sequere aut sibi conuenientia finge.*[2] Much of the narrative of Books 7 to 12 can only be Virgil's, even if it is spangled with colourful details from tradition, meant often to be recognized as such; but often too, one supposes, more recondite details, the result of Virgil's zealous research. Moreover, where Virgil uses traditional material, he often welds it to fresh material of his own that sets a new slant upon what he has taken over.

Frequently, there is a sustained technique of allusion,[3] one aspect of the play of the intellect that lights up the sober and occasionally sombre epic narrative. The reader who catches the echo enjoys the pleasure of recognizing an old phrase embedded in a new context and

---

[1] The story is of course found elsewhere—in Arctinus, etc. See Austin on 2.403.
[2] Cf. *Ars Poetica*, 129 ff.
[3] On allusion see *Latin Explorations*, pp. 216–20.

Part 1: Form

is often thereby protected as well from a too facile commitment to the story told (Distancing). It is a game Virgil plays constantly with fragments of Homer (see Chapter 6). But the post-Homeric tradition is drawn upon as well. For example, when Aeneas in Book 1 in the depth of despair attempts a pathetic assertion of his lost dignity to the unknown huntress, who is in fact his divine mother in disguise (1.378–85), the reader who catches in his words *sum pius Aeneas* an echo of Oedipus' words to the Theban elders at the beginning of Sophocles' play (*Oedipus Tyrannus* 8: ὁ πᾶσι κλεινὸς Οἰδίπους καλούμενος) senses better the sudden stylization of Aeneas at this point. The famous echo of a line of Catullus (Catullus 66.39: *inuita, o regina, tuo de uertice cessi*, a translation presumably of Callimachus— it is a lock of hair cut from the queen's head that is speaking) in Aeneas' words to Dido when he meets her in the Plains of Grief (6.460: *inuitus, regina, tuo de litore cessi*), often assumed to be stridently inappropriate, is part of the same technique.[1] Narrative material can also be used allusively (as opposed to structurally)—for example, the cry of Eris (*Iliad* 11.1–14), taken over by Virgil at 7.511–22, can hardly be said to contribute to any assertion of Homeric form in Book 7—apart from the collective contribution of such echoes to a kind of mosaic effect (see Chapter 2); it is simply an allusion which may or may not be caught.[2] Virgil, in other words, does not just take over traditional material that is convenient or congenial. Often, while remaining recognizable, what he borrows serves as the starting point for a new idea. Virgil's characterization of Dido (the woman who is only passion) and Aeneas (the man who can thrust passion into the background) obviously owes a lot to Euripides' study of Medea and Jason. But to point out Virgil's debt involves no repudiation of his originality. Turnus, as Virgil himself emphasizes (6.89), is another Achilles; but he is also another Menelaus and another Hector; above all he is a coherent character of Virgil's own imaginative creation. Or take the scene when Aeneas returns to a Troy now in ruins and sees first the pile of loot (2.760–6) and then the long queue of women and children (2.766–7):

[1] On this and other echoes of Catullus in the *Aeneid* see Agathe Thornton, 'A Catullan quotation in Virgil's *Aeneid* Bk VI', *Aumla* 17 (1962) 77–9. In some cases it is perhaps over-subtle to see more than an attempt to secure the reader's pleasure in recognition—and an acknowledgment by Virgil of his indebtedness to a poet he admired.

[2] Cf. Virgil's use of a detail of the wounding of Hector (*Il.* 14.433–9) in his beautiful scene of Mezentius by the river, 10.833–40.

> pueri et pauidae longo ordine matres
> stant circum.

What reader familiar with classical literature does not feel scenes from Euripides' *Trojan Women* flash before his mind—and know therefore, without Virgil pausing to tell him, what lies in store for the terrified women and children who stand lined up, waiting?[1]

Euripides' chorus of Trojan women appear in fact, transformed, at many points in Virgil's poem as the *matres* who are sometimes the helpless victims of war hysteria[2] and sometimes caught up themselves in that hysteria: we see the mothers of Pallanteum watch alarmed the preparations for war and the departure of their young prince with Aeneas (8.556 and 592), and we see them lament when Pallas' dead body is brought back (11.147); the *matres* are prospective spectators of the duel (12.131); one, the mother of Euryalus, is assigned a whole Episode in which to lament the death of her son (9.473–502). Observe too the progression in the following series of glimpses: the Italian *matres* admire Camilla as she flashes by (7.813); later they join their daughters in execration of war (11.215); when war starts again after the truce, they are swept along by the emotions it generates and pray for the overthrow of Aeneas (11.481); then at the end of the book, after the death of Camilla, we see them in despair, convinced the Trojans are upon them (11.877). In all these scenes, in which groups of *matres* (not the same groups, of course) keep reappearing like a chorus, we may see Euripides as the starting point.[3] What he has contributed is less a literary idea than a component of Virgil's sensibility.

Sometimes the process of making traditional material his own involves Virgil in a synthesis. If Dido is in part Euripides' Medea, she is also Apollonius' Medea: from Euripides comes the working out of searing, irresistible, almost repellent passion; from Apollonius the sympathetic study of passion's first onset.[4]

---

[1] Cf. the glimpses of the women kissing the doorposts of the invaded palace, 2.490. For a remarkable exploitation of the single word *Iliades* see 11.35.

[2] Cf. Catullus 64.349–51 and Horace's *bella matribus detestata* (*Odes* 1.1.24–5).

[3] The *matres* also assemble with their menfolk for exile at 2.797, set the ships on fire in Book 5, and join in fighting from the walls at 11.891.

[4] This is perhaps the place for a word on a hoary controversy. Servius, with that insensitive pedantry of which he is sometimes guilty, begins his commentary on Book 4 with the assertion that *Aeneid* 4 was wholly taken over from *Argonautica* 3: 'Apollonius Argonautica scripsit et in tertio inducit amantem Medeam: inde totus hic liber translatus est'. (He is followed by Macrobius, *Sat.* 5.17.4.) Servius is rather prone to this kind of remark, but

Part 1: Form

Here are three examples of Virgil's synthesis of material, to correct any impression that his narrative is almost wholly Homer. In *Aeneid* 1 the Homeric parallels are obvious: the storm scene resembles the storm scene in *Odyssey* 5; Aeneas' opening words echo Odysseus' words when he sees storm and death all around him; Aeneas' encounter with Venus and the magic cloud in which she envelops him are based on *Odyssey* 7; the *Iliad*, too, is drawn upon—Venus' intercession with Jove is based on the intercession of Thetis with Zeus in *Iliad* 1. But the storm and the colloquy between Jove and Venus are also taken from Naevius.[1] Lycophron too is present, as we saw above, in Juno's speech (1.39–41). Similarly, the pictures on the wall of Dido's temple are a direct challenge to Homer, but they incorporate non-Homeric material—for example, the references mentioned above to Troilus, Memnon and Penthesilea. And not only do the pictures imply a reassessment of Homer's judgments (Virgil's reference to the horses of Rhesus, 1.469–73, implies an attitude quite different from that in the *Doloneia*); the scenes chosen are a kind of foreshadowing of Virgil's own story: Achilles on his chariot foreshadows Turnus, whose symbol is also the chariot (especially in his fugue in Book 12); the horses of Rhesus foreshadow the escapade of Nisus and Euryalus in *Aeneid* 9; the brutal murder of Troilus foreshadows the murder of Polites in *Aeneid* 2; the temple of Pallas is prominent in *Aeneid* 2; the confrontation of Priam and Achilles foreshadows the confrontation of Priam and Neoptolemus in *Aeneid* 2; Penthesilea foreshadows

---

fortunately for once we have Virgil's source to refute him. Yet though he has often been rebuked (e.g., by Austin, *Aeneid* 4, p. xvi) the smear still lingers. Apollonius' description of Medea falling in love (it begins at 3.444–70 and continues at 616–824 and at 948–1162) is detailed, realistic, based on shrewd psychological observation, but it is diffuse, less poetic than Virgil and therefore less pathetic: too much dramatic energy is dissipated on the whimsical observation of accurately observed trifles. We might suppose that Servius was thinking only of the narrative framework (the divine plots to make Medea and Dido fall in love and the use of Eros and Cupid) if he had not added the heavy-handed observation that Virgil's tragic queen is almost a figure of comedy: 'nam paene comicus stilus est: nec mirum, ubi de amore tractatur'.

[1] Servius once again is categorical (*Servius auctus* on 1.198): 'Totus hic locus de Naeuii Belli Punici libro translatus est', and once again he is backed up by Macrobius (*Sat.* 6.2.31):

In principio Aeneidos tempestas describitur et Venus . . . queritur. . . . Hic locus totus sumptus a Naeuio est ex primo libro Belli Punici. Illic enim aeque Venus Troianis tempestate laborantibus cum Ioue queritur et sequuntur uerba Iouis filiam consolantis spe futurorum.

But though we must take their *totus* with a grain of salt, there must have been something in Naevius to justify their assertion.

Form and Technique

Camilla in *Aeneid* 11.[1] A final example: Virgil takes from Apollonius (2.178–300) the story of Phineus and the Harpies and the sons of Boreas (connected with the islands of the Strophades by Apollonius at 2.296–7, as in Virgil) and weaves into it Homer's story of the stealing of the cattle from *Odyssey* 12—Homer's explanation of the divine wrath that fell upon Odysseus and his men; he then transposes the prophecy which Phineus makes to the Argonauts in Apollonius and assigns it to one of the Harpies; in that prophecy he attributes to the Harpy Celaeno the famous prediction,[2] found first in Lycophron, about the tables which the Aeneadae must eat when they arrive in their new home.

II. DIFFERENCE IN ATTITUDE BETWEEN VIRGIL AND HOMER

The poem remains none the less manifestly, *in form*, a Homeric epic. Virgil makes of course no particular effort at accurate reconstruction of Mycenaean times. From the point of view of the archaeologist or the historian, his narrative is full of anachronisms.[3] What matters a good deal more is that, while he adopts Homer's *form*, Virgil does not adopt Homer's *attitude*. Quite apart from the shift of sympathies imposed by telling the story of the Trojan War from the Trojan point of view, an intellectual gulf separates Virgil from Homer.

For Homer the legend he narrates is essentially a story, told for its own sake. The story is told larger than life, but we have little reason for supposing that Homer or his audience were conscious of a deliberate departure from the world in which they lived—the things narrated might not actually have happened, but it would not have seemed *impossible* that they should have happened. Homer's heroes perform feats of strength beyond the reach of ordinary men; but the poet who

---

[1] See R. D. Williams's excellent study, 'The pictures on Dido's temple', *CQ* 10 (1960) 145–51.

[2] The prophecy was well known in Virgil's day—see Williams on 3.256 f.

[3] See R. E. Anthony, *Anachronisms in Virgil's Aeneid* (1930). Anthony's lists of anachronisms are mostly, of course, beside the point. In some respects Virgil was perhaps deliberately anachronistic. See F. H. Sandbach, 'Anti-antiquarianism in the Aeneid', *Virgil Society Lectures* No. 77 (1966) 26–38, who argues that Virgil makes use of anachronism to 'underline the continuity between the men about whom he wrote and those for whom he wrote' (p. 36).

spins a tale of stirring times to a patriotic audience easily makes his heroes braver and stronger than the men his audience see about them. Nor are Homer's gods and goddesses treated as supernatural in our sense of the supernatural. Within the limitations of an overriding fate they intervene at will in the affairs of men; but their intervention is most often physical rather than what we should call divine or magical. They are more super-men and super-women—indeed Homer's heroes often have a god or goddess for father or mother. Even those attributes which seem fantastic to the modern reader—their ability to hurtle through the air at great speed, to assume an identity other than their own, or to envelop a hero in a protective cloud of invisibility—are treated with an ingenuous matter-of-factness; the same is true of miraculous events, such as the preservation of Hector's body. In this we may see the first germ of Greek rationalism; but we should relate it too to the easy, intimate, anthropomorphic attitude to the divinity, and still more to the saints, prevalent today among unsophisticated people in many parts of Europe. The Homeric bard, if we were able to question him, might admit that his gods and goddesses were probably not quite as he had painted them; but he would see in his treatment of them no more than the friendly disrespect of the genuinely religious in moments of relaxation.

When we come to Hesiod, we find this atmosphere of casual, unsophisticated yarn-spinning supplanted by the beginnings of an intellectual awareness of the limitations to be placed upon what can happen in the world as we know it. Hesiod offers us a systematic doctrine of a Heroic Age:[1] it came fourth in his series of five ages and suspended for a time the progressive decadence from Gold to Silver and Silver to Bronze—and then things got much worse with the coming of the Iron Age, in which men now live. In the Heroic Age gods and goddesses still moved freely among men, whereas in the Iron Age they have deserted us—a detail of Hesiod's rationalization used by Catullus in Poem 64 and by Virgil in the fourth *Eclogue*. In Hesiod the term 'hero' acquires precise definition: a hero is the descendant of one mortal and one immortal parent.

The Greek tragedians show a further progress in sophistication, an increasing suppleness and subtlety of the intellect. Where Hesiod had attempted to explain away what he could not believe by rational but gratuitous hypothesis, the Athenian tragedians developed a capacity for conscious fantasy. Legend is treated as an imaginative fiction.

[1] Hesiod, *Works and Days*, 109–201.

whose improbabilities caused no concern. By a conscious act of the imagination poet and audience were able to pretend for a time that things happened which they knew, or were pretty sure, could not have happened so. The story, in short, is no longer told for the story's sake; it becomes a hypothesis. The audience are confronted with a familiar situation—they know the legend—and are invited to look at it anew in the light of a moral awareness and a capacity for analysis which the contemporaries of Sophocles and Euripides had only recently acquired. Their passion for dialectic made them almost impatient with story: the old stories were good enough as raw material, even better than new ones because they were more economically productive of dramatically interesting situations. (Compare Platonic myth—for example, the myth of Prometheus in Plato's *Protagoras*.) When they were interested in the story itself, it was a more sophisticated interest—not for its narrative excitement, but to see the way things would work out (Tragic Suspense).

The Hellenistic Age, while it preferred comedy and realism on the stage, in bookish circles possessed, in an even more refined degree, the Athenian fascination with the legendary story that is simultaneously true and untrue to our human experience. For Callimachus it becomes a kind of game to pretend to take legend *au pied de la lettre*, in order to derive sophisticated, intellectual irony from sharpening its implausibilities. The old stories were worn threadbare—no one could take them seriously; so he amused himself by *pretending* to take them more seriously than ever.[1] In Apollonius the conflict between reality and fantasy is less strident. In his narrative of Medea and Jason in particular we see all the psychological realism of New Comedy: Medea is a real girl in love, studied with acute psychological sympathy, like any heroine of Menander, we may suppose—or Plautus—and quite unheroic. But at the same time the atmosphere is one of fantasy: this charming, young, lovesick girl is also a witch with the terrifying resources of magic at her command, and the whole story unfolds within a framework which is strictly legendary and unrealistic.

We can suppose an innocent poetaster in the age of Augustus attempting to write an epic poem that was not only Homeric in form and in technique, but completely Homeric in spirit also, that cheerfully accepted the limitations of moral and psychological insight of archaic times. Virgil, as we know from the *Eclogues* and the *Georgics*, was not

[1] See K. J. McKay, *The Poet at Play* (1962) and *Erysichthon: a Callimachean Comedy* (1962).

Part 1: Form

the man—unless his object were some *tour de force* incompatible with serious literature—to shut his eyes to the spectacular development of the Hellenic intellect during the seven centuries that separated him from Homeric times. Instead we find, as we should expect to find, that the *Aeneid*, though in form and technique a Homeric epic, revitalizes form and technique with the spiritual acquisitions of the whole Greek tradition. Where Homer exaggerates, Virgil tells a conscious fairytale.[1] Compare, to take an extreme case from Homer, Homer's Book of the Dead (*Odyssey* 11) with *Aeneid* 6. Homer's tale is ingenuous fiction intended for an audience half disposed to believe. Virgil makes belief in his stylized fantasy impossible by interspersing among the parts we might be prepared to believe passages so patently ironical in intent (for example, Charon) or allegorical (for example, the vestibule of the underworld) that the question of belief hardly arises.

From Hesiod (a poet much cultivated in the Hellenistic Age and one Virgil had studied carefully in writing the *Georgics*) Virgil took over the intellectual recognition of legend as moving in an age fundamentally different from our own. From the Athenian tragedians he learnt what could be gained by transferring the emphasis from story to situation: his story is quick-moving, businesslike, selective; a framework, constructed almost impatiently, for a series of scenes upon which he lavishes his real sympathy and his acute dramatic sense. The Hellenistic Age also makes its contribution: more important than the scenes Virgil takes from Apollonius, is the interest he owes to Apollonius in psychological realism. The contribution of Callimachus is more elusive, but we see it in certain stylized Tableaux (e.g., the catalogue of ships, 10.163–214—see Chapter 4; or the description of Atlas as simultaneously giant and mountain, 4.246–51) and in a prevailing note of irony and detachment, what I have called the play of the intellect upon the narrative.

Greek philosophy too leaves its clear imprint on the pages of the *Aeneid*. Plato figures most obviously in the myth of Anchises in Book 6, but in a sense the whole poem is (like Cicero's *Somnium Scipionis*) a Platonic myth, a story told to help us sense a moral truth. Of Stoicism and Virgil's concept of fate much has been written. Epicureanism also

---

[1] Pöschl, Eng. edn, p. 96:
Homer stays within the limits of the natural even though his heroes' deeds border on the miraculous. Vergil exceeds that limit.
We must take care, however, to put the matter in its proper intellectual context: Homer's awareness of the 'limits of the natural' is very ingenuous, Virgil's acute.

Form and Technique

finds its place, though a minor one—the study of Dido in Book 4, for example, is almost as much a study in Lucretian Epicureanism as it is a study of love as a tragic passion.

Nor should we neglect the contribution of Ennius and the Roman epic tradition of simple, dignified terseness. Though this is something that will be dealt with more fully in the chapter on style (Chapter 6), it is relevant here to remind ourselves that style can express attitude and tone and serve as an index of sophistication and intellectual stature. No less than its greater intellectual maturity, this characteristically Roman grave urgency, strengthened rather than weakened by a constant, subdued, subtle irony (introduced into Roman literature by Catullus and the *poetae novi*, but applied to a new end—to show that sustained high seriousness is a deliberate decision of earnestness of purpose, not simplemindedness) stamps Virgil's epic as fundamentally different in attitude from Homer.

III. THE EXPLOITATION OF FORM

The fact remains, despite the difference in attitude and a free submission to intellectual influences from every department of Greek literature, that the form of the *Aeneid* is strictly that of Homeric epic. Virgil's spiritual superiority over Homer is not, therefore, a guarantee of artistic superiority—some of the highest examples of poetic art are the product of quite unsophisticated cultures or individuals. Indeed his maturity was liable to prove more irksome than helpful if his choice of Homeric form meant a conscious struggle to assume limitations of insight which might put him out of sympathy with his form.

One of Virgil's greatest interpreters, John Conington, maintained, indeed, that Virgil's modern spirit, as he called it, kept intruding on an archaic form, to involve Virgil in a conflict between form and attitude which he was often unable to control; a striking case, according to Conington, was Dido: Virgil's mature sympathy for a woman in love caused him inadvertently to transform into an appealing heroine a character he had cast in a minor role.[1]

[1] In 'Virgil's Tragic Queen', *Latin Explorations*, Chapter 2, I have tried to show that Conington misunderstands Dido and does less than justice to Virgil.

Part 1: Form

While it is a superficial reading of Virgil's poem which fails to detect this conflict, I feel we misunderstand Virgil's intentions totally if we suppose that the conflict is inadvertent, or that it frustrates Virgil's purpose. One of the fundamental features of the poem's structure, it seems to me, is a conscious, carefully organized conflict, or tension, between the ways in which Virgil makes every effort to identify himself with Homer (by adopting Homer's form, a story that attaches itself directly to Homer, a way of telling it that adheres closely to Homeric conventions, an allusive technique that constantly evokes Homer) and the ways in which he makes no effort to limit himself to Homer's intellectual, moral or psychological standpoint. What we have, in short, is not an unsuccessful attempt to accept the limitations of an alien form, but the *exploitation of form*.

It is not uncommon for an archaic, ingenuous poetic form to be invested, in a more sophisticated age, with a fresh depth of content; Horace's *Odes*, Coleridge's 'Ancient Mariner' or Keats's 'La belle Dame sans merci' are examples. What I have called 'exploitation' of form is something rather less straightforward, however.

We may, if we choose, read the *Aeneid* as a story told for the story's sake. Most of those who today read the poem in a prose translation read it for the story and enjoy it. Presumably a majority also of Virgil's contemporary audience accepted his poem in this spirit. The more discerning reader, however, is soon troubled by a feeling that the story lacks qualities which well-organized, first-rate narrative should possess. It is too plain from the beginning of the contest in Books 7 to 12 that Aeneas must win and Turnus must lose—a feeling that troubles us particularly when we come to the duel in Book 12: however exciting each phase, the end is obvious. There is too much, moreover, that is hard to swallow: the battle scenes, to take an example, though conventionally Homeric in what they narrate, often seem disturbingly far-fetched. Because these are reasonable reactions to Virgil's text, many have been inclined to believe they are valid strictures on the poem.

A Rolls-Royce will not take corners at high speed as successfully as a well-designed sports-car; in a sports-car that is by common consent well designed the occupants are less comfortable than in a Rolls-Royce. But though these are reasonable reactions to a ride in each, they do not express relevant criticisms of the structural properties of the two vehicles. In any complex structure, mechanical or artistic, we can always point to things that could have been done better—if it were not that excellence of the whole structure as a structure is only to be achieved by abandoning the attempt to provide in some respects what might well be considered indispensable in a different structure; desirable qualities can be mutually exclusive; the motor designer who attempts to provide all equally must content himself with a vehicle that is outstanding only in its mediocrity.

Few people make this kind of irrelevant criticism of motor-cars because a general understanding exists of the different intentions of designers. (The fact, of course, that a designer has successfully realized his intentions does not exempt his product from censure: his intentions may be meretricious—to produce a shoddy, showy product that will sell—or out of touch with developments in engineering. But it is a good idea to begin by asking ourselves what the designer set out to do.) In literary criticism the mistake is comparatively common. We are in danger of making it if we condemn Virgil's story out of hand as rigged and far-fetched, instead of asking ourselves if anything has been gained by doing the thing the way it has been done.

Virgil's use of form is one for which parallels exist in most literatures. The modern novel, for example, readily lends itself to structural exploitation. Such an attitude to form seems to me characteristic of the novels of Mr Graham Greene, to be seen most clearly in *The Power and the Glory*, the story of a broken-down, whisky-drinking priest in a Central American military dictatorship where the Roman Catholic religion has been banned, who continues reluctantly to exercise his priestly functions until eventually arrested and executed.

Any wide-awake reader of this novel knows he can rely on Mr Greene not to cheat: the lieutenant of police will get the whisky-priest in the end; and, having got him, he will send him to the firing squad—just as, in the *Aeneid*, we know all along that the story must work out the way it does. When the priest makes his spectacular escape over the mountains, when he is captured quite early in the novel by an unprepossessing half-breed, and then captured again about two-thirds of the way through for carrying liquor—but under a false identity which is not penetrated—a mood of suspense is built up that both holds the attention and *fails to convince*: we know as we read that the story cannot end the way it pretends for a moment to end—because it is the wrong ending, or the right ending too soon. The priest's apparent escapes provide a relief that we accept while knowing it to be artificial —compare Turnus' escape from Aeneas in Book 10 when he is whisked away by Juno (10.633–88) and in Book 12 when a fresh outbreak of fighting puts an end to the preparations for the duel (12.216–613); we all accept the trick, but nobody is hoodwinked by it.

So much for the structure of the narrative. Consider now Mr Greene's *attitude* to his narrative. The description of the night the priest spends in prison after being arrested for carrying liquor is laid on with a trowel: he is thrown into an unlighted cell filled with people excreting and fornicating in the dark; the air is alive with mosquitoes. (We have the comparable feeling that what we are reading is almost an ironical caricature, a parody, of narrative excitement on reading Virgil's description of the duel—when eventually it takes place.) And yet in *The Power and the Glory* we feel this sacrifice of plausibility is justified by the symbolism (compare the symbolism of the duel, heightened by the introductory similes 12.684–703), however manifest and trite the symbolic statement appears if we formulate it explicitly—the prison is a microcosm, Aeneas and Turnus symbolize incompatible ideals. Or compare Mr Greene's picture of the night in prison with Virgil's battle scenes, where all that is conventionally expected of a heroic battle occurs and is described with a luridly graphic attention to gruesome detail that seems incompetent lack of restraint till we sense Virgil's purpose.

Turn now to the main characters. The lieutenant of police is the representative of an evil power, but there is good in him and refinement—it is almost with reluctance that he sends the priest to his death. The priest, on the other hand—the representative of good—is coarse and degraded. It is a most unsubtle working-out of the elementary precept that an evil character must have good in him and a good character evil. (Here Virgil perhaps shows more restraint. All the same, Turnus is a very conventional embodiment of an evil force—discord—whom we none the less admire; Aeneas the representative of right who is by no means wholly admirable.)

Taking it as a story, we must admit that *The Power and the Glory* holds the attention of the reader by blatantly conventional tricks. Yet it does not occur to us to condemn the novel as a result. The tricks are justified somehow by the novel's evident serious purpose and by the quality of the experience it offers the reader, often at the very moment when we are on the point of revulsion at the tawdriness of the thriller form which Mr Greene has chosen to exploit.

For *The Power and the Glory* is not just a story to be read quickly in a mood of uncritical suspense. It can be read as a satire, though the satire is not easily pinned down: is it aimed at the godless police state—

or at established religion? The priest, though degraded, seems capable still of discharging his priestly functions, but one is never quite sure whether it is religion or superstition that is at work; when his time comes at last, a successor unexpectedly appears, but it is such a *coup de théâtre* one can see mere coincidence in this, or the writer's irony at the expense of the priest's—or our—credulity, if one prefers. Or the novel can be read for its seamy characters, as a slice of a corrupt world, appealing to those who feel cynical about the world. Yet it is evident that the objective Mr Greene has set himself and the basis of the novel's artistic success are remote from what the novel offers us on any one level; it is a distorting limitation of the novel's possibilities to assume that any one way of looking at it is the right way.

There are points of resemblance here with most good novels. But *The Power and the Glory* is quite different from the usual adventure story that offers the reader more than narrative excitement—such as, say, Hemingway's *For Whom the Bell Tolls*. Mr Greene's familiarity with the thriller form has led him to exploit that form. The reader is invited to enter into a kind of compact not to take the story at its face value, to regard it as a kind of sustained, richly-textured, fundamentally ironic parable—not one in which the writer's beliefs are rammed down our throats, but an imaginative invitation to have another look at the world in the light shed on it by acceptance of certain beliefs about it.

We must naturally be chary of pushing comparisons with the *Aeneid* too far. It is not profitable to suggest, between two works of art which are so different, more than a general, overall comparability of intent. Of both we must say that the story is not just done badly; neither is the work of an incompetent botcher. On the contrary, both are brilliant pieces of writing. Their very brilliance should warn us that they are not meant to convince on the level to which we are inclined at first to assign them. Somehow both gain by the conflict or tension between the conventionality of the genre to which they purport to belong and an evident, not easily defined, purpose which is alien, and superior, to this genre.

There exists of course some measure of agreement among critics about what Mr Greene is up to, but it is a necessary consequence of an artist's intellectual maturity that the contours of his intent are not easily traced. What concerns us for the moment is the fact that it is precisely because *The Power and the Glory* is not just another crime thriller that Mr Greene stresses his adherence to the traditional plot

Part 1: Form

and sensational techniques of the crime thriller. I suggest that when we consider the intellectual context in which the *Aeneid* was written, when we realize the maturity of the poet who wrote it, when we read the poem itself with a sharper critical attention, we see it is precisely because the *Aeneid* was intended not to be just another heroic epic that Virgil went to such trouble to stress his adherence to Homeric form.

IV. IMPURE POETRY

To this planned tension between conventional form and the re-assessment possible in a more mature intellectual context of the attitudes implicit in that form I have given the name 'exploitation of form'. It is of course a kind of writing that has its origin in Alexandria. But in a way James Bond, modern pop art, the intellectual wild western are more or less pure Alexandrianism—they represent an ironical deployment of talent on a form the artist cannot accept at its face value. Some writers—Virgil and Greene among them—carry the process a stage further: they have a purpose more serious than exhibitionism.[1]

But if the story of the *Aeneid* is not told for its own sake, what is Virgil's object in telling it? Clearly it is not simply parody or satire. If maturer attitudes are brought to bear upon a story that is Homeric in form and essentially Homeric in substance and the manner of its telling, what are the reactions the poet hopes to produce by exploiting that form? What are the reflections his new way of telling an old story is meant to inspire?

To answer these questions we must remind ourselves of the special status of the *Aeneid* and the special circumstances of its genesis, for it is these that justify the special use of form.

The *Aeneid*, as we saw in Chapter 2, is a poem tied to an occasion—the battle of Actium, taken as the symbol of the victory of Augustus in the civil war, a victory which Virgil invites the reader (in Book 8) to

---

[1] I am pretty sure the attitude of Milton to his form was different. The term 'literary epic' seems to me applicable to 'Paradise Lost' in a way it is not applicable to the *Aeneid*: 'Paradise Lost' is an epic poem filled with echoes of the *Aeneid* (and therefore of Homer) because Milton believed this was the proper way, the artistically right way, to write a long poem on a grand theme. For Virgil it was a matter of rules that had no inherent rightness about them.

regard as the culmination of a historical process whose beginnings can be traced back to the establishment of Trojan civilization in Italy by Augustus' ancestor Aeneas.

This occasional status of the *Aeneid* is an essential, fundamental aspect of the poem, though it is one that is often disregarded (many preferring to love the poem for the beauty of its imagery, its sensitive, telling pathos, or even its grandiloquence, its rhythmical grandeur, or its magnificence as verbal poetry) or evaded by those who feel the less said about Virgil's patriotic or propagandist intentions the better they will enjoy the poetry.

Those who are more uncompromising or more forthright complain the propaganda in the *Aeneid* sticks in their throats. If they are themselves poets, they are particularly apt to feel that the artistic integrity of a work of art is indivisible and that there is no such thing as a poem which is good in parts. It is for reasons of this order that Ezra Pound and W. H. Auden have spoken harshly of the *Aeneid*,[1] though T. S. Eliot has defended the poem with his usual austere urbanity as the work of a mature mind.[2] The most violent of Virgil's detractors among modern poets is Mr Robert Graves, in whose eyes Virgil has compromised his integrity beyond forgiveness and is to be ranged among the Apollonians, is even to be regarded as the type of anti-poet to be despised by the true free poets, the Dionysians, who follow only inspiration and the dictates of the Muse.[3]

To hold that, because the *Aeneid* is an occasional poem (using this term in a somewhat special sense—it is usually confined to trivial compositions), it is therefore fundamentally dishonest is, I feel, to misunderstand the basis of the poem's artistic integrity. The question is less straightforward than Mr Graves makes it appear.

In the first place, there is nothing underhand about the propaganda; Virgil makes no bones about it. His patriotic purpose is announced in the opening sentence of the poem. If we call the poem a propaganda poem, we must add that the overtones of covert, surreptitious action which the word 'propaganda' evokes are inappropriate.

Second, we should remember that, if the *Aeneid* is tied to an occasion, that is not in itself anything very unusual. The same is true of

---

[1] See, e.g., W. H. Auden, 'Secondary Epic', in *Homage to Clio* (1960) 34–5.
[2] T. S. Eliot, 'What is a Classic?', in *On Poetry and Poets* (1957) 53–71.
[3] Robert Graves, 'The Anti-poet', in *Oxford Addresses on Poetry* (1961) 27–53, repeated in 'The Virgil Cult', *Virginia Quarterly Review* 38 (1962). Mr Graves' Apollonians and Dionysians are the descendants of the two types of poetic intellect described by Nietzsche in *The Birth of Tragedy* (1872).

Part 1: Form

Pindar's *Odes* and many other poems, of musical compositions such as the Eroica symphony, and of many paintings and pieces of sculpture that are widely admired. Then there is the larger group of works of art not specifically tied to an occasion, which none the less are felt by all to comment on an occasion, or to inspire reflections which are appropriate to a particular set of circumstances. Dramatists especially often take advantage of the interest they can arouse by their fiction to explore with their audience a problem which is in the air. Euripides' *Medea* is intended to arouse reflections about the status of women in Athens, his *Trojan Women* to present his audience with an imaginative realization of some of the horrors of military conquest by a ruthless power. There is no formal, stated reference, but that does not make the poet's intention to comment on contemporary events less certain, or less obvious—compare Arthur Miller's *The Crucible*. In a more general sense, *Macbeth*, *Othello*, *Tartuffe* and many other plays deal with situations which prompt questions about what was the right thing to do or the right way to behave. To arouse these questions may well not be the main purpose of the dramatist, but it is one component of his total purpose. So that if we are uncompromising about the purity of poetry, we must regard such works as impure. They have an intent outside art; the dramatist wishes, in addition to creating a work of art, to affect the opinions or beliefs of his audience; the interest he arouses by his fiction arouses interest in the problem it presents.

In modern times the whole controversy of the rights and wrongs of *littérature engagée* threatens to flood in at this point. All I want to show is that the fact that the *Aeneid* is tied to an occasion and intended to arouse reflections about a set of circumstances (the civil war) does not damn it at once as a poem. When we come to novels, the mixed work of art is probably met with even more frequently than it is in plays. It is clear, therefore, that mixed status cannot of itself mean condemnation of a play or a novel; it is equally clear that the degree of purity is no index of artistic quality.

To come back to poems: we find that the purity of a poem, in this sense, varies with the social and intellectual context in which the poem was written. In the seventeenth and eighteenth centuries, poems which are tied specifically to an occasion but claim none the less to be taken seriously as poetry (and are so taken by modern critics) were comparatively common—Marvell's 'Horatian Ode upon Cromwell's Return from Ireland', Dryden's 'Song for St Cecilia's Day' or his

'Astraea redux' are obvious instances. In modern times such poems are less common, though still written—examples are Yeats's 'Easter 1916', or Auden's 'In Memory of Sigmund Freud'. Poems whose relevance to a special set of circumstances is apparent but not specifically acknowledged in the poem are found in all periods.

In our own day the commonest form for a poem to take is the short meditative lyric in which the poet takes no apparent account of his eventual audience. His poem explores an essentially private problem. It is understandable if the mixed or impure work of art is misunderstood by poets like Graves, jealous of the hermetic integrity of personal meditative lyric; and equally understandable if such poets do not always remember that the independence they claim is possible only in a social context where the kind of poem they write is appreciated, and their anti-social behaviour not held censurable, however much we continue to expect—and to receive—the traditional compromise between art and social function from those who work in other departments of literature, or in music and the plastic arts.

The poet who disregards his eventual audience is the product of a special set of social circumstances. Between the poet whose poem is tied to an acknowledged occasion and the poet whose comment upon a set of circumstances is unacknowledged, the difference is much less one of intention than of what was usual in the society in which the poet lived. In Virgil's day, the occasional poem (in our sense) was a very usual function to expect a poet to discharge; indeed, as we saw in Chapter 2, it was a function poets felt self-conscious about evading. Accepting that function need not mark them off as inferior to the modern kind of poet, any more than, say, the specific acknowledgment of a task accepted by the Flemish portrait painters of the seventeenth century (for example when Van Dyck painted Charles I) necessarily puts their art on a lower level than that of those modern artists who refuse commissions: art is not compromised by having a customer, though it is usually necessary for the artist to give the customer more than the customer has bargained for.

For in such a mixed work there is apt to be an unresolved conflict between what the occasion superficially requires and what the artist offers. Although this is a concept with which Romanticism and its doctrine of unshackled inspiration could not cope, modern critics have no difficulty in accepting the notion that poetry is the product of the intellect as well as what for convenience we may still call inspiration. Even if certain modern poets reject outright the idea of

Part 1: Form

poetry as a social activity, it remains the business of all good impure poetry, and perhaps of all serious literature generally, to suggest reservations and complexities which the writer is wise to leave unresolved—not regarding himself as a philosopher, but as a person whose unusual sensitivity compels misgivings, revulsions, regrets (and, of course, the opposites of these) where we do not have these reactions.

Impure art can achieve its object simply by the imaginative reconstruction of the circumstances upon which it offers comment. This is the course often followed by novelists, for example Arthur Koestler in his *Darkness at Noon*. Or the story may have no explicit connexion with the events towards which the writer wishes to suggest an attitude: for example, Camus' *La Peste*. In this case something is desirable to make the reader aware that more lies in the story than meets the eye. Irony is one way of detaching the reader from the narrative in order to invite him to look at it more quizzically and see in its absurdities a hint of the absurdities in the more familiar world about him. This is the method of Swift. But the ironical exploitation of form can take many shapes. A familiar one is that of the modern pseudo-classical French dramas of Giraudoux and Anouilh.[1] Anouilh's *Antigone* is almost a modern version of Sophocles' play. Giraudoux's *La guerre de Troie n'aura pas lieu* (translated as *Tiger at the Gates*) is a synthesis (what the Roman comedians called a *contaminatio*) of parts of the *Iliad* and parts of *Aeneid* 7. But the spirit in which these plays were written is completely out of sympathy with the classical works the dramatists took as their formal models. What Giraudoux and Anouilh are doing is quite different from the use of Greek and Roman themes by the classical French dramatists of the seventeenth century; one would be tempted to say they are parodying their originals, if it were not plain that they meant serious business. An important component of these dramatists' total purpose is to prompt reflections that have nothing to do with Homer or Virgil or Sophocles, but much to do with the social circumstances in which the plays were first offered to their audience— Giraudoux's play (first produced in 1935) is intended (if we choose to single out this component of a complex work of art) to make us think about the problem of war hysteria;[2] Anouilh's *Antigone* (first produced

[1] Cf. J.-P. Sartre's *Les Mouches*.
[2] Virgil, too, in *Aeneid* 7 is concerned with the problem of war hysteria and it is possible that Giraudoux read Virgil this way; but the part of *Aeneid* 7 which he makes his own (that dealing with the opening of the Gates of War) makes

in 1942) to make us think about some of the problems that faced the French under the German occupation.

The *Aeneid* is probably less extreme, less strident in its exploitation of form than the work of these modern dramatists. It is after all a poem, whereas Giraudoux and Anouilh write in racy, often colloquial prose—though, in our insensitivity to a dead language, we may well miss Virgil's irony, the studied stylization of his imagery (which emphasizes his non-realistic intent) and the calculated colloquialism of many of his lines. All the same it is profitable to conclude by a loosely formulated comparison. In the *Aeneid* and in Anouilh's *Antigone* (to take a specific example) there is the same atmosphere of detachment or distancing, the same play of the intellect: in Anouilh it amounts almost to a debunking of classical tragedy; in Virgil to a more discreet underlining of the impossibility of full emotional commitment to Homeric ideals.[1] The relationship of both to a situation upon which they comment is also similar: neither works like a *roman à clé*; in both there are clear transfers of significance to current events, but it would be idle to push these too far (Anouilh's Créon is no more Pétain than Aeneas is Augustus—and as much), and there is much that is not intended to be directly transferable. Both works, as it happens, compel reflection upon similar problems: the problems of leadership in emergency and the corruption of human nature in war. But whereas Anouilh is concerned as well with the problem of the irresolvable antagonism between unswerving, unpractical idealism and the collaborator who believes collaboration not merely the expedient, but the right course of action, Virgil is concerned with the

---

this point less clearly than the scenes which precede (see the Analysis of Book 7 in Chapter 4).

[1] This is perhaps the place to mention Brecht's famous theory of alienation, described by a critic as follows:

> The destruction of stage illusion, however, is not an end in itself. The 'Verfremdungseffekt' has its positive side. By inhibiting the process of identification between the spectator and the characters, by creating a distance between them and enabling the audience to look at the action in a detached and critical spirit, familiar things, attitudes, and situations appear in a new and strange light, and create, through astonishment and wonder, a new understanding of the human situation. The great discoveries of mankind, Brecht points out, were made by men who looked at familiar things as if they had never seen them before—Newton at the falling apple, Galilei at the swinging chandelier—and in the same way the theatre public should be taught to look at the relationships between men with the critical 'estranged' eye of the discoverer. 'The natural must be made to look surprising.'

Martin Esslin, *Brecht: A Choice of Evils* (1959) 114.

Part 1: Form

problem of unthinking courage, the need to show that the standards of the Heroic Age are no longer applicable.[1]

It is important to stress how easy it is to distort Anouilh's *Antigone* by making it appear to be 'about' these things in too simple-minded a sense, if only to warn the reader against supposing that I intend a similar simplification of Virgil's purpose in exploiting Homeric form. The issue is not a simple one, and it is agreeable to be able to quote a critic of classical literature who has expressed it well:

> A work of art is not a vehicle with interesting merchandise inside it; it is a ζῷον. If it is alive, its soul and its body are inseparable. The living thought and the living form each explain the other; each exists, indeed, for the sake of the other.[2]

PART 2: TECHNIQUE

When we talk of technique, we usually mean the special uses poets make of the words they choose—the flavour of the words, the associations they evoke, the rhythmical and other auditory properties of the words, by themselves or as units of a phrase or sentence. This aspect of Virgil's technique will be dealt with in Chapter 6. But technique can cover too the ways in which a poet manipulates the conventions of the form he has adopted.

He may accept them quite uncritically and write an epic poem or a sonnet that reads in all respects as much like a Homeric epic or a Shakespearean sonnet as the writer can make it, adopting not only the form of his model, but also his model's way of putting things, adjusting his thinking till it fits the conventions of his model, rejecting thoughts for which no appropriate conventional expression is available; he may, as it were, pour his thoughts through a sieve before pouring them into a mould. Or he may press his unsieved thoughts into the mould;

---

[1] Despite the debunking, Anouilh is not so far, of course, in spirit from Sophocles as Virgil is from Homer: Anouilh's play suggests a different historical context for a problem in some respects similar to Sophocles' problem; Virgil suggests problems where Homer saw no problems.

[2] H. D. F. Kitto, 'The Idea of God in Aeschylus and Sophocles', Fondation Hardt, vol. 1: *La notion du divin* (1954) 169.

Form and Technique

each great English sonnet writer, for example, has, as we say, 'made the form his own'. The former course usually results in pastiche; the latter is the course usually followed by serious poets.

What Virgil does is more complicated. His object is not pastiche, but the creation of an illusion—a poem that looks and sounds like Homer, though completely different in attitude and spirit. Exploitation of Homeric form necessarily involved strict adherence to conventions which normally a creative writer conscious of the difference in attitude and sensibility between him and his model would reject as needlessly inhibiting. Virgil had to use the sieve as well as the mould. It had at any rate to look like Homer's sieve, though it had been adapted to withstand a new pressure of thought. Homer's conventions, in short, are made to serve fresh ends.

An apparently rigid observance of the conventions of Homeric form confronted Virgil with two major problems. The first was the problem of Homer's gods. Homeric epic is almost inconceivable without them. But Virgil wrote for a more sophisticated age. No cultivated reader, even if he were not a sceptic or a thoroughgoing materialist, as many were, could take Homer's gods very seriously. Acceptance, therefore, of Homer's divine machinery was likely to prove a serious nuisance. The second problem was that of motivation. Virgil's audience were keenly interested in *why* people did things and able to discuss people's motives with some subtlety. Homer, writing in a much less sophisticated age, allots very little space to the discussion of motivation—it was not something he thought much about. If Virgil confined himself to Homeric conventions in this respect, his audience were likely to find their curiosity about motive and the reasons for behaviour left unsatisfied. The two problems are, of course, related, as we shall see.

I. GODS[1]

We may begin by saying that Virgil keeps Homer's divine machinery. It is a hypothesis of his poem that actions and events are caused by gods, though this is not asserted of every action and every event. The gods may act on a physical level (do things themselves), or on a

[1] For a useful introduction to the question of Virgil's gods, see Boyancé, Chapter 2.

Part 2: Technique

psychological level (put ideas in people's heads). Within the limitations of a framework of fate, by which events are determined rather than the actions of individuals (though fate determines the allotted span of individuals), Virgil's gods, like Homer's, seem to have a free hand to interfere.

The divine machinery is tidied up a good deal, however. In the first place there is less of it. Virgil has only one divine Council of War (10.1–117), for example, into which he gathers material from four meetings of the gods in the *Iliad* (*Iliad* 4.1–72; 8.1–40; 15.1–167; 20.1–40). Moreover Virgil's council is accorded a rather different status. Jove's decree that the participants in the forthcoming battle must be left to work out their own destiny (10.104–13) echoes Zeus' decree of non-intervention in *Iliad* 8.1–40. But Zeus' decree is a temporary measure followed by the bickering at the meeting in *Iliad* 15 and eventually rescinded at the meeting in *Iliad* 20, where Zeus gives the gods *carte blanche*. Jove's decree, delivered with a detachment and a dignity that are Roman and Virgilian, puts an end to argument. It is not merely a matter of difference in style or outlook. Virgil, while filling his one council of the gods with patent reminiscences of Homer, has made it subserve his tragic purpose.

Of Jove's other major appearances, two show a similar exploitation of Homeric convention: his interview with Venus (1.223–304), modelled on Zeus' interview with Thetis in *Iliad* 1 and Athena's conversation with Zeus in *Odyssey* 1, culminates in Jove's long prediction to Venus of the future destiny of Rome; his conversation with Juno (12.791–886), in which Jove warns Juno that future resistance to fate is idle and assures her that the war will end in a peaceful union of the two peoples, is likewise an exposition of fate's purpose. Both Episodes, moreover, serve a useful structural function—the first sets Virgil's legendary story, at the moment when it is beginning to unfold in an atmosphere of fantasy, against a panorama of Roman history that acts as a corrective to the intellectual play of the long opening storm scene; the final conversation between Jove and Juno permits a spectacular magical ending to the duel (the dispatch of the uncanny invisible bird, the beating of whose wings against his face paralyses Turnus into inactivity) and permits the poem to end with a *coup de théâtre* (the killing of Turnus) by getting out of the way beforehand a statement of the consequences of Aeneas' victory. The other Episode in which Jove makes a major appearance is that which relates his conversation with Juno during the battle (10.606–32), as a result of which

Juno is allowed to spirit Turnus away from the fighting (after *Iliad* 18.356–67, where Zeus and Hera watch Achilles).

Jove makes as well a number of minor appearances. One is to brief Mercury (4.219–37); another is his conversation (in a flashback) with Cybele (9.82–106); in another he consoles Hercules who cannot intervene to save Pallas (10.466–72); in a fourth he sends Tarchon into battle at 11.725–8; in a fifth we glimpse him, scales in hand, weighing the destinies of Aeneas and Turnus (12.725–7).[1]

Leaving Book 6 out of account, there are something like nine major divine scenes in which Jove makes no appearance: (1) the storm sequence (1.34–156); (2) the meeting between Aeneas and Venus (1.305–417); (3) the conspiracy between Venus and Cupid (1.657–90); (4) the intervention of Venus to prevent Aeneas killing Helen and to reveal to him the gods engaged in destroying Troy (2.588–623); (5) the conspiracy between Juno and Venus to stage a marriage between Dido and Aeneas (4.90–128); (6) the colloquy between Venus and Neptune and the pageant which follows (5.779–826); (7) the sequence of scenes in which Allecto carries out the instructions she receives from Juno (7.286–571); (8) the bedroom scene in which Venus prevails upon Vulcan to make armour for Aeneas and Vulcan's early morning visit to his workshop (8.370–453); (9) the magical healing of Aeneas by Venus (12.411–29).

Apart from these, Virgil's use of the Homeric divine machinery is sparing. We have half a dozen references to divine messengers, apart from Allecto's meddling in Book 7: Mercury (1.297–304, 4.219–78); Iris (4.693–705, 5.605–58 and 9.1–15); Opis, who kills Arruns on instructions from Diana (11.836–67); Iuturna (12.134–60); one of the Dirae (the invisible bird) (12.843–86).

Then there are occasions where mortals see gods in visions (Aeneas sees Mercury, 4.556–70, and Tiber, 8.31–65) and occasions where gods assume human shape in order to intervene (Iris becomes Beroe, 5.618–58; Somnus becomes Phorbas, 5.838–61; Iuturna becomes Metiscus, 12.468–886). In addition there are a number of miscellaneous references to divine machinery: Portunus, appealed to by Cloanthus, helps him win the naval race (5.239–43); Neptune gets the Aeneadae safely past Circe (7.23–4); Juno opens the Gates of War (7.620–2); Venus hands Aeneas the magic shield (8.608–25), protects Aeneas from a hail of arrows (10.331–2), and wrenches free his spear during the duel (12.786–7) after Iuturna has handed Turnus his

---

[1] We should perhaps add fleeting references like 4.331 and 10.689.

sword. In two places the gods watch without intervening: Hercules (at Jove's side) listens tearfully to Pallas' prayer for assistance (10.464–5); the gods watch the battle in progress (10.755–61). We may perhaps add miscellaneous manifestations of the divine will, such as Laocoon's serpent and the flaming head of Iulus in Book 2, the miracle of the arrow of Acestes in Book 5, the miracle of the saving of the ships in Book 5, and the miracle of the ships that became sea nymphs in Book 9 (they appear again in Book 10).

The full list is a fairly long one. Virgil makes a much less perfunctory use of divine machinery than Apollonius. If the reader's first impression is that the human action is dominated constantly by a divine machinery designed strictly in the Homeric tradition, we need not doubt that this is the impression Virgil wished to produce: the exploitation of technique, like the exploitation of form, depends on an illusion of strict adherence. A little reflection shows, however, how much Virgil has pruned his divine machinery. There are fewer big scenes and less incidental, arbitrary interference. (The interference of Venus at 10.331–2 and 12.786–7 is exceptional.)

At the same time it is plain that the actions of Virgil's characters make sense psychologically even when the gods interfere. Not only, moreover, do their individual actions make psychological sense in the immediate context in which they act: the whole complex of the actions of a character suggests a coherent personality.

It is not simply that the characters in Virgil's fairy-tale behave emotionally like real people (physically their actions are sometimes superhuman). Homer's characters strike us as real people too: if their emotional make-up is unsophisticated, we accept this as part of the process of tuning in to the poem which our historical sense imposes. But Homer's characters are quite unlike Virgil's characters. Virgil's are created for a public interested in what goes on in a man's mind when confronted with an emergency or a moral decision, by a poet whose intellectual formation and genius equip him for this kind of analysis.

There is, in short, no reason to regard Virgil's characters as exempt from the moral judgments we make of real people, or of the characters in a serious modern play or novel. The accusations which have been levelled at Virgil that his characters are mere puppets[1] not only

---

[1] See, e.g., G. Boissier, *La religion romaine d'Auguste aux Antonins*, vol. 1 (1874) 244–5:
Enée est tout à fait dans la main des dieux et tient toujours les yeux fixés sur

exaggerate the extent to which Virgil superimposes on a heroic action (fundamentally different in spirit from Homer) a divine machinery in which his adherence to Homeric conventions is apparent; they also simplify the relationship between the two, as a result of a failure to realize that acceptance of Homer's techniques does not necessarily imply identity of outlook and purpose.

What then is the function of Virgil's divine machinery? If it is only the assertion of his adherence to Homeric convention, our first impression is, surely, that Virgil stands to lose more than he gains. It is usually assumed that this is the case; that Virgil must have found his divine machinery an embarrassment. In fact Virgil achieves, I think, several objectives by exploiting Homeric technique.

The most obvious is to suggest the tragic and philosophic viewpoint, to prompt in the reader the reflection that Virgil's tale is a parable or a myth of real life, that we should judge real people too with more compassion, regarding them as less responsible for their actions than the everyday need to censure and approve makes us apt to assume. Virgil possibly believed in fate; he believed certainly that we are less than fully responsible for our actions, while in no way intending his divine machinery as an accurate picture of the forces that control the world and us. The philosophical standpoint of the poem, at all events, is pretty much conventional Stoicism. Though in his youth an Epicurean, he had perhaps come to adopt Stoicism himself. But his own beliefs really matter little; for Virgil is not, I am sure, aiming at serious or creative philosophical or theological exposition. The Stoic view of the world was a prevalent one. It fitted in with the story of the *Aeneid*; indeed, it was essential to its plot. (See the discussion of these questions at the end of the Analysis of Book 1.) So long as Virgil did not believe the Stoic philosophy palpably false, he could without any loss of artistic integrity employ it as the philosophic hypothesis upon which he constructed his poem.

---

cette force supérieure qui le mène. Jamais il ne fait rien de lui-même. Quand les occasions sont pressantes, et qu'il importe de prendre un parti sans retard, il n'en attend pas moins un arrêt du destin bien constaté pour se décider.

Cf. H. E. Butler, *The Fourth Book of Virgil's Aeneid* (1935) 24:
Dido ... is the sport of circumstances, the victim of two designing goddesses, and the poet never seeks to evoke any emotion in our hearts save pity.

Cf. W. S. Maguinness, *Aeneid* 12, p. 12:
The actions of the human characters are, in fact, so restricted and dictated by divine will, and by the destiny which rules both gods and men, that they sometimes seem like puppets moved by invisible hands.

Part 2: Technique

But this is not the whole answer. The other part of the answer is, however, more difficult to state. The divine machinery is also a device to keep Virgil's story formally within the framework of fantasy. The *Aeneid* is not a narrative of the past, but a tale in which Aeneas, or Turnus, is hardly more to be taken *au pied de la lettre* than Jove or Juno. In Homer there is always a certain casualness in the narration of the miraculous which is quite different from Virgil's terse stylization. Compare, for example, *Iliad* 13.23–31, where Poseidon comes to the help of the Achaeans, with Virgil's narrative of Neptune (1.145–7). Basically it is the difference between a man who is something of an agnostic but still close to an age that believed, and a man for whom there is no question of belief in gods who look and behave like this. One can point also to the difference between Greek intellectualism and its tendency to explain the supernatural away by rationalizing it and anthropomorphizing it, and Italian imaginative readiness to accept the mysterious.

We find occasionally in Virgil the good-natured realism with which Homer treats his gods: Jove's pronouncement from the chair in Book 10 (10.104–13) easily reads as a gentle caricature of a dignified, slightly pompous real-life chairman anxious to be fair to both parties. But almost everywhere an undercurrent of ironic, distancing fantasy is present. When the brusque, athletic huntress is transformed before Aeneas' eyes into his divine mother, the skirt which she had been wearing hitched above her knees (1.320) flowed down to her toes, while the very way she held herself revealed the goddess (1.404–5):

> pedes uestis defluxit ad imos;
> et uera incessu patuit dea.

Frequently this is the dominant note of whole scenes: the entire storm sequence in Book 1 thrusts credulity aside in all but the most insensitive reader, as surely as the ironic portrait of Charon puts uncritical acceptance of Virgil's picture of the underworld out of the question.

This is not to say that Virgil's gods are conceived in a spirit of irreligious mockery. They are rather the embodiment, in a form that is vivid and intellectually pleasurable, of all those genuinely mysterious forces in the world of which the Roman mind possessed a profound if confused awareness. Many of Virgil's contemporaries would have been content to talk of gods, rather than in abstract terms, meaning by gods something at once more real and less precise than Virgil's fairy-

Form and Technique

tale figures. It is even possible up to a point to argue that Jove is the embodiment of fate, Juno the embodiment of some irrational principle of discord that creates havoc and hatred in the world, and Venus perhaps some embodiment of an irrational impulse to avoid the consequences of discord at whatever cost. Neither Juno nor Venus seems to have any clear foreknowledge of what is fated or even a sure grasp of what has happened.

Still less are the gods conventional transpositions from a purely behaviourist view of the universe. Heinze held that Virgil simply represented psychological phenomena in terms of divine interference, expecting the educated reader to translate his divine machinery back into psychological terms; but this is a misrepresentation of Virgil's attitude to the world, as Professor Pöschl warns us—a simplification which falsifies the way poetry works.[1]

The ironic fantasy of the divine scenes is in fact a pointer to the spirit in which we should take the more delicately stylized fantasy of the heroic narrative. Virgil's purpose in creating this atmosphere of fantasy we have discussed in Chapter 2: the moral comment of his story is rendered more effective if there is a gap, which the reader must bridge for himself, between the fairy-tale and the reality of recent events. Somehow, if the reader is left to put two and two together, the conclusion he draws impresses itself more deeply upon him.

Virgil, then, has consciously adopted a convention that might seem to stand in the way of a serious purpose and attempted to exploit that convention. But here, perhaps more than in any other single aspect of his structure, success has eluded him. His attempt to restrict the divine machinery so that it will not overshadow the heroic action has resulted in a serious loss of dramatic plausibility. Intellectually we can accept that the gods interfere on certain occasions only and not on others. But in a poem in other respects as sophisticated as Virgil's the reader

---

[1] Heinze, p. 305:
Was dies betrifft [das Eingreifen der Götter], so bin ich in der Tat geneigt, viel mehr, als man das heute meist tut, bei Virgil symbolisierende Absichten anzunehmen, d.h. eine bewusste Umsetzung einfacher psychologischer Vorgänge in die Form göttlicher Einwirkung, wobei darauf gerechnet ist, dass der gebildete Leser diese Götterszenen 'allegorisch' deuten werde.
Pöschl, Eng. edn, p. 72, comments:
It is a mistake to assume that Vergil 'translated psychological facts and the "educated" reader retranslates them into psychological terms because he understands, e.g., the appearances of the gods "allegorically"' (Heinze). Such a game cannot be reconciled with the religious spirit of the poet, nor is it fair to the nature of poetry.

should feel that the occasions when the divine machinery intervenes stand out, and that the reasons for the gods' intervention, and above all the reasons for their abstention on so many occasions when intervention seems so easy, are made convincing. It cannot be said that Virgil has managed this. Why *should* Juno intervene only when she does? Why should Venus not realize till Aeneas is already in Carthage, a city protected by Juno, that her protégé is in critical danger (1.671–2) and cheerfully allow him to make his way to Carthage, even describing what he will find there?

Moreover his attitude to his own fiction is not wholly consistent. The Venus who keeps Aeneas from killing Helen in Book 2 (2.588–621) is created in a very different spirit, for example, from the Venus who, in a scene shot through with playful irony, heals Aeneas in Book 12 (12.411–24) when his wound proves beyond mortal surgery.[1] Above all, there is an awkward clash between his Homeric gods and his Roman gods. The Penates who figure so prominently in the actions of Books 2 and 3 are plainly on an entirely different footing. Worse still, Apollo, though one of Homer's gods, is treated throughout, with the reverence the Romans paid their shadowy abstractions, as the powerful god of prophecy. Virgil's difficulty here, of course, is the cult of Apollo by Augustus and the official assertion that the battle of Actium was won with Apollo's assistance.

It must have been a task of immense difficulty to reconcile three things that were so incompatible—Homer's gods in the new spirit in which Virgil conceived them, the kind of genuine Roman religious belief sincerely entertained by many thinking men, and the apparatus of the official Roman State religion, to which Augustus was determined to give fresh impetus and stringency. The fact remains that the gods of Virgil's poem, though not the failure they are often represented to be, are not the success Virgil must have hoped.

II. CHARACTERIZATION AND MOTIVATION

An example will show the problem that confronted Virgil. Let us take the lines which precede Drances' speech in the Italian Council of War (11.336–42):

---

[1] Actually even Venus seems unable to effect a complete cure, and during the duel Aeneas' game leg causes him some embarrassment.

> tum Drances idem infensus, quem gloria Turni
> obliqua inuidia stimulisque agitabat amaris,
> largus opum et lingua melior, sed frigida bello
> dextera, consiliis habitus non futtilis auctor,
> seditione potens (genus huic materna superbum
> nobilitas dabat, incertum de patre ferebat),
> surgit et his onerat dictis atque aggerat iras.

*Then Drances—hostile as ever, but jealousy of Turnus'
glory made him sly, irked him with bitter goads;
a generous man, better as a speaker, for in war his
right hand froze, reckoned a sound leader in debate,
powerful in intrigue (his mother's noble birth
gave him pride of race, though his father was, they say, obscure)
—rising, vents his anger with these words.*

As usual, it is possible to point to a Homeric parallel—the description of Thersites as he rises to speak in the Greek Council of War (*Iliad* 2.212–19). But this kind of straightforward, detailed analysis of the interplay of character and motivation—the way the sort of man Drances was made him act the way he did on this occasion—is not something we should expect to find in the *Iliad* or the *Odyssey*. Homer merely gives Thersites the character of a talker and troublemaker. Drances is a complex, intriguing character (see analysis of the passage in Chapter 4). And where Homer devotes half his description to Thersites' misshapen, uncouth appearance, Virgil says nothing of the way Drances looked; he concerns himself only with character and motive.[1]

Homer appeals, in short, to the appetite for narrative excitement, naturally keener in an audience that has never experienced the more refined pleasures of reflection and analysis. Even if the interest had been there, Homer would have lacked the philosophical and linguistic equipment to satisfy it; his insight into individual motivation is rudimentary. Bruno Snell claimed that the very concepts of individual decision, and therefore of responsibility, upon which we base moral judgments, are not to be found in Homer, but first occur in Athenian tragedy.[2] That is probably an oversimplification which does Homer

---

[1] Ennius' description of Geminus Servilius comes a little closer (epic fragment 210–27W); but his portrait, though shrewd, altogether lacks Virgil's subtlety.

[2] Snell's thesis, formulated in his *Aischylos und das Handeln im Drama* (1928), has been contested by many, most recently by Albin Lesky, 'Göttliche und menschliche Motivation im homerischen Epos', *Sitz. der Heidelberger Akad.*

less than justice; all the same, Homer's idea of man as an individual and Virgil's are radically dissimilar.

The audience for which Virgil wrote was also a different audience. Interaction of character and motivation was a thing they understood: for centuries the problems of human conduct had had brought to play upon them the brilliant light of the Greek intellect, on the stage and in the schools of philosophy and oratory. They were problems in which the Romans themselves were passionately interested: their deeply moral temperament, whetted by the day-to-day routine of the law courts, had recently begun to find expression in their own native literature (in Cicero's philosophical treatises, in Horace's satires and epistles, for example). Here lay the dominant interest of their better historians: if Livy is an old-fashioned storymonger in the epic tradition, Sallust and Tacitus are more interested in character and motivation than in recording the past, acute in observation and skilful in the expression of what they have observed and deduced. Naturally, it was an interest for which imaginative literature also was expected to cater—recall Horace's precept on the need to give dramatic characters philosophical depth (*Ars Poetica* 309-18 and 343-4).

Clearly then Virgil must do better than Homer. He will disappoint his audience otherwise; his own sensitive, discerning understanding of human nature, sensed by every reader of his poem, will feel constantly frustrated. We might expect, therefore, that here if anywhere he will find himself forced to depart from the conventions of Homeric technique.

In fact, the analysis of Drances' character and motives is wholly exceptional. Elsewhere, Virgil conforms rigidly to the techniques of Homer: he resigns himself to a minimal amount of comment on character and motive, combining techniques of expression which are characteristically Homeric with others where he adheres to the letter rather than the spirit of Homeric technique. But into these narrow, inhibiting conventions he infuses a richness of psychological observation and comment utterly alien to Homer. It is a remarkable achievement, the starting point, because of the response this terse, penetrating comment arouses in the reader, for a fully rounded picture in the reader's mind.[1]

---

der Wiss., Phil.-Hist. Kl. (1961) 4. On the other hand Otis's theory (pp. 48-61) of a high degree of moral awareness in Homer (which Homer chooses to leave implicit) seems to me anachronistic.

[1] Otis (p. 77 and elsewhere) calls this kind of comment 'editorial intrusion'.

Form and Technique

Let us look at the slender equipment with which Virgil has chosen to arm himself. Linguistically speaking, his techniques of direct statement are strictly Homeric. States of mind are expressed by a single word—a verb (e.g., 9.197: *obstipuit*), an adjective (one that he is fond of is *amens*, e.g., 2.314: *arma amens capio*), a short phrase (e.g., 9.740: *sedato pectore*), or a more ornamental phrase, occupying a whole line perhaps, but strictly in the Homeric tradition as far as style and diction are concerned, and therefore pictorial rather than analytic—the most famous is 2.774: *obstipui, steteruntque comae et uox faucibus haesit*, which Virgil, in Homeric fashion, repeats several times in different contexts, slightly altered or augmented (3.48, 4.280, 12.868). Less straightforward emotions are briefly delineated within the space of a few lines, with occasional recourse to the simpler abstractions, but the words preserve always the ring of traditional epic—though what they convey may be infinitely more subtle. A simple example is 9.342-4:

> nec minor Euryali caedes; incensus et ipse
> perfurit ac multam in medio sine nomine plebem,
> ... subit.

The lust for slaughter that comes over Euryalus as he watches his companion cut down the sleeping Italians is suggested rather than analysed by the two words *incensus* (which makes use of metaphor: Euryalus is set on fire) and *perfurit* (where the metaphor—Euryalus' mood is a kind of madness—is sharpened by the preverb: Euryalus' madness sends him charging *through* the sleeping Italians). A slightly more compact example is 10.813-14:

> saeuae iamque altius irae
> Dardanio surgunt ductori.

Virgil sets out from the Homeric convention of the stock epithet—*all* anger is savage in a sense. But Aeneas' anger on this particular occasion is particularly savage because it thrusts aside the compassion he first felt for Lausus; and then the welling-up of rage is expressed by the metaphor in *surgunt*.

A conflict between emotions can equally be expressed within the same framework of technique. We have an example in 10.397-8:

> Arcadas accensos monitu et praeclara tuentis
> facta uiri mixtus dolor et pudor armat in hostis.

Pallas has just upbraided his men for hanging back, then hurled him-

Part 2: Technique

self at the enemy with a fine display of reckless courage. They feel resentment (*dolor*) at his words, but are shamed (*pudor*) by his example. Aroused (*accensos*) equally by the rebuke (*monitu*) and by Pallas' example (*praeclara tuentis facta*), they face the enemy.

Now something more complicated: when Virgil wishes to analyse the sudden crisis that causes Dido's resolution to falter on the night before her suicide, he presents first a picture of a world in which all else is asleep, and then continues (4.529–32):

> at non infelix animi Phoenissa neque umquam
> soluitur in somnos oculisue aut pectore noctem
> accipit: ingeminant curae rursusque resurgens
> saeuit amor magnoque irarum fluctuat aestu.

The first two lines strike the epic manner, but *infelix*, which again looks at first like ornament, is given a fresh, puzzling depth by *animi*—'ill-starred in her thoughts' is an example of the new tough, un-Homeric precision with which Virgil invests traditional vocabulary: Dido's thoughts are ill-starred because they are leading her to destruction; then in the next line, *animus* is contrasted with *pectore* in words that might come straight from Lucretius (cf. 4.3–4): because these thoughts dominate her *animus*, Dido cannot 'let night into her eyes' (shut her eyes in sleep)—and thus black out the thoughts in her *pectus* (according to Lucretius, the site of the *animus*). The first sentence resorts therefore more to suggestion than analysis. The second offers an undisguised analysis of the conflict produced in Dido's mind by the fact that she is still passionately attracted to Aeneas, but no longer feels any affection for him. Now that she is about to be separated from him for ever, her love for him becomes again as intense as it was in the beginning (*rursusque resurgens*). But love brings her no comfort, only torture (*saeuit*); instead of affection, she feels a sudden burst of anger that becomes more violent as she sees that the alternatives to suicide will only expose her to humiliation and ridicule. To convey this complex mood Virgil resorts to metaphor—a sea that is stormy again after an interval of calm (*rursusque resurgens*): Dido is on that sea; her passion, the waves that strike furiously against the vessel's side (*saeuit amor*) while she is tossed (*fluctuat*) upon a great swell of anger (*magno irarum aestu*).[1]

By exploiting Homeric technique, an effective economy and

[1] Cf. 7.344–5; 9.44, 717–19, 760–1; 10.515–17, 810–11; 11.451–2, 709–10; 12.667–9.

Form and Technique

simplicity can be achieved where we might expect only an inhibiting naïveté. In contexts where a responsive interest in motivation has been established in the reader's mind by such techniques, the reader can often be left to himself to supply the state of mind in which an action is performed, guided by no more than the general tone of a passage. Take 9.375-80:

> haud temere est uisum. conclamat ab agmine Volcens:
> 'state, uiri. quae causa uiae? quiue estis in armis?
> quoue tenetis iter?' nihil illi tendere contra,
> sed celerare fugam in siluas et fidere nocti.
> obiciunt equites sese ad diuortia nota
> hinc atque hinc omnemque aditum custode coronant.

> *It was not idly seen. From the line Volcens called,*
> '*Halt, there! Why are you out, why armed,*
> *whither bound?' They made no rejoinder,*
> *but fled quickly into the woods, trusting themselves to night.*
> *The horsemen block the bypaths they know well*
> *on either side and cut them off with a cordon of guards.*

Virgil's crisp rapidity is sufficient key to the emotions of his characters —the brusque, soldierly reaction of the Italians to something untoward, the sudden panic of Nisus and Euryalus. Or a state of mind may be left to be inferred from a brief description of appearance, or reaction to situation. We see both in 12.219-21:

> adiuuat incessu tacito progressus et aram
> suppliciter uenerans demisso lumine Turnus
> pubentesque genae et iuuenali in corpore pallor.

No analytic comment is needed to explain how much Turnus' state of mind has changed since the previous evening (see 12.81-106, discussed below). One word suffices now to state that the reaction of the Italians to his appearance contributed (*adiuuat*) to a complex change in their attitude to the duel (217: *uario misceri pectora motu*). At the beginning of the book, when their morale was low after the battle of Book 10, they were impatient for Turnus to fulfil his promise to meet Aeneas (12.1-3); now a change of heart has set in, they feel Turnus has taken on too much; then the sight of him, walking silently up to the altar, eyes downcast, so pale, so young, so humble in his supplication of the gods (compare the majesty and confidence of Aeneas, 175-94), completes the transformation of their attitude to Turnus from indignation to pity.

Part 2: Technique

These techniques can be used in conjunction with dialogue. A passage of a few lines can serve as the equivalent of stage directions, sketching in the tone in which a speech is to be read, so that the speech can itself more fully reveal character or state of mind. This device is commonest in Book 4, the most dramatic of the twelve, e.g., 4.474–7:

> ergo ubi concepit furias euicta dolore
> decreuitque mori, tempus secum ipsa modumque
> exigit et maestam dictis adgressa sororem
> consilium uultu tegit ac spem fronte serenat.

Dido, tortured beyond endurance by her passion (*euicta dolore*), feels within her a mad impulse to take her life (*concepit furias*—the crazy plan lay in her thoughts and then sprang to life like seed in the womb). The decision taken (*decreuitque mori*), she works out her plan in detail and then goes to her sister. Anna is gloomy (*maestam*), but Dido assumes an expression that conceals her plan. She 'makes expectation bright with her look' (*spem fronte serenat*). The reader is not only put on his guard by this stage direction, made ready to detect the overtones in Dido's opening words (see below under 'Tragic Irony and Insight'); he can sense, too, the effort Dido makes to control herself, the mad calm with which she speaks.

An analysis of motivation that has been compressed to keep it within the limits of Homeric convention can be expanded by a simile or an image. This use of imagery as an illustration of mental states is one of the main themes of Professor Viktor Pöschl's *Die Dichtkunst Virgils*. He discusses, for example, the following lines (4.68–73):

> uritur infelix Dido totaque uagatur
> urbe furens, qualis coniecta cerua sagitta,
> quam procul incautam nemora inter Cresia fixit
> pastor agens telis liquitque uolatile ferrum
> nescius: illa fuga siluas saltusque peragrat
> Dictaeos, haeret lateri letalis harundo.

The simile illustrates, first, how Dido looks and behaves (*tota uagatur urbe* is rendered more vivid by *illa fuga siluas saltusque peragrat Dictaeos*); then, second, how Dido feels (*uritur* is made more vivid by *coniecta cerua sagitta*); moreover the relative clause (*quam . . . nescius*), which looks on the surface like Homer's technique of picturesque expansion of the simile, reminds us of another component of Dido's dilemma: Aeneas has no inkling that she has fallen in love with him,

Form and Technique

and this of course is why Dido must roam the city helpless 'carrying in her flank the shaft that will bring death'. Finally, *letalis*, again ostensibly the ornamental epithet, is in fact the first hint to the reader that Dido will die of her passion, alone and in anguish, as surely as the deer will die from its physical wound.[1]

Let us conclude by studying a somewhat longer passage (12.81–106):

> haec ubi dicta dedit rapidusque in tecta recessit,
> poscit equos gaudetque tuens ante ora frementis,
> Pilumno quos ipsa decus dedit Orithyia,
> qui candore niues anteirent, cursibus auras;
> circumstant properi aurigae manibusque lacessunt   85
> pectora plausa cauis et colla comantia pectunt.
> ipse dehinc auro squalentem alboque orichalco
> circumdat loricam umeris; simul aptat habendo
> ensemque clipeumque et rubrae cornua cristae,
> ensem, quem Dauno ignipotens deus ipse parenti   90
> fecerat et Stygia candentem tinxerat unda.
> exin quae mediis ingenti adnixa columnae
> aedibus astabat, ualidam ui corripit hastam,
> Actoris Aurunci spolium, quassatque trementem
> uociferans: 'nunc, o numquam frustrata uocatus   95
> hasta meos, nunc tempus adest: te maximus Actor,
> te Turni nunc dextra gerit. da sternere corpus
> loricamque manu ualida lacerare reuulsam
> semiuiri Phrygis et foedare in puluere crinis
> uibratos calido ferro murraque madentis.'   100
> his agitur furiis totoque ardentis ab ore
> scintillae absistunt, oculis micat acribus ignis:
> mugitus ueluti cum prima in proelia taurus
> terrificos ciet atque irasci in cornua temptat
> arboris obnixus trunco uentosque lacessit   105
> ictibus aut sparsa ad pugnam proludit harena.

After a passionate scene, in which Turnus refuses to let Latinus and Amata talk him out of his abrupt decision to face Aeneas, Turnus stalks off (*rapidus recessit*) to an inner courtyard in the palace to ask for his precious white horses; he finds them being groomed and pauses to enjoy the spectacle (81–6). The point of his action has often been missed. There can be no question, commentators complain, of horses in a duel. But if we assume Turnus' frame of mind is rational, we must

[1] See Pöschl, Eng. edn, p. 81.

wonder too why he troubles to test his equipment (87–94): he has been fighting all day, he must know that his armour fits and that his weapons are in good condition.

What Virgil offers us is a study in three successive states of mind. Turnus' horses represent the kind of fighting he understands best, the kind he glories in during his long fugue in which he escapes from the realities of the duel (12.324–613). He wants to see them now because it makes him happy to look at them. Virgil leaves to the single, quite imprecise verb *gaudet* (82) the task of asserting Turnus' state of mind, leaving us to infer from the scene which follows (the magnificent white horses, the charioteers grooming them) the precise quality of Turnus' happiness. There is in it an element best left unstated: we have just had a hint that Turnus feels he will die in the duel (74: *neque enim Turno mora libera mortis*); we readily imagine, as Virgil's words evoke the happy, routine scene before Turnus' eyes, so irrelevant to the turn of events which has wrenched routine aside, that Turnus wants to see his horses now because he half feels that after tomorrow he will not need them again.[1]

It is in something like this frame of mind that Turnus returns to reality. The testing of his equipment is more a dress rehearsal, a way of alleviating a fresh surge of impatience to get on with the duel now that he has made up his mind, than the practical action of a professional soldier. He begins, however, calmly enough: *circumdat* and *aptat* in 88 are neutral words—they denote action with no comment on the way the action is performed.

But then the calm vanishes and he 'snatches up with a violent gesture' (93: *ui corripit*) his great spear and brandishes it so that it quivers (94: *quassat trementem*). The dress rehearsal has become indistinguishable from the real thing: the urgent, repeated *nunc* in 95–6 suggests Turnus half imagines Aeneas already before him as he abuses, and tries to make sound contemptible, the enemy he subconsciously fears. The final sentence (101–6) is Virgil's subtlest stroke. It begins on a note of magic: Turnus is a fairy-tale figure whose eyes actually flash fire in his rage and from whose mouth sparks actually fly. And then the sympathy we start to feel for this fantastic yet pathetic figure is cruelly undercut by the earthy simile (103–6) and the fresh evaluation

---

[1] The horses are of course used to draw Turnus' chariot as he rides out for the ceremony (12.164). Heinze (p. 229, note 1) and Pöschl (Eng. edn, p. 113), though they correctly interpret the function of the arming scene (Mackail, on 12.81–106 and Maguinness, p. 73, do not), miss the function of the horses in it.

it imposes of Turnus' emotions: his flamboyant rhetoric is no more sublimely pathetic than the blood-curdling roar (103-4: *mugitus terrificos*) of a bull working up his anger by driving his horns against the trunk of a tree in preparation for battle. (Compare the simile at 12.715-22.)

In this whole scene we have been told almost nothing about Turnus' state of mind, and yet clearly the purpose of the scene is to convey his state of mind to us in all its complexity. By the very simplicity of the techniques to which Virgil has limited himself, an atmosphere has been created which renders the reader sensitive to every hint. The techniques employed are fundamentally different from those employed in describing Drances' state of mind when he rose to address the Italian assembly, but can we maintain they are less effective? Drances' state of mind, though complex, is not hard to describe (provided one allows oneself the resources of sophisticated Latin prose): both the situation and the character are within the bounds of an educated Roman's everyday experience; little harm is done, therefore, by stating them precisely. Evaluation of Turnus is more tricky: he is neither wholly admirable nor wholly ridiculous; heroically impulsive, but not without a confused awareness (which we shall see clarify as the action of the book moves to its conclusion) that destiny has cast him in the losing role. The very limitations of Homeric technique, by the artificial restraint they impose, necessitate a subtlety in their manipulation of which Virgil in scene after scene shows himself triumphantly master.

III. PARALLEL DIVINE AND PSYCHOLOGICAL MOTIVATION

Virgil's analyses, explicit and implicit, of his characters strike us as so thoroughly acceptable in terms of our own notions of how people feel and behave, and his techniques for presenting his analyses—though puzzling till we realize the basis of the rules which he has set himself—so thoroughly in keeping with what, and how, and how much, we want a good poet to tell us, we might expect to find that the role assigned the gods in the *Aeneid* (leaving aside what we may call their actual physical intervention in the heroic action) limited to providing the external circumstances, the web of fate and chance in which the characters are entangled. It would certainly have been neater if Virgil had done it that way. But this is not the way Homeric epic works. In Homer the rudiments of a concept of independent human motivation have to jostle for a place with older strata of thought which attributed to the gods—to put the distinction with a clarity which is, of course, an anachronism—not only the things that happened to men in the world, but the things that happened in men's minds as well.

In the *Iliad* and the *Odyssey* the confusion between traditional belief and man's new awareness of himself as an individual settles down into a rather ill-defined parallelism in which mental events tend to be presented on two levels.[1] C. H. Whitman put the matter perhaps just a little too strikingly when he claimed that 'everything in the *Iliad* happens twice, once on earth, and once in the timeless world of deity'.[2] For we must remember that, however fascinating we may find the conflict in Homeric epic between primitive habits of thought and the first beginnings of mental processes resembling those of modern man, a need to reconcile the two was not something the composer of the *Iliad* and the *Odyssey* can have kept very clearly or very conspicuously before him.

We might expect Virgil to avoid this conflict of attitudes, however characteristic of the Homeric poems. In fact he accepts it. The parallelism had perhaps become too deep-seated in tradition for him to ignore it. For we find it also in Athenian tragedy, though for the tragedians it is not the result of different strata of thinking, but an artistic stylization of something really felt—that, however much our decisions seem our own, we are not free agents.[3] This is, of course, one of only two or three frameworks of belief within which tragedy is possible; if man is not, in some measure, the victim of gods or chance, or his genes, then his moral responsibility is complete and tragedy becomes melodrama—those who suffer only get what they deserve. Tragedy, like pity, implies consequences out of proportion to responsibility.

Occasionally we may feel that Virgil's object is simply to assert his adherence to Homeric technique. A number of times an impulse to action has a divine origin ascribed it in a way that strikes us as purely formal. Examples are Aeneas' sudden realization (as we should put it)

---

[1] See M. P. Nilsson, *Geschichte der griechischen Religion*, vol. 1 (2nd edn 1955) 365–6, and Lesky, op. cit., p. 17.

[2] C. H. Whitman, *Homer and the Heroic Tradition* (1958) 248.

[3] See Kitto, op. cit. Cf. E. R. Dodds, 'On misunderstanding the *Oedipus Rex*', *GR* 13 (1966) 37–49.

Form and Technique

that he must leave Carthage before it is too late (ascribed to the message brought him by Mercury from Jove, 4.265–82), and his final decision to depart (ascribed to a dream in which Mercury visits him a second time, 4.556–70). In other cases the touch seems even more perfunctory—for example, Aeneas' determination to depart when confronted by Dido is ascribed to the warnings of Jove (4.331—a phrase that is used again of Mezentius when he takes Turnus' place in the battle, 10.689); or when the prophecy of the tables is inadvertently (as we should say) fulfilled (7.110), the Aeneadae do what they do because *sic Iuppiter ipse monebat*.

A little thought shows point in what we might first take to be no more than the adoption, for stylistic purposes, of a Homeric tag. Virgil makes his tag serve a new purpose—compare his exploitation of stock epithets. It is a reasonable fancy that Jove should stand by to prompt Aeneas when he is exposed to the sudden onslaught of Dido's misunderstanding anger; an ironical fancy that Jove should send the rabid atheist Mezentius to his death in battle (and it prepares for the irony we sense in Mezentius' words to Orodes, 10.742–4—see Chapter 4, and compare 11.725–8); and almost a necessary fancy that Jove should prompt the fulfilment of the oracle (otherwise the fulfilment of the prophecy becomes a matter of chance; compare 11.901). But before we persist in making things neater than Virgil wants them, we should remind ourselves of Nisus' words to Euryalus—Virgil's dramatic presentation of the hesitancy which lingered on in men's minds, perhaps in his own, between two explanations of the impulse which comes unheralded and is not a decision reached after conscious thought (9.184–7):

> Nisus ait: 'dine hunc ardorem mentibus addunt,
> Euryale, an sua cuique deus fit dira cupido?
> aut pugnam aut aliquid iamdudum inuadere magnum
> mens agitat mihi nec placida contenta quiete est.'

> *Nisus spoke: 'Is it the gods set men's minds on fire,*
> *Euryalus, or do we make gods our own imperious desire?*
> *To fight, to undertake some great deed, this is the thought*
> *that stirs in my mind impatient of idleness and calm.'*

But there are passages too, and they are apt to seem more puzzling, in which a mental event is related more explicitly on both levels. Dido provides an instance that is famous because of the misunderstanding it has produced of Virgil's intentions. She falls in love because Venus

Part 2: Technique

sends Cupid, disguised as Aeneas' son Ascanius, to the banquet and he sets her on fire. That is one level; on the other level she falls in love because she is a passionate woman who has till now resisted passion in her widowhood, but finds her infatuation with Aeneas, the handsome adventurer who has aroused her pity (1.630), impossible to resist (4.22–3):

> 'solus hic inflexit sensus animumque labantem
> impulit. agnosco ueteris uestigia flammae.'

> '*He alone has bent my feelings, sent my resolution tottering. I acknowledge the trace of a fire that burnt of old.*'

Or take Amata: it is the Fury Allecto who maddens her by slipping a magic snake between her breasts and sends her on her wild fugue into the mountains (7.346–53); but Amata is already seething with anxiety and anger (345: *curaeque iraeque coquebant*); it is only to be expected if she attempts some crazy plan (see Analysis in Chapter 4). Or Aeneas, engaged in his fruitless pursuit of Turnus in Book 12: Venus sends him the idea of an attack on the Latin city (12.554–6); but an alternative explanation on the other level immediately follows: as Aeneas casts an eye around, he sees the city and realizes the opportunity it presents for a sudden, spectacular stroke (557–60). We have a longer example in the incident of the stag in Book 7. Again things are presented first on the divine level: Allecto makes the dog scent the stag (7.479–82); some lines later the same event is recounted on the other level (493–5); whereupon Ascanius takes a shot at the fleeing stag—and Allecto ensures that he scores a hit (497–8).

Then there is the death of Palinurus (5.833–63). The god of sleep comes in disguise to Palinurus, casts a spell on him with his wand and tosses him overboard. But, though this time the expression of the parallelism is more subtle, it is equally clear that Palinurus was drowsy, fell into a half-sleep, and still in that half-sleep he fancied he saw Phorbus at his side and then fell completely asleep and tumbled overboard still clutching the rudder in his hands.

We occasionally find in Apollonius this apparent intrusion of the divine motivation that puzzles us because it seems superfluous. For example, 3.817–19: after a beautiful passage in which we see Medea tempted to poison herself from her own poison casket (this lovesick girl is also a witch), then reflect on the joys of life, 'as is natural in a young girl' (οἷά τε κούρη), then realize that she cannot let them go, her decision to put the casket down is ascribed to Hera, who needs Medea in order to save Jason. But Apollonius' fairy-tale, by comparison with Virgil's, follows the older tradition of motivation by anthropomorphic gods only casually.

Once we accept the hypothesis that the destiny of Aeneas is controlled by fate, the situations which arise are always such that it is reasonable to fancy that fate steps in. But it is important to keep saying 'to fancy', in order to remind ourselves that Virgil's whole story is fanciful, a fairy-tale which offers important insights into reality, but is not in any sense intended as a record of what actually happened. We must remind ourselves too that Virgil, despite his extraordinarily modern interest in human behaviour, was not what we should call a behaviourist, but a man whose view of the world was tinged with mysticism and religious belief. He is most unlikely to have believed that men were free agents. He was an ancient Roman, still close to ways of belief that thinking men have long discarded—or sought to discard; for even to us the phenomena of impulse and decision, of thoughts that flash through the mind, remain ultimately mysterious; we have not so long emerged from a mental climate in which certain thoughts at any rate were widely believed to be the work of the devil.[1]

IV. FATE[2]

The idea that certain things must happen is deep-rooted in the most ancient strata of belief. It is well established in Homer, along with the idea that the time and manner of their happening may *not* be fixed; or that something which is fated can only happen as a consequence of a particular action by a human being; there was, for example, the old legend of the *fata Troiana* (Troy would not fall until the Palladium had been stolen, a particular son of Priam killed, and so on).

Here too Virgil adopts the conventions implicit in his form, though with an altered emphasis. The concept is stressed of fate as a general plan in which man participates by his labours, rather than by

---

[1] For parallel divine and psychological motivation in Catullus 64 see my study of the poem in *Critical Essays in Roman Literature*, ed. J. P. Sullivan, vol. 1: *Elegy and Lyric* (1962) 55–9.

[2] See Boyancé, Chapter 3.

Part 2: Technique

the inadvertent commission of predetermined acts. He speaks both of *fatum* and *fata* (the plural easily comes to mean a prophecy, a pronouncement about what is fated, because of the etymological connexion with *fari*). Among older beliefs, one to which he gives some prominence is the idea that the time and even the manner of a man's death could be fated. Alongside these ancient beliefs we find the Hellenistic rationalization of fate as chance (τύχη)—the way things will turn out. Virgil does not concern himself with distinguishing clearly between fate and chance (*fortuna*). When he uses the word *infelix* in connexion with Dido and Turnus ('ill-starred' is a less misleading translation than 'unhappy' or 'unfortunate', though it introduces an irrelevant metaphor) his object is to assert the tragic view of the world; Dido and Turnus are to be pitied because things turned out for them the way they did. (See, later in this chapter, 'Tragic Attitude'.)

Fate, as has been said, is a necessary component of Virgil's poem; the *Aeneid* depends on the hypothesis that Aeneas has a destined mission to found a city which will one day be the Rome his audience knew, and Virgil takes full advantage of this hypothesis in his three great cadenzas—Jove's prophecy to Venus, Anchises' prophecy to Aeneas, and the vision of the future worked by Vulcan upon the shield of Aeneas. But the concept of an overriding fate involves him in situations that call for delicate handling. Take Jove's prophecy to Hercules that Turnus' end is at hand (10.471-2). We might perhaps say that Turnus was fated to die young and in battle (he was that sort of person, to reinterpret fate in terms of character) and that the actual time was fixed by a combination of that character and the way things chanced. Or take Vulcan's remark at 8.398-9: Virgil perhaps believed that cities, like men, are fated to die, but that the fall of Troy could be hastened or retarded by the behaviour of the Trojans. Once again, however, we must warn ourselves against treating Virgil as a philosopher. Who searches Shakespeare for a philosophy of predetermination because of the witches in *Macbeth*? Or for a belief in individual survival because of the ghost in *Hamlet*? Virgil, likely enough, gave more serious thought than Shakespeare to the way the world worked. But there are dangers in fussing too much about, say, Jove and the scales in 12.725-7.

Consider the famous curse that Dido pronounces as she sees Aeneas' fleet sailing down the harbour of Carthage. She understands at last that it is fated that Aeneas should reach Italy (4.612-14):

Form and Technique

> 'si tangere portus
> infandum caput ac terris adnare necesse est
> et sic fata Iouis poscunt, hic terminus haeret.'

But she goes on (615–20):

> 'at bello audacis populi uexatus et armis,
> finibus extorris, complexu auulsus Iuli
> auxilium imploret uideatque indigna suorum
> funera: nec, cum se sub leges pacis iniquae
> tradiderit, regno aut optata luce fruatur,
> sed cadat ante diem mediaque inhumatus harena.'

Her curse is, of course, answered—these things do happen. The exile Aeneas is involved in a war with a courageous people in Italy; he is separated from his son; he has to look to others for help; he sees his own men die in battle; he is destined, we are told (1.265–6), to survive the final victory by only three years. And Juno (one of the divinities entreated by Dido) is instrumental in bringing about the war when all seemed set for peace. So that in a sense Dido is avenged and Aeneas punished. But the war is already predicted by Jove to Venus in 1.263–4:

> 'bellum ingens geret Italia populosque ferocis
> contundet moresque uiris et moenia ponet.'

What Dido has asked for is already part of the divine purpose, part somehow of the *labor* of Aeneas. And when she goes on to demand undying hatred between the peoples of Tyre and Troy (4.622–9), Virgil clearly is only placing the Carthaginian wars within a fated framework.[1]

A further example may help us to gauge the spirit in which to take the example just considered. When Dido kills herself, Juno has to send Iris down from Olympus to release her soul from her body which holds it prisoner—a fanciful representation of an idea that is characteristically Platonic. Iris' intervention is necessary because Dido is dying 'not by fate nor by deserved death; but before her time in a sudden access of madness'—and therefore Proserpina had not had time to cut from her head the lock that condemned her to the underworld (4.696–705). This is the nearest we get to a plain statement from Virgil of Dido's responsibility for her suicide. Obviously Virgil wants

---

[1] What disturbs us is that Virgil tries to distinguish this war from the war in Italy by making Jove call the former a just war (10.11–14).

the story of Dido to end as it began, in an atmosphere of fairy-tale: Iris is no more to be taken at her face value than Cupid. Isn't it, then, a mistake to look for a statement of Virgil's concept of fate in the beautiful fantasy of these lines, beyond perhaps the simple meaning that Dido had brought it all on herself?

Part 3: THE CONTRIBUTION OF TRAGEDY

The stress we have laid on Virgil's adherence to epic form and technique must not blind us to an aspect of the poem that strikes any modern reader who comes directly to it, unprejudiced by what he knows of its traditional allegiances—the intensely dramatic character of the *Aeneid*. As far as the structure of the poem is concerned, this is a matter which has been dealt with in Chapter 3, Section III ('The Episodes'). It is not so much the fact that dialogue makes up more than a third of the poem which marks Virgil's debt to tragedy, as his use of dialogue and situation to reveal character. Aeneas' reply to Dido in the quarrel scene, as we said in Chapter 3, is not intended as Virgil's exculpation of Aeneas, but to show the man Aeneas is: decent, honest, aware of his share of blame, unwilling to be drawn into rancorous argument, but no more able to see Dido's point of view than she is to see his. The quarrel scene dramatizes this clash of personalities, so little equipped to understand one another, torn apart after their brief happiness by incomprehension of each other's basic assumptions. It is one of many Episodes that possess the proportions, the tenseness, the internal unity of true drama.

Yet here too Virgil avoids open rupture with the epic tradition. Homer makes even freer use of dialogue (and in the speeches Virgil assigns his characters echoes of characteristic Homeric conventions are common—the heroic exchange, for instance, before one character kills another on the battlefield) and often presents situations dramatically, as a series of long speeches linked by brief comment (e.g., the quarrel scene, *Iliad* 1.53–305).

The difference, however, is striking. Partly, it is the result of Virgil's keener sense of objective, and his superior technical skill: where Homer's speeches are apt to ramble, to be filled out with the formulae of bardic poetry loosely strung together, Virgil's manner is intense,

Form and Technique

concentrated on the building-up of character and motivation through dialogue and the incisive narrator's comment which precedes or follows the speaker's actual words. Though it is a commonplace, from Aristotle onwards (for example, *Poetics* 1459b), that the elements of tragedy can be found in the *Iliad* (by a reader of a more sophisticated age who is looking for them), they are the result of the natural instinct of the story-teller to tell his story, as far as possible (even at considerable loss of economy), in the direct speech of the participants, guided by an ill-defined awareness (which the modern reader easily makes sharper) of the pathos inherent in human suffering. They are not the result of a clearly thought-out tragic attitude and a technique evolved for the express purpose of exploring motivation and personality.

I. TRAGIC ATTITUDE

If much of the story of Dido is as strictly tragic in form as it is in spirit, it is in a somewhat different sense that the story of Turnus is commonly spoken of as tragic.[1] For obviously, if the story is spread over six books, is not continuous and is told in narrative form as much as in dialogue form, we can scarcely talk of a transposition from tragic to epic form.[2] But to talk of 'the tragedy of Turnus' is none the less meaningful, just as it is meaningful to talk of the tragedy of Mezentius or Camilla, though Mezentius and Camilla are less frequently spoken of in this way. Sentimental critics in all these cases are apt to talk in terms of Virgil's instinctive, impulsive sympathy for the losing side, not realizing his determination to create something more than storybook heroes and heroines, to create complex characters worthy of a sympathy that can be intense but is not uniform, for as the story advances our sympathy changes direction.[3]

---

[1] See W. S. Maguinness, 'The tragic spirit of the *Aeneid*', Presidential address to the [British] Virgil Society (1955).

[2] Though J. B. Garstang, 'The tragedy of Turnus', *Phoenix* 9 (1950) 47–58, has attempted to tabulate the actions of the Turnus Episodes as if they were the acts and scenes of a formal tragedy.

[3] I borrow the phrase 'our sympathy changes direction' from L. C. Knights' study 'On the tragedy of Antony and Cleopatra', *Scrutiny* 16 (1949) 318–23:

> That relationship of Antony and Cleopatra is evoked and defined with a variety of resources that has behind it almost the whole of Shakespeare's working lifetime. Different and apparently irreconcilable evaluations are

Part 3: The Contribution of Tragedy

But there is a more precise sense in which Dido, Turnus, Mezentius and perhaps Camilla can be spoken of as tragic characters. It is a sense which involves our recognition of them as characters created by a poet whose outlook on life has been deeply influenced by Athenian tragedy. The characters in Virgil's poem, both major and minor (though this is obviously something that is not made invariably explicit—one can ram a point home too often), are caught up in a pattern of events constructed according to a concept of the world upon which Greek tragedy virtually depends. True tragic plot represents the interaction of personality and circumstances—the way things worked out. In this sense Dido is as strictly a tragic figure as Oedipus.

It is an attitude which can confuse us until we do come to understand it. The modern reader (as was remarked in the Analysis of Book 1) is apt to want Dido to be to blame, and is upset because it all seems not her fault. She could not be blamed for falling in love—either on the divine or on the human level of motivation. As for what happened in the cave, she seems exculpated on the divine level and very forgivable on the human. The answer is that she could have resisted passion more successfully; she could have known, or learnt, to put duty or *pudor* before infatuation; and after yielding to infatuation she could have been honest enough with herself not to pretend she had marriage in her grasp. It is the interaction between these elements in her character and the way things worked out that involve her in tragedy. It needn't have happened; it was her bad luck that she became embroiled in fate's plans for Aeneas; but having become embroiled, the consequences *are* her fault. She is as little entitled (and as much) to enter a plea of

---

explicit in commentary and implicit in direct speech and action: as we move from point to point in the play our sympathy changes direction, and as a result of recurrent shifts of the emotional current, 'judgment' becomes more complex. No single statement that we are given concerning the central love-relationship or the individual lovers can be taken as summing up what the play as a whole has to offer, and it is a task of no little difficulty (though not, for the reader of Shakespeare, an unfamiliar one) to expose oneself to the whole experience rather than to some selected part of it (p. 318).
Later in the same article (p. 322) Knights says:
It is, of course, one of the signs of a great writer that he can *afford* to evoke sympathy or even admiration for what, in his final judgment, is discarded or condemned.
—a phrase first brought to my attention by Professor R. G. Austin's quotation of it (*Aeneid* 4, p. xiv). I doubt, however, whether in the case of Virgil we can speak of discarding and condemning: he points to the flaws in his characters, and as a result we can feel our sympathy change direction, but condemnation is another matter—Virgil is too gentle for that.

force majeure as Oedipus—or the Helen of Euripides' *Trojan Women*.

The superiority of this attitude to our modern, instinctively moralizing attitude to literature is evident. In literature *we* want people to be to blame. Yet if we are honest we must admit that most often people are punished in this world mainly for being the people they are, that what people suffer bears little correlation to the degree in which they appear morally deserving or admirable. The tragic view imposes a detachment which accords well with the universality of Virgil's sympathy—always veering but never finally withheld.

Let us return, to make things clearer, to Turnus. Why does he die? Because he killed Pallas, we may say, and Aeneas kills him in return—it is Virgil's version of the story of Achilles' killing of Hector in revenge for Patroclus. This is true, of course. But it is an answer that takes no account of the internal, tragic logic of Virgil's story. Turnus killed Pallas in fair fight: Pallas was creating havoc among the Italians, and it was reasonable for the Italian leader to take on himself the task of removing him. Having killed him, he treated his body only as Pallas had prayed *he* might be allowed to treat the body of Turnus if he had won (10.462: *cernat semineci sibi me rapere arma cruenta*). True, Turnus strikes his young victim down in an ugly hybristic mood: he wishes, he says, Pallas' father were present to watch his son die (10.443); and when he has killed Pallas, he hands over the body with a contemptuous message to Evander—'I restore Pallas,' he says, 'in the condition he has asked for' (10.492: *qualem meruit, Pallanta remitto*). But Evander was an old enemy of the Latins (8.55), and we can easily suppose Virgil wants us to imagine that Turnus feels old enmities fanned to fresh flame at the sight of Evander's son ranged against him. We are told that Turnus was excited and—as men do—went too far (10.501–2: *nescia mens hominum . . . seruare modum, rebus sublata secundis*). The context, however, connects the words with the action of taking the belt, not that of killing Pallas—either the deed itself, or the words Turnus used.

Virgil's attitude is clear. Turnus committed no monstrous crime that, more than the other killings in the poem, cried out for vengeance; but having killed Pallas, he did something he need not have done: he stripped from the body a belt that he coveted, one that was easy to recognize. The act was characteristic of the man; but by it he was to prove 'unwittingly' (501: *nescia mens hominum*) the agent of his own destruction. It is the fatal slip of tragedy, committed in a mood of unthinking, insensitive contempt for his victim—one form of hybris;

Part 3: The Contribution of Tragedy

but Turnus' death is no *punishment*, it is merely the way things worked out, and when death comes we can sympathize with him and regard him as *infelix* (12.941) because things worked out the way they did.[1]

II. TRAGIC SUSPENSE

In the simpler forms of story the reader's eagerness to know what will happen keeps him alert and pleasurably excited. Even the simplest tale can provide more than this, of course: if it is well told, we read it again and again, not just because we like the writer's style, but because our pleasure in the tale itself, the excitement even, can somehow be recaptured.

Suspense is something different. It is aroused by the reader's feeling that certain things will happen. In more sophisticated forms of story the reader often knows in a general way what to expect—somebody will be killed, a villain unmasked, a beautiful girl married; the suspense arises from *waiting* for these things to happen; a kind of tension is created, offsetting the risk of boring us which the writer must run if he attempts to give breadth and depth to his story and make it more than a recital of exciting events.

Rather different from this feeling that particular things will probably happen is the kind of suspense we find in still more sophisticated forms of story, where the suspense is provided by our interest in *how* the thing we expect to happen will come about. It is, to use Coleridge's terms, the superiority over surprise of expectation.[2] Elements of puzzlement and reflection are introduced and a more refined form of satisfaction aroused when things click at last into place.

Most good detective stories provide both kinds of suspense. The

---

[1] Strictly speaking, it is the belt which is called *infelix*. J. Ashmore, in a lecture to the [British] Virgil Society, 1953 (published in summary form, referred to by W. S. Maguinness, 'The tragic spirit of the *Aeneid*', 3–4) seems to have made this point.

[2] Coleridge, in *Essays and Lectures on Shakspeare*, etc. (Everyman edn 1907) 52–3, puts first in his list of characteristics which distinguish Shakespeare from other dramatists:
   Expectation in preference to surprise. . . . As the feeling with which we startle at a shooting star compared with that of watching the sunrise at the pre-established moment. such and so low is surprise compared with expectation.

reader knows when he begins that pretty soon somebody will get killed, and he enjoys being on the alert for the murder to happen; there is little point in puzzling over who will be killed, because often the corpse proves to be that of somebody not previously mentioned in the story. This is the tension kind of suspense. After the murder the puzzling, reflective kind of suspense can begin: the reader is invited to work out, from the clues provided, how the story will end. Careless readers of course often read the second, major part of a detective story in the same spirit of tension-suspense as the first part—merely waiting for the dénouement, without attempting to anticipate it or concerning themselves greatly with how it is contrived.

Homer's *Iliad* offers primarily the pleasurable excitement of a well-told story. There is a limited amount of tension-suspense: we know Achilles must return to help the Greeks; we know after the death of Patroclus that Achilles must kill Hector. We may even take an interest in how these things come about. But this is not really an interest for which Homer caters: the plot is too loosely constructed to provide much reward for reflection. Nor is the story designed to provide any particular insight into human nature or to bring us to accept a particular view of the world. The reader may have such reflections, but they are hardly aroused by the structure of Homer's story, and certainly the story does not depend for its success on arousing them.[1]

Tragedy, however, at any rate Athenian tragedy, is written for an audience with a different kind of interest. The story is designed to stress the interplay of human personality and fate—the way the sort of people we are is apt to prove our undoing. To cater for this kind of interest the story must be constructed differently, to reveal (with appropriate subtlety) the sort of people the characters in it are, to foreshadow (often simply by retelling a known tale) what is going to happen to them, so that we are put on the alert to see how things will work out the way they must. We may then be drawn into reflections upon how it all came about, which is why the climax of a Greek tragedy seems sometimes to us, unaccustomed to this preference for dialectic over tragic spectacle, oddly premature.

Writing in this tradition of tragic suspense, Virgil makes little attempt at narrative excitement. Even in Book 2, the most continuously exciting of the twelve, the primary emphasis remains on *how*

---

[1] See G. E. Duckworth, *Foreshadowing and Suspense in the Epics of Homer, Apollonius and Vergil* (1933).

Part 3: The Contribution of Tragedy

things will work out the way they must. Troy's fall is fated, the wooden horse the known stratagem by which the Greeks gain entry to the fortress they have besieged for ten years. But how will fate work upon the minds of the Trojans to make them the instruments of their own destruction? Aeneas is cast from his first appearance in Section 2 of the book as the man fated to save his people. But how can this be brought about when his impulse is only to squander his life uselessly?

Even where he might easily create excitement out of uncertainty about what will happen, Virgil discards the opportunity. We might have been left to guess that Turnus will be killed in the end. Virgil leaves us in no doubt. We get the first intimation at 10.471–2 as Turnus faces Pallas; there is a clearer hint at 10.503–5; the whole narrative of the duel is constructed in such a way as to make it clear that it will end with Turnus' death. Dido's fate is likewise made easy to anticipate. Obviously she must lose Aeneas. But the reader could not be sure that her death would form part of Virgil's story. The deer simile (4.68–73) is the first hint; throughout Sections 2 and 3 it becomes increasingly clear that the narrative must end with her suicide.[1]

When the movement of the battle in Book 10 seems to sweep Pallas towards Lausus, we are told at once that Jove will not allow the two to meet because each is fated to die at the hands of a greater enemy (10.436–8):

> ipsos concurrere passus
> haud tamen inter se magni regnator Olympi;
> mox illos sua fata manent maiore sub hoste.

The reader is not entitled at this stage to form any expectation about what will happen to Pallas and Lausus; so Virgil forewarns him, in order that he can watch the march of events over the next 400 lines (Lausus is killed at 10.820), alert to see *how* what he has been told to expect will come about and *who* the greater antagonist is that awaits each; being forewarned, he can observe more readily how Pallas and Lausus, by being the persons they are, reject the loopholes fate leaves them—Pallas accepts the challenge to meet Turnus; Lausus throws himself in Aeneas' path to save his father.

Virgil's determination to reveal his hand in advance becomes at times almost a mannerism, one aspect of his constant technique of Suspended Narrative. Take the truce which is arranged for the duel between Aeneas and Turnus, and broken after the conclusion of the

---
[1] See *Latin Explorations*, Chapter 2.

opening ceremony by the intervention of Iuturna on the initiative of Juno. The description of the opening ceremony and the narrative of the briefing of Iuturna by Juno might very well come in that order. Instead Virgil reverses the order so that the reader comes to the description of the opening ceremony knowing that the duel will not follow it. Virgil is careful, however, to gratify our interest in seeing *how* what we know will happen comes about: it is the reaction of the Italians to the spectacle (Aeneas calm and majestic, Turnus pale and tense) that facilitates the intervention of Iuturna.

III. TRAGIC IRONY AND INSIGHT

A story based on the interplay of character and circumstances readily invites us to contrast our understanding of what is happening to a character with the character's own awareness of his predicament (as revealed by his actions or his words). In the simpler forms of story this is something we can only conjecture about: we may be moved by the story, feel that it is convincing. But we are influenced more by our own intuitive realization of an author's characters—what it must have felt like to be those characters—than by evidence in the text. In Virgil, as in Athenian tragedy, the author makes it his business to cater for this interest—and not to cater for it crudely.

Let us turn to the point in *Aeneid* 12 where Turnus realizes the duel with Aeneas can no longer be evaded (12.665–80):

> obstipuit uaria confusus imagine rerum   665
> Turnus et obtutu tacito stetit: aestuat ingens
> uno in corde pudor mixtoque insania luctu
> et furiis agitatus amor et conscia uirtus.
> ut primum discussae umbrae et lux reddita menti,
> ardentis oculorum orbis ad moenia torsit   670
> turbidus eque rotis magnam respexit ad urbem.
> ecce autem flammis inter tabulata uolutus
> ad caelum undabat uertex turrimque tenebat,
> turrim, compactis trabibus quam eduxerat ipse
> subdideratque rotas pontisque instrauerat altos.   675
> 'iam iam fata, soror, superant, absiste morari;
> quo deus et qua dura uocat Fortuna, sequamur;

Part 3: The Contribution of Tragedy

> stat conferre manum Aeneae, stat quidquid acerbi est
> morte pati; neque me indecorem, germana, uidebis
> amplius: hunc, oro, sine me furere ante furorem.' 680

Virgil begins with a fairly full analysis of a complicated state of mind—Turnus' reaction to Saces' news that disaster has struck the city and that the queen is dead; lines 665–8 ensure that we come to Turnus' words prepared to lend them the significance they deserve. Moreover, the preceding narrative of Turnus' exploits in the chariot was constructed in such a way as to suggest that his exploits were an evasion of reality. When, therefore, Turnus, stung by Saces' last words (664: *tu currum deserto in gramine uersas*), reproaches himself—shame is one element in the complex of seething emotions (665–8) aroused by Saces' words; the others are mad grief, wild affection for Lavinia, and the feeling that he can play a man's part—we feel begin a process of self-criticism dramatically and psychologically more effective than any that open accusation could have elicited. Then reason takes control (669) and Turnus wheels round to appraise the situation at the city (670–1). He sees enveloped in a column of flame the tower whose construction he had himself supervised (672–5). The symbolism is plain. And to Turnus too (such is the clear implication of the stress Virgil lays on Turnus' share in the building of the tower) some sense of a destruction of his own work, of lost purpose, precipitates the decision he now takes.

Against this background are set Turnus' words to his sister (676–80). Hardly less moving than the pathos of Turnus' recognition of his powerlessness against fate is his realization of how little there is to be proud of in his decision to meet Aeneas: the duel will be no more than a final act of madness; the best Turnus can hope is that it will seem less shameful (679: *indecorem*) than his empty heroics in the chariot. The double entreaty of *oro* and *sine me* in 680 fix the tone: there is no stridency or bitterness; only recognition of the pointless pettiness of the wish to cut a better figure in death than in life.[1]

---

[1] Pöschl comments, p. 185:
 . . . je näher die Niederlage heranrückt, desto mehr wächst seine innere Grösse. Je mehr er erkennt, dass die Götter ihn verlassen, umso stärker wird seine Entschlossenheit, der Ruhmesverpflichtung bis in den Tod treu zu bleiben.

But though this is an accurate appraisal of the gradual nature of Turnus' increasing awareness of his predicament, it seems to me too grand a way to talk about the quality of Turnus' insight—so grand that Turnus ceases to be truly heroic.

Form and Technique

Let us, as an initial assessment of stature, set Turnus' words as he faces death alongside the familiar words of Sidney Carton in a situation sufficiently similar to be of use to us:

> It is a far, far better thing that I do, than I have ever done; it is a far, far better rest that I go to, than I have ever known.[1]

What Dickens offers us is sentimental rhetoric: Carton, the waster who gives his life for Darnay because his devotion to Darnay's wife has morally redeemed him, achieves a certain dignity in death and has some right, therefore, to contrast his present sacrifice with his past life, and his words are dramatically convincing. But there is nothing we should call insight. I am not concerned with the evident difference in quality, but with an ingredient present in Virgil which is absent in Dickens. For Carton this is a moment of triumph; the prospect of death is made less grim by the thought of noble action. For Turnus it is a moment, not merely of defeat, but of the first confused onset of a humiliating comprehension. And because he at last understands himself, Turnus lays in the moment of defeat that special claim upon our sympathy prompted by our recognition that there is more to someone than we had supposed.

Rather closer to Dickens, perhaps, is Mezentius' soliloquy as he prepares to ride out to face Aeneas a second time, after his dead son, killed by Aeneas, has been brought to him as he rested wounded by the river[2] (10.846–56):

> 'tantane me tenuit uiuendi, nate, uoluptas,
> ut pro me hostili paterer succedere dextrae,
> quem genui? tuane haec genitor per uulnera seruor,
> morte tua uiuens? heu, nunc misero mihi demum
> exsilium infelix, nunc alte uulnus adactum!   850
> idem ego, nate, tuum maculaui crimine nomen:
> pulsus ob inuidiam solio sceptrisque paternis,
> debueram patriae poenas odiisque meorum:
> omnis per mortis animam sontem ipse dedissem!
> nunc uiuo neque adhuc homines lucemque relinquo: 855
> sed linquam.'

---

[1] Charles Dickens, *A Tale of Two Cities*, Chapter 15.

[2] Mezentius' frame of mind is the same as Turnus'—Virgil uses the same words (10.870–1):
                                  aestuat ingens
uno in corde pudor mixtoque insania luctu.
(12.668, found in some MSS. after 10.871, has probably no business there.)

Part 3: The Contribution of Tragedy

> '*Did such love, lad, for living hold me
> that, in my stead, I let face a foe's right hand the son
> that I begot? By these wounds of yours is a father saved,
> alive by your death? Alas! now I feel in my misery
> how ill-fated exile is, how deep the inflicted wound.
> And I have made dull, son, with blame the name you bear:
> robbed of throne and ancestral sceptre by those who hated me,
> I had owed hatred's retribution to my country;
> would that I had given up unnumbered times my guilty life!
> Now I live, I have not left mankind and the light of day behind,
> but I will!*'

The accusation (851: *crimine*) with which Mezentius has tarnished his son's name is not one that arises from his past conduct (as in the punctuation of some editors) but the accusation of cowardice—his failure to face death at the hands of Aeneas—he owed his fellow-countrymen his life for the way he had treated them; instead he allowed his son to die.[1]

At this point it is necessary to distinguish carefully between two dramatic devices which are subtly interwoven in a good writer, but none the less dissimilar. We may use for them the common terms Tragic Insight and Tragic Irony, so long as we are clear what we mean by each.

We may say we have Tragic Irony when a speaker's words have one sense for the person addressed and another, usually more telling, sense for the speaker, and for us, the audience or reader. In moments of great emotional tension, thoughts, like murder, will out. We all know the complex satisfaction it gives us then to find words that in fact express our meaning, while concealing it from the person we are speaking to. The exploitation of this in literature involves a special kind of Ambiguity. A good example is provided by Dido's words to her sister when her decision to commit suicide is at last taken. She needs her sister's help to prepare the funeral pyre, but she must hide from her sister the pyre's real purpose. Her speech to Anna begins (4.478–9):

> 'inueni, germana, uiam, . . .
> quae mihi reddat eum uel eo me soluat amantem.'

---

[1] Virgil and Dickens both build, of course, upon an ancient tradition of story-tellers—that which gives dramatic prominence to a man's dying words. It is human nature to feel a man more interesting when he is about to step into death, particularly if he dies by choice, or in some other way that makes it easy for us to feel that his life has at its close transcended the common lot.

> '*Sister, I have found a way* . . .
> *to bring him back to me, or stop me loving him.*'

For Dido's sister, the discussion of magic which follows fixes the meaning of the opening words: some kind of spell will either literally bring Aeneas back, or free Dido from her passion—a witch might do either. But we have read the lines with which Virgil introduces Dido's speech (474–7):

> ergo ubi concepit furias euicta dolore
> decreuitque mori, tempus secum ipsa modumque
> exigit et maestam dictis adgressa sororem
> consilium uultu tegit ac spem fronte serenat.

> *So once, overcome by grief, she has conceived her act of madness and determined on death, she fixes with herself the time and way of it and, when she goes to her sister to speak of her plan, she hides it by her look and makes expectation shine upon her countenance.*

The emphasis these lines lay on her decision to commit suicide enable *us* to sense, as Dido speaks, that her words have a very different meaning for her: she hopes perhaps that she and Aeneas will be united in death (as for a moment they are in Book 6); death will anyway put an end to her passion.[1]

A related kind of Tragic Irony occurs when the words spoken have one meaning for the speaker and another for the audience, which the speaker misses, and which gives *us* the thrill of perceiving that the speaker has inadvertently said more than he meant, or said something which is true but not in the sense he intended. The best example I know in the *Aeneid* is found in Aeneas' words to Magus, who has asked if Aeneas will spare his life for ransom. Aeneas, mad with anger, replies (10.531–3):

> 'argenti atque auri memoras quae multa talenta,
> natis parce tuis. belli commercia Turnus
> sustulit ista prior iam tum Pallante perempto.'

---

[1] The ambiguity is achieved by *reddat* and *soluat*, each of which is to be taken in two ways. Note how *amantem* helps to hold the line together—it may go either with *eum* or with *me*. Two pun ambiguities therefore and one syntactical ambiguity in this line. There are many examples of the same device in Book 4. E.g., 436, where irony turns on the syntactical ambiguity of *morte*: for Anna the word means 'I will repay the favour when I die'—obscure, but too vague to be alarming; for Dido and for us *morte* is not locative ablative but instrumental: the repayment will be made ample *by* her death. Another example in Dido's words to Barce (639).

Part 3: The Contribution of Tragedy

> '*Keep for your sons all these gold and silver talents
> you talk about. Such bargaining in war Turnus put
> an end to before I did, at the time Pallas died.*'

Aeneas throws on Turnus the responsibility for Magus' death—he killed Pallas instead of sparing him. But Pallas did not ask to be spared; he would have killed Turnus if he had had the chance; nothing occurred between Pallas and Turnus which need preclude ransom now. Take Aeneas' words in the sense in which he means them, and what he says is untrue. But give them an ironical twist, and what he says is true after all: because Pallas is dead, Aeneas' lust for revenge is so strong he will not accept ransom; he wants to *kill*. It is an early hint of the mood of self-righteousness, of a failure of insight, which we see again when Aeneas stands over the body of Lausus.[1]

For this second form of Tragic Irony can combine with Tragic Insight to produce an effect more subtle, and more telling, than that produced by Tragic Insight in its straightforward form, such as the example considered earlier of Turnus' words to his sister (12.676–80). The basic requirement of insight is that a character should come to understand himself; our understanding of what has gone wrong is accompanied by a special kind of pleasure aroused by the realization that *he* understands, too. It may be our only bond of sympathy with a character whom on other counts we should condemn. But there is a danger in making this too clear-cut: self-understanding should not seem easily won, however ready we may be to believe that the imminence of death can throw light on what was dark. It is important, in fact, that we should not be too sure; if we are not sure, scope is left for giving a character, at the moment when we want to be on his side, the benefit of the doubt. Plays, or poems, in which what goes on in a character's mind is made plain are not likely to be good plays or poems.

When Aeneas, near the end of the duel, mocks Turnus, who stands irresolute and afraid (12.867: *illi membra nouus soluit formidine torpor*) because he hears a sound that terrifies him and which *we* know to be the beating against his shield of the wings of the bird of death, Turnus replies (12.894–5):

> 'non me tua feruida terrent
> dicta, ferox; di me terrent et Iuppiter hostis.'

---

[1] Other examples of this second kind of irony are: 4.321–2, 374, 379–80, 384; 10.743–4 (cf. 10.689).

Form and Technique

> '*Your hot words, your fierce airs*
> *do not fright me; the gods fright me and my enemy Jove.*'

We know from the preceding narrative that Turnus' words are more completely, more literally, true (in the sense that one can speak of literal truth in a fairy-tale) than Turnus can know them to be. We know that the dreadful, uncanny bird has been sent by Jove to hasten the fulfilment of fate; but Turnus cannot even see the bird, he can only hear the beating of its wings.[1] This is the element of *irony*: what is inference or rhetorical simplification for Turnus is sober fact for us. But the element of *insight* is present also: Turnus realizes with increasing fullness that he is fighting against fate and the utter hopelessness of the struggle. He now faces, therefore, the enemy he was so nervous of meeting (219–21) with the indifference of one who recognizes a greater enemy.[2]

Let us take as a final example a less straightforward mixture of these elements—the words with which Dido convinces herself she must go ahead with her plan for suicide (4.547–52):

> 'quin morere, ut merita es, ferroque auerte dolorem!
> tu lacrimis euicta meis, tu prima furentem
> his, germana, malis oneras atque obicis hosti.
> non licuit thalami expertem sine crimine uitam
> degere, more ferae, talis nec tangere curas.
> non seruata fides cineri promissa Sychaeo.'

> '*Nay, die as you deserve, dismiss grief with steel!*
> *You it was, sister dear, vanquished by my tears, who first*
> *loaded my madness with misfortune, exposed me to my foe.*
> *I was not allowed to leave marriage out of it, to live innocent*
> *of reproach, as wild beasts do, untouched by cares like these.*
> *The promise made to Sychaeus' dust was not kept.*'

One reason for the extraordinary power of the lines is that Dido makes us understand what has gone wrong while not fully understanding herself—insight is mixed with the failure of insight, conscious truth

---

[1] Turnus' sister, being divine, recognizes the sound of the wings (869); Turnus is merely terrified by the sound. It might be argued that he learns from Iuturna's words (875–7) what the sound is, but I do not think Virgil intends us to take her long aside in this way: observe that Aeneas, who does not apparently either hear or see the bird, does not hear Iuturna either.

[2] Contrast Turnus' understanding now with the brash, misplaced confidence he showed on our first meeting with him, when he laughed in the face of Juno's messenger with the words (7.438–9) *nec regia Iuno immemor est nostri*—a simple example of tragic irony.

Part 3: The Contribution of Tragedy

with unconscious truth. Like Aeneas in his words to Magus (10.531–4), Dido tries to escape full responsibility for her own actions. She first unloads some of the responsibility on to Anna (548–9). Then she attributes the rest to a fault the responsibility for which is more easily borne—she broke her promise to her dead husband that she would not remarry (552: *non seruata fides cineri promissa Sychaeo*). It is a pathetically shallow explanation to herself of what went wrong: there is little insight here—honesty is too circumscribed by a wish to lighten the burden of blame: breaking a promise not to remarry hardly sounds a grievous fault, so long as the admission is formulated to exclude consideration of why the promise was broken.

But in the preceding lines, before she retreats to the chill comfort of a half-truth, we see Dido fumble with the question of why. To us it is apparent that, if Dido broke her promise, it was not because she wanted remarriage, but because she wanted Aeneas. Only, if she were to get Aeneas, it seemed to her that marriage could not be left out of it. Here we feel the beginning of insight, though a more limited insight than that granted to Turnus.[1] So that when Dido says (550–1):

> 'non licuit thalami expertem sine crimine uitam
> degere, more ferae, talis nec tangere curas',
>
> '*I was not allowed to leave marriage out of it, to live innocent of reproach, as wild beasts do, untouched by cares like these*',

we sense, along with the insight, the kind of dramatic irony we saw in Aeneas' words to Magus. Dido takes it for granted there had to be marriage and that marriage took place. The reader has his reservations on both scores: for all her talk of marriage, what took place was the most abject surrender to passion. Her words point to a truth none the less, though not the one Dido intends: they reveal her obsession with marriage; they make us feel it was her conviction that marriage would put things right which brought her where she is, even persuaded her marriage was hers when it was not.[2]

---

[1] The reason is obvious: if Dido is to persist in her resolution to take her own life, she must not be allowed now too lucid an understanding of her own measure of fault for what has happened; she must go on believing that she is a woman piteously wronged whose despair only death can cancel. For the marriage, to the reality of which she continues to cling, is, as I have tried to show elsewhere, largely a fiction of her own mind (*Latin Explorations*, Chapter 2). No one except Dido can seriously suppose that in fact a marriage exists.

[2] The ambiguity of *thalami expertem* (which I have discussed in *Latin Explorations*, p. 55) emphasizes that Dido's concern is for the look of things:

Form and Technique

The reader wonders, perhaps, if I do not attribute to Virgil a degree of psychological acuity that is historically improbable. How can Virgil have had our modern understanding of mental processes, or our interest in these processes, which is largely a consequence of the understanding of them won in quite recent times?[1] There are two things which can be said, I think, in answer. First, it is easy to point to passages where Virgil's interest in motivation is explicit (see earlier in this chapter)—to say nothing of the complex and convincing motivation revealed implicitly by the way a character reacts to a situation. More remarkable still, perhaps, is the almost incredibly modern sound of Dido's dreams (4.465-8). Second, the claim made for Virgil's subtlety in revealing character through dialogue is not inconsistent with the intellectual climate in which he lived. His understanding of *what* made people do things was perhaps unsubtle and expressed in terms of a fairly traditional repertoire of emotions, based mainly on Plato, Aristotle and Lucretius. But his understanding of what people *said* about what they did can reasonably be supposed to have been sophisticated and acute. Their skill in rhetoric equipped the Romans to recognize a man who was making the best of a bad case. Knowing how to do it themselves, they would have been quick to spot the technique in others. And knowing how it was done consciously by the skilful orator, they could hardly have failed to recognize the same thing done *un*consciously—a man assembling crooked arguments to justify himself and not fully realizing that they are crooked. It does not seem implausible to suppose that an intelligent Roman could even spot an impulse to argue crookedly in this way in himself.

What Virgil is doing is rather different, but different essentially in the ways in which the representation of reality in art differs from reality. Virgil consciously constructs, using the tricks of the professional orator, as has often been pointed out, the crooked arguments he attributes to his characters. But that does not mean we are always to think of his characters as orators consciously or cynically taking advantage of the rhetorical tricks. We are to think of them instead as the victims of a pattern of crooked thinking apparent to any intelligent observer with the sort of everyday knowledge of rhetoric an educated Roman possessed. The satisfaction such a Roman derived

---

she regrets now the necessity, as it seemed to her, to demonstrate respectable marriage (by cohabitation in the royal *thalamus*); she neither repents of her surrender to passion, nor sees in that the reason for disaster.

[1] See G. H. Gellie, 'Character in Greek tragedy', *Aumla* 20 (1963) 241-55.

from an intellectual analysis of how Cicero pulled the wool over the eyes of a gullible jury must have equipped him to enjoy a comparable analysis of the way Dido, for example, blinds herself to the true rights and wrongs of her predicament.

Nor should we miss the interaction in Virgil of the tragic and the Stoic concepts of life. The Stoics, preoccupied with the paradox that 'fate will find a way' whatever we do (Virgil's *uiam inuenient fata*), were apt to emphasize the ineluctability of fate and underplay the psychological element which Virgil, following tragedy, stresses—how fate, in finding its way, takes advantage of the sort of people we are. The Stoics added, however, a psychological dimension of their own: the importance of *awareness*, of making oneself the willing instead of the unwilling instrument of destiny: *ducunt uolentem fata, nolentem trahunt*. In Virgil these two traditions are interwoven and supplement one another. If Turnus had recognized sooner the inevitability of the historical processes he was resisting, he might have yielded before the pattern of events was set in train that led to his destruction; his awareness came too late; he was not the sort of person to see things clearly in time. If Dido had acted more prudently—if she had realized in time that her objective was a hopeless one, she could have avoided humiliation. But she was too impulsive, too stubborn—so much so that, when fate has found a way to rescue Aeneas from her, she kills herself in a final upsurge of wounded pride.

IV. IMPLICIT COMMENT

Dryden remarked that Virgil says 'much in little and often in silence'.[1] I use the term 'Implicit Comment' to denote Virgil's curious, characteristic technique, not of understatement, but of non-statement. An explanation, an interpretation of an action or a situation, a connexion between two events, a judgment that what a character says is false, inadequate, or misleading, or reveals something which it is important to note, stares the reader in the face; but Virgil leaves the obvious, expected—we are tempted to say, obligatory—comment unspoken.[2]

[1] Mackail on 8.531 remarks that Dryden may have drawn the suggestion for his often quoted aphorism from Servius' note on this line.
[2] See Heinze, pp. 362–3.

Form and Technique

The device occurs as commonly in the narrative sections of the poem as in dialogue. But it is likely that Virgil got the idea from a necessary feature of tragedy. The dramatist cannot always make his characters explain their actions, or transfer to their lips the comment he wishes his action to arouse; for in any complex situation it is necessary that we, the audience, should feel that the characters, the participants in the action, do not clearly understand what is going on, cannot clearly analyse their own motivation, have failed to appraise the significance of what has happened. Indeed (as we have seen in our discussion of Tragic Irony and Insight) the impact of a situation upon us often depends on a hiatus between the assessment of the facts made by the characters involved and our assessment of them. The dramatist, therefore, the ancient dramatist at any rate (for some modern dramatists build a good deal of explicit comment into their parenthetical stage business), must arrange his facts so that the facts appear to speak for themselves—though naturally, if he is a good dramatist, the facts will not speak unequivocally.

Virgil has narrative, of course, at his disposal as well as dialogue; even in the Episodes of the poem which are essentially dramatic in structure a certain amount of narrative accompanies the dialogue. We have seen, however, that in this case Virgil limits strictly the use he makes of narrative as a vehicle of comment upon motivation and emotion, in order to remain within the conventions of Homeric form —while exploiting this self-imposed limitation by making his restricted comment subtle and close-packed.

His concentrated, intense exploitation of epic technique cannot meet all situations. A technique, moreover, must not become stereotyped—we do not want the poet all the time telling us in an urgent, ingenious stage whisper what we are to make of a situation or a speech. Virgil assumes therefore the obligation, which the classical dramatist cannot evade, of constructing situations and speeches in such a way as to force us to make for ourselves the comment he wishes to prompt.

He works to clear-cut rules—which is not to say, of course, that he consciously enunciated them for himself; he may simply have developed an instinct for the proper point at which to leave things to the reader. While formally the narrative is spoken by the traditional narrator of epic, the confidant of the Muse and as omniscient, therefore, as the Muse chooses to make her confidant, Virgil usually adopts a more restricted role. Comment is kept down to what the

Part 3: The Contribution of Tragedy

astute neutral observer could reasonably be expected to see, or feel willing to infer: the actual events that take place, the actual words of the characters, the appearance of the characters as they speak or listen to others speak, the frame of mind (the emotional state) in which they can be reasonably supposed to act or speak. Beyond this, apart from little flashes of omniscience which are partly an epic mannerism (for example, 7.756-7, 10.435-8 or 11.759) or a trick of plot construction (for example, the comment after Turnus takes the belt off Pallas, 10.501-5), Virgil normally avoids explicit comment upon his own fiction.

Until he grasps the rules, the modern reader often wants to accuse Virgil of carelessness, of forgetting in one place what he has told us in another. We notice that what Palinurus tells Aeneas (6.347-71) does not square with what the narrator told us at the end of Book 5. (For a discussion of this see the Analysis of Book 6 in Chapter 4.) We notice that when Latinus in Book 12 tells Turnus that he will speak frankly to him about how the war has come about (12.25-33), Latinus proceeds to assume a responsibility for starting the war which clashes violently with the narrative of the same events in Book 7. (For a discussion of this see the Analysis of Book 12 in Chapter 4.) More disturbing than these—apparent—lapses of memory, are the occasions where we feel that the poet has failed to notice the moral comment implicit in his own narrative, so that he seems to have exposed one of his own characters to our condemnation without realizing it.

Take the moment when Aeneas stands over the body of Lausus, killed when he interposed himself between Aeneas and his father Mezentius. The scene is one of intense pathos (10.821-32):

> at uero ut uultum uidit morientis et ora,
> ora modis Anchisiades pallentia miris,
> ingemuit miserans grauiter dextramque tetendit
> et mentem patriae subiit pietatis imago.
> 'quid tibi nunc, miserande puer, pro laudibus istis,
> quid pius Aeneas tanta dabit indole dignum?
> arma, quibus laetatus, habe tua, teque parentum
> manibus et cineri, si qua est ea cura, remitto.
> hoc tamen infelix miseram solabere mortem:
> Aeneae magni dextra cadis.' increpat ultro
> cunctantis socios et terra subleuat ipsum
> sanguine turpantem comptos de more capillos.

But when he saw Lausus' dying face and lips,

the lips so strangely pale, Anchises' son
groaned sore pitying and reached his right hand out,
and a picture of duty to a father done filled his thoughts.
'What now, unhappy boy, in return for such glorious deeds,
shall good Aeneas give you, what gift worthy of such greatness?
Keep the arms that brought you joy; you yourself I cede
to ancestral ghosts and tomb, whatever their concern avails.
But though ill-fated, you will be consoled by this for an unhappy death,
that you fall by great Aeneas' hand.' He speaks sharply to the
boy's comrades to make haste and raises Lausus from the ground,
his carefully combed hair all foul with blood.

At first we may think Virgil makes Aeneas react as we must react—makes him not merely feel the pathos of Lausus' death, but see in it a parallel too close for comfort with the death of Pallas. But though no reader can fail to connect the two events, nothing Virgil says connects them; nothing shows he wants us to think that Aeneas' reaction is impelled by the thought that the pursuit of revenge no longer makes sense when it leads to an action no less horrible than that for which revenge is sought. For though Aeneas hesitated to attack Lausus (whereas Turnus sought out Pallas, intending to kill him and bragging he would do so), Aeneas in the end kills Lausus in a sudden surge of anger (10.813–14: *saeuae... altius irae Dardanio surgunt ductori*) with a cruel blow, the effects of which are described in detail (815–20). Aeneas' anger subsides at once. But he seems affected only by pity for Lausus' sacrifice of his life to save his father. More disconcerting still, there is no sign that any connexion between the death of Lausus and the death of Pallas is present in Virgil's own mind.

If we are less than convinced of Virgil's competence as a poet, it is easy to feel that Virgil has muffed things; that something which could have been made memorable and telling has misfired because the poet has not realized the implications of his own fiction. But if we look back over the structure of the book, we see that the narrative of the battle is laid out to highlight the deaths of the two young men Pallas and Lausus, whose parallel destinies are insisted upon at the moment of their confrontation at 433–6. Once we take in the care with which the structure is put together, we realize there can be no question of an oversight by Virgil: 362–605 lead up to the death of Pallas, followed by the reaction to it of Aeneas; then after the interlude in which Turnus is spirited away by Juno, 689–908 lead up to the death of Lausus, followed by the reaction to it of Mezentius. The narrative in

Part 3: The Contribution of Tragedy

fact is planned to bring out the connexion between the two deaths with a clarity which renders explicit statement of the connexion superfluous.

Virgil loses nothing by refraining from making the obvious point. The reader can be relied on to connect the death of Lausus with the death of Pallas unprompted. But, the reader's active participation having been thus elicited, more can be achieved. The reader can be relied on, too, to notice (after his first puzzlement at Virgil's failure to voice the thought that springs to his own mind) that *Aeneas* does not seem to connect the death of Lausus with the death of Pallas; to notice the irrelevance, almost, of Aeneas' words. Aeneas feels pity for the young man he has killed where Turnus felt none. But some failure of awareness, some residue of the righteous anger in which he launched himself upon his blind pursuit of revenge after the death of Pallas, still clouds his moral vision.

For Virgil to point this out would be heavy-handed: one does not underline a hero's defects. No good writer can allow his fiction to degenerate into a series of situations in which motivation and moral responsibility are precisely measured. Why should Aeneas' thoughts be open for our immediate scrutiny? Perhaps he *does* connect the death of Lausus with the death of Pallas, for after this his appetite for battle is lost—the mood of the concluding Episode of the book, when Mezentius challenges Aeneas and is killed by him, stands in marked contrast to the earlier fighting. Perhaps he tries now to cover up his shame as best he can. Or perhaps he only half admits to himself the significance of what he has done. We can only be sure what goes on in the mind of a character if the author stands nudging us with his elbow explaining all uncertainties away. How much better, if Virgil had decided precisely what his Aeneas felt, for him to keep it to himself.

When Aeneas is warned by Mercury that he must leave Carthage without delay, he is at first in an agony of indecision. One thing is uppermost in his thoughts: how can he face Dido, how begin to tell her he is going (4.283–4)?

> heu quid agat? quo nunc reginam ambire furentem
> audeat adfatu? quae prima exordia sumat?

The ensuing situation is presented by Virgil very briefly in indirect speech (4.287–95):

> haec alternanti potior sententia uisa est:
> Mnesthea Sergestumque uocat fortemque Serestum,

Form and Technique

> classem aptent taciti, sociosque ad litora cogant,
> arma parent et, quae rebus sit causa nouandis, 290
> dissimulent; sese interea, quando optima Dido
> nesciat et tantos rumpi non speret amores,
> temptaturum aditus et quae mollissima fandi
> tempora, quis rebus dexter modus. ocius omnes
> imperio laeti parent et iussa facessunt. 295

Aeneas has hit on what seems 'a better plan'. But better than what? Better, presumably, than telling her at once. In short, he procrastinates. But what then is *alternanti*? The word implies Aeneas has been vacillating between two possibilities: what are they? To go or not to go? But there can be no question of his staying. To tell her now or later? But the idea of procrastinating has only just occurred to him. Till now the only two feasible courses were to tell Dido ... or not to tell her at all; *alternanti* hints in short that Aeneas has considered the possibility of going without telling Dido; each time he felt tempted to take the easy way out, he rejected it, perhaps, and then found himself confronted with the disagreeable alternative—facing it out with her.

He calls his captains together, and tells them to get everything ready and to invent some pretext that will disguise the fact they are leaving (288-91). We can imagine the raised eyebrows, the questions that rise to their lips—and are quickly suppressed: why the secrecy? hasn't he told the queen? Aeneas attempts to meet their questions: the queen does not know (292: *nesciat*), he says; she has no inkling (292: *non speret*); she is terribly in love (292: *tantos amores*); the right way round this (294: *quis rebus dexter modus*) will have to be found, an opportunity for breaking it as gently as possible (293-4: *mollissima fandi tempora*). Note the uneasy formality with which Aeneas speaks to his own men about his royal mistress—she is *optima Dido*.[1] Then how double-edged *mollissima* is! Aeneas pretends—even to himself—that he wants to spare Dido. But the earlier lines describing Aeneas' anguish of indecision suggest a different reading of *mollissima*: Aeneas tries to persuade himself that, if he procrastinates, somehow he will be able to tell her without getting involved in an unpleasant scene; somehow he will find an easy way out.

Though nothing is said explicitly, the implication is plain: Aeneas

---

[1] The meaning of *optima* has caused a good deal of argument among commentators who have felt the common honorific use of the word inappropriate. I follow Mackail, rather than Austin. It is the term used by Horace of Maecenas before they became close friends, *Sat.* 1.5.27. Rather like our 'noble'.

Part 3: The Contribution of Tragedy

would probably have gone on pretending the time was not ripe (if Dido had not found out first and come to confront him) until the preparations for departure were complete—and found some way of leaving after all without facing Dido. A great deal more is implied, with sensitivity and economy, by providing only the bare essentials of a scene of unusual tenseness, and leaving us to draw our own conclusions. Note the implication of *laeti* in 295. It looks like the routine epic epithet: Aeneas' men spring happily, with alacrity, to do their commander's bidding. But if *they* are *laeti*, it is patent that Aeneas is not. And is it not equally patent that one element in their alacrity is the feeling that a situation they did not like is over? The lines are full of implicit comment—on Aeneas' attitude to the liaison, on the way his relations with his own captains have become stiff and uneasy, on the weaknesses uncovered in Aeneas by an uncomfortable situation that is largely of his own making.

The funeral procession that takes the body of Pallas back to his father is described in elaborate detail (11.59-99). Two very light implicit comments should be noted. Virgil describes the body of Pallas as it lies upon the bier through a simile, and then narrates how Aeneas places upon it one of the two richly ornamented cloaks, presents to him from Dido who had made them with her own hands (11.67-77):

> hic iuuenem agresti sublimem stramine ponunt,
> qualem uirgineo demessum pollice florem
> seu mollis uiolae seu languentis hyacinthi,
> cui neque fulgor adhuc nec dum sua forma recessit:
> non iam mater alit tellus uirisque ministrat.
> tum geminas uestis auroque ostroque rigentis
> extulit Aeneas, quas illi laeta laborum
> ipsa suis quondam manibus Sidonia Dido
> fecerat et tenui telas discreuerat auro.
> harum unam iuueni supremum maestus honorem
> induit arsurasque comas obnubit amictu.

> *Here they place the youth high on a rural couch,*
> *like a flower a girl has plucked with her thumb,*
> *a soft violet or a languid hyacinth, perhaps,*
> *that has not yet lost its glow and its shape,*
> *though mother earth feeds it no more or gives it strength.*
> *Then Aeneas brought out two cloths stiff with gold*
> *and purple, which for him once, happy in the task,*

*with her own hands Sidonian Dido had
made, dividing the web with thread of gold.
One of these he drapes sadly round the youth, a final
honour, shrouds with it the hair destined for the pyre.*

On the surface the passage is purely, if richly, descriptive. But the simile is concentrated on building up an image of innocence and fragility, of something that has nothing to do with war. Then the cloaks. A verbal echo establishes the cross-reference to 4.261-4—Aeneas dressed in the cloak that Dido had given him, wearing the sword that she had given him, in evident acquiescence in the role of consort which she has thrust upon him:

> illi stellatus iaspide fulua
> ensis erat Tyrioque ardebat murice laena
> demissa ex umeris, diues quae munera Dido
> fecerat et tenui telas discreuerat auro.

It is hard to resist a comment which we may frame perhaps like this: here is another life destroyed, like Dido's, by contact with Aeneas; somehow it is part of a leader's destiny to bring disaster to those who surround him.[1]

After a long description of the procession as it gets under way, Virgil ends with the words (11.94-9):

> postquam omnis longe comitum praecesserat ordo,
> substitit Aeneas gemituque haec addidit alto:
> 'nos alias hinc ad lacrimas eadem horrida belli
> fata uocant: salue aeternum mihi, maxime Palla,
> aeternumque uale.' nec plura effatus ad altos
> tendebat muros gressumque in castra ferebat.

*After his comrades had all passed by in a long line,
Aeneas paused a moment, then added these words with a deep groan:
'Me the selfsame awful fate of war calls to other
tears: mighty Pallas, I bid you evermore farewell,*

---

[1] The passage is an interesting example of Virgil's exploitation of tradition. The Homeric starting point is *Il.* 24.580, where the body of Hector is wrapped in two cloaks, a passage also evoked by Apollonius 3.1205-6. Virgil does not tell us what happened to the second cloak. Conington is surely right in stating that only one was used to wrap the body of Pallas, despite the use of two cloaks in Homer. Only one cloak is mentioned in 4.261-4 because obviously Aeneas can only wear one at a time. Is the mention of two here simply to get in the Homeric echo, or to suggest the comment that Aeneas was given two and kept them and cannot bear to part with both?

Part 3: The Contribution of Tragedy

for evermore adieu.' *He said no more but was on his way, bending his step toward the high walls of the camp.*

Aeneas has a valid excuse for not accompanying the procession—he must attend to the burial of his comrades who have fallen in the battle. And we can readily imagine that the grief he feels at Pallas' death makes him break off abruptly (98: *nec plura effatus*) at the moment of final separation. But it is easy to feel an additional, implicit comment: that Aeneas can no more face Evander than he could face Dido when he was about to leave her, and that he grasps the excuse which duty offers him to avoid the encounter. Nothing prompts this judgment except the abruptness with which Aeneas breaks away (95: *substitit*) from the procession and the hint conveyed by the words *nec plura effatus* that what Aeneas has said is somehow inadequate, that he has said less than was in his thoughts. But the reader who has become accustomed to Virgil's manner—the way in which he creates between us and his characters the intimacy of understanding that exists in real life between people who know one another so well they can, as we say, read one another's thoughts—comes to understand that, when Virgil says nothing or little, it is not always because there is little or nothing to say.

We must beware, of course, of treating the *Aeneid* as a kind of puzzle in which there are always right answers to be uncovered. It is necessary that we should remain unsure that our answers are right answers, or even that an answer is needed at all. Let us conclude this section with a few easier examples of the sort of answer that springs none the less to our minds as we read carefully.

Sometimes it is merely Virgil's use of the word which is formally right but so obviously inadequate that touches off our reaction. The most striking example I know is in the narrative of the death scene in Book 4. Dido stabs herself with Aeneas' sword as she makes her own little formal funeral oration. When it is over, the narrative resumes; her attendants arrive and take in the bloody scene (4.663–5):

> dixerat, atque illam media inter talia ferro
> conlapsam aspiciunt comites ensemque cruore
> spumantem sparsasque manus.

The pluperfect *dixerat* ('she had spoken') is the traditional cliché for picking up narrative after direct speech; it is used like this some twenty times in the poem. But what sensitive reader can fail to feel that Virgil has chosen it here as a precisely gauged understatement,

Form and Technique

avoiding the obvious comment ('these were the last words she would ever speak') which a lesser writer might feel compelled to add but which a good writer leaves to our private thoughts?

We have seen with what sensitivity Virgil uses the mothers of the young men who fight or are about to fight (the *matres*) like a chorus, perhaps, in Euripides' *Trojan Women*. But when the war hysteria breaks out again, interrupting the Italian Council of War, we see them in a rather different light as they make their way in a procession to the temple of Minerva led by Amata and Lavinia (11.477–85):

> nec non ad templum summasque ad Palladis arces
> subuehitur magna matrum regina caterua
> dona ferens iuxtaque comes Lauinia uirgo,
> causa mali tanti, oculos deiecta decoros.   480
> succedunt matres et templum ture uaporant
> et maestas alto fundunt de limine uoces:
> 'armipotens, praeses belli, Tritonia uirgo,
> frange manu telum Phrygii praedonis et ipsum
> pronum sterne solo portisque effunde sub altis.'   485

And to the temple, to Minerva's highest citadel,
the queen is escorted by a great host of mothers,
bearing offerings; with them goes the maiden Lavinia,
cause of so much evil, her pretty eyes downcast.
Arriving, the mothers fill the temple with incense,
pour out their sorrowing voices from the high doorway:
'Mighty in arms, our leader in war, Tritonian maid,
smash with your hand the spear of the Phrygian brigand,
cast him face down on the earth, sprawled by our high gates.'

Note the tone of aggressive hatred of the enemy in their words as they approach their patron goddess to ask for victory. The comment that is withheld is plain: this is what war does even to these pathetic, defenceless women who normally command our pity. And note the taste with which Virgil avoids overplaying even this slight hint. How easily he might have used some adjective to underline the hatred in their voices; instead the formal *maestas* (482)—it is their unhappiness he wishes to bring out, for of that unhappiness their hatred of Aeneas is only an incidental consequence.

Sometimes Virgil's interpretation of a character can be assembled from scenes in none of which judgment is passed, though all point to an implicit collective judgment. We see Camilla first as the glamorous Amazon whom the older women (the *matres*) and the young men

Part 3: The Contribution of Tragedy

freshly marshalled for war admire as she flashes by (7.812–14). We see her again at 11.498–506, when she rides up to Turnus full of the joy of battle. This atmosphere of innocence, happiness and magic is then heightened in the charming story of her upbringing in the woods (11.539–84). But when we come to her exploits in battle (11.648–831), the narrative begins, after a general description of scene, with a rapid recital of Camilla's victims, the tempo of which is slowed down while Virgil dwells upon a detailed revolting description of the first victim doubled up on his wound and chewing the ground while he vomits a torrent of blood (11.668–9):

> sanguinis ille uomens riuos cadit atque cruentam
> mandit humum moriensque suo se in uulnere uersat.

It can hardly be accidental that this is one of the most horrible death scenes in the *Aeneid*. But if we seek to make explicit the comment which Virgil wishes to imply, we are likely to render it crudely insensitive. Virgil is not debunking Camilla, this attractive, impulsive, courageous young girl who deals in bloodshed and is then affronted when death strikes *her* down (11.831). He wishes rather to draw attention through her to aspects of heroism that the common, narrow view of bravery neglects. First, its unthinking insensitivity (in a person we might not at first think of as insensitive). Second, how comparatively easy it is to be brave: Camilla's courage serves as a kind of comment on Turnus' courage, which we might otherwise accept quite uncritically. Yet it is a kind of courage that acts unguided by common sense. When Turnus learns, for example, of the death of Camilla, he immediately abandons the ambush which he had prepared for Aeneas and which might well have won the war. Virgil, almost obstinately, avoids all comment, contenting himself with a simple juxtaposition: no sooner has Turnus deserted his position than Aeneas advances through the fork (11.901–5).

6

Style

1. WORDS ALONE

Even in the hustle and bustle of everyday prose, words play an essential part: they are the writer's messengers; their business is to carry the writer's thoughts to us unobtrusively, impersonally, without comment. But it is not a task that brings them much honour or attention; as we reach out to grasp the proffered message, we have time for no more than a quick glance at the familiar, nondescript ciphers who bear it. In more careful prose, on the occasions when, as we say, we weigh our words, it is another matter. Though words remain the writer's servants, their appearance, their behaviour tell us something now about their master. If he is a pompous fellow, he will choose and groom his words accordingly, anxious to ensure that we are given a proper sense of the importance of his message; if he is thoughtful, witty, eccentric, he may choose less showy messengers, but they will reflect the tastes and quirks just the same of the man who employs them. By themselves, out of context, words are the raw material of structure, form and also style.

In poetry words are the writer's friends, the recipients of his confidence more than his employees. They deserve, invite, provoke a second look. If the message is a tricky one, one beyond the ordinary run of messages sent, the messengers may be expected to help, expanding statement by innuendo, or ensuring that the jest or mystification the poet planned does not misfire. These subtler roles are hard

Words Alone

to classify, but there are kinds of poetry in which words are called upon to play them all the time.[1]

Latin possesses a limited vocabulary. The language cannot match the almost inexhaustible fund of words, the undisciplined host of synonyms, we find in Greek or English. It is more like French. But where the limitations of literary French are the result of a deliberate, ruthless pruning (carried out by the literary mandarins of the seventeenth century, determined to strip away the luxuriant wild growth of the Middle Ages and to restore to French the well-ordered sobriety of classical Latin), the lexical poverty of Latin is original and primeval; the literary instrument that Virgil wields with such subtlety had not long ceased to be a language of peasants, the tongue of a people born, like Remulus' Italians (9.603-13), to a life of tough, rustic simplicity.[2] Beneath the urbanity thrust upon Latin by Rome's spectacular rise to political greatness, the language bears still the marks of its humble origin: Latin is heavy, rugged and alliterative. Where a Greek is loquacious, interested in details because the words to describe them come easily, always ready, and able, to make his meaning abundantly clear, a Roman's natural cast of expression is reticent and aphoristic.

However, the quality of a literary language is decided less by its origins than by the intellectual calibre of those who employ it: poverty can be overcome, wealth misspent. An educated Roman in the time of Augustus was able to profit from the determined onslaught made during the previous half-century, above all by Cicero, on the problems of abstract thought.[3] He could deploy a complicated sentence like a well-disciplined army with a clearly understood chain of command, instead of allowing his thoughts to stumble on like a crowd of untutored peasants. At first sight these may not seem spectacular achievements—any educated Athenian of the fourth century could have done as well—but to have done it in Latin was something remarkable: it gave the contemporaries of Virgil a pride in their language denied Lucretius;[4] where Ennius must have approached Homer feeling rivalry with Homer was out of the question—all he

[1] For an excellent introduction to this whole question see Winifred Novotny, *The Language Poets Use* (1962).
[2] See J. Marouzeau, 'Le latin, langue de paysans', in *Mélanges J. Vendryes* (1925) 251-64. It is true that the Latin of Plautus shows a measure of exuberance, compared with literary Latin of the classical period.
[3] See J. Marouzeau, 'La conquête de l'abstrait', in *Quelques aspects de la formation du latin littéraire* (1948) 107-24.
[4] Lucretius, as is well known, complained (1.832) of the poverty of his native tongue (*patrii sermonis egestas*).

Style

could hope was that his second-best might acquire some distinction from a careful exploitation of limited resources—Virgil was in a position to approach Homer aware that he could say what he wanted to say with a sharpness and a penetration which, though in fact no recent acquisition of the human intellect, seemed fresh and exciting in Latin, and were, of course, wholly beyond Homer.

But before we turn to what Virgil does with words, let us look at the words out of context.[1] Even for a Latin writer his total vocabulary is small. Many Latin words, of course, just could not be used because Virgil's metre ruled them out: any word, for example, in which a short syllable was enclosed by long syllables was precluded.[2] Not a few of the commonest Latin words fall under this or similar metrical bans, or are limited by them to certain forms. Nowhere in Virgil's poem can 'soldiers' (*milites*) do anything; Virgil must either use the singular, or cast his sentence in the passive, or in some other way turn his thought differently. Less rigid limitations are imposed on Virgil's choice of words by the fact that Latin words tend to be clumsy: long polysyllables need not be excluded, but they must earn their keep.

Virgil shows a fondness for certain words—the most notorious is *ingens* which occurs 168 times;[3] another is *immanis*. His guiding principle seems to be a desire for simplicity of diction which led him to prefer simple verbs to compound verbs and to weed out superfluous words (prepositions and conjunctions, for example, could often be easily dispensed with—see below, under 'A Common Style'). But this desire for simplicity is coloured by a consciously sought note of archaism, secured by a limited use of obsolete words and to a greater extent by the employment of normal-sounding words in combinations that draw out old meanings (see below, under 'Words in Action'). Another principle he seems to have followed was the avoidance of needlessly specific descriptive words: Virgil's Vignettes

[1] For a detailed study of Virgil's vocabulary in the *Aeneid* see A. Cordier, *Etudes sur le vocabulaire épique dans l'Enéide* (1939). Much of Cordier's study consists of lists designed to distinguish words Virgil took over from his epic predecessors, including archaisms (such as *fragmen* and *uirago*), and words introduced into epic by Virgil; the latter comprise mainly compounds (e.g., *praediues, irremeabilis*) and derivatives (e.g., *pugnator, litoreus*) apparently invented by Virgil, but include also such natural-sounding words as *nimbosus* and *spumeus* and unusual synonyms of common words (called 'gloses' by Cordier, after Aristotle's classification, *Poet.* 1457b) such as *crispo* or *coluber*.

[2] If the word ended in a long vowel, the vowel could be elided before a following short vowel and a dactyl thus constructed—a clumsy expedient, which was avoided.

[3] See Austin on 4.89.

and Tableaux are usually evocative rather than precise; only occasionally is the narrative tightened by the use of the rare or technical term (4.259: *magalia*, 6.412: *foros*), or by description as detailed or as exact as the word-picture of the snakes advancing to attack Laocoon (2.203–19).[1]

So long as we confine our inspection to individual words, the arsenal on which Virgil draws hardly looks exciting. It contains, admittedly, a high proportion of solid, useful-looking words that feel nice on the tongue and please the ear. But if we turn our attention from sound and appearance to meaning, they are apt to lose their businesslike air. To some extent it is the inevitable result of the conscious pursuit of classicism—one notices something of the sort in literary French: despite the clarity of good French prose, it is often oddly difficult to pin a writer down. In some ways, too, the spectacular development which the Romans underwent during the last century B.C. in sensibility and sophistication imposed an almost intolerable strain upon their lexical equipment. The basic concepts are well catered for: even in the limited Latin vocabulary, ideas like 'seeing', 'killing', 'burning' are represented by a multiplicity of synonyms. To cope with new ideas, however, the areas of meaning of words had often to be expanded, by a process of metaphor and association, to the point that, taken by themselves, the words seem to mean so many things they become woolly and characterless.

II. WORDS IN ACTION

Words acquire character from the company they keep. Merely to organize words into statement in an inflected language is often to lend them a new vitality: stolid, heavy monosyllables and disyllables can acquire a lilt that sends them tripping off the tongue; *urbs* can become *urbibus*, *tango* can become *tetigere*. Or inconspicuous words can acquire a new dignity: *asper* can become *asperrima*. Or the whole vowel structure of a word can be transformed: *facio* can become *fecerunt*.

In the turning of a phrase, the whole gamut of phenomena which we

[1] Compare, e.g., the detailed, specific realism of the pseudo-Virgilian *Moretum*.

call style is involved. The moment you put words together, you create a new unit with its own internal organization and its own character. The vagueness of words can disappear as if by magic. In action, only the wanted meanings emerge; the others fade away because nothing calls them forth when the words are pronounced or read in their context. (In poetry it is sometimes effective to preserve a conflict of meanings—see below under 'Ambiguity'.)

We might fancy that in a highly developed language there is practically no end to the number of such units that can be created, even though we keep within the limits of meaningful statement. Actually no language comes near exhausting the possibilities which vocabulary offers. We have all met the educated foreigner whose statements make good sense and are grammatically watertight but odd, or even ridiculous, because the words have been put together in a way no native speaker would think of putting them together. We say that such unpermitted statements are unidiomatic. But no individual makes use even of all the possibilities permitted by idiom; each of us makes his own selection, overworking some, neglecting others, so that we all differ in our vocabulary of idioms just as we differ in our verbal vocabulary. Moreover, each individual is guided in his choice of idioms by a sense of what the occasion demands; on one occasion he will turn his phrase in a way that he would not on another because it would seem to him out of place. Individuals differ too in the degree to which they resist idiom, because the ready-turned phrase does not fit their thoughts or their personalities. The man who thinks in clichés offers little resistance to idiom. A creative writer may offer a great deal of resistance; he may even do violence to idiom. But when he does, it is not the inadvertent violence committed by the educated foreigner; it is an act of calculated violence, designed to strain or distort idiom for a particular purpose.

In a conscious, intelligent artist like Virgil the conflict between linguistic convention and the writer's personality is subtle, complex and intense. Virgil is not the sort of poet who rides roughshod over idiom, either the idiom of his language or the idiom of his form. His Latin is simple compared with the Latin of Propertius or the Latin of Juvenal. He adopts the patterns of natural, everyday literary Latin imposed by literary tradition upon his form, while vitalizing those patterns constantly, by giving them a new freshness, by investing them with an unexpected depth of content, or simply by turning a phrase in one of the ways that are distinctively his own.

Words in Action

(i) The Tradition

(a) Ennius and the Old Poets

We saw in the previous chapter how diligently Virgil observes Homer's formal conventions without limiting himself to the attitudes and resources of insight of an archaic, intellectually unsophisticated society with whose ideals he had little in common. Given this exploitation of Homeric form, we naturally expect a re-evocation of Homer's style—Virgil's turn of phrase should somehow remind us of Homer. But the extent to which this can be achieved is limited. Nothing Virgil can do will ever make Latin really sound like Homeric Greek. Even when the echo is clear, the new medium must distort it. In any case, it is not desirable that the echoes of Homer's actual words should be too frequent or too prolonged: Virgil is not translating Homer, and he must avoid the subservience to his original which a translator accepts.

His style, in fact, gets its Homeric colouring more by a process of transference. Virgil's *dixerat*, to take a simple example, only recalls Homer's ὣς φάτο because Virgil uses it, as Homer used his phrase, to mark the conclusion of a passage in direct speech. His descriptions of dawn, his similes, most of the other formulae which remind us of Homer, recall Homer because the content is Homeric, not the turn of phrase. It is only as the result of a philological tradition that has too much regard for the content of what is said, and too little for the actual words, that we have got into the habit of taking it for granted that Virgil's poem is a patchwork of literal translations of Homer.

Take Virgil's beautiful lines describing the death of Orodes (10.745–6):

> olli dura quies oculos et ferreus urget
> somnus, in aeternam clauduntur lumina noctem.

It is not hard to catch, in the concluding phrase, an echo of Homer's description of the death of Democoon (*Iliad* 4.503):

> ... τὸν δὲ σκότος ὄσσε κάλυψε.

There is also an echo of Homer's description of the death of Iphidamas (*Iliad* 11.241):

> ὣς ὁ μὲν αὖθι πεσὼν κοιμήσατο χάλκεον ὕπνον.

The situation moreover is Homeric—the climax of the death of an epic hero. And, as happens regularly in Homer, Virgil's formula

Style

occurs more than once—lines 10.745–6 are repeated, slightly altered perhaps (there is a variant reading), in describing the death of Alsus at 12.309–10. Despite all this, it is misleading to say that Virgil has translated Homer. What Virgil says is different in so many ways. Even where the echo is clearest, we catch new overtones—*ferreus* suggests quite different connotations from χάλκεος.[1]

The stylization, the epic flavour, which we detect in those turns of phrase we call Homeric belong in fact to a tradition that is Roman, not Greek, and must have touched off in Virgil's contemporaries reactions and associations we can easily miss—inattentive as we are to the words, so hard always to gauge in a language we cannot speak. There is a strong tendency to conservatism in the language of poetry, though it cannot for ever exclude reform, or even revolution. The language of Latin poetry still retained in Virgil's day much of the simplicity, the natural directness and dignity of the poets of the third and second centuries B.C.: Livius, Naevius, Ennius, their lesser contemporaries and successors, remained still the obvious, almost the obligatory basis of style for an epic poem. However you wrote in prose, your turn of phrase in verse was guided by an affectionate respect for the voices of poets who had been dead for a hundred and fifty years or more. You might not take them very seriously as poets, but you felt the appeal of their way of talking. For the contemporaries of Augustus the attraction lay partly, no doubt, in their strong historical sense, partly in the flavour this style possessed for them of wholesome directness—a quite unhistorical reaction, because Ennius' style must have seemed, to *his* contemporaries, elaborate and ornate.

But this was also a style which had been devised originally, not so much to translate Homer, as to represent him in a more limited tongue; it must have possessed, therefore, for the contemporaries of Virgil (who still read Livius' *Odyssey*) instinctive emotional associations with the world of Homeric epic equally difficult for us to catch. On the other hand, the same style had been used by the old Roman poets to recreate Athenian tragedy. To judge from the surviving fragments (which may misrepresent them), the old tragedians had, it is true, a fondness for aphorism and the sententiously rounded phrase. But as far as the organization of words into statement is concerned, Roman epic and tragedy together form the

---

[1] See Maguinness on 12.309–10. The second part of Homer's description of the death of Democoon is discussed below, in connexion with Ennius' adaptation of it.

basis of a grand manner that became, and remained, the normal form of expression for serious poetry.

In directness, in its ability to suggest a careful refinement of living speech, this style was actually closer to the language of Athenian tragedy than to the highly artificial language of Homeric epic, and utterly remote from the sham-antique archaism of Apollonius. Greek literature with its multiplicity of conventional literary dialects has no equivalent of this single, natural, almost timeless, grand manner. Metre, of course, separated drama from epic poetry in Latin as it did in Greek, but not the turn of phrase—a fact that made Virgil's synthesis of epic and tragic ideas and structural techniques easier: if he had been writing in Greek, he would have had to embody the conventions of one style in the characteristic expression of another.

Of the eighteen books of Ennius' *Annals*, only some 565 lines survive; of his twenty or more tragedies, rather less; the longest epic fragment (a description of the taking of the auspices by Romulus and Remus, 80–100W[1]) comprises 21 lines; there are four other passages of some length (32–48W, 186–93W, 210–27W, 409–16W); the remaining fragments are made up of short passages (two to six lines), single lines or phrases, or even paltry two-word tags. It might seem hard to form any worthwhile impression from such limited evidence of the extent to which Virgil drew directly on his famous predecessor. But, as it happens, many of the fragments have survived precisely because Virgil embedded them, or a recasting of them, in his poem. Macrobius quotes about 65 lines or parts of lines (including one passage of eight lines) which, he says, Virgil imitated; Servius quotes another 40 or thereabouts. In some cases the line of Ennius and the line of Virgil are substantially the same; most often there is an identical phrase; occasionally the parallel is a little far-fetched. In addition, we have a number of lines or parts of lines quoted by grammarians from the *Annals* of Ennius (usually because of some verbal peculiarity) clear echoes of which *we* can detect in the text of the *Aeneid*—a fact which lends support to the conjecture we should be inclined to form anyway, that the lists given by Macrobius and Servius are not exhaustive.

Sometimes Virgil goes to Ennius merely for help in turning a phrase in a simple, dignified, slightly archaic manner. No doubt many of these phrases had become the common stock of the epic style; but it is likely, too, that Virgil wanted to set a *cachet* of authenticity upon a passage of his own making by weaving into it an actual phrase from Ennius.

[1] Unless otherwise specified, references are to the epic fragments.

Style

The narrative, for example, of the scene of war hysteria which follows Allecto's exploits begins with a rugged, strongly alliterative sentence that is wholly Virgilian in its artistry (7.519–21):

> tum uero ad uocem celeres, qua bucina signum
> dira dedit, raptis concurrunt undique telis
> indomiti agricolae.

But at the same time the manner suggests Ennius—the formula *concurrunt undique telis* is lifted directly from Ennius (161W), rhythm, syntax, and sense all subtly altered by the addition of *raptis*. Or take the lines that conclude the narrative of the pitched battle which followed the breaking of the truce (12.552–3):

> pro se quisque uiri summa nituntur opum ui;
> nec mora nec requies, uasto certamine tendunt.

Once again Virgil's deftness and sureness of phrasing guarantee weight without clumsiness, while picking up what was perhaps a well-known Ennian tag (it is quoted by Macrobius from two different contexts in Ennius, 164W and 394W): *summa nituntur opum ui*; as in Ennius, the phrase concludes a hexameter, but in a poet whose rhythmical sense is more acute the jerkiness gains a new effectiveness.

Or take the description of the Italians settling down for the night before the blockaded Trojan camp—a closely wrought Vignette (9.159–67) which caught our attention in the Analysis of Book 9. As in the previous examples, the evocation of archaic scene and archaic manner is authenticated by actual quotation (164–5):

> fusique per herbam
> indulgent uino et uertunt crateras aenos.

The phrase *uertunt crateras aenos* (552W) is one of Ennius' greater achievements, but it is incorporated here in a context whose economic elegance both recalls and outdoes Ennius. Compare the phrase *labitur uncta carina*, used to describe the movement of a ship's pitch-caulked hull through the water and quoted from Ennius in two different contexts (374W and 442W). Virgil borrows the phrase twice, modifying it slightly each time: once to pick out a detail of the scene of the Trojans preparing their ships for departure in Book 4 (4.398: *natat uncta carina*), the second time to describe the uncannily smooth movement of Aeneas' ship up the Tiber to the site of Rome (8.91: *labitur uncta uadis abies*).

Words in Action

If we had more of Ennius, we should doubtless find Virgil more often refashioning material which he has taken from the ancient quarry in the spirit of the craftsman who is conscious of the traditions of his art. We must bear in mind that we can really only see him at work in this way when an ancient critic happens to have caught him on the job. But this means neither that Virgil is guilty of plagiarism, nor, often, that he intends any specific recall of his original. The line he uses to describe Aeneas' reaction when the Penates of Troy come to him in a vision, bidding him forsake Crete and seek out the land in the west, can fairly be taken, I think, as representative of Virgil's unobtrusive indebtedness to tradition. Ennius wrote (424W):

> tunc timido manat ex omni corpore sudor.

Virgil recasts the line, introducing several minor differences and one real improvement (3.175):

> tum gelidus toto manabat corpore sudor.

His *gelidus* is more graphic than Ennius' *timido* and avoids an awkwardness present in Ennius' line—*timido* is presumably dative, but it seems at first to go with the following ablatives. Or take these lines from Virgil's narrative of the burial of Misenus (6.218–19):

> pars calidos latices et aena undantia flammis
> expediunt corpusque lauant frigentis et ungunt.

Servius comments that 219 is a line of Ennius' (*uersus Ennii*), quoting the original (157W):

> Tarquinii corpus bona femina lauit et unxit.

But that is really not the way to put it. In a similar situation Virgil has turned his phrase more or less as Ennius did, introducing a brilliant touch of his own—the extraordinarily effective pathos of the participle *frigentis* (see the Analysis of Book 6). The same is true of the famous lines (9.503):

> at tuba terribilem sonitum procul aere canoro

and (8.596):

> quadripedante putrem sonitu quatit ungula campum

(which occurs again in slightly different form at 11.875). Each time Virgil adapts a phrase from Ennius (143W; 283W, cf. 204W and 429W).

Style

The result in all these examples is a line written in the Ennian tradition rather than one intended specifically to recall Ennius. If the ancient critics had not told us, we should not feel entitled to suspect an Ennian antecedent. Virgil, we may believe, had so saturated himself in Ennius that, in a similar situation, Ennius' turn of phrase, or something like it, would often come to his mind; moreover he liked the phrase or the half-line that carried the clear imprint of the tradition in which he wrote; at the same time he developed to the full his capacity to make the phrase strikingly and unmistakably his own.

In so self-conscious a poet, however, there is apt always to be an element of allusiveness, a Hellenistic spirit of rivalry, if the original is at all memorable. Consider, for example, how Virgil adapts a famous line—it looks the sort of tag that was often quoted out of context (24W):

> est locus, Hesperiam quam mortales perhibebant.

Virgil's line introduces a four-line passage, put on the lips of Ilioneus in Book 1 and on the lips of Helenus in Book 3 (1.530, 3.163):

> est locus, Hesperiam Grai cognomine dicunt.

Not only is the re-formulation neater metrically, the statement is more exact (*Hesperia is* a Greek word) and it is used to introduce a piece of sophisticated didacticism; and yet the line has a personality that survives recasting.

Ennius hit upon a happy phrase to describe the appearance of the stars in the night sky: *caelum stellis fulgentibus aptum.* In a fine line he makes a god, Jove perhaps, the wielder of the firmament studded with gleaming stars (59W):

> qui caelum uersat stellis fulgentibus aptum.

He uses the phrase again (162W, of Lucretia, some suggest, as she lies on the roof after her violation):

> caelum prospexit stellis fulgentibus aptum.

Echoes of the same phrase occur in 205W:

> uertitur interea caelum cum ingentibus signis

and, of night, in 332W:

> hinc nox processit stellis ardentibus apta.

It is interesting to observe how Virgil works over this material. He takes *ardentibus* from Ennius' description of night in 332W to replace *fulgentibus* of 59W, makes Atlas the subject, substitutes *axem* for *caelum* and *torquet* for *uersat*, and sharpens a vague personification into a clear-cut image by the introduction of *umero*. This new line:

> axem umero torquet stellis ardentibus aptum

is put on Dido's lips (4.482), and on the lips of Anchises at 6.797. Then the Ennian material is broken up and fitted together afresh of night at 11.201–2:

> nox umida donec
> inuertit caelum stellis ardentibus aptum

which in point of statement sets out from 332W, but as a piece of verbal poetry is greatly improved by the material adapted from 59W.[1]

Take another famous tag (258–9W):

> postquam Discordia taetra
> belli ferratos postes portasque refregit. . . .

Horace quotes it (*Satires* 1.4.60) as an example of a phrase that would continue to bear the indelible stamp of the elevated style even if one jumbled the order of the words. We cannot be certain of the context; *Discordia* may be no more than rhetoric, or the fragment may come from the proem to Ennius' narrative of the outbreak of the Second Punic War and Discordia may be the allegorical figure partly described in another fragment (260–1W)—the ancestor, presumably, of Virgil's Allecto. But when Virgil took over the *disiecta membra* of Ennius' majestic phrase to describe the throwing open by Juno of the Latin Gates of War, we have rhetoric or allegory no longer, but a *coup de théâtre* within the narrative (7.620–2):

> tum regina deum caelo delapsa morantis
> impulit ipsa manu portas, et cardine uerso
> belli ferratos rumpit Saturnia postis.

The gates of war are actually flung open by Saturnian Juno (it is no figure of speech) as she sweeps down from on high to strike at them with a great gesture that sends them swinging back on their hinges, shattering the iron-clad rails.[2]

[1] See J. Sparrow, *Half-lines and Repetitions in Virgil* (1931) 101.
[2] For this interpretation of *postis* see Mackail and Austin on 2.480. For Virgil's use of Ennius' phrase see E. Norden, *Ennius und Vergilius: Kriegsbilder aus Roms grosser Zeit* (1915) 18–33.

Style

This last example brings us to passages where Virgil is concerned not merely with turning a phrase according to the conventions of a traditional style, but also with the creation of epic atmosphere. In the earlier examples his object was, as it were, to catch the epic poet's speaking voice, to talk as an epic poet was expected to talk. Our attention turns now to examples that show him talking of things that an epic poet was expected to talk about; the situation too, not just the phrase, is characteristically epic.

In creating an epic style, Ennius and the other old poets had to evolve appropriate Latin turns of phrase for the stock situations of epic. Take a line like this from Homer (*Iliad* 1.544):

τὴν δ' ἠμείβετ' ἔπειτα πατὴρ ἀνδρῶν τε θεῶν τε.

It is made up of two epic tags or formulae—the one a honorific periphrasis for the name of Zeus, the other the formula for marking the transition from one speaker to another. Such clichés help the epic poet in two ways: their repetition can create atmosphere (this is the function of the formula πατὴρ ἀνδρῶν τε θεῶν τε); or the clichés can provide the basis of a rudimentary narrative structure (this is the function of the formula τὴν δ' ἠμείβετο—it provides an easy transition from one speaker to another). When the Roman poets set out to devise an epic tradition in their own language, they had to find equivalents for both types of cliché, though it seems clear that even from the beginning they made more discreet use of them than Homer. Homer's periphrasis for Zeus becomes in Ennius *diuum pater atque hominum rex* (207W) and Virgil picks up that formula (1.65, 2.648, 10.2, 10.743); in 1.254, however, he goes back directly to Homer for a slightly closer translation of his own (*hominum sator atque deorum*).[1] For a change of speaker Ennius devised (presumably among other formulae) the terse, characteristically Latin *olli respondit* (31W and 124W, each time at the beginning of a line with inversion of the subject). Virgil avails himself once of Ennius' formula at 12.18 (preserving the archaic *olli*), but usually prefers to incorporate his formula for change of speaker in a phrase that makes some terse comment on the speaker's appearance, or the speaker's reaction to what has just been said.

Take three rather more complicated characteristic epic situations. Each time, though the situation is Homeric, the solution of the linguistic problem involved in re-formulating the situation in Latin

[1] See Conway on 1.65.

has already been evolved by Ennius.[1] Virgil's re-use or adaptation of the formula must necessarily, therefore, have touched off in his contemporaries a double process of association—on the one hand with Homer, on the other with their own literary past.

The first situation is that moment in a pitched battle where the two sides stand firm in close-packed formation, each individual hard against his neighbour in order to leave no opening for the adversary. The spectacle is an exciting one and it is natural for the epic poet to want to communicate this excitement by detailed description. We have such a moment in Homer when the Greeks rally to beat back the Trojan attack upon their fleet (*Iliad* 13.128–31):

> οἳ γὰρ ἄριστοι
> κρινθέντες Τρῶάς τε καὶ Ἕκτορα δῖον ἔμιμνον,
> φράξαντες δόρυ δουρί, σάκος σάκεϊ προθελύμνῳ·
> ἀσπὶς ἄρ' ἀσπίδ' ἔρειδε, κόρυς κόρυν, ἀνέρα δ' ἀνήρ.

Homer repeats line 131, in which both rhythm and syntax so effectively describe the spectacle of effort unaccompanied by movement, in a different context at *Iliad* 16.215. Understandably Ennius is prompted to describe this spectacle in Latin. Unfortunately only a fragment of his description survives (507–8W):

> ... pede pes premitur, armisque teruntur
> arma. ...

But we may feel sure his description ended with an equivalent of Homer's climactic 'man against man'. And we may even be fairly sure that his equivalent was *uiro uir*, because a minor epic poet of the generation before Virgil, Furius Bibaculus, set out in his turn to describe this spectacle and his hexameter, with an obvious echo of Ennius, is quoted by Macrobius:

> pressatur pede pes, mucro mucrone, uiro uir.

Virgil takes the tail end of Furius' hexameter (or, more likely, he went directly to Ennius) and combines it with a version of the first half that differs slightly from both Ennius and Furius, while preserving the Ennian *pede pes*, which is not in Homer, to conclude the description

---

[1] This point was made by Macrobius (*Sat.* 6.3.1):
Sunt quaedam apud Vergilium quae ab Homero creditur transtulisse, sed ea docebo a nostris auctoribus sumpta, qui priores haec ab Homero in carmina sua traxerant.

Style

of the struggle between the two sides, locked for the moment in even combat, that followed the Etruscan landing near the besieged Trojan camp (10.355–61):

> certatur limine in ipso
> Ausoniae. magno discordes aethere uenti
> proelia ceu tollunt animis et uiribus aequis
> (non ipsi inter se, non nubila, non mare cedit;
> anceps pugna diu, stant obnixa omnia contra):
> haud aliter Troianae acies aciesque Latinae
> concurrunt; haeret pede pes densusque uiro uir.

Note Virgil's sureness of touch. The rallentando of the last line effectively expresses the slowing down of the two armies after their rapid advance (361: *concurrunt*). The excitement is all in what precedes—the striking *certatur limine in ipso Ausoniae* (355–6), the simile describing the uneasy calm that follows the massing of storm clouds. After the final line, the spotlight switches to a different part of the battlefield; Virgil, as it were, withdraws from the scene before the dramatic tension is dissipated by a stalemate, making a formal bow to the epic tradition as he does so.

The death of a warrior in battle presents the epic poet with another stock situation. Sometimes the man killed need figure only as one of a string of names, suggesting the magnitude of the slaughter. At other times individuals have to be picked out: if the effect aimed at is excitement, the emphasis then will fall on the way in which the death-blow is delivered; if pathos is desired, the emphasis will fall on the manner of the warrior's death. We have a typical Homeric formulation of the latter in the description of the death of Democoon (*Iliad* 4.503–4). Ennius' re-formulation of the final hexameter is (417W):

> concidit et sonitum simul insuper arma dederunt.

If we compare Virgil's description of the death of Pallas, the linguistic debt to Ennius is obvious (10.488–9):

> corruit in uulnus, sonitum super arma dedere
> et terram hostilem moriens petit ore cruento.

There is a clear verbal echo of Ennius' *et sonitum simul insuper arma dederunt*. But Virgil has tidied up the clumsy *simul insuper* (two adverbs in a row) and taken advantage of the space gained for the vivid *corruit in uulnus* where Ennius, despairing of finding an equivalent for the economical verb plus participle of the Greek (δούπησεν πεσών), had contented himself with translating the participle.

What counts after all in this cliché of battle is the success with which words express (by connotation, sound, rhythm—all the resources that words possess) such ingredients of the spectacle as can be effectively expressed within the framework of the cliché; the rest may be left to the reader's imagination. The sound of a particular word, the convenience of a particular construction, led Homer to concentrate on the thud of the dying man as he fell, followed by the crash of his shield, sword, etc., upon his body. The linguistic battle to get something equivalent to this into a single line led Ennius to omit explicit reference to the thud of the falling body—the Latin *concidit* copes with this adequately by its sound and leaves him space to grapple with the second part of Homer's line. Virgil, having taken over Ennius' *concidit* on other occasions (2.532, 5.448), hits here on a vivid detail of his own: the way a man wounded in the chest doubles up upon his wound—a detail not available to Homer because Democoon was wounded in the head, and taken over by Virgil from Lucretius 4.1049.[1] Compare a slight variation on the same situation in Virgil's description of the death of the giant Bitias (9.708–9):

> conlapsa ruunt immania membra;
> dat tellus gemitum, et clipeum super intonat ingens.

Here the clichés are adapted to their context by the adjectives stressing size (*immania, ingens*); and instead of the thud of the falling body, the earth groans beneath the weight of the falling giant.

A third stock epic situation is the dawn of a fresh day. The action of three books of the *Iliad* and five books of the *Odyssey* begins with dawn. One of the Homeric clichés is (*Iliad* 11.1–2, *Odyssey* 5.1–2):

> ἠὼς δ' ἐκ λεχέων παρ' ἀγαυοῦ Τιθωνοῖο
> ὄρνυθ', ἵν' ἀθανάτοισι φόως φέροι ἠδὲ βροτοῖσιν.

For a Latin formulation of the first part of the cliché prior to Virgil we have again to turn to Furius Bibaculus; instead of Tithonus, we have Oceanus (cf. *Iliad* 19.1):

> interea Oceani linquens Aurora cubile....

We cannot tell how Furius went on to complete his version of Homer's

---

[1] For the following line in Virgil's description of the death of Pallas (10.489), compare *Il.* 11.749, etc., and *Od.* 22.94. Note how the one word *hostilem* adds a new pathos to these echoes of epic tags.

Style

cliché. Perhaps, like Homer, he placed his principal verb at the beginning of the following line and then left his image of Dawn rising at that. At any rate Virgil, on an occasion when he wants no more than a curt evocation of the epic atmosphere before passing on to the brilliant pageant of the Carthaginians and Trojans assembling on the morning of the hunt, by a slight modification of Furius' line completes the sense within a single hexameter (4.129):

> Oceanum interea surgens Aurora reliquit.[1]

Elsewhere Virgil amplifies tradition with fresh imagery. He is interested in the poetry of dawn. At the beginning of Dido's last day on earth, for example, he picks up the second half of Furius' hexameter, but goes back to Homer for the name Tithonus and the flash of saffron (e.g., *Iliad* 19.1), characteristically transferring the epithet as he does so and applying it to the bed instead of Aurora's dress. He precedes this line (which he had already worked out in *Georgics* 1.447) by a naturalistic hexameter underlining the ambiguity of *Aurora*, the phenomenon of dawn and the goddess—the adjective *prima* can only apply to the natural phenomenon—as he does so (4.584–5):

> et iam prima nouo spargebat lumine terras
> Tithoni croceum linquens Aurora cubile.

The couplet is repeated at 9.459–60. At 12.113–15 Virgil combines naturalistic statement with another traditional image of dawn, the horses of the sun-god rising from the sea:

> postera uix summos spargebat lumine montis
> orta dies, cum primum alto se gurgite tollunt
> Solis equi lucemque elatis naribus efflant.

Here too his approach to a recurring image in Greek poetry (e.g., Pindar, *Olympian* 7.70–1) is through Ennius, from whom Servius quotes the original of Virgil's concluding phrase (560W):

> ... funduntque elatis naribus lucem.

But he replaces the faded metaphor of *fundunt* with the more precise and more challenging *efflant*.[2]

---

[1] The Latin tradition had firmly established Oceanus as Tithonus, the husband of Aurora, so that *surgens* is sufficient to evoke the matrimonial Tableau rather than the naturalistic imagery of *Il.* 19.1–2, etc.

[2] See Maguinness on 12.113–19. For other striking formulations of the dawn cliché see 4.6–7 and 7.25–6; cf. 3.521, 5.42–3, 5.104–5, etc.

Words in Action

So much for Virgil's indebtedness to that part of the early Roman poetic tradition on which he would most naturally draw in the turning of a phrase or the formulation of an epic cliché.[1] The phrases and clichés are, of course, the components of larger structures. They may unobtrusively assume their task of conveying the poet's meaning alongside all the components Virgil did not take from Ennius but contrived for himself in conscious adherence to the Ennian tradition; or they may catch our eye a moment as they fall into place—because Virgil has turned his phrase in a spirit of allusiveness hoping his readers will recognize the compliment, or the challenge, to his predecessor.

In the larger structures Virgil is naturally much more distinctively himself, but there are occasions too when he subordinates his own personality to tradition. Analysis of the Virgilian sentence and paragraph is something we must leave till later in this chapter; but a comparison is worth attempting, even though the evidence is woefully limited. Of the five passages of some length that have come down to us, the episode in which Ilia relates her dream (32–48W) and the narrative of the taking of the auspices by Romulus and Remus (80–100W) probably give the best idea of Ennius' style when writing carefully. The reader who has studied these will be better able to sense the extent to which Virgil's narrative of the felling of the trees for the funeral pyre of Misenus, for example, is organized in a spirit of conscious pastiche. Ennius' lines read as follows (181–5W):

> incedunt arbusta per alta, securibus caedunt.
> percellunt magnas quercus, exciditur ilex,
> fraxinus frangitur atque abies consternitur alta,
> pinus proceras peruortunt; omne sonabat
> arbustum fremitu siluai frondosai.

They are a re-write of part of the description in *Iliad* 23 of the preparations for the funeral of Patroclus, and we need only turn to Homer's lines (*Iliad* 23.114–22) to see how the different linguistic equipment at Ennius' disposal and his limited command of its potentialities have forced upon him a rugged, robust, highly alliterative concision very different from Homer's easy, confident, flowing description. Homer can fit in without effort any detail that interests

---

[1] The reader who is interested may further compare 1.254–6 with 450–1W, 5.241 with 541W (cf. *Il.* 15.694–5), 6.625–6 with 547–8W (cf. *Il.* 2.487–9 and *Georg.* 2.42–4), 7.295–6 with 349–50W, 9.528 with 173W.

Style

him; Ennius has to discipline his lines or they will get out of hand, and content himself with weight and directness in order to avoid that sprawling gaucheness which is too often the mark of his imperfect competence. The result is a brilliantly successful piece of writing, but its structure is dictated by limitations from which Virgil was exempt. If, therefore, Virgil in describing a similar scene imposes on himself the same limitations, it is because he wishes the weight of his lines and their rudimentary syntax to evoke Ennius more sharply than usual, partly to draw out our memory of a famous passage and thus set himself alongside Ennius and against Homer, and partly to establish through words and syntax an archaic atmosphere (6.179–82):

> itur in antiquam siluam, stabula alta ferarum,
> procumbunt piceae, sonat icta securibus ilex
> fraxineaeque trabes cuneis et fissile robur
> scinditur, aduoluunt ingentis montibus ornos.

This atmosphere of austere, primeval simplicity will dominate the description of the ceremony which follows (6.212–35).

In less extreme form, this trick of discarding his own lithe, fast-moving narrative manner for the slower, plodding tempo of Ennius is one to which Virgil resorts not uncommonly, in order to suggest by linguistic and syntactical archaism the remoteness and the simple grandeur of the Heroic Age. One naturally compares with the funeral of Misenus the funeral of Pallas in Book 11 (11.135–8). But we catch the same note in the opening lines of Book 6 (see Analysis in Chapter 4), and, in many other places, the device forms the basis for a more sophisticated heavy style which is one of Virgil's characteristic manners (for example, 4.1–5 or 4.86–9; 7.170–6).

Let us conclude with a final comparison. We are told a number of times by the ancient critics that a whole passage in the *Aeneid* has been taken over from Ennius, and on one occasion the original has come down to us.[1] It is Virgil's description of the expulsion of Turnus from the Trojan camp at the end of Book 9. Ennius' lines are quoted by

[1] Servius says of the description of Romulus and Remus and the she-wolf on the shield of Aeneas, 8.630–4, 'sane totus hic locus Ennianus est'. On 2.486 ff. he says, 'de Albano excidio translatus est locus'. Macrobius (*Sat.* 6.2.32) makes a similar comment about the Episode of Pandarus and Bitias, 9.672 ff. In addition the Allecto Episode in Book 7 and the boat race in Book 5 seem to have had Ennian antecedents. In the absence of the originals one must be a little chary, for this is a matter on which the ancient critics are prone to wild pronouncements—remember Servius' remark that *Aeneid* 4 is wholly modelled on Apollonius.

Words in Action

Macrobius, who tells us they refer to the stand of the tribune C. Aelius in the Second Punic War (409–16W):

> undique conueniunt uelut imber tela tribuon:
> configunt parmam, tinnit hastilibus umbo,
> aerato sonitu galeae, sed nec pote quisquam
> undique nitendo corpus discerpere ferro;
> semper abundantes hastas frangitque quatitque;
> totum sudor habet corpus multumque laborat,
> nec respirandi fit copia; praepete ferro
> Histri tela manu iacientes sollicitabant.

Virgil's reason for recasting them is probably that Ennius himself, as in our last example, was attempting to paraphrase Homer (*Iliad* 16.102–11—Ajax is driven back while defending the Greek ships). The spirit of rivalry is plain—Virgil's paraphrase is closer to Homer than Ennius could achieve. He makes, therefore, no attempt this time at pastiche (9.803–14):

> ... aeriam caelo nam Iuppiter Irim
> demisit germanae haud mollia iussa ferentem,
> ni Turnus cedat Teucrorum moenibus altis.   805
> ergo nec clipeo iuuenis subsistere tantum
> nec dextra ualet, iniectis sic undique telis
> obruitur, strepit adsiduo caua tempora circum
> tinnitu galea et saxis solida aera fatiscunt
> discussaeque iubae capiti nec sufficit umbo   810
> ictibus: ingeminant hastis et Troes et ipse
> fulmineus Mnestheus, tum toto corpore sudor
> liquitur et piceum (nec respirare potestas)
> flumen agit; fessos quatit aeger anhelitus artus.

Ennius' lines are not particularly admirable. He is unable to cope with fast-moving narrative and the dominant note becomes a kind of breathless clumsiness: his lines move stumblingly, the ideas are too much watered down; one feels how grateful Ennius would have been if he had had space for more of Homer's adjectives. Virgil's lines, while the turn of phrase follows the same stylistic tradition, are remarkable first of all for being totally different from Ennius: verbatim echoes are cut to a minimum. And the lines move with unruffled grace. There is time for the effective (808: *adsiduo*; 809: *solida*), even the telling (812: *fulmineus*; 813: *piceum*) epithet, or verb (808: *obruitur*; 809: *fatiscunt*).

Style

The right words seem to fall effortlessly into the right places in the line. Even where there is an echo of Ennius' words, the echo is transformed (*tinnit* becomes *tinnitu*; *nec respirandi fit copia* becomes the neater *nec respirare potestas*). The lines are in fact a useful indication of the relative competence of the two artists.

(b) Catullus and the New Poets

As well as a new formal sophistication (see Chapter 2) and a new attention to the interaction of syntax and metre within the hexameter (see later in this chapter under 'Metre') Catullus and the new poets whose names we associate with his represent a way of writing which revolutionized the Roman tradition. Virgil's debt to the older poets lay chiefly in the turning of a phrase and in the striking of a basic style. To Catullus and the *poetae novi* he owes a subtler understanding of the role words can play in poetry.

The older poets use language as an instrument for the effective communication of relatively unsophisticated ideas and straightforward, uncomplicated attitudes to the situations and personalities of the poet's fiction; the function of words is to create atmosphere. The new poets use language as a challenge to the reader: mostly it is a result of the battle the poet is waging to put into words things not easily expressed in words—the poet's words take the reader as far as words can; at other times style becomes a battle of wits in which the reader is invited to join. The older attitude may be described as essentially *rhetorical* (using that term descriptively, not pejoratively) and the new attitude as essentially *intellectual*—except that the term 'intellectual' is apt to slight the contribution of the imagination. Neither attitude to words necessarily guarantees high poetic quality; either may bring the practitioner success with a particular audience. But from Catullus to the end of the Golden Age, the pleasure Roman classical poetry offers its audience becomes more and more a refined pleasure, dependent on the subtlety of the audience's response to words, and less and less one derived from broad, uncomplicated emotional stimulation and stock response to conventional situations.[1] Cicero, on the whole, was for the latter—he understood rhetoric

---

[1] It is important to remember that, though the new poets belong to a different social epoch, they stand close in time to Virgil. Catullus was perhaps hardly more than ten years older than Virgil and likely enough still writing when Virgil first came to Rome. At any rate the experiments of the new poets must have been very much the talk of the literary world.

better;[1] so was that plain man Agrippa who objected to Virgil's tricks with words.[2]

What we are speaking of is easiest described as the difference between the first acquisition of competence in a literary tradition and the attainment of a vigorous, self-conscious maturity. To that extent it is a natural, almost inevitable, development. But there are other factors. The two attitudes are separated also by their social context. Ennius lived in a society where the poet's task was to put well for a large audience sentiments readily comprehended and acquiesced in—again, of course, the function of rhetoric; Dido's *non ignara mali miseris succurrere disco* (1.630) is a rare example of this in the *Aeneid*;[3] the audience whose approbation Catullus and his followers desired most to win was an exclusive, critical audience, on its guard against facile emotional incitement. The audience for which Virgil wrote a generation later was an unusually competent one. As a result of its literary background (the interest of the well-read of the time in writers like Callimachus and Euphorion), it possessed a highly refined appreciation of verbal ingenuity. As a result of its interest in moral philosophy (whetted by writers like Cicero and Horace) it was aware of the many-sidedness of moral situations. As a result of its own everyday familiarity with the manipulation of words it had some understanding of the inadequacy of language—how, often, what one wants to say is ultimately ineffable.

The new poetry may fairly be described as intellectual on two levels, which are historically separable. Verbal dexterity in the handling of a theme from legend was not an invention of the new poets—they had Callimachus and his followers as their models; the problem was only to discover how to emulate such verbal pyrotechnics in Latin. But the verbal dexterity of Hellenistic writers was largely expended on themes divorced from reality. It became an end in itself, not the

---

[1] See, e.g., Cicero *Orator* 68:
   Ego autem, etiamsi quorundam grandis et ornata uox est poetarum, tamen in eis cum licentiam statuo maiorem esse quam in nobis faciendorum iungendorumque uerborum, tum etiam non nulli eorum uoluntati uocibus magis quam rebus inseruiunt. . . .

[2] For Agrippa's famous complaint, quoted by Suetonius 205–7R, see below under 'Innovation—*callida iunctura*'.

[3] An interesting case is 2.354:
   una salus uictis nullam sperare salutem.
We admire the rhetoric while dissociating ourselves from the sentiment—Aeneas' surrender to the heroic impulse.

expression of a refinement of the moral sensibility; as there was nothing in particular to say, verbal brilliance was apt to run riot. The *poetae novi* set out seriously to explore the problems of human relationships in verse. They began with self-analysis. Having new, exciting things to say, they evolved deft, precise, probing ways of saying them. Because they were talking about themselves, they avoided grandiloquence, substituting for it a crisp, understating directness as close as possible to the everyday speech of the sophisticated set to which they belonged; in poetry as in social behaviour, their ideal was *urbanitas*.[1]

They did not see immediately the extent to which these interests and techniques could be transferred to their larger-scale poetry on fictional themes. In Catullus' Poem 64 there is too much brilliance, too little restraint, and only the first stirrings of a new sensibility, a new capacity for intellectual analysis of fictional situations. It was left for Virgil to complete the synthesis of the world we know and the world of legend.

Virgil's actual verbal debt to the new poets is comparatively slight. We can point to the occasional phrase lifted from Catullus, but the strained manner of Poem 64 is reserved, like pastiche of Ennius, for special effect: it is too strident, too flamboyant for a poem on the scale of the *Aeneid*.[2] When Virgil strikes this note himself, it is to exploit the interplay between two intellectual components—the verbal element (the straining to dazzle us with words) and an element of hard sense. The two are made to work together to produce the distancing tone, the quizzical, ironical verbal fabric that warns us against too facile a commitment to a fairy-tale not told merely to entertain.

What Virgil has learnt from Catullus more than anything is to write with a lightness of touch, an unostentatious economy of words enlivened by a wry irony. It becomes, indeed, his normal manner wherever we feel the narrator advance (dropping for the moment the epic poet's pose of unhurried earnestness) for the exposition of something that must be dealt with briskly or probed with a new acuteness. Consider, for example, how the poem begins. First an elaborate opening sentence full of echoes of Homer (see the discussion of the opening sentence in Chapter 2), followed by the formal invocation of the Muse.

[1] See my *The Catullan Revolution*, pp. 58–64.
[2] Some examples: cf. 4.10 and Cat. 64.176; 4.21 and Cat. 64.181; 4.316 and Cat. 64.141 (Dido has something of Ariadne about her); 6.27 and Cat. 64.115; 6.460 and Cat. 66.39.

This is Virgil's grand manner: tougher, more close-packed than Ennius, but equally grave and impressive. Then at line 12 the epic solemnity is dropped, tone and tempo change for a fast-moving, clipped prologue. With apparently effortless rapidity the basic facts are sketched in, the emphases deftly distributed (14: *studiisque asperrima belli*; 22: *sic uoluere Parcas*) with a detachment that becomes increasingly ironical. One moment we are speaking of Rome's destiny; the next of Juno's pique over failure in a beauty competition and her husband's infatuation with Ganymede; at line 29 the long parenthesis comes to an end and the poet resumes his grand manner for a suitably solemn ending to his prologue. Mackail is scandalized by what he can only regard as a lapse into Alexandrianism.[1]

It would be a gross simplification to say that Virgil tried to write an epic poem in the style of the new poets, or even that he used features of their style in order to bring the style of Ennius up to date. Virgil's epic style varies constantly and over a wide range. At the extremes we find the manner of Ennius or the new poets plainly evoked. More frequent than either extreme is a contrapuntal effect, produced by an unresolved mixture of styles. And if we take the poem as a whole, the grand manner, or rather Virgil's more compact, more intense version of it, clearly preponderates. The poem's ostensible status demands sparing use of the informal manner of personal poetry, however elegant the understatement, however penetrating the softly spoken comment, just as its scale precludes sustained use of the stridently intense tone of the sixty-third and sixty-fourth poems of Catullus.

In the speeches Virgil assigns his characters it was especially important not to try too hard. There are speeches, like Aeneas' reply to Dido in the quarrel scene (see Chapter 5), where nearly every word tells. But often the function of a speech is to create atmosphere. Virgil's characters must continue to behave like epic characters, even if our attitude to them has become more subtle; in fact, as Catullus sensed in drawing Ariadne, the effect of distancing depends on the poet's ability to provoke conflict between the simple-minded grandiloquence, anger or pathos of a character's words and our more complex assessment of the situation.[2]

[1] Mackail, p. 1:
So prominent a mention of the Rape of Ganymede in the prologue of the epic is an unhappy concession to Alexandrianism.
He would wish line 28 away, regarding it as typical of some half-dozen in the book which 'are open to exception as irrelevant or superfluous'.
[2] Cf. Horace *Odes* 3.27 and *Latin Explorations*, pp. 263–6.

Style

Moreover a long poem means a multiplicity of situations. What makes the situations memorable and interesting tends to be what the characters say in them. Often they need only talk long enough to establish the situation in the reader's mind. What Evander says in his farewell speech to his son (8.560–83) matters less than that he speaks long enough for these very obvious old man's sentiments ('I wish I were younger—I pray you come to no harm—if anything happens to you, may death spare me knowledge of it') to have their impact upon us, to draw out the pathos inherent in the situation. Though expressed with unobjectionable epic propriety, the sentiments are only those of a very conventional old man about to send his son off to the wars. Their purpose is twofold: to make dramatically convincing the old man's final collapse, overwrought by his own words, and to embed the scene in the memory of Aeneas, as in our memory, so that it contributes later to his savage reaction to the death of Pallas. It is equally of no great consequence what Iuturna says when she is forced to abandon her brother to his fate (12.872–84). But she must talk long enough for the essentially selfish reaction of this frightened, helpless girl, abruptly stripped of her supernatural power to protect her brother, to establish itself in our minds sufficiently for us to feel that it is a convincing, forgivable reaction.

Often a rhetorical line, essentially declamatory in its effect, is sharpened by a new attention to precision. Consider, for example, how in the line with which Aeneas dismisses the Italian ambassadors (11.119):

'nunc ite et miseris supponite ciuibus ignem'

the one word *ciuibus* vitalizes what would otherwise have been no more than cursory rhetoric. Or a cliché may be revitalized by building fresh poetry into it. Take these lines from Aeneas' first words to Dido as he jumps forward from his place of concealment to thank her for her offer of help and protection (1.603–10):

'di tibi, si qua pios respectant numina, si quid
usquam iustitia est et mens sibi conscia recti,
praemia digna ferant. quae te tam laeta tulerunt
saecula? qui tanti talem genuere parentes?
in freta dum fluuii current, dum montibus umbrae
lustrabunt conuexa, polus dum sidera pascet,
semper honos nomenque tuum laudesque manebunt,
quae me cumque uocant terrae.'

Words in Action

The basis is a fabric of clichés—three of them: (1) the appeal to whatever in this world rewards right action; (2) the question, Where can such unprecedented excellence (or whatever the quality designated is) have originated? and (3), commonest of all, the assertion that the natural phenomena of the world will be subverted before a particular statement ceases to be true. Virgil subjects the first cliché to intellectual analysis (what are the possible sources of reward for right action?) and then re-formulates it like a trained philosopher, making Aeneas appeal first for divine beneficence, then for human justice, and finally for the reward that comes from one's private sense of virtue—subordinating the second and the third along with the first to ultimate divine control. The second cliché he is content to state in clear-cut, pleasing form (note the declamatory effect of the sharp alliteration of t's and l's and the ringing assonance in the three ae's). The lead-in of the third cliché is pure formula (607: *in freta dum fluuii current*); but it is followed by a piece of fresh verbal poetry—two striking phrases that hold the attention: *lustrabunt* is not the verb one expects to find associated with *umbrae*; *polus dum sidera pascet* is even more startling.

In more than one way essentially rhetorical material has been given an intellectual flavour. The first cliché has been submitted to the scrutiny of an inquiring mind. The second has been stated precisely, economically, with a minimum of declamatory rhetoric. In the third we see the method of Pindar and, on a more trivial level, the Hellenistic poets: a dynamic quality is imparted to a phrase by bringing together words that seem to want to spring apart (*sidera* and *pascet*). It is also the method of Shakespeare and modern poetry, a phenomenon to which Mr F. W. Bateson has given the name of the 'semantic gap'.[1] It differs fundamentally from the method of Homer who takes his phrases ready-made, or sought like Aeschylus in framing them for the rhetorical qualities of majesty and sonority ('towering proud words aloft'[2]) rather than hard, fresh sense and deft, unfussy craftsmanship.

(c) A Common Style[3]

One debt to tradition cannot be overstressed: it is the contribution

---

[1] F. W. Bateson, *English Poetry* (1950) 50–2. Cf. W. H. Auden's re-formulation of this third cliché in 'As I walked out one evening'.

[2] Aristophanes, on the style of Aeschylus, *Frogs* 1004.

[3] I take the concept of a 'common style' from T. S. Eliot, 'What is a Classic?', in *On Poetry and Poets* (1957) 63.

Style

made by tradition to a distinctive style common to all Augustan verse. Virgil, the elegists, even Horace, all write in an idiom marked off by certain distinctive features of syntactical practice from contemporary prose. The keynote is a hard-hitting compactness, suggestive of a past age in which men spoke more simply. In fact, however, this common style is a highly self-conscious, carefully polished artefact. Some of its features are archaisms inherited from Ennius and the old poets, others turns of phrase launched by Catullus and the new poets, others deliberate strainings of language for which the past offered little warrant. In a sense this is classical eclecticism, rationalized by the pursuit of defined objectives—to cut out the needless word; to avoid the jaded turn of phrase and the increasingly clumsy constructions of contemporary prose; to fabricate instead a syntax compact, fresh to the point of being exotic, and at the same time traditional.

A simple and obvious feature of the common style is its avoidance of prepositions. The main constructions involved are:

(*i*) *Locative ablative.* In classical prose, the use of the preposition *in* had become customary, to distinguish the locative function of the ablative from its other functions, except with those old friends of schoolboys, the names of towns and small islands (where there was little risk of misunderstanding) and in a few other instances (of which the commonest is when the noun is accompanied by a form of the adjective *totus*). (We are not here discussing the *temporal* functions of the locative ablative.) Unlike other prepositions used with the locative ablative (*sub, super*), the preposition *in* rarely kept its original force (to emphasize the concept 'upon'), becoming merely the sign of the locative ablative. This generalization of *in* is resisted in the common style of Augustan verse; the preposition is regularly, though not invariably, omitted. For example, 4.133–4:

> reginam *thalamo* cunctantem ad limina primi
> Poenorum exspectant,

or 12.24 (where ablative blends into dative):

> sunt aliae innuptae *Latio* et *Laurentibus agris.*[1]

(*ii*) *Ablative denoting movement from a place.* In classical prose the prepositions *ab*, *de* or *ex* are customary. More often than *in*, those prepositions retain their original force and cannot therefore be

---
[1] Cf. 1.52, 56, etc.

omitted; but where a prose writer would feel obliged to use them merely as a sign of a particular case-function, they are often omitted—even at the risk of some slight obscurity—in the common style of verse; for example, 2.8–9:

> et iam nox umida *caelo*
> praecipitat suadentque cadentia sidera somnos.

Where the verb on which the ablatival phrase depends was compounded with one of these prepositions, prose usage varied. But in an example like the following (4.152–3):

> ecce ferae saxi deiectae *uertice* caprae
> decurrere *iugis*,

idiom would probably require *de uertice* and *de iugis*.[1]

(*iii*) *Other ablative constructions.* Similarly we find instrumental ablatives like *luctu*, 'in grief' (2.12), *metu*, 'in fear' (3.213), and *quo numine laeso* (1.8), and locative ablatives like *terris* (1.3) in contexts where—if the context itself had been normal prose—we might expect *propter luctum* or *ob luctum, per terras*, etc.

(*iv*) *Lative accusative.* With the exception again of towns and small islands, etc., prose usage required the preposition *ad* or *in*. But in the common style of verse the preposition is often omitted, as in 3.254:

> ibitis *Italiam* portusque intrare licebit.[2]

So far we have only the conscious retention of a syntactical archaism, though we may suppose that some of Virgil's turns of phrase (those involving the lative accusative in particular) are wholly synthetic products and never natural Latin. We come now to two usages whose pedigree is more complicated.

(*v*) *Dative denoting motion towards.* The starting point for this interesting construction seems to lie in contexts where a metaphor (expressed or latent, but of a kind hardly admissible in prose) can be felt to authorize a dative in a context where a prose writer would

---

[1] Cf. 1.125–6, 679, etc.
[2] Cf. 1.512; 2.781; 3.293, 440, 507, 601; 4.106; etc. Where these prepositions retain their original force, they naturally remain in verse: e.g., in 1.24, 4.133, etc., *ad* = 'close to', 'beside'; in 1.161, etc., *in* = 'into'. The more meaningful prepositions *sub, super, circum*, etc., are therefore not omitted.

Style

naturally use the accusative with *ad* or *in*.[1] We can easily feel such a metaphor implicit, for example, in 12.263–4:

> petet ille fugam penitusque *profundo*
> uela dabit.

(Contrast 1.34–5: *in altum uela dabant laeti*.) It seems a mannerism of Virgil to substitute in such cases for the word that would draw out the metaphor a synonym that does not; perhaps the construction could be felt to reinstate the metaphor, in examples such as 12.513–14:

> ille Talon Tanaimque *neci* fortemque Cethegum,
> tris uno congressu, et maestum mittit Oniten

by suggesting that *neci* is equivalent to *Morti* (as a personification) or *Orco*.

But this construction, which is alien to normal prose, becomes involved in a general tendency (affecting contemporary prose also in a limited degree) to extend the use of the dative at the expense of *ad* or *in* with the accusative—a reaction, perhaps, against a contrary tendency of everyday speech to use *ad* with the accusative even where grammar clearly called for the dative. Examples such as 4.391–2:

> suscipiunt famulae conlapsaque membra
> *marmoreo* referunt *thalamo*

probably depend more on this extension of the *datif de rapprochement* than on a latent metaphor;[2] this seems also the best way to look at the famous *it clamor caelo* (5.451, cf. 11.192).

This construction has no precedent in archaic speech. As a feature of the common style it is best described as an artificial development whose origins lie partly in metaphor and partly in hyperurbanism— the tendency of literary language to react against innovations of colloquial style. The construction is much commoner in Virgil than the lative accusative without preposition (to some extent its rival); in Virgil's use of it, it merges into the locative ablative without preposition, particularly when the noun in the dative (or ablative) depends on a compound verb. In 1.44–5 (a good example, in any case, of the concentrated use Virgil makes of the ablative):

---

[1] This is the explanation given by E. Löfstedt, *Syntactica*, vol. 1 (2nd edn 1942) 180 ff.

[2] The term *datif de rapprochement* is taken from Ernout-Thomas, *Syntaxe latine* (1951) 56–8—a useful account of this remarkable extension of the dative, which seems to grow out of a synthesis of constructions involving the dative with verbs like *appropinquare* and adjectives like *similis*.

> illum exspirantem transfixo pectore flammas
> turbine corripuit *scopuloque* infixit *acuto*

it hardly matters whether we call *scopulo* . . . *acuto* ablative or dative.[1] Virgil was no grammarian and we are dealing with artificial turns of phrase outside prose usage.

Other constructions favoured by the common style are partly exotic —based to some extent on Greek syntax. One of these, the dative of the agent, may be considered here since it supplants the common ablative of the agent which requires the preposition *a* or *ab*.

(*vi*) *Dative of the agent*. This is a way of putting things just possible in Latin (supported by the use of the dative with the gerund and the gerundive—where the dative does not really express an agent, since no action actually takes place), but used much more widely in the common style of verse than in prose, in conscious imitation of Greek syntax. As in Greek, the dative of the agent is commonest with perfective forms of the verb, for example 3.13–15:

> terra procul uastis colitur Mauortia campis
> (Thraces arant) *acri quondam regnata Lycurgo*,
> hospitium antiquum Troiae sociique penates.

But it is also found with other tenses (3.398):

> cuncta *malis* habitantur moenia *Grais*.[2]

It must be emphasized that the normal constructions with prepositions are just as common in the *Aeneid* as the constructions with-

---

[1] Cf. 1.79, 97, 112, 377, 512, 538, 627; 2.36, 186, 688; 3.89, 131, 338, 410, 569, 715; 4.613; 5.34, 93, 176, 203, 233, 346, 434, 451, 805; 6.178 (= 2.186); 11.192 (= 5.451); 12.255–6, 319, 380, 417, 555, 681. (See Austin on 2.186, Williams on 5.34, and Conway on 1.627; on the overlap of dative and ablative see Ernout-Thomas, § 83.)

[2] Other examples: 3.275, 412; 5.305 (also ethic dative), 360, 610; 12.391; etc. Other Graecisms of case syntax found in the common style are:
Accusative of respect. A construction wholly alien to Latin, perhaps not found earlier than Lucretius (3.489), but well established in the common style though never frequent, probably supported by a confusion with the use of the accusative after a past participle. We see both these constructions in 1.320:
> nuda genu nodoque sinus collecta fluentis.

Other examples: 1.589; 2.381; 3.594; 4.558; 5.97; 12.5. (See Austin on 4.558 and Williams on 5.97.)
Genitive of respect. This is a convenient term for a number of uses of the genitive (a case whose functions notoriously resist classification), many of them Graecisms. For example 5.73: *aeui maturus Acestes*.

out prepositions—some of them more common. The prepositional constructions are used sometimes for the sake of emphasis or clarity, sometimes for metrical convenience, but often, no doubt, merely because the gain to be derived from the use of the more compact (and less precise) constructions would have been nullified by abuse. All the same, the prepositionless ablative word or phrase becomes, along with the free use of the infinitive (see below), one of the most striking characteristics of the common style of verse. The extensive, often strained, use by Virgil of the ablative of description is part of the same tendency.[1]

At times dative and ablative seem almost to fuse into a single grammatical category. But while even the educated Roman was perhaps no more than dimly conscious of the distinctions which we, who learn the language from grammar-books, make as a matter of course between the different functions of a single case, his instinctive feeling for grammatical category must have been a good deal sharper than ours.[2] Virgil, therefore, in these borderline examples is probably exploiting a tension the reader feels in his mind as he tries to hold two grammatical categories (dative and ablative) separate, comparable to the tension created by a planned conflict between two meanings of a single word (see below under 'Ambiguity'), or to the tension the careful speaker of English feels when he is in danger of mixing up in the same sentence a past participle, say, and a past tense identical in form. Take 11.646–7:

> dant funera *ferro*
> certantes pulchramque petunt per uulnera mortem.

The reader's first instinct is probably to take *ferro* as instrumental ablative with *certantes* ('they deal death fighting with steel'). But a meaning different from the obvious one is drawn out from this highly mannered, wholly artificial phrase by the process of Theme and Variation (see below) by which the idea is restated in 647 after the second-foot caesura. When we get to the end of 647, we feel we want to take *ferro* with *dant* (which means, in grammatical terms, regarding it as dative instead of ablative): 'they make to steel an offering of death as they fight.' (Cf. 8.570. For a fuller discussion of this tension

---

[1] For a good study of Virgil's experiments with the descriptive ablative see Mackail, Appendix A.
[2] The fact that dative and ablative were sometimes distinct in *form* would naturally underpin the feeling that they were separate grammatical categories.

between grammatical categories see below under 'Syntactical Ambiguity'.)

Economy can, of course, be achieved in other ways besides cutting down on prepositions.

(*vii*) *Final dative.* The use of the dative to express the objective of an action is a Latin construction, but never one that became common until the mannered style of Silver Age historians. It offers one way of avoiding the more clumsy Latin mechanisms for expressing purpose. For example, 1.21–2:

> hinc populum late regem belloque superbum
> uenturum *excidio* Libyae.[1]

(*viii*) *Freer use of the infinitive.* One of the most striking features of classical Latin prose is a strong tendency to circumscribe the use of the infinitive; apart from its use in reported statement, the infinitive is hardly found except in association with a number of common verbs (*cupio, iubeo,* etc.). The common style of verse reverses this tendency, preserving an older state of affairs in which the infinitive was used with great freedom. The remarkable flexibility of Greek syntax and a desire to achieve a comparable economy and simplicity of statement in Latin doubtless prompted this reaction as much as any spirit of archaism.

In the common style the infinitive is used, for instance, to expand the meaning of a noun in ways impossible in prose. In 2.10:

> sed si tantus amor casus *cognoscere* nostros

the infinitive provides an alternative to one of the clumsiest of Latin syntactical idioms, the gerundival phrase—Lucretius might have written cheerfully: *casus nostros cognoscendi.*[2] A rather less extreme use of the infinitive is with the noun phrase that can be felt as equivalent to a verb, as in 1.703–4:

> quibus ordine longam
> cura penum *struere* et flammis adolere penatis.[3]

Less commonly the infinitive is found with adjectives, as in 4.563–4:

---

[1] Other examples: 2.798; 3.540.
[2] Cf. 2.451; 3.60–1, 670–1; 5.183–4; 6.134; 7.393; 8.163–4; 9.757–8; 12.282. Virgil does not, of course, deny himself the gerundival construction—e.g., 2.137–8.
[3] Cf. 2.575–6, 585; 3.294–7, 682–3.

Style

illa dolos dirumque nefas in pectore uersat
certa mori.¹

The infinitive is also used with a great variety of verbs. Aeneas' words (3.363-4):

'cuncti suaserunt numine diui
Italiam *petere* et terras *temptare* repostas'

represent a construction impossible in classical prose.² Where the circumstances are sufficiently comparable for us to speak of a prose equivalent, the equivalent is normally a subordinate clause.

(*ix*) *Accusative noun, etc., dependent on passive participle, etc.* This construction, a regular feature of verse style from Catullus onwards,³ is explained in different ways by modern grammarians. The most popular explanation is to speak of a direct object after a verb which has kept its middle force. This can be expressed in terms of normal Latin grammar by saying that a transitive verb is treated as though it were deponent instead of active. Examples similar to 2.274-5:

quantum mutatus ab illo
Hectore qui redit *exuuias indutus* Achilli

with the participle *indutus* are indeed found in early Latin. The construction, in other words, can just be felt as Latin.⁴ Undoubtedly, however, an awareness of Greek syntax, where the middle voice is an active grammatical category (and not a vestigial survival as in Latin) and regularly co-exists with an active form of the same verb, contributes a good deal to the frequency in the common style of verse of examples such as 3.63-5:

stant manibus arae,
caeruleis maestae uittis atraque cupresso,
et circum Iliades *crinem* de more *solutae*.

But in examples like 3.47-8:

[1] Contrast 4.554: *iam certus eundi.* Cf. 12.290.
[2] Cf. 1.527-8; 2.64 (cf. Ennius, epic fragments 432W, 444W), 627-8; 3.4-5, 31-2, 77, 134, 144, 257, 415, 465, 608-9, 700; 5.21-2, 29, 69, 155, 194, 247-8, 262, 342, 485-6, 509-10, 666; 12.344-5.
[3] See, e.g., Catullus 64.64-5.
[4] One or two examples from Ennius are sometimes quoted to show that this idiom had native sources. These may have added a faint archaic flavour to the construction in the Roman reader's feeling for it.

> tum uero ancipiti *mentem* formidine *pressus*
> obstipui steteruntque comae et uox faucibus haesit,

where we feel we want to accord the participle its passive force ('oppressed by fear in my mind'), it is more usual to describe the construction of the noun as an accusative of respect. Some grammarians even prefer to treat all these accusatives as accusatives of respect.

As we are dealing with grammatical categories that lack a living identity in Latin, argument about labels is unrealistic. Doubtless Virgil sometimes associated what he wrote with the Greek syntactical idiom we should call accusative of respect, sometimes with what we should call the middle voice, though probably it is upon his reader's ability to feel his innovations as a kind of archaism, sufficiently underpinned by the Latin construction with deponent verbs to make them intelligible, that Virgil depends in devising these departures from normal syntax. The construction is very much commoner with past participles than with finite verbs.[1]

Other features of the common style are:

(x) *Omission of parts of* sum. In both Greek and Latin traces remain of an archaic form of syntax in which a simple juxtaposition of subject and predicate sufficed to form a statement. Such statements were later felt to be anomalous and were usually adapted to what had become the normal pattern by connecting subject and predicate with a suitable verb. The older aphoristic form of statement never, however, lost its appeal to the Roman mind—as in 2.354:

> una salus uictis nullam sperare salutem.

The idiom is frequently extended to more complicated statements; in particular the periphrastic tenses, formed by adding a form of *sum* to the past participle, are very commonly left without a verb; for example, 4.552:

> non seruata fides cineri promissa Sychaeo.

Historically speaking, it is misleading to say that a form of *sum* is to be 'understood' in such cases. Even though the verbless form of proposition was undoubtedly chosen in pursuit of economy and compactness, it could still be felt in all probability by Virgil's contem-

---

[1] Page, *Aeneid I–VI*, pp. 505–6, quotes 26 examples from Books 1 to 6. See Austin on 2.57, Williams on 3.65 and 5.135, and my *The Catullan Revolution*, pp. 66–7.

poraries as an artistic development of archaic style. Virgil frequently leaves subordinate clauses also without the courtesy form of *sum*, as in 2.10:

> sed si tantus amor casus cognoscere nostros.[1]

(*xi*) ne *with imperative*. This is an archaism not found in classical Latin prose, though it occurs occasionally in post-classical prose. In Greek, of course, imperative forms may be negativated. E.g., 2.48: *equo ne credite, Teucri*.[2]

In the syntax of the common style we keep finding two factors at play: conscious revival of archaic usage, and conscious innovation based on Greek precedent. Virgil's objective, however, is not so much a flavour of archaism or exoticism as the moulding of a direct, compact style. The impetus to create such a style seems largely to have been a reaction against the increasing wordiness of classical prose and its tendency, at times almost perverse, to consecrate clumsy syntactical idioms; perhaps they were felt to be more impressive than the older, simpler forms, or perhaps they result from a wish to build up a prose syntax that was distinctively Roman. But more is involved than reaction: the poets sought clearly to create a way of writing that, with the help of metre, should bear the imprint of verse statement as plainly as a rhetorical period bore that of the forum or the law courts.

(ii) *Innovation*—callida iunctura

The principle of the *semantic gap* was well understood by Virgil and his contemporaries. Horace, with that sensitive grasp of current literary ideas which is the real merit of the *Ars Poetica*, formulated the principle as follows (46–8):

> in uerbis etiam tenuis cautusque serendis
> dixeris egregie notum si callida uerbum
> reddiderit iunctura nouum.

Be careful of your diction, avoid the heavy hand.

---

[1] Other examples with *si*: 2.349; 4.319; 5.363. With *quoniam*: 12.647; with *quia*: 12.808; with *cum*: 6.125; with *dum*: 8.580; with *postquam*: 1.216, 520, 723; 3.1–2, 212–13; 4.151; 6.226; 7.406, 709; 8.184; 10.298; 11.248; with *ubi*: 1.81; 2.634; 4.80; 5.32, 315, 362; 8.175; with *ut*: 8.362; in relative clauses: 1.602; 4.59.

[2] Cf. 2.606–7; 6.544 (on which Servius remarks '*antique dictum est, nam nunc "ne saeuias" dicimus*'); 12.72–3, 875, 938. See Austin on 2.48.

Words in Action

The perfect turn of phrase is one where crafty placing makes an old word new.

Put like that, the precept sounds unexciting. Horace intends it, however, as a carefully worded statement of an attitude to style—what we should now call Augustan classicism: avoid the new poets' weakness for strident, showy effects, yet keep their sensitive alertness to freshness of diction.[1] But where Horace is content to operate at an essentially rhetorical level, even in his most striking phrases (*splendide mendax, palluit audax, simplex munditiis,* etc.), Virgil is both less obtrusive and more daring in his experiments with the common style.

The result was apt to seem objectionable to those of his contemporaries who preferred straightforward rhetoric. Marcus Vipsanius Agrippa, who won the battle of Actium for Augustus, complained of a new kind of affectation, one that was hard to spot because it consisted in playing tricks with ordinary words.[2] His annoyance shows the extent to which Virgil was prepared to neglect the audience at which a national epic would traditionally have been directed, in order to concentrate on a narrower audience more sensitive to poetry, more likely to understand what he was trying to do. Agrippa, though the elder Pliny (hardly an *avant-garde* intellectual) described him as too much of a country-bumpkin to appreciate sophistication,[3] was not an uneducated man; a leading politician, the commander of Augustus' fleet, could not be without education. He does not even seem to have been an uncompromising philistine, for he had expressed interest in an epic poem on the battle of Actium.[4] Yet we can well imagine him putting down Virgil's account of the battle (8.671–713) puzzled and annoyed (see the discussion of the lines in the Analysis of Book 8).

For a simple example of *callida iunctura* we may take the words Virgil uses to describe the steady glare of fire in Charon's eyes (6.300: *stant lumina flamma*)—a phrase acutely analysed by W. F. Jackson Knight.[5] Observe first the innocent air of the three words. All are

---

[1] For examples of this kind of *callida iunctura* see L. P. Wilkinson, 'The language of Horace and Virgil', *CQ* 9 (1959) 181–92.

[2] Agrippa blamed Maecenas (whose surviving scraps of verse undoubtedly display a tasteless affectation), Suetonius, 205–7R:
> M. Vipsanius a Maecenate eum suppositum appellabat nouae cacozeliae repertore, non tumidae nec exilis, sed ex communibus uerbis atque ideo latentis.

[3] Pliny, *NH* 35.26: *uir rusticitati propior quam deliciis.*

[4] Assuming, as I have argued in Chapter 2, that it is a poem about Actium that Horace declines to write (*Odes* 1.6).

[5] W. F. Jackson Knight, *Roman Vergil* (1944) 209.

everyday Latin, though *lumina* is used in a sense more characteristic of the common style of verse than of prose. They do not challenge our rhetorical sense by a direct semantic clash, like, say, Horace's *palluit audax*. They simply refuse, until we have pondered over them, to assemble into an intelligible meaning.

Or take the words Virgil uses to describe Dido's appearance as she comes to explain her mad plan to her sister (4.477):

> consilium uultu tegit ac spem fronte serenat.

The first half of the line helps us with the second; even so it requires a conscious effort on the part of the responsive reader to hold the phrase ('she makes expectation bright upon her face') together until meaning is extracted from it. When we have made the effort and successfully resisted the apparent tendency of the words to spring apart, we experience not only the intellectual pleasure of triumph over hard sense, but also a more subtle poetic pleasure, one that is not easily explained, which resides perhaps in the feeling that the three words *spem fronte serenat* provide an imaginative realization of the poet's meaning by a technique different from, and superior to, the normal processes of communication.

Let us take a rather more complex example. After the fine Tableau with which Book 5 begins (see Analysis of Book 5), the narrative moves on (5.8–11):

> ut pelagus tenuere rates nec iam amplius ulla
> occurrit tellus, maria undique et undique caelum,
> olli caeruleus supra caput astitit imber
> noctem hiememque ferens et inhorruit unda tenebris.

The lines are a repetition, slightly altered, of 3.192–5, where they follow their Homeric original (*Odyssey* 12.403–6) more closely. Odysseus goes on to relate how he lost his pilot in the storm, which is perhaps what reminded Virgil of Homer's lines when he was laying out the structure of his own narrative of the loss at sea of Palinurus. Our interest here is not in Virgil's vigorous version of the first half of Homer's sentence, but in what he has made of the second half (5.10–11). It is commonly assumed that in cases like this we can use Homer as a crib.[1] But a moment's attention to Virgil's words shows that *imber* is

---

[1] Cf., however, Warde Fowler's remarks, *The Death of Turnus* (1919) 127–8, on 12.727:
   I turn to the Latin, which is difficult. The usual way of interpreting it is by turning out two passages of Homer, . . . and then proceeding to adapt

not a cloud (νεφέλη), though Latin dictionaries (more concerned with helping us translate Latin than with fixing the denotations of Latin words) quote this passage as an example of *imber* in the sense of 'cloud'. The Latin word can only denote 'rain',[1] and it is combined with *caeruleus* (which *does* translate Homer) in a *callida iunctura*. We normally think of rain as colourless, and this contributes to our first careless assumption that Virgil must be talking about a *cloud*. In fact, he is describing a squall that suddenly appears against a cloud-filled western sky (19: *uespere ab atro*), blotting out the setting sun (*noctem hiememque ferens*). Under such conditions a heavy squall assumes a curiously sinister indigo colour.[2] The column of rain is so sharply localized that it appears to tower over (Virgil's *astitit*—instantaneous perfect) the spectator in its path. Next consider *inhorruit tenebris*, with which Homer offers us no help. The phenomenon Virgil describes is, of course, the roughening of the water as the squall approaches. But Virgil has chosen the word to suggest that the thrill of dismay Aeneas feels is shared by the sea itself: 'a shudder ran through the sea' (instantaneous perfect) 'in the darkness'—because except in the west all is already dark. Finally observe that *supra caput* (Virgil again departs from Homer) is less innocent than it appears—as Servius saw.[3] In this highly pregnant context it suggests a kind of personal menace—as though the storm that stood over Aeneas' head were about to exact retribution for Dido's death.[4]

The night Troy fell, Anchises refuses at first to leave the burning city,

---

Virgil's words to Homer's. This method is nearly always misleading: Virgil takes the idea of his image or simile from Homer, Apollonius, or another poet, but almost always adapts that poet's words to his own poetical needs, or to the ideas and beliefs of his own time. It is therefore putting the cart before the horse to adapt his words to his predecessor's; it is misleading to talk of his 'copying', a process of which a mind like his would never be guilty. Yet commentators go on fancying that when they have quoted Homer they have explained Virgil.

[1] Mackail on 3.194, after correctly defining *imber* as 'a downpour or rainburst from a cloud' and supporting this sense from 11.548 and *Georg.* 4.312, oddly goes on to say that the word 'is here used of the cloud itself from which the downpour comes'.

[2] For a similar transference cf. 2.113: *toto sonuerunt aethere nimbi* ('the clouds resound' for 'the thunder resounds among the clouds'); cf. also 4.120.

[3] Servius remarks: '*nec enim simpliciter dictum est, cum omnis imber supra caput sit*'.

[4] W. F. Jackson Knight's translation, though it makes explicit the sense that Virgil's words appear to strain to convey, comes near to Virgil's meaning:

an inky squall gathered above the prince's head, bringing night and storm, and the waves shuddered in the darkness.

Style

unmoved by the entreaties of Aeneas and Creusa. Two signs from the gods are needed to shake his resolution. The first is a strange flame that encircles the head of Ascanius (2.679–84):

> talia uociferans gemitu tectum omne replebat,
> cum subitum dictuque oritur mirabile monstrum.
> namque manus inter maestorumque ora parentum
> ecce leuis summo de uertice uisus Iuli
> fundere lumen apex, tactuque innoxia mollis
> lambere flamma comas et circum tempora pasci.

A furious debate has raged round the meaning of *apex*. Mackail, in a somewhat careless paraphrase of Servius, asserts that Ascanius was wearing the *pilleus* which later became the official head-dress of certain Roman priests; actually, Servius says only that this is the proper meaning of the word (*proprie dicitur*)—implying it is not the meaning here. Virgil, as Servius saw, is building in a little history as he goes (*tangit latenter historiam*), for the reference is as much to the flame that played round the head of Servius Tullius, the sixth king of Rome (also mentioned by Servius) as to the head-gear of the *flamen dialis*; Austin and other editors have insisted therefore that *apex* means 'a tongue of flame', a meaning easier reconciled with *leuis* and imitations of the passage in later writers. The debate depends for its heat (if not for its light) on the assumption that *apex* has here a clear-cut meaning; the only question, as editors see it, is which meaning. Poets, however, even when not describing miracles, often deal with things beyond normal experience and normal vocabulary; to make the unfamiliar vivid, they are drawn to approximations; and often on such occasions, to avoid beating about the bush, they reach across the semantic gap. In Virgil's day, *apex* commonly meant something worn on the head—a crown (as in Horace *Odes* 1.34.14 and 3.21.20), a helmet (such as that of Aeneas at 12.492), or, in technical contexts, a cap (cf. 8.664). If he had been writing prose, Virgil might have said that the light playing round Ascanius' head looked like some kind of head-gear; in poetry, such caution is superfluous, even disastrous. Moreover, it presupposes a logical, detached narrative fundamentally different from Virgil's technique of Projected Narrative (see Chapter 3). What first strikes the narrator about this *apex* is its lack of weight. On top of the head of Ascanius something appeared that to the observer seemed best described as a 'buoyant crest' (or 'crown'); the word *apex* is delayed, as if it took the narrator a moment to find the most appropriate word to describe the phenomenon; then he realizes it is a flame, though a miraculous one, and he calls it that in the second half of the sentence—the narrator's second shot at description, after he has got over his surprise.

Often Virgil strains language almost to breaking point. The tantalizing quality of some of his *callidae iuncturae* has resulted in their becoming notorious cruces: the words all look straightforward, but they refuse to combine in any straightforward meaning. (A number of examples have already been considered in their context in Chapter 4.[1]) Nothing, for example, obviously marks off the last four words of Diomede's reference to Agamemnon (11.266-8):

> 'ipse Mycenaeus magnorum ductor Achiuum
> coniugis infandae prima intra limina dextra
> oppetiit: deuictam Asiam subsedit adulter.'

But what do they mean? Servius, unable to tease intelligible statement out of what Virgil wrote, accepted an easier reading (*deuicta Asia*) and lame sense: after the conquest of Asia, 'an adulterer succeeded' to Agamemnon's kingdom. To get at Virgil's meaning we must allow an employment of words outside the normal limits of grammatical statement. We can put it like this. Just as a king may personify his kingdom, so, in a more audacious figure, Agamemnon returning from the Trojan war can personify the land he has conquered. Giving *subsedit* its common meaning, we then have, 'an adulterer lay in wait for conquered Asia'. But why should Virgil resort to this odd substitute for plain statement? The question is not really hard to answer. Agamemnon appears in Diomede's speech as the last of a series of instances of how retribution overtook the Greek leaders for their sin in destroying Troy. The facts are well known. To avoid prosiness, Virgil elicits them by a variety of oblique techniques. Line 268 forms the climax of this mannered, allusive passage—the list builds up to the commander-in-chief and then passes to lesser names. For his climax Virgil wants a concentrated, ironical expression of the cliché, 'how are the mighty fallen!' Basically the device has much in common with the familiar two-word oxymoron such as Horace's *splendide mendax*: two concepts are juxtaposed and the reader left to effect a reconciliation between them and ponder on its significance. The linguistic processes involved here are more complicated, of course. Virgil wants to suggest so many things: the contrast between the hybristic arrogance of the

---

[1] E.g., the scales of Jove (12.725-7).

conqueror and the contemptible underhand method of his assassin; the abruptness of Agamemnon's fall and the bathetic triviality of the way death came—the judgments, in short, any intelligent person might make reflecting on the story of Agamemnon's fate. Judgment is not, however, the poet's business. His function is to touch the process of judgment off in us by a striking, compact, challenging form of words.

Virgil naturally cannot often push words in this way to the limits of intelligibility. On the other hand the responsiveness created in the reader by such hard combinations can be drawn upon in quite dissimilar contexts. Studied understatement can then be as effective as challenging obscurity. The problem set the reader is not that of battling with words till he can extract sense from them, but that of finding the point in an apparently obvious remark, instead of allowing it to collapse into bathos. After describing Turnus' last desperate attempt at resistance to Aeneas in the duel, Virgil goes on (12.913-18):

> sic Turno, quacumque uiam uirtute petiuit,
> successum dea dira negat. tum pectore sensus
> uertuntur uarii: Rutulos aspectat et urbem
> cunctaturque metu letumque instare tremescit;
> nec quo se eripiat, nec qua ui tendat in hostem,
> nec currus usquam uidet aurigamue sororem.

At first the final line seems platitudinous and verbose after the penetrating concision of what precedes. Turnus abandoned his chariot at 12.681; obviously it is now some distance away, certainly nowhere in the open space between the two armies in which the duel is taking place. We know equally that Iuturna is no longer present—she left Turnus at 886. Why waste time at what should be the climax of an important passage telling us that Turnus cannot see his chariot or his sister? We need only ask the question to sense the answer. As Turnus looks about him, helpless, cornered, near despair, he loses rational control of his thoughts. One moment it is: 'If only Iuturna and my chariot were here' (he felt so happy, so much in command of the situation when he was in the chariot with Iuturna at his side; if only he could escape back into that happiness . . .). The next moment he is actually looking for them.

It is also possible to utilize on a more modest level the responsiveness aroused in the reader by such highly tensioned contexts. We have spoken already of the use of a stock epithet in a context that reinforces or appears to challenge its appropriateness (see Chapter 5, 'Characterization and Motivation'). Let us consider another example here (4.574–6—Aeneas is giving orders for a hasty departure):

> 'deus aethere missus ab alto
> festinare fugam tortosque incidere funis
> ecce iterum instimulat.'

On one level *tortos* is the ornamental epithet of traditional epic—all ropes are twisted. On another level the ropes Aeneas is commanded to cut are the tangled bonds of passion that hold him to Dido and make him reluctant to leave Carthage, even though the decision to depart has been taken and all the preparations for departure are complete.

The most famous instance of a context that appears to challenge a stock epithet occurs also in Book 4. When Dido faints after her denunciation of Aeneas in the quarrel scene and is carried away by her attendants, Virgil concludes the scene with these lines (4.393–6):

> at pius Aeneas, quamquam lenire dolentem
> solando cupit et dictis auertere curas,
> multa gemens magnoque animum labefactus amore,
> iussa tamen diuum exsequitur classemque reuisit.

Our first reaction is: how can Virgil go on calling Aeneas *pius* after the way he has treated Dido? It is, of course, the reaction Virgil wants, for it focuses our attention on the effort it costs Aeneas to thrust passion aside (see line 395) and remain faithful to his concept of duty. Compare 10.591:

> quem pius Aeneas dictis adfatur amaris.

The scene is the fugue that follows the death of Pallas; Lucagus taunts Aeneas, goading him to an angry rejoinder. There is an ironical tension between *pius* and *amaris*. The implication is: look how Aeneas, for all his *pietas*, is losing control of himself.

The heightened status won for a word by its context need not always have this structural purpose. Often the reader is offered merely the intellectual pleasure that comes from being invited to look at a familiar word a second time and see in it a depth, a layer of meaning, which had not occurred to him before.

(*a*) *Latent Metaphor*

A feature of rhetorical style is its tendency to abuse metaphor. Words or phrases are used with only casual attention to the metaphors they imply, their function being not to make meaning fuller or more precise but to add dignity to the obvious. The orator says 'I marshalled my thoughts' because it sounds more impressive than saying 'I thought'. Some increase in stature accrues no doubt to the person who is doing the thinking. But not because we have a mental image of soldiers on a parade-ground or railway wagons in the marshalling yards of a station. It is not the speaker's intention to elicit an actual image. Nor, usually, does it make his meaning clearer or more profound if we do have this reaction. His meaning is clear in the first place; no particular profundity was intended. We may even lose the thread of the argument if we indulge an over-sensitive response.

Poetry often reverses this degradation of language, restoring to a phrase which has become jaded its original imaginative content. This is particularly a feature of what I have called the intellectual style. A poet might, for example, pick up the phrase, 'he marshalled his thoughts', and draw out the latent metaphor with a second phrase, such as 'with a clank of rusty couplings'. In the *Aeneid* the device is commonest perhaps in Book 4—another sign of the book's technical perfection. Take these lines describing the achievements of Iarbas, the builder of temples (4.198–201):

> hic Hammone satus rapta Garamantide nympha
> templa Ioui centum latis immania regnis,
> centum aras posuit uigilemque sacrauerat ignem,
> excubias diuum aeternas.

We should probably be content to take *uigilem* on a rhetorical level— if the latent metaphor were not drawn out by the words following. The ancient belief that the gods actually inhabited their shrines is made more vivid by a military metaphor: the altar flame is their camp-fire, near it are the unseen presences of the gods, eternally vigilant over mankind, like the sentinels (*uigiles*) who stand guard in a camp at night to protect their sleeping companions. The conceit hardly deserves a full-scale simile. By a turn of phrase that elicits the metaphor latent in *uigilem* and *excubias*, Virgil has expressed the idea more economically and more effectively. He has also kept the reader's mind on the alert for more important occasions.[1]

[1] See Maguinness on 12.327, Conington on 1.381.
For other examples of latent metaphor see 4.1–2, 4.63 (discussed in the Analysis of Book 4). Cf. Catullus, 64.1–2:
> Peliaco quondam prognatae uertice pinus
> dicuntur liquidas Neptuni nasse per undas

Words in Action

(b) Archaism brought out by Context
In rather similar fashion an archaic, half forgotten meaning of a word may be drawn out by the context given it. Take, for example, the description of Antony at Actium (8.685):

> hinc ope barbarica uariisque Antonius armis.

Here *ope* has the archaic meaning 'troops' (a meaning taken over in classical Latin by the plural of *copia*; cf. Ennius, tragic fragment 103W). An archaism Virgil is rather fond of is *adnare*, not in its classical sense of 'swim to' but with a meaning something like 'make one's way to'. Ilioneus says, for instance (1.538):

> 'huc pauci uestris adnauimus oris'.

Compare Dido's words (4.612–13):

> 'si tangere portus
> infandum caput ac terris adnare necesse est'.

Virgil's use of *adnare* might puzzle us if we did not have two lines of Ennius (epic fragments 20W and 247W, using the forms *transnauit* and *nare* respectively) and the comments of ancient grammarians upon them.[1]

(c) Etymological Puns
Related to this use of archaism is the trick of using a word in a context that draws out the etymological meaning, or what Virgil supposed was the etymological meaning, instead of the meaning the word possessed in current usage. Take Aeneas' prayer to Jove (5.689–92):

> 'da flammam euadere classi
> nunc, pater, et tenuis Teucrum res eripe leto;
> uel tu quod superest infesto fulmine morti,
> si mereor, demitte tuaque hic obrue dextra'.

The context of *letum* requires the meaning 'destruction' and precludes the meaning 'death' (the only meaning of the word in classical Latin), except as a rather pointless metaphor. Undoubtedly Virgil connected

---

where the latent metaphor in *prognatae* is drawn out by the following phrase—the ships are living creatures. Cf. Francis L. Newton, 'Recurrent imagery in *Aeneid* IV', *TAPhA* 88 (1957) 31–43.

[1] Curiously enough, the sense Virgil gives the word seems to square neither with Servius' comment on *Georg.* 4.59 ('*nare pro uolare*') nor with the dictum of Festus, 170.28 (' "*nare*" *a naue ductum Cornificius ait*'). In 6.358 Virgil seems to be attempting a pun ambiguity.

letum with the past participle *deletum*, perhaps also with *Lethe*. Both these etymologies are suggested by ancient grammarians, though neither is accepted by modern scholars.[1] Or take Aeneas' words describing his departure from Troy (3.11–12):

> 'feror exsul in altum
> cum sociis natoque penatibus et magnis dis.'

Here the normal meaning of *exsul*, 'an exile', remains, but the context (the implied antithesis with *altum*) touches off simultaneously a second meaning suggested by the supposed etymology of the word, 'a man without a land' (*solum*).[2]

While Virgil occasionally uses *infandus* in contexts that do not challenge the meaning the word had acquired in current usage of 'monstrous' or 'unnatural' (4.613 and 8.483), he is fond, too, of incorporating it in contexts which force us to restore to it the meaning 'not to be spoken of'. When Aeneas says to Dido (2.3):

> 'infandum, regina, iubes renouare dolorem',

the primary sense, that Aeneas is reluctant to speak of the past and does so only because Dido asks him to, overrides, as it were, the meaning of *infandum* in current usage, though this subsists as a secondary meaning. The original sense of *infandum* is reinforced by *fando* in line 6. Compare 4.84–5:

> aut gremio Ascanium, genitoris imagine capta,
> detinet, infandum si fallere possit amorem.

The context from line 76 onwards underlines the sense 'not to be voiced': it is for Aeneas to speak first of love; till he does Dido cannot voice her passion. Again, of course, the normal meaning subsists as an overtone.[3]

(iii) *Ambiguity*

This incipient conflict between the meaning of a word determined by its context and a secondary meaning subsisting, or obtruding, as an overtone brings us to a more fully developed exploitation of a property

---

[1] See Ernout-Meillet, *Dictionnaire étymologique de la langue latine* (3rd edn 1951). Priscian suggests the connexion with *deletum*, Varro the connexion with *Lethe*. According to Cordier, op. cit., 38, *letum* is an archaism taken over by Virgil from Ennius (epic fragment 385W).

[2] Servius remarks: '*quasi trans solum missus, aut extra solum uagus.*'

[3] Compare the use of *latronis* in 12.7 and Maguinness' note.

of words in action. While we read often in ancient literature of men deceived by prophecies whose double-edged character they had missed, in most everyday uses of language ambiguity is inadvertent, a failure on the part of the speaker or writer to reckon adequately with the many-sidedness of words. Occasionally circumstances force evasiveness upon us; it may then require considerable linguistic skill to skate over the thin ice, to find a formula that avoids definite commitment to an opinion by seeming to mean different things to different people. But we are more inclined to consider such a formula a misuse of language than a stylistic achievement to be proud of. In normal prose ambiguity is a danger to be guarded against (unless it is our object to raise a laugh by a *jeu de mots*), one that was perhaps particularly acute in classical Latin prose because of the wide areas of meaning developed by key-words as a limited vocabulary struggled to cope with an increasingly complex culture. Ordinarily if the reader allows his mind to dwell upon meanings other than the one obviously intended, he loses sympathy with his author; the impact of the words upon him is weakened by irrelevant associations.

But when we read Virgil a quite different frame of mind is called for. The disciplined precision of prose of which we have been speaking was a recent acquisition by a people whose habits of thought felt still the influence of a time when words were mysterious things, more the stuff of magic than an instrument of the reason. What Virgil offers us is a highly intellectual exploitation of this state of mind. It is something with which all readers of modern poetry are familiar. Yet this exploitation depends at the same time on an irrational surrender, which the modern reader of poetry has to re-learn, to the power of words.

But while the poet relies on the complexity of his reader's reaction to his words, it must, of course, be a well tuned, accurate reaction. An undiscriminating determination to welcome every possibility of ambiguity may do more harm than an unresponsive adherence to the surface meaning. What is needed is a congruity of response, a sensitive alertness to the reactions the poet wants, guided by an intimate knowledge of the language, the literary tradition in which the poet writes, and the workings of the poet's own mind. Naturally these are desiderata with which no modern reader of Virgil is perfectly equipped. Often we must remain unsure about the admissibility of an ambiguity which an intelligent contemporary reader would have accepted or rejected instinctively.

There are many lines or phrases in the *Aeneid* where the ancien

Style

commentators or modern editors, or both, find it impossible to fix on one meaning of a key-word to the exclusion of another meaning, since both make equally good and equally relevant sense. Their reluctance to grapple with the possibility that both meanings were intended by Virgil appears curious, until we remember that commentators are apt to regard it as their function to provide unequivocal right answers, and that even the ancient commentators on the *Aeneid* belong to an age dominated by the practice of rhetoric, and separated from the Augustan age by an interval of several centuries during which no first-class poetry had been written in Rome.

Numerous examples of cohering complexity of statement in Virgil have already been considered.[1] Before we begin a systematic study, it will help if the procedure adopted is made clear. The presence of an ambiguity and its effect are best explained by a reduction of the ambiguous word or phrase to two (or more) separate, clear-cut statements. Logical analysis provides, in short, a convenient technique of interpretation. It represents in no sense, however, a reversal of the thought process in the poet's mind which produced the words we are analysing. Nor is it a particularly accurate representation of the effect the poet desires to produce in the reader's mind.

The best point, probably, to begin is with that form of ambiguity which is the result of a planned clash between different meanings of a single word. Such poetic puns depend on a shift in the relationship of the key-word to the other words which form its context. Two ideas or two images are presented. Sometimes the conflict between them is evenly balanced. At other times one is paramount while the other lurks in the background, daring us to admit it to our thoughts. Naturally a context is required that stimulates the reader's responsiveness. This may be achieved by a simple fracture of a normal idiomatic pattern. We have an example in Aeneas' words to his mother (1.381):

> 'bis denis Phrygium conscendi nauibus aequor'.

The conflict of meanings in *conscendi* is well analysed by Conington, though he does not use the term 'ambiguity':[2]

> Here as elsewhere... it seems that Virg. while he secured the sense 'embark' by the use of 'conscendo', arranged his words so as to give

[1] See Index under 'Ambiguity'.
[2] The term 'ambiguity' owes its popularity to modern critics (see Novotny, Chapter 7), but it is used too by older commentators (see, e.g., Orelli on Horace *Odes* 1.5).

him the advantage at the same time of some other ideas, of which that of climbing the wave ... may have been one, and the notion opposed to 'demittere' ('quove magis fessas optem demittere navis' 5.29), whether of actual ascent or of effort, may have been another.

The effect of the ambiguity here is to strengthen a word, and therefore a statement, by drawing attention to different facets of its meaning and to the different metaphors latent in it and drawn out when combined with different direct objects—*conscendere nauem* on the one hand, *conscendere aequor* on the other.

Or take the following lines—Turnus' charioteers are exercising his horses (12.85–6):

> circumstant properi aurigae manibusque lacessunt
> pectora plausa cauis et colla comantia pectunt.

The tone of these lines, suggesting detailed visual description of a routine operation, makes us want to assign to *lacessunt pectora* a meaning on the same level as *colla pectunt*. We can get such a sense if we assign to *lacessunt* its less common meaning (though one apparently well established in poetry from Lucretius onwards) of 'hit' or 'strike'. On this level, *lacessunt* describes the slapping of the horses' chests by the charioteers.

But the sense 'slapped' is 'secured' (as Conington would put it) by *plausa*; moreover, idiom works against this unusual meaning of *lacessunt* to suggest a sense in which *lacessunt* bears its ordinary meaning and *pectora* is used figuratively—as though Virgil had written *lacessunt animos*: 'they arouse the spirits of the horses'—by slapping them of course; this second meaning depends on the continuing presence, in the background, of the other meaning. The reader feels the tension between idiom and context but stops short normally of complete analysis, content with the pleasurable sensation that he has apprehended something complex compactly stated.[1]

Most often, however, no warning is provided, by a departure from normal idiom or syntax, of the presence of an ambiguity. Only our sense of congruity can set limits to the subtlety of our reaction. In 5.350:

> 'me liceat casus miserari insontis amici'

our recognition of a pun is validated by the appropriateness of a pun

---

[1] See Maguinness on 12.85–6.

Style

to the situation; clearly the object of Aeneas' remark as he awards a consolation prize to Salius is to play upon the two meanings of *casus*: (1) 'let me show my sympathy with your misfortune' and (2) 'let me sympathize with you for falling'.[1]

Virgil's use of the word *inanem* in 5.672–4:

> 'en, ego uester
> Ascanius!' galeam ante pedes proiecit inanem,
> qua ludo indutus belli simulacra ciebat

has provoked debate from Servius onwards.[2] Clearly the meaning 'empty' cannot easily be ruled out. An equally strong case for the meaning 'idle' or 'useless' is presented by Virgil's fondness for using *inanis* in this sense in other contexts where the meaning 'empty' is inadmissible (e.g., 4.449, 10.465). Our inability, of course, to decide between the two meanings is not in itself any guarantee that Virgil intended both. If there is an ambiguity it must have point; if the ambiguity is well planned, the context should pull both ways in order to draw out both meanings.

What, then, is happening in these lines? Ascanius' words suggest that his reason for tearing off his helmet is to proclaim his identity. But having removed the helmet he does not merely throw it on the ground, as some commentators (for example Henry) make him do: he casts it at the feet of the women (*ante pedes*; the feet can only be those of the women—Ascanius is on horseback) in a gesture of remonstrance. Our attention is thus focused on the moment of impact: the women are pulled up short by the clang of the empty helmet as it lands at their feet. But we can also feel in Ascanius' gesture an element of exasperation: the impulse to pluck off the helmet is provoked by his sense of the irrelevance to the present emergency of the mock battle in which he has been participating. To ensure that we attach this second meaning to *inanem* Virgil devotes a whole line to drawing it out (*qua ludo indutus belli simulacra ciebat*).

Our analysis of the emotions that prompt Ascanius' action is necessarily artificial. Its object is to point to the complexity of feeling inherent in the situation and the role of the ambiguity of *inanem* in suggesting that complexity. Consider the following example (4.447–8

---

[1] See Williams on this line. Compare the pun on *rostris* (in a highly-mannered context) in 9.119.

[2] See Williams on the passage.

Words in Action

—Aeneas has just been likened, in a simile, to an alpine oak in a storm):

> haud secus adsiduis hinc atque hinc uocibus heros
> tunditur, et magno persentit pectore curas.

The effect of the ambiguity in the last four words depends less on our sense of the simultaneous appropriateness of two meanings than on an unresolved conflict between them. Our first impulse is to take *magno pectore* as a variation on *magno animo* and to assign to the phrase the meaning 'he feels fully the impact of grief in his great heart' ('great' in its capacity for compassion and affection). This is the meaning required by the immediate context. Simultaneously the larger context of the tree simile suggests giving *magno pectore* the conflicting meaning 'throughout his great chest' ('great' this time in the sense of 'of heroic dimensions', cf. line 11, and 447: *heros*). As the great trunk of the oak is buffeted by the storm, so Anna's words beat against the great chest of Aeneas, provoking the emotional stresses which he feels deep within himself—or rather 'throughout his being' (an altered emphasis this time on the *per* of *persentit*).

Rather different from these evenly balanced ambiguities, in which the reader's mind oscillates between two meanings, logically exclusive but poetically complementary, is the type of ambiguity in which a secondary meaning is imposed as an overtone upon the obvious, straightforward or literal meaning clearly required by the context. In 12.166–7:

> hinc pater Aeneas, Romanae stirpis origo,
> sidereo flagrans clipeo et caelestibus armis

we naturally first attach to *sidereo* the meaning 'star-like', i.e., Aeneas' shield shines like a star; this is the meaning drawn out by *flagrans* and the emphasis on light (e.g., 163: *fulgentia*) and visual description in the preceding lines. But *caelestibus* then draws out a secondary meaning, 'having its source in the stars' (a reference to the divine origin of Aeneas' shield), a meaning which would seem recherché without the support of *caelestibus*, an epithet more readily taken figuratively than graphically.

Or take Virgil's description of the entrance to the underworld (6.273):

> uestibulum ante ipsum primisque in faucibus Orci.

The opening *uestibulum* at first restricts our reaction to *faucibus*, drawing out the technical meaning (entrance, passageway, i.e., in a house) and inhibiting our response to the normal meaning of the word. Then, remembering that *Orcus* in classical Latin poetry is not so much a place as a vaguely sinister personification (cf. Horace *Odes* 2.3.24: *uictima nil miserantis Orci*, etc.), we feel the non-technical sense, 'jaws' or 'gullet', half re-establish itself (the epithet *primis* works against full establishment, like *prima Aurora* in 4.584–5) as an effective overtone or latent image.

More poetically effective are examples in which the latent image firmly establishes a level of figurative statement transcending the plain or obvious sense of a phrase. Let us start with simple examples. Third in the catalogue of Etruscan commanders in Book 10 comes the augur Asilas (10.175–7):

> tertius ille hominum diuumque interpres Asilas,
> cui pecudum fibrae, caeli cui sidera parent
> et linguae uolucrum et praesagi fulminis ignes.

Common sense requires us to take *parent* as equivalent to *apparent*—Virgil's normal preference for the more archaic, more epic, simple verb form over the compound: the stars in the sky, lightning, and the tongue of birds 'are clear' to Asilas in the sense that their significance is clear—he knows what they presage. But in this highly mannered context we entertain, too, for a moment the fancy, touched off by the normal, everyday meaning of the simple verb, 'obey': Asilas is so much the intimate of these sources of prophetic wisdom, has mixed so much with stars, birds and thunderbolts that he has won some kind of control over them.[1]

Compare the description of Pandarus and Bitias throwing open the gates of the Trojan camp (9.675–8):

> portam, quae ducis imperio commissa, recludunt
> freti armis, ultroque inuitant moenibus hostem.
> ipsi intus dextra ac laeua pro turribus astant
> armati ferro et cristis capita alta corusci.

---

[1] The meaning 'obey' is probably emphasized by the repetition of *parent* in hat sense in 179. Somewhat surprisingly Mackail follows Servius' prosaic ejection of this poetic fancy:

> The note of Servius, '*parent* est, peritissime agnoscuntur', is certainly right; it means 'lie open to him'. The ordinary interpretation 'obey', as Servius goes on to say, 'non procedit; nam quomodo sidera vel fibrae vel aves vel fulgura possunt obtemperare?'

The two brothers take up position on either side of the entrance defying the Italians to advance. It is the technical, straightforward sense of *pro turribus* that is paramount: they station themselves 'in front of the towers' that frame the entrance. But the stress laid in line 674 on the gigantic proportions of the brothers elicits as a fleeting overtone the meaning 'instead of towers', i.e., Pandarus and Bitias are themselves towers.

Take Apollo's prophecy to the exiled Trojans (3.94–6):

> 'Dardanidae duri, quae uos a stirpe parentum
> prima tulit tellus, eadem uos ubere laeto
> accipiet reduces. antiquam exquirite matrem. . . .'

We naturally accord *ubere laeto* the obvious sense of 'with its rich land' (cf. 1.531: *ubere glaebae*), dismissing the latent metaphor, and accepting *laeto* in the sense (well enough attested in reference to land) of 'rich'. But the firm wording of the injunction *antiquam exquirite matrem* conjures forth the metaphor, which we now see was first hinted at by *tulit*; whereupon *laeto* resumes its ordinary meaning, 'happy', and upon the image of rich fields is superimposed the image of a mother welcoming her child 'with glad breast'.[1]

Or take Virgil's description of Cupid sitting on Dido's lap disguised as the boy Ascanius (1.718–19):

> . . . et interdum gremio fouet inscia Dido
> insidat quantus miserae deus. . . .

It is the normal, literal meaning of *insidat* which the context elicits first. At the same time the reader's foreknowledge of the trap Venus has laid for Dido touches off associations with *insideo* and *insidiae*, suggesting the meaning, supported by the dative *miserae*, 'unaware how great the god that lays siege to unhappy Dido' or '. . . that plots unhappiness for her' against the sense 'unaware, poor woman, how great the god that sits on her lap'.

Now a rather more subtle and more powerful example, in which the reader is given the same pleasurable feeling of seeing behind the surface meaning of the words. After the detailed description of Aeneas' magic shield, the eighth book concludes with the following tailpiece (8.729–31):

[1] See Williams on 3.95 on the double ambiguity. Cf. 4.88: the obvious meaning of *pendent* is 'are suspended', but the meaning 'droop', i.e., in the lethargy of inactivity, is also half present, the way having been prepared for it by *adsurgunt* in line 86.

> ... talia per clipeum Volcani dona parentis
> miratur, rerumque ignarus imagine gaudet
> attollens umero famamque et fata nepotum.

In this highly allusive context we can hardly talk of *literal* meaning. Who can set limits to the implications of the phrase *rerum ... ignarus imagine gaudet*? We associate *rerum* first with *imagine* and then with *ignarus*, so that there are two interwoven statements: (1) 'in his ignorance he takes pleasure in the representation of things' (cf. 1.464: *animum pictura pascit inani*); (2) 'he delights in the picture ignorant of the reality'. As for the last line, the meaning most obviously to be drawn from it is—in paraphrase—that Aeneas lifts on to his shoulder the shield on which is depicted the glorious destiny of his descendants. But Aeneas knows and we know what the shield is for: it is to protect him in the coming war (cf. 8.532–6 and his mother's words at 8.612–14). The gesture of raising the shield on to his shoulder is therefore symbolic: the act represents acceptance of responsibility for what is to come. Virgil puts it more compactly when he speaks of Aeneas 'taking on his shoulders the glorious destiny of his descendants'—a sense supported by association with idiomatic phrases embodying a common rhetorical metaphor (e.g., Cicero, *Pro Flacco* 37.94: *rem publicam umeris sustinere*).

Consider the lines with which Virgil concludes his narrative of the reception by King Latinus of the embassy sent him by Aeneas on arrival in Italy (7.280–5):

> ... absenti Aeneae currum geminosque iugalis
> semine ab aetherio spirantis naribus ignem,
> illorum de gente patri quos daedala Circe
> supposita de matre nothos furata creauit.
> talibus Aeneadae donis dictisque Latini
> sublimes in equis redeunt pacemque reportant.

The first four lines provide a context of fancy and magic that brings us to the last line disposed to accord it a status beyond plain, factual narrative. Let us begin with *sublimes*. The primary meaning is 'on high': the Aeneadae came to Latinus on foot; they depart riding the horses Latinus has given them. The second part of the line, *pacemque reportant*, also can have an obvious, everyday meaning: 'they bring back peace', i.e., they report the terms Latinus has offered (cf. 2.115). At this point the two halves of the line begin to interact. The fact that the Aeneadae are bringing back peace invites for *sublimes* the meaning 'in high hope', 'elated' (cf. 12.788). Simultaneously the literal meaning of *sublimes* invites for *pacemque reportant* a meaning something like 'they carry peace back'. What they carry back is, of course, the visible evidence of peace, the gifts that Latinus has lavished upon them; but in the highly active context of this passage we can take 'they bring peace back' as a compressed statement of the significance of the Tableau in which we see them returning laden with gifts; we perhaps toy even with the fancy that peace *is* something tangible that could be carried back. At the same time we feel a sense of ironic detachment from their joy and their belief that peace is within their grasp, knowing that war and suffering hang low over the Aeneadae.

Finally in this section on ambiguities that turn on the different meanings of words, let us consider some passages where Virgil offers us more than the simple pleasure in verbal complexity which the reader of intellectual poetry expects. In the following examples the function of the overtone or less straightforward meaning is to serve as a substitute for statement: to suggest an idea that it would take too long to put into words, or an idea which Virgil does not wish to put into words—because doing so would be heavy-handed or commit him to an attitude to his narrative which he does not wish to adopt openly.

The Tableau of the Trojans sailing out into the unknown from the ruins of Troy concludes with lines which we have already quoted (3.11–12):

feror exsul in altum
cum sociis natoque penatibus et magnis dis.

One purpose of these lines is to situate an ancient, primitive legend within the framework of a more sophisticated concept of the nature of the gods and of human destiny. According to the legend Aeneas took with him the images of Troy's gods and carried them to their new home. Those among whom the legend first took shape would have accepted without question that where the images went the gods went also; they would not have troubled themselves with, or perhaps been able to grasp, a clear-cut distinction between the gods and their images. But if Virgil is to make a fusion of the two ideas acceptable to his contemporaries, he must handle things delicately. There is a first hint of the fusion in 1.6 (*inferretque deos Latio*); the time has come for a plainer statement of it. Of the four ablatives dependent on *cum*, the first two represent beyond question actual occupants of the ships; in that context *penatibus* must also refer to the actual images, leaving us

Style

to attribute what symbolic significance we choose to their physical transfer. But the word *penatibus* is given a fresh context at the turn of the line, and its association in this fresh context with *magnis dis* involves a shift in meaning: the Penates are now associated with the other divine powers that watch over and protect the Aeneadae on their journey. An echo of Ennius (epic fragment 193W) helps to bridge the gap between the two levels of statement.[1]

Or take the famous lines from Dido's second speech in the Quarrel Episode (4.384–6):

> 'sequar atris ignibus absens
> et, cum frigida mors anima seduxerit artus,
> omnibus umbra locis adero.'

Here the nearest we can get to plain statement is that Dido after her death will follow Aeneas wherever he goes, like some kind of avenging fury. That is more or less what the words must mean for Aeneas as he hears them. But the puzzling compactness of *sequar atris ignibus absens* will not let us rest content with this meaning. We sense a second and a third meaning. Each is an example of Tragic Irony (see Chapter 5)—a special form of ambiguity—and each loses a good deal of its poetic force upon reduction to plain assertion. The second hints at a plan for revenge, never perhaps clearly formulated by Dido; somehow, though Dido will not be present herself, the murky flames of her own destruction will pursue Aeneas and exact revenge. She means that the manner of her death will weigh on Aeneas' conscience, or perhaps that he will be troubled by a ghost of her in her death agony; but she makes the threat not really intending him to understand it. Finally, a third meaning of the phrase makes Dido the dupe of her own statement. For Dido has not yet really decided to take her life, still less how she will commit suicide; and when she does kill herself, Aeneas has fled and is not there to witness the spectacle. But for the reader her words serve as an inadvertent prediction that the flames of the funeral pyre will follow Aeneas, i.e., be visible to him, when he is far from Carthage —the scene that in fact forms the opening of Book 5.[2]

---

[1] In the echo of this line at 8.679:

> cum patribus populoque, penatibus et magnis dis,

all four nouns dependent on *cum* have the same status: all describe the backers of Augustus in the battle rather than his actual companions. For a similar play on two levels of statement cf. 3.154–9, especially 157–8.

[2] All three meanings, the Furies, revenge, the flames of the pyre, are recognized by Servius, who plumps for the third.

Words in Action

(iv) *Syntactical Ambiguity*

As well as the different meanings of individual words a poet may exploit the ability of the words in a phrase, or the phrases in a sentence, to assume different relationships. Ambiguities of this kind are apt to seem more forced to us than the pun type because we are less familiar with them in our own language. One reason is our modern habit of punctuation, which causes us to expect phrases and sentences to be self-contained. Roman punctuation was rudimentary: the grammatical structure of a sentence usually removed any uncertainty about the relationship of its parts; a free use of connecting words and particles marked off sentences, as well as indicating the logical connexions between them. Where uncertainty remained, a careful writer could remove it by such rhetorical devices as repetition and anaphora, periodic structure, or starting a new sentence or phrase with a word that could not be connected by the reader or listener with what preceded.

Rhetorical structure, however, is a good deal more fluid than the logical structure of our modern formal punctuation. Virgil often takes advantage of its flexibility to make the flow of ideas more lively or more dramatically convincing. In such cases modern punctuation compels a decision that is unreal, or even misleading. Take Aeneas' opening words as he rises to begin his tale to Dido (2.3–8):

> 'infandum regina iubes renouare dolorem—
> Troianas ut opes et lamentabile regnum
> eruerint Danai quaeque ipse miserrima uidi
> et quorum pars magna fui—quis talia fando
> Myrmidonum Dolopumue aut duri miles Ulixi
> temperet a lacrimis?'

Modern editors debate whether the *ut* clause depends on *dolorem* or on *fando*; some put a full stop after *dolorem* and a comma after *pars magna fui*, others reverse this punctuation. Logically, of course, one cannot have it both ways. Rhetorically, and psychologically, one can. The relationship of the phrases to one another shifts in the speaker's mind as his thought takes shape. It is this natural fluidity of thought that Virgil has tried to capture.[1]

---

[1] I have suppressed as well the commas isolating the vocative *regina* (cut off in reading the line from *infandum* by the secondary caesura) and the comma after *Danai* (where the pause is again sufficiently indicated by the metre).
   One may compare a trick of Plato's conversational style, sometimes called **palindroma**, where a demonstrative clause belongs to a preceding relative

Style

Let us look again at the opening sentence of the poem, leaving out the punctuation (1.1–7):

> Arma uirumque cano Troiae qui primus ab oris
> Italiam fato profugus Lauinaque uenit
> litora multum ille et terris iactatus et alto
> ui superum saeuae memorem Iunonis ob iram
> multa quoque et bello passus dum conderet urbem
> inferretque deos Latio genus unde Latinum
> Albanique patres atque altae moenia Romae.

Logically, the phrase *saeuae memorem Iunonis ob iram* must belong either to what precedes or to what follows. Rhetorically, it may belong equally to both; and this is what Virgil wants—Aeneas' *Iliad* and Aeneas' *Odyssey* are both the result of Juno's unrelenting ire. Punctuation confuses, as much as it helps, by leaving the phrase in mid-air.

Mr Robert Graves, taking as his example the sonnet 'Th' expense of spirit in a waste of shame', has shown how our response to the interplay of different strata of meaning in Shakespeare is deadened if we break up the flux and reflux of the sense with the apparatus of formal punctuation required by modern printing conventions.[1] Much of what he has to say is equally applicable to Virgil (particularly in dialogue passages)—or to any other ancient writer whose ideas flow out of one another, connected psychologically rather than logically. We cannot abandon our modern habits of punctuating Virgil, without increasing unnecessarily the difficulties that face the reader coming to him for the first time. But we should remember that the punctuation is not Virgil's, can never be more than tentative, and is likely to stand in the way of appreciation if we continue to respect it after it has served its purpose.

Here are five lines, as punctuated by Mackail (6.40–4—Aeneas and his companions enter the shrine of the Sibyl):

> talibus adfata Aenean, nec sacra morantur
> iussa uiri, Teucros uocat alta in templa sacerdos.
> excisum Euboicae latus ingens rupis in antrum,

---

clause, and also to a further explanatory relative clause following. See W. J. Verdenius, 'Notes on Plato's *Phaedo*', *Mn* 11 (1958) 196.

[1] Robert Graves, 'A study in original punctuation and spelling', in *Modernist Poetry* (1926), reprinted in *The Common Asphodel* (1949) 85–95, especially 88–92.

> quo lati ducunt aditus centum, ostia centum,
> unde ruunt totidem uoces, responsa Sibyllae.

We might equally well punctuate rhetorically as follows, gaining a good deal in liveliness at the sacrifice of a little clarity:

> talibus adfata Aenean—nec sacra morantur
> iussa uiri—Teucros uocat alta in templa sacerdos—
> excisum Euboicae latus ingens rupis in antrum,
> quo lati ducunt aditus centum ostia centum,
> unde ruunt totidem uoces, responsa Sibyllae.

For what is the status of lines 42–4? Are they separate statement (with *est* or *erat* 'understood' after *excisum*), or are they an expansion in apposition of *templa*? The answer must be—both: what starts by being an explanation of *templa* then flows on in its own right, until by the end of the double relative clause the original grammatical status of the phrase has been lost sight of; a full stop after *antrum*, though tempting as a substitute for the full stop after *sacerdos*, would impose a rigid interpretation on the reader that robs the lines of some of their vitality.

Modern punctuation can be particularly misleading in cases such as the following (1.459–63—Aeneas' reaction on seeing the pictures on the wall of Dido's temple):

> constitit et lacrimans 'quis iam locus,' inquit, 'Achate,
> quae regio in terris nostri non plena laboris?
> en Priamus. sunt hic etiam sua praemia laudi;
> sunt lacrimae rerum et mentem mortalia tangunt.
> solue metus; feret haec aliquam tibi fama salutem.'

The traditional punctuation given above has led countless readers to take line 462 as a generalization (Arnold spoke of 'the Virgilian cry, the sense of tears in mortal things'), undefined by the previous line, to which it is related rhetorically by the anaphora of *sunt*. Moreover, if we break up the flow of the sense in this way, the relevance of the last line is lost. We should perhaps punctuate 461–3 as follows:

> 'en Priamus! sunt hic etiam sua praemia laudi,
> sunt lacrimae rerum et mentem mortalia tangunt:
> solue metus—feret haec aliquam tibi fama salutem.'[1]

Or take these lines (5.613–17—the Trojan women, alone on the shore, are mourning Anchises):

[1] See E. J. Kenney, *CR* 14 (1964) 13.

Style

> at procul in sola secretae Troades acta
> amissum Anchisen flebant, cunctaeque profundum
> pontum aspectabant flentes. 'heu tot uada fessis
> et tantum superesse maris!' uox omnibus una;
> urbem orant, taedet pelagi perferre laborem.

The punctuation given breaks the sense up into a series of jerky, detached units. In fact the words in direct speech belong as much to *flentes* as to *uox omnibus una*, while *uox omnibus una* belongs equally to what precedes and to what follows.[1]

Another reason for our insensitivity to syntactical ambiguity in Virgil is that the relationships between words are much more firmly fixed in English by prepositions, auxiliary verbs, and so on, than in the common style of Augustan verse. We have also lost the habit of regarding words as slippery customers; the Romans knew you could be tricked by oracular pronouncements, for instance, through failing to observe an ambiguity. Moreover there is less intellectual pleasure to be derived in English from the manipulation of words in a phrase. Fewer words are needed usually in Latin to express a given idea, and in poetry they may all be bulky words; the manipulation of the meaning of a phrase made up of such large units locked in a metrical pattern must have provided an aesthetic satisfaction for which we have no equivalent. When Virgil writes, for example (12.264–5—Iuturna's instructions to the Rutuli, to rescue Turnus):

> 'uos unanimi densete cateruas
> et regem uobis pugna defendite raptum'

any simple grammatical analysis of the second half of the sentence is impossible. We may take *uobis* with *defendite* ('defend *your* king') or with *raptum* ('the king that has been taken *from you*'—still dative of course); similarly we may take *pugna* with either the verb ('defend by fighting') or the participle ('taken from you by the fighting'). A second-foot caesura before *uobis* and a fourth-foot caesura after *pugna* hold the two words together and isolate them from what follows.[2]

Whichever of the four possible ways we plump for in translating, the meaning of the line is not greatly affected. But no translation can recapture a quality of the Latin words that makes us feel them a

---

[1] See Williams on 5.615–16.
[2] Mackail recognizes the ambiguity of *pugna* in 12.265, remarking: 'It is impossible to convey this nuance exactly in English.'

convincing, stirring climax to Iuturna's exhortation; that quality resides in the cohering complexity of the words and in the collaboration between metre and syntax. The effect is essentially a rhetorical one: nothing meaningful or particularly subtle is added by the syntactical ambiguity, yet somehow we feel that a turn of phrase has been found which is adequate to the dramatic occasion.[1]

On this level the device is common enough and need no longer delay us. Other examples are: 1.130 (where *Iunonis* belongs equally to *fratrem* and to *doli* and *irae*); 12.235 (where *fama* belongs equally to both verbs); 4.634 (where *mihi* belongs equally to *cara* and to *siste*); 10.867 (where *tergo* belongs equally to *exceptus*, to *consueta* and to *locauit*); and—a slightly more complicated example—11.495–6 (where *perfundi* may be taken either with *adsuetus* or with *emicat*; in the first case *aquae* depends on *flumine*, in the second on *adsuetus*).

In all these examples grammatical analysis is artificial: no decision is forced upon the reader. When there is a significant conflict of meanings, however, the reader must make up his mind, and his decision may involve an inflection of the voice in reading aloud that rules out one of the two meanings. In Aeneas' words to Evander (8.532–4):

> 'ne uero hospes ne quaere profecto
> quem casum portenta ferant—ego poscor Olympo
> hoc signum cecinit missuram diua creatrix'

it is just possible to preserve the flow of sense and take *Olympo* both with *poscor* and with what follows (though a modern editor is forced to punctuate before or after *poscor*). In 4.381:

> 'i sequere Italiam uentis pete regna per undas'

the pause in the flow of Dido's words necessitated by the third-foot caesura detaches *uentis* sufficiently from *sequere* for us to feel that *uentis* belongs equally to *pete*, though once again modern punctuation cannot represent the ambivalence.

A more interesting example is 4.124–5—compare 4.165–6, where Juno's prophecy is fulfilled:

---

[1] The older commentators were ready to admit that a word or a phrase could be equally divided (ἀπὸ κοινοῦ) between two contexts. This liberality was discouraged by a new fashion, about the end of last century, for rigid grammatical analysis, which popularized the doctrine, often taken for granted by modern commentators, that only one of the possibilities could have been intended by the writer, our uncertainty being the result of his incompetence, or our ignorance of idiom. See my article, 'Syntactical ambiguity in Horace and Virgil', *Aumla* 14 (1960) 36–46.

Style

'speluncam Dido dux et Troianus eandem
deuenient'.

The primary meaning is, 'Dido and the Trojan leader will make their way down into the same cave'; if we read the line with a third-foot caesura it is indeed the only meaning. But if we read the line with a fourth-foot caesura and a secondary second-foot caesura, the effect is not quite the same. We catch now a second meaning: 'Dido leading, she and the Trojan will find their way down into the same cave.' We feel we should reject this second meaning; yet at the same time we feel the hint of truth in it—as though Juno's words give the game away and are then picked up ironically when the line is echoed by the narrator (after the prophecy has become a fact), with the second meaning underlined this time a shade more prominently.[1]

By far the commonest form of syntactical ambiguity is that which turns on the grammatical status of a noun or an adjective or participle. Latin case-endings are often not an unequivocal indication of grammatical status. Some forms are common to genitive and dative, others to genitive and nominative, others to dative and ablative—to name only some potentially ambiguous forms; the ablative is a combination of three separate cases that originally expressed quite different concepts; as the language developed the other cases developed functions which, though related historically, are often as apparently unrelated in meaning as the different meanings of many important Latin words. To cope with the dangers of misunderstanding, Latin prose had evolved a system of prepositions (originally adverbs that simply reinforced an idea already present in the case-ending) to mark off different functions of the one form. But this is a development which was resisted, as we have seen, in the common style of verse. The Augustan poets were anxious to avoid cluttering up their lines and obviously welcomed at the same time the contribution to coherence and density of a turn of phrase that felt compact and many-sided without seriously impairing intelligibility. From there it was only a step to the conscious exploitation of ambiguity—the added meaningfulness to be derived from an interplay of meanings.

[1] For *dux* of Dido, cf. 1.364: *dux femina facti* (followed by *deuenere*—is there an inadvertent verbal reminiscence in 4.125?); for *Troianus* = 'a Trojan', cf. 12.359. Note too the implication of the emphatic *eandem*. As well as the idiomatic meaning of 'together', pointed out by Austin, it implies that Dido and Aeneas were separated when they fled for cover in the storm, and then 'found their way down into' (*deueniunt*) the entrance to the *same* cave; Aeneas hesitates a moment perhaps, then Dido takes the first step into the cave.

Words in Action

There are two types. In the first we are simply left in doubt about the status of a word. Take 5.740—Anchises' ghost departs:

> dixerat et tenuis fugit ceu fumus in auras.

Grammatically speaking, *tenuis* may be nominative, describing Anchises or the smoke to which he is likened; or it may be accusative plural, describing *auras*. Clearly the adjective is equally appropriate to Anchises, smoke, and the thin air into which he vanishes. The word lingers, as it were, in the reader's memory to become available afresh as each noun occurs. In reading aloud, a decision between nominative and accusative is forced upon the reader: if he wants to take *tenuis* with *auras* he must lengthen the final vowel; even then, as the syllable is closed and in arsis, the vowel can perhaps be felt as long by the time the last word in the line is reached, though one took it first as short.[1]

Such examples hardly count as ambiguities; indeed we should perhaps rule out those dependent on doubt about the length of the vowel in final *-is*—there is some evidence that long *i* was distinguished in writing from short *i*. A more certain example of intentional ambiguity is 4.681 (Dido to Anna):

> 'sic te ut posita crudelis abessem?'

Here *crudelis* may be either nominative or vocative.[2] Or 10.404 (Rhoeteus tumbles from his chariot as he dies):

> caedit semianimis Rutulorum calcibus arua.

We may take *semianimis* as nominative or as ablative plural with *calcibus* (both the second-declension and third-declension forms of the adjective occur).

In the second type of case-ambiguity a word, or more often a phrase, may combine with other words or phrases in either of two grammatical constructions—or in both. In 1.75:

> 'exigat et pulchra faciat te prole parentem'

pulchra prole may be either instrumental ablative with *faciat* or descriptive ablative with *parentem*.[3] In 2.631:

> congemuit traxitque iugis auulsa ruinam

---

[1] Cf. 4.66: *est mollis flamma medullas*; etc.
[2] See Austin on 4.681.
[3] See Conway on 1.75.

Style

iugis may be either locative ablative with *traxit* or ablative of separation with *auulsa*. In 4.611:

> 'accipite haec, meritumque malis aduertite numen'

Dido may invite the gods either to 'turn their attention to her misfortunes' (taking *malis* as dative); or she may ask from them 'the attention she has earned by her misfortunes' (taking *malis* as instrumental ablative).[1] When Aeneas says to his men as he stands by the trophy of Mezentius (11.15-16):

> 'haec sunt spolia et de rege superbo
> primitiae manibusque meis Mezentius hic est',

though the primary meaning of *manibusque meis* is probably 'here in my hands' (locative ablative), the prouder assertion 'by my efforts' (instrumental ablative) is apparent beneath the surface meaning of the words.

In all these instances, the double allegiance merely adds an element of pleasurable complexity to the line. Because the bonds that hold the structure together seem to intertwine, the individual words are less easily prised out of their context; we feel that what is said is immutable or inevitable. There are, however, cases where we may feel that the doubtful status of a word significantly affects the meaning. It introduces a note of wry irony, for example, into Aeneas' description of his fellow Trojans gaping at the monstrous horse which led them to disaster (2.31):

> 'pars stupet innuptae donum exitiale Mineruae'.

Is *innuptae Mineruae* dative or genitive? The horse perhaps bore the inscription *innuptae donum Mineruae*, 'a gift for the maiden Minerva' —*innuptae* has an epigraphic ring about it, while *exitiale* represents Aeneas' interpolated proleptic comment. *Mineruae* is dative, then. But the Trojans in their folly accept the present for themselves, and it turns out to be a gift from Minerva (she helped the Greeks construct the horse, see line 15)—a gift that brought ruin upon the recipients; if we take it that way, *Mineruae* is genitive.[2]

Take Dido's words to her sister which we have already discussed as an example of Tragic Irony (4.478-9):

[1] Cf. 3.279 and Williams's note.
[2] See Austin on 2.31. Laocoon's famous cry, 2.49: *timeo Danaos et dona ferentis*, rules out neither sense—if he takes the horse as a gift *to* Minerva, then the idea that the horse is a gift *from* Minerva subsists as Tragic Irony.

> 'inueni, germana, uiam—gratare sorori—
> quae mihi reddat eum uel eo me soluat amantem.'

Though, as we come to the end of the line, *amantem* attaches itself more directly to the phrase just concluded (agreeing in that case with *me*), we feel it attach itself also to the echo of the first half of the line in our mind (agreeing in that case with *eum*). Observe also the ambiguity of *reddat*: (1) 'bring back to me in Carthage'; (2) 'restore to me in death'. Likewise *soluat* is ambiguous: (1) 'release', i.e., from my passion; (2) 'put an end to'. This sudden unexpected intensity of meaning after the pretended matter-of-factness of the previous line is extraordinarily effective.

Or take the lines which describe Dido as she comes to Aeneas at the beginning of the quarrel scene (4.296–9):

> at regina dolos—quis fallere possit amantem?—
> praesensit motusque excepit prima futuros
> omnia tuta timens. eadem impia Fama furenti
> detulit armari classem cursumque parari.

Here *tuta* may be both neuter plural accusative with *omnia* ('fearing all things though they offered no appearance of danger'; or perhaps, 'fearing all things that seemed safe'—because they seemed too good to be true) and nominative singular feminine ('fearing all things though safe herself'; or perhaps, 'already fearful while she was still safe'). Of course the effect of the ambiguity is more discreet than rigid analysis suggests. The phrase, one might say, instead of falling into two separate statements, is more closely welded together, because the words interlock more intimately than logical statement allows. The next sentence contains a similar ambiguity, coupled with a construction-ambiguity. We may understand *eadem* as nominative with *impia Fama*, when *detulit* is constructed only with the following accusative and infinitive ('this same mischievous Rumour', i.e., the same divinity as was described in 173 ff.). But the position of *eadem* strongly suggests, as well, a neuter plural sense: 'Rumour reported to her the same things she had already noticed for herself' (*praesensit*); now *eadem* is the direct object of *detulit* and *armari classem cursumque parari* an explanatory apposition. Apart from the intellectual pleasure the apprehension of this pattern of ambiguities offers, the movement in the syntax brings out the working of Dido's mind: she keeps

Style

putting two and two together, everything fits, everything points to the same conclusion: Aeneas' fleet is preparing to depart.[1]

III. THE VIRGILIAN SENTENCE

Our concentration upon the turning of a phrase has not been wholly artificial. It is true that phrases represent only the fragments of a poet's sense; true also that his decision to shape a phrase one way rather than another depends on factors unlikely to be revealed by any examination of his words, however close, unless we take into account the larger structures of which they were chosen to form a part, and the run at this juncture of the poet's intentions. There is abundant evidence, all the same, that poets work in phrases. Round the formulation of a phrase must take place the struggle, in which every poet engages, to accommodate the emerging, still inchoate thought to the words and syntax which will give that thought the degree of urgency, dignity or pathos the poet wants; or compress, or reflect, his meaning without distorting it. If he is a conscious artist like Virgil, he will persist with the struggle, moulding and remoulding his phrase till the words assume the relationship he desires to the conventions of his chosen medium. He may wish to evoke tradition by the flavour of his words, by syntax, or by direct allusion. Or he may wish to press upon a traditional turn of phrase an imprint that will suggest the force or the subtlety of his personality. Only rarely will he content himself with the anonymity of the common style.

Such struggles are, of course, only the incidental skirmishes of the pitched battle to subjugate form and structure to the poet's ultimate design. In this chapter we are less concerned with Virgil's final goal than with the ways he uses words to achieve it. All the same, it is time to move on from a consideration of the warp and woof of the verbal fabric to the basic patterns whose repetition builds up the picture on the tapestry. In Chapter 3 we dealt with the units of the narrative: Books, Episodes, Tableaux and Vignettes. In the concluding section

---

[1] For a further discussion of ambiguity in Latin see W. Wimmel, 'Doppelsinnige Formulierung bei Horaz?', *Glotta* 40 (1962) 119–43, and Mark W. Edwards, 'Intensification of meaning in Propertius and others', *TAPhA* 92 (1961) 128–44.

The Virgilian Sentence

of this chapter the limits we shall set ourselves are those of the line, the sentence and the paragraph.

(i) *Metre*[1]

Before we step from phrase to sentence we must remind ourselves that as well as its syntactical structure the verbal fabric possesses a structure of a different order—that imposed by metre. The metrical structure of a statement can lend it a vitality and an illusion of rightness or inevitability often imperfectly felt by the modern reader. Consider the effect of metre on the following lines, which—unlike the *disiecta membra* of Horace's line from Ennius—would seem without metre nothing more than simple, elegant, unexciting historical prose (1.418–20—Virgil is describing the arrival of Aeneas and Achates in Carthage):

> corripuere uiam interea qua semita monstrat,
> iamque ascendebant collem, qui plurimus urbi
> imminet aduersasque aspectat desuper arces.

Or take 2.634–8 (Anchises refuses to leave Troy):

> atque ubi iam patriae peruentum ad limina sedis
> antiquasque domos, genitor, quem tollere in altos
> optabam primum montis primumque petebam,
> abnegat excisa uitam producere Troia
> exsiliumque pati.

Note here, in addition to the vitality lent the sentence by the metrical structure, the emphasis thrown by their position in the line on the keyword *abnegat* (the first dactyl in the line) and the repeated *primum* (after the second-foot caesura and again after the fourth-foot caesura).

We may without excessive unfairness describe the verse of Ennius and the older practitioners of the grand manner as rhetoric which scans. When Horace invites us to agree that a line and a half he quotes from Ennius is so unmistakably poetry that the poetry will survive though we change the order of the words and remove the metrical pattern, what he is pointing to is essentially a kind of rhetorical

[1] This section is concerned with the relationship of metrical structure to syntactical structure. For a detailed study of the metrical structure itself, see W. F. Jackson Knight, *Accentual Symmetry in Vergil* (1939), and L. P. Wilkinson, *Golden Latin Artistry* (1963), who deals as well with the relationship os sound to sense and similar matters (also very fully discussed by Austin in hif commentary on Book 2).

imagery which the exalted style of the grand manner can affect—one too bold for prose rhetoric (except in an impassioned purple patch) and one even less appropriate to the conversational tone of Horace's hexameter verse—except where he strikes a pose and consciously evokes this style (e.g., *Satires* 1.5.51–6; 2.6.93–4, 100–1; etc.).

Horace exaggerates of course to make his point. Not all of Ennius is as grand as the fragment he quotes, nor is the metrical structure of Ennius' phrase really negligible. We may detect the beginnings, particularly in tragic verse, of a consciousness of the line as a structural unit of sense as well as a metrical unit. But in the epic-tragic style collaboration between sense and metre is rudimentary and precarious. Any consistent collaboration and all subtlety are ruled out by inadequacy of technique. Too often the poet has to stretch the sense by padding till it fits the metre, or allow metre to dictate the order of the words. The very real success achieved by Ennius and the early writers depends in a large measure on the impression of directness produced by the simplicity of their syntax.

A century and a half after Ennius the writer of verse found himself confronted with a problem that did not exist for Ennius. The development of prose oratory had been spectacular; a highly organized, impressive syntax had been evolved to cope with the increasingly sophisticated needs of prose expression. To adapt this new syntax to the grand manner of verse was tempting. It proved intractable: the new syntactical rhythms were too characteristic—a periodic sentence made to scan remained a periodic sentence; the syntactical pattern dominated the metrical one, imposing its own tempo and a tone of calculated, measured thought—the unmistakable atmosphere of prose. What makes much of the hexameter verse of Cicero grotesquely prosy is that the syntactical rhythms suggest the wrong associations. Even Lucretius sometimes flounders when his argument becomes too complicated for enunciation in the simple rhythms of Ennius. The clumsier rhythms imposed by new habits of formulating thought keep involving him in syntactical patterns that straddle the principal caesurae and cut across the natural phrasing of the verse.

Clearly verse had to break free from the rhythms of periodic prose. The rupture was effected by Catullus and the new poets.[1] At the same

---

[1] It is interesting to compare the elegiac verse of Catullus with Poem 64. Narrative is easier to handle. In his elegiac verse, when he has something complicated to say, the lines often lapse into the pattern of a periodic sentence that has been made to scan.

time they achieved a degree of collaboration between metre and syntax without precedent in Latin.[1] Their most lasting contribution to the development of Latin verse style probably lies here—if these reforms are less often associated with the *poetae novi* than the abuse of one or two details of rhythm which later became notorious, it is because their more important innovations, though not applied by their successors with the same stringency, won general adoption.

The hexameter now became a syntactical unit as well as a metrical unit—hitherto there had been no more than a tendency for the two to coincide. More important than this was the care expended on making the hexameter internally coherent in its syntax. One way to do this was to make the line start with an adjective and conclude with the noun with which that adjective agreed. Such lines occur occasionally in our fragments of Ennius and occasionally in Lucretius; in Catullus' Poem 64, however, the pattern occurs 21 times in 408 lines. Another way was to place the epithet at the principal caesura and the noun it agreed with at the end of the line; often this resulted in an internal rhyme. Still more showy was a line the first half of which contained two adjectives and the second half the nouns agreeing with them. Perhaps more important than these patterns, which quickly become monotonous if abused, was the consciousness created of the possibilities of a new kind of verse syntax, distinct from that of prose, in which the syntactical units did not merely coincide with the metrical units but repeated or echoed the phrasing of the verse.

As a result of this collaboration between syntax and metre, adjectives acquired a new importance. In prose, adjective and noun naturally most often occur side by side; at any rate they are not usually separated by more than a word or so. But in this new verse syntax they are often widely separated. Moreover the adjective now very frequently precedes the noun—an order found in prose with colourless adjectives such as *omnis* and *totus*, but not otherwise common; if it does occur, the adjective, instead of discharging its normal function of distinguishing by description, serves to remind us of something we already know or to invite our acquiescence.[2] It is this *affective* use of the Latin adjective rather than the stock epithet of epic which the

---

[1] To some extent their innovations represent an adaptation of Hellenistic experiments. See H. Patzer, 'Zum Sprachstil des neoterischen Hexameters', *Museum Helveticum* 12 (1955) 77–95.

[2] See Marouzeau, *Traité de stylistique latine* (2nd edn 1946) 325–9. Rather similar principles decide the position of the epithet in modern French.

Style

poetae novi regularized, as a structural device, to the point where practically every noun has its adjective.

It is not always realized how the Latin usage differs from the ornamental adjective which became a mannerism of English eighteenth-century verse, as a result, of course, of conscious imitation of Latin verse—largely misguided, since the structural effects obtainable in Latin cannot be reproduced in English, where the order of words is less flexible.[1] The English adjective normally precedes the noun; it may have an affective flavour if it follows the noun ('battle royal', etc.), but this order is seldom possible. Moreover the English adjective is not inflected: it cannot be separated from its noun (unless it is used predicatively) or the sense of the phrase is lost. Nothing in English can correspond to the expectation (comparable psychologically to the expectation aroused by a subordinate clause preceding its main verb) created in Latin by the case-ending of an adjective used attributively but separated by a phrase from its noun. The adjective bears, say, the distinctive ending of the feminine accusative plural; in the mind of a reader trained to think in an inflected language this ending is stored up without conscious analysis; a feeling that there is something still to come persists until the noun with which the adjective agrees is reached.

The main types used by Virgil in the *Aeneid* are as follows:[2]

(*a*) *Adjective-* (*or participle-*) *noun enclosing line.* Though used more sparingly than in Catullus' Poem 64, this type is fairly common. For example, 2.168 (affective adjective):

    uirgineas ausi diuae contingere uittas.

Or 1.91 (participle):

    praesentemque uiris intentant omnia mortem.[3]

(*b*) *Adjective, etc., at principal caesura, noun at end of line* (8.2):

    extulit et rauco strepuerunt cornua cantu.[4]

(*c*) *Patterns involving two adjectives, etc., and two nouns* (1.492):

    aurea subnectens exsertae cingula mammae.

Or 10.887:

---

[1] On collaboration between syntactical and metrical structure in English verse, see Donald Davie, *Articulate Energy* (1955).
[2] See Norden, Anhang III.
[3] Cf. 1.74, 128, 551; 10.245, etc.; 12.286, 386, 484, 487.
[4] Cf. 1.36, 86, 134, 291, etc.

The Virgilian Sentence

> immanem aerato circumfert tegmine siluam.[1]

A particularly balanced effect is produced by a chiasmus such as the following (1.53—adjective-noun noun-adjective):

> luctantis uentos tempestatesque sonoras.

(d) Rather more common than these patterns involving whole lines is a version of (a) confined to the first half of the line. For example, 1.472:

> ardentisque auertit equos....[2]

This type depends on a much greater flexibility in the placing of the principal caesura than we find in either Virgil's predecessors or his contemporaries. They depart comparatively seldom from a third-foot principal caesura, whereas Virgil very frequently places his principal caesura in the fourth foot: if there is a third-foot caesura as well, it is often obscured by the syntactical phrasing of the line.[3]

It should not, of course, be assumed that every adjective in the *Aeneid* precedes its noun, or that an adjective accompanies every noun. Virgil in fact makes more discriminating use of adjectives in the *Aeneid* than in the *Eclogues* and *Georgics*. There are fewer of them naturally in narrative than in descriptive writing—where, in addition to their structural function, they have an evocative function, amounting to a condensed form of description. The following comparatively dense descriptive passage illustrates Virgil's restraint (12.161-74):

> interea reges: ingenti mole Latinus
> quadriiugo uehitur curru, cui tempora circum
> aurati bis sex radii fulgentia cingunt,
> Solis aui specimen; bigis it Turnus in albis,
> bina manu lato crispans hastilia ferro;
> hinc pater Aeneas, Romanae stirpis origo,
> sidereo flagrans clipeo et caelestibus armis,
> et iuxta Ascanius, magnae spes altera Romae,
> procedunt castris, puraque in ueste sacerdos
> saetigeri fetum suis intonsamque bidentem
> attulit admouitque pecus flagrantibus aris.
> illi ad surgentem conuersi lumina solem

---

[1] For the pattern two adjectives, verb, two nouns ('golden line') see Williams on 5.46 and 3.152.
[2] Cf. 1.484; 2.28; 3.420; etc.
[3] See Williams on 5.1.

Style

> dant fruges manibus salsas et tempora ferro
> summa notant pecudum paterisque altaria libant.

Of the 40 nouns in this passage (including proper names) 19 are accompanied by an adjective; 14 adjectives precede and 5 follow their noun.

It was Virgil's interest, perhaps, in the half-line and the metrical variety to be obtained by a much freer use of a fourth-foot caesura emphasized by the syntactical phrasing which led him to experiment with lines held together by a syntactical pattern in the form of a chiasmus. The leaner, less showy rhythms of these lines follow the verse phrasing closely. Because they do not depend on the use of adjectives, they appear closer to the rhythms of conversation. At the same time they break away from the periodic patterns of prose, introducing an artificiality of their own.

These chiastic patterns are much more distinctively Virgilian than those based on the affective use of the epithet. The latter represent a refinement upon the practice of the *poetae novi* and Virgil's contemporaries, the former set the stamp of Virgil's personality upon the common style. The basis, however, of the chiastic patterns is a stylization of a form of expression characteristic of Homeric epic— the expression of a sequence of events or a complex idea through reiterated parallel statement instead of by the more analytical subordinating syntax of classical prose. (See below under 'Theme and Variation'.) The main types are:

(*e*) *Line enclosed by two verbs*. This pattern, which is very common in the *Aeneid*, is rare outside Virgil. The sense, as it were, runs up to the principal caesura and then retreats from the caesura in reverse order; the two verbs may be separated by their direct objects as in 12.130:

> defigunt tellure hastas et scuta reclinant

or by any other form of predicate, e.g., 4.76:

> incipit effari mediaque in uoce resistit.

Or we may have a chiasmus involving two dependent infinitives as in 4.112:

> misceriue probet populos aut foedera iungi

or 12.2:

> defecisse uidet, sua nunc promissa reposci.

The Virgilian Sentence

Naturally many other variations on the basic type are possible. The turning point of the sense may be either at a third-foot caesura as in the second and fourth examples just quoted, or in the fourth foot as in the first and third examples.[1] This type with its economical, stylized simplicity is eminently suited for narrative writing. A more showy version is appropriate to similes. In the following passage we have the chiastic pattern in three out of four lines, the other line (379) being enclosed by a participle and its noun (2.378–81):

> obstipuit retroque pedem cum uoce repressit,
> improuisum aspris ueluti qui sentibus anguem
> pressit humi nitens trepidusque repente refugit
> attollentem iras et caerula colla tumentem. . . .

(*f*) *Line enclosed by two nouns.* This rather less common type is best suited for a succinct summing-up of a situation, as in 1.209:

> spem uultu simulat, premit altum corde dolorem

or 4.55:

> spemque dedit dubiae menti soluitque pudorem.

Or for graphic description, as in 12.102:

> scintillae absistunt, oculis micat acribus ignis.

(*g*) *Line enclosed by two adjectives* (*or participles*). When the two epithets are syntactically parallel, this type imposes a more languid rhythm, as in 4.26:

> pallentis umbras Erebo noctemque profundam.

Or a more ornamental effect, as in 4.75:

> Sidoniasque ostentat opes urbemque paratam.

A less showy version of the same type, in which the adjectives are not syntactically parallel, simply involves a juxtaposition of opposing word-orders, as in 12.8:

> impauidus frangit telum et fremit ore cruento.

(*h*) *Over-flow.* So far we have dealt with types where the hexameter can be taken in isolation as an independent, if sometimes complex, unit of sense—not necessarily a complete sentence. The *poetae novi*, to

---

[1] Cf. 4.135, 142; 12.55, 66, 85, 133, 235, 246, etc.; there are 17 examples in Book 6 alone.

Style

judge from Catullus' Poem 64, favoured an end-stopped style—it drew attention to the architecture of a line; another reason, perhaps, was that if they allowed the sense to flow on through several lines, they were apt to find themselves writing in prose periods. But even in a short poem a break in the sense at the end of every line quickly becomes monotonous. In a poem on the scale of the *Aeneid* it is obviously even less desirable. Virgil took pains to work out a way of writing in units of sense larger than the individual hexameter, and sometimes spreading through several hexameters (*over-flowing* from one line to the next) in syntactical patterns quite unlike those of contemporary prose.[1]

One way of securing over-flow was to use an affective epithet to bind two lines together, as in 4.158–9:

> *spumantem*que dari pecora inter inertia uotis
> optat *aprum*. . . .

Or the over-flow from one line to the next could be secured by separating a verb from its predicate, as in 4.22–3:

> solus hic inflexit sensus animumque labantem
> impulit . . .

or by delaying the subject of the sentence, as in 10.238–9:

> iam loca iussa tenet forti permixtus Etrusco
> Arcas eques. . . .

Sometimes three or more successive lines may be bound together in this way; the effect is of a surging forward of the narrative. This is done by means of epithets in 12.121–3:

> procedit legio Ausonidum, pilataque plenis
> agmina se fundunt portis, hinc Troius omnis
> Tyrrhenusque ruit uariis exercitus armis . . .

by delaying the verb in 12.131–3:

> tum studio effusae matres et uulgus inermum
> inualidique senes turris ac tecta domorum
> obsedere. . . .

Sometimes a verb forms an isolated dactyl at the beginning of a line (a rhythm Virgil is very fond of); sometimes the over-flow carries on to the caesura in the second or third foot. This suspension of the sense cannot, of course, be continued indefinitely—sentences must stop

[1] See D. S. Raven, *Latin Metre* (1965), section 77.

somewhere. They need not, however, stop always at the end of a line; and in fact Virgil is careful to vary the points at which definite breaks in the sense occur (as the famous half-lines show).

(i) *Superflux.* But these definite breaks between sentences are not the only points at which the sense can be felt to be complete. A marked feature of Virgil's style is what Mackail called *superflux.* A statement which seems complete at the end of a line flows on again in the next. Whereas in *over-flow* the line ends with an onward pressure of sense that appears irresistible, in superflux there is a pause, followed by a fresh wave of sense, creating an effect of fullness; or else the tempo is relaxed, to describe a detail of scene or an incident of narrative more completely. The superflux may consist of a whole line, as in 2.293–5:

> sacra suosque tibi commendat Troia penatis:
> hos cape fatorum comites, his moenia quaere,
> magna pererrato statues quae denique ponto.

Or it may consist of a half-line, as in 12.887–8:

> Aeneas instat contra telumque coruscat
> ingens arboreum.

(ii) *Theme and Variation*

A feature of Virgil's style, so common it quickly attracts the reader's attention, is what is apt at first to appear an odd fondness for repeating himself. Words, phrases, half-lines, even complete lines hunt in couples with a regularity we feel out of place in a writer so plainly sensitive elsewhere to the importance of economy, so keenly aware of the effectiveness of an incisive phrase, the impact of a telling word. Even where the alternative word or phrase adds something to the meaning, we are surprised that a second stab at the same idea was necessary; surely a practised writer should be able more often, by taking better aim, to secure first time a direct hit.

There is more to this trick of style than can at once meet the eye. Closer examination reveals the mixture we have found so often already in Virgil of traditional turn of phrase and modern artefact. Repeating an idea for rhetorical emphasis or for rhythmical effect is as old, probably, as the first awakening of man's pleasure in words. It is a prominent feature of early Roman poetry.[1] The word or phrase may be simply repeated; or a phrase may be followed by a variation of it (to

[1] See Eduard Fraenkel, *Plautinisches in Plautus* (1922) 361–4.

Style

give the idea amplitude, dignity, or pathos—or poetic beauty). But side by side with these are repetitions which are the result of a more primitive habit of thought in which the components of a complex situation or idea are juxtaposed instead of being gathered together in a syntactical synthesis that extracts the most important element and subordinates the others to it.

We should not, therefore, be surprised to find similar repetitions in the *Aeneid*. Like Virgil's other evocations of the past they contribute to the poem's atmosphere, the constant assertion, implicit in Virgil's choice of words, phrases and syntax, of adherence to a traditional form of speech most easily definable in terms of its detachment from the present. The mere renunciation of subordination in favour of parallel statement in itself involves an assertion of pastness. But once again we shall expect a traditional element to earn its keep, the employment of it to be more refined, more carefully calculated. And once again we shall expect to find developments of it which are wholly Virgilian.

We have, in fact, already studied two of these. One is the use of a chiastic parataxis to impose a syntactical pattern upon a metrical pattern. The other is the use of *over-flow*, the apparent flowing over of a phrase into a reiteration of that phrase or a variation upon it.

Our concern now is not with repetition as a structural device, but with the characteristic patterns formed by the elements that compose it. To this end we shall disregard repetitions which are mere reiterations —the same word or phrase or an exact equivalent repeated—in order to concentrate on what I shall call Theme and Variation.

In the simplest form of theme and variation two words only are involved, linked by a connecting particle. The traditional grammatical label for this phenomenon is *hendiadys*. The Greek word implies two shots at the same thing, and it is of course true that in all forms of writing a word may be backed up by a near-synonym, either because the right word cannot be found or because an unfamiliar idea seems easier grasped when put two ways. Virgil's very frequent use of hendiadys represents almost always a refinement upon this simple phenomenon. In his practice, the second noun sharply limits or corrects the first (e.g., 1.2–3: *Italiam . . . Lauinaque uenit litora*), or approaches the problem of statement from another direction or on another plane (e.g., 3.222–3: *uocamus in partem praedamque Iouem*).[1]

[1] For an excellent account of hendiadys in the *Aeneid* see C. G. Cooper's excursus in *Journey to Hesperia* (1959).

The Virgilian Sentence

When two phrases are involved, they are seldom exactly parallel in sense. A common type presents side by side two successive steps in a narrative. Take the opening lines of Book 2 (2.1–2):

> Conticuere omnes intentique ora tenebant.
> inde toro pater Aeneas sic orsus ab alto.

Expressed in English prose, this amounts to something like: 'There was a sudden hush, followed by an expectant silence; then Aeneas began to speak from the high couch, as follows.' Virgil gives us a highly selective, almost impressionistic description of a familiar situation—the reaction of an audience when a well-known figure rises to speak. As usual, he is more interested in the emotions inherent in the situation than in the details of the scene—the only detail picked out here is the vague *toro ab alto*. He concentrates on the sudden hush (*conticuere*, instantaneous perfect) that fell upon the buzz of conversation, the silence that followed, the sea of expectant faces turned towards the speaker, waiting to size him up from his first words (the imperfect *tenebant* describes a situation, not an action). A prose writer, not interested in this kind of psychological reconstruction, would probably content himself with some formula such as *silentio facto*, and then introduce Aeneas' speech—passing into a reported version of it in *oratio obliqua* after citing the opening phrase. If for some special reason he chose to describe the silence which followed the lull in conversation, he would probably try to organize these two ideas and the verb introducing Aeneas' words into some kind of syntactical hierarchy. This, however, is just the kind of syntax Virgil prefers to avoid.[1] He leaves it to the difference in tense to indicate that

---

[1] Conway on 1.90 remarks:
Starting from an observation of Mr T. E. Page (*Cl. Rev.* VIII (1894), p. 203), in his *Aeneis*, VI (Anhang II, 2) Norden has shown that V.'s dislike of subordinate clauses has led him again and again to replace what in prose would have been put into a clause introduced with *cum*, *simul*, or the like, by one connected with the main statement merely with *et* or *-que*; and that he often does this deliberately to imply that the clause so connected is part of the main action and not to be distinguished from it in point of time, or, if distinguished at all, that it was prior; as in VI. 567 *castigatque auditque dolos* 'after hearing their guilty ways, he chastises them'; VI. 226 *conlapsi cineres et flamma quieuit* 'the ashes fell in when the flame died down'. Other examples in 43, 123, 398; II. 353 and 749; VI. 115, 331, 365 f., 543, 545; VII. 7. Sometimes the arrangement is complicated by an Interweaving of the order (V. 731 ff.). How strongly V. preferred this simpler form of narrative to the subordination which is natural in Latin prose, Norden illustrates happily by contrasting five lines from Lucretius (VI. 58–62) which contain four sub-

the second half of his first line is not just a repetition of the first. His syntax involves an immediate assertion of a style fundamentally different, in structure as well as technique, from that of normal prose. At the same time he has evoked a characteristically epic structural pattern (Theme and Variation), but with a new precision in the choice of significant detail.[1] In addition the chiastic arrangement of the two verbs and the placing of his principal caesura (it falls between the two arms of the parataxis) give him a syntactical pattern that underlines the metrical phrasing.[2]

A further type, to which the name 'Theme and Variation' applies better than to paratactic statements in a narrative sequence, occurs more often in descriptive passages than in narrative passages. The basis of the theme and variation is some kind of contrast, two ways of dealing in words with the same phenomenon or situation. Virgil is here sometimes accused of elegant variation by critics, unaware that he is relying on his readers to recognize the exploitation of a traditional syntactical pattern, and insensitive to the differing flavour of his words in the two arms of the parataxis. The argument that time and space are wasted by the parataxis is often raised, as though a poem were a means to some end or had an objective other than to be itself.

The contrast may be between intellectual and rhetorical statement of the same idea, as in 2.10–11 (Aeneas to Dido):

'sed si tantus amor casus cognoscere nostros
et breuiter Troiae supremum audire laborem. . . . '

The first line is precise, mannered (*tantus amor* is not natural Latin and still less natural when followed by an infinitive), carefully eschews grandiloquence; the second line (a Superflux) makes an immediate claim upon our feeling for pathos by a rhetorical flourish. What Virgil is after is the pleasure produced in the reader by the contrast in emotional appeal of two statements of the same idea; a pleasure, in

---

ordinated clauses with the opening of Book VI, where there are two periods each containing three clauses which would have been subordinated in prose, but which in V. are connected merely by *et*, *-que* and *tum*.

[1] On the theme and variation pattern as a feature of the appositional style in Greek and Roman writers see Harry and Agathe Thornton, *Time and Style* (1962).

[2] Mr Robert Graves, *Oxford Addresses on Poetry* (1962) 45, missing Virgil's exploitation of the epic manner (and his reasons for it), and assuming that one past tense is much the same as another for Virgil, roundly castigates Virgil for amateurish reiteration of the same idea in this line.

fact, strictly comparable to that offered by the statement of a musical idea followed by a variation upon the same idea.

Or the contrast may be not so much between levels of emotional appeal as between tight sense and full sense—the compact presentation of an idea, followed by its repetition in fuller form. Here is an extreme example (8.26–7):

> nox erat et terras animalia fessa per omnis
> alituum pecudumque genus sopor altus habebat.

The theme is reduced to its barest essentials—the two words *nox erat*; the variation upon it is full and flowing.[1] In 1.546–7:

> quem si fata uirum seruant, si uescitur aura
> aetheria, neque adhuc crudelibus occubat umbris ...

the initial statement of the theme in compact form is followed by a fuller, more pathetic statement of it and then capped by a second variation upon the initial theme.

Or the contrast may be between abstract or matter-of-fact statement of an event, and the presentation of that event in visual or dramatic terms, as in 8.7–8:

> undique cogunt
> auxilia et latos uastant cultoribus agros.

Or a piece of imagery may be built up for a purely poetic effect, as in 11.573–5:

> utque pedum primis infans uestigia plantis
> institerat, iaculo palmas armauit acuto,
> spiculaque ex umero paruae suspendit et arcum.

A prose writer might say simply, 'when Camilla was old enough her father taught her to hunt'; or if he were making a short story long he might say, 'taught her to use the javelin and the bow and arrow'; no useful purpose would be achieved by drawing out the imagery latent in the words 'javelin', 'bow' and 'arrow'. Virgil perhaps started with the phrase *iaculo palmas armauit acuto*. Then, feeling that *acuto* was likely to be taken merely as a colourless stock epithet, he made his sense flow over in a full-line Superflux; the result is a charming three-line Vignette.

Finally the variation may take the form of a kind of pathetic echo, as in Dido's words (4.24–7):

[1] Compare the even fuller variation in 4.522–7, and the shorter version in 3.147.

Style

> 'sed mihi uel tellus optem prius ima dehiscat
> uel pater omnipotens adigat me fulmine ad umbras,
> *pallentis umbras Erebo noctemque profundam,*
> ante, pudor, quam te uiolo aut tua iura resoluo.'

Compare 10.821–3 (Aeneas looks down on Lausus, whom he has just killed):

> at uero ut uultum uidit morientis et ora,
> *ora modis Anchisiades pallentia miris,*
> ingemuit miserans grauiter dextramque tetendit.

(iii) *Subordinate Clauses*

The syntax of classical Latin prose allots a dominant part to the subordinate clause, but in the *Aeneid* the subordinate clause plays a comparatively minor role. Its importance is limited by many factors, often complementary. Two have been discussed: an avoidance of the syntactical patterns of contemporary prose, and an evocation, as constant as it is discreet, of a past literary tradition.

The two grammatical systems, that of prose and that of verse, are the product of, and in their turn produce, different attitudes of mind in the narrator—the one detached and analytical, reporting things over and done with, the other intimately involved in the enactment of the story, offering us a flowing description of events as they occur. (See Chapter 3, 'Projection of the Narrator into his Narrative'.) Take 5.101–3 (the Aeneadae are sacrificing at the grave of Anchises):

> dona ferunt, onerant aras mactantque iuuencos,
> ordine aena locant alii fusique per herbam
> subiciunt ueribus prunas et uiscera torrent.

There are six separate statements (all historic present) in the space of three lines, no subordinate clauses and only one participial phrase.[1] Where a prose historian or an orator, in giving an account of something, would feel obliged at every turn to explain the motives of his actors, larding his narrative therefore with causal clauses, Virgil's chosen *persona* allows only the briefest comment on motivation (see Chapter 5, 'Characterization and Motivation'). At the same time it enables him to sidestep one of the most characteristic syntactical patterns of contemporary prose, the explanatory *cum* clause with the

---

[1] See Williams on 5.101–3.

The Virgilian Sentence

pluperfect subjunctive.[1] What first strikes the reader reared on prose about the Virgilian sentence is its directness and its simplicity,[2] features not always absent of course from contemporary prose. There are occasions, however, where a subordinate clause, or something equivalent to it, is called for. Clauses expressing a temporal relationship between events are probably, after relative clauses, the type most often met with. The commonest conjunction is *cum*. Despite Virgil's avoidance of *cum* with the pluperfect subjunctive, *cum* is used 66 times with the present indicative and pretty freely also with the imperfect subjunctive (26 examples, of which 5 are in reported speech). He is fond of the 'inverted' *cum* construction (a syntactical pattern in which the *cum* clause follows the principal clause and is only as a result of a grammatical convention regarded as subordinate to it),[3] which occurs 44 times, and avoids flouting what had become established usage: there are only a couple of examples of the pre-classical use of the perfect indicative with *cum historicum*, and an isolated example (5.42) of the pluperfect indicative.

Next in frequency comes temporal *ubi* (59 examples, most with the perfect indicative) and temporal *ut* (or *uti*) (58 times, 53 times with the perfect indicative, 5 times with the historic present); whereas temporal *ubi* is found in good usage from early Latin onwards, temporal *ut* is uncommon in early verse (it is not found in Lucretius) and not so very common in classical prose. Virgil's fondness for coupling *ut* with the verb 'to see' or the like is worth noting (19 examples with *uidere*, 17 more with an equivalent verb or phrase). The effect is that of a disguised comment on motivation, as in 12.1–4:

Turnus ut infractos aduerso Marte Latinos

---

[1] The conjunction *cum* with the pluperfect subjunctive does not occur in the *Aeneid*; it is also very rare in later epic writers (who doubtless follow Virgil). See B. Axelsen, *Unpoetische Wörter* (1945) 87–8.

[2] Eduard Fraenkel, 'Vergil und Cicero', *Atti e Memorie, Reale Accademia Virgiliana di Mantova* 19–20 (1926–7) 217–27, remarks (p. 226):

[Vergil] manzipiert sich von der Alltagssprache ohne doch gegen ihren Geist zu verstossen, das heisst er führt keine Kategorien ein, die in der lebendigen Rede nicht mindestens dynamisch schon vorhanden waren, bewegt sich jedoch innerhalb der einmal zugelassenen Kategorien viel freier als das eine nicht stilisierte Prosa vermocht hätte. Das aber ist genau das Verfahren das Cicero an den im hohen Stil gehaltenen Stellen seiner Reden, Briefe und theoretischen Schriften befolgt.

[3] The status of an inverted *cum* clause is very much that of a sentence beginning with a continuing relative pronoun. On this construction see Williams on 5.84–5.

Style

> defecisse uidet, sua nunc promissa reposci,
> se signari oculis, ultro implacabilis ardet
> attollitque animos.

If we are told that Turnus became angry when he saw the reaction of his men to defeat, the implication is that what he did is a reaction to what he saw.

After these comes *postquam* (30 examples, chiefly with the perfect indicative). In meaning *postquam* provides an alternative for *ut* or *ubi*, but its greater weight makes it more appropriate for resuming the narrative after a clear break;[1] it then commonly occupies the first position in a hexameter (14 examples); a particular mannerism is the coupling of *postquam* with a perfect participle without a finite verb (12 examples).

The conjunction *dum* occurs nearly a hundred times, mainly with the present indicative, and mostly with the meaning 'while' or 'as long as'. For the notion 'until', a more sophisticated temporal relationship which it is naturally less often necessary to express, Virgil is also fond of *donec* (14 examples); the *donec* clause always follows the principal clause, an order which perhaps had a characteristic epic flavour—it is found in one of Horace's parodies of the epic style (*Satires* 1.3.103–4).

While relative clauses remain very common in the *Aeneid*, it is apparent that Virgil sought to reduce their incidence by a free use of forms of *hic* and by simpler syntactical patterns, such as the accusative with a past participle.[2] Two patterns are worth noting. The first involves a phrase (sometimes a complete line) built on to a vocative noun or adjective—an artificiality of the grand manner quite foreign to prose. The prose equivalent, for example, of Aeneas' farewell to Palinurus (5.870–1):

> 'o nimium caelo et pelago confise sereno,
> nudus in ignota, Palinure, iacebis harena'

would have to begin something like, '*O Palinure, qui nimium caelo et pelago sereno confisus es . . .*'. In 1.664–5, 8.36–8 we find the artificial and the normal prose syntactical patterns side by side. This construction, also found in Catullus (e.g., 64.215, 77.1), was part of the common style.[3]

---

[1] See Austin on 2.90.
[2] An obvious prose equivalent, for example, of 3.65:
> et circum Iliades crinem de more solutae

is '*et circum Iliades, quibus crinis de more solutus erat*'.
[3] Other examples in Virgil are 3.475; 5.389, 724–5; 12.947; etc.

The Virgilian Sentence

The second pattern is seen in examples such as the simile in which Dido is likened to a wounded deer (4.68–72):

> uritur infelix Dido totaque uagatur
> urbe furens, qualis coniecta cerua sagitta,
> quam procul incautam nemora inter Cresia fixit
> pastor agens telis liquitque uolatile ferrum
> nescius.

The words which follow the relative clause (*liquitque uolatile ferrum nescius*) appear at first to disrupt the syntactical structure of the sentence. We expect a second relative clause. But to make the second relative clause grammatical, we should have to have *et in qua*, or something similar. That would give us, of course, an irremediably prosaic syntactical pattern, but it is sometimes said of passages like this that a second relative pronoun, in a different case if necessary, is 'to be understood'. The phenomenon is more accurately explained if we describe the words *liquitque uolatile ferrum nescius* as an Over-flow. Compare 1.469–73 (Aeneas contemplates the picture of Diomede driving off the horses of Rhesus):

> nec procul hinc Rhesi niueis tentoria uelis
> agnoscit lacrimans, primo quae prodita somno
> Tydides multa uastabat caede cruentus,
> ardentisque auertit equos in castra prius quam
> pabula gustassent Troiae Xanthumque bibissent.

In these and similar examples, the sense flows over because Virgil is imitating an archaic habit of thought which allows the spontaneous tangential expansion of an idea in a way not permitted by the more strictly logical discipline of classical prose.[1]

(iv) *Imagery*

Imagery, in the largest sense of the term, denotes any use of words specifically designed to elicit a mental picture. For this some suggestion of a dramatic setting is necessary: we have to be invited by the words to *visualize* the thing happening. Take the following lines, in which Virgil passes from his formal hypothesis to the beginning of the narrative proper (1.29–35):

> his accensa super, iactatos aequore toto

---

[1] Cf. 12. 943–4; etc.; and Thorntons, op. cit.

Style

> Troas, reliquias Danaum atque immitis Achilli,
> arcebat longe Latio, multosque per annos
> errabant acti fatis maria omnia circum.
> tantae molis erat Romanam condere gentem.
> uix e conspectu Siculae telluris in altum
> uela dabant laeti et spumas salis aere ruebant.

The first five lines contain no verbal imagery, though they may touch off private images in the responsive reader. The last two lines are different: they provide specific, if impressionistic, details for a particular picture.

The term 'imagery', however, is commonly confined to a more restricted sense, to denote the verbal representation of an idea in terms of a visual image often in no way accurately descriptive of the person or thing being illustrated, but aimed at making some feature of the person or thing clearer by means of an imaginative word picture. Similes and metaphors (including Latent Metaphors—the potentiality of a word to evoke visual overtones) are the commonest form of imagery in this sense.

There are of course short similes in Homer (e.g., *Odyssey* 5.281); but when we speak of a Homeric simile, we normally mean an elaborate yet loosely organized syntactical pattern, flowing out from an initial point of similarity, adding detail after detail to the imagery. Homer's narrative is often a fabric of clichés, deftly adapted by an experienced hand to fit a limited range of narrative and emotional situations, and made vivid by the mass of detail; his tone is leisurely and matter-of-fact—compare the intense, evocative selectivity of Virgil's narrative. It is Homer's similes that mark the transition from craftsman to creative artist. In some ways they are like the choruses of a tragedy: the action stops while an idea suggested to the poet by the context is explored at a more poetic level. Often there is little organic connexion between them and their context. Indeed one modern translator, Robert Graves, has been prompted to represent Homer's similes as short lyric poems embedded in a translation otherwise in prose.

Many poets, before Virgil and after him, have attempted to recapture the atmosphere of Homer's full-blown similes. None, however, has shown quite the same pertinacity as Virgil in the pursuit of this objective. Many of his similes follow a Homeric original closely; in others a fusion of two originals is easily recognized. Where no model exists, the simile still follows the syntactical layout of Homer's similes. Virgil's similes in fact represent his most direct challenge to

The Virgilian Sentence

Homer, the detailed working-out on a small, more intense scale of Virgil's technique of exploitation of form.

If we compare Virgil's similes with their originals we quickly see that the apparent over-flow of imagery and syntax is in fact a carefully organized structure. Take for example the simile Virgil uses to describe the troops of Messapus on the march (7.698–702):

> ibant aequati numero regemque canebant,
> ceu quondam niuei liquida inter nubila cycni—
> cum sese e pastu referunt et longa canoros
> dant per colla modos, sonat amnis et Asia longe
> pulsa palus. . . .

The general run of the lines, which substitutes vividness and spontaneity for rigid observance of the syntactical structure, is entirely in the Homeric tradition.[1] If we look, however, at the Homeric original (*Iliad* 2.459–66—the Achaeans assembling for battle), the difference is obvious. First, Virgil has sharpened the focus: where Homer has geese, cranes and swans, Virgil concentrates on swans. Second, though there is sufficient general resemblance to evoke the Homeric original in the mind of a cultivated reader, the intent of his imagery is quite different: Homer's birds illustrate the organized complexity of a body of men engaged in the preparations for battle—the noise of units forming and re-forming; Virgil's swans illustrate the purposeful, relaxed advance of soldiers singing on the march. Third, Virgil's description is much more selective; his adjectives are carefully chosen and carefully placed —even though *longa... colla* is an exact rendering of Homer's δουλιχόδειρος, it acquires a new freshness from its context: the swans' necks are not just long, they are stretched out in flight; notice, too, Virgil's attention to sound and rhythm—how *pulsa palus*, for example, suggests the reverberation of the swans' cries. Virgil's simile shows in fact that concentration on bold, clear strokes which is so characteristic of his imagery, amounting sometimes to a degree of stylization that suggests he is describing a work of art rather than reality.[2]

In the first book of the *Aeneid*, we find three such formal similes.

---

[1] R. D. Williams, 'The function and structure of Virgil's catalogue in *Aeneid* 7', *CQ* 11 (1961) 151, has suggested that these lines contain a compliment by Virgil to Ennius who, according to Servius, claimed to be a descendant of Messapus.

[2] Often we may suspect an actual work of art is at the back of Virgil's mind. In one or two cases we have evidence. The image of Madness chained behind the Gates of War in 1.294–6 seems to have been inspired by an actual picture in the Forum of Augustus, based perhaps on a detail of a painting by Apelles

Style

The first (1.148–56) renders more vivid the picture of Neptune calming the storm by a characteristically Roman reinterpretation: Neptune is like a statesman calming a noisy assembly. Not surprisingly, there does not seem to exist a Homeric original for this simile.[1] The second (1.430–6) describes the Carthaginian workmen around Dido's temple in terms of bees at their manifold tasks around the hive (an elaboration of *Iliad* 2.87–90, of which we find a first version in *Georgics* 4.162–9). In the third (1.498–503) Dido is likened to Diana leading a dance on the banks of the Eurotas or in the hills of Cynthus (based on *Odyssey* 6.102–8). In a fourth shorter, un-Homeric simile (1.592–3) Aeneas at the moment of his epiphany before Dido is likened to a work of art in ivory, or in gold and silver. Of six full-scale similes in Book 2, three have clear Homeric antecedents (2.304–8, 379–82 and 470–5).[2]

Virgil's similes are occasionally strictly Homer's; for example, the simile which likens the destruction of Troy by angry gods to the felling of a great mountain-ash by woodsmen (2.626–31). Even in such cases the image is apt to be an unexpected one or even startlingly fresh—the result of 'a leap in the poet's imagination',[3] as in the following (10.262–6—compare *Iliad* 3.2–6):

(see Chapter 4). The image of Cupid on Dido's lap in 1.717–19 resembles that on a fourth-century south Italian *crater* representing Eros on Helen's lap (A. Lesky, 'Amor bei Dido', *Beiträge zur älteren europäischen Kulturgeschichte, Festschrift R. Egger*, vol. 2 [1953] 169–78). Cf. his descriptions of temples in 1.455–93 and 6.20–33.

[1] Dryden's comment on this simile is interesting:
This I have observed of his similitudes in general, that they are not placed, as our unobserving critics tell us, in the heat of any action, but commonly in its declining. When he has warmed us in his description as much as possibly he can; then, lest that warmth should languish, he renews it by some apt similitude, which illustrates his subject, and yet palls not his audience. . . . This is the first similitude which Virgil makes in this poem, and one of the longest in the whole; for which reason I the rather cite it. While the storm was in its fury, any allusion had been improper: for the poet could have compared it to nothing more impetuous than itself; consequently he could have made no illustration. If he could have illustrated, it had been an 'ambitious ornament' out of season, and would have diverted our concernment: *nunc non erat his locus*; and therefore he deferred it to its proper place. Ed. John Carey: *The Works of Virgil, translated into English Verse* by John Dryden, vol. 1 (1819) 288–9.

[2] Austin is particularly good on the relationship between these similes and their Homeric originals. See also his comments on 2.516.

[3] I take this attempt to describe the vital element in a successful image from Cleanth Brooks and Robert Penn Warren, *Understanding Poetry* (3rd edn 1960) 89.

The Virgilian Sentence

>   clamorem ad sidera tollunt
> Dardanidae e muris, spes addita suscitat iras,
> tela manu iaciunt, quales sub nubibus atris
> Strymoniae dant signa grues atque aethera tranant
> cum sonitu, fugiuntque Notos clamore secundo.

There is no particular difficulty in visualizing the scene: the morale of the Trojans besieged in their camp is suddenly raised at the sight of Aeneas returning with reinforcements, and they redouble their efforts to repel their attackers. It can hardly be said that the picture is made clearer by comparing them to cranes in flight before a storm. Virgil's imagination, however, as he visualized the scene for himself was captured apparently by two details: the straining forward of the Trojans as they hurl their missiles and the cry that accompanies this action; stimulated by these details his imagination leaps forward in a piece of poetic fancy aimed at prompting a similar leap in the reader's imagination. The effect resembles that produced by the semantic gap between words unexpectedly brought together in a poetic context. Compare 5.213-19:

> qualis spelunca subito commota columba,
> cui domus et dulces latebroso in pumice nidi,
> fertur in arua uolans plausumque exterrita pennis
> dat tecto ingentem, mox aere lapsa quieto
> radit iter liquidum celeris neque commouet alas:
> sic Mnestheus, sic ipsa fuga secat ultima Pristis
> aequora, sic illam fert impetus ipse uolantem.

and 5.273-80:

> qualis saepe uiae deprensus in aggere serpens,
> aerea quem obliquum rota transiit aut grauis ictu
> seminecem liquit saxo lacerumque uiator;
> nequiquam longos fugiens dat corpore tortus
> parte ferox ardensque oculis et sibila colla
> arduus attollens; pars uulnere clauda retentat
> nixantem nodis seque in sua membra plicantem:
> tali remigio nauis se tarda mouebat.

The function of these two similes is to elicit the reader's recognition that Mnestheus' ship as it rounds the rocky turning point close in and then crowds on sail can be thought of as a dove, flapping its wings frantically as it flies out of a cave and then planing low across the open sea; and Sergestus' crippled ship, struggling to get free of the rock with

Style

half its oars broken, as a snake whose back has been broken by a chariot wheel. What Virgil offers the reader is not greater clarity but the poetic experience involved in bridging the gap across which the poet's imagination has leapt.

Commoner than this challenge to the reader's responsiveness is Virgil's technique of representing mental states in terms of visual or aural imagery. This function of simile is, of course, not unknown to Homer—e.g., *Iliad* 9.4–8, where the consternation in the hearts of the panic-stricken Achaeans is likened to a storm at sea.[1] Virgil's use, however, of imagery to explore the emotions of his characters is both more frequent and more systematic. We have discussed several such similes already—for example, the simile in which Dido in love is likened to a wounded deer (see Chapter 5, 'Characterization and Motivation') and the simile in which Aeneas tossed between love and duty is likened to an alpine oak in a storm (4.441–6).[2]

Subtlety as well as precision often characterizes the transfer of significance. Turnus, for example, is likened to a wounded lion at bay (12.3–8):

> ultro implacabilis ardet
> attollitque animos. Poenorum qualis in aruis
> saucius ille graui uenantum uulnere pectus
> tum demum mouet arma leo, gaudetque comantis
> excutiens ceruice toros fixumque latronis
> impauidus frangit telum et fremit ore cruento.

How is he like a wounded lion? Or are the details of the imagery purely picturesque as in the Homeric model (*Iliad* 20.164–73)? The clue lies in the opening lines of the book (studied in the Analysis of Book 12 in Chapter 4). It is not just Turnus' attitude of angry courage that we are asked to visualize. The wound he suffered is to his pride: he feels the hostility of his own men, though they dare not openly confront him—like a wounded lion that has rounded on its pursuers, faces them, sullen and dangerous, then charges forward in a sudden mad impulse to hurt back.[3] This exploration of emotion often has an ironical flavour. Compare Homer's simile likening Paris on his way to battle to a horse just given its liberty (*Iliad* 6.506–14) and Virgil's re-

---

[1] An image used by Ennius (epic fragment 430–2W) for a purely visual comparison; cf. Virgil 2.416–18.

[2] See *Latin Explorations*, p. 41.

[3] I cannot agree with Pöschl, p. 184, that the wound Turnus has suffered is the Italian defeat in Book 10.

The Virgilian Sentence

modelling of this simile in 11.492–7 (discussed in the Analysis of Book 11, Chapter 4). Or take the simile that likens Pyrrhus at the entrance to Priam's palace to a snake (2.470–5):

> exsultat telis et luce coruscus aena,
> qualis ubi in lucem coluber mala gramina pastus,
> frigida sub terra tumidum quem bruma tegebat,
> nunc, positis nouus exuuiis nitidusque iuuenta,
> lubrica conuoluit sublato pectore terga
> arduus ad solem, et linguis micat ore trisulcis.

The Homeric model is *Iliad* 22.93–6 (Hector holding his ground as Achilles advances; the detail of the evil herbs helps the reader's recollection). Virgil's simile, however, has a sharply ironical purpose: the evil herbs hint that Pyrrhus, this glittering, warlike figure, is also evil. The simile tells against him more effectively than open comment.[1] Compare the simile of the two bulls at 12.715–24 (see discussion in Analysis of Book 12, Chapter 4).[2]

It must not be supposed that we have had space for more than a sketchy account of some of the more important principles that guided Virgil in the shaping of his sentences. Naturally a formulation of basic principles gives little hint of the variety and subtlety that can result when the principles are manipulated by a skilled and careful craftsman. The enormous range of Virgil's syntactical patterns cannot be overstressed. At one extreme his style is abrupt, staccato—more like notes for sentences than completed sentences. Take 2.13–30 (Aeneas is telling Dido about the wooden horse):

> 'fracti bello fatisque repulsi
> ductores Danaum tot iam labentibus annis
> instar montis equum diuina Palladis arte   15
> aedificant, sectaque intexunt abiete costas;
> uotum pro reditu simulant, ea fama uagatur.
> huc delecta uirum sortiti corpora furtim
> includunt caeco lateri penitusque cauernas
> ingentis uterumque armato milite complent.   20
> est in conspectu Tenedos, notissima fama

---

[1] Austin on 2.471 ff. comments:
The passage is close to Homer, superficially—but Homer is concerned with externals only, Virgil is depicting Pyrrhus' evil heart.

[2] For a detailed discussion of Virgil's imagery (in particular of Books 2, 5, 8 and 12) see Michael C. J. Putnam, *The Poetry of the Aeneid* (1965).

> insula, diues opum, Priami dum regna manebant,
> nunc tantum sinus et statio male fida carinis;
> huc se prouecti deserto in litore condunt.
> nos abiisse rati et uento petiisse Mycenas.   25
> ergo omnis longo soluit se Teucria luctu.
> panduntur portae; iuuat ire et Dorica castra
> desertosque uidere locos litusque relictum.
> "hic Dolopum manus, hic saeuus tendebat Achilles,
> classibus hic locus, hic acie certare solebant." '   30

Aeneas' narrative begins with a series of terse, carefully worded phrases (13–20) that focus his story upon the horse and its contents. Then he leaves the horse (Suspended Narrative)—he will come back to it again in a moment at line 31. The function of the intervening lines is to sketch in the dramatic occasion with the maximum of economy and the minimum sacrifice of vividness.

Or the object of syntactical simplicity may be to create an atmosphere of slow-moving understatement, as in 4.685–92:

> sic fata gradus euaserat altos,
> semianimemque sinu germanam amplexa fouebat
> cum gemitu atque atros siccabat ueste cruores.
> illa grauis oculos conata attollere rursus
> deficit; infixum stridit sub pectore uulnus.
> ter sese attollens cubitoque adnixa leuauit,
> ter reuoluta toro est oculisque errantibus alto
> quaesiuit caelo lucem ingemuitque reperta.

Dido's last moments require an unobtrusive, subdued style; none the less the narrative must move smoothly, carefully avoiding the stridency of antithesis and asyndeton—except for the stark *infixum stridit sub pectore uulnus*.[1]

A fast-moving sequence of actions demands a more tight-lipped, connected series of simple statements, as in 12.509–12:

> Turnus equo deiectum Amycum fratremque Dioren,
> congressus pedes, hunc uenientem cuspide longa,
> hunc mucrone ferit, curruque abscisa duorum
> suspendit capita et rorantia sanguine portat.

Turnus dismounts from his chariot to confront the two brothers Amycus and Diores as they ride towards him; he unseats Amycus, then dispatches him with his sword, having meanwhile disposed of

---

[1] For the syntax of this passage see *Latin Explorations*, p. 201.

The Virgilian Sentence

Diores with a spear shot before he can approach; he cuts off their heads and ties the heads to his chariot, then remounts. All this is packed into four lines, and then Virgil moves on, deliberately underplaying the barbarity of Turnus' final action.

At the other extreme are occasions which demand more elaborate syntax. Take this flowing sentence (4.522–7—Dido's last night on earth):

> nox erat et placidum carpebant fessa soporem
> corpora per terras, siluaeque et saeua quierant
> aequora, cum medio uoluuntur sidera lapsu,
> cum tacet omnis ager, pecudes pictaeque uolucres,
> quaeque lacus late liquidos quaeque aspera dumis
> rura tenent, somno positae sub nocte silenti.

Here we have a world peacefully asleep; the syntax is diffuse, therefore, almost ornate. In the following sentence comes the bald statement that unhappy Dido cannot shut her eyes in sleep or receive the night in her heart (4.529–31):

> at non infelix animi Phoenissa: neque umquam
> soluitur in somnos oculisue aut pectore noctem
> accipit.

The function of 8.1–6 is to summarize the consequences of the action of the previous book:

> Ut belli signum Laurenti Turnus ab arce
> extulit et rauco strepuerunt cornua cantu,
> utque acris concussit equos utque impulit arma,
> extemplo turbati animi, simul omne tumultu
> coniurat trepido Latium saeuitque iuuentus
> effera.

First, recapitulation—an intellectual activity, hence subordinate clauses; then at *extemplo* we pass to description and a more animated syntax. Observe the effective Over-fiow of the single word *effera* which sums up the mood of hysteria that has led to the outbreak of war.

What all these sentences have in common is conscious control, an alert attention to the appropriateness of the effect produced, and a versatile deployment of the resources of Latin syntax, exploiting the many facets of a complex tradition, yet distinctive and above all efficient. Much harm has been done to Virgil's reputation by Tennyson's often quoted compliment.[1] No one reading Tennyson's poem ('To Virgil, written at the request of the Mantuans for the nineteenth century of Virgil's death') would suppose that the elderly laureate (he was in his early seventies) had in mind accurate critical assessment. The occasion called only for memorable platitudes. But because the line

> Wielder of the stateliest measure ever moulded by the lips of man

is memorable, it has been quoted till we have come to attribute to it the ring of authority. Against it we may set the more carefully weighed opinion of T. S. Eliot, a better critic than Tennyson and a poet whose own practice equipped him better to understand Virgil:

> I do not think that any poet has ever developed a greater command of the complex structure, both of sense and sound, without losing the resource of direct, brief and startling simplicity when the occasion required it.[2]

[1] ... I salute thee, Mantovano,
   I that loved thee since my day began,
   Wielder of the stateliest measure ever moulded by the lips of man.
[2] T. S. Eliot, 'What is a Classic?' in *On Poetry and Poets* (1957) 63.

List of Passages Discussed

Note: A reader interested in a particular passage should consult first the Analysis of the relevant book in Chapter 4. Passages discussed elsewhere than in Chapter 4 are grouped together in the following List according to the Episodes in which they occur. Passages only briefly alluded to are not included. Passages quoted out of context (mostly individual lines) are given separately at the end of the List.

Book 1
1–7:   40–3, 406.
12–33:   373, 431–2.
84–123:   90–1.
124–56:   305, 434.
223–304: 35, 47–8, 75–6, 112, 322.
305–417: 75–6, 305.
418–519: 76, 82, 91–2, 407, 415, 431, 434.
520–636: 75, 374–5, 434.
697–796: 87, 401.

Book 2
1–13:   405, 425–6.
13–39:   412, 437–8.
57–198:   61, 85.
199–233: 82.
298–369: 11–12, 17, 20–1.
434–505: 5–6, 437.
506–58:   3–8, 75.
559–87:   17–18, 62–3.
634–704: 387–9, 415.

Book 3
1–12:   88, 394, 403–4.
73–120:   401.
472–505: 88.
588–691: 61–2.

Book 4
1–89:   313–14, 319, 394, 427–8, 431.
90–128:   409–10.
173–94:   82–3.
195–218: 392.
219–78:   346.
279–95:   343–5.
296–396: 74, 88, 391, 404, 413–14.
397–449: 398–9.
450–503: 313, 333–4, 386, 412–13.
504–52:   311, 336–7, 439.
553–629: 321–2, 391.
630–92:   56–7, 94, 347–8, 438.
693–705: 322–3.

Book 5
1–41:   386–7.
42–103:   428.
104–285: 80–1, 435–6.
604–99:   15, 72, 393–4, 398, 407–8.
827–71:   95, 319.

Book 6
9–155:   406–7.
156–82:   368.
294–425: 79–80.
426–547: 10.
752–892: 48–9, 112.

List of Passages Discussed

Book 7
1–36: 93.
170–285: 402–3.
341–405: 319.
475–539: 319, 358.
601–40 (*see also* Gates of War): 361.
647–817: 433.

Book 8
1–17: 439.
18–78: 427.
184–305: 93.
370–406: 321.
407–53: 69.
541–84: 374.
608–731: 22, 35, 49–51, 84, 112, 401–2.

Book 9
77–125: 123.
159–75: 358.
176–223: 318.
224–313: 95–6.
314–66: 12, 310.
367–458: 13, 14, 16, 312.
525–68: 10.
569–89: 13.
672–818: 365, 368–70, 400–1.

Book 10
163–214: 400.
256–307: 434–5.
308–61: 363–4.
362–425: 69–70, 310–11.
426–38: 329.
439–509: 326–7, 364–5.
510–605: 18, 334–5.
689–761: 44–5.
762–832: 11, 85, 310, 341–3, 428.
833–70: 86, 332–3.
870–908: 14, 16.

Book 11
1–99: 345–7.
225–444: 14–15, 307–8, 389–90.
445–85: 348.
532–96: 427.
648–724: 94–5, 349.
759–835: 10.
896–915: 13, 349.

Book 12
1–80: 8–9, 15, 74–5, 86–7, 429–30, 436.
81–112: 314–16, 397.
113–33: 96–7, 366.
161–215: 419–20.
216–76: 312.
324–82: 11.
383–467: 307.
500–53: 68–9, 438–9.
554–613: 19–20.
614–80: 15, 330–1.
791–886: 374.
887–952: 335–6, 390.

Lines quoted out of context

1.53:	419.	4.22–3:	422.
1.75:	411.	4.26:	421.
1.91:	418.	4.55:	421.
1.209:	421.	4.75:	421.
1.381:	396–7.	4.76:	420.
1.492:	418.	4.88:	401.
1.546–7:	427.	4.112:	420.
2.1–2:	91, 425–6.	4.129:	366.
2.3:	394.	4.158–9:	422.
2.10–11:	426.	4.381:	409.
2.49:	412.	4.584–5:	366.
2.168:	418.	4.611:	412.
2.293–5:	423.	4.681:	411.
2.378–81:	421.	5.350:	397–8.
2.631:	411–12.	5.740:	411.
3.65:	430.	5.870–1:	430.
3.175:	359.	6.219:	359.

List of Passages Discussed

6.273:	399–400.	11.119:	374.
6.300:	385–6.	11.831:	59.
6.889–901:	65.	12.2:	420.
8.2:	418.	12.8:	421.
8.7–8:	427.	12.102:	421.
8.532–4:	409.	12.121–3:	422.
8.679:	404.	12.130:	420.
8.685:	393.	12.131–3:	422.
9.119:	398.	12.167:	399.
10.238–9:	422.	12.265:	408.
10.870–1:	60.	12.666–8:	60.
10.887:	418–19.	12.852:	59.
11.16:	412.	12.887–8:	423.

Index

Actium, battle: 22, 26, 27, 34, 47, 197–8, 293, 385.
adjectives: 417–20.
Aeschylus: 267, 375.
Aesop: 53.
Agrippa: 29, 371, 385.
Alexandrianism: 373 (*see also* Hellenistic poetry).
Ambiguity: *main ref.* 394–414; 32, 102, 126, 177, 180, 195, 197, 221, 248, 274, 275, 334, 337; Syntactical Ambiguity: *main ref.* 405–14; 136, 195, 224.
Analysis: *refers to the prose restatement of individual books in Chapter 4.*
Anderson, W. S.: 46, 162, 163, 193, 267.
Anouilh, Jean: 297–9.
Anthony, R. E.: 284.
Antony, Mark: 55, 152.
Apelles: 105, 433.
Apollonius: 109, 123, 132, 278, 279, 282, 284, 286, 287, 319–20, 346.
Arctinus: 279.
Aristophanes: 267.
archaism: 393.
Aristotle: 137, 324, 352.
Arnold, Matthew: 407.
Ashmore, J.: 327.
Auden, W. H.: 50, 294, 296, 375.
Augustine, St: 135.
Augustus (*including references under name Octavian*): 24, 26, 32–3, 34, 39, 40, 54, 104, 106, 153, 173, 253, 259, 275, 298, 307.

Austin, R. G.: 18, 63, 325, 434, 437, and *passim.*
Axelsen, B.: 429.

Bateson, F. W.: 375.
Bevan, E.: 58.
Boissier, G.: 303.
Bowra, C. M.: 18, 58, 124, 223.
Boyancé, P.: 300, 320.
Brecht, B.: 298.
Bridge Passage: *main ref.* 72; 65, 67, 74, 85, 87, 94, 102.
Brooks, C.: 434.
Büchner, K.: 62, 63, 217.
Butler, H. E.: 304.

Caesar, Julius: 31, 39, 55, 152, 172, 259, 264.
callida iunctura: *main ref.* 384–91; 138.
Callimachus: 44, 286, 287, 371.
Camps, W. A.: 33, 46.
Camus, Albert: 297.
Catullus: *main ref.* 370–5; 30, 37–8, 102, 109, 206, 217, 281, 282, 285, 288, 320, 392, 416–17, 422, 430.
Characterization and Motivation: *main ref.* 307–16.
Choerilus of Iasos: 27.
Choerilus of Samos: 37, 278.
Cicero: 27, 36, 54, 111, 115, 195, 241, 287, 309, 339, 351, 370–1, 402, 429.
Clark, M. L.: 111.
Clausen, W.: 174.
Cleopatra: 55.
Coleridge: 110, 289, 327.

Index

collage: 43-4, 53.
Common Style (of Augustan verse): *main ref.* 375-84; 80, 352.
Conington, J.: 148, 248, 249, 250, 288, 346, 396-7.
Conway, R. S.: 48, 223-4, 425, and *passim.*
Cooper, C. G.: 424.
Cordier, A.: 352, 394.
Crump, M. M.: 65.

dative and ablative, fusion: 380-1.
Davie, D.: 418.
determinism (in the *Aeneid*): *see* fate.
Dickens, C.: 332.
Dickson, T. W.: 27.
Distancing: 281, 373.
divine machinery: *see* gods.
divinity, imperial: 39.
Dodds, E. R.: 317.
Donatus, Aelius: 63-4.
Donatus, Tiberius: 63.
dramatic technique (in the *Aeneid*): *main ref.* 323-49; 74-6, 77-83.
Dryden: 21, 141, 295, 339, 434.
Duckworth, G. E.: 67, 73, 328.

Edwards, M. W.: 414.
Eliot, T. S.: 43, 170, 294, 375, 440.
Ennius: *main ref.* 355-70; 35-6, 38, 42, 126, 164, 165, 184, 207, 236, 263, 264, 277, 288, 308, 351, 382, 404, 415, 417, 436.
Epicureanism: 111, 287.
Episode: *main ref.* 71-6; dramatic and narrative structure in: 74-6.
epyllion: 37.
Esslin, M.: 298.
Euphorion: 371.
Euripides: 114, 128, 148, 282, 348.

fairy-tale, the *Aeneid* considered as: *main ref.*: 110; 219, 228, 259, 268, 303, 305-6, 315, 320, 323.
fantasy: 305 (*see also* fairy-tale).
fata Troiana: 115, 320.
fate: *main ref.* 320-3; 109-12, 118, 124-5, 213-15, 301, 339.
fighting (in the *Aeneid*): 68-71.
Fordyce, C. J.: 37.
Fowler, Warde: 266, 386.
Fraenkel, Eduard: 33, 423, 429.
Furius Bibaculus: 27, 365.

Gardner, H.: 226.
Garstang, J. B.: 324.
Gates of War: 105-6, 184.
Gellie, G. H.: 338.
Giraudoux, Jean: 297.
gods: *main ref.* 300-7; 109-12, 285.
Graecisms: 379, 381-2.
Graves, Robert: 43, 206, 294, 406, 426, 432.
Gray, Thomas: 261.
Greene, Graham: 290-3.
Groningen, B. A. van: 41.
Guillemin, A.: 63.

half-lines: 61.
Heinze, R.: 85, 113, 134, 306, and *passim.*
Hellenistic poetry: 30, 37, 44, 216, 286, 371, 417.
Hemingway, Ernest: 292.
hendiadys: 424.
Heroic Impulse: Chapter 1; 118-20, 181-2, 208.
Hesiod: 285, 287.
historical epic: 37.
Homer (*see also* Virgil, relation to Homer): 8, 9, 45, 59.
Horace: 10, 28, 29, 30, 31-2, 34, 43, 45, 49, 53-4, 73, 100, 104, 197, 229, 260, 266, 280, 282, 289, 309, 344, 361, 371, 373, 385, 388, 400, 415-16, 430.
Housman, A. E.: 208.

imagery (*see also* Latent Metaphor): *main ref.* 431-7; 57, 101, 139, 313-14, 427.
Implicit Comment: *main ref.* 339-49; 61, 70, 156, 189, 192, 205, 245, 261.
impressionistic narrative (in the *Aeneid*): 101.
inconsistencies: 63.
intellectual poetry: *main ref.* 370-5; 102, 216-17, 280-1.
Interweaving: 178, 229.
irony: 61, 194, 436.

Juvenal: 354.

Keats: 289.
Kenney, E. J.: 407.
Kitto, H. D. F.: 299, 317.
Klingner, F.: 50.
Knauer, G. N.: 42.

Index

Knight, W. F. Jackson: 101, 165, 166, 188, 385, 387, 415.
Knights, L. C.: 324.
Koestler, Arthur: 297.

labores of Aeneas: *main ref.* 123–4; 113, 132.
language: Chapter 6; 310.
Latent Metaphor: *main ref.* 391–2; 138.
Lesky, A.: 278, 308, 317, 434.
littérature engagée: 295.
Livius: 356.
Livy: 35, 38, 244, 309.
Löfstedt, E.: 378.
Lowell, Robert: 235.
Lucan: 36.
Lucretius: 39, 59, 70, 101, 137, 209, 276, 288, 311, 351, 379, 381, 417, 429.
Lycophron: 179, 279, 283.

McKay, K. J.: 286.
MacKay, L. A.: 174.
Mackail, J. W.: 61, 62, 117, 373, 387, 400, 408, and *passim*.
Maguinness, W. S.: 273, 304, 324, 327, and *passim*.
Macrobius: 25, 60, 283, 363, 368.
Maecenas: 385.
manuscript tradition: 62.
Marouzeau, J.: 351, 417.
metre: *main ref.* 415–23; 352.
'*metri causa*': 92.
Miller, Arthur: 295.
Milton: 293.
Mohler, S. L.: 154.
motivation: *main ref.* 307–16; 111, 338, 428.
Mountford, J. F.: 64.
mythological epic: 37–8.

Naevius: 35–6, 38, 42, 277, 283.
Newton, F. L.: 393.
Nietzsche: 294.
Nilsson, M. P.: 317.
Nordon, E.: 361, 418, 425.
Novotny, W.: 351, 396.

objective correlative: 79, 103.
Octavian: *see* Augustus.
oral and litearry epic: 278.
oratory: 308, 338.

Otis, Brooks: 25, 27, 30, 35, 36, 88, 174, 219, 278, 309, and *passim*.
Over-flow: 421–3, 424, 431, 439.
Ovid: 135, 148.

Page, T. E.: 425.
Palladium: 39, 115.
Palmer, L. R.: 18.
Parallel Motivation: *main ref.* 316–20; 115, 140, 159, 180–1, 259.
Parallel Narrative: *main ref.* 84–7; 65, 116, 170, 265.
Patzer, H.: 417.
Perret, J.: 51, 55, 60, 61, 98, 262, and *passim*.
Petrarch: 241.
pietas: 111–12, 391.
Pindar: 295, 366, 375.
Plato: 22, 54, 287, 405.
Pliny (the Elder): 60, 105, 385.
Plutarch: 7.
Pöschl, V.: 55, 56, 108, 180, 188, 189, 226, 287, 306, 313–14, 331, 436, and *passim*.
post-Homeric epic: 279.
Pound, Ezra: 294.
Probus: 63.
Projected Narrative: *main ref.* 77–83; 155, 184, 388, 428.
propaganda: 31, 105, 257, 294.
Propertius: 27, 28, 32–3, 37, 40, 45, 354.
punctuation: 405–9.
puns, etymological: 393–4.
puns, poetic: 396.
Putnam, M. C. J.: 56, 437.

Racine: 129.
Raven, D. S.: 422.
Reinmuth, O. W.: 86.
repetitions: 59–60.
revenge: 225–6, 335.
rhetoric: 236, 370–5, 391–2, 423.
rhetorical structure: 405.
Richter, G. M. A.: 115.
Rostagni, A.: 24.

sacrifice of live prisoners: 225, 272.
St Denis, E. de: 122, 159.
Sallust: 130, 238, 309.
Sandbach, F. H.: 284.
Sartre, Jean-Paul: 297.
Section: *main ref.* 71.

447

Index

Seneca: 7, 225.
Servius: *main ref*. 63–4; 60, 62, 64, 157, 165, 194, 200, 241, 249, 282, 283, 368, 388, and *passim*.
Servius Danielis: 64.
Shakespeare: 321, 324, 327, 375.
Shipley, F. W.: 61.
simile: *see* imagery.
simile, Homeric: 432–7.
Slicher, J. J.: 99.
Snell, B.: 308.
Sophocles: 104, 114, 279, 281, 297.
Sparrow, J.: 59, 61, 361.
Stallworthy, Jon: 73.
Statius: 7.
Stoicism: 57–8, 111, 124–5, 174, 214, 287, 304, 339.
structure, function of: 73.
Suetonius: 24–5, 36, 39, 40, 60, 61, 225, 234, and *passim*.
Sulpicius: 24.
Superflux: 423, 426, 427.
surprise: *main ref*. 327; 113.
Suspended Narrative: *main ref*. 85; 105, 113, 116, 146, 162, 166, 177, 184, 236, 248, 329.
suspense: *main ref*. 327–30.
suspension of disbelief: 110.
symbolism: 55, 108, 117, 158–9, 166.
syntax: *main ref*. 375–84; 428–31.
syntax, influence of metre on: 415–23.

Tableau: *main refs*. 72 and 65–6; 66, 78–83.
Tacitus: 309.
Taeger, F.: 39.
Taylor, L. R.: 39.
tempo, narrative: 88–97.
Tennyson: 440.
tenses: *main ref*. 88–97; 268; historic present: 77–8, 165; instantaneous perfect: 102, 165, 177, 236, 272, 425.
Theme and Variation: *main ref*. 423–8.
Theocritus: 133.
Thornton, A. H. F.: 53, 271, 281, 426, 431.

Thucydides: 214, 238.
Tibullus: 31.
Tracking Away: *main ref*. 94–5; 65–6, 258.
Tracking Forward: *main ref*. 94–5; 66, 165.
tradition, Virgil and: 350–70, 414, 424.
tragedy: 5, 317.
tragedy, Greek, Virgil's debt to: *main ref*. 323–49; 279, 285–6, 308.
tragedy, Roman, Virgil's debt to: 356.
Tragic Attitude: *main ref*. 324–7; 111–12, 137, 214, 273.
Tragic Irony (and Insight): *main ref*. 330–9; 118, 120, 131, 256, 340.
Tragic Suspense: *main ref*. 327–30; 109, 221, 246, 253.
tripartite structure: 67, 71.
Trojan horse, the: 115.
Tyrtaeus: 4–5.

Van Dyck: 296.
Varius Rufus: 29.
Verdenius, W. J.: 406.
Vignette: *main ref*. 72; 86.
Virgil, *Eclogues*: 28, 36, 285.
Virgil, *Georgics*: 28, 34, 36, 38, 434.
Virgil, relation to Homer: *main refs*. 41–7 and 284–8; 5, 53, 70, 102–3, 106–7, 122–3, 205, 238–9, 308–9, 317, 323, 346, (linguistic debt) 355–70, 386–7, 432–7.

wanderings of Aeneadae, chronology: 122.
Warren, R. P.: 434.
Wells, H. G.: 110.
Whitman, C. H.: 317.
Wilkinson, L. P.: 385, 415.
Williams, R. D.: 46, 55, 107, 151, 173, 174, 184, 186, 284, 433, and *passim*.
Wimmel, W.: 35, 414.

Yeats, W. B.: 73, 296.